Praise for *Australians: Origins to Eureka*

'When it comes to writing page-turning narrative no one does it better than Thomas Keneally . . . no doubt about it, *Australians* is a corker.'
— Cassandra Pybus, *Weekend Australian*

'. . . the story of Australia and the Australians could be in no better hands than Keneally's.' — *West Australian*

'Keneally evokes these distant lives with concrete detail and vivid sympathy . . . his people inhabit the same world we do —we meet them without the hesitation of reaching across voids of space and time.
— Marian Quartly, *Sydney Morning Herald*

'[*Australians*] will appeal to the general reader and the avid historian alike, and this is only the first volume. This reader can't wait for the second.'
— *Bookseller + Publisher*

'Volume one of *Australians* builds a sense of historical wonder.'
— Stephen Wilks, *Canberra Times*

'This new perspective on Australia's founding fathers is truly fascinating.'
— Sandy McCutcheon, *Courier-Mail*

THOMAS KENEALLY
AUSTRALIANS

THOMAS KENEALLY

AUSTRALIANS

FROM EUREKA TO THE DIGGERS

ALLEN&UNWIN

First published in Australia in 2011

Allen & Unwin
Sydney, Melbourne, Auckland, London

83 Alexander Street
Crows Nest NSW 2065
Australia
Phone: (61 2) 8425 0100
Fax: (61 2) 9906 2218
Email: info@allenandunwin.com
Web: www.allenandunwin.com

Cataloguing-in-Publication details are available from the National Library of Australia
www.trove.nla.gov.au

ISBN 978 1 74237 448 2

Typeset in 11.5/15pt Minion by Midland Typesetters, Australia
Printed and bound in Australia by Ligare Pty Ltd, Sydney

10 9 8 7 6 5 4 3 2 1

To my brother, John Patrick Keneally, honoured medical specialist, with whom I have shared nearly seven decades of Australian history

CONTENTS

ACKNOWLEDGEMENTS

These are the generous people who proved essential to this book but who bear no blame for its faults and are responsible for any of its virtues.

Firstly, Jo Kildea, the chief researcher, shows herself so highly accomplished at the task, and indeed is such a good writer, that maybe I should have left the entire task to her. She also compiled the chronology which appears in this book.

Before Jo Kildea joined the project, my skilled and generous daughter Margaret Keneally hunted down the correspondence of the Dickens' brothers and other figures who appear early in the narrative.

With my editor Rebecca Kaiser at Allen & Unwin, I enjoyed a relationship which seemed to consist of as much laughter as effort. Rebecca knows how to anaesthetise the writing process, to take the edge off the pain and add to the pleasure.

Patrick Gallagher, head of Allen & Unwin, thought up this series in the first instance, and so it is my wish that he is as pleased with this volume as he kindly professed himself to be with Volume I.

My agent Fiona Inglis has been an impeccable representative and dear friend. Her advice is measured and always effective, her championship of her authors and her loyalty to them is of such a high order that it bespeaks high character as well as high professionalism.

The copy editor Ali Lavau was as perceptive and tactful as she had been on other works of mine, and the photo editor, Linda Brainwood, seems to have the same taste as myself for pictures rarely seen in standard texts and which will thus help the reader see Australia anew.

My wife Judy, who has lived with me through this berserk career, is a natural editor, a first port of call for my early ill-formed chapters, who tells the truth about failed passages and phrases with tact, and is wonderfully enthusiastic for what all writers want to produce—the good bits.

May all of you flourish!

FROM 1860 TO THE DIGGERS

If you are like me, you do not always read author's notes. So I had better tell you at the start of this story what you can expect, and what I am trying to give you through the lives of the remarkable Australian women and men we will meet here.

A character in one of my novels says, 'History is a bugger when you're in it.' So what I am trying to present in these pages is the narrative of men and women struggling with the histories in which they are stuck, histories in which some perish, histories through which others endure, histories through which some dance. Sometimes, as happened in the first volume, I introduce more obscure Australians, but at other times take a fresh look at the Australians most intelligent readers think of as settled in dour civic memory, but who were men and women of vivid dreams and complicated ambitions. I cannot cover the careers of all those Australians, well-known or not, who would be eligible for inclusion. And there are some figures I intended to include but who do not appear here except perhaps by occasional mention. Amongst these is the remarkable Daisy Bates, early champion of Central Australian Aboriginals; the great diva Dame Nellie Melba; and Victor Trumper, the splendid cricketer. To illustrate the phenomenon of banditry in Australia, the story of some bushrangers is told in preference to others. Not every Aboriginal resistance fighter is mentioned, nor every social reformer, nor every high ranking digger nor valiant nurse. Some early film entrepreneurs and actors are dealt with in preference to others.

But I believe I have chosen a formidable group of people who are entirely appropriate to the purpose of the book. And that purpose is to attempt to place the reader inside the very flesh and breath and passion of Australian life in the past. The people of this book are the lenses through which—at least I hope—you will more than adequately see Australia's history play itself out. If the author does not succeed in doing this, he extends his sincerest apologies.

So let us begin with these people.

From 1860 an era commenced in which Australians pursued glimmering visions of equity but also engaged in savage class conflict; became a place of cities but 'unlocked' the land to redeem the immigrant and native-born from urban squalor; dreamed of the illimitable continent whose limits painfully revealed themselves; became a nation but retained provincial objectives; was independent and craftily subservient; made a legend out of bushrangers, industrial fights and brutal wars, but underestimated how, beneath these things, the living flesh of ordinary men and women shuddered and trembled; honoured anti-authoritarianism but saw no revolution arise; saw the immigrants increase and the indigenes diminish; planned big for the Australian North but could barely populate it; sought racial whiteness as the sole possible condition of its life yet spent an era quaking at the closeness of Asia and the militancy of Japan; became in the mind of the world, and in its own mind, the Working Man's Paradise, but retained what Lawson called 'the armies of the rear', the regiments of want; and was a nation of both vision and earthy pragmatism. This was the country of the larrikin and the emergent artist; of the prophetic and the hard-nosed; of radical oratory and ultimate respect for society's structures; the Promised Land and the land the immigrant would have left had he owned the fare home. Suffusing it all was the idea that, although provincial, we were an especial people; that although distant, in our social experiments and reforms, we were a society the world had much to learn from; that we were better than those who thought us crass and that, unleashed, we would show them a thing or two. The thunderclap of a world-wide war reinforced the mythology of Australian uniqueness even while helping create a world that widened class schisms and bespoke unresolved and coming peril.

It can be asserted again, in the hope that the book confirms the assertion, that none of this was dull.

CHAPTER 1

Old and new faces in a colonial society
1860s to 1870s

POST-TRANSPORTATION CONVICTS

Conviction was at an end in Eastern Australia, but because of its shame it had induced in the white community a tendency to pretend that all convicts ceased breathing and vanished utterly at the date of the abolition of transportation. Much later in the nineteenth century, the *Bulletin* wrote that the day 'among all others which has been forced upon us as the natal-day of Australia is that which commemorates her shame and degradation'. Nowhere was the taint, and the desire and impossibility of forgetting, more intense than in Tasmania.

The convicts, however, were in many cases still serving sentences, or else living in the community, some of them lost souls, some cherished by families, some treasured even by society at large. The lost souls were numerous, though it can be argued these were far from being the majority.

At Port Arthur, in the era of transportation, a separate prison had been built to impose on prisoners a soul-scarifying form of solitary confinement: the Pentonville system, in which convicts worked in silence and had no contact with each other. Silence, solitude and lack of stimulation were considered the new cure for criminality. At their brief exercise in the yard, men wore masks. Even in the chapel each worshipper was screened off from every other, so that glances could not be exchanged. The system made the criminal more criminal, the deranged more deranged still. Perhaps these results can be seen in the case of two convicts who experienced the old system and the separate, Pentonville system as well. Mark Jeffery, a burglar when transported in 1850, had experienced this separate prison before his release in 1870. After a fight in a pub in which a man was killed, he was convicted of manslaughter and sent back to Port Arthur for life, where again he experienced the separate prison. There he tried to murder the doctor and, seeing that he was both unstable and dangerous, the authorities sent him to the Isle of the Dead off Port Arthur as the grave-digger. There the devil himself, 'His Satanic Majesty', appeared in Jeffery's hut and spoke to him. Jeffery begged to be released from the island and was sent to Hobart gaol in 1877, being guilty there of more assaults. Photographed in the 1890s, the former hulking terror of a man supports himself on two sticks. He ended in the Launceston Invalid Depot, where he died in 1903. Like a number of other male convicts he left no recorded Australian family behind him.

Richard Pinches had spent fourteen years on Norfolk Island for stealing shirts, and then served time in solitary in Port Arthur after the convict establishment in Norfolk Island was moved there in 1853. Released, he was tried for stealing pigs in 1860 and sentenced to four more years at Port Arthur. Then, at large after an escape, he broke into a building and was sent back to Port Arthur again for five years. By 1875 he was freed with a ticket of leave but then received a further sentence of fourteen years for larceny and a burglary in Hobart. For all his impulse to flee prison, he devoted his life to ensuring his return to it.

There were happier stories. An old lag named Jack Best worked as a guide at Port Arthur after it was closed, and was a favourite with Tasmanians and other visitors to the haunted place, having the last word on what had happened there.

Margaret Dalziel had arrived in Hobart from Glasgow in 1851 under a ten-year sentence for the highway robbery of a tin case and registered papers. She was a small woman, barely 5 feet, who was assigned as a convict servant to a number of masters—including James Hirst, overseer of the coal mines—but absconded and ended up in the Female Factory. In 1857 she was at Impression Bay Probation Station, where Scottish immigrants stricken with typhus from the immigrant ship *Persian* were quarantined. Perhaps she was selected because she could speak Gaelic and the ship was full of Highlanders. Margaret received her ticket of leave for her work there. In 1860 she was living with a former convict, Robert Carter, and had a son named James. Having begun a free life, she then disappeared from the record.

Mary Witherington, born in England in 1805, died in the town of Ross in Van Diemen's Land in 1890. She had been transported for stealing a blanket while working as a housemaid in London. In 1835 she married a convict stone-mason, Daniel Herbert, transported for life in 1827 for highway robbery. He was subjected to severe punishments for idleness, insolence, drink and absconding. But he worked as an overseer on the Ross Bridge, a fascinating little sandstone arch which is decorated with the faces of many of the citizens, convict and free, of Tasmania, as well as those of classic and Celtic mythology. One of the faces is of the Viking of Van Diemen's Land, briefly a former President of Iceland, Jorgen Jorgensen. Another is Herbert's wife, Mary.

Most former convicts came from the labouring classes but there were, as there had been from the beginning, the bourgeois ex-convicts. Francis Abbott had been a watchmaker transported for seven years in 1844 for acquiring watches by false pretences. He had a wife and seven children for whom his arrest and sentencing must have been a great crisis, but all of them would follow him to Van Diemen's Land. He not only ran a successful jewellery business in Hobart but by 1860 was a member of the Royal Society of Tasmania and a fellow of the Royal Astronomical Society, London, and was made a fellow of the Royal Meteoro-logical Society in 1869. He contributed meteorological data to the Papers and Proceedings of the Royal Society of Tasmania from 1873–74.

Even more notable was the career of the Irish political prisoner and surgeon, Kevin Izod O'Doherty, involved in the abortive Irish Famine uprising of 1848 and transported to Van Diemen's Land the following year. Pardoned in 1856, by 1862 he had settled in the new colony of Queensland, doing so partly under the influ-ence of his friend Bishop James Quinn, whose desire was to populate Queensland with the Irish. O'Doherty moved there with his young wife Eva, a notable Irish poet. By the mid-1860s O'Doherty was one of the two most esteemed Brisbane surgeons, founding president of the Queensland Medical Association, a member both of the militia and of the Queensland parliament, and a pioneer of public health and quarantine in that city. Though tragedy would take his two brilliant sons from him, and liquidity problems and anti-Irish bigotry later blight his life, he was for many decades, a model of the successful ex-convict.

Anthony Trollope, visiting his son in Australia in 1871–72, felt that the fact that New South Wales had such a vast hinterland in comparison to Tasmania allowed people in the founding colony to believe that former convicts 'have wandered away whither they would. Now and then a good-natured reference is made, in regard to some lady or gentleman, to the fact that his or her father was "lagged", and occasionally up in the bush a shepherd may be found who will own to the soft impeachment of having been lagged himself.' Although many families kept quiet about their connections to convictism, there was a less frantic attitude to the matter.

Some children of convicts had great longevity. Jim Kelly, surviving brother of Ned Kelly and son of the Vandemonian convict Red Kelly, was a boy in prison in Wagga at the time of the Kelly outbreak in 1880. When released, he worked as a farmer on the family's small block at East Greta, not far from Glenrowan, and under a reformed administration, was never in trouble again. (In the late 1930s he attended the opening of Woolworths in Benalla.) Significantly he died a hundred years after the great anti-transportation protests of 1842, and after the fall of Singapore. The eldest son of Irish convicts Hugh Larkin and Mary Shields, born in a bush hut at Coolringdon Station in 1845, worked long after the end of transportation as a blacksmith in Gundaroo and was still alive in 1920.

Did former Vandemonian and New South Wales convicts settle in South Australia? It would be remarkable if they did not, thus rendering the colony less pure than it chose to think itself. The South Australian Act of 1838 excluded them, and Adelaide's first execution, in 1839, was of an escaped Irish convict from New South Wales named Michael Magee. Other convicts and ticket-of-leave men came as members of droving parties, and some settled in shacks in the Adelaide Hills and were referred to as Tiersmen, fearless, lawless Irish who lived on the tiers of the hills above the Anglican plain of Adelaide. One of these men, Tolmer, was hanged for bushranging and outraged decent citizens by smoking his pipe on the scaffold. Other ex-convicts worked for the South Australian Company itself at its Encounter Bay whaling station, again as early as 1839. That some of them did not marry or beget young South Australians is improbable.

Western Australia remained the only Australian colony accepting convicts in the 1860s. From a want of labour, and under the aegis of Earl Grey, the British Secretary of State, in 1849 it had adopted the practice it once renounced, just as the other colonies were abandoning transportation. It wanted only those convicts whose prison record was good. The first load of seventy-five sailed for Western Australia in March 1850 on the *Scindian*, and on that and later ships the prisoners were guarded by military pensioners—that is, veterans who travelled with their families to Western Australia, where they were contracted to spend a number of years as penal guards in return for an ultimate land grant. Few of them, of course, went back. Even in the convict system, population building was the primary concern in Western Australia. And there was evidence that, having served in the ranks of the British army, the guards had a good sense of how men behaved under humiliation of sentence and were often less authoritarian and more compassionate than professional gaolers.

There was a pattern from the start to issue tickets so that convicts could work for private employers, and the system was more successful than assignment had been in the east, in part because there were no women convicts transported to Western Australia. A Visiting Magistrates Board was established in 1850 to hear any complaints from either side of the contract. By the 1860s the convicts were building prisons at Perth and Fremantle, a new Government House, the Pensioner Barracks at Fremantle and the Perth Town Hall. Ships running between the east and Western Australia preferred the southern town of Albany as a port, but the road between the south coast and Perth remained primitive. Further roads closer in, however, were built by convict labour. Around York to the east of Perth and southwards towards Bunbury the new thoroughfares were hacked out by convicts amongst the huge shafts of native hardwood. The York pastoralist, landowner and merchant John Henry Monger would employ in all sixty-three ticket-of-leave men up to 1871. He was the largest exporter of sandalwood and so an important generator of capital for the under-capitalised west. Monger was a relatively rare native Western Australian, having been born in the Swan River colony in the misery days of 1831.

Western Australia had trouble getting all those it wanted. The number of statutory transportation sentences had diminished since the high days of eastern convictism. Only 300 British were so sentenced in 1860 and another 300 the following year. The Western Australian administration wanted 1000 a year and could not get them. Later in the decade some 600 a year would be sentenced—in large part due to republican offences in Ireland.

J.S. Hampton, who had been a feared controller-general of convicts in Van Diemen's Land, came to Western Australia as governor in 1862, and in 1866 scandalously appointed his son Comptroller-General of Convicts in Western Australia, a lucrative post. The son's severity was not far removed from the harsh conditions then being promoted at British prisons such as Pentonville. His thinking was influenced by an 1863 British Committee on Prison Discipline, which recommended that there should be a far more severe experience of punishment than that which transportees underwent. Transportation was no good for punishment, since Western Australian property owners wanted as many of the convicts working out of prison as possible. Young Hampton managed at least to abolish the Board of Visiting Magistrates in March 1867. Convicts no longer had any right of complaint. If they were guilty of misdemeanours they found themselves on bread-and-water diets in darkened cells in grim Fremantle gaol, backed up by flogging and banishment to chain gangs as distinct from mere work gangs. Attempts at escape tripled under Hampton junior.

But a new comptroller named Fauntleroy arrived from England in that year, and Hampton senior left office in 1868. Fauntleroy at once established a more humane, though still severe, regime and reduced the number of chain gangs. The British government was about to announce that transportation would end, and the last ship, the *Hougoumont*, arrived in January 1868 with convicts and an especially recognised and quartered group of Irish political prisoners, or Fenians. They were young men, self-taught, often middle class, who had observed the Famine in their childhoods and believed that Ireland must be freed from the Crown to be run equitably. They were also physical force men, who drilled, however ineffectually, in the hills outside Irish cities—and some were British soldiers who rebelled from within the ranks.

Throughout the history of convictism, except perhaps for some gentlemen prisoners after the Irish uprising of 1798, there had not been any accommodation of the idea of separating the politicals from the 'common criminals' as on the *Hougoumont*. The civilian Fenians aboard had access to paper and books and produced a handwritten newspaper edited by a young Fenian named Cashman. One of their leaders was a young man named John Kenealy, their spokesman when Prime Minister Gladstone pardoned four dozen of them in 1869. Kenealy was a young man who in time would repent of physical force but who would nonetheless invest in a Yankee whaling ship, the *Catalpa*, to rescue the last of the unpardoned life-sentenced Fenian soldiers on Easter Monday in 1876.

The transportation of these young men caused a great deal of anxiety amongst the Western Australian establishment, and a body of citizens sent a delegation to Earl Grey begging him not to send the Fenians. The concern in Perth was characterised by the Crown Solicitor, George Leake, who warned citizens that America too was full of Fenians and that it would take only one American Fenian vessel 'merely armed with one long 18 pounder to lay Fremantle in ashes in a few hours'. The commodore of the British Naval Station in Sydney, Commodore Lambert, told Governor Hampton that to allay the fears of citizens he would send him HMS *Brisk*, a corvette of sixteen guns. Two companies of the 14th Regiment would also be temporarily brought from Tasmania.

A large number of these Fenians, when landed, worked in road and timber gangs. One convict, the Irish political prisoner John Boyle O'Reilly, a poet whose reputation would become international, would write of the country he worked in on a road gang:

Here the aisle
Moonlit and deep of reaching Gothic arms,
Realmed for towering gums, mahogany and palm,
And odourless jam, and sandal;
There the growth
Of arm-long velvet leaves grown hoar in calm—
In calm unbroken since their luscious youth.

He also called Western Australia 'the Cinderella of the South'. A soldier Fenian, he was to serve a life sentence, but escaped on a Yankee whaler in 1869 and became a noted Bostonian newspaper editor and literary figure, once reading his verse in a three-hander literary session with Mark Twain and Walt Whitman. Some of his verse concerned the penal station for Aborigines on Rottnest Island. He would also write a highly popular novel named *Moondyne* concerning the convict Joseph Bolitho Johns, or Moondyne Joe, who was probably a better escapologist than bushranger.

Many of the civilian Fenians were pardoned by Prime Minister Gladstone in 1869 as a gesture towards Ireland, and most of them settled in the United States, though those who fell in love with Australian Irish girls on their way through Sydney—such as John Feehan, who married a dairy farmer's daughter from Gerringong, and John Flood, who would become for many decades the newspaper editor and owner in Gympie—stayed in Australia. Some of the civilian Fenians whose names were inexplicably not on Gladstone's list had to serve out their terms.

Most ex-convicts of either criminal or political origins remained labourers or became small farmers after their release but there were the normal convict success stories. One was that of Daniel Connor, a labourer's son from County Kerry transported for sheep stealing. On his release he peddled goods out of a backpack he carried along the country roads around Perth and Fremantle. He began to speculate in livestock and bought land at Guildford, an area in which he had laboured as a convict, and married an Irish servant girl from his home county. In Toodyay he acquired property, a flour mill and hotel, and began to advance money under mortgage to other farms. He became a stern forecloser when drought or the reluctance of banks struck those he had lent to. He also ran illegal gambling in Toodyay from his hotel. His son-in-law, Timothy Quinlan, who managed his father-in-law's Shamrock Hotel in Perth, would become a member of the Legislative Assembly. Two of his sons studied medicine at Trinity College Dublin and returned to Perth to practise.

DESOLATE IN THE EXTREME

It was in this era that Australians had it confirmed to them that at the country's core lay no mothering wellsprings, no surging waters. Dryness was to be destiny. There could be no American-style rush to the centre, and no cities of the central plains. In 1862 John McDouall Stuart, a small-statured Scot tormented by alcoholism and driven on by that ruthless Presbyterian deity who drove the Scots in their prodigious endeavours worldwide, reinforced in his journal on crossing the Australian continent the water poverty and relentless geography of Central Australia. 'I have searched every place where I think there is a remote chance of finding water, but without success.' He encountered for days the 'same open plains, with forest beyond', the forest being stunted eucalypt and mulga, 'sheltering no stream'. The fact that he had, in the northwest coastal area, found the Daly River very promising country, and had had pleasant times while camped in Newcastle Waters, a freshwater lagoon south of the Roper River, echoed only in the minds of those with pastoral ambitions in the north. Newcastle Waters on its own was not enough to compensate for the general dryness at Australia's Centre.

The message was that the interior of Australia would be hard on its children. The generation of the 1860s and 1870s was the one which had to accommodate itself to the idea of a desiccation lying at Australia's core. No great spine of water favoured the continent as the Mississippi did the United States. There was no Ohio, no Missouri, no Cumberland, along whose banks Jeffersonian farmers might settle. The vicious country let the explorers down and then tried to kill them. The serpentine water ran underground, was richly envisaged by the original race, but denied the explorer a sight of it.

Combined with the idea of blistering, stony emptiness was the idea that the explorer must suffer inordinately, and indeed, to enter the pantheon, should perish or disappear. Stuart, in many ways a paragon of Australian exploration, evaded death in the Centre only by his skills of organisation and his wisdom, but is not honoured as are the bumbling Burke and Wills. Stuart was a Scot born in 1815 and full of vigour when he first undertook his journeys in Australia.

In 1844 he had travelled with Charles Sturt into the centre of the continent and saw the effects of scurvy on members of the expedition. There were other members of *Homo sapiens sapiens* out there who did not suffer from scurvy and had lived there for millennia, but they knew the country in a different way. In May 1858, with the help of William Finke—a South Australian merchant who would have the supposed oldest river on earth named in his honour—Stuart moved out of Adelaide with a companion, an Aboriginal tracker and provisions for four weeks to explore beyond Lake Torrens and Lake Gardiner and to look for grazing land. He got as far as Coober Pedy before turning south and then west.

In 1859, he went out again, financed by Finke and a colleague, James Chambers. Stuart always travelled swiftly, with small parties and without any Burke and Wills panoply or over-expenditure. He came back saying that he had found waterholes to provide the basis for a permanent route northwards. But his pace was frenetic, and he never allowed much time between expeditions. On 4 November that year he set out with his third expedition, and then was off again on 2 March 1860 with two men and thirteen horses. Most of their provisions were soon spoiled by floods and it was now that the party reached a channel temporarily full of water, which Stuart named the Finke.

Despite Stuart's careful preparations and stress on travelling lightly and efficiently, the party began to suffer from scurvy and Stuart lost the sight in his right eye. They followed the Finke to the mountains that Stuart named after the Governor of South Australia, Sir Richard MacDonnell, the barren but beautiful range which stretches westward from the present site of Alice Springs. They headed north and on 22 April 1860 camped at a place that Stuart's readings told him was the centre of the continent. Nearby he named Central Mount Sturt, later changed to Central Mount Stuart, and planted a flag as 'a sign to the natives that the dawn of liberty, civilisation and Christianity were about to break on them'. After a futile attempt to go to the north-west, he found a creek which he named Tennant's Creek and travelled on north 200 miles (320 kilometres) before he turned around, though not entirely because of an onslaught by the natives at Attack Creek, more than two-thirds of the way across the continent. Starting again on New Year's Day 1860 he got 100 miles (160 kilometres) beyond it but met impenetrable scrub and himself began to die of dietary deficiency. Water was ever the problem—his horses on one occasion were 106 hours without it. Two months later the party dragged itself back into Chambers Creek Station in South Australia. The Centre had almost done for Stuart again.

At the end of 1860 the South Australian government voted £25 000 to equip a large expedition to be led by Stuart. This time he penetrated further but provisions ran out, clothes shredded, and he gave in. He got back to Adelaide on 23 September 1861. He received the 1861 gold medal of the Royal Geographical Society, but crossing the continent was still his furious ambition and he was quick to apply himself to it again and was ready to leave by the end of October. These quick turn-arounds after bouts of dietary disease and exhaustion seem ill-advised to a modern reader.

This time he took a botanist, Frederick Waterhouse, with him, and nineteen-year-old John Billiatt, future stalwart of Glenelg, Paraguayan adventurer, owner of a fencing school and enlightened student of the desert Aborigines. Early in that last expedition, Stuart was knocked down by a horse which then trampled his right hand, dislocating two joints of his first finger, tearing the flesh and injuring the bone. He rode back to town for treatment, evaded amputation, then took off in pursuit of his party.

Months later, he penetrated the scrub that had defeated him beyond Sturt's Plain, and reached Daly Waters, named to honour South Australia's new governor. Stuart thought that in the Roper River area he had encountered 'the finest country I have seen in Australia'. He admired the Adelaide River too, though fire burned along it. The party rested at Daly Waters for two weeks, then on 24 July 1862 they forced their way through a tangled mass of vegetation and saw the Indian Ocean on the coast of Kakadu. 'I advanced a few yards onto the beach, and was gratified and delighted to behold the water of the Indian Ocean . . . before the party with the horses knew anything of its proximity. It was not an idyllic beach but one of soft blue mud, typical of the tropic, the mud from which mangroves rose.' The next day they fixed a Union Jack embroidered by Elizabeth Chambers in Adelaide to a tall bamboo stalk and had a modest celebration.

On the return journey, Stuart was ill with scurvy and became nearly blind, almost an exemplar of explorers' failure to find in this zone landscapes softer on the eye. He could not eat much because the condition of his teeth prevented him from chewing. He declared that he was 'very doubtful of my being able to stand the journey back to Adelaide; whatever may occur I must submit to the will of Divine Providence'.

As the party continued south, Stuart found it hard to endure the motion of the horse for twelve hours a day. On Tuesday 7 October he wrote, 'What a miserable life mine is now! I get no rest night nor day from this terrible gnawing pain;

the nights are too long, and the days are too long, and I am so weak that I am hardly able to move about the camp.'

By 16 October things were worse. 'I am now nearly helpless; my legs are unable to support the weight of my body.' He was taking potassium bicarbonate, which was recommended for his condition, but it was having little effect. By 27 October he was vomiting blood and mucus. The next day he lost the power of speech for a time. He was living on a little beef tea and some boiled flour. He could see nothing at night, and one of his party 'informed me that my breath smelt the same as the atmosphere of the room in which a dead body had been kept for some days'.

He had been carried on a stretcher, slung between two horses. But now he found his health improved a little. At Polly Springs on the Finke River on the edge of the Simpson Desert he was able to walk two or three steps leaning on members of the party. But the strength was soon diminished by an attack of dysentery. At last, on 26 November and on a stretcher again, he was carried into Mount Margaret Station, the northernmost settled point in South Australia and the point at which all his expeditions, including this one, had begun. While still far from Adelaide, he wrote, 'I am very doubtful of my being able to reach the settled districts. Should anything happen to me, I keep everything ready for the worst. My plan is finished, and my journal brought up every night, so that no doubt whatever can be thrown upon what I have done.' The willpower required to keep his journal up to date must have been of an astounding scale.

The party arrived in Adelaide on 17 December 1862. Stuart had assiduously observed the Sabbath throughout his treks and had lost not a single man. He was able to report that the country from the Roper River to the Adelaide River, and thence to the shores of the Gulf, was 'well adapted' for the settlement of a European population, 'the climate being in every respect suitable, and the surrounding country of excellent quality and of great extent. Timber, stringy-bark, ironbark, gum, etc., with bamboo fifty to sixty feet high on the banks of the river, is abundant, and over convenient distances.' These reports were not lost on enterprising pastoralists, though some of those who took him at his word would end by feeling as disappointed as, long before, Phillip had been at Cook's report on Botany Bay. As Stuart's party entered Adelaide, people lined the streets to cheer him and he was awarded £2000. But on that he was permitted only the interest to sustain a life now broken. He was white-haired, exhausted and nearly blind. He returned to Scotland to see his sister and his journals were published in 1864, but his health was ailing and he died of swelling of the brain—very likely cerebral meningitis—in June 1866. Some questioned whether he had reached the Indian Ocean in 1862 and others spoke of his alcoholism, but the tree on the Indian Ocean shore which he had marked with the initials JMDS was rediscovered in 1883 and photographed two years later.

SENIOR INSPECTOR BURKE

When the Royal Society of Victoria had decided that the golden pre-eminence of Melbourne warranted that it put together the first exploring party to cross the continent, they chose as its leader Senior Inspector Richard O'Hara Burke, a man born of a genteel Galway Protestant family in 1821 who had never been beyond the settled regions. Burke combined in his character the stereotypical stage-Irish virtues and flaws—a yearning for the beyond, a Celtic romanticism about death, a volatile temperament balanced by charm and humanity. His posting was to Beechworth but in the pre-Ned Kelly era, when new land laws initiated by the Irish patriot Charles Gavan Duffy in the Victorian legislature were just beginning to trouble the squatters. Amongst other things, Burke was meant to prevent squatters using fake agents—dummies to select lands—but he was forgetful enough in his duties that he is said to have papered the walls of his Beechworth residence with reminders and documents to be dealt with.

When young he had served in the Austrian army as a hussar, but in 1848, the year of European revolutions, when the Austrians were fighting the Italian nationalists for possession of Milan and Rome, some shadow had fallen over his career, perhaps gambling debts. He was allowed to resign—a form of shame. He served in the Irish constabulary before emigrating to Victoria in 1853 with a promise of patronage and good hopes of promotion. Waiting for a posting, he ran up gambling debts at the Melbourne Club. He wanted to transcend that sort of social meanness by some transcendant deed. His young brother James had entered the pantheon by being the first British officer killed, in his case in hand-to-hand combat, in the Crimea in 1854. Burke too was looking for a place in the pantheon.

The name of William Wills, the expeditionary surveyor and astronomer, is a paler though perhaps more admirable presence in the expedition. He was in fact third-in-command. Second-in-command was George James Landells, who had both aquired and was responsible for the camels. But since it was Wills who struggled with Burke through the mangroves of the Flinders River to within reach of the Gulf of Carpentaria, tasted the water there and found it salty and suitable to validate their claim of a first crossing, and because they then died at Cooper's Creek, their names are cemented together. Burke'nwills is an Australian term for bad luck, admirable but futile effort, and—despite the fact that they died by a flowing creek amidst Aborigines who were celebrating a good season—death in the desert.

The Royal Society of Victoria, consumed by civic ambition, wished to forestall the proposed third expedition of John McDouall Stuart, which sought to cross the continent (but which did not manage to). In making that journey, great natural resources might be found. Burke and his lieutenant Wills managed the south-north crossing in February 1861, while McDouall Stuart did not make the transit till July 1862. It would be a painful triumph though, since Stuart's would be the route used forever more and serve as the route for the Overland Telegraph Line, and Burke and Wills gave their lives for their success.

From the beginning of the expedition Burke quarrelled with the English camel expert, Landells, and shed men and equipment as he went. He used his generous but aging meteorologist-naturalist-geologist, Ludwig Becker, for menial jobs such as loading the camels. While Burke was plunging northwards with Wills, the Irishman and former soldier John King, survivor of the Indian Mutiny some four years before, and a sailor named Gray, Becker would die near Cooper's Creek (near the junction of present day New South Wales, Queensland, the Northern Territory and South Australia) in the spring of 1861.

Burke and Wills struggled over the Selwyn Ranges, past the present site of Cloncurry, and on into a Carpentarian wasteland of mud and mangrove and bewildering watercourses. In the better parts of this country they had sighted Aboriginal huts. But at the height of this triumph of European transit, all they could do was to taste the brackish water whose salt showed that they had reached the fringes of a shore they lacked the strength to struggle through and find. The place where they tasted the water of the Gulf is obscure to this day—no notable road is laid down to terminate there, or to follow their course across the continent.

At the same time, Burke and his three began their return journey wasted emotionally and physically not only by the conditions of travel but by scurvy. Gray died—foreshadowing Scott's scurvy-ridden Antarctic expedition. They reached Cooper's Creek depot, and the tree marked DIG, to find that the party that had waited there for them for over three months had ridden out just hours before and left a cache of supplies buried in the soil beneath it! Then came Burke's decision, after rest, not to follow the track of the departed depot party but to strike out south-westwards towards a station in South Australia. And then, that proving hopeless, they went back to Cooper's Creek for the last time.

King would prove to be the survivor, fed in particular by a woman named Carrawaw with fish and the edible grass seed named nardoo, prepared in the native fashion. Burke and Wills too had both eaten nardoo, which before they died they prepared with King by grinding it and mixing it with water. It is fashionable to believe they ignored native food sources. They obviously did not. Wills said they ate three to four pounds of it a day. Only when King was a near-helpless survivor did Carrawaw begin to feed him with nardoo prepared in the native way, from roasted seed. Without the roasting the nardoo did not provide thiamine. Burke and Wills, having unwittingly omitted one step in preparation, were somewhat amazed they were failing despite the use of the great Aboriginal staple. Wills found, unlike the experience of famine victims, that nardoo appeased his appetite. 'Starvation on nardoo is by no means very unpleasant.'

While John McDouall Stuart was still crossing the continent on his last journey, the bones of Burke and Wills and the living survivor, King, were retrieved from Cooper's Creek by a party led by William Hallett. Hallett, the survivor and the remains all reached Melbourne just before Christmas to be greeted by the Exploration Committee and Ellen Dougherty, Burke's former nurse, now elevated to new status as nurturer of the immolated Burke. As one historian, Michael Cathcart, justly says, the exposing of the remains of Burke and Wills was a Victorian-age necrophiliac orgy.

When the remains arrived in Melbourne in a tin box, they were taken to the Royal Society Hall and examined (fragments of bone and tooth were stolen as civic relics). They were then displayed for fifteen days in a raised catafalque on which stood glass-topped coffins.

In black, Julia Mathews, the adolescent actress Burke had fallen in love with and to whom he had left all his goods, visited the bones. Those with influence were actually permitted to handle them. Treating bones as if they contained some relevant magic was something the good Protestant gentlemen of the Royal Society generally associated with Papism, but now it was practised in full and barely inhibited mode. Volunteer regiments accompanied the hearse on the way to burial, and houses and shops along the way to interment were draped in purple and black. The *Age* claimed 40 000 people wept. Stuart's interment was a far less crowded affair at London's Kensal Green cemetery.

The death of the explorers had redeemed all their failures. The fact that the country they had travelled was of little economic promise was forgotten in a paroxysm of grieving. They had sacrificed all to find the undefined and to know the as-yet-unknown. But while Stuart's expedition had practical results, there was nothing practical to be gained from Burke and Wills' journey. Even the long rectangle of desert and tropics that then lay between the western border of Queensland and the eastern border of South Australia and the Northern Territory was not acquired, since Queensland was permitted to subsume that sliver of country to complete its mass.

The funeral of Burke and Wills was a massive recognition of the idea that Australia's core was malign and unfair. The Royal Commission of Inquiry began its sittings in late November 1861 but found very little to blame in either the planning or execution of the expedition.

GENTLEMAN TRANSPORTEES

By 1860 the idea of Australia as the place for the less talented or more disreputable young Briton was well established in British culture. It would long continue to be so. In Oscar Wilde's *The Importance of Being Earnest* (1895), a wastrel young man named Algernon is told that his uncle 'said at dinner the other night that you would have to choose between this world, the next world, and Australia'.

Charles Dickens can be seen as typical of a number of nineteenth-century bourgeois Englishmen who saw Australia as offering possible redemption for unsatisfactory sons. Sometimes young gentlemen were sent for moral turpitude. Joseph Furphy would give voice to a young man of this type in *Such Is Life* (1903). At a camp in the Riverina a group of bushmen, drovers and bullockies hear a young English gentleman tell how he was detected 'in a liaison with a young person who resided with my uncle's wife as a companion. Whereupon my lady used her influence with the demd old dotard, and I was cut off with a shilling. However, he gave me a saloon passage to Melbourne . . .'

It is famously known that as a boy Charles Dickens worked in a so-called blacking factory—that is, a factory which made shoe polish and dispensed it in bottles. Surrounded by squalor and coal barges, he had yearned for beauty and education and, when he came to affluence and success, he was pleased to be able to send his own sons and daughters to good schools—three of his sons attended a fashionable boarding school in Boulogne—and to share with them a series of increasingly fine residences from Devonshire Terrace to Tavistock

House and the beloved Gad's Hill Place in Kent. In these transits of success, Dickens picked up from meetings with such folk as Caroline Chisholm, the great promoter of emigration to Australia, a particular view of the distant colonies. In the last issue of his magazine *Household Words* in May 1859, he wrote an article on Chisholm's schemes, and published a number of letters from emigrants to Australia. He himself wrote, 'It is unquestionably melancholy that thousands upon thousands of people, ready and willing to labour, should be wearing away life hopelessly in this island, while within a few months' sail—within a few weeks when steam communication with Australia shall be established—there are vast tracts of land, of country where no man who is willing to work hard . . . can ever know want.'

He exploited that destination in his imaginative work as a place to send a failed gent such as Mr Micawber, the hapless debtor in his novel *David Copperfield* (1850). Aboard the emigrant ship, Micawber cried, 'This country I am come to conquer. Have you honours? Have you riches? Have you posts of profitable pecuniary emolument? Let them be brought forward. They are mine!' Micawber rises in Australia to become a magistrate at a fictional place named Port Middlebay. In *Great Expectations*, which Dickens began writing in 1860, Magwitch, a transported convict who returns to England illicitly but as a wealthy man, was also indicative of popular British belief in Australia's being a less mentally and morally testing environment for success. If former convicts could do well in Australia, young gentleman should have no trouble at all.

Dickens' tenth child and youngest son, Edward Bulwer Lytton Dickens, and his sixth son, Alfred D'Orsay Tennyson Dickens, were both future Australian immigrants. Alfred acquired the family pet name Skittles, and the younger Edward was called Plorn. But despite the fond nicknaming of his children, Dickens could often think he had too many of them—ten, of whom nine survived to adulthood. Dickens said of Alfred that, 'I have always purposed to send [him] abroad.'

Dickens' interest in Australia had been piqued again when in 1862 he met Sir Charles Nicholson, who had served as a doctor in New South Wales and whose interest in archaeology led to his name being attached to a museum of archaeology in Sydney University. He had published a book, *The Australian Colonies, Their Condition, Resources and Prospects*, which Dickens devoured with his customary energy. Enthusiasm for Australia was also at work in the mind of the novelist and British Post executive (inventor of the red post-box) Anthony

Trollope, when he gave permission for his son Frederic to emigrate to Australia in 1863. Young Frederic wrote back enthusiastic reports of station life which might well have reached Dickens through his friendship with his fellow novelist.

These factors caused Dickens, with whatever degree of enthusiasm from his son, to decide on Australia as a place for Alfred. Alfred had been working at an importer's involved in trade with China, but now he was off to a place of greater opportunity. Like many notable Britons sending their sons to Australia, Dickens wrote to a friend, Sir Charles Layard, undersecretary in the Foreign Office, to ask him for references for Alfred, and supplied some of his own. At the time of his departure Alfred was twenty years old and a man of fashion; after his son's departure, Dickens received bills for eleven pairs of kid gloves and other items Alfred had taken to Australia. His ship arrived in Melbourne in early August 1863. An English friend of Dickens, the Reverend G.K. Rusden, had worked on bush stations before becoming Clerk of Parliament in Victoria. Rusden and Sir Charles Nicholson took an interest in young Alfred, and advised him on possible employment in the bush. He became manager of Conoble, a sheep station nearly 100 miles (150 kilometres) north of Hay, in flat, drought-prone country, a planet away from the England of Dickens' novels. He wrote from there, as plucky British lads were meant to, that he was 'as happy as a king'.

In 1867 Dickens withdrew young Plorn from school, telling his headmaster that he intended for him 'an active life', and determining that this should be in Australia. Dickens had already suspended Edward's study of Latin and said that the boy should apply himself to 'a general improvement of his acquaintance with the properties of the things he will have to subdue to his use in a rough wild life'. At the boat train at Paddington, bound first for Plymouth, with his brother Henry travelling with him to that port to see the sixteen-year-old Plorn off, Dickens was distraught. 'I shall never forget, so long as I live, the parting that took place between my father and my brother Edward, his youngest and best loved son,' Henry would later report. Dickens would never see either Alfred or Plorn again. Indeed, thanks to the relentless pace of his work, he was eroding his health and had only two more years to live. As for his sons—whom we shall revisit later—they would suffer many Antipodean tests and tragedies of a kind Dickens could not have anticipated, and one can see through them the gulf between what Europeans expected of Australia, and what Australia was. In the meantime, his Australian sons would demonstrate, at the peril of their very souls, that in Australia rainfall was destiny.

BEING BLACK AND WHITE

By the 1860s, the Bible, newspaper editorials and various branches of science seemed to underpin the potent belief that to be white was to be God's elect. Across the north of Australia, the battle for land between the two races was in full flower. In the southern regions of Australia, the battle had already been won. People in cities and 'settled districts' were already finding evidence in science, the Gospels and social science that the conquest, if regrettable, was inevitable. First of all, the concept of the Great Chain of Being, a proposition deriving from Aristotle, was a given in the European view of the cosmos. One of its main planks was the principle of gradation. At the base of being were rocks, at the apex was God, beneath him angels, and beneath angels, man. Inevitably Christians stood highest amongst mankind's creeds, and Europeans highest amongst the races of man. Aborigines were thought lowest. Phrenology, the science of grading humanity by studying the shape of the head and the size of the brain inside it, had been used to explain the criminality of convicts. But it also explained the low state of Aborigines. Founded by the Australian physician Franz Joseph Gall in the 1790s, and adapted by the Scottish brothers George and Andrew Combe, phrenology had such respectability that men with high qualifications could assure audiences in the south-eastern cities that, scientifically, the Aboriginal skull showed deficiencies in morality and brain power, and an excess of aggression and powers of observation (hence their capacity to track animals and men).

The Aborigines also had reason to fear certain colonial interpretations of Darwin's *The Origin of Species*. More in sorrow than in hate, the *Age* declared in January 1888, 'It seems a law of nature that where two races whose stages of progression are brought into contact, the inferior race is doomed to wither and disappear . . . in accordance with a natural law which, however it may clash with human benevolence, is clearly beneficial to mankind at large.' Thus, too much kindness only delayed an inevitable obliteration.

It would be wrong to see such opinions as deliberately malign. They were taken as science by decent people, on the basis of expert ideas powerfully arrayed to support them. It was phrenology which made Truganini, the Tasmanian Aborigine, very nervous of what would happen to her body after her death. William Lanney, her husband, seen as the last surviving full-blood Tasmanian Aborigine, had died in 1869 and his corpse had been immediately dismembered and beheaded. 'I know that when I die the Museum wants my body,' Truganini told a clergyman. She had good reason to be fearful that her head would join the hundreds on display for the use of scholars in museums in Australia and throughout the world. Indeed, after her death in 1876, the Dandridge family, who had protected her in life, buried her at midnight in the remains of the old Female Factory at the Cascades. It was scientific men from the Royal Society of Tasmania, not ghouls, who exhumed her body in December 1878 and kept it in a secure part of the museum for study by scientists. But ultimately, in the early twentieth century, as she had feared, she was placed on public display. She would again be buried—with honours and more publicly than the first time—a hundred years after her death.

This premise of God-given white supremecy influenced not only settlers but began to penetrate some Aboriginal minds as well. One of the most tragic cases was that of a young man named Harry Bungaleenee.

In 1846 a story arose in Gippsland that a white woman had become a captive of the natives. One of three expeditions which set out from Melbourne to find her carried with them handkerchiefs with advice about escape printed in English on one side and, since the Port Phillip region was pervasively Scottish, Erse, the tongue of the Highlands and Islands, on the other. In fact this white woman was utterly mythical, but one of the Aborigines persecuted for concealing her was a man of the Kurnai people named Bungaleenee, who was for a time captured and held in prison in Melbourne.

Bungaleenee's children, Harry and Tommy, were educated at the Baptist School for Aborigines at Merri Creek near Melbourne, and then were sent to Coburg National School and its hard-fisted teacher Mr Hinkins. Tommy died at the age of eleven in 1856. Harry was praised for his intellect but tended towards truancy, and at one stage attacked Hinkins with an iron bar. Nevertheless, the teacher was determined to transform him, and by the early 1860s places were sought for him at Scotch College and Melbourne Grammar, but he was not accepted by either. He became a messenger in the Department of Lands and was then implicated by white youths in an attack on a young girl, and sent to the training ship SS *Virginia*, the equivalent of a juvenile detention centre. He was part of the crew when it searched for Burke and Wills in the Gulf of Carpentaria, and by then he had settled to the discipline of being a sailor, and seemed to enjoy it.

At the age of eighteen, Harry was back working as a map tracer at the Department of Mines, where he showed gifts for literacy, a good copyplate hand and competent drawing. He had entered a phase in which he wished to a demented degree to be saved from his own blackness, and had told his fellow sailors on

Virginia that his parents were white. While washing his hands one day, he said to his old mentor and punisher Hinkins, 'I think they are getting a little whiter—are they not, father?' When someone suggested that he might like to marry a well-educated Aboriginal girl from New South Wales, he was outraged. 'A black girl indeed! It's like their impudence to speak to me about a black girl as a partner for life.' While still eighteen, he asked Hinkins to sponsor him for membership of the Society of Oddfellows. The Oddfellows had derived their curious name from the fact that they accepted men from a number of trades, not simply one. Their self-help organisation stressed temperance, and their lodges had been erected all over Britain and in the colonies, where most towns of any size had an Odd-fellows hall. The regalia involved in their ceremonies was somewhat like that of the Freemasons. Into this society, the son of Bungaleenee was duly inducted.

In front of a crowded lodge in Melbourne, he declared, 'Though I am the first of my race to receive this high honour, I sincerely hope I shall not be the last.' Having achieved one of the marks of the white fellow, membership of a lodge, he died before he could achieve others. A month after his induction, he perished of gastric fever. By the time of his death the Kurnai, his people, were being rounded up into a mission named Ramahyuck, outside the Gippsland town of Sale, run by the Moravian Methodists. From south-east Queensland to South Australia some 4000 squatters and their 20 million sheep occupied an extraordinary swathe of land, massive by European standards, of almost a billion acres (400 million hectares, or 4 million square kilometres). It was not that native land had been taken over which concerned most liberal-minded people, but that it had not yet been unlocked. And when it was unlocked, it would not be unlocked for the Kurnai at Ramahyuck.

POLITICS AND BANKRUPTCY

By 1860 Henry Parkes, the ivory-turner immigrant from Birmingham who had espoused republican politics and promoted them in his liberal newspaper *The Empire*, was concerned with matters other than the principles implying white supremacy. An activist whose eloquence had helped put a final end to the trans-portation of prisoners to eastern Australia, he was a politically adept member for East Sydney in the Legislative Assembly of New South Wales at a time when the seats were large but were able to return a number of candidates, following the English pattern. He embarked upon becoming a consummate politician, but remained a bad businessman, a writer of poor verse, and a fancier of women.

He had already met the other great colonial politician, Charles Gavan Duffy, when Duffy first arrived from Ireland, ultimately to settle in Melbourne, and had seen at once that he was a man of similar skills. 'I do not profess to enter into the spirit of Mr Duffy's public life in his native country, I yet know this of Irish history and Irish wrongs, that had I been myself an Irishman, with Mr Duffy's temperament and his principles, I believe I should have been a rebel like him.' Like Duffy, he was already a convinced Federationist. 'The time is coming,' he said in the early 1860s, 'when we must all be Australians.'

Governments of the time were unstable entities. When in New South Wales the first true ministry, led by the Sydney merchant, landowner and self-proclaimed liberal conservative Stuart Donaldson, lasted only two months, Parkes, one of his radical democratic opponents, claimed Donaldson resigned 'in a fit of petulance' over not being permitted to appoint judges to the Legislative Council, the colonial Upper House. The short life of Donaldson's government was merely an omen of short-lived administrations to come throughout the early decades of self-rule.

Always over Henry Parkes, as he participated in these unstable arrangements, there was the shadow of debt. William Bede Dalley would declare of the middle-aged Henry Parkes in 1872, 'If he lives long, he will rule over a nation, not of admirers and friends, but of creditors.' Said another contemporary, 'The very ring of his voice has a promissory note in it.' A prodigious liability of £50 000 had been built up by *The Empire*, and Parkes had been forced by it to quit politics in 1856. In the same year he published his second volume of poems, *Murmurs of the Stream*. This book was 'dedicated to the 3057 electors of Sydney who returned the author to the Legislative Assembly, March 13th, 1856'.

His verses were undistinguished but had an idealistic ring:

Poor land! Of what avail for thee
Thy summer wiles and skies resplendent,
If all this light still lifeless be,
And man grow here a thing dependent.

As Sir Charles Wentworth Dilke, an English politician who travelled extensively in Australia, said of Parkes, 'His debts, his poetry, are powerless to sink him.'

The extolling of the 'liberty' side of the British tradition, that almost theological belief that emerged from Thomas Paine's work and would be a founding principle of the civil life of the United States, was very strong in Parkes too.

But small issues of business woe dragged him down from transcendence of Australian vision. He wrote of, 'Disappointment's pain and trust deceived, and efforts foiled.' His heart bled under 'misery's fang'. But Australia, he said in a poem to his son, 'the little southerner', 'shall startle the world from its pomp of old sins'.

In a letter he wrote in March 1857 to his friend Jacob Levi Montefiore, a nineteenth-century entrepreneur in that colonial mode that stretched from insurance to manufacturing to pastoral interests, and a forgiving creditor of Parkes, he related that Sir Daniel Cooper, another of his creditors, had told him to his face that he would rather crush *The Empire* than suffer personal annoyance from his connection with it. 'In ordinary cases this might be borne—if the ends in view were only the accumulation of money.' But Parkes believed that 'to infuse fire and vigour into the political life of the country', he needed to be free of money worries.

Wisely or not, he re-entered Parliament for the North Riding of the County of Cumberland in 1858, and declared his support for Charles Cowper's Electoral Law Amendment Bill, introduced to the Legislative Assembly in May 1858, proposing representation on the basis of equal population per seat, manhood suffrage and vote by ballot. The Lancashire-born Cowper was a strange—some would say wonderful—combination of progressive businessman and radical. According to the conservative John Hay, the bill was likely to lead to mob chaos. 'It left the good old English path . . . and was an indication that the Government of the country was on a downward course towards democracy and the tyranny of an unthinking majority.'

Supporting such reforms, Parkes still had to resign when Sir Daniel Cooper struck again, demanding repayment of £11 000 with which Parkes had bought *The Empire*'s premises. The matter went before the Supreme Court, and possession of the property was taken and *The Empire* was advertised for sale. A meeting of creditors was held. Embarrassingly, there were wages owing to staff. Parkes faced insolvency. There were attempts by Parkes' political supporters to take up the mortgage. The paper closed down, leaving his house in Ryde threatened and forcing him 'to begin life afresh with a wife and five children to support, a name in a commercial sense ruined and a doubt of the practical character of my mind'. But through help from friends, he had at least avoided bankruptcy. But he had to surrender his estate, the liabilities being estimated at £50 000 and the assets at £48 000.

Though completely exonerated by the judge, Parkes had given his opponents a stick to beat him with. When he appeared before the electors of

South Sydney at the general election of 1859 he was 'vilified, oppressed, penniless', but by the time the 1860s dawned he was the member for East Sydney, and economically but not politically humbled. He was still considered a radical, since he told the House that the parliament of a new country 'has no graver duty to perform than guarding against the accumulation of special enactments which . . . are often at variance with the maxims of common law'. The common law favoured the rights and freedoms of citizens, not those of special interests or large landholders.

The issues which were to make him unpopular with Catholics were already arising—state-aided religious schools were adverse to his belief that all religious bodies in the colony should work on a voluntary and self-supporting principle. Catholic priests denounced his secularism, and to some extent what they saw as his sectarianism, from the pulpit. He was already worried about the scale of Irish immigration. He complained that in the period 1860–69, 15 000 out of 20 000 assisted immigrants were Irish, and he saw the Irish Catholics as representing one solid priest-ridden political force alien to British progress. This assumption would in time make him behave obsessively towards the Irish, as when he opposed an assisted-immigration bill in 1869 because he 'had no desire that his adopted country, the birth place of his children, should be converted into a province of the Pope of Rome'. Such talk made him a darling of the Orange Lodges, however, lodges inherited from Ulster whose mandate was to counter 'Romish' influence. Conflicts between 'Green' Irishmen and 'Orange' Irishmen were bitter.

It was true that the Irish clergy sought to corral their flocks from other influences, so that the 'One, True Faith' remained unpolluted. There was also a tendency within Catholic schools to emphasise Irish history and to distinguish Australianness from Britishness. Mainstream prejudice against them cemented their Irish Catholics' attachment to each other in any case. That aside, they were like everyone else trying to make their way in the suburbs, generally the industrialising ones, or often in the shabbier reaches of the bush. Unlike in Boston or New York they did not live in ghettoes, and their allegiance to Australia was unquestioning. In any case, the factory conditions in the cities and drought and low prices imposed a common Australian experience on everyone, without sectarian favour, though there were companies, such as Frederick Cato's, the wholesale grocers, which would not employ Catholics. During the 1860s, signs reading No Irish Need Apply were placed at the doors of many businesses and factories. (Ulster Protestants were exempt from this exclusion.) In response, Irish

Catholics began to organise through the Hibernian Association and the Knights of the Southern Cross to take workplaces over for their own kind. Catholic children in Melbourne schools in the 1890s would be told that members of the Holy, Catholic and Apostolic Church had 'taken over' the city's tramways, and so they could always get a job there.

Early in 1861, under the sting of want, Parkes accepted an invitation by Cowper to tour Britain with W.B. Dalley as an official government lecturer on immigration at a salary of £1000. His objective, he said when he was leaving, was to attract rich men as well as poor men to Australia. Some believed that he was offered this job, and its accompanying welcome salary, as a means for his enemies to get him out of Parliament. Cowper knew Parkes needed the money and, as William Lyne said, thus 'in the course of a few days, one of the most prominent and consistent of the radical party ... was removed from the arena'. When he sailed in May Parkes left behind his wife Clarinda and his children impoverished on their rented farm at Werrington.

Dalley and Parkes opened offices in London, and described their official position—New South Wales Government Immigration Agents. They had letters of introduction to Mr Gladstone, Lord Brougham and the Duke of Newcastle. In dispatches home, they said that they were having problems because of 'the indisposition of the wealthy classes to immigration'. Manufacturing was booming and the larger employers of labour were for the present in need of workers, and did not want to see a haemorrhaging of people to any of the new world countries. The 'humbler walks of life' were more interested in emigration but were put off by the New South Wales plan. Each emigrant, unless able to pay the whole of his passage money, was required by law to lodge the partial payment with the Colonial Treasury in Sydney, and this was a rigmarole for ordinary people not used to dealing with banks. (Queensland, Victoria and South Australia offered more attractive and less bureaucratic terms.) It was difficult to arrange ships until a certain number of passengers were guaranteed, so that many emigrants, like Parkes himself and Clarinda in 1838–39, had to wait around in London or Liverpool, Glasgow or Cork until the required number of emigrants were signed up.

Though touring for money in an era before the payment of members, Parkes lost none of his sense of destiny, and during the progress of his journey he was able to meet and converse with such literary stars as Thomas Carlyle, renowned writer of *The History of the French Revolution* and the wit who called economics 'the dismal science', and Richard Cobden, advocate of peace and free trade. Going to Birmingham, the city of his birth, to lecture—travelling first class in contrast to the third-class unglazed carriage in which he and Clarinda had made their initial journey to London twenty-two years before—he took the opportunity to come to a business agreement with a fancy goods exporting business. He hoped (in vain) that this might guarantee his family's affluence for the rest of their lives.

Back in Sydney, he was delayed in his return to politics but there was no thwarting him permanently. In January 1864 he returned to the House at a by-election for the seat of Kiama, which he would hold until 1870. He was helped not only by his repute but by the fact that Kiama was the headquarters of the anti-Catholic Orange Lodge. He opposed both the Martin and Cowper ministries and built his own free trade radical faction.

In 1865 Cowper tried without success to buy the ever cash-strapped Parkes off with an offer of the post of Inspector of Prisons, and when Parkes rebuffed that he offered him a ministry portfolio. But when Cowper lost the confidence of the House in early 1866 and the more conservative Cork-born James Martin was commissioned to form a ministry, he valued Parkes' alliance and made him his colonial secretary. The alliance between Martin and Parkes was characteristic of nineteenth-century politics. Though raised Catholic, Martin—a liberal conservative with a passion like Parkes' for state education—was agnostic enough to be attacked from the pulpit of St Mary's Cathedral by Archbishop John Polding. Martin and Parkes collaborated to have the bushrangers of the time hunted down and, when successful, wanted some of their death sentences commuted.

Parkes' portfolio of Colonial Secretary made him responsible not only for internal New South Wales administration but also for liaising with the Colonial Office in Whitehall. Of Parkes as a minister, the *Sydney Morning Herald* would declare that, 'No man among us knows better where to find the heart of the dark-browed and the rough-handed'—that is, of what would come to be called the proletariat. As for his passion for state schooling, Parkes declared, 'My motto has always been, fewer gaols and fewer policemen, more schools and more schoolmasters.'

Parkes was now equipped with the gifts—being visionary, ambiguous and cunning—to take him to his coming eminence.

PLORN TRIES TO DO A MAGWITCH

The story of Plorn Dickens in Australia would be characteristic of that of a number of genteel young Britons, in a class of more elevated self-transportees.

His elder brother, Alfred, had left Conoble for a new job as manager of Corona, a station in the barren Barrier Hills north of the site of what would be Broken Hill, and when in December 1868 young Plorn arrived, just sixteen, Mr Rusden organised a job for him at Eli Elwah, a large sheep station near Hay in New South Wales. Ten days after Plorn left for Eli Elwah, he turned up again in Melbourne, declaring that the resident owner was not a gentleman. Whatever had happened, Rusden wrote to Dickens that Plorn was lacking in resolution. Now it began to occur to Dickens that it might have been a mistake to commit Edward to such a wild and demanding colonial life. Dickens, having suffered a stroke, or a series of small ones, wrote to Rusden in early 1869 both warning his Australian friend not to believe the dire news about his health, and also declaring Edward to be 'a queer wayward fellow with an unformed character . . . I still hope he may take to colonial life. I know that it is an experiment which may not succeed, and I know perfectly well that if it should not succeed, the cause of the failure will be in himself alone.' One wonders how many young men of a nature like Plorn's, dispatched to Australia, felt the same alienation and bewilderment when a kindly person in Sydney or Melbourne found them a position in some remote place full of rough-handed, harsh-souled men.

Plorn's new post was even more remote. Momba Station, 80 kilometres north-west of Wilcannia on the Darling, was in country marked by stony hills and lagoons and waterholes. Nearly 2 million acres, Momba carried 353 cattle and 75 000 sheep. Rainfall was meant to be 25 centimetres annually but did not always oblige. The other Australian reality was that millions of rabbits infested the pasture. The rabbit had taken only a few short decades to colonise the remotest Australian pasture land.

The storekeeper at Momba Station was W.H. Suttor, who would later be a member of the Legislative Assembly of New South Wales. He himself had had hard times in 1868–70 on a station of his own in this country of saltbush and cottonbush, and he was in heavy overdraft when he took the job of store-keeper at remote Momba. Suttor told young Plorn that he was enjoying John Forster's *The Life of Charles Dickens*, a work which was based on the great writer's conversation and anecdotes. He thought Charles Dickens one of 'the Great Magicians' able to distract from the harshness of station life. 'A man must read out there—or drink', a man of the west told the journalist C.E.W. Bean a quarter of a century later.

To the family back in England, looking at a map of New South Wales, Corona, Alfred's station, and Momba looked close, and they surmised that Alfred would be able to give emotional support to Plorn. In fact, over 200 kilometres of rough terrain separated the brothers. On the day before his death in 1870, Dickens addressed a letter to Alfred at Corona and the subject was in large part Plorn. 'I am doubtful whether Plorn is taking to Australia. Can you find out his real mind?' But Plorn endured life there, amongst the stockmen of Momba, in country an Englishman who had never seen it could barely imagine. It provided for young Plorn an experience which was sometimes exciting and sometimes the Australian equivalent of his father's blacking factory days.

C.E.W. Bean described the country of western New South Wales as 'beautiful, endless, pitiless'. Sheep could live there, he said; men couldn't. It was a landscape of stunted trees, blue clumps of applewood, needlewood, belar, grey-blue mulga, leopard tree, saltbush and spear grass. When water filled the lagoons near Momba, Plorn would have found duck, teal, swans, brolgas, pelicans, ibis, kangaroos and emus coming in to drink. But rain also isolated him and his fellows, making the track to Wilcannia a soup of red mud into which horses sank to the fetlocks and beyond. Ration carts came round about every six weeks to two months, selling supplies the manager or owner might need. The table Plorn sat at in Momba offered a raw cuisine—limitless mutton, damper and golden syrup in 2-pound tins. Since Plorn had gone to Momba as an apprentice, he received no wage, or only a very small one, for all his work.

The store Suttor ran was like those on all the big stations, where drovers bought their tobacco and other needs. Distance made the prices high. But Suttor the storekeeper remained a bush patron to the younger Dickens and helped him with advice about horses he wished to buy with the money he had brought from England. Before he died Dickens was pleased to hear about Plorn's ventures into Australian horseflesh. Plorn, he wrote—approvingly now—was taking 'better to the bush than to books'. Horse racing was often the only communal sport for these widely spread people and Edward would enjoy it all his life. Throughout the nineteenth century, gentlemen often raced their own horses in bush and city race meetings, as would the poets Adam Lindsay Gordon and Banjo Paterson.

Dickens suffered a severe stroke, and died on 9 June 1870. It was August before the news reached the boys on their remote stations. Edward's resolve to stick to the business of being a bushman was nevertheless reinforced. After his father's death, Aunt Georgie, Dickens' executor, sent him a yearly allowance of £100, enough to buy horses with. But he was not yet twenty-one and able to inherit. He wrote asking for a larger part—for, despite what Suttor, other drovers and the country itself could tell him of the hardships, he wanted to become an

Australian pastoralist. As it would for many others, the land would grind him on the anvil of its drought years.

In December 1872, however, four months before his inheritance would be released to him, Plorn and two partners bought a small part of and took a lease on the rest of Yanda, a station of 300 000 acres along the banks of the Darling on the road from Bourke to Wilcannia. From its homestead a particularly beautiful bend in the deep-banked river was visible, and standing by the shearing shed above the water, Plorn must have felt that he had joined the world of men and validated his father's memory.

One of the partners, William Hatton, undertook to live on the property, an arrangement the Land Act required of partners in pastoral leases. But the fare by riverboat from Wilcannia to Bourke, the nearest town to Yanda, was over £12, which was 12 per cent of Plorn's annual endowment. Plorn was fortunately promoted by the pastoral company, E.S. Bonney and Company, to manage the neighbouring station, Mount Murchison, which was about half a million acres with a 25-mile frontage on the Darling.

He was closer to Wilcannia at Mount Murchison, and became a young Justice of the Peace in the area and sat as a magistrate. He was a member of the committees of both the Church of England and the Wilcannia Jockey Club. His horse, Greytail, was second in the Wilcannia steeplechase. Later in his career, his horse Tam O'Shanter won by a length, while his Murky Morn won the squatter's purse of £15 at the Mena Murtee Station races. He scoured local stations to create a cricket team to play the township, and he was captain of it.

Plorn met a girl named Constance Desailly, whose father ran a station named Netallie west of Wilcannia. The marriage was to take place in July 1880. Though there was a week of feasting, dancing and celebrations at Netallie Station, he and Constance did not go on a honeymoon but instead headed straight back to Mount Murchison, to the demands of running a station in hard country. Plorn told Rusden in a letter that he was in receipt of £300 a year for running Mount Murchison and thus he would have no difficulty in supporting a wife. He had moved to a new house, the old homestead, spacious enough for a woman to put her mark on it.

Now Momba and Mount Murchison were bought by the South Australian firm Elder, Smith & Company, and Mount Murchison was absorbed into Momba. It became a property bigger than Ireland, 2 million acres carrying 190 000 sheep. But Yanda, Plorn's leasehold, was not flourishing. His partner, Hatton, who managed Yanda and to whom Plorn and his wife were now heading, complained of the drought and wished them a happy trip on their way to him 'and a wet one'. Pastoralists in that area did what they could to retain the yearly rain, building dams and high mounds to stave off the wind, planting trees and covering the tanks with water weeds to protect them from the sun. But the evaporation was furious, and only 9 to 12 inches fell on the plain around. There would be three straight years in which only 7 inches of rain fell. Magwitch had not made his fortune in country like this—he had been transported early enough to find the pasture lands further in. But the Dickens boys were struggling to survive on the edges of desert.

SOCIAL BANDITS

At the other end of the pole of social aspirations and pastoral dreams lay the bushranger, generally a selector of land, or a selector's son. Bushranging had begun with absconding convicts such as Martin Cash in Tasmania and bold Jack Donohue in New South Wales. But in the second half of the nineteenth century it was influenced by the movement of gold around the countryside from regions not yet serviced by railways and, above all, despite the land laws—by land discontent and a dark sense of rancour towards the law and the squatter. Children of small settlers who grew up before land acts in communities where former convicts were plentiful and where the attitudes of dispossession associated with both convicts and the Irish seemed to form an amalgam of resentment, often took to bushranging or supported the concept.

The high standing of the bushranger in popular imagination has been, despite the disapproval of authorities, enduring. Ned Kelly remains fabled, where the man who condemned him to death, Redmond Barry, despite being a great Victorian in both senses of the word, despite his statue outside the State Library of Victoria, despite being one of the creators and Chancellor of Melbourne University, despite his brilliance as judge and classicist, despite his being bravely loyal to a long-term partner named Mrs Barrow, despite his being a defender of Aborigines, is unknown in popular legend. Even the students who pass Redmond Barry Hall at Melbourne University are probably ignorant of his record. Search the streets of the cities and one finds statues of forgotten monarchs and unspecified colonial politicians, and scarcely a marker to bushrangers. Glenrowan, scene of the last stand of the Kelly Gang, goes unmarked and unexplained by anyone other than local entrepreneurs. Yet the bushrangers' monuments have existed since their day and until now in the Australian imagination. When the bullet-ridden corpse of Ben Hall was buried in Forbes in 1865, respectable girls and women attended the gravesite, on the grounds of his gallantry to those he held up or detained as temporary prisoners, though they were secretly attracted by his glamour and daring. They were not alone in that.

The bushrangers got all the popular ballads too.

> *Oh come all you Lachlan men, and a sorrowful tale I'll tell*
> *Concerned of a hero bold who through misfortune fell.*
> *His name it was Ben Hall, a man of good renown*
> *Who was hunted from his station and like a dog shot down.*

In the 1860s remoter rural areas such as the Fish River district between Goulburn and Bathurst had a high number of ex-convicts, predominantly Irish Catholics, illegally occupying small holdings and having little contact with people beyond their district. Here an Irish farmer named Coffee was arrested in 1864 for receiving part of the ransom paid to the Gilbert–Hall gang for the life of the captured gold commissioner, Henry Keightley. A dispirited policeman named H. Master reported that it was impossible to get information on bushranger movements out of people like Coffee in the bush, not because of fear of the miscreants but because 'the population in this District would sooner screen the Bushrangers than put the police on their tracks, and I have no hesitation in saying that one half of the inhabitants of the Burromee and Fish Rivers does harbour and assist them at times'. A local magistrate in the wild Wollombi district, hunting William White, alias Yellow Billy, the part-Aboriginal bushranger who flourished between 1863–66, declared, 'Nearly every settler . . . is a sympathiser with this vagabond.' As well as that, these were men who, as the *Sydney Morning Herald* put it, 'Rode like centaurs and ran like kangaroos'. The police had to use black trackers to get anywhere in a landscape that was familiar to the bushranger.

Ben Hall, most renowned of all 1860s bushrangers, was born at Breeza Station, west of Tamworth in New South Wales, on 8 March 1838, his father a convict from Bristol, his mother one from Dublin. The family settled on the Hunter. According to the morality of many hand-to-mouth smallholder former convicts and immigrants, cattle, sheep and horse theft was no sin. Cattle duffing and gully-raking for wandered livestock were in some cases a prelude to bushranging. There were many small landholders who boasted that they never ate their own meat, and indeed butchering a neighbour's cow was tolerated by the owner as long as large numbers of livestock were not slaughtered. Horse stealing was a very important activity to the flash sons of small farmers. Young bushrangers knew every horse in their district, and who owned them. The native-born bushranger Frederick Ward, also known as Captain Moonlight, was shot dead while trying out a horse at Kentucky Creek near Uralla in the New England area of New South Wales. Sometimes bushrangers borrowed horses and tack from their supporters in the bush population. Ben Hall walked with a limp as a result of a friend trying to set a broken leg for him, but on a good horse he was lightning.

When New South Wales established a new centralised police force in 1862 it was modelled along the lines of the British and Irish constabularies, and staffed by men from both these forces. Fear of corruption meant that those who had served in the old New South Wales police forces were given no encouragement to join the new one. Though corruption was avoided, valuable knowledge of rural areas was squandered. Telegraph stations were too far apart, police weaponry was inferior and the centralised nature of the force required any officer pursuing bushrangers to report first to Sydney. To deal with the outlaws, if they were brave enough, the bush policemen rode the cheapest horses the government could acquire, on which they had no chance of capturing the bush-crafty renegade on his stolen thoroughbred. The law's reach was so poor that in December 1864 Ben Hall threatened that he and his accomplice, Johnny Gilbert, could capture the attorney-general, James Martin, and an Anglican archbishop, both of whom were travelling in the vicinity at the time. Hall said he was 'quite amused at the thought of making the Attorney-General his humble and obedient servant'. Nothing came of the plan, and indeed Hall and Gilbert were soon to be dead, but the bush, which the bushrangers knew and the attorney-general did not, made such threats plausible.

Under the reign of bushrangers, there were periods of lawlessness when central government seemed at peril. The mails on the southern roads beyond Goulburn were stopped and plundered day after day, locals complained. The roads around Mudgee and Bathurst were almost as dangerous, and the police seemed helpless to prevent crime or to detect offenders.

The Empire newspaper wrote in 1864 that it was no exaggeration to say 'that a large portion of the South-Western and Western Districts of the interior of this colony has been under the control of robbers rather than the Government'. In October 1863 Ben Hall's gang went into Bathurst one Saturday night, bought oranges, visited a gun shop and took over the public house. There was no intervention by the police. With John Gilbert, Hall held up the town of

Canowindra, some 50 miles (85 kilometres) west of Bathurst, for three days. They offered hospitality in a pub, in what does appear to be a benign sort of hostage taking, at Robertson's Hotel; stopping each dray and team that passed through town, they lodged and fed the passengers and supplied them with drink free of charge. Townspeople who wanted to move about the town were given signed passes by Ben Hall. It was this power and stylishness that resonated with the sons of small selectors. The *Herald* even suggested that the solution would need to be a treaty between the government and the bushranger, as disgraceful a thing as that would be for a British territory; under an arrangement, travellers in the bush could pay a sort of toll to the bush bandits. The fight was unequal both in material and mythic terms.

It was on the road from Binalong to Goulburn, where the Halls were taking horses of sundry origins for sale, that Ben first met the bushranger Frank Gardiner, alias Christie, a charismatic scoundrel of Scots descent. It is harder to attach the social bandit label to Gardiner. One could make a stronger case for his being, even in his own mind, a criminal and nothing more, but he had a certain way about him. He had already served a sentence at Cockatoo Island for horse theft before getting a ticket of leave. Later, in the early 1860s, the young Ben would link up with Gardiner in one of the famous Royal Mail gold escort raids.

Ben had never intended to become a bushranger. He settled on his own small station outside Forbes while managing a larger one which belonged to a squatter, Hamilton. He had met a young woman, Bridget Walsh, who, according to fellow bushranger John Bradshaw, was a disgrace to her sex, a curse to her husband, a woman more vicious than the Empress Messalina. While Ben was away mustering, she left him, taking their infant son with her, to run away with a man named Taylor. Her departure, together with the financial stress of keeping a small farm going in the Weddin Mountains, and then the burning of his homestead by the police, are said to have turned the genial Hall into a professional bushranger in a colony where great unpoliceable stretches of track existed.

Hall's native hills were placed in the midst of a series of gold-mining and pastoral towns—30 miles (50 kilometres) from Forbes, 40 miles (60 kilometres) from Lambing Flat, and only 15 miles (25 kilometres) from Grenfell. All portable wealth which travelled these roads was, by the authority of his whimsy and sense of grievance, potentially forfeit to him. So he began to fulfil the bushranger destiny whose phases were, in the imaginations of people in the bush, as definite as the phases of the Stations of the Cross, and which all ended at Golgotha.

*

The hold-up of the Eugowra gold escort in April 1862 was an extraordinary feat of bushranging, the hold-up par excellence. The location was a steep gully where the coach had to both slow and pass a rock outcrop. The bushrangers—including Ben Hall, Frank Gardiner and John Gilbert, a Canadian-born expert horseman and model of boldness—persuaded some bullockies to block the road with their wagons and to pretend to be drunk or sleeping. At the appearance of the bandits, the horses bolted and the coach turned on its side, the driver and four police fled for the bush, one of the police being shot in the testicles. A fabulous £14 000 in gold and bank notes were taken.

The association between Ben Hall and Gilbert was informal—any attempt to see bushranger gangs as a fixed set is not viable even in the case of Ned Kelly. But Gilbert was with Hall in the hold-up of the entire town of Bathurst, in the raid on Canowindra, and the kidnapping of Gold Commissioner Henry Keightley, who had shot the young bushranger Mickey Burke at his property, Dunn's Plains. An undaunted Mrs Keightley rode alone through perilous territory to her father's property to get the £500 ransom.

In November 1864, while holding up the Gundagai–Yass mail with Hall, Gilbert killed Sergeant Parry, and then burned down a store in revenge for an attempt by one Morris, the proprietor, to hunt them down. Social banditry was starting to get bloody. In all, between 2 February 1862 and 10 April 1865, Gilbert had a part in at least forty-four armed hold-ups in New South Wales, including the theft of five racehorses. Outlawed under the Felons Apprehension Act, Gilbert was shot by Constable John Bright on 13 May, and buried in the police paddock in Binalong. Hall had earlier been shot dead in a police ambush near Forbes.

Yet, once again, the bushranger triumphed at the level of legend. The respectable Sydney solicitor and journalist Banjo Paterson, who first heard of Gilbert's death as a child in the bush school at Illalong near Yass, would write:

There's never a stone at the sleeper's head,
There's never a fence beside,
And the wandering stock on the grave may tread
Unnoticed and undenied;
But the smallest child on the Watershed
Can tell you how Gilbert died.

*

There were bushrangers who, by their savagery, attracted no songs, no curious maidens.

John and Thomas Clarke were, like Ned and Ben, the children of an emancipist father in the Braidwood district. Clarke senior's lease was a small holding in hilly, scrubby country—probably about 40 or 50 acres. He was a seller of sly grog and a cattle thief. He had never forgiven a nearby pastoralist who had not renewed an earlier and better lease he held, and for twenty years until his death in prison in 1866 (on a charge of murdering an Aborigine) he would school his sons in stealing livestock from the man responsible. It was perhaps a good year for him to die, in that it was also the year of the Registration of Brands Act which made cattle duffing a much harder trade.

In 1864 his relatives had organised Thomas Clarke's escape from Braidwood gaol where he was awaiting trial for stock theft. He took to the bush imbued with the characteristic hatred of the establishment and the police. With various members of his clan, he held up mail coaches and post offices and shot dead a constable, Miles O'Grady. His brother joined him in 1866. Henry Parkes appointed special police to hunt down the Clarkes but they were called off for being ineffectual. He then created what would now be called a task force of four special police led by a gaol warden named John Carroll. In 1866 that party, walking along a bush track, was surrounded by the Clarkes and were all shot dead with far greater ruthlessness than Ned Kelly would show in his later tragic showdown with the Victorian police at Stringybark Creek in 1878. Parkes now poured police into the area, and the horrifying repute of the Clarkes was not improved by the fact that the opportunistic Frank Gardiner used the name 'Clarke' and introduced himself as such to some of his victims. The founder of Presbyterianism in Australia, that turbulent and wonderful citizen John Dunmore Lang, would show how even for killers of police like the Clarkes there was a public sympathy, and some romance still attached to them. Held up by the Clarkes while travelling in a coach near Goulburn, Lang created a public controversy by saying he was not molested by the young men and could understand the attraction of such a life to them.

An inquiry into the crisis represented by bushranging was held and it was discovered that magistrates were not brave enough to send them to trial, many squatters collaborated with them to save their properties from raids, and the Irish of the ex-convict and small landholder class were their protectors. The authorities of course won in the end. Led by an expert bushman, Senior Constable William Wright, and a black tracker named Sir Watkin, the Clarkes were captured in April 1867, and despite the defence by the eloquent Irish lawyer and politician Bede Dalley, they were both hanged in Darlinghurst gaol in June.

The young man whom some named Mad Dog Morgan or 'the travellers' friend', the latter name attaching to his treatment of ordinary travellers not large pastoralists, had operated on both sides of the Murray and had raided stations whose owners had a reputation for severity. At Burrumbuttock Station he made the owner write out cheques totalling £400 for the station employees. He was an energetic ambusher of coaches, where he behaved with the same sort of gallantry as his contemporary Ben Hall. But his volatility and mental instability, and two murders he was guilty of (in 'fair fights' he would have said), explained the nickname which would attach to him in bushranging history. In 1865 he crossed to Victoria to work above the King River, and a station owner named George Rutherford and five station hands were able to ambush him and shoot him dead.

It might be from the treatment of his body that the awe for the bushranging phenomenon can be judged. Hair was cut from his head and beard as souvenirs, and after his body was displayed in Wangaratta, his head was removed and sent to Melbourne University. There were rumours lasting to this day that his scrotum was fashioned into a tobacco pouch.

CULLIN-LA-RINGO

In October 1861 a victim of frontier warfare, the highly entrepreneurial Victorian landowner Horatio Wills, son of a convict transported for life for highway robbery, lay dead and badly hacked with eighteen other European corpses in the tall grass of a run named Cullin-La-Ringo, near the present town of Springsure, inland from Rockhampton. The Kairi people had killed Wills and his stockmen and their families. This party had travelled for three months by ship and then overland to reach these natural pastures. It was a notable case of a worthy from the south expanding his interests into the fresh pastures of Queensland, but it set a tone for relations, black and white, in north Queensland.

Horatio Wills had been born in Sydney in 1811 and was at the height of his powers by 1860. From the 1830s onwards, after a period in which he edited his stepfather George Howe's renowned *Sydney Gazette*, he had shown a capacity to move cattle and sheep over great distances. In the 1840s he had taken up a run of just under 125 000 acres in western Victoria, a property he named Lexington. Horatio experimented with breeding and with wheat, and Lexington became a model station. After he sold it and took up residence near Geelong on a smaller property named Bellevue, he was able to travel, live graciously and educate his sons in England and Germany.

In the Western District of Victoria inland from Portland, where Horatio Wills had established Lexington, the squatters, including Wills himself, had been concerned by the Aborigines and their attacks on shepherds and settlers. Augustus Robinson, the famous Protector of Aborigines, had listed Horatio Wills as having shot a number of Aborigines. On the other hand, Horatio would have argued he got on well with the non-predatory Aborigines who lived close to his homestead, and fed them rations twice a day. Rations were a form of peace-making, and for the natives a pleasant break from the arduous work of hunting and the gathering and grinding of seeds. This combination of Christian charity to nearby genial and non-combative natives contrasted with feelings towards abominable Aboriginal raiders who struck from a distance away.

The large pastoral stations once available by squatting and then by lease in Western Victoria were by 1860 hard to come by, but inland Queensland offered the same promise the Western District once had. In 1860 Horatio Wills had taken over the lease of four blocks, each of 16 000 acres, the whole going by the title Cullin-La-Ringo. The previous owner, Peter Macdonald, had become so short of rations on one of his sweeps of the country that he tried to survive by eating tadpoles and drinking the blood of emus. But Wills had the resources of capital to ensure he was never himself in that situation.

In January 1861 he left his wife behind at Bellevue and set off with his son Thomas and a group of his stockmen, wagon drivers, shepherds and servants, along with their wives and children, by ship to Brisbane, where they would buy livestock and drove it to the station. By taking his son Tom on this journey Horatio hoped he would be able to introduce him to a more serious world of frontier business, since the convivial twenty-five-year-old, whom his father had taken the trouble to educate at Rugby School in England, had until now pursued no career except as a sportsman, playing in intercolonial cricket matches where he had a reputation as an intimidating bowler. Twenty months before the Cullin-la-Ringo massacre, he had helped codify for his cricket club a most remarkable code of football.

In early February the party set off from Brisbane, with five bullock wagons, part of whose space was taken up by the wives and families of the men, and moved over the coastal range to the Darling Downs where Horatio assembled a herd of ten thousand sheep. From here it was a 600 mile journey on rationed food, but the native-born Australians and the peasant immigrants who now populated the continent were rugged people used to short commons. They reached Rockhampton in seven weeks, and then turned west.

At the time Horatio Wills' party turned inland from Rockhampton, Lieutenant Powell of the Native Mounted Police had recently been through the region of Cullin-La-Ringo with George Dalrymple, former Sri Lanka coffee planter and now Commissioner for Lands. The pair had made unrecorded punitive raids on the Aborigines. By the time the Wills party arrived, both sides were committed to ferocity and, on the Aboriginal side, to vengeance.

The people who settled central and northern Queensland, the Territory and Western Australia possessed an acquisitive and martial spirit. They were not timid folk. But the splendidly built natives of Queensland had convictions about the landscape and their right to it as much as any grazier. Being human, they were not above attacking pastoral or mining parties for the goods on their wagons as well as from outrage at their unthinking trespass. As distinct from the defence of their livestock and homesteads, the frontier settlers already saw punitive excursions as a necessity, and any native raids on Europeans as nothing more than treachery. They also were appalled at the softer attitudes of people in more settled regions along the coast and in Brisbane, who argued that Aboriginal attacks arose from earlier deadly Native Mounted Police and posse-based raids on their own people.

It was into this hostile atmosphere that confident Horatio Wills rode, ignoring his son's advice about being watchful, his suggestion that they broach the cases of arms and distribute weapons amongst the men of the party. Now, from Wills' campsite on Cullin-La-Ringo, in between flat-topped hills, as the men set to cutting slabs of wood for a new series of huts, Horatio had the heady experience of seeing his grassland stretching away without apparent limit. Horatio—or, more correctly, whatever overseer he intended to leave here when all was set up—would live the same sort of harsh life that the squatters had lived in the 1830s in New South Wales and Victoria. Perhaps he hoped that Tom Wills, the arrant sportsman and intercolonial cricketer, might take on that job.

The Aborigines could be heard in the bush shouting to each other but Horatio was not concerned. Seven days after arriving at Cullin-La-Ringo, he ordered Tom to take two empty drays and two men to Albinia Downs Station 50 miles (80 kilometres) south for a load of supplies. The journey to and from Albinia Downs took a full week. As Tom and his drays returned and neared the proposed homestead site at Cullin-La-Ringo, the stench of corpses drifted out to meet them. Riding nearer he found scattered the victims of retaliatory slaughter—nineteen dead, including his father. It was clear the dead had been taken by surprise. Women still had sewing in their hands. They had not been violated. The cook was by his fire, the children by their mothers. Three of the men had been erecting a tent at the time of the attack. The warm spring weather now made burial imperative—Horatio in his own grave and the others in a mass grave.

This would prove to be the largest massacre of settlers on the frontier. It would be used to justify untold slaughter of natives. Occurring early in the settlement of the region, its impact on future contact between the races was enormous even if it cannot be exactly measured. There was a belief that the attack was motivated purely by greed rather than as a form of resistance to invasion, and it is true, since Aborigines are not different from other humans, that desire for plunder was a factor. Blankets, crockery, tools of all kinds, knives and clothing had been taken, and some thought all this property had been too clearly displayed and had tempted the Aborigines.

There was a tendency to blame Horatio for his lack of prudence. But even so, to edgy men on a perilous frontier the massacre was an act of war. Punitive expeditions, one of them assembled by the station owner Jesse Gregson, set off almost at once. Daniel Cameron on Planet Downs Station wrote disapprovingly, 'Bloodshed, terror and anarchy, retaliation and revenge will be quick and sharp . . . the innocent and guilty alike will disappear.' Another contemporary source, F.H. Grundy, declared 'the greatest punitive expedition in pioneering history gathered in force from points north, east, south and west. Hundreds of blacks were slaughtered.' It is not mentioned whether Tom Wills rode with any of these parties. His brother wrote from Germany to ask him: 'Were you one of the eight who attacked the blacks' camp the Tuesday after it happened?'

Peter Macdonald, former occupier of Cullin-La-Ringo, convened a meeting to form a second posse to hunt down the attackers and add to Gregson's first reprisal raid. Tom's godly sister, Emily, would write from Victoria to her young brothers in Germany that 300 blacks, 'gins and all', had been slaughtered. Tom certainly expressed anger with anyone who recorded that they had come across a group of Aborigines and not exacted revenge. Charles Dutton of Bauhinia Downs felt sorry for the Aborigines' destiny as fair game, but was attacked by Tom in a letter to the colonial secretary. Tom felt the most savage war had been waged against him and his family. But his attitude was reflected too in others who were miles from the disaster.

Meanwhile, Tom's first and most pressing need was to find a knowledgeable man to help him at Cullin-La-Ringo. He would honour his father by giving up cricket and running the place. He had a hard time recruiting stockmen to this accursed and vulnerable place. By November, some Queensland papers, as if the massacre had provided a sporting windfall, suggested that since Tom was now in Queensland he might be recruited for the state team.

There was another aspect to the Aborigines of the frontier though. They made fine stockmen and readily took to the horse as an extra dimension to the skills they already possessed of reading country, identifying tracks and silent pursuit. Oscar de Satgé was another Rugby Old Boy drawn to the pastoral life. With his brother, he drove livestock from Melbourne to Queensland's Darling Downs, crossing rivers and open pasture. Even in drought it was a delight to Satgé to scout for water in billabongs along the Lachlan looking for somewhere for the cattle and/or sheep to take their once-in-thirty-six-hour drink. In this he used Aboriginal stockmen. And later, on his property on the Darling Downs, he would say, 'I sometimes thought the black boys could see through a ridge,' when it came to sighting wild horses and tracking them to where they could be surrounded and mustered into the homestead yards.

Satgé, having taken up a property at Peak Downs in the Central Highlands, heard the news of the Cullin-La-Ringo slaughter after one of his own black drovers met a group of fleeing Aborigines with blankets, moleskin trousers and blue shirts. He came to consider the revenge expeditions of Patten, Gregson, McIntosh and others regrettable in scope, and the arrival of a detachment of the Native Police under Lieutenant Love led to a further tracking down and thorough punishment of the Aborigines within a 100-mile radius of the massacre. Horatio Wills had always argued that after long experience in Victoria, he was prepared to civilise and make use of the Aborigines, and had made friends with them from the start. 'Poor Wills,' wrote Satgé, 'paid the penalty of his kindness and over-confidence.' Satgé said that he interpreted the lesson of Cullin-La-Ringo to be never to have blacks 'in'—that is, within reach of the homestead.

The realities of bush life ultimately defeated Tom Wills. Given his failures of competence, the trustees of the company his father had founded to oversee the affairs of Cullin-La-Ringo removed him from its management in 1864. Travels from Queensland to Melbourne to take part in interstate games or intercolonial games of cricket had in any case distanced him from the management of the place.

THE ABOMINABLE CRIME

One of the motives for putting an end to transportation had been the knowledge that a penal life involved the likelihood of sodomy. When the young Benedictine priest William Ullathorne heard the confessions of Irish convicts condemned to death after an uprising on Norfolk Island, he is said to have been so shocked that, balancing a fear of revealing the secrets of the confessional with his outrage, he published an 1838 pamphlet, *The Horrors of Transportation Briefly Unfolded to the People*, in which he decried the unnatural acts the convict system drove men to.

In nineteenth-century Australia, as in the rest of the English-speaking world, sodomy—'the abominable act of buggery'—was a capital offence. In the imaginations of many members of the heterosexual majority, it was also associated with men dressing as women for depraved purposes. In the theatres of the colonies and for the purposes of vaudeville men frequently dressed as women. That was then, as it had been for many centuries, one of the staples of popular entertainment. But it was not acceptable or legal unless done in fun.

In 1863 a police constable in Fitzroy apprehended what appeared to be a woman talking to a man on a corner. The woman took off when the policeman approached but was run down after a block and a half. At the police station the apparent woman confessed to being a man, John Wilson. His offence of dressing as a woman for apparently sinister purposes attracted a charge of vagrancy, but Wilson gave the policeman a key to a house which he shared with a man named Moody who would be locked out if the key was not passed to him. The police took the key to the premises and inspected them. Inside they found there was only one bedroom, and a search turned up some pornographic photographs of men. Within hours Wilson was charged with sodomy, and thus faced the possibility of the gallows, the first non-convict to be in that situation for that crime.

It took some months for the authorities to gather depositions from a number of men who had had sex with Wilson as paying clients—these men were granted immunity so that they could testify that they had paid Wilson for fellatio, but under the sincere belief that he was a woman. The trial took place before Sir William Stawell, Chief Justice of the Supreme Court, and on his being found guilty, Wilson was condemned to death. After some weeks the sentence was commuted to life. Wilson was very unfortunate in the timing of his supposed crime. In 1861, under the Crimes Against the Person Act in the United Kingdom, the death penalty for sodomy was abolished and substituted by ten years' imprisonment. But it was not until 1864, the year after Wilson faced his judge, that Victoria passed the Criminal Law and Practice Act. This Act still prescribed the death penalty for persons convicted of the abominable crime either with a person under the age of fourteen, or 'with violence and without consent'. But otherwise the maximum sentence was fifteen years, no bagatelle from a Victorian life span, especially since it might involve flogging as well, but better than the whole of life. A tragic figure, Wilson wasted and died after serving six years in Pentridge Prison.

No similar legal severity existed in the case of lesbianism. While Wilson was being charged and condemned, a young woman from Adelaide named Anne Jones, who had worn male attire for five years, claiming that she had begun the practice 'as a frolic', was not further investigated. When a man named Jorgenson died in Elmore in Melbourne in 1893 he was found to be a woman. The newspapers claimed he had done service in the Victorian Mounted Rifles and had tried for some time to find a wife, despite facial damage caused by a kick from a horse. The public reaction to the Jorgenson story—her real name being Joanna— and her attempts to marry a young woman seemed to create public amusement rather than the sort of moral outrage which Chief Justice Stawell expressed against Wilson. Lesbianism had never had the press, judicial attention, the condemnations from pulpits and public forums, that male homosexuality attracted.

Another much later case of a woman masquerading as a man with the apparent purpose of same-sex marriage was that of Harcourt Payne, who in 1939 collapsed in the street in Lidcombe in New South Wales. He was taken to the Lidcombe Old Men's State Hospital. When he was bathed he was found to be a woman. Immediately he was dressed as a woman and transferred by ambulance to a nearby psychiatric hospital. His real name was Annie Payne and he had been twice married and widowed. Harriet, his first wife, had known of his gender when they were servants in Newcastle, working in houses across the road from each other. Harcourt was married to Harriet for seventeen years, and his second wife, Louisa, for ten.

The universal enforcement of the various colonial enactments adopted from Britain controlling homosexuality was generally ineffective. Between 1871 and 1900 only 356 men were arrested in Victoria for 'unnatural offences', a class of crime which included bestiality as well as homosexuality. Homosexual men frequenting 'beats'—such as parks and beaches—were generally charged with loitering or offensive behaviour and appeared before magistrates. Despite the statute against it, paedophilia did not seem to preoccupy the law as did sodomy. For example, when James McFadden, a station manager at Beechworth, attempted to have sex with his thirteen-year-old male cook while out droving, he was charged with assault with intent to commit sodomy, not with sexually assaulting a minor.

One reason law enforcement often subjected homosexual men to warnings and misdemeanour charges was in part an attempt to draw public attention away from the existence of gays. The question of whether there was a self-aware homosexual community in the big cities and towns, and how early in Australian history, is debated. In the 1860s and 1870s there still existed in Australia an imbalance between the sexes, and many itinerant former convicts were accustomed to homosexual sex from their experience of imprisonment. The extent to which they were 'committedly gay', as the modern phrase has it, is a mere surmise.

CHAPTER 2
Taking further shape
1860s to 1870s

THE SQUATTER GRANDEE

It would not be until the mid-1870s that the price of wool declined. The graziers of the 1870s pushed out into saltbush and mulga country, trying to increase production. The mulga was a desert form of acacia, a robust tree good for campfires and making fences, but its very name became synonymous with infertile and remote places. Settlement pressed unviably forward in New South Wales and Queensland in the 1860s and into the desert regions of South Australia in the 1870s.

While the fleece was golden, the squatters were flush and enthused enough to employ architects and craftsmen the gold rushes had brought to Australia to build country houses which mimicked those found in the English countryside. Horatio Wills' Lexington was one. In remoter Queensland, the slab timber house made of bark and branches, all pegged down with lengths of timber, was still the characteristic homestead, but such rough materials would no longer suffice for the grandees of Victoria and New South Wales. The old shacks of the early years had gone hand in hand with casual sexual associations—the companionship of the convict or ex-convict servant woman or the Aborigine had been good enough then. There had been exceptions. William Adams Brodribb had brought his wife Eliza Matilda Kennedy to Coolringdon station near Cooma in 1844, and nine years later John Kennedy had married Brodribb's sister Lavinia. These wives bore, at least for a considerable part of their marriage, elementary food served on a slab of bark amidst the din of Aboriginal marital arguments from beyond the door. Add to their woes the severe seasons, the mutton-fat smokiness, the uninhibited clouds of insects, the earthen floors, the bushfires, the dust storms, the loneliness, the lack of entertainment and the dearth of medical attention for themselves and their young children. These old days are evoked by the song 'The Squatter's Warning':

> Dwell not with me,
> Dwell not with me . . .
> Our dwelling place a hut would be,
> Half shaded by a blackbutt-tree.
> Aah, then you'd mourn the soft woodbine,
> Which round your lattice now doth twine . . .

But by the 1860s these old features of the squatter's life were giving way to elevated architecture and comforts. He could marry now at an age he chose and did not need to endure a long celibacy. The Married Women's Property Act of Victoria in 1870 probably found its way through the conservative Legislative Council because it enabled squatters' wives to acquire their share of their parents' land and add it to the holdings of their husbands.

Sir Samuel Wilson, a Northern Irishman, married Jeannie Campbell, daughter of another wealthy squatter. During the gold rushes, he had brought supplies by bullock team to the gold diggings, and the miners knew him as 'Bullocky Sam'. His later photographic portrait in the suit, buttoned britches, long hose and buckled shoes of his knighthood, his sword clasped by the blade diagonally in his gloved hand, has nothing of the bullocky about it. Wilson came to acquire many squatting properties in the Wimmera, to which he added many more in other parts of Victoria and at Yanco in New South Wales. He had the characteristic land obsession of the Irish and would acquire eighteen stations by the end of his life. In 1874 he would endow the University of Melbourne with £30 000 to build Wilson Hall.

Charles Ebden of Carlsruhe in Victoria earned the nickname 'The Count' because he refused to talk to any except the most important visitors to his property and consigned the rest to a slab cottage or the workers' quarters. Robert Barton, an overseer on Gurley Station near Moree, New South Wales, found that the owner's wife and her sister were determined to exclude him from the dining room by not setting a place for him at the table. Barton determinedly went on fetching his own cutlery from the kitchen, but ultimately he had to eat in the kitchen along with the 'colonial experiencers', the young men sent by their families in Britain to gain experience of Australian stations.

Rachel Henning on Exmoor Station in Queensland required men to dress in suits when sitting in the parlour. White employees ate in the kitchen, black stockmen and servants on a bench outside the back door. She did not mix with any of the local farmers for fear they would borrow tools, horses or oxen, and become unduly sociable.

Barwon Park near Winchelsea, south-west of Melbourne, built in 1869–71 by the pastoralist Thomas Austin, who would introduce the hardy rabbits which would infest Australia for the rest of its history, was an extraordinary pile. Austin's wife, Elizabeth, had been mortified by her sister-in-law's grand house and had been ashamed to receive the Duke of Edinburgh in her own homestead, which she considered of inferior quality, when he was visiting Victoria in 1867. The result of her ambition was a massive bluestone house with forty large rooms, an entrance hall and a staircase. Her husband died, but Elizabeth lived in the palazzo for forty years and finally endowed the Austin Hospital in Melbourne. The central staircase of Barwon Park is worthy of an ascent by any duke, and its columns, mouldings and balustrades are of a quality fit for the grandest British house.

Werribee Park was a similar house near Melbourne, built by the squatter Thomas Chermside, son of an East Lothian farmer. While still showing the rough edges of his earlier squatting life, Chermside, a bachelor, built a mansion containing sixty rooms in two wings. The old bark homestead was permitted to stand on in the grounds as a reminder of humbler origins.

In 1874 Sir William Clarke, in his sixties, a Van Diemen's Land settler who then moved his operations into the Port Phillip region, built a mansion named Rupertswood near Sunbury. He had a private railway platform built to receive house guests arriving by rail.

At Birksgate near Adelaide, Thomas Elder, a Scot who would create one of the biggest wool-buying and-selling companies in the world, and who bred camels for transportation in the hinterland of Australia and shipped in Afghans to manage them, acquired the mansion of Birksgate near Glen Osmond and installed his own gas plant to light up the house and conservatory. On the grounds he stocked a zoo and built a tower from which he could signal to yachts racing on Gulf St Vincent. He was also a massive endower of the University of Adelaide.

Bonthorambo in northern Victoria was a particularly fine house with a tower, owned by Joseph Docker, a minister of religion and former rector of

St Matthew's in Windsor, New South Wales. He had crossed the Murray in 1838 looking for land, and had shown some sympathies for the native inhabitants. He occupied the splendid house built in 1864 for only one year before his death.

OTHER PASTORAL ORPHANS

What Elder and Docker were, Alfred d'Orsay Tennyson Dickens wanted to become. While at remote Corona, Alfred Dickens was host to an expedition which had been surveying the exact boundary between New South Wales and South Australia. They were astonished to find in this harsh, stony country the son of the famed novelist. But now he had opportunities he did not have before his father's death. He had received £7000 as his share of his father's inheritance. Dickens had expressed the hope that each boy would use the money from his will to become 'proprietors'. By 1872 Alfred had taken up a property further east, Wangagong near Forbes in New South Wales.

But it was a year of drought, and in such a time money evaporated. Nearby, in the same hard season, Anthony Trollope was visiting his son on his property, Mortray, and declared that, 'I never knew a man work with more persistent honesty.' Trollope himself had invested some thousands into Frederic's property, but just before his visit to Australia, the New Zealand Loan and Mercantile Company took the property over and employed Frederic as the manager.

Alfred, having lost a great part of his inheritance in western New South Wales, went to Melbourne to take up a job with the London and Australian Agency Corporation Limited in their wool warehouses and office in Collins Street. He became engaged to Augusta Jessie Devlin, the daughter of a master mariner. They were married at St John's Church of England in Toorak on 13 March 1873. Alfred gave his occupation as 'gentleman'. He told his relatives that his wife was 'beautiful and accomplished'.

Misfortune struck again, but he could barely be blamed for his next disaster—the company he worked for went bankrupt itself. Drought had snuffed them out too. It was as if the country kept saying, *Drought!*, but people did not quite believe it. In 1874, as part of his new work—acting secretary to the Deniliquin and Moama Railway in New South Wales, though still domiciled in Melbourne—Alfred came to the Western District of Victoria, and Hamilton in particular. There he made such an impression as a good fellow that they selected him as a member of their cricket team to play a neighbouring town. By January 1874 he was in partnership with Robert Bree as a stock and station agent of Hamilton, within energising sight of mountains named the Grampians. Clearly intending to settle permanently in Hamilton, Alfred bought a nine-room house and furnished it in a way which must have impressed his neighbours. He and Jessie possessed oil paintings, Wedgwood statuettes and a piano. There were stables, an underground watertank and a pony carriage in which his wife went driving. Jessie gave birth to two girls, members of the group immigrants called 'natives'.

Was this the Australian success his father had imagined? Had Alfred become safe from the bullyings of Australian seasons? He pursued the Dickens' passion for cricket as a member of the Hamilton Cricket XI and secretary of the Cricket Association. He also joined the racing club and the whist club. He attended balls and civic events. Then, in 1878, Jessie was thrown from her pony cart and killed. There was grief for Alfred. A young townswoman named Polly McLellan moved in to the Dickens' house as housekeeper, an event which would have been considered by some as faintly improper.

The year after his wife's death, the partnership with Bree was dissolved and Alfred d'Orsay Tennyson Dickens returned to Melbourne to work in his own right as a stock and station commissioner and a general financial agent. With Yanda sold to pay debts, Plorn also came to Melbourne and they ran the company as partners, though, for reasons unknown, the company bore Plorn's name alone—E.B.L. Dickens and Company.

THE DUKE, LOYALISM AND PISTOLS

Prince Alfred, Duke of Edinburgh, the second son of Queen Victoria, was just twenty-four when he visited Australia in the ship he commanded, HMS *Galatea*. After bypassing a disgruntled Western Australia, he reached Adelaide at the end of October 1867. To his own mind he was just a young man looking for a good time, but in the mind of the parliaments and populists he was an embodiment of that Crown which stood at the apex of all Australian law, civic piety and even land use. In Melbourne his visit was attended by a riot, or more accurately an Orange Protestant versus Irish Republican brawl, but the prince was not distracted by sectarian fury amongst the lower classes. It was possible for gentlemen to be entertained by a better class of prostitute in the private boxes in theatres, and Prince Alfred was accommodated by one nicknamed Psyche, a famous woman of the demimonde. It was also rumoured that Police Commissioner Standish introduced him to an establishment in Lonsdale Street.

In Sydney a royal charity picnic, open to the public, was to be held at Clontarf—a delightful beach Sydneysiders could reach by ferry—on 12 March 1868. The name may have seemed symbolic to some of the more passionate Irish since Clontarf was the site of the medieval Irish king Brian Boru's final battle against the Norsemen and the place of his death. Amongst the public who crossed to Sydney's Clontarf by ferry that day was a young mentally deranged man named Henry O'Farrell, a self-appointed Fenian—not a member of the official organisation. He carried two weapons, a Smith & Wesson and a Colt, concealed in his clothing. Most of the rest of the Irish community, remembering the famine, remained behind in Sydney, murmuring about the event's perceived silliness and mocking the lickspittles who had gone.

At Clontarf, O'Farrell manoeuvred himself behind the prince and the Governor of New South Wales, Lord Belmore, a liberal-minded Irish landowner who like many of his class took colonial jobs as a way of partly financing their encumbered estates back in Ireland. The bullet O'Farrell fired entered to the right of the prince's spine and lodged in the flesh on the right side of the chest. O'Farrell was wrestled to the ground, yelling, 'I'm a Fenian—God save Ireland!'

The prince was taken back to Sydney, the bullet was removed from the chest—according to some without his taking anaesthetic—and the wound pronounced non-fatal. Young and robust Prince Alfred would recover, later giving his seal of approval to the founding of two hospitals, one in Sydney, one in Melbourne, in his name.

When questioned by the police O'Farrell told them that he had been authorised by the international organisation of Fenians to kill Prince Alfred, a statement which created hysteria amongst some loyalists—though not with Lord Belmore, who could see O'Farrell was mad. O'Farrell withdrew the statement on the eve of his execution at Darlinghurst gaol, but many throughout Australia believed his original statement and chose further to believe that he represented in his actions the desires of all Irish Catholics.

Sir Henry Parkes, Attorney-General of New South Wales, was a competent stoker of the frenzy. He even let a convicted confidence man out of gaol to go into the bush, to such places as Grenfell, and track down Fenian cells amongst the Irish. It was believed too that Fenian cells were working on the state railways. Lord Belmore warned Parkes of the dangers of provoking sectarianism, but Parkes had found hysteria too useful a political asset. Even in the police force Irishmen were under suspicion and any item of reported pub gossip was likely to attract an energetic investigation. Throughout all the colonies, many Irish Catholics were immediately sacked, creating generations of bitterness. A Bellevue Hill milkman who had said the prince deserved punishment for being a philanderer was investigated by all the forces of the law.

Prince Alfred would marry a daughter of the Russian Tsar and live until 1900. On both sides of the sectarian divide, the bitterness would last longer.

SECTARIAN VITUPERATION

After Catholic bishops from all over the world voted in the Vatican Council of 1869–70 to acknowledge the sovereignty and infallibility of the Pope in matters of faith and morals, the Irish Catholics of Australia accepted the dogma without much fuss. In America, there had been many bishops who believed that the final arbiter of faith and morals was a council of the church's bishops meeting under the aegis of the Pope, rather than the authority of the Pope alone, but this position was outvoted in the Council. The future Catholic Archbishop of Sydney, scholarly, austere Patrick Francis Moran, had attended the Vatican Council as a proxy for an Irish bishop, and he had no doubt about papal infallibility and, after his appointment to Sydney in 1884, vigorously espoused it. Like most Irish church leaders of his generation, he had been educated not in France, like the priests who took part in the Irish uprising of 1798, but in the Irish College of Rome, where the centrality of the papacy was everywhere accepted and visible.

The tendency of the majority to see the Catholic Australians as utterly Pope- and priest-ridden was enhanced by the newly defined doctrine. Ordinary Catholics sometimes thought that any directive from Rome was binding, and that any bishop seeming to speak for Rome could utter binding judgments covering the whole of life. But the irony was that far from intending his primacy as a tool to make Irish Catholics disobey civil power, Pope Pius IX and his followers wanted them, for the sake of good relations with Britain, to be less politically engaged in the Irish question, the question of Irish independence. The Vatican wanted, for diplomacy's sake, the Irish to exhibit loyalty to Crown and Empire.

A Catholic colonial politician like the eloquent and prodigiously gifted Gavan Duffy abominated the Vatican's interference in Irish politics and in Irish nationalist causes espoused in America, Canada and Australia. Monsignor Barnabo of the Vatican had written from Rome forbidding priests in County Meath from attending anti-landlord Tenant League meetings without the Archbishop of

Dublin's express permission. Duffy wrote of this, 'The Lord God be thanked I am living amongst Irish Catholics [in Victoria] who would go to the stake, rather than deny their faith, but who would sling that insolent missive into the Yarra Yarra. It makes my blood boil to think of a peasant in a mitre, a shallow, conceited dogmatist, a dense mass of prejudice and ignorance, squatting down upon the Irish cause and smothering it.'

These subtleties were lost on the mainstream, who having mistrusted papists earlier now had an added prejudice—in a contest between civil authority and the Vatican, who would the Irish obey?

A CHILDHOOD IN THE CITY

Alfred Deakin was born of English immigrant parents in George Street, Fitzroy, in August 1856, a year after an entirely different species of Australian, the son of a convict, was delivered of his mother Ellen Kelly in a hut in Avenel, and less than two years after Eureka. It was a characteristic of the 1860s and 1870s that one child might live a life appropriate to that of a significant British city and all its enriching institutions, while another might still be a product of slab huts and hessian sack beds, of land and livestock hunger (and theft), and frontier hardship. The childhoods of Alfred Deakin and Ned Kelly might have been lived in parallel universes. In a different sense than in previous decades, Australian life had become diverse. The city intellectual, not utterly lacking before in the person of the soon-to-die (1865) orator, writer and child of convict Daniel Deniehy, and in his friend the cultivated Scottish lawyer and booklover Nicol Stenhouse, now became a more numerous breed. So did the angry sons and daughters of small selectors.

Alfred's father William was a partner in a cab, coach and dray business, which was taken over in 1857 by a syndicate led by a young American, James Ruther-ford. The company secured a monopoly on mail delivery and would come to be known as Cobb and Co. But despite the romance which attaches to that name, the evocations of gold escorts and bush banditry, the Deakins were genuine Melbourne suburbanites, and Deakin's young life was that of any British boy growing up in a British provincial city. Though blasts from the direction of Antarctica gave a grim bite to his winters, and the ferocious breath of the desert descended on him in summer and ringed the civic enthusiasm of the citizens with bushfires, the growing Deakin saw himself not as remotely placed on earth, but as the citizen of a great city of Empire.

When Alfred was six the family moved to South Yarra and lived in what might be called 'frugal comfort' by biographers. In the cottage in South Yarra he was towelled by the fire after his bath and presented by his father with books to enrich the intensity of his imagination. He and his older sister Catherine were sent out to Kyneton 50 miles (80 kilometres) from Melbourne to attend a little boarding school run by two sisters, the Misses Thompson. The Misses Thompsons' establishment seems to have been more a well-regulated country holiday house than one of those fierce rural schools the young Deakin would read about in English children's literature. The Misses Thompson in any case soon transferred their school to South Yarra.

To a stricter teacher he would have seemed talkative and a little distracted—in modern times his behaviour might even have carried a psychiatric tag. But all such flaws of concentration then were considered to arise from the devil's influence, and when for the first time in his life he was clapped around the ears by a male teacher, his parents removed him to a nearby school, one within walking distance, the Melbourne Church of England Grammar School.

The city in which Melbourne Grammar was an estimable institution had reached a population of 140 000, such a population comparing notably with that of many major provincial cities in the United Kingdom and the United States. It was a city too which had a university, libraries, theatres and all the facilities appropriate to a community anywhere on earth possessing ambitions to be notable.

The school was, of course, like similar ones founded by Presbyterians, Methodists and the Jesuits, a version of Rugby, Eton, Harrow and Winchester. But instead of holding a quotient of the offspring of hereditary peerages and earldoms, it had sons of squatters, of city merchants much wealthier than the Deakins, and of aspiring (though not rich) families like Alfred's. The staff of such colonial schools were generally graduates of the major British universities: Oxford, Cambridge, Edinburgh or Trinity College, Dublin. An assumption might have been made that these men were rejects from the British public school system but that would have been unjust to many of them, and to none more so than the headmaster, the Reverend John Edward Bromby, who had once competed for the Cambridge Chancellors' Medal—as William Charles Wentworth had also done in his youth—against Alfred, Lord Tennyson. He had been recruited while working for his father, a vicar in Hull, but he had earlier been a young headmaster in Bristol and at a private school in Guernsey, and had been University Preacher at Cambridge. He had arrived in golden Melbourne in 1858. Since his manner was never vicious, his sense of humour was advanced, his learning carried lightly, and his cane rarely plied, he was beloved by Deakin as by most of his students. Deakin, a gifted verbal thumbnail sketcher, later said of him that he was 'breezy, humorous, prompt, passionate and impressive'. He would give boys informal instruction while he chopped wood with them.

Deakin would later regret that he had been too concerned with adventure books and had left his interest in Latin and Greek too late. But a younger teacher, J.H. Thompson, an athlete and a scholar, gradually turned Deakin into 'a passable student'. There had been apparently some doubt, not least in his own mind, as to whether he would attempt to try to matriculate for entry into the University of Melbourne. But then a forceful boy, one who had quarrelled with his headmaster at another school, turned up as a classmate of Deakin's. Theodore Fink was the son of a Jewish family who had emigrated from Guernsey and who were merchants in Melbourne. Fink was tall and full of vivacity, and chose to respect only those teachers who had intellectual gifts. Deakin said later that through meeting and conversing with the precocious, happy, mature Fink, he ceased to be a wandering imagination and became a person. And so he passed the matriculation exam in 1871, algebra, Euclid (geometry) and history being the subjects in which he shone. Surprisingly— given his eloquence as a politician—English and Latin were not amongst the subjects at which he excelled.

MAKING GAMES

Tom Wills, son of the massacred Horatio, arrived back in Melbourne, having first created confusion by promising New South Wales that he would play for them in their next intercolonial. But in Melbourne he disavowed the undertaking. The game in the new year of 1863 was, as usual for Sydney intercolonial matches, played in the Domain. Ill feeling was expected, and in fact there was great bitterness between the teams and great complaints about bowling and umpiring. Whatever the rancour, cricket was sucking Tom back to the southeast of Australia.

Around 1860, the cricket clubs of Melbourne (the MCC), Richmond, St Kilda and Corio (Geelong) were well-established entities with both gentlemen (players who played for nothing) and professionals (paid players). The paid players were eternal schoolboys without inherited wealth and eventually, despite his father's success, Tom Wills would have to become a professional. Cricket at Rugby had involved underarm or round-arm bowling, with the arm not to rise above the shoulder. The young Tom Wills was a ruthless round-arm bowler in intercolonial cricket and was accused of being a thrower and of raising his arm above the shoulder, and of displaying visible joy when he struck a batsman on the body. In one intercolonial match, 'the Hobart crowd observed with distaste Tom jump about exultantly when the cricket ball hit the batsman'.

But he is remembered for more than his version of bodyline bowling. A letter Tom Wills wrote to the magazine *Bell's Life* in early winter 1858 suggested that now cricket had been put aside for the season, rather than allow 'this state of torpor to creep over them, and stifle their new supple limbs', the Melbourne Cricket Club should form a football club and appoint a committee of three or more to draw up a code of laws.

There was already football in Australia, of course, both uncodified versions and ancient ones. Various witnesses in the west of Victoria had seen the Aborigines there playing a form of football with a ball made out of tightly rolled plant roots. Did Tom see the game as a child and, if so, did it contribute to the new game? That is, is Australian Rules millennia-old, or simply a post-gold rush phenomenon, a creation of the sporting fever which kept step with other Melbourne enthusiasms in the Golden Age? Irish Australians often assume that the game derived from the then chaotic Gaelic football, which was not codified until 1880, but which in its essence resembled the Melbourne game. But none of the men who devised the first rules had an Irish background, and Gaelic football may have been simply a parallel tendency of sportive humanity.

In any case, advertisements for an initial and experimental game appeared in the *Argus* and *Herald*, and on Saturday 7 August 1858 on Richmond Paddock, by the Melbourne Cricket Ground, the first game was played under uncertain laws but roughly on the pattern of football which would increasingly capture the passions of the southern and western regions of Australia from that day on. The first game of the new as-yet uncodified form was primal, contested by forty Scotch College boys against the same number of Melbourne Church of England Grammar boys. Tom Wills was one of the umpires. The game was robust and much 'rabbiting' occurred (the bringing down of an opposition player running with the ball by bending down in front of him). The game lasted three hours and ended in a score of one goal each.

On the night 17 May 1859, Tom and four other enthusiasts from the Melbourne Cricket Club met at the Parade Hotel on Wellington Parade, up the hill from the Melbourne Cricket Club. During games there had been by now too many fist fights about rules, and nose-breaking and limb-fracturing confrontations. The men who joined Wills at the Parade were themselves interesting. Newspaper man William Hammersley, Oxford-educated and a cricket fanatic, had first played against Tom Wills during a cricket match when the latter played for the Gentlemen of Kent against the Gentlemen of Surrey at the Oval three years before. Hammersley would later flay Tom in the press, in part because of an unfairly afflicted injury Hammersley suffered from Tom's play in a football game. But tonight the two men were of one purpose. So was another attendee, Thomas Henry Smith, the classics master at Scotch College. James Thompson, the sporting editor of the *Argus*, was the fourth member of the party. He too was English-born and studied at Cambridge University. Thus only one of the four men was a native-born Australian, and either meritoriously or not, in part because of his earlier letter to the newspaper, it was Wills' name which would always be honoured with initiating of one of the earliest codifications of any game on earth.

Wills advised against a slavish imitation of the game then known as Rugby, but to work out 'a game of our own'. Ten rules were established. Some of them are irrelevant to today's game but all of them were aimed at preventing chicanery and violence, and promoting fluidity. There were arguments about the taking of penalty goals—Tom desired that the best kicker be given them (as at Rugby), but the others disagreed. The mark, at least in its modern codified form, was sanctioned in rule six that night. Wills wanted an ovoid ball, Thompson a soccer ball.

During a Richmond and Melbourne game two weeks later, in which Wills captained Richmond and Thompson led Melbourne, Wills made it a condition that the ovoid ball be used. Thompson would write in the *Argus*: 'Another drawback to an otherwise almost perfect afternoon's enjoyment was the objectionable shape of the ball.' There was an argument, too, about a cross bar being placed between the goals. Thus, barely more than three and a half years after the battle of the Eureka Stockade and some three years before Cullin-La-Ringo, Tom helped or—according to many—led the process of codifying a game which, to the new and massively ambitious city, would become its divine frolic, its identifying mark, its focus of civic cohesion between native and newcomer, between Irish minority and British majority, and its map of the world.

FIRST TOURERS

By 1865, when he captained Victoria and scored a then unprecedented 58 runs against the New South Welshmen on the Melbourne Cricket Ground, Tom Wills was at the peak of his authority, having walloped a team which included two All-England players, one of them the Sydney sporting man and cigar parlour owner Charles Lawrence. It did not seem to trouble Tom the cricketer that it was his brothers Cedric and Edgar who were left with the running of haunted Cullin-La-Ringo for the trustees.

The Melbourne Cricket Club passed a motion in January 1866 which raised the possibility of bringing an Aboriginal team to the Melbourne Cricket Ground to play against the Melbourne club. The event would be a splendid fundraiser and, for some of the chief promoters, profitable. Tom Wills, though in theory a gentleman player, was receiving payment in kind and cash from the Melbourne Cricket Club, and he was certainly offered a worthwhile contract when he was appointed coach of the proposed Aboriginal team.

To recruit his team, Tom left for Lake Wallace, near Edenhope, west of the Grampian Mountains. Tom still thought of the Aborigines of his childhood, the Jardwadjali people of the Djabwurrung language group, as substantially different from the murderous crew who had slaughtered his father. The Aborigines he was to coach were the Jardwadjali whose relatives he had known as a boy. He called in young Aboriginal males for trials and found that a young man named Johnny Mullagh, Oonamurriman, was a fine batsman. The team was to play on the Melbourne Cricket Ground on Boxing Day 1866. Tom would play with them.

They attracted a crowd even when they arrived at the Melbourne Cricket Ground for their first practice. Aborigines had become a rarity in the Melbourne area, and the western Victorian players had novelty value.

It proved to be very important to the Melbourne Cricket Club that, as Britons, they should not be defeated by the Western District's semi-civilised natives, as good as those same cricketers were for the gate takings that day. They stacked their team with players from other clubs, and won by seventy runs, after Mullagh and tall, sturdy Harry Bullocky top-scored for the natives, and the slighter Johnny Cuzens took most of the white wickets. Bullocky was later arrested for drunkenness, but both he and Cuzens were chosen to play for Victoria against the Tasmanians.

A Melbourne entrepreneur of questionable honesty, Captain W.E.B. Gurnett, was now planning to take over the team and bind them to a contract to tour the colonies and England. When the players signed Gurnett's contract on 8 January 1867 their Aboriginal and European names were both listed. From this document we learn that Jemmy Tarpot's real name was Murrumgunarriman, that Harry Bullocky's name was Bullenchanack, that Johnny Cuzens' name was

Yellanach and Dick-A-Dick's name was Jungagellmijuke. Wills' name was not on the contract but Gurnett engaged him as coach.

After a series of poorly attended matches in Melbourne and Victorian towns, Captain Gurnett, Tom Wills and the Aborigines left for Sydney by steamer. There they stayed at the Manly hotel of Charles Lawrence, a former English professional who had settled in Sydney. Sadly, the team had been late arriving in Sydney and the grandstands and booths which had been erected in the Domain for the game had had to be taken down. When the game, which was attended by the governor, was finally played against the Albert Cricket Club at Redfern—a strong team, captained by Lawrence—Tom Wills was arrested as he walked onto the ground under a writ brought by those who had suffered economic loss by the cancellation of the Domain event. He would spend a day in gaol before coming to terms by paying £35 to the claimants. During the game at Redfern that day, as was by now the set program, the Aborigines were required not only to play cricket but to give exhibitions of boomerang and spear throwing, and to ward off thrown cricket balls with shields.

Within a day or so Gurnett was arrested on far more serious fraud charges, since the Victorian leg of the tour had left him virtually bankrupt and he had spread bad paper all over the colony. He was imprisoned in Darlinghurst gaol. There had been criticism anyhow, notably by the secretary of the Aboriginal Protection Board, R. Brough Smith, that the whole business was exploitation of innocence. Smith suggested the Victorian government should prohibit the tour planned for New South Wales and Britain. Now the promoter was in gaol, so the tour was off in any case. The team returned to Melbourne with Wills, and thence to their country near Edenhope in the Western District. On the way back to his homeland, Bilayarrimin, also known as Wattie, died in a cart from lung congestion worsened by intoxication.

Meanwhile, the Central Board in Victoria failed to have legislation passed to look to the welfare of Aborigines contracted for tours, so Charles Lawrence travelled to Edenhope to re-recruit the former team and add some newcomers for a tour of Britain. Thus the first major team to represent Australia internationally was made up of old Australians, not settlers. While the settlers looked upon the northern hemisphere as home, for the Western District cricketers the centre was there, west of Mount William, and all else was the increasingly grim outer world.

The team left for England in February 1868 on the *Parramatta*. The base of the team was in Kent, but after their first match at the Oval, attended by

7000 spectators in picnic mood—and which the Australians played with loud enthusiasm, and lost—their journeying became hectic. They travelled on most of their rest days and had little time for practice. In mid-June they played the MCC (Marylebone Cricket Club) at Lord's, the MCC declaring it wanted no athletic feats performed in the intervals. But here too, at public demand, the team was required to participate in shows of native skill. A poster for the game at Trent Bridge in Nottingham shows us what some of these were. There were eleven events in which amateurs could pit themselves against the Aborigines, including feats such as the standing high jump and throwing the cricket ball, at which Dick-A-Dick excelled, just edged out on three occasions by the famous Englishman, W.G. Grace. Mock battles were also fought in which three of the team spear throwers would accurately hem in but miss three others standing nearly 90 yards (about 80 metres) distant. Dick-A-Dick could also parry cricket balls thrown from fifteen to twenty yards away with a narrow native shield.

A conscientious sergeant of police from Edenhope had warned before the team left Victoria that some of them had chest problems. Not long after the Lord's game—during which Yellanach was again the star bowler, taking ten wickets in the MCC's two innings, including those of an earl and a viscount—King Cole (Bripumyarrumin) died of tuberculosis at Guy's Hospital in London and was buried at the Victoria Park cemetery. The impact of this on the other players is not recorded, but their fear of the naming of the dead, and of what damage a disgruntled spirit far from home might wreak, must have been intense.

After their ten games in the south of England, of which they won only one, they moved northwards, beginning to achieve success as they went, winning fourteen matches, losing an equal number and drawing nineteen. They were sensitive to racial slurs and Mullagh, after being insulted at York, played sullenly. When less discontented, he and Cuzens, together with their white captain, Lawrence, were the best bowlers and batsmen. Cuzens' score of 87 at Norwich was typical of his skill. At Reading, Mullagh scored 94, in an age when centuries were rare.

The players returned home on two ships which left England in October. On their arrival in Australia in February 1869, they played one of their final matches against a combined team from the sailors of Prince Alfred's HMS *Galatea* and the Victorian garrison. The prince, recuperating from being wounded by an Irishman in Sydney, himself attended. Even as they played that game, the Protection Board was in the midst of founding four reserves for Aborigines, including one named Flamlington near Warrnambool, which was meant to contain the Jardwadjali players and their clansfolk.

Mullagh and Cuzens returned to their home country after playing for the Melbourne Cricket Club and tried not to be gathered into the reserve. Mullagh would play for Victoria in 1879 against Lord Harris's touring English XI. He became a rabbit-trapper and died a respected man in 1891. Other Aborigines disliked the new reserves, and Hugh McLeod of Benayeo and A.A. Cowell of Brippick Station permitted groups to live on their properties and supplied them largely from their own pockets. The former members of the cricket team, Peter (Arrahmunyarrimun) and Tiger, lived on these stations. Dick-A-Dick, who also played professional cricket in Melbourne, eventually returned to Mount Elgin Station and worked as a drover. He would ultimately be awarded a 'king-plate'—a gorget for wearing round the neck—which proclaimed him to be King Billy. (Kingship was of course a concept unfamiliar to Aboriginal culture.) He adopted the name Kennedy after the Edenhope police constable who had helped him since his boyhood.

OVERLAND TELEGRAPH

The Northern Territory was the preserve of South Australia until 1910. In 1870 the South Australian government sent a party to the north coast by ship to select a port for a settlement. The port named Palmerston near Escape Cliffs was created with a small staff of administrators, six officials and thirty-eight men under the management of Dr J.S. Millner. A less-than-gifted South Australian official named Captain William Bloomfield Douglas soon took over as permanent Government Resident and hoped to become a local satrap in the manner of his grand relative, Sir James Brook, who had ruled as the white Rajah of Sarawak. By his lordly manner Bloomfield alienated all the Darwin officials he had to deal with, and by his financial incompetence lost favour in Adelaide.

The local Larakia tribe, who had encountered Europeans earlier through a party led by the South Australian surveyor George Goyder, looked upon the settlement with curiosity and were attracted and pacified by gifts of food and axes. Axes transformed a man from a warrior of stone to a warrior of iron, and as everywhere else created immediately a temporary elite of hatchet-men, at least until everyone acquired one. Flour was a deliverance from the time-devouring business of harvesting and pounding native grasses. It must have seemed a miraculous 'convenience food'. It was the Woolna people further to the east who would prove, in European terms, intractable and 'mischievous'. But for most of the perhaps 50 000 natives of the Territory, the European intrusion was for the moment too minuscule to make a dent in their lives. An overland telegraph would be the beginning of change, however.

The small, vigorous, stubborn English astronomer and telegraphic expert Charles Todd had come to South Australia in 1855 to build the telegraph lines throughout that colony, having been nominated for the job by his superior, the astronomer royal, Sir George Airy. Even in the late 1850s, Todd, still in his early thirties, began to plan for a telegraph connection between South Australia and Melbourne and Sydney. Todd had also created a series of meteorological stations in South Australia, which began operating in the early 1860s. He made friends with the Victorian Superintendent of Electric Telegraphs, Samuel McGowan, and together they persuaded South Australia and Victoria to finance a line laid down under Morse's system. The British themselves were recommending telegraph connection to Australia—it had already been established between England and India, and it could be extended south to Singapore and the Dutch East Indies. A sea cable could be laid around the east coast of Brisbane then, and thence a land line to Sydney. Todd, who showed great skill when it came to dealing with decision makers, assessed all these plans. But John McDouall Stuart's crossing of the continent in 1862 made Todd think of a telegraph overland all the way from Adelaide to the northern coastline of Australia.

Early in 1870 the British Australian Telegraph Company, which was laying cable from its ships in the seas north of Australia, sought permission from the Premier of South Australia, Henry Bull Templar Strangways, to land the line at the barely peopled little port of Palmerston, and Strangways decided that an overland line should be built from Adelaide to meet it. For this task Todd—now Postmaster-General as well as Superintendent of Telegraphs—needed more survey time than the politics of the situation and the urgency of the British Australian Telegraph Company would permit him. He had to fall back on the maps and documents of Stuart's expedition.

He divided the work of creating the line into three sections, the southern and northern being let out to contractors under the supervision of Todd's overseers, and the central to be done by government labour under his direct management. The Aborigines through whose land the line passed looked at it with some interest but did not seem to see it as representing the same scale of intrusion new pastoral stations had. Occasionally they set fire to the poles, since they were good sources of fuel in a land of mere undergrowth, and the porcelain conductors looked fascinating. The repeater stations, placed every 180–300 miles (300–500 kilometres) to on-forward messages down the line, were now built with materials available in the region (often of stone) and staffed by telegraphists. The telegraph was completed in 1872 and for the first time created an expensive but as good as immediate communication with Europe.

The repeater stations along the line began to change native life by serving as bases for gold prospectors and pastoralists—as was the case at Pine Creek, where a gold rush began almost simultaneously with the building of the Pine Creek repeater station. Other repeater stations to pass the communications of Australian businesses and governments northwards to the greater world were based at Tennant Creek and Alice Springs to the south, where further settlement gathered.

GOYDER AND ALL THAT

To emphasise the matter of dryness and the limitations it placed on colonial expectations, in South Australia young surveyor George Goyder adjusted to what had been found, and what had not been, and in 1865 drew a line across the southern reaches of the colony, in substance following the 10 inch isohyets beyond which less than 25 centimetres of rain fell a year. North of the line was country where the droughts had already destroyed many prospective settlers and where no one could expect to grow cereals or pursue other agriculture. In the mid-1870s, when South Australia experienced higher than average rainfall, settlement extended over Goyder's Line, and the South Australian government helped farmers to settle nearly as far north as Lake Eyre, the great salt lake many considered the abomination of desolation at Australia's heart. Whenever the lake was flooded it fed rivers, including the Georgina, the Diamantina and the Cooper. But in bad times, the validity of Goyder's Line became tragically apparent to all.

It was thought that artesian water would be the answer to the Australian reality. Artesian wells, which had been first dug in Artois in northern France, tapped water lying beneath the earth, often between layers of impermeable rock. In 1879 Ralph Tate, professor of palaeontology from Adelaide University, travelled to Lake Eyre and found water gushing from hummocks. This was artesian water, closer to the surface here because this was the western outer rim of a huge saucer, the Great Artesian Basin, most of it lying beneath Queensland but also beneath parts of the Northern Territory, South Australia and New South Wales. The other side of the saucer on whose rim Tate stood lay on the western side of the Great Dividing Range in Queensland. The basin would prove to contain over 650 000 square miles (1.7 million square kilometres) of submerged water. So there might be no desolation at all—the much-needed living water ran beneath the rock!

At this stage a pair of Vandemonian brothers, Charles and Suetonius Officer, were running cattle at Killara near Bourke, close to the centre of the Great Artesian Basin. When in 1878 their cattle trampled down a mound spring and reduced it to a morass, the manager David Brown used a mechanical rig to drill 1800-feet (550-metre) bores. One of them spouted up 13 000 gallons (58 000 litres) per day. Near another mound spring Brown sank a second bore and hit water at less than 20 feet (6 metres).

Stockmen on neighbouring country taken over by the technically minded cattle king Samuel McCaughey also struck water. In that same year, the Victorian government began to drill in the Western District. The news that there was artesian water beneath the ground provided the Australian pastoral and agricultural imagination with a subterranean Mississippi, a redemptive lake. God had veiled the true promise of Australia and destroyed the unwise, but now promise was revealed. In Queensland, in the drought of the early 1880s, the government began to build tanks and dams on the stock routes throughout the bush, with government engineers sinking wells in such places as Winton, a town that was barely self-sufficient in water. Simon Fraser, grandfather of the twentieth-century politician Malcolm Fraser, had been running cattle in Queensland since the 1860s and did not consider the conserving of water to be entirely the government's responsibility. He had heard of artesian finds from his brother-in-law and he engaged a Canadian well borer named J.S. Loughead to drill on his company's Thurulgoona Station, 50 kilometres from Cunnamulla. Loughead's machinery could drill nearly 1600 metres into the earth. In the summer of 1886 he discovered a submerged reservoir of water at just under 520 metres and from it came 2.1 million litres per day. Loughead drilled similar deep bores at Barcaldine in January 1888 and at Blackall. Grazing could now be extended into country that had previously proved untenable, and squatters poured into the Artesian Basin country in Queensland, New South Wales and South Australia. By the early 1900s, when there were 1500 bores, some of the disadvantages became apparent. So much drilling released pressure in the hidden water and flows became more modest.

Though artesian water extended pastoral possibilities, and allowed cattle to degrade an even larger part of the surface of remoter Australia with their hard hoofs, it did not make the wilderness bloom and did not generate cities. Artesian water also meant that more Aborigines, accomplished in living in arid regions kept safe from intrusion by their very dryness, were now driven off land they had thought till now they securely possessed.

THE ASIAN SOUTH AND NORTH

North or south, the Asian miner attracted rancour. One of the many grievances white miners had against the Chinese is that they did not participate in the struggle for miners' rights. It was true that there had been no Chinese miners at Eureka, though the question arises as to whether they would have been welcomed into the rebel ranks. The first wide-spread outbreak against the Chinese had occurred in 1861 at Lambing Flat, the future town of Young, where 13 000 diggers had gathered. Two thousand Chinese joined the Europeans and were described by the Lambing Flat paper as a 'swarm of Mongolian locusts'. After a large meeting at which there was a great deal of inflammatory rhetoric, the miners from Tipperary Gully marched into Lambing Flat, collecting men as they went, and then moved on towards Victoria Hill where the Chinese were working. The physical harm to the Chinese was not as extreme as the oratory which preceded the riot, but it did involve the riding down of Chinese and whipping them. Their tents were burned, however, and much of their gold, dredged by great labours, was plundered.

At Back Creek 500 more Chinese were attacked. The bank clerk Preshaw in Kiandra wrote of a white woman married to a Chinaman who was 'maltreated by the mob'; her child narrowly escaped death when miners set fire to the infant's cradle. According to the *Sydney Morning Herald*, some attackers cut off Chinese pigtails 'with the scalp attached'.

On 14 July 1861 a party of constables arrested three of the rioters, whereupon 3000 miners marched on the police camp with guns and sticks. One white miner was killed in the attack and others were wounded when a detachment of mounted troopers charged the mob with drawn swords, forcing them to flee, some of them bleeding from wounds to their faces and heads. The fury this created amongst the miners and the risk of retaliation drove the police and troopers to retreat to Yass to await reinforcements. Soldiers and artillery were sent from Sydney and, arriving on the goldfields, imposed a sullen order. Eleven miners were charged but acquitted by juries who favoured them. The Chinese of the area hid or left for other goldfields, or in many cases took up other occupations, as reapers, shearers, carters of wood and water, tailors, carpenters or hawkers of fish, vegetables and fancy items.

The Yass Chinese merchant Lowe Kong Meng wrote, 'If such a thing had happened in China—if a number of English miners had been subjected to such cruel and wanton outrage—every newspaper in Great Britain would have been aflame with indignation.' The reaction in New South Wales was, however, the passing of the Chinese Immigration Restriction Act of November 1861, which imposed a Chinese residency tax similar to one already in place in Victoria.

Northern Australia was considered an unfit territory for European women, a zone of degeneracy and fever. Metropolitan Australia accepted that but it also harboured a considerable anxiety about what was happening up there and the dangers of tropical Australia becoming 'Mongrelia' and 'Piebald Australia'. On the Great Chain, the external racial challenge was still, above all, the Chinese. The Chinese had arrived in small numbers in Queensland by 1860, at gold diggings at Gympie but further north as well, at Cape River, Crocodile Creek and the Gilbert River. Although by 1870 there were only 2000 Chinese, the Palmer River goldfield near Cooktown would attract 1000 a week during April 1874 and there were 18 000 miners from southern China on the Palmer goldfield alone by the middle of 1877. An anonymous poet in *Queensland Punch* expressed the standard hostility.

> *Though we annoy them as much as we dare*
> *Fair play or foul, they are more than a match for us . . .*
> *They'll be our bosses and we'll grow their cabbages*
> *If they go on the way they've begun.*

In 1874, the South Australian government had entered a contract with the Netherlands India Steam Navigation Company to include Adelaide in their route to China and back a stop in Port Darwin. This created further editorialising and concern. The *Cooktown Courier* declared, 'In a very short time the Great Wall of China will encircle the Palmer, and the "outer barbarian", the unfortunate digger, will have to look for fresh fields.'

An editorial in *Northern Miner* on 26 May 1877 pushed the would-be scientific line. 'Kanakas [indentured Melanesian labourers] and Chinese are distinct types of the genus *Homo*—some would go so far as to deny that they belong to the human family at all. There is no affinity between them and men of the

Caucasian race, and miscegenation of races so physically antagonistic must inevitably degrade the higher race.'

The Ingham Hospital publicly declared that it excluded from its admittance lists:

An African because he is black;

A Malay because he is Asiatic;

A Native of New Caledonia because he is a South Sea Islander.

The Chinese were in Cairns from 1877 when the town started, having moved there from the Palmer River goldfields up the coast. In the hinterland they made up almost half the population in tropical North Queensland. Many of them worked under contract to clear the tropical rainforest on blocks selected by Europeans under the Queensland Land Acts of 1876 and 1884, acts which excluded the Chinese themselves from land ownership. Chinese workers cleared land energetically by a method called 'scarfing', setting up a domino effect in the trees. Once the clearance work was done, they often hired land back and grew plantations of bananas. The Hop Wah plantation was established outside Cairns in 1879 by a syndicate of 100 Chinese. These growers shipped the bananas down to the coast on sampans and then transferred them to junks, which took them into Cairns. About fifteen junks operated in the area of Trinity Bay north of Cairns, where rivers such as the Barron, flowing down from the Atherton Table- lands, entered the sea. The junks themselves were made from cedar logs felled in the rainforest by full-time Chinese boat builders.

The relationship of the Chinese and the Aborigines, involving Aborigines work- ing for Chinese enterprises, led to sexual contact between the Chinese men and Aboriginal women, sometimes resulting in marriage. The Chinese were accused not only of sexual predatoriness but also of providing opium to the European and Aboriginal communities. In a region where opium moved freely from China to Australia, white employers also gave opium to their black workers.

There were a number of Chinese merchants in Cairns by 1890—a hat maker, a jeweller, a watchmaker. The Chinese lived in their own Chinatown around present-day Grafton Street, and if they fell ill were treated in an aliens' ward in the hospitals. The Chinese contributed to local charities and institutions in towns like Innisfail and Cairns. Though there was a ban on Chinese travelling first class on coastal steamers, the rule was ignored for the more prosperous

Chinese. Wealthier Chinese merchants invited Europeans they knew—generally lawyers, bankers, the local newspaper editor, the inspector of Polynesians and so on—to Chinese New Year banquets. A dinner given by Willie Ming and Ah Young in 1897 was attended by all the white worthies of Cairns.

Stories of similar successes abound. Leon Chong was the leading Chinese citizen in Cairns in the 1890s. He was the manager of the Hop Wah plantation and then founded a citrus growing enterprise. Tam Sie was another prodigiously enterprising merchant. The news of Queensland gold reached his village in southern China magnified by its passage over the wires and from mouth to mouth. He came to the Palmer River goldfields in 1876. After a brief time he took a voyage on a junk to New Guinea to collect the shellfish named trepang or bêche-de-mer, a prized Asian delicacy and aphrodisiac. He returned to Cooktown and sold the bêche-de-mer for an excellent return. Sick from some tropical fever, he was lucky to miss out on the junk's next journey, for most of the crew were killed by Papuan villagers. He was involved in various enterprises in the chief gold towns of the interior and in the coastal sugar towns. Colonial Sugar Refinery contracted him to clear land for them and he employed 500 men to do it. In December 1887 he left for China, taking some of his profits but leaving behind £4000 worth of property. Back in his home village, Tam Sie found that 'the lure of Queensland' took him again, and he returned and even grew rice in the Daintree Forest. He entered into partnership with Sun Kwong Key, the chief banana-exporting company, formed a partnership with Innisfail merchants, and then began his own banana-shipping company. He bought real estate in Cairns and experimented with the growing of rubber and cotton in the hinterland.

To the white community, however, the chief threat remained not only to prosperity or wages but to racial purity. If Europeans were the highest form of humanity, any dilution of whiteness was a violation. William Lane, the great Labor leader and editor of Brisbane's *Boomerang*, declared in 1888 that he would rather see his daughter 'dead in her coffin than kissing a black man on the mouth or nursing a little coffee-coloured brat that she was mother to'.

Travelling from Innisfail to Cairns, a *Bulletin* commentator who described himself as 'Bluey' declared he was forced to journey with two 'Chows', a Japanese and six Kanakas. He was horrified to find the port at Cairns full of Chinese sampans selling fruit to the people on the steamer. Cairns was in fact considered a disgraceful town, where white men ate with Chinese, slept with Japanese prostitutes who had been recruited from Nagasaki, and let themselves be outwitted by the Asians. As late as 1941, forty years into the white Commonwealth, the Queensland census showed that 40 per cent of Cairns and nearby Cardwell were still Chinese, Japanese, Manilamen (Filipinos), Sri Lankans and Kanakas.

THE ENNOBLING LAND

To Australians 'the land' bespoke sturdiness and fulfilment and a form of holiness. Immigrants from land-starved northern Europe, particularly peasants and working-class people, were infatuated with the promise of land. While industry debased the soul and injured the body, the land would exalt the soul and invigorate the body. Yet though the fable-making of Australia was so preoccupied with 'the man on the land' and his family, by 1891 more than half of Australia's people were living in the cities. This remained the unarguable truth of Australia despite the intent of the Eureka rebels and progressive law makers in the nineteenth century to 'unlock the land'.

In Victoria, after the fall of the pro-squatter Nicholson government in 1861, a group of reformers led by Richard Heales (a temperance leader slowly dying of tuberculosis) and John Henry Brooke (another Englishman, who was popular for granting annual occupation licences to selectors) won twenty-two of the twenty-seven goldfield seats and were able to form a government. In this government Charles Gavan Duffy, the former Irish rebel so often charged with sedition and tried for it in his own country, but now an urbane member of the Victorian Legislative Assembly, framed a Land Act which became law in 1862. City workers, former miners, shearers and landless labourers could select a minimum 40 acres (just over 16 hectares) of land that was not designated as gold-bearing or did not have stands of red gums. They were required to occupy such land, live on it, put at least 10 per cent of it under crop and build improvements equivalent to £1 ($2) per acre. The annual lease payments were high enough to allow the land to be handed over by the Crown to the selector outright at the end of eight years.

Throughout the bush in New South Wales and Victoria people crowded into the land offices set up by the colonial governments in all the major centres—in Yass in New South Wales, in Hamilton in the Western District. Here the former Scots crofter or factory labourer, the Irish bounty emigrant in whom the appalling land system of his country had induced a ferocious thirst for land, and the English from the Midlands and north and poorer parts of London crowded in, acquiring maps, hungrily eyeing them, getting on horseback to inspect the available lots. How bright futures must have looked then, in the early 1860s, with the land laws passed, and men possessing the franchise. And the residency requirement would surely prevent the squatters from using proxies or dummies. Duffy, always a city dweller himself, whether editing the rebellious *Nation* newspaper in Dublin or shining as an urbane Melburnian, hoped to open up 4 million acres (1.6 million hectares) in the first three months. Ireland could not be reformed. Victoria seemed gloriously reformable.

Most land acts passed in other colonies partook of similar clauses, and were motivated by the same intent as Duffy's. Under later acts, for example, selectors were able to claim land that had not yet been surveyed and thus was not in the squatters' sights, and call for it to be surveyed after they had taken it up. But successive land acts in all the colonies were never able fully to thwart the squatters or, above all, help selectors come to terms with the fierce demands of the selected land. Steele Rudd, selector's son, would give the reader an idea of how hard it was even to clear land in his Dad and Dave stories set on a selection on the Darling Downs in Queensland. When north-east Victoria (or Kelly Country, as it would become) was opened up for selection, three squatting partnerships or families increased their holdings by a total of 210 000 acres through using proxies and moving quickly to claim the best 'unlocked' land. In their minds, they had been the first there, had borne the dangers and discomforts, so why not tie up what interlopers would otherwise take?

Sir Charles Wentworth Dilke, a future British radical politician and visitor to Australia, would write, 'The squatter is the nabob of Melbourne and Sydney, the inexhaustible mine of wealth. He patronises balls, promenade concerts, flower shows, he is the mainstay of the great clubs, the joy of the shopkeepers, the good angel of the hotels; without him the opera could not be kept up, and the Jockey Club would die a natural death.' Dilke found that squatters were quite willing to read about democracy as long as it happened elsewhere. 'Democracy, like Mormonism, would be nothing if found among Frenchman, or people with black faces, but it is at first sight very terrible when it smiles on you from between a pair of rosy Yorkshire cheeks.'

Duffy's successor, the Melbourne solicitor James Grant, had the same experience as Duffy and his good intentions were also frustrated. He guided a law through both houses which gave him administrative power to cancel any suspect selection. Generally amiable, Grant had a weakness for drink that drove him to heights of reckless passion, and perhaps drink as well as conviction had a hand in a speech he gave at Camperdown, Victoria in 1865. As reported by a journalist, he declared 'that he carried a guillotine in his heart—and swore by his Maker that he would cut off the heads of the squatters rather than that they should have the land'.

Jack Robertson, the New South Wales Minister for Lands, was himself a considerable landowner. A large earthy Scot, this aficionado of the profane joke, who was described as drinking, swearing and dressing like a man from the bush, was the leader in the fight for Free Selection in New South Wales. As a tall, red-haired young man he had been an explorer of the Namoi and Darling rivers, and set up as a squatter on the Namoi. Unlike many of his brethren, he realised that the land he leased belonged to the Crown and thus to the community.

In March 1860, all the candidates who openly opposed land reform were defeated in a colonial election and Robertson came to the premiership. This election was considered the end of the old colonial order of things, when former colonial officials and their friends, such as Edward Deas Thomson, Colonial Secretary from the old quasi-autocratic days, and Stuart Donaldson, squatter and friend of squatters, dominated Parliament. Robertson was in his own way an enlightened conservative, however, like so many progressives in the nineteenth century. He believed that if miners in particular did not get land, they 'might become dangerous to the public's safety'.

Robertson would deliberately retire from the premiership in 1861 so that he could further concentrate on getting his land bills through the House. When he could not persuade the Legislative Council to pass them, he resigned from the Assembly so that he could be appointed to the Council and argue the bills through, and persuaded the governor, Sir John Young, to appoint like-minded people to the Council or else his cabinet, still in place, would have to resign. When it seemed that Sir John Young might appoint wild radicals to the Council, nineteen conservatives furiously resigned, and left the Council without a quorum. But the new members were appointed, and the land bills were passed and came into operation in October that year.

Very few of Jack Robertson's supporters understood the complexity of what was going to happen as a result of the bills, which allowed that unsurveyed land could now be selected and bought freehold in 320-acre (130-hectare) lots at £1 per acre on a deposit of 5 shillings per acre, that is, for £80, the balance to be paid within three years on the basis of an interest-free loan of three-quarters of the price. Again, those who acquired the land had to take up residence on it.

*

Queensland introduced selection to pay for the railways it had to build. In this state, too, the normal pieties about the holiness of the land were uttered. The Brisbane *Courier* of 23 March 1872 believed that farmers 'lived nearer God', and the Anglican Archbishop of Brisbane said that a man with a few acres was less likely to turn into a socialist. The best land for selection was on the Darling Downs, where conditions seemed better than in most of that either too-dry or too-tropical colony. The Selection Acts produced a great number of selector families in the region.

The importance of land in the mind of South Australians had the added sanctity of having the old Edward Gibbon Wakefield vision of land settled by godly yeoman added in. In South Australia there had always been a concern in the city that pastoralism would prevent the growing of enough food. But through selection, South Australia became in fact an exporter of wheat to South Africa and England, as well as to other Australian colonies. Henry Strangway was a Somerset man who as a boy had visited an uncle in South Australia and then, having been admitted to the Bar at the Middle Temple in London in 1856, returned to Adelaide in early 1857. His legislation, which was passed in January 1869, provided for the creation of agricultural areas and of purchases on credit of up to 640 acres (259 hectares) with a deposit of 25 per cent and with four years to pay. He was applauded in his colony as the 'St George of Land Reformers', and selectors took up blocks, particularly along the Murray River.

Subsequent history tells how resistant to Strangway's idea South Australia's rainfall and topography were. Into the 1880s, the movement would be further influenced by Wesleyan temperance progressive George Witherage Cotton of the Legislative Council, and by his book *Small Holdings: The Mainstay of Individuals and Nations*. Witherage believed there were still not enough South Australians on the land. He founded a Homestead League which bought up blocks for occupation by settlers. He was backed up by favourable legislation to make it all more possible, but by 1896 only 4 per cent of the state's population, about 13 000 people, were 'block holders', that is, people who had received the Homestead League's loans to start small farms.

ON OUR SELECTION

Henry Lawson, a selector's son from Eurunderee in the Central Ranges of New South Wales, knew something of the reality of selecting, the husband often having to go away droving to supplement income. He wrote of a 'Land where gaunt and haggard women live alone and work like men/Till their husbands gone a-droving will return to them again'.

Another who knew of that reality was the Queenslander Steele Rudd. His true name was Arthur Hoey Davis, his father a Welsh blacksmith and his mother, Mary Green, one of the Irish orphan girls shipped to Australia in the late 1840s from the workhouses of famine-stricken Ireland, in her case from the Tuam workhouse in Galway. Arthur—or Steele Rudd, as he is known to history—was born in 1868 in Stanthorpe, where his father mined for tin. Under the Land Settlement Act the Davises took up a selection of 160 acres north of Toowoomba in country heavily covered by timber. The setting-out of the family for their selection must have been a thousand if not ten thousand times repeated in Australia. 'We came from Stanthorpe on Jerome's dray—eight of us, and all the things—beds, tubs, a bucket, the two old cedar chairs with the pine bottoms and backs that Dad put in them, some pint pots.' The house they built was 'slabbed', with a shingled roof, and was divided into two rooms. 'The floor was earth, but Dad had a mixture of sand and fresh cow dung with which he used to keep it level. About once every month he would put it on; and everyone had to keep outside that day till it was dry . . . [The] slabs were not very close together, we could easily see through them anybody coming on horseback.'

The requirement for secure title to the farm involved improving the land, and thus felling the box and ironbark trees which rose all around the hut. This timber was the reason the land had not been selected earlier. The first objective was to clear some 4 acres and put in corn, but this turned into fierce labour and the trees, once felled, 'lost all their poetry'. When the character Dave (often depicted as a buffoon in standard Australian jokes but taken seriously enough in Rudd's work) asked his father why they 'didn't take up a place on the plain, where there were no trees to grub and plenty of water, Dad would cough as if something was sticking in his throat, and then curse terribly about the squatters and political jobbery'.

In the world according to Rudd, the women laboured like drudges and were afflicted by loneliness, want and fear of losing the place. Concern about money was constant. 'I can remember how Mother, when she was alone, used to sit on a log, where the lane is now, and cry for hours.' If Rudd is writing about his own mother—and why would he not?—he is not depicting some pampered woman, but a woman who had known since childhood nothing but a succession of harshness. Yet selection was nearly too much for her.

Children laboured at blistering work, such as shelling corn. Dad went to the produce merchant to sell it and found the lot, after his bill for food and stores was deducted, was worth £3. 'Dad went home and sat on the block and got depressed. Ultimately he showed the invoice to Mum and she did the same.' So kangaroo stew became the staple. Dad was reduced to roasting a slice of bread on the fire till it was like a coal, then pouring boiling water over it and letting it draw. 'That served as coffee for a time.' At the right time Dan, an older son, turned up with money earned in shearing. Child labour on and outside the farm was so desperately needed by the family that it was remarkable if a child could be spared many years for education. Rudd attended Emu Creek school and, because he was a clever boy, was able to stay till he was twelve.

In Rudd's world, the real world of the Queensland selection, Rudd's family were, like their class, an enduring people. But frequently endurance was not enough. Australia ate people like the Rudds alive. 'You'll ride all over it filled with the proud spirit of ownership,' wrote Rudd, '. . . even the wild flowers and darn stones'll be yours! How you'll admire it all!' But possession of it hung by a thread.

NORTHERN TERRITORY PASTORALE

Patterns of settlement in Northern Australia were unique. Wentworth D'Arcy Uhr had never been a lover of the Aborigine, and an uncle of his had been murdered by natives a year after his birth. While overlanding cattle and horses to meat-hungry and horse-needy Palmerston from Rockhampton in 1872, Uhr and his companions had three clashes with natives, the first near the Territory border west of Bourketown. The next tribe encountered to the west, the Garrwa, were more amenable to the passage of the cattle and horses through their country and did not have to confront the Snider and Westley Richards guns of the party. Passing west into the country of a different tribe, the Yanyuwa, the party kidnapped a black child they named Pilot. This was a common means of recruiting a pliable guide. Further on, the party saw their leading cattle begin to stampede back on them, and on galloping to the front they were attacked with a shower of spears. They retaliated with brisk fire, but even then the natives were not easily persuaded to retire.

Led by Pilot, the party crossed the McArthur River. Here they released the little boy and left him in negotiations with the tribe in whose country he had been dumped, the Wilangarra, who would later become extinct. At Limmen

71

Bight, in the western corner of the Gulf of Carpentaria, the overlanders ran into 130 blacks dressed as if for a ceremonial occasion 'with feathers and down of all kinds of birds tufted on their breasts and all over their bodies', and believed as many settlers did that feathers bespoke hostile intentions. This was a fatal misconception, for the arduously collected feathers were always used for ceremonial purposes. Uhr arranged his companions in pairs, telling each of them to shoot in sequence at his command, so that there were always two rifles ready to fire at any time. The overlanders fired their weapons, which the people of the area were unlikely ever to have seen before. Uhr and the others were surprised that the natives went on throwing spears and boomerangs for a full half-hour despite their brethren 'who writhed or lay forever motionless among them'. Eventually the Aborigines retreated a short distance and turned the points of their spears downwards, surrendering. To deal with the wounds, some of them tore bark from ti-trees for bandages, while others used fragments of broken spear, retrieved from the fire, for splints for shattered limbs.

One of the party, Cox, now rode ahead, and would reach the Overland Telegraph depot near the junction of Hodgson and Roper rivers, near Miniyeri, on 17 August, five days before the telegraph wires from Palmerston (later to become Darwin) to Port Augusta were finally joined up to transform communication between Australia and the world. Uhr's cattle—not many of the horses survived—were sold along the way at the new goldfield near Pine Creek telegraph station, a field to which some prospectors had walked from Charters Towers. After all that damper, the miners were hungry for beef. With what was left of the mob, the first overlanders from Queensland turned north to Palmerston, which was in similar need.

The first permanent pastoralist settlement in Central Australia was not founded until 1876, when Owen Springs and Undoolya south-west of Palmerston were taken up by Irish-born Ned Bagot, who had copper-mining and pastoral interests near Kapunda in South Australia, and who was the contractor who had built the southern section of the Overland Telegraph from Port Augusta to just north of Lake Eyre. In 1877 Glen Helen, named for the niece of the pastoralist Alexander Grant, west of Alice Springs, and Henbury, south of the telegraph station at the Springs, were established. By 1884 there were thirty-two stations in the Territory, although most of them were in the north.

The sturdy Tiwi people of Melville and Bathurst islands resisted every attempt to turn their country into cattle stations. Any whites landing on the islands were prevented from going inland by tall, well-built angry natives. In 1895 Joe and Henry Cooper established a buffalo-hunting camp on Melville Island but Harry was killed by the Tiwi two years later, and Joe was forced to escape to the mainland, taking with him two kidnapped Tiwi women. Five years later he went back to the islands with a group of the warlike Iwaidja people from the Cobourg Peninsula east of Palmerston and set up a permanent camp. He remained the only European resident until the remarkable Father Francis Xavier Gsell set up a mission on nearby Bathurst Island in 1911.

John MacCartney, another of those thrustful Irish-born Protestants, who would own twenty-five stations in Queensland, set up Florida Station in 1892 on the Goyder River in Eastern Arnhem Land under the management of Wentworth D'Arcy Uhr. Not only did the tropical climate prove testing for livestock but Uhr, a tough overlander who strong-armed the local tribes, was forced out by Aboriginal attacks within a year. He wisely took up a hotel at Yam Creek and made a living out of, amongst others, thirsty gold-seekers. Indeed Arnhem Land would prove so unsuitable to the purposes of settlers that it was ultimately returned, freehold, to Aboriginal ownership.

KANAKA DAWN

For sixty years the native races of Polynesia and Melanesia were kidnapped from their homes and then enslaved, murdered, or simply left to their own devices on the edge of the towns and settlements of Australia. There were two periods of Kanaka 'immigration', of plantation labour that cost about sixpence per head per day. The first Kanakas were brought to Australia from 1847 onwards by the New South Wales pastoralist and trader Benjamin Boyd—not without peril, since his first recruiting vessel, the *British Sovereign*, was wrecked and the crew killed by native Melanesians and devoured. Boyd offered the recruited islanders supposed contracts, signed indecipherably by them. Their pay was to be 26 shillings a year plus food and clothing. Boyd kept three of them in Sydney as a walking advertisement which might attract orders from other grandees.

But their work as shepherds in the bush was not successful. They became targets for Aborigines, and if they wandered onto other stations they were driven away and persecuted by white agricultural labourers, who did not want their wages undermined. Many of Boyd's Kanakas absconded anyhow; some even reached Melbourne, others Sydney, where they squatted on the pavement outside Boyd's metropolitan offices and were a negative presence. Ultimately he had to return them home at his own expense. When they got back to the New

Hebrides, the Kanakas discovered that during their absence their wives had been put to death according to custom because they had been presumed dead.

Financially overstretched, Boyd's companies ultimately failed in 1849, after something like an insurance scandal involving damage to his ship the *Seahorse* and the failure of Boyd's Royal Bank. On an expedition to Guadalcanal, he went ashore alone, at his own insistence, and vanished. No trace of him was ever found.

Kanakas (the word means 'human being' in Polynesian language) became fashionable again in the 1860s, when northern Queensland was subject to energetic settlement. Entrepreneurs began to look again to the New Hebrides as a possible source of labour. A lugger, *Don Juan*, arrived in Brisbane in August 1863 with a cargo of sixty-seven Kanakas ordered by Robert Towns, a robust Geordie who had married the half-sister of William Charles Wentworth and who had interests in banking, land and trade. He was exactly the sort of man who was now expanding his interests into both the Darling Downs and those northern regions of Queensland already named to honour the martyred explorer Edmund Kennedy.

In the small city of Brisbane, there was much press and public condemnation of *Don Juan* and Towns. In North America, Gettysburg had been fought in the name of the liberation of black races, and there were clergy and professionals in Brisbane who knew that, and were appalled that Towns was making an opening bid on a new form of slavery. An uneasy Queensland Legislative Assembly ordered Towns to submit to them the written instructions dated 29 July 1863 he had given his 'blackbirding' captains, Grueber and Ross Lewin.

These letters of course emphasised the care the captains and supercargoes (managers of the shipped labourers) were to take to allow the native to make an informed choice, and on general welfare of those shipped. But Ross Lewin was a sadist who had been cashiered from the Royal Navy after the first China war, had worked as a 'slave driver' in the sandalwood trade for Towns, and was troubled by the concept of kindness for South Pacific Islanders. The reality was that only a few of those who sickened on board were returned home, as promised, within the stated period, and the healthy were kept in Queensland for three years or longer. Towns had asked Grueber to make friends of any missionaries he met and to use them to help recruitment. Not quite disarmingly, Towns' circular to be issued to the missionaries read, 'I, with my cotton emigration . . . will do more towards civilising the natives in one year than you can possibly in ten.'

Towns' ships the *Uncle Tom* and the *Black Dog* could carry more than 100 Kanakas and the *Spec* sixty-three. When the Kanakas arrived, Towns sold their labour to other planters but maintained 300 himself on his own cotton plantation on the Darling Downs. Towns ran a nineteenth-century version of a Potemkin village, Townsvale, 40 miles (60 kilometres) from Brisbane, and used it as a model farm for exhibition to the governor, Sir George Bowen, and other influential colonials. After a visit in which Bowen saw well-clothed and well-fed Kanakas attending to duties that did not demand severe labour, Sir George congratulated Towns on a 'splendid example of colonial enterprise'. But not all was splendid.

Ross Lewin was charged at Brisbane Police Court in 1867 with the rape of a girl whom he had dragged aboard his boat at Tanna in the New Hebrides, but there were no white witnesses and the magistrate refused to commit Lewin for trial. When Towns dismissed Lewin in any case, Lewin set up in business for himself and said he would be happy to receive orders for the importation of South Sea natives at £7 a head.

Meanwhile, sugar plantations were proliferating in north Queensland and sought Kanaka labour as well. Captain James Louis Hope, like Towns a member of the Legislative Council of the colony, had been experimenting with the growing of sugar on his property at Cleveland, south of Brisbane, and built a sugar mill in 1864, buying up the labour of fifty-four Kanakas from Towns' schooner *Uncle Tom*. It was Hope who showed how efficiently Kanakas could be made to work on sugar plantations. Shortly after, Hope entered directly into the Kanaka trade himself. He took some of his expired three-year men to Brisbane, where they spent their entire wages on such goods as Jew's harps, grindstones, beads, gunpowder and silk umbrellas to take home. He then purchased a 130-ton schooner and took the men to Tanna. There they showed the goods they had brought back and explained that these could be earned by '39 moons' service in Queensland.

Some masters were conscientious in their treatment of islanders, others behaved more questionably. But the evil was that a plantation aristocracy was emerging. Sometimes wooden buildings were provided for the incoming labour-ers, sometimes the Kanakas were allowed to build their own conical grass or cane huts on the edge of the plantation. In all cases, sanitation and water supply were poor and disease common. Anthony Trollope, who visited Queensland in 1871, wrote that the Kanakas were 'badly fed, and worse cared for. They received nominally ten shillings a month. I say, nominally, because instead of actually getting it, they get a small allowance of tobacco ... and a supply of clothing which they would rather be without.' He observed that their diet consisted chiefly of pumpkins, damaged corn and corncobs, 'and when a bullock was killed they got the head, entrails and other reject parts'.

Nineteen natives employed by George Raff MLA absconded from his plantation early in 1868, complaining they had not been given sufficient food during their twelve-month service. They also alleged ill treatment by George Raff's son, Robert. The party, including a woman, made their way to the Brisbane Immigration Depot and asked to be returned home. Instead, they were brought before the Brisbane Police Court. No interpreter was available. The magistrates ordered the men to return to the plantation. They refused to go, and so were again brought before the magistrates and had their agreements cancelled with the loss of twelve months' wages.

Later in the same year twenty-three Kanakas employed by the Maryborough Sugar Company went on strike, claiming they had been promised a passage home within twelve months. The company relied on the alleged existence of three-year contracts. The men, who had been subsisting on the edge of town by eating grass, were arrested and sentenced by Maryborough justices to seven days' imprisonment.

In at least one case Kanakas supplemented their diet with cannibalism. Charles Eden, a planter—of whose book, *My Wife and I in Queensland*, an English critic declared it was 'enough to warn honest men away from Queensland for some time to come', and who would be accused of libelling Queensland society—employed twenty natives from Tanna and Lava. The Tanna men ate several Aborigines. They also adopted a young boy of the Lava tribe, and one day Eden and his wife were invited to attend a ceremonial feast at which the boy was to be cooked and served up. The Edens adopted the boy instead.

The next legislative councillor to apply himself to the Kanaka trade was Captain Claudius Whish, formerly an officer in the British army serving in Persia, who planted sugarcane on the Caboolture River north of Brisbane in the mid-1860s. While still a member of the Legislative Council, Whish formed the Sugar Planters' Association, which possessed powerful magic in its relations with government. A premier of Queensland, Sir Robert Ramsay Mackenzie—son of a baronet, conservative politician and friend of squatters, as well as an auctioneer and stock and station agent and commission broker in Brisbane—joined a ring of cabinet ministers and members of the Legislative Assembly and Council who chartered the 240-ton *King Oscar*. Mackenzie was exactly the sort of man for whom Queensland was a good place to make money and exercise power but not to settle for good. He had every intention of going back to Scotland rich. The consortium advertised:

> South Sea islanders: The *King Oscar* has arrived, and will be again despatched to the islands without delay. Parties wishing to engage South Sea islanders for employment on stations, plantations, & C, are requested to apply immediately to the agents, FENWICK AND CO.

The group employed Ross Lewin as its recruiting agent. Lewin sailed to the New Hebrides on the *King Oscar*, shot some Islanders who resisted recruitment, burned villages, collected a cargo and sailed back to Queensland, where the Kanakas' services were sold for £9 per head. Thus he and others earned nearly £2500 for a fortnight's work. Missionaries in the islands began sending outraged reports to the Anti-Slavery Society in London.

In the end some 67000 Kanakas would be recruited over nearly forty years. Some of them came on the collier *Syren*. After her captain had unloaded his load of Australian coal at New Caledonia in 1867, he called all hands together and announced that he intended to fill up with a cargo of Kanakas for the return journey. His men invited natives aboard, cut their canoes adrift and then set sail—the Kanakas being now locked up in the hold amidst coal dust-coated walls. Their wives swum after the ship for more than three miles, 'crying loudly for the restoration of their kidnapped husbands'. At a nearby island, natives were invited aboard and their canoes then sunk by gunfire. Of the 110 natives conscripted by the *Syren*, twenty-one died of dysentery before the ship reached Queensland. Earlier in the same year, one of Robert Towns' ships, the *Curlew*, had been attacked and destroyed by natives in the New Hebrides. Three of the crew were killed, in part because the islanders knew Towns had failed to repatriate natives within the three years he had earlier promised.

The Royal Navy was now ordered to deal with the kidnapping and murder of natives. The Admiralty, however, doubted the Royal Navy could end the practice, since it felt it could not interfere with Queensland legislation in the matter, and only one warship could be devoted to the policing action. Captain George Palmer of HMS *Rosario* would write an outraged account, *Kidnapping in the South Seas*, of his patrols in the region.

In March 1869 the *Rosario*, at the orders of Commodore Lambert of the Australia Station of the Royal Navy, made inquiries throughout the South Seas of the kidnapping of natives by vessels flying the British flag. His first stop was New Caledonia. Here he found that French vessels were also kidnapping natives from the New Hebrides or the Gilbert group of islands for work in the colony. The French offered Captain Lambert little aid. They took some vengeance for Australian intrusions by implying that the London Missionary Society was involved in recruiting. 'The truth', wrote Palmer, 'is that the French Government had got the opportunity of returning us tit for tat. We expostulated with them ... a few years ago, and now they return the compliment, and accuse us [the Society] of kidnapping, and we can do nothing but point to the Queensland Labour Act—that very interesting document'. Indeed it was interesting enough to hamstring Palmer and make his work impossible.

The French administration of New Caledonia imposed stringent regulations which did not exist in the case of Queensland. For example, French government agents travelled on board and no natives were, at least according to the rules, to be taken away from their homes except of their free will. On their arrival in Noumea they were inspected by a number of government officials whose job it was to ascertain if the natives were there by their own choice, whether they were in good health and whether they understood the contract read out to them. In Queensland none of these measures were taken.

Palmer found that in the recent past no less than thirteen Australian vessels had been engaged in illegally taking natives from Lifou and Maré in the Loyalty Islands, French-controlled islands north of New Caledonia, and nearly all these vessels were from Sydney though they delivered their cargo of islanders to Queensland. Their documents, when inspected, declared they were picking up cargoes of bêche-de-mer and coconut oil.

A native who Captain George Palmer respected on Tanna in the New Hebrides was the orator Yaufangan, also called the Washerwoman because he organised the washing of the laundry of the officers of various visiting British ships. He told Captain Palmer that he himself had helped procure twenty-four Tanna men for a ship named the *Young Australia*, and they had all agreed to go for one yam season—that is, for one year. Palmer asked him had he ever seen violence done to Tanna people and Yaufangan readily answered yes, he had seen men dragged from the shore, he had seen men hauled up on ships by the hair of their heads, and forced along by musket. He had seen girls kidnapped to be sold in Australia, generally to Kanaka men who wanted wives. During Palmer's conversation with the orator, a man came up and complained that his son had been engaged for one year but had never come home. The more Captain Palmer investigated, the more appalling the news was.

The next island the *Rosario* touched at was Erromango, north of Tanna. Long before blackbirding, the recruitment of natives, by force or inducement, for indentured labour in Australia, it had been the scene of many depredations by sandalwood traders, and its natives had struck back with intermittent murder. It was here a chief told Palmer of the kidnap more recently of ten natives, who were lured aboard a ship with a promise of tobacco. Another ship took five. One captain got nine Erromangans aboard by telling them he could supply them with pigs for a coming feast. And so it went, a regular attrition of small numbers of men. Palmer discovered that not a single native that had been taken from Erromango had ever come back.

Captain Palmer came to despair of Queensland legislators and officials. Many others in Brisbane and other cities were similarly outraged. The Sydney *Empire* wrote, 'The more inquiry into the Polynesian Labour question is prosecuted, the clearer it becomes that nothing less than a species of slavery is intended to be perpetrated by the planters of Queensland.' The Governor of Queensland, Sir George Bowen, son of a Donegal rector and described as 'a good trumpeter' for Queensland, was told by the Colonial Office that the traffic in islanders was one 'in respect of which ... you are under the most serious responsibility'.

The Queensland government was thus forced in 1869 to appoint a Select Committee to inquire into the operations of the Polynesian Labour Act. Six of the seven members appointed either favoured the indenture system or used Kanaka labour themselves. The Methodist preacher William Brookes told the select committee that 'husbands were separated from wives, thousands of children left without their natural protectors, homes desolated, villages ransacked and burned, drunkenness, fraud, and every dishonest artifice employed in order to procure these men who were to add so immensely to our comfort'. The witnesses summoned consisted mainly of planters and government officials, though Robert Short, the Queensland correspondent of the Anti-Slavery Society, was also summoned; his evidence would prove so damning that it was not included in the printed document sent to London.

The committee reported there was no evidence of kidnapping, no abuses during voyages and no complaints received about conditions on the plantations. The members of the committee further ruled the reports of brutality were entirely due to the behaviour of slavers from Noumea and Fiji. Queensland recruiting vessels were 'in nearly all cases humane and kind'. The implication that this was slavery was denied, Captain Palmer lamented, 'and even sleek oily men in sable broadcloth are found to stand forth in defence of the man-stealers'. He quoted an unnamed 'late Governor of Queensland', almost certainly Sir George Bowen, as saying that many of the indentured Kanakas serving in the colony had returned to Queensland after revisiting their homes. But much evil had been done, and would now continue to be done, said Palmer, under the Polynesian Labour Act of 1868.

The Queensland Parliament ultimately amended the Act in 1870 to allow for government agents. The salary offered was just £10 per month and was likely to attract men who were not necessarily accomplished at other trades. It was also enacted that recruiters, as blackbirders were called in the legislation, were to take out a government licence and lodge bonds of £500 to refrain from kidnapping and 10 shillings per recruit to return him to his home within three years. The master of each vessel had also to obtain a certificate from a prominent white man on the island of origin of the recruited native stating that the recruits understood the agreement and consented to it. The planters who purchased islander labour were to keep a register showing the names and condition of all natives employed, reporting any deaths to the local magistrate. And so on. Yet there were many ways to evade the pieties of this law. Captains could sail from distant parts of Queensland, recruit their natives and then land them back in unsupervised stretches of the Queensland coast. Even vessels that docked at Brisbane found enforcement of the Act was not strict. Captain Palmer initiated prosecutions for kidnapping against the schooners *Daphne* and *Challenge*, but despite powerful evidence against them the masters and owners of both were found not guilty. Even in the one successful prosecution for 1869, where it was proven that the officers of the Sydney schooner *Young Australia* had fired rifles into the hold and killed three rebellious natives, the murderers served only short sentences in Sydney and Melbourne gaols.

One government agent who did not shut his eyes was John Meiklejohn, stationed at Maryborough in Queensland. He alleged that John Michael Coath, captain of the *Jason*, had kidnapped several natives in the New Hebrides. Coath threatened Meiklejohn that he would shoot him if he recorded the incident in his log. A few days later, claimed Meiklejohn, he was given a powerful drug in a glass of wine, chained up in the hold of *Jason*, and left delirious and starving for five weeks. Friends of his who boarded the *Jason* at Maryborough found him hollowed out and demented. An official inquiry was called, but this time all three members were nominated by the Minister for Works, W.H. Walsh, a man who was accused of 'monomania' in his campaign against mistreatment of blacks. He was considered 'soft' on Aborigines by many members of the Parliament, but his campaign secretary, Travis, was the registered owner of the *Jason*, and so Captain Coath was exonerated.

The radical politician William Brookes was a gifted member of the early Queensland Parliament who had moved a message of condolence be sent from that body to Abraham Lincoln's widow and who stood for a great deal of the opinions one founds in 'towns'. He had recently lost his seat in Parliament, but still he continued calls on the British government to apply their anti-slavery laws to Queensland, and in this he worked with his friend Short, of the Anti-Slavery Society. He had attempted to move an anti-slavery bill in the House of Representatives but the fact it came from him foredoomed it. The British Parliament in 1872 passed the first Pacific Islanders Protection Act, which empowered Australian courts to accept native evidence and try any British subject caught blackbirding. Until then only the evidence of another European was admitted. But the blackbirders were barely incommoded by this new enactment.

One of the worst cases had occurred in 1871 with the brig *Karl* when Dr James Patrick Murray quarrelled with two of his partners in a Fiji plantation. Put ashore by him in the New Hebrides, they were killed and then cannibalised. Dr Murray sailed on to Bougainville and captured eighty natives with the inventive measure of dropping lumps of iron through their canoes as they came alongside. During the voyage, when the natives tried to escape from the hold, Dr Murray and the crew drilled holes through the bulkhead and fired their revolvers into the natives below. About seventy natives were shot and thrown overboard whether dead or wounded. But when word got out, Murray turned Queen's evidence and saw many of his associates sentenced to long terms of imprisonment in Sydney. Murray, returned to Melbourne, would vanish from history.

Naturally, blackbirding put Europeans living in the islands in danger. Anglican Bishop Paterson of Vanuatu knew his life was in constant danger from natives because blackbirding ships often impersonated missionary ships. In October 1871 when he landed alone on the island of Nukapuj, he was clubbed to death by the inhabitants, and two of his companions waiting offshore in a boat were killed with poisoned arrows.

KIPLING OF THE PACIFIC

Louis Becke, once hailed as the 'Rudyard Kipling of the Pacific' and read by Mark Twain and Joseph Conrad, was typical of the raw entrepreneurship trading in natives in the South Pacific. Born in Port Macquarie in 1855, before he was out of his teens he stood trial in a Brisbane court as the accomplice of the notorious Captain 'Bully' Hayes, a piratical American blackbirder.

William Henry Hayes had been born in Cleveland, Ohio and was in his robust late thirties when Becke first joined the crew of his vessel *Leonora* in the Marshall Islands. Before taking to the trade in natives, Bully had been in Darlinghurst Gaol for debt, had involved himself with a minstrel troupe in the Hunter Valley, sailed around New Zealand in various craft, and then in May 1866 acquired the *Rona* and became a trader and blackbirder. The *Rona* was sunk off the Cook Islands, a disaster in which Bully lost his wife Amelia and his children, but in 1874 he was given the command of the American blackbirder *Leonora*, on which Becke travelled as supercargo, that is, as the manager of the ship's store which exchanged manufactured goods for island products.

The *Leonora* was the most notorious blackbirding vessel in history. A brilliant white, beautifully trim yacht, she was armed with two guns on each side and carried a sizeable crew of thirty men. But it was in her dark forehold that true crowding occurred—as many as 200 kidnapped natives could be stowed there at a time. In the main cabin Bully Hayes entertained the most attractive of the captured native girls. Becke would claim that he rejected Hayes' offer of one of these women. The government agents Becke met on the blackbirding vessels he sailed on were no better than the rest of the crew. 'Drunk nine days out of ten, did as much recruiting as the recruiters themselves, and drew . . . thumping bonuses from the planters sub rosa!'

The *Leonora* at last sank on a reef off Kosrae in the present Micronesia, stranding the survivors there. *Leonora* had been swiftly abandoned by the crew, but islander men and women were left to their own devices in waters which were reputed to be plentiful in sharks. Ashore, writes Becke cryptically, '[m]any a tragedy resulted, for . . . mutiny, treachery, murder, and sudden death was the outcome of the wreck of the *Leonora*'. Hayes and Becke set up a station on the island and collaborated with King Togusa in a palm-oil extraction business. But the routine bored young Louis. After a fight with Hayes, Becke went to live on the other side of the island in a native village.

When the British warship *Rosario* arrived six months later, Bully escaped action by Captain Palmer by flitting on a fourteen-foot boat heading for the open ocean. Young Becke was arrested on a charge of stealing a competing ketch, the *E.A. Williams*. Acquitted in Brisbane, he took a number of jobs, working variously as a bank clerk and Palmer River prospector, but by 1880 he was in the Ellice Islands (now Tuvalu), had married an islander and was trading in his own store at Nukufetau. For him as for Bully Hayes it was not a business bereft of peril. Later that year he lost everything in a shipwreck.

Hayes, meanwhile, set up a trading station in the Caroline Islands and terrorised the natives, again escaping an inspection by the *Rosario* in a small boat with one companion. He was picked up by an American whaler and landed in the North Pacific at Guam in February 1875. In April 1877, commanding the *Lotus* in the Marshall Islands, he was killed by a mutinous sailor with an iron bar and his body was cast overboard. His tale would attract Rolf Boldrewood, who would recount it in a novel named *A Modern Buccaneer* (1894), based on one of Louis Becke's manuscripts. He would later feature as a principal character in Becke's own *Tales of the South Seas*.

Becke had a further significance when it came to the relationship of the Australian colonies to the South Sea islands. While working as a storekeeper in Rabaul, he became conscious of the activities of a fraudster of heroic scale, the Marquis de Rays, a Frenchman who had begun advertising a Nouvelle France on the island of New Ireland, declaring himself King Charles over an unclaimed archipelago, and attracting 570 German, Italian and French settlers to buy unsuitable sections of land in what he named—to honour his Breton birth— the Colonie Libre de Port Breton. The colonists arrived in 1881 and 1882 and realised that the land they had bought had been fraudulently described to them. The realities of malaria and swamp-dwelling quickly drove most of them to flee to New Caledonia or Australia. De Rays would first be imprisoned and then perish in a French asylum, but his activities might have helped motivate Queensland to seize New Guinea.

Becke returned home in 1886. His island wife having been lost at sea, he married Bessie Maunsell, daughter of a Port Macquarie settler. He became subject to recurrent fevers and could no longer find work in the islands. He was labouring in Sydney, digging up tree stumps, when he met the editor of the *Bulletin*, the eccentric but passionate J.F. Archibald, and began to tell him some of his stories about life in the South Seas. Archibald urged him to write them down. Though Becke objected he had never written a story, Archibald advised him, 'Write just as you are telling me the tales now.' When he died in 1913 at the Hotel York in Sydney, Becke was penniless, however. Though he had a literary repute, his rampaging in the Pacific had availed him little.

STEAMING TO AUSTRALIA

Immigration to Australia, and mail and freight to and from Australia, had become more predictable because of steamships. The first regular steamship to Australia was the *Chusan*, which had come to Melbourne in 1852 after a seventy-five-day voyage from Southampton. In 1857 the new iron steamship *Royal Charter* established the record for the England–Australia run, fifty-nine days. When the Suez Canal opened in 1869 steam voyages of thirty-three to thirty-five days became normal. In 1877 the Orient line's new steamer *Lusitania* brought 1000 passengers—more than Phillip's 1788 penal fleet transported—in forty days. The new ships offered better accommodation too. On the *Orient*, a 9500-ton iron ship, even the third-class accommodation had only two berths to a cabin, allowing for an incredible amount of personal room by comparison with the cramped space, the crammed-together bunks, the staleness of the bilges experienced by steerage passengers such as young Henry Parkes and his wife Clarinda only a decade or two before.

On the new steamships morality was honoured in a way that might have bemused the pragmatic captains of a previous generation. Single women had the exclusive use of the after cabin and the poop deck and were not permitted to mix with the crew or the single males on board. On arrival, free passes were given to those immigrants who wished to travel inland to take up advertised jobs. When arriving at the country town to begin his employment, the immigrant was to hand in the pass at the police station and receive in return free board and lodging for at least two days.

In Sydney many single women immigrants were still accommodated at the Hyde Park Barracks, part of which was also being used as an asylum for aged women. Generally, the girls quickly found jobs as servants to middle-class families. Their job conditions varied according to the temperament of their employers, but if they dreamed of going home again even in this age of steam, it was often a futile hope. Of the hundreds of thousands of migrants who came to Australia in the nineteenth century, as little as one in ten ever got to see 'Home' again.

In the early 1860s the new Queensland government had found it hard to persuade ships to sail to that colony instead of to the more profitable southern ports. The Queensland agent-general in London was able to organise two shiploads of immigrants, but to attract shipping, conditions imposed on ship owners as regards space and diet were eased. When the mortality aboard ships in the early

1860s was high, the requirements hammered out over more than two decades by the gentlemen of the London-based British government Colonial Land and Emigration Commission to recruit and ship off colonists to Australia were reimposed. So the commission was able to charter only twenty-seven ships for Queensland between 1860 and 1867, but the Queensland government showed its spirit of independence in working independently of the Colonial Land and Emigration Commission and continuing to charter its own ships as well.

Two shipping groups, James Baines and T.M. Mackay & Company, both agreed to transport immigrants to Queensland according to the rules and free of charge in return for a land grant to them of 18 acres for each person landed. The migrants recruited were offered not only a free voyage but they themselves were promised by the Queensland government a grant of 12 acres after a period of continuous residence. Hence, 11 000 immigrants, many of them laid-off hand-loom weavers from Manchester, arrived in Queensland over two years, and the ship owners acquired 200 000 acres.

On arrival in Queensland in the mid-1860s, the migrants were put in the old military barracks in Brisbane. Many families found it so uncomfortable and unclean, and the sewage so bad, that they moved away and camped under trees. Their rations in the meantime were of very poor quality—flour, 'salt chunk of a consistency of the material comprised of a blucher boot', and tea. Tradesmen and professional men had to go on the road looking for agricultural work. Of one such family an immigrant wrote, 'That is what too many of our poor English come to . . . he, and other deluded villagers, agree to rush out to Australia, only to scrape on as best they can . . . little better all of them than walking skeletons, living in a mere log hut, and lamenting having left their English home.' Some accounts give the impression that Australia could never have been populated if the journey back home had been affordable.

In the early 1860s a number of English railway workers and their families were brought to Queensland to build the coastal lines, but in 1867, due to recession, the men were dismissed. They descended on Brisbane in protest and the authorities defused potential revolution by giving them free passage to Rockhampton and other coastal towns. For the length of the depression the assisted-migration scheme was dropped. Nonetheless, Queensland advertised in 1868 for migrants who could pay their own way and offered in return 80 acres of 'best agricultural land', or 160 acres of pastoral land at a nominal rent for five years, after which they would be granted the freehold. Assisted migration resumed in the 1870s and a new immigrant depot was built, with sub-depots in ports such as Maryborough, Rockhampton and Townsville and even at some inland towns.

Many immigrants to the colonies brought the latest industrial and technical crafts with them, which helped accelerate Australian industrial growth. But the return of disappointed gold diggers to the cities put pressure on jobs. Former officers and clergymen who had immigrated could be found labouring on the roads, the clergymen insisting still on wearing their white neck cloths. One of the friends of the diarist C. Stretton, brother of a member of the House of Commons, worked on the roads for two months to earn his fare home. An immigrant named William Howitt scarcely recognised another of his fellow passengers, a doctor and biologist, now in rags, nearly blind and with a running ulcer on his nose.

THE REFRIGERATION WARS

It was ever the concern of Australian colonies to shrink time and space. Refrigerated ships were like the telegraph. In an iced hold time and distance were nullified since all spoilage was halted. To ship frozen Australian meat and keep it frozen all the way to Britain presented the consummate challenge for a Lancashire-born hyper-businessman named Thomas Mort. Mort had emigrated to Australia to escape the Dickensian drudgery of life as a clerk in Manchester. He had made his fortune as an auctioneer and a wool buyer, and, most notably, he created the first market in Sydney where wool could be sold and bought in an orderly manner. This replaced the old haphazard system by which wool buyers rode out beyond the limits of, say, Liverpool in New South Wales to intercept the owners of the wagons of wool coming down along the roads from the bush, then haggled with them over a glass of spirits at such public houses as the Woolsack.

Mort acquired pastoral properties, a tin smelter and mines, and built at Balmain, with the help of Captain Thomas Rowntree, a ship-graving dock so large that it could take the steamers which first arrived in Australia in 1853, and the ships of the Royal Mail. What a gift for innovation would have been smothered had he remained a Manchester clerk. He knew that Great Britain offered substantial business to any exporters of meat who could get the produce to them, the Britons being Europe's only incessant beef eaters. In the decade 1851–1860 the average production of meat in Britain was 910 000 tons, or 72 pounds (33 kilograms) per head of population, which was not sufficient for the British appetite, which was closer to 110 pounds (50 kilograms) per person.

Many had been trying to solve the refrigeration challenge. As early as 1846 the husky, Canadian-raised Sizar Elliott made his first attempt to ship Australian meat by canning it in Sydney. Israel Joseph then opened a factory, and so did the Dangar brothers, New England pastoralists, in Newcastle. Their motivation was the doubling of Australian sheep numbers in the eight years from 1860 to 1868, which was too many for the local market and live export. The boiling down of both sheep and cattle in large stinking vats in the bush resumed on a large scale, animal tallow selling for more than meat.

The results of early refrigeration experiments were small-scale. Sizar Elliott went broke. In the early 1870s small quantities of hard frozen beef reached Britain from the USA, the meat being frozen by a mixture of natural ice, cut from rivers and lakes in the north-eastern USA, and salt. But this method worked only because of the shorter distance the American meat had to travel, and in any case the climatic conditions of Australia did not favour natural ice.

In 1855 James Harrison, Scots printer and publisher of the *Geelong Advertiser*, self-educated at such institutions as the Glasgow Mechanics' Institute, created an ice-making machine in Geelong. It was said to be able to manufacture 3 tons of ice per day. He experimented with ether to produce a practical refrigerating machine in which the ether vapour was condensed to a liquid again and recycled. Harrison applied for British patents in March 1856. While Harrison was distracted by refrigeration and ice-making, his newspaper was losing money, and he was declared insolvent in 1861 and the assets of the publishing company sold. In 1866 he was employed by David Syme, proprietor of the Melbourne *Age*, and was left with little time to devote to refrigeration schemes.

In 1865 a refrigeration-minded pastoralist named Augustus Morris, who had been mocked by his peers for trying to raise money to back Harrison, met up with a fellow enthusiast, Eugène Nicolle, in Sydney. Nicolle was a Frenchman, a graduate of the University of Rouen employed on engineering projects in England and then in Australia, and the holder of a patent for his own refrigerating machine developed in 1861. Nicolle's Darlinghurst plant was opened in 1863. His machine depended on the cooling effect which arose from ammonia being absorbed in water. In 1866, with the backing of Augustus Morris, he called a public meeting to raise money for an experiment which would demonstrate the feasibility of exporting frozen meat. The meeting was held in the rooms of the merchant Thomas Mort, who was not in Sydney at the time and had up till now shown little interest in Nicolle. But when Mort returned and met Nicolle and Morris, he offered to finance further experiments in refrigeration.

The experimental machinery was built at the Sydney Ice Company's works in Paddington and was demonstrated to an invited audience in September 1867. Samples of frozen meat from Nicolle's new refrigeration machine had already been served at Government House and elsewhere and been approved of and, above all, afflicted no one with food poisoning. Mort bought the rights to the new machine and was granted a patent in November 1867. He called a meeting on 2 February 1868 to raise funds of £10 000–15 000 for a trial shipment of around 200 tons of frozen meat to Britain. A large committee was gathered and included pastoralists and merchants. But even so, the subscriptions came to only £2500. Nicolle, after attempting to work on refrigeration based on air, returned to improving his ammonia heat-absorption machine. The progress was so slow that Mort apologised to his subscribers in 1869. Meanwhile, Mort was becoming interested in the refrigerating machines built in Britain by Rees Reece which, like Nicolle's, were based on ammonia absorption. Mort wrote to his brother William asking him to obtain a model of Reece's machine.

Mort's sense of urgency was due to the fact that sheep numbers had continued to increase so significantly and at the same time wool prices were still falling disastrously. Mort was auctioning off many pastoral properties and at the same time waiting for the right equipment to save the bush by refrigerating meat. By 1872 he had become disillusioned with the international possibilities, but decided to use Nicolle's refrigeration system on land. He would build an abattoir at Bowenfels, 150 kilometres from Sydney, where he could buy stock cheaply, chill the meat there and transport it by railway wagons, refrigerated with a mixture of ice and calcium chloride, to a cold store in Darling Harbour. By the time it was all working properly and profitably, he was approached again on the question of whether he would make a trial shipment of meat to Britain. He said he could not finance it alone; but if £20 000 was subscribed, he could ship between 300 and 500 tons of meat overseas.

Mort trialled Nicolle's shipboard ammonia refrigeration in 1875, but before it left Sydney Harbour, the ship's vibrations strained the pipes and the fluid flooded the meat. By March 1876, most of the money had been subscribed or promised and the project went ahead. The problem was that though the ammonia plant worked well on land, ships' masters and insurers were unwilling to accept the hazards of having ammonia on board their ships. Nicolle adjusted his scheme to use the cooling effect produced when salts such as ammonium chloride were dissolved in water. The salt solution could then be boiled on board the ship to recover the salt crystals that would then be recycled into the refrigerator. The engineering workers at Mort's dock had a lot of difficulty making the equipment, since they had to use exotic metals to resist corrosion. But by 1877 it was working well.

Then, in 1878, Mort, full of schemes at sixty-two years of age, fell sick while at his property at Bodalla in southern New South Wales and died of pleuropneumonia. Nicolle retired with the great endeavour unfinished. Harrison, having been sent broke by his refrigeration schemes nearly a quarter of a century before, continued with his work in Melbourne and had overcome the scepticism of his friend the Reverend Doctor John Ignatius Bleasdale, a remarkable Catholic priest with a passion for chemistry who was Harrison's confidant. Harrison conducted experiments and, until his health failed, Bleasdale reported on them. Harrison exhibited his products at the Melbourne exhibition of 1872–73, showing fresh meat frozen and packed 'as if for a voyage, so that the refrigerating process may be continued for any required period'. A group of pastoralists had subscribed £2500 to enable Harrison to prepare and take to Britain a parcel of 25–50 tons as a demonstration. Thus the *Norfolk* sailed from Melbourne on 22 July 1893 with Harrison and two tanks of frozen meat on board. Before departure, David Syme, Harrison's editor at the *Age*, a gaunt, reserved man but one who had backed with the power of his paper all colonial innovation, provided a champagne lunch for Harrison.

The experiment proved to be a fiasco, the tanks leaking shortly after leaving Melbourne. The rotting meat had to be thrown overboard off Cape Horn. Meanwhile, new refrigeration schemes were used to cross the Atlantic and led to the successful delivery of meat from New York, but again they did not have to deal with the challenges the longer haul from the Antipodes involved. In 1877 the first successful shipment of frozen meat from the southern hemisphere took place when a ship from Montevideo, the *Paraguay*, took mutton to France. The Grand Hotel in Paris served the meat for a whole week.

Thomas McIlwraith, a Scot, ultimately to become a controversial premier of Queensland, hearing of the *Paraguay*, asked his brother Andrew and Andrew's English partner Malcolm McEacharn to inspect the *Paraguay* at its mooring in France and report on whether the refrigeration system would work in shipping meat from Australia. McIlwraith and McEacharn then chartered the ship *Strathleven* and set up a refrigeration plant like the *Paraguay*'s inside the hold. None of the ill omens and misfortunes which had plagued the other apostles of refrigeration intervened now. The ship left Melbourne on 6 December 1879, and arrived in London on 2 February 1880 with its meat still frozen. The refrigeration machinery was absolutely adequate to the task and indeed so effective it could be shut down for part of the day even in the tropics. Neither Andrew McIlwraith nor Malcolm McEacharn followed up the success of the voyage by engaging in the meat trade. But by 1882 eight ships had been fitted with refrigerating machinery for the Australian and New Zealand meat trade.

A huge offload of protein to the northern hemisphere began.

MINERAL DREAMS

By the 1860s the gold rush was turning into a mineral industry. The joint stock company was replacing the individual red-shirted miner. Naturally the sentimental alcoholic Henry Lawson remembered from his childhood the days that mattered to him, the early golden years that were somehow less mercenary than the later ones.

> *The night too quickly passes*
> *And we are growing old,*
> *So let us fill our glasses*
> *And toast the Days of Gold.*
> *When finds of wondrous treasure*
> *Set all the South ablaze*
> *And you and I were faithful mates*
> *All through the roaring days.*

But the Roaring Days, if they had ever been so fraternal, were no longer like that. The prospector had become an employed miner, and the world of the miner was an early catalyst of industrial action. A young Orkney Islander named William Guthrie Spence, who had arrived in Melbourne with his parents in the Roaring Days, specifically 1852, had created a Miners' Union which he united with the Amalgamated Miners' Association in 1878 in the first coup of a career devoted to industrial action. A vigorous Presbyterian and temperance man, he was characteristic of those practical Scots who believed that the deity helped those who took action rather than passively awaited His will.

Throughout the 1860s he might be found addressing miners across Victoria, in Clunes and Ballarat and Castlemaine, and with equal eloquence preaching to Presbyterians, Primitive Methodists and Bible Christians on Sundays. The gold-mining business was a matter of industrial equity for him, not of memories of old mateships.

In the early 1860s, 40 000 miners left eastern Australia for the Otago gold rush in New Zealand's South Island, but to compensate that loss, an increasing number of women and families came to join husbands and fathers in Australian gold-mining areas. The women humanised the gold towns, introducing sheets to go with the blankets, serving meals on china and putting muslin curtains in the windows. Even so, Anthony Trollope found the store tents and shops in the valley at Bendigo, which ran for seven miles, 'dirty, uncouth, barren, and disorderly'. He declared the hospitals excellent, however, and charitable welfare, in his conservative view, so good as to almost encourage poverty.

Well-ordered cottages, broad streets and stone churches were by now the mark of Ballarat. Later goldfields, such as Lambing Flat in New South Wales, still possessed the old rawness, the hotels and boarding houses being large tents, and at the dances miners in muddy clothes and heavy boots 'solemnly danc[ed] the Mazurka' with each other. The pubs, when they were built—477 public houses and hotels in Ballarat alone—were numerous and sometimes remarkably elegant compared to the shebeens and grog tents of the first days. The gold buyers often built their fortunes here, buying cheaply on the fields, sending the portion they bought off to Melbourne by gold escort.

Not all the goldfields had achieved sophistication. Young diarist G.O. Preshaw joined the Bank of New South Wales and was sent to the remote goldfield of Kiandra, a later field than Ballarat, Bendigo or Ophir. The bank was still located in a calico tent with a stream of melted snow running in a channel down the centre of the mud floor. Preshaw had to carry all the gold deposits of the day nearly a mile to the small military and police camp where they were stored under the commandant's bed. He and his fellow clerks tried to supplement their wages by sinking a shaft inside the bank, but it yielded them little.

Indeed, to get enough gold on some of the goldfields now, diggers had to buy and install quartz-crushing equipment, great machines called 'batteries'. Several such machines had been in operation at Bendigo as early as 1855, but their use accelerated from the 1860s onwards. By 1864 the number of small miners in Bendigo had dropped to 83 000, of whom a third were Chinese, and average earnings were about £70 a year. Machine drills now came into use and took the mining underground, and the typical lung diseases of miners began to be seen, including 'black spit'. Individual prospectors might still be found in places like Ararat, Stawell and Rutherglen, but when they eventually went they often left a mining ghost town in their wake.

In a Queensland depression in 1867 James Nash found gold at a place named Gympie, north of Brisbane. Gympie's white reefs of gold helped create the standard mining town with wooden fronts and canvas posteriors. Charters Towers' gold was discovered by men who were too late to Gympie to cash in on its wealth. Gold was located behind Cooktown on the Palmer River and at Hodgkinson in the hinterland behind Cairns; James Venture Mulligan was said to have had a hand in both. It happened thus: Mulligan was an Irishman who on arrival in Melbourne in 1860 had tried to join the Burke and Wills expedition, and had been lucky enough not to be accepted. He subsequently settled in Armidale in New South Wales, where he opened a butcher shop and prospected on the Peel River. He followed the gold to Gympie in 1867, Gilberton in 1871 and the Etheridge, or Charters Towers, in 1873. That year Mulligan led a party of six from Georgetown to investigate a gold discovery by William Hann in the Cape York Peninsula near the Daintree and Palmer rivers. He had unspecified problems with Aborigines but came out to Cooktown with 102 ounces of gold. After the proclamation of the Palmer goldfield by the governor, Mulligan's party received a £1000 reward. He discovered gold at Hodgkinson near Cairns, but since Hodgkinson was mainly a reef requiring crushing and there was little alluvial gold to be found, many miners were furious at him for attracting them there. He had lived by the gold frenzy and now died of it. A drunken prospector who was assaulting a woman by the Hodgkinson River was interrupted by Mulligan. The drunkard beat him and Mulligan died the next day in the rough hospital at Mount Molloy.

The biggest company involved in the Northern Territory in the early 1870s was the Northern Territory Gold Prospecting Association. In their prospectus they declared that the Northern Territory was an extension of the rich goldfields of Queensland, which was not the truth. The company's party had arrived in Palmerston (later Darwin) in February 1872 and went south with equipment and horses and men, following the trail of empty meat tins and medicine bottles along the telegraph line. One of the principals of the company was John

Chambers, an Englishman long settled in South Australia who with his friend William Finke (whose name John McDouall Stuart would attach to the river of that name in Central Australia) had in 1857 found copper and had formed the Great Northern Mining Company. The mine had been found to be grossly overvalued, but Finke had survived the scandal.

The Overland Telegraph had created relay stations at a site named the Shackle and at Pine Creek, 121 and 150 miles (200 kilometres and 240 kilometres) from Palmerston respectively, and as John Chambers and others surveyed the geology of the Pine Creek area, excited telegraphs were sent down the line to Adelaide offering mine sites for sale or investment. Agents in Adelaide would buy the so-called mines without having even seen them. Sixty companies having been floated by May 1874, Northern Territory gold shares were bought up in the Brisbane stock exchange. The stock exchange was busy until after dark, and the cafe nearby was full of men smoking cigars and bubbling with speculative fervour about some Northern Territory rock outcrop.

Men with less capital actually marched to the far-off fields equipped with a broad hat, Holloway's Ointment (a universal cure for cuts, bruises and 'inveterate ulcers'), quinine, tent, hammock, mosquito net, revolver and breech-loading gun. At Pine Creek, coloured flags marked the borders of mining claims where men were digging or plugging dynamite into holes in reefs to blow up the quartz. Pine Creek was a rough settlement, devoid of women. Relatively nearby Yam Creek was famous for being 'the place where resides an actual, real, live young lady'.

But there were great problems impeding the mining process itself, either by individual prospectors or by companies. There were no nearby vegetable gardens or stations to supply the fields with fresh food. Perhaps the desperate isolation of the field is best encapsulated in a recipe for liquor drunk there consisting of gin, kerosene, sugar, Worcestershire sauce and ginger. More refined goods could come in only by long-distance carriage or by ship to Palmerston. The long journey to the Northern Territory inflated the price of everything and in the rainy season the mines could not be reached anyhow because of the morasses which lay between them and the port to the north. Hence, in November 1873, D'Arcy Uhr's journey with cattle 600 miles from Normanton in Queensland to sell the meat on the hoof on the goldfields! Others who tried the same journey came to disaster—William Nation lost his cattle and nearly starved to death after getting lost along the track from North Queensland by way of the Gulf of Carpenteria. He had £29 in his pocket and no food to spend it on. 'Farewell, dear friends, all,' he wrote at one stage.

The mercy of fresh food was occasional, and there were deaths at Pine Creek and elsewhere from that terrible dehumanising disease, scurvy. The conclusion was reached that only Asians could put up with the hardship and Captain Bloomfield Douglas chartered a ship in Singapore to bring 186 Chinese and ten Malays to Palmerston on two-year indentures. They were paid rice and preserved fish and £8 a month to work at Pine Creek and elsewhere. The Northern Territory attracted Chinese diggers from other colonies as well, and Julian Tenison Woods, Adelaide geologist, Catholic priest and confidante of Mother Mary Potter, wrote in 1886, 'At present the whole gold-mining industry of the Northern Territory is bound hand and foot and handed over to the Chinamen. I have seen something of China and much of the Chinese, and I say we will one day regret any supremacy we give them.'

SOCIAL BANDITS II

Far to the south, Victoria had been transformed by new railways. The wheat farmers of the Wimmera—if they were able promptly to get a machine contractor to strip their crop—could send it to Melbourne on a train regardless of road conditions and without the high cost of road transport. To look a little way into the future, in 1887 the Victorian and South Australian rail systems met up, and in 1888 New South Wales and Queensland met at Wallangarra on the border. In their own way, the railways federated Australia, despite the different widths between rails which meant trans-shipping at the border, as it would become possible for a citizen to travel from Brisbane to Adelaide by rail. Borrowing heavily from London financiers, the Victorians built 2400 kilometres of rail lines by 1885. But even in the 1870s the railways and the telegraph made it easier for a centralised police force to deal with the bush riffraff, though the disgruntled small settler still had the advantage of knowing the remoter bush.

Red Kelly, Ned's convict father, who had served his time in Van Diemen's land before coming to Melbourne and marrying Ellen Quinn, the daughter of free settlers, was continuously anxious about police attention. While farming at Avenel, north of Seymour, he was arrested for cattle stealing and having in his possession illegally one cowhide. His sentence was a £25 fine or six months in prison, and although £25 was an enormous sum for people like the Quinns and Kellys, the money was raised before he had served the full six months. He died soon after his release, 'of dropsy', or congestive heart failure, and was buried at Avenel in the last days of 1866.

The Quinns were a large bush clan, wanted at various times for horse theft, and characteristic of the small, alienated selector and farmer to whom stock theft came naturally and was, if Ned Kelly's Jerilderie letter can be believed, in the case of the Irish in particular, seen as an extension of vengeance on the stock of landlords in Ireland. So pervasive was the problem that Mr McBean, a squatter from Kilfera Station in north-east Victoria, grew disgusted at the lenient sentences the magistrates handed down and posted an advertisement in a newspaper addressed to sheep stealers.

> In consequence of the decision of the magistrate in the Benalla Court, the undersigned would be obliged if sheep stealers would take only what mutton they require for private use.

Under the Land Act of 1865, the widowed Mrs Kelly took up a small area at East Greta in north-east Victoria close to the main Melbourne–Sydney road, a location which she hoped might help in the success of the farm. But it was poor country and Mrs Kelly found it hard to fulfil the cultivation requirements. The Kelly boys grew up as part of a group of wild locals known as the Greta Mob.

As a selector, Ellen Kelly—like the men who married her daughters, such as William Skillion—was hampered in the taking out of acreages by the squatters' stratagems known as peacocking, dummying, and the use of Duffy Certificates. Duffy Certificates were issued as compensation to those who purchased land at auction in the 1850s and had paid more than £1 per acre. They were used by pastoralists as proof of title to good land and so to frighten selectors away. And the demand that the police deal strenuously with all stock theft led ultimately to a relentless and vengeful bullying of the Kelly clan.

Ned Kelly's famous Jerilderie letter, detailing all his complaints against the established world and started in Euroa when he had held up the bank there in December 1878 and finished in the virtual capture of the town of Jerilderie in the Riverina of New South Wales in February 1879, was written to justify his path. By the time he crossed the Murray, his mother Ellen, with babe in arms (the father, her partner George King, an American), had been arrested by Sergeant Steele at the Kelly farm. After being handcuffed she was charged with aiding and abetting one Edward Kelly in a murder attempt. She had been sentenced by Redmond Barry at Beechworth to three years' servitude. What else would be needed to enhance a young man's sense of being engaged in civil war?

The death of policemen at Stringybark Creek barely delayed the popular imagination when it applied itself to Ned. At an official and establishment level, though, Stringybark was seen as demonstrating Ned's true nature as an irremediable killer. Sergeant Michael Kennedy, who had earlier in the month assisted in the court proceedings against Ellen Kelly, created a police camp at Stringybark Creek in the melancholy bush outside Mansfield in late October 1878. The detachment stationed there were all Irish themselves. On the afternoon of 26 October 1878, the Kelly gang were attracted to the place by tracks they spotted and because one of the constables, McIntyre, fired at some parrots and gave away the police position. The Kellys bailed up McIntyre and Lonigan, the other policemen then in the camp, late in the afternoon. Constable Lonigan, who in helping to arrest Ned the previous year on the charge of riding a horse across a pavement in Benalla and had resorted to twisting Ned's testicles, began firing from behind a log and was shot dead. McIntyre, unharmed, became a prisoner. The gang then concealed themselves until Kennedy and Scanlon arrived back from their patrol at 6 p.m. McIntyre rose to advise his colleagues to surrender. Kennedy at first thought him joking, then drew his revolver and slid down off his horse, which McIntyre took hold of and immediately escaped on. Kennedy was mortally wounded and, in bloodlust or mercy or an instinct partway between, Kelly shot him dead through the chest. Scanlon too had been killed in the exchange. McIntyre rode into Mansfield to warn of what had happened.

There are signs that Ned, who was not a killer by nature, became fatally haunted by the men murdered at Stringybark, and from then on set about, however aggressively, seeking forgiveness before man and God. Yet the events of the Euroa hold-up were still considered by his supporters as consummate bushranging accomplishments, Euroa itself being achieved with style and a considerable amount of tactical planning, and possessing a romance that the killing of the policemen at Stringybark Creek had lacked.

At lunchtime on 9 December 1878, a party of four men had sauntered into the yard of Faithfull's Creek station a few miles to the north of Euroa. The gang at that moment consisted of twenty-three-year-old Ned, his seventeen-year-old brother Dan, Steve Hart and Joe Byrne (both selectors' sons from the Beechworth district). The manager and the whole workforce were 'bailed up', and when at dusk a hawker drove up to the station, Ned and the gang took him and his assistant prisoner and fitted themselves out from his stock with new suits, boots, hats and magenta Tommy Duds (neckties). Mrs Fitzgerald, the station cook, and other women were allowed to move about the station as they pleased, but the male prisoners were kept in the storeroom, where they played cards and talked to Ned about the killing of the policemen at Stringybark Creek six weeks before. Ned insisted that it had not all been deliberate murder.

Euroa, like other of Ned's acts of hostage-taking, was in part a kindly affair, and some of the men, without being pressured, even offered him money for his cause. The next day Ned's lieutenants cut the telegraph wires north of town, and the hostage numbers increased with the arrival of some sporting kangaroo hunters and telegraph-wire repairers.

In Euroa, the two bank tellers and a manager opened the safe and over £2000 in cash, gold and jewellery was removed. The outlaws, as was always their custom, also took mortgage papers held by the bank against local selectors, an act which further enhanced the sympathies between the gang and the small farmers. The bank manager's family, the Scotts, were gathered up from the bank residence at the rear of the bank for transport back to Faithfull's Creek station. Since it was a busy day in town, with people having come in from their selections to renew their licences, Mrs Scott insisted on wearing a new dress just sent from Melbourne. The Scott family having been taken to Faithfull's Creek station, Ned sat down to write a detailed letter to Donald Cameron, MLA, member for West Bourke, who in the House had asked the Premier of Victoria to look into the issue of whether the behaviour of policemen in Benalla had provoked the Stringybark Creek murders. Then the outlaws, who as a result of these and other raids and acts of self-justified depredation had become known as 'The Gang', issued graphic threats against any of their captives who tried to leave the station before 11 p.m., and departed, shouting and jumping their horses over fences, in the direction of the wild Strathbogie Ranges. As the Kelly Gang crossed the Murray and rode to New South Wales and their consummate raid on Jerilderie, Ned carried in his pocket the pages of what would become his Jerilderie letter, over 8000 words long when finished, a document in which his denouncement of police competed with his plea for absolution for the Stringybark killings.

In Jerilderie, late on a Saturday in early 1879, Ned captured the police station and Senior Constable Devine, whom he locked up. Next day, dressed in Devine's uniform and posing as a visiting trooper, he would accompany young Mrs Devine to Mass, treating her entirely as the good, devout Irish young woman she was, but letting her know her husband's survival depended on her behaviour. The other constable, Richards, was more easily cowed than Devine and took the uniformed Ned Kelly and his brother Dan, similarly attired, to the Royal Hotel, the Bank of New South Wales being located within the building.

They held up the Royal Hotel, including any customers who happened to be there, then went on to the bank. There they found the manager, John Tarleton, having a bath. The safe was opened and over £2000 was taken along with all the papers, including mortgages. Once the robbery was over, Ned Kelly went to find the town newspaper proprietor, Samuel Gill, to give him his letter for printing in his *Jerilderie and Urana Gazette*. However Gill had left town on hearing of the gang's arrival, and was hiding in a drain in the countryside. Ned instead handed his manifesto to Samuel Gill's assistant, Living.

At an unspecified time that day, the child John Monash, some ten years old, was in town from boarding school and visiting his parents, who ran a store there. Ned chatted with him on the street, meeting through him the Diggers who in World War 1 would attempt to re-produce his, 'Tell them I died game' style of gallantry in a chaos of high explosive and gas.

When it was time to leave, Ned gave the normal fiery and eloquent speech about what had turned him into an outlaw. His anxiety to justify himself is telling. No other bushranger sermonised to pubs full of citizens or went searching for someone to publish his apologia. The gang then gave an exhibition of rough and skilful riding in the main street before vanishing, back across the Murray and into the mountains of north-eastern Victoria, the country in which they were utterly at home.

At the time of the Jerilderie raid, despite the fact that under the Outlawry Act the Kelly brothers and their companions were considered to be beyond the normal protection offered by the law, but could be shot at any time by anyone, though twenty-three Kelly relatives and associates were in gaol in Beechworth and though a fabulous reward sum for turning the Kellys in was on offer, information and aid continued to flow to the gang. Seven of the twenty-three gaoled men were Kelly relatives; contrary to the view of Kelly's support being entirely Irish-based, three were Scottish and the rest were English. For every man locked up there were now even more willing to defy the police.

The Jerilderie letter Ned had left with Living seems to come directly from the language of Irish protesters, and of Irish transportees who saw themselves as victims of a system rather than, as the authorities would have it, criminals. There existed a pernicious system which had not let him live in peace, Ned claimed. The Victorian police were successors of those Irish who were willing to serve 'under a flag and nation that has destroyed, massacred, and murdered their fore-fathers'. In his view an Irish policeman was 'a traitor to his country, ancestors, and religion'. He had 'left the ash corner, deserted the shamrock, the emblem of true wit and beauty'. The persecution had extended to Ned's family. 'Is my brothers and sisters and my mother not to be pitied also who has no alternative only to put up with the brutal and cowardly conduct of a parcel of big ugly fat-necked wombat headed big bellied magpie legged narrow hipped splay-footed sons of Irish bailiffs or English landlords which is better known as officers of Justice or Victorian police?' One aspect of Ned's instinctive republicanism emerged in the universal Irish peasant hope that America would declare war on Britain, 'as it is all Irishmen as has got command of her armies forts and batteries . . . would they not slew around and fight her [Britain] with their own arms for the sake of the colour they dare not wear for years and to reinstate it and rise old Erin's isle once more from the pressure and tyrannism of the English yolk which has kept it in poverty and starvation and caused them to wear the enemy's coat.'

Then the letter takes on a manic tone. 'I give fair warning to all those who has reason to fear me to sell out and give £10 out of every hundred towards the widow and orphan fund and do not attempt to reside in Victoria . . . Neglect this and abide by the consequences, which shall be worse than the rust in the wheat in Victoria or the druth of a dry season to the grasshoppers in New South Wales.'

In fact Ned's justification, threats and appeal for absolution would not be published in the time left to him. It was suppressed. The New South Wales attorney-general sent a cable to Jerilderie warning Living against selling it to Melbourne papers who clamoured for it. Instead the manuscript was seized by the New South Wales police and sent to the government of Victoria.

On a weekend in June 1880, Ned put into action a plan that centred on the town of Glenrowan. Ned had brought to Glenrowan the famous armour hammered out of ploughshares which he and the others would wear at various stages during the coming siege.

At pistol point on Saturday night, he made several railway platelayers lift segments of the line by a steep embankment just north of Glenrowan. He had reason to believe a police special would come up from Benalla pursuing him. Had Ned passed over into a state of nihilism in which death-dealing was the chief principle of his life? If so, he had not displayed that tendency at Euroa or Jerilderie—and he was so haunted by Stringybark that it was unlikely.

According to a kinder view of Ned, and that of eminent historian John Molony, as the train arrived from Benalla he would have the stationmaster flash a danger signal, and the occupants would be informed by an emissary, a Kelly supporter, of the situation they were in and warned that if they tried to reverse, the line behind them would be blown up by blasting powder. Indeed, had Ned intended loss of life by train wreck he would surely have derailed the line to the south of Glenrowan. He wanted to use the captured police, including Super-intendent Francis Hare, Kelly-hunter-in-chief, as hostages to exchange for his mother's freedom. He expected the police to come post-haste during Saturday night, resulting in an early Sunday morning confrontation. Instead the police in Melbourne and not Benalla put together the response. Everything would be delayed a day.

Ned expected police to come to Glenrowan from Benalla because he had organised an event to attract them. While Ned was attending to pulling up the rail, he had sent his brother Dan and his lieutenant Joe Byrne to threaten a police informer who had grown up with the Byrnes, Harts and Kellys in the Beech-worth area, one Aaron Sherritt, who was sheltering in his hut under a guard of five police. Unfortunately, words which Sherritt, in a fit of guilty anger, had uttered to Joe Byrne's mother—'I'll kill him and before he's cold I'll fuck him'—provided Joe Byrne with an absolute warrant for Sherritt's death. Despite the five police guards hidden in the bedroom, Aaron Sherritt was shot dead by Joe. The outlaws then rode away to meet Ned at Glenrowan. To acquire some hostages the gang took over Mrs Anne Jones' Glenrowan Inn, where some sixty people were detained, including a local schoolteacher named Thomas Curnow.

Ned's expectations grew in grandeur during that Sabbath. He would capture the train, its police and horses, and with them as his bargaining pieces, advance down the line raiding banks, perhaps even kidnapping the ultimate hostage, the Governor of Victoria.

In Mrs Jones' pub there was singing—even a Kelly ballad was performed by one of Ned's guests. 'Ned would go through the waltzes, he was laughing and amused all around him,' Mrs Jones later told the police. Mrs Jones said that not everyone approved of the idea of derailing trains—a sign that in the eyes of the hostages Ned did contemplate a train wreck. 'But the devil was in us. We had to be looking at the darling man, but sure Ned was a darling man.' Towards three o'clock on the Monday morning it was decided that all the women at the pub could go home, but first Ned gave his obligatory self-justifying speech, and while he was still speaking, a train was heard.

Curnow, having been released on the plea that his wife was expecting a baby, returned home southwards along the line, collected a red scarf to screen a candle, and bravely signalled the train to stop at the station rather than thunder through to Beechworth. Ned's idea of taking those on the train hostage was stymied.

Amongst those held at the Jones inn was Constable Bracken, a local policeman, who when the train pulled up and the bushrangers began armouring themselves escaped and ran to the station to join up with the disembarking party, whose passengers included Superintendents Hare and Nicholson, Stanhope O'Connor, the officer in charge of the black trackers specially brought along, and two women who had come as spectators. In all, fifty-seven police would be involved in the siege.

Dan Kelly, Joe Byrne and Steve Hart, confronted by the police, left a bonfire blazing in the open and used Mrs Jones' hotel as a flimsy fortress. Ned was in the bush nearby. The police fire led to Byrne being wounded in the thigh and bleeding to death. Ned was wounded in the foot, hand and arm. At about 5 a.m. Ned, looming through the early mist in his armour and rapping its steel plates to attract police fire, made his way to join his confederates in the hotel, and on the way took many wounds in the legs. More police arrived half an hour later. Inside the hotel Ned could not find Dan or Steve because they were in one of the back rooms. He assumed they had already escaped on horseback, and walked into the backyard of the hotel to find his horse. It had fled.

It was dawn when the police at the northern end of the hotel saw Ned emerge from the mist again, a terrible figure in his armour. 'Come on,' he called, 'and we will lick the lot of the bloody police.' Ned fell with a total of twenty-eight wounds in his extremities, and the police moved in and removed his helmet. Sergeant Steele wanted to kill him as he lay there, but Constable Bracken, who had been Kelly's hostage, prevented him. Around 10 a.m., by which time the morning passenger train from Wangaratta had arrived by way of the now-repaired rail, civilian spectators were calling on the police to grant a truce and stop firing on the hotel, where there were still hostages. Superintendent Sadleir, who had taken over from Hare when Hare was wounded in the hand and would be demoted for his inflammatory part in the whole Kelly business, allowed a ceasefire. The hostages came out and were forced to lie on the ground until their identity was checked. By now Ned's sister Maggie Skillion and Father Matthew Gibney, who earlier had given the last rites to Ned, offered to act as intermediaries to get Dan and Steve to surrender, but the police threatened to shoot Maggie if she went near the building. At 2.30 p.m. the hotel was set alight by a policeman under covering fire. Father Gibney protested to Sadleir, ignored his orders and ran into the burning hotel. He found Byrne's dead body where it had fallen by the bar, and in the back room Dan Kelly and Steve Hart lying side by side, their heads on rolled blankets, their armour by their side, a dead dog at their feet. He presumed they had suicided but in fact it seems they had been laid out in that dignified manner by one of the Kelly supporters who had broken into the inn, a friend known to and ever after cherished by the Kelly clan. Flames drove Gibney out of the hotel, and the police dragged Byrne's body free and rescued the wounded Martin Cherry, last of the prisoners, who died almost immediately.

When Dan Kelly's body, consumed by fire to below the knees, was drawn out of the ruins, Maggie Skillion and her sister Kate Kelly leaned over it keening. Ned, with two dozen or more wounds to the arms and legs, was transferred south to Benalla with the body of Joe Byrne. And so on to the 'Such is life' consummation, the trial in Melbourne and the hanging in Melbourne Gaol.

As far as south-eastern Australia was concerned, bushranger-ism died with Ned. No later outlaws seized the popular imagination in that way and to anything like that extent. When Ned died in 1880, the Melbourne establishment were beginning to develop financial structures which would operate so fraudulently that Ned's raids on banks would be modest by comparison.

CHAPTER 3

One hundred years complete
1880s

THE BROKEN HILL

Charles Rasp had been born in 1846 at Stuttgart and became a chemical technologist in Hamburg. When in 1868 he suffered a serious lung infection, it was decided he should move from Germany to a warmer climate. When he first arrived in Melbourne in 1869 he pruned vines before becoming a boundary rider on Walwa Station and then on the Mount Gipps Station in the Barrier Ranges in the far west of New South Wales. There had been discoveries of silver at Silverton and a place named Daydream and now every station hand was searching for indications of the metal.

When the shearing season occurred at Mount Gipps in September 1883, twenty shearers worked in the long stone shed and the boundary riders trotted in with the sheep from distant paddocks. Thirty-seven-year-old Charles Rasp, who was fetching sheep in from 12 miles out to the south end of the run, carried with him a book on prospecting and began to chip at the rocks and gather samples at the site known as 'the broken hill'. The samples were very black and heavy for their size and Rasp thought that perhaps they were tin. On the advice of his station manager, George McCulloch, a syndicate of seven was formed and seven blocks were pegged out across the whole ridge. McCulloch, a university graduate who had tried to farm in Mexico, was a heavy-built Scot, loud-voiced and genial, who delighted in feats of strength and practical jokes, but who was hard up from long drought. The broken hill would transform his fortunes and, like Rasp, he too would live a rich man—in his case until 1907.

Each of the seven members of the syndicate invested £70 in the Broken Hill Mining Company which was now formed, though without official registration. Each partner also paid £1 per week so that the claim could be worked. An analyst's report done in Adelaide was disappointing but it was found the analyst had only tested for tin. When the rocks were tested for silver the results were different. Rich silver ore was found and a Broken Hill Proprietary Company was set up, and 16 000 £20 shares sold. Within five years Rasp had made his fortune. When dividends were declared, he was able to move to Adelaide, marry there and buy a house, Willyama, where he and his wife Agnes lived as grandees. Agnes entertained and Rasp amassed a huge library of French and German books. The man with the weak chest would also live until 1907.

MORE KANAKA SCANDALS

In 1880, two Queensland government health officers, C.K. Hill-Wray and John Thomson, carried out a full statistical investigation of ten large plantations in the Maryborough district. They found that the death rate of Kanakas was up to twenty times greater than among white men of similar age groups. Nearly 500 native deaths had occurred on the ten plantations in the previous five years, yet not one death certificate had been forwarded to the registrar of Births, Deaths and Marriages. When the largest plantation was inspected by the two doctors, twenty-six Kanakas were lying in their huts sick, with four of them close to death, yet no medical aid had been summoned. Some planters were accused of letting Kanakas die towards the end of their indenture, so that their wages were forfeited. One observer, William Thomas Reay, a Melbourne *Herald* journalist, said that Kanaka women were forced to work late into their pregnancies and then came back to work a few days after giving birth, often with a half-caste baby.

The Melbourne journalist George Ernest Morrison, who would later achieve fame as 'China' Morrison, posed as an ordinary seaman aboard the *Lavinia*, out of the port of Mackay, when it took about twenty natives who were too ill for further plantation work back to their homes in the New Hebrides. On his first night aboard the *Lavinia*, he heard someone groaning by the windlass. He found a boy of about fourteen. The boy stood—'his withered little frame, already in the hands of death . . . and tottered down to his bunk and the first night at sea he died and his body was let into the deep'. Morrison was appalled that a health official in Mackay, Dr Robert McBurney, part-owner of the

Lavinia, had let this mortally ill boy undertake an impossible voyage. Morrison's later article for the *Age* mentioned amongst other things the impact upon women—'whose presence aboard turns the ship into a "brothel" and whose experience on the mainland almost invariably transformed a pretty, chaste girl into a diseased hag within the three years ashore'. Native hospitals were built in some areas and a tax of £1 per labourer was levied to pay for them. Nevertheless, the overall death rate of Kanakas in Queensland was reduced only to eight times that of white men.

By the early 1880s the profits to be made out of an industry employing islander labour had begun to attract the attention of many of the devout Presbyterian capitalists of Melbourne and Sydney. Pioneer planters now sold out their sugar plantations to the capitalists from the south, the original owner sometimes staying on as supervisor. The 6000-acre Hambledon estate near Cairns, for example, was sold to Thomas Swallow, founder of Swallow & Ariell, the biscuit manufacturer seeking sugar to sustain his industry.

The blackbirders had by now been driven out of the New Hebrides by the Royal Navy, and so turned to New Guinea as a source of labour. Premier Sir Thomas McIlwraith, who would temporarily annex New Guinea to Queensland, was a partner in the North Australian Pastoral Company, which was at this stage transforming pastoral land into sugar plantations. He needed Kanaka labourers and had the ships to bring them to Queensland.

The island trading company Burns Philp was also involved in blackbirding in the 1880s. The *Heath*, the *Hopeful* and the *Minny* were amongst the Burns Philp vessels used for recruiting. The *Heath* was the oldest of the fleet, and had been rejected by insurance companies as unseaworthy, but still managed to bring back several cargoes of Kanakas. Late in 1883, when Premier McIlwraith was defeated at the polls, the new premier, Samuel Griffiths, prosecuted the master of the *Heath* for recruiting islanders under false pretences. The master served a gaol term. Burns Philp sued the government for the financial loss involved, losing the case only after years of legal manoeuvring. The captain, recruiting agent, government agent, mate, boatswain and two crew members of the *Hopeful* were prosecuted for kidnapping and murder. All were found guilty on the kidnapping charges, and the recruiting agent and the boatswain were also found guilty of having shot dead two natives. A boy of five had two empty coconuts tied under his arms and was thrown overboard. The crew saw him drown in the surf. Two crew members, McNeil and Williams, were sentenced to death, later commuted to life imprisonment, and a petition on their behalf was later organised and signed by 28 000 supporters of the Kanaka industry in Queensland. When in 1888 the Griffith government lost office and Boyd Dunlop Morehead became premier, he ordered the release of the two murderers and four kidnappers and they were carried through the streets of Brisbane by cheering crowds. The import of Kanakas was nonetheless suspended.

As depression hit in 1890, many of the mills and plantations were closing. But in 1892, Samuel Griffith rose in Parliament to announce the 'temporary reintroduction' of the Kanaka trade to enable sugar growers to cut their costs and survive. The reformer William Brookes, dying, had himself carried to the Queensland Parliament on a stretcher to oppose the bill in the Legislative Council, and spoke for an hour. The proponents of White Australia opposed the new Kanaka bill too, complaining that imported native labourers worked for fourpence a day, and white men could not compete. The British government also protested. But a further 11 000 natives were recruited.

The activities of the Queensland government were not acceptable to the Commonwealth Parliament when it met in 1901. A Pacific Island Labourers Act was quickly passed prohibiting the importation of natives after 1904, and arranging for the repatriation of survivors in Australia. Robert Philp, who was now Premier of Queensland—on being offered a seat in the first federal parliament he had declined because he was too busy with trade—warned Prime Minister Barton of the attitude of Queensland people. For the huge plantations were now a vested interest not only for Colonial Sugar Refinery's many shareholders but for almost every other white resident. Queensland fought a rearguard action, asking the British government to disallow the Commonwealth Act. The final Commonwealth Act allowed natives who had lived in Australia for more than twenty years to continue to do so, as well as those who owned land, and those who were too old and sick to return. Even with these wide exceptions only about 1300 natives remained. So did the unmarked graves of the island recruits to Queensland labour.

DROUGHT AND BISHOP MOORHOUSE

The second Bishop of Melbourne, James Moorhouse, born in England in 1826, was a very modern churchman. He did not believe in the literal interpretation of the Bible and, in nineteenth-century Victoria, asserted that the laws of God now operated in the sphere of morals and belief, but could not prevail against natural law. He was enthusiastic and amiable, and travelled the farming areas for two or three months a year.

A great controversy arose in 1882 over his attitude to drought, and the extent to which prayer could deliver the drought-bullied farmer. Travelling through the Mallee to Kerang, he had been shocked by the desiccated country-side, and by the sight of abandoned and boarded-up farmhouses. When he reached Kerang, a town surrounded by dried-up lakes and lagoons, Anglicans from that region asked him to institute a special day of prayer. From that request came his famous aphorism, 'Don't pray for rain, dam it.' He was aware, he said, that there was terrible distress, but while miracles had been essential in the church's early days to attract converts, they would not occur now. Climatic laws were what now operated. If God intervened as a result of prayer, it would militate against that foresight, industry and prudence that farming in Australia demanded and which sensible farmers should display. 'Prayers for rain may indeed be pressed out of my heart by anguish . . . but I cannot say, because I do not think, that such a prayer is that of an instructed and spiritually-minded Christian.' The aridity of the continent of Australia was not a problem for God but for man.

His views outraged many, both in the region in which they were uttered and, via a report in the *Argus*, in Melbourne as well. The bishop's arguments seemed heartless to some. Dean Slattery, an Irish-born priest in Geelong, argued, with considerable respect for Moorhouse's reputation and gifts, that prayers against natural disasters existed not only in Catholicism but in the Church of England's Book of Common Prayer. The bishop was forced to reply to his critics and did so vigorously but stood by his principles. 'Let a man be ever so righteous and prayerful, if he neglect to comply with the order of nature, he will be unprosperous.'

THE END OF DICKENS' ORPHANS

At the time of this controversy, the stock and station agency E.B.L. Dickens and Company, founded by Plorn and Alfred Dickens in Melbourne in 1882, operated as a realtor for the pastoral industry, but also offered to purchase goods in any city for transportation to stations. Plorn Dickens promised that he and Alfred would personally supervise the buying and packing of these supplies. The *Australasian* wrote, 'How the Dickens can I put it? Best plainly. Two sons of Charles Dickens are about to commence business as station agents in Melbourne.' But the conditions to which Bishop Moorhouse had reacted would continue to shape the fortunes of the Dickens boys.

Still the ambition to be more than an agent existed. In September 1882 that year, Plorn invested £2000 on leases for South Australian land, 2000–3000 square miles (approximately 5000–8000 square kilometres) in country north of Lake Eyre. Why Plorn would buy into land beyond Goyder's Line is hard to discern. Despite rumours of a copper find in the near-desert, he would never mine or run livestock in the country. The leases would in any case be cancelled in 1885.

He returned to Wilcannia in 1883 to begin a Wilcannia branch of the company, leaving Alfred to run the company in Melbourne. He folded his own company into a Western Pastoral Agency he founded with two other Wilcannians, one of whom would soon go south to the emergent silver settlement of Broken Hill, which was the coming town in the region. Shares in the Broken Hill Proprietary Company would rise from a preposterous £175 in January 1888 to £409 in February that year. Within seven years the mining population of Broken Hill would reach 20 000.

His partners in the agency went under and he was left on his own. The town of Wilcannia endured. It had 2000 people and its warehouses and stores withstood both heat and cold. The Athenaeum Club and Library of Wilcannia was opened in a torrid January 1884, and the Druids and Oddfellows and Masonic Lodges honoured it with a procession through town. On that same hot day in January three large stations were auctioned by a larger brokerage, but in collaboration with E.B.L. Dickens and Co. Two of these properties had been put up for sale by Plorn's father-in-law and one by his brother-in-law, all as an attempt to rationalise their holdings on account of the drought. The April 1884 Jockey Club meet had to be cancelled because of dust storms, which the writer Tom Collins described as 'Wilcannia showers'. Barges and steamers were stranded at various places along the river as it dried out.

Before the end of 1884, drought or not, Edward had fulfilled the duty of any robust colonial gentleman, being elected president both of the Jockey Club, though his own fine horses had been sold by then, and the Cricket Club. He also began to take an interest in land legislation made in Parliament in Sydney's Macquarie Street for regions many of the politicians had never clapped eyes on. Out in this dry country, Edward considered the selectors 'not farmers but blackmailers'. That is, they selected or threatened to select a farm of 320 acres, the legislatively decreed size of a selection, knowing it could not sustain them, and waited for the pastoralist to buy them off. Edward was elected honorary secretary of the Land Bill Opposition Society and was even involved in a Separation League which threatened to cut the west off from the state of New South Wales and make it its own colony. On the day he attended the first meeting of the Separation League in 1884, the land gave its own comment on the separatist dream by sending a dust storm which enclosed the town in an orb of red dimness. Edward remained a secessionist and moved the proposal that a petition on the matter be sent to the British government.

It was true that when the legislators in Macquarie Street thought of the impact land laws were making, they tended to have in their minds the better-watered central-western regions of the state, places where a prudent selector might survive. But, as Edward argued of the legislators, 'They knew no more of these parts than we know of the moon.' He emphasised that the proposed new colony would be about 60 000 in population, more than Victoria's population when she separated from New South Wales and more than twice Queensland's. The colony's revenues would be drawn from the Barrier silver mines to the south. Only water was needed to develop the rich resources of the area, he said, and to him as to many colonists the water problem was half beaten by water conservation and the sinking of more wells.

Dickens also felt that the existence of a new colony would hasten Federation, which he felt was impossible while petty jealousies prevailed. The new western state would build bridges and roads which would knit together the region with other states. The Federation Convention held in Sydney in 1883 had been merely an excuse for delegates to journey to beauty spots and to engage in after-dinner oratory, he said. But the new colony he foreshadowed would be devoted to cooperating in a genuine way in the Federation project. The more realistic delegates from the river port of Bourke were not in favour of separation because of the lack of a seaport, and so the separatist dream remained unresolved and, under the breath of the drought, withered away.

During the drought and the separation debate, Edward's company was in great need of funds and he needed £800. Some claimed that as well as suffering the impact of the drought, he had been gambling. He wrote a begging letter to his Aunt Georgie but was refused. Next he appealed to his brother Henry, the successful London barrister. Though dubious, Henry at last sent the money.

A new Land Act for New South Wales was to make special provisions for the far west of the state. According to the act, the minimum homestead lease was for a 'run' of 5000–10 000 acres. The owner had to live on the property for at least six months of every year and fence the outer boundaries within two years. Most westerners still considered such an area would not be viable. But Edward—to his own relief, since he needed the income—was appointed an Inspector of Runs. The Chairman of the Wilcannia Board, equally anxious to earn an income now that he had lost all, arrived in December 1884. It was Frederic Trollope, son of Anthony. Thus the sons of the two most notable English novelists of the nineteenth century were at the same time living in this small and inaccessible town far in the interior of Australia and just scraping by. No Barchester Towers were visible in that country. The towers there were pillars of sand moving on an arid wind.

The long drought ended in January 1885, with floods in the Darling and Paroo rivers. The result, as so often when droughts broke, was damaging floods which swamped many houses. Plorn, having himself taken up a homestead lease of 10 000 acres—a great reduction on the square mileages in South Australia on which he had lost money—led a delegation to Sydney to talk about the realities of life in the west. Like all Wilcannians, he felt the threat of extinction in the fact that the railway had reached Dubbo to the east and was proposed for Bourke, further up the river, bypassing Wilcannia. As well as that, a tramway was being built to connect Menindee in the south with Silverton, the mineral town near Broken Hill. It seemed that Edward's beloved town was being abandoned.

In 1886 Fred Trollope left town to take up full-time employment in the Lands Department in Sydney. Plorn replaced him as a member of the Wilcannia Licensing Court, an assistant to the Chairman of the Land Court. He was elected alderman and was still playing cricket, honoured by his fellow Wilcannia players after a game against stockmen from Nuntherungie station. A new electorate of Wilcannia was established in 1888 to send a member of the Legislative Assembly to Macquarie Street, and Plorn was asked to stand as the Protectionist candidate. He was attracted to Protectionism, even though many pastoralists were Free Trade, for the way it had kept the prices of grain and livestock high and thus profitable in Victoria, which he believed was outstripping New South Wales in wealth and power. Many New South Welshmen thought their colony would benefit from a similar policy, and a National Protection Association was formed.

A bill to establish payment of members had been supported by all parties and passed early in 1888. Since Plorn was now a man of scant resources, a few of his friends collected money for him to last him till the legislation came in, and payment of members began. Five days after Dickens' nomination, Mr Charles

Fartiere of Maryfields Station was persuaded to stand as a Free Trader. Dickens' policy speech declared that 'the splendid position and general prosperity of the neighbouring colony of Victoria' was the outcome of Protection. But he would also campaign for a new Land Act, the present one being a dismal failure. Nine out of ten homestead lessees, he asserted, would clear out tomorrow if they could get even nine-tenths of their money back. But the government would not compensate graziers for improvements on their properties, and people did not want to walk away and let a new leaseholder have the benefit. The rabbit was an essential part of his platform too. As an example of the sort of cost to pastoralists that Plorn was struggling to explain to urban legislators in Sydney, Momba Station spent up to £3000 a month on rabbit extermination.

The election was held. There was a time lapse while votes were retrieved from all over the huge, 200 000-square-mile (500 000-square-kilometre) electorate. But it emerged that Dickens had won by a two-to-one majority. At the end of summer, Plorn departed with his wife Connie by coach on the first leg of his journey to Macquarie Street, and on 5 March 1889 was introduced to Parliament. Sir George Dibbs, the Protectionist, was temporarily in power. Dibbs would be defeated as soon as Parliament convened when some of his own Protectionists dissented from a proposed severe Protection law, disapproved of his lack of interest in Federation, and crossed the floor to vote with Sir Henry Parkes. Such fluidity was characteristic of the loose groupings of colonial politics. Dibbs and Parkes would exchange the premiership a number of times during Plorn's incumbency.

The Sydney the Dickenses came to had a population of 350 000 and must have seemed a metropolis indeed to Edward and Connie, who took up residence at a hotel in Gresham Street. During his time in Parliament, Plorn took the opportunity to found an office of E.B.L. Dickens in Sydney. Dickens' six years in the Legislative Assembly came at a time when the collapse of the land boom brought desolation to the finances of the Australian colonies, and he must sometimes have thought himself fortunate to be receiving a parliamentary salary. But from the first, he campaigned as promised, not least attacking the unsatisfactory reaction of Macquarie Street to the great degrader of the pastoral landscape, the rabbit. Apart from certain bacteria which reached the indigenous peoples even before they had so much as seen a white man, the rabbit had been Australia's most successful European explorer, having, while retaining perfect health, conquered Australia to its very core within less than a hundred years of settlement. As we shall see, they had their abettors. In 1892 Beatrix Potter would rivet British children with *The Tale of Peter Rabbit*, but to the children of the bush and their parents the rabbit was not a charming mischief-maker in a blue coat but a consumer of futures and destinies. Stock riders on the stations herded thousands at a time into a 'battue', a trap with calico wings which funnelled the pests into a small yard where local children clubbed them to death. But that was not adequate. A Rabbit Department had been set up by the New South Wales government to administer a system under which bounties were paid for the scalps of dead rabbits, but some squatters began to suspect that rabbiters employed under it left enough of their prey behind to ensure a recurrent plague. It was believed that men looking to make a living might release rabbits in an area, and then go to the farmers and be paid to kill them. John Reid, manager and part-owner of Tintinallogy, a station between Wilcannia and Menindee, said that the first thing trappers did in an area was not to kill rabbits, but their natural enemies, the goanna, hawks, feral cats and dingoes. Samuel Hubbe, German-born Chief Vermin Inspector for South Australia, said that rabbits had been liberated in 1874 in the Barrier Ranges in New South Wales, and at Campbell's Creek on the Darling. He believed they had been deliberately released in South Australia as well.

Needless to say, by the time Plorn got to Macquarie Street, the government had received many complaints of the ineffectuality of the eradication scheme. In his maiden speech in the Legislative Assembly, he would announce that, in some cases, the capacity to carry livestock had been reduced by half through the rabbit plagues.

Being a political novice, Edward Dickens was soon trapped into indiscretions. From his earliest speeches he suffered from being both Dickens' son and a man from dry Wilcannia. The editor of *Haynes Weekly*, John Haynes, the co-founder with J.F. Archibald of the *Bulletin* and a Parkes disciple now in the House, orchestrated a campaign which implied that Edward had achieved his seat purely because he was the son of Charles Dickens. This led to Plorn declaring in the House that Haynes was 'a servile supporter of Sir Henry Parkes'. Dickens pointed out that in 1884 Haynes had attacked Parkes in print over land policies. He read the text of Haynes's eloquent attack: 'It would be dangerous to give him the reins of government again ... Over and over again he has told us that he was the architect of his own fortune. And over and over again we have thought he ought to have prosecuted the aforesaid architect.'

The Speaker objected to Dickens' use of the word 'servile'. Dickens made an apology and declared that he was only a young member of the House and that 'sons of great men are not usually as great as their fathers. You cannot get two Charles Dickens in one generation.' Ambiguously there were calls of 'Hear! Hear!'

Dickens as a speaker held out no vision of future grandeur for the colonies. In his maiden speech he explained how the present Land Act, though framed with good intentions, was a failure.

> I took up 100,000 acres as a homestead lessee. I spent about £250 cash upon it and it was one of the best areas available, being close to a town. I thought it better eventually to sacrifice the £250 and to allow the lease to be cancelled than to spend more money on it . . . The proportion of good seasons to bad seasons is about one in four. Therefore if these unfortunate men do get their heads a little above water in one season they are dragged down again.

Dickens' speech was met with contempt. One pro-Parkes member said that the Honourable Member for Wilcannia 'must lament the misery he has brought on the House tonight by bringing forward at such an untimely period the grievances of his constituents'. But, he said, Dickens should not underestimate the number of friends the far west had on the other side of the House.

Dickens mentioned that Parkes too had attacked the men of that western region because they didn't buy their necessities from and sell their produce in New South Wales. They would be glad to, said Plorn, but they could not get their goods to or from Sydney cheaper than they could to and from other places. Then he made the point that Sydney had received in rain in March 1889 an inch more than Wilcannia had received in the whole year of 1888.

Dickens' speech yielded no fruit and when he next rose, on the night of 23 May 1889, it was to comment on a new Crown Lands Bill, introduced by James Nixon Brunker, a stolid Maitland butcher and Parkes' Minister for Lands. Dickens' speech took for granted—as the man himself did—that these far western leaseholds could be made fruitful, an idea of which he, along with his fellow Britons, would never be cured despite all the evidence about rainfall and pasture he himself presented to the House. However, if a man had to abandon his lease, 'Compensation for water improvements is a right'. If this were done, said Dickens, hundreds of men walking around the country with swags on their shoulders would find employment, apparently because new lessees would take up the improved land and make further improvements and would need labour. But if men were not able to take over abandoned leases at a fair price, 'the Government will find that they will have on their hands a lot of silted up tanks, a lot of fences tumbling down, and wells falling in.' If members would look at the government astronomer's rainfall map, they would get some idea of the difficulties which the tenants in the western country faced. He then quoted the rainfalls for 1884—Milparinka 2.18, Bourke 6.83, Wilcannia 3.23, Wentworth 4.59, Menamurtie 1.86, Pack Saddle 2.11. For brave leaseholders who tried to conserve water under such conditions, compensation from the state should be automatic.

The Governor of New South Wales, Lord Carrington, said Dickens 'had the pluck last year' to take a land trip from Bourke to Broken Hill, and had said at Wilcannia that he thought he had seen some of the most miserable country in the world. The governor said he had been to the second cataract of the Nile, but he could not have believed, if he had not seen it, that there was so much desolation and misery within 50 miles of Wilcannia.

Dickens knew of this desolation. He told Parliament the story of a man who drove 32,000 sheep towards market in Cobar, of whom 14,000 to 15,000 perished on the road. He sold the rest at a lesser price because of their condition, and after paying all expenses had lost £993 and also was lacking his 32,000 sheep. 'Here is the case of a man who started in 1880. In 1883 and 1884 he lost 80,000 sheep, in 1885 he had a fair season, in 1887 he lost 7,000 lambs and spent £27,000 in restocking his country. In 1888 he lost 50,000 sheep, in 1881 he had 2,000 bales of wool and in 1884, 700.' Hence, marginal returns.

Members seemed to be getting sick of being lectured by Plorn Dickens. The new Land Bill, with fewer blemishes from Dickens' point of view, was passed in the Assembly on 18 December 1890 and was rushed through the Council, its speedy passage there being guided by Edward's old friend the storekeeper from Momba, W.H. Suttor, who believed it a great improvement over the previous Act.

As for the issue of the rabbit, we know Plorn was just as persistent. During an adjournment debate he heard members cry, 'Hang the rabbits, we are sick of rabbits!' to which the Minister for Lands exclaimed, 'Hear! Hear!' If Parliament had been a schoolyard, Plorn would have been one of the bullied boys. But his younger brother Henry, a barrister soon to be a judge in England, reported the story that his little brother had routed the Member for Bourke, W.N. Willis, with the sally, 'Mr. Speaker, my late honoured father once wrote. "Barkis is willing". If he had been here tonight, he would have said, "Willis is barking." '

Early in the next session Edward asked if plans to extend the railway line from Cobar to Wilcannia would be introduced during that session of legislation. (He had earlier written to Parkes on the matter: 'At the present time we are alienated from Sydney and are forced to deal with South Australia [and sometimes Victoria when the Rivers Darling and Murray are navigable].') The minister told him it would not be. The truth was both that the railway would save Wilcannia from its crippling and expensive isolation, but also that with the depression having bitten, the great age of governments building railways on money borrowed in London were gone. British financial institutions with money to invest in ventures in far places were turning their attention to South America and to a Western Australia transformed by the desert gold reefs of Coolgardie and Kalgoorlie.

Edward and Sir Henry were together in Broken Hill on 4 April 1890, looking on its changing landscape, pastoralists now outnumbered by industrially militant miners. Along the Barrier the union organiser was replacing the drover, and he was likely to travel on bicycle rather than by a Waler, the sturdy hybrid horse ridden in the wilderness. Edward went on ahead to Wilcannia to prepare for a visit by Sir Henry, and civic groups began planning the reception on the Darling's august banks where the powerful old man would be presented with the town's, the region's special needs. But the seventy-five-year-old Parkes found Wilcannia a reach too far and a session of the House in Macquarie Street was about to begin. He left for Sydney via Adelaide and Melbourne without visiting the town.

So Edward ploughed his lonely parliamentary furrow, and no one took any notice.

THE GREAT RABBIT PRIZE

It was believed that the initial rabbit infestation of Australia began not with the less hardy species brought on earlier ships but with the consigning of two dozen grey European rabbits in 1859 from James Austin in Glastonbury, Somerset, to his brother Thomas Austin, a Geelong district pastoralist, who wanted to use them for hunting and eating. (His crime of folly is partly expiated by his widow's ultimately endowing the Austin Hospital in Melbourne.) The rabbits swiftly spread to neighbouring properties, and Austin spent a considerable sum trying to exterminate them to appease outraged graziers. One of them, John Robertson of Wando Vale, spent more than £30 000 trying to wipe them out.

The rabbits reached the Murray River by 1872, and by 1884 had appeared along the Lachlan and Darling. They somehow crossed the central deserts and could be found in Western Australia by 1894, having by then also infested Queensland and South Australia. Government and private expenditures applied to hunting and poisoning having failed to diminish the population, New South Wales under the premiership of Sir Henry Parkes, now eighty-one years old and enjoying a fourth term, had decided in 1887 to offer a reward of £25 000 for the biological obliteration of the rabbit. To claim the prize devised by Parkes and Minister of Mines Francis Abigail, the saviour of pastoral Australia would need to prove the efficacy of his method to an Inter-Colonial Royal Commission on Rabbit Destruction (itself, in being intercolonial, a harbinger of Federation), and the eradication process would need to operate successfully for twelve months.

The advertisement of the New South Wales prize was published in Europe, and the great French chemist and microbiologist Louis Pasteur had it pointed out to him at a friend's dinner table. He ordered his nephew Adrien Loir, barely twenty years of age, to prepare flasks of virulent cultures of chicken cholera, cultivated in water in which beef had been boiled, to take to Australia. The Pasteur Institute was cash-poor, but Pasteur was so confident as Loir departed with two small boxes of chicken cholera flasks that he assured his bankers that Loir would soon be back with the £25 000 reward.

Accompanied by two doctors who worked at the Pasteur Institute in Paris, Loir arrived in Australia in 1888 to begin work on the issue. But he faced the immediate problem that New South Wales had passed a law forbidding the introduction of foreign microbes and that Victorian law forbade experiments by people who were not doctors. Just the same, he was able to earn some revenue for the Pasteur Institute by advising Thomas Aitken, owner of the Victoria Brewery, on developing brewing cultures for the manufacture of Victoria Bitter.

In Sydney there was a meeting between Mr Abigail and the French, from which Loir got the impression that the chicken-cholera method was being ruled out by the government. But soon Loir and the others were called to appear before the Commission on Rabbit Destruction. The owner of Tarella Station near Wilcannia had offered his property as a testing ground. Pasteur thought that the prize should be awarded after four to six weeks, whereas it became apparent at this meeting that the commission intended a year's trial.

By now Dr Archibald Watson, Professor of Anatomy at Adelaide University and a competitor for the prize, was selling rabbits infected with a fatal disease named 'rabbit scab' to South Australian farmers in the belief that, once introduced, it would kill all the other rabbits. Overall there were 1500 entries into the contest for rabbit eradication. Most of them were complicated machines for rabbit trapping. There were 115 biological submissions, of which forty-two came from the Australian colonies, six from New Zealand, and the rest from Britain and Ireland, the United States, France and from nearly every country in Europe.

The Pasteur men were treated with widespread suspicion. A suggestion was made that Pasteur's methods should be tried experimentally on an island. The young Dr Henry Allen, Professor of Medicine at Melbourne University, declared that one could not predict the direct or indirect impact of Loir's chicken-cholera cultures. There was a perception amongst the public—which the anti-Pasteur people were willing to spread—that chicken cholera was a close relative of the fatal human disease just now being defeated in the cities by sanitary engineers. Allen cited all the latest research from Germany and France to attack the French plans.

Loir and his team were sidelined into trying to find a cure, working with diseased sheep from a property in the Riverina owned by a pastoralist named Arthur Devlin. In a Sydney laboratory, Loir made cultures from the lesions on the dead sheep and tested them on mice. Loir declared that Cumberland disease was in fact anthrax. He tried it out on rabbits, which quickly died.

Despite the prejudices against them, Parkes himself was anxious to keep the Frenchmen in Australia, and ordered the construction of a research station on Rodd Island near Iron Cove in the Parramatta River for them to carry out their research projects. But Parkes' government showed no understanding of intellectual property and had the Experiment Committee of the Rabbit Commission performing the same experiments as the Pasteur team virtually as soon as Loir had reported them home. This was possible because Parkes had every telegram that came to Pasteur's representatives in Australia, and every one they sent, presented to him and made available to cabinet and the bureaucracy. Parkes therefore saw that Pasteur had ordered his people by telegram not to proceed with any more anthrax research until they had solved the rabbit problem and won the prize. Since he thought that anthrax could more promptly be cured by the French to the colony's great benefit, Parkes retained this telegram and did not pass it on to Loir, and ordered the Stock Department as well to carry on with anthrax trials in the Riverina, even as the French continued to research it at Rodd Island.

Eventually William Lyne, a Protectionist, future premier and future federal member of Parliament, who himself owned a rabbit-infested station named Tyrie in the central west of New South Wales, asked Parkes in Parliament whether any communications from Pasteur to his representatives had been interfered with. Parkes admitted some early ones had been opened at the Colonial Secretary's office by mistake, but had since been let go to Loir unopened.

Loir and his Pasteur Institute colleague Dr Germont kept on carrying out animal anthrax experiments in an enclosed pasture on Yarah Station in the Riverina, near Junee. Soon 260 000 sheep were available for inoculation, but Pasteur had a better sense of intellectual property than Henry Parkes did, and on 20 October 1888 Pasteur sent a telegram to Loir telling him to instruct the New South Wales government that a supply of the anthrax vaccine could be purchased at a cost of £100 000. 'Wait for payment of that sum by the Government before proceeding to the first practical experiment on the 100 000 sheep.'

Parkes intercepted the telegram as usual, and was outraged that Pasteur was asking for a sum for anthrax eradication that was four times the amount of the rabbit eradication prize. In the meantime, the Queensland government invited Loir and Germont to Brisbane to produce the pleuro-pneumonia microbe and make cultures for injecting livestock. A four-man Pleuro-Pneumonia Commission was set up in Queensland on 16 November. The young Henry Lawson in New South Wales also encountered pleuro-pneumonia in cattle and 'used to bleed them by cutting their tails and ears in the sickening heat—and was often sick over the job—and inoculate them with a big needle'. Soon there might be a less squalid and more effective means.

Pasteur was now complaining to the British government and even the Prince of Wales, an acquaintance of his, about the interception of telegrams. A member of the Legislative Council and former *Bulletin* editor named William Traill had already attacked Parkes for the damage done to New South Wales in the international press.

In 1889 Parkes, threatened with insolvency once more and under suspicion from his followers that he was not a true Free Trade man, was the victim of defections that enabled Sir George Dibbs to become premier again. Pasteur was delighted that Parkes was gone, and in hope of a big sale posted off to Australia further tubes of anthrax. Even as he did so, the preliminary report of the Commission on Rabbit Destruction was being written on the Pasteur scientists' chicken-cholera scheme. It read, 'The Commission cannot recommend that permission be given to disseminate broadcast throughout Australasia a disease which has not been shown to exist in these colonies.'

When Loir left Australia in February 1892, he took with him 250 000 French francs from the sale of cultures, but not the prize money. Pasteur told a French journalist that his representatives had 'clashed with the malevolent intentions of the Commission appointed by the Australian Government'. Parkes, yet again returned to government, engaged Loir's services once more and brought him back to Australia in 1890. Loir had convinced Pasteur to let him go ahead with the anthrax vaccination scheme. Arthur Devlin, the Riverina pastoralist, was again a great customer of the vaccine. By the end of the year pastoralists had made the anthrax and the pleuro-pneumonia vaccine so popular that Loir was able to send back a further 700 000 francs to the Pasteur Institute. Loir was beginning to like the country as well, and the laconic landowners and lessees of the bush—and in any case he had the company of Sarah Bernhardt during her 1890 tour of Australia. The great actress both lunched, dined and, for some nights, stayed on Rodd Island. Sarah's last Sunday in Australia was spent on Rodd Island.

Loir, returned to France again, achieved his doctorate with a thesis entitled 'Microbiology in Australia'. This document achieved great currency amongst scientists and was used by Pasteur to get even with the Commission on Rabbit Destruction. Loir, with his new wife, boarded the steamer *Australien* for Australia and New Caledonia. Arriving in Sydney in August 1892, he found that public opinion was starting to run in Pasteur's favour. Abigail, the former mines minister, who Pasteur saw as having played games with his nephew, was now one of those bankers destroyed by the depression and had been sentenced to five years' hard labour for issuing a false balance sheet.

The powerful had been chastened by the great collapse and in this new and more genial atmosphere, Loir announced that he intended to stay in Australia permanently if he could get the right backing. The *Sydney Morning Herald* supported the idea that Pasteur should be given the prize, and Premier Sir George Dibbs, being Parkes' political enemy, was not unsympathetic. Loir was able in the meantime to go ahead with testing the vaccine of a student of Pasteur's. Professor Saturnin Arloing's black leg (anthrax) vaccine was designed to protect Australian cattle against an affliction endemic in Australia. But when Loir's thesis, now translated into English, was published in excerpts in the Australian newspapers, many colonial scientists were enraged. It was, in particular, Pasteur's own inserted commentary on colonial biological ignorance which created the most anger. Loir departed Australia for good in 1893 to run the Pasteur clinic in Tunis. Though he would never see the rabbit prize awarded, he would live until 1941, nine years shy of the introduction of the organism myxomatosis into Australia's enduring rabbit population.

IS ART POSSIBLE?

Could the Australian harshness and otherness permit poetry, and could the light and strangeness permit painting? Henry Kendall, struggling with alcoholism, former shepherd, gold commissioner on the New South Wales South Coast, and finally a New South Wales inspector of forests, was a notable Australian lyric poet at the beginning of the 1860s. Indeed his 1869 book, *Leaves from Australian Forests*, derived from his penetration of the coastal bush on horseback throughout that period. Generations of children in schools learned his gentle, celebratory and subtly nationalist 'Bell-birds'.

> *Through breaks of the cedar and sycamore bowers*
> *Struggles the light that is love to the flowers;*
> *And, softer than slumber, and sweeter than singing,*
> *The notes of the bell-birds are running and ringing.*

Adam Lindsay Gordon, twenty-seven in 1860 and with only another ten years to live, was no tender philosopher-poet—he was a boxer, a mounted trooper, a horse breaker and an extraordinary horseman in all ways. He too had something wayward in his soul, and in that was characteristic of a number of well-bred Britons who brought their flaws to Australia, a place that was well designed to magnify them. A graduate of the Royal Military Academy, Gordon came to Adelaide in 1853, at first serving in the police and then becoming a horse breaker and steeplechase rider. In 1862 he married Margaret Bark, a girl of seventeen. His first poem, 'The Feud', was published in March 1865, at a time when he was a member of the South Australian House of Assembly. He gave that up to settle on land in Western Australia but returned to South Australia, impoverished, and lived in Mount Gambier in 1867. His poems showed his classical education even in their titles, such as 'Finis Exoptatus', 'Quare Fatigasti?' and 'Exodus Parthenidae'.

'I've had an interview with the banker,' went his lament for broke squatters in 'Exodus Parthenidae',

And I found him civil, and even kind;
But the game's up here, we must weigh the anchor,
We've the surf before, and the rocks behind.

Throughout this time he was publishing verse in the *Australian* and *Bell's Life* in Victoria. He tried to run a livery stable at Ballarat, but again went broke. He had a bad riding accident in 1868—jumping fences and barriers in his enthusiasm for steeplechase training. His only child Annie died, and his wife left him. Yet for all this bitterness, Lindsay Gordon seemed a romantic figure. At Flemington he won three steeplechase races on one afternoon, two of them on his own horse.

There were bookmakers, trainers, touts,
Heavy swells and their jockeys light,
The man that drinks and the man that shouts,
Carrier pigeon and carrion kite.

In March 1870 he fell badly in a steeplechase and suffered a head injury. The day before he shot himself on the beach at Brighton in June 1870 he published his *Bush Ballads and Galloping Rhymes*. To a reader of his best-known extended poem, 'The Sick Stockrider', it seems as if he had always expected to be destroyed by the bush.

There was Hughes, who got in trouble through that business with the cards,
It matters little what became of him;
But a steer ripp'd up MacPherson in the Cooraminta yards,
And Sullivan was drown'd at Sink-or-swim.
And Mostyn—poor Frank Mostyn—died at last a fearful wreck,
In 'the horrors', at the Upper Wandinong;
And Carisbrooke, the rider, at the Horsefall broke his neck,
Faith! the wonder was he saved his neck so long!

Lindsay Gordon's death from the head injury evoked extraordinary tributes from sources as diverse as the Archbishop of Canterbury, Arthur Conan Doyle, and the Governor of Victoria. Oscar Wilde said he was one of the finest poetic singers the English race had ever known. 'A shining soul,' said Kendall, 'with syllables of fire who sang the first songs this land can claim to be its own.' In

1934 his bust would be placed in Westminster Cathedral to represent Australian poetry. For Australians and many Britons his poem 'Froth and Bubble' took on the moral force Kipling's 'If' would later exert.

Life is mainly froth and bubble,
Two things stand like stone,
Kindness in another's trouble,
Courage in your own.

Oscar Wilde, in reviewing an early Australian anthology, gave a withering judgment. He described Australian versifiers as 'poets who lay under the shade of the gum-tree, gather wattle blossoms and buddawong and sarsaparilla for their loves, and wander through the glades of Mount Baw Baw, listening to the careless raptures of the mopoke'. Wilde did, however, have regard for Kendall and Lindsay Gordon.

At the same time Adam Lindsay Gordon died, twenty-five-year-old immigrant Marcus Clarke was putting the last touches to the novel *His Natural Life*, which was first, in the style of the time, published in serial form and which raised the embarrassing questions of British brutality and convict endurance. In 1856 the journalist Frederick Sinnett, writing in the *Journal of Australasia*, said that it was not possible to write Australian novels because Australian life, scenery and settings were unsuitable for the purpose. Although time would prove him wrong, it was clear that many Australians, native-born and immigrant, felt the same. Immigrants and people who thought of the northern hemisphere as their true home sought their literature from that source. As they believed colonial policies coincided with that of Great Britain, so they believed should their taste in books. Thus the impact of Clarke's Australian novel on liberal-minded colonists was enormous, and though its purpose was not necessarily national-ist, it was the sort of book which gave wings to the desire for the distinctness of the native-born Australians. Sadly, Clarke would not write a corpus of novels because he died in 1881 at the age of only thirty-five, after a career first with the *Argus*, then at the Melbourne *Herald*, and finally at the *Age*.

Rolf Boldrewood (the pseudonym of Thomas A. Browne), author of *Robbery Under Arms*—which was first published in the *Sydney Mail* over late 1882 and early 1883—enhanced the image of the bushranger as 'iron-barked within and without' and thus thoroughly Australian, badly used and striking back with skill. As a struggling pastoralist himself—he had whimsically called his pastoral lease on the Eumeralla River Squattersea-sur-mer—perhaps Boldrewood's novel was his extended daydream about getting even with banks and other forces of authority, even though he had been a gold commissioner and Gulgong magistrate. Until now heroes in novels published in magazines had been gentlemen Britons colonising Australia. The stylish rebel bushrangers of Boldrewood's novel were emphatically Australian. The reality that the bushranger was often Irish was avoided for the sake of mainstream sympathy, and the central character was true-blue Briton hero Ben Marston.

Between 1890 and 1905 Boldrewood would write a number of other novels, short-story collections. He also helped Louis Becke write and publish his famous South Sea 'blackbirding' stories involving the piratical Bully Hayes, with whom Becke had sailed. But *Robbery Under Arms* would earn Boldrewood/Browne an international reputation; on their journeys to Australia Mark Twain and Rider Haggard would seek him out.

Writing remained a particularly hard option for colonials and one not everyone understood. The reason for coming all this way was inevitably, and in the huge majority of cases, to acquire the wealth to justify the journey. In this atmosphere Kendall found it impossible to work full-time as a writer, and Henry Lawson, considered a prodigious success by Australian standards, earned only £700 pounds from writing in his first twelve years—far less than most labourers' wages. In 1899 he would write, 'My advice to any young Australian writer whose talents have been recognised would be to go steerage, stowaway, swim and seek London, Yankeeland, or Timbuktu.' Failing that, he suggested, study anatomy and thus know where to shoot oneself dead accurately. From several editions of *My Brilliant Career*, Miles Franklin would earn a mere £24. That seemed to prove the point.

Painters, particularly painters from elsewhere on earth with an established reputation, brought a worldliness with them when they turned up for the Australian phase of their careers. Louis Buvelot (1814–88), born in Switzerland, served as the bridge between the colonial and the Heidelberg paintings of Tom Roberts and others. He was a painter of huge, exotic landscapes who arrived in Melbourne in 1865 at the age of fifty-one with a young female artist, Caroline-Julie Beguin. (The place of Australia and New Zealand as places for sexual new starts is a subject which might one day attract an historian.) Buvelot had taught at a Swiss art school near Bern after earlier spending eighteen years in Brazil, where his uncle owned a coffee plantation. He would paint Australian material for the next twenty years, concentrating on Australian light. There is a resemblance between Buvelot's paintings and those of Conrad Martens (who had sailed as artist on the famous *Beagle* and whose landscapes concentrate on Sydney Harbour) and those of the Viennese landscapist Johann von Guerard, who would paint in Australia for sixteen years. The work of these three artists was commonly accused of stressing the similarities between Australia and Europe instead of facing up to the unique demands the Australian environment made on the European sensibility, the demands which Tom Roberts and his Heidelberg School camping companions are seen as addressing.

Buvelot's paintings of cattle grazing at Templestowe and Coleraine, and also his 1869 waterpool near Coleraine, do seem European in landscape, but looked to his contemporaries like an exciting blend of northern Europe and the Antipodes. Frederick McCubbin felt that *A Summer Afternoon near Templestowe* was 'thoroughly Australian' despite the fact that it did not look anything like the bush McCubbin himself would paint. Buvelot was the Melbourne painter of his day who was most likely to be exhibited (and bought), and his work was shown at the Intercolonial Exhibition of 1866. Julian Ashton and Tom Roberts knew him when they were young and were impressed by his resemblance to Leonardo da Vinci.

Julian Ashton, father of art in Sydney for more than half a century after he moved there in 1883, claimed in Melbourne in 1882 that he was the first Australian painter to complete a painting in the open. John Ford Paterson and John Mather, both Scots and friends of Alfred Deakin, liked the outdoors and sketched in the Healesville district and along the eastern shores of Port Phillip Bay in the Heidelberg area. But it was the four major figures of the Heidelberg School—Tom Roberts and Frederick McCubbin, who at the end of Australia's first century were in their early thirties, and Arthur Streeton and Charles Conder, who were just twenty—whose paintings would convey powerfully the sense of being in the bush. Ironically their adventures in the wilderness, as rich as they were in paintings, involved a journey of perhaps at most 20 kilometres from Melbourne.

IRRIGATION AND THE REDEMPTION OF AUSTRALIA

In 1884 Alfred Deakin, a visionary young Liberal, was put in charge of a Victorian Royal Commission into matters of irrigation.

Alfred Deakin was then a young barrister of twenty-eight years of age, the son of one of those who had gone to the goldfields in 1851. He had a restless intelligence and embraced theosophism and spiritism, believing that even contact with the dead could be achieved by scientific means and could be proven to be governed by natural laws. In 1882 he married nineteen-year-old Elizabeth Brown, the daughter of a wealthy Melburnian who was also a prominent spiritualist. If there was a solution to spirit contact, there certainly was a solution to the problem of water. And so the idea of irrigation did not daunt Deakin—like others, he was excited and relieved by its prospects.

Irrigation was for Deakin almost the sister dream to that of Federation. He had been inflamed by stories of Californian irrigation schemes which he heard from one Steven Cureton, an Australian newly home from Los Angeles, during a train journey in which he happened to share a train compartment with the young man. Deakin and others thought that in the irrigation of the arid Central Valley of California lay a technology which could be applied to Australia. On Christmas Eve 1884 he left for California with an engineer who had some experience of irrigation work and two newspaper correspondents, E.S. Cunningham representing the *Age* and J.L. Dowell of the *Argus*. He wished them to be promoters of his discoveries in California.

In Los Angeles, Deakin and his party met George Chaffey, a Canadian who, with his brother William, was a citizen of Ontario—not the province of Canada, but an irrigation settlement in the desert 40 miles (64 kilometres) east of Los Angeles on the Santa Ana River. It had been settled by Canadians in planned temperance communities. The settlements of Ontario and Etiwanda, which the Chaffeys founded between them, had been based upon the purchase of land and water rights by the Chaffey family at a low price, the land being resold to settlers in 10-acre blocks, with a mutual irrigation company being formed to distribute water as a non-profit enterprise. Cement pipes were used in the main water channels.

George Chaffey impressed Deakin with the force of his own character and with the technological change he had brought to irrigation. In the copious notebooks the Australian brought back to Melbourne lay the means, he believed, for 'the conquest of those areas hitherto regarded as worthless'. Only irrigation could provide 'her arid districts a permanent prosperity'. In the meantime,

George, the elder and more restless of the brothers, decided to go to Melbourne and pursue irrigation works in the colony of Victoria. When he arrived in February 1886, full of the zeal for temperance, righteousness and water technology, he had already been warned by Deakin and others that he would not be able to obtain a land grant on terms identical to those in California, but that something favourable could be worked out. Nonetheless, Chaffey did not understand that Australians looked more to government to provide major public works, unlike the Americans, who looked to free enterprise. But George did a tour of the Murray Valley and became excited by its capacity to support irrigation.

Deakin was able to assure George Chaffey that the government would make available a quarter of a million acres of Crown land on favourable terms, and George at once sent a cable to his brother William telling him to sell up all their interests in California and follow him to Australia. George selected the desolate region of an abandoned sheep station, Mildura in the Mallee, for his first irrigation settlement. It had the disadvantage of being hundreds of miles from the railway at Swan Hill. But the Chaffey brothers signed a compact with the Victorian government guaranteeing that it would spend at least £300 000 on permanent improvements in Mildura over the next twenty years.

The bill which Deakin introduced to the House to confirm the arrangement was opposed, and the Chaffeys were described by some as 'cute Yankee land grabbers'. Sir John Downer, Premier of South Australia, hearing of this opposition to the Chaffeys, steamed to Melbourne and offered them 250 000 acres in his colony, and soon the Chaffeys had selected Murray River frontages in the Renmark area. In any case, since no competing tenders for Mildura had been received, the Chaffeys went ahead there too. For the next four years, George worked at an astonishing pace, overseeing and developing both areas as irrigation centres. William remained at Mildura and a younger brother, Charles, arrived to manage the Renmark area.

By December 1890, 3300 people had settled at Mildura and 1100 at Renmark. The towns were well surveyed and shaded by trees planted in the manner of Ontario and Etiwanda. But the settlers became disgruntled at the Chaffeys' Mildura Irrigation Company's charges for water, and the Crown Law Department told the Chaffeys that the subdivisions were entitled to free water. Many attacks on the Chaffeys were made in the Victorian Parliament, and even more so when the economy collapsed in the 1890s. The settlers themselves were offended by the brusqueness and officiousness of the Chaffeys and combined to try to get rid of them and substitute the Victorian government as their landlord. So, in

August 1895, the colony's Mildura Irrigation Trust took over the functions of the Chaffeys' Mildura Irrigation Company.

On 10 December 1894 Chaffey Brothers Limited went into liquidation with assets of 438 acres of unsold land at Mildura and Renmark. The Bank of Victoria, which had earlier supported the Chaffeys' endeavour, foreclosed on the mortgages of hundreds of settlers along the river, but in the end the irrigation schemes survived under government supervision. In 1896 Premier Sir George Turner, Victoria's first native-born premier, a shabbily dressed but urbane Federationist, appointed a Royal Commission to inquire into the Mildura matter. The report, which was tabled in 1897, blamed the Chaffeys for the Mildura failure, citing their lack of planning and their dependence on finance. All this, however, left the belief in the holiness and God-ordained quality of irrigation undaunted in Alfred Deakin.

In August that year, as the report was being presented to the premier, George Chaffey had sailed to the United States where he tapped underground water to revive the Ontario settlement and diverted the water of the Colorado River to irrigate the desert west of San Diego. He named the region Imperial Valley, and it was successful. William Chaffey, on the other hand, remained at Mildura, working an orchard of 81 hectares and establishing the Mildara Winery Pty Ltd. He died there in June 1926, having been Mildura's first mayor, and long after his death the belief that irrigation was the answer to Australia's disappointing inland rainfall remained powerful. His son was killed in the AIF in World War I.

BUSHRANGERS, TIME, ART

There is a picture that most people interested in bushrangers are familiar with. It is taken on a winter's morning in 1880 by the side of Benalla police barracks, and it shows the body of a young man strung up in a doorway, stricken rigid by death. His body had been transported here from the place he fell dead from a gunshot wound, Glenrowan, Victoria, while calling on his saviour for forgiveness. He seems to stand in the photo but the stance is crumpled. His name was Joe Byrne, who came from the area named Woolshed near Beechworth, and he was Ned Kelly's lieutenant. He had been dead about a day at the time the photograph was taken.

To me this is more than a photograph of a bushranger's body and yokel onlookers, but is a point of juncture between worlds, and between visions of

Australia. And it is strangely post-modern as well—the photographer has photographed yet another photographer who is photographing the dead bushranger. Photographers in that age tried not to acknowledge the presence of their own camera, let alone that of others.

This was certainly the case with the man who took the Joe Byrne photograph, J.W. Lindt, a German photographer whose prints were very popular in Australia. He had created a successful studio photograph entitled *Aboriginal Man and Woman with Kangaroo*, involving an Aboriginal male with a kangaroo-skin skirt, his wife, seated, holding a large boomerang, and a dead kangaroo, the work of a taxidermist, lying with its head on a log in front of them and with a boomerang between its paws. The picture of Joe Byrne taken by this vigorous young German, using the wet plate process since he had rushed up from his society studio in Collins Street, was astoundingly impromptu therefore. One of the bush bystanders, shirt-sleeved this cold morning, is scratching his nose as he talks to others. A boy child moves and his face becomes a blur on the plate. Someone, maybe the photographer being photographed—the government photographer A.W. Berman, who is up much closer to Joe's body—has slung his overcoat in the fork of a bare tree. And on the left of the camera, in a bowler hat and a good overcoat, taking no direct interest in what Lindt is doing, a man with a pad under his arm is turning away, having finished his sketches of the aftermath of the Kelly climax in Glenrowan.

This man is a young Englishman, Julian Ashton, artist, up from Melbourne to make sketches for David Syme, the editor of the *Age* and of an illustrated paper, the *Australian News*. Ashton looks like a robust young man, even though he has asthma and has immigrated in a mistaken belief that Australia will be good for it.

Julian Rossi Ashton, having finished with poor Joe and turned away, was a different sort of Australian beast. In his early twenties he had studied painting at the Académie Julian in Paris, and had his work accepted by the Royal Academy of Arts. He would ultimately move to Sydney and, through his presidency of the Art Society, establish a tradition of professional art and found his own painting school, whose students would include George Lambert, Thea Proctor, Sidney Smith and William Dobell. On their way to the future Ashton and his younger brother, who also worked for David Syme, brush past a limping, sturdy block of a young man escorted by two policemen. Ned Kelly. Though severely wounded, Kelly amazed all with the strength of his constitution, though he would be borne from the train, once it arrived in Melbourne, on a very elaborate litter. Julian Ashton would similarly amaze men with his endurance.

The hunters and police would have their picture taken too by that door once Byrne's body is taken down. In their midst is Superintendent Sadleir, whose fire on a Glenrowan hotel full of civilians had been so reckless that the question of criminality had become a sliding term that night. By the time that photo was taken, Ashton was well and truly gone. He had turned his back on all that. He was heading in the direction of his own regimen of sketching and, at least through later artist friends, Impressionism.

A RUSSIAN IN NEW GUINEA

It could meanwhile be argued that one of the influences on Australia's early concentration on New Guinea was a Russian naturalist. Nicholai Nicholaievich Miklouho-Maklai (Maclay), born in July 1846 in Novgorod province, was an extraordinary Russian natural scientist who, in his labours, concentrated on the Torres Strait region. As a result of training in Leipzig and Jena, he was motivated to study the natural history and ethnography of New Guinea, and first settled near Astrolabe Bay in what is now north-east Madang province in 1871, and lived there for two years. With the characteristic and unthinking hubris of the Europeans of his day, he named the stretch of coastline extending 320 kilometres east from Astrolabe Bay 'Maklaya' or, as it became known, the Maclay coast. On 20 January 1880, Maclay joined the London Missionary Society missionary James Chalmers on a mission schooner to visit the southern coast of New Guinea. By now, said Maclay, there were a dozen pearling-shell stations operating eighty-eight vessels in the Torres Strait—the captains working for Sydney companies and often exploiting native divers. He sought to advise the natives at Kalo Kalo near Milne Bay on how to deal with the realities of European justice.

Though during his absence in Batavia local natives destroyed his hut and killed his native supporters, Maclay remained a passionate advocate against their exploitation by Europeans, and would appeal on their behalf for their protection by Dutch, British and German authorities, pleading with them to prevent Australian blackbirding in the region, and the trade in guns and liquor. On a visit to Australia he investigated further the trade in Kanaka labour, but also the comparisons between Aboriginal, Chinese, Malay and New Guinean skulls. Maclay visited Mer, Murray Island, the home of people from whom eventually Eddie Mabo would be born. Here he was appalled by the activities of a London Missionary Society native teacher named Josiah and his use of the lash. He was so uncomfortably vocal about all this that some Queensland politicians justified the seizure of New Guinea by Queensland in 1883 by arguing that proposals had been made to the Russian government by a certain Baron 'Maclay-Miklouho' to annexe New Guinea and to establish a Russian naval, coaling and trading station there.

Maclay was involved in petitioning the Colonial Office to grant land rights to the natives of Maklaya when in November 1884 the Germans annexed north-east New Guinea. In that same year he had made a robust Australian connection through his meeting with the widowed daughter of prominent New South Wales politician Jack Robertson. Maclay would marry Margaret in Vienna on the way to visit his family estates in Russia. Nursed by her, he would die in Russia in 1888, at the age of only forty-two, his purpose to return to Australia and New Guinea to continue both his studies and his advocacy unfulfilled.

CELESTIALS IN SOUTHERN AUSTRALIA

In 1871 a sergeant of police in Ballarat took Anthony Trollope on a tour of the Chinese quarter. The novelist was shocked by what he saw in the hovels and opium dens. 'Boys and girls are enticed among them, and were with them, and become foul, abominable, and inhuman.' But white people were polluted by the Celestials in other ways. Eighteen white prostitutes lived at the Chinese camp in Narrandera amongst 303 male Chinese residents. A survey of the biggest Chinese camps in the Riverina in 1883 showed that out of 800 Chinese males living in the region, thirty-six were married to white women. Some clergy refused to conduct the marriage ceremonies. It was said that one 'Highland clergyman' married a China man to a white woman with the words, 'You two I declare one mutton.'

As well as for their supposed hunger for fair flesh and opium, the Chinese developed a repute for gambling and sometimes found themselves locked up for playing Fan-tan, a relatively harmless card game. To help their brethren in the face of threat, the Chinese in Australia, particularly the merchants, set up societies and self-help clubs. The oldest, the Csee Yap Society, was founded by Louis Ahmouy in 1854. The Csee Yap rules were that all Chinese who came to seek gold 'must love and help each other'. The society favoured the idea that its members would find gold, then go home with it rather than settle locally. One of the tasks of the society was to bury those who did not get home in the appropriate manner. The Chinese practices of 'feasting the dead', funeral feasts where chickens were devoured and firecrackers let off, seemed outlandish to white miners and townspeople. The dead were buried with such goods as would see them through eternity—roasted fowls, rice and money. In Melbourne twenty or thirty horse cabs were loaded with Chinamen and set off every third Sunday of the month, the day for visiting the dead, in procession to the cemetery. Once every two years, the coffins of those long buried were dug up, the bones washed, sometimes in creeks, and shipped back to China in cases or carpet bags.

Though the Chinese were condemned for smoking opium in Chinese opium dives, the reason opium was not legislated against was that it was a major ingredient in patent medicines, including those which tuberculosis sufferers ingested to help them through their last days. The New South Wales government permitted the unrestricted importation of opium at a duty of 10 shillings per pound, raising considerable revenue. It was not until 1893 that H.W. Hunt, Secretary of the Victorian Society of the Suppression of the Opium Traffic, was able to get a bill through the Victorian Parliament banning the free use of opium.

GRANDMOTHERLY LEGISLATION AND THE PRIVILEGES OF DISEASE

Melbourne's weak point as it grew into a city of pretentions was the Yarra itself, apparently so poisonous in odour that no one could work near it without smoking tobacco to mask its stench. The *Bulletin* referred to Melbourne as 'Marvellous Smelbourne', for the Yarra was the Melbourne sewer into which liquid refuse from buildings, stables, factories of all kinds and urinals made their way by channels, constructed and informal, into the river. Some compared it to Port Said, and on 24 January 1889 the *Argus* quoted an observer as saying, 'I never saw a dirtier city than Melbourne, not even among the Heathen Chinee.' As late as the 1890s Michael Davitt, travelling in Australia to raise money for Irish Home Rule, found the approaches to Melbourne unfortunate. 'To see it without your prejudices being excited, through gasworks and tanneries on the one hand, or the Liffey-like odour of the channel of the Yarra river . . . you would have to drop in upon the city in a balloon sailing down from the region of Mount Macedon.'

In the 1880s, night cart men were cutting their working hours short by dumping the human waste they were supposed to dispose of in distant sand dunes within the city itself. Typhoid and diphtheria were thus large killers and Melbourne, in its mere sixty years of existence, had managed to achieve a level of pollution and peril to health which was more akin to the public image of Manchester than of the golden city it had been and still wanted to be. In 1889, for example, there were 910 deaths from typhoid fever in Victoria, over 550 of those in Melbourne, mainly in the typhoid season from February to May. A doctor at Prince Henry's Hospital declared in February 1888 that every time a typhoid death occurred a mayor should be hanged.

Adelaide and Sydney were healthier since they had each begun construction of a city-wide sewerage system. But the city authorities and the legislators of Melbourne were too busy with land shares to concentrate on installing similar schemes in the complicated urban topography. At the Intercolonial Medical Congress in January 1889, Charles Pearson, reforming Premier of Victoria, declared bitterly: 'We value so highly our constitutional rights—the rights of a man to pollute running water ... that many of us would oppose to the death any interference with ... the vested right of every Englishman to carry death into his neighbour's household.' However, any attempt to attack the matter of public health on a broad front was often patronised in the legislature as 'grandmotherly legislation'.

At last, in 1889, James Mansergh, a renowned sanitary engineer, was brought to Melbourne to consult on the idea of a deep sewerage system. He had devised a plan to supply Liverpool and Birmingham with unlimited clean water, had devised sewerage systems for a number of British cities and had been honoured with a Fellowship of the Royal Society. Mansergh visited Melbourne for a ground survey and ordered all the survey maps the colonial and city authorities had. He was shocked by Melbourne in comparison even to the worst British cities. 'Open gutters conveying chamber slops and other foul liquids' into the Yarra and Hobsons Bay were normal, and the yards of houses were sodden with human and other wastes. He submitted a plan by which street gutters would carry only rainwater to the rivers, and all other water would be carried by pipes to land treatment plants on the outskirts of Melbourne. He factored into the equation the high propensity of Melbourne people for baths and allowed in his plans for a population of 1.6 million people using over 400 litres per day. The press was outraged by the proposed price, £7 million, and so he adjusted the plan and cut out one of the treatment works.

Mansergh seemed to be the Empire's favourite improver of water supplies and sewerage. After the Melbourne plan he worked on the water system of

Toronto and sewerage schemes for Colombo and the lower Thames Valley. There can be no doubt that his involvement in Melbourne would save the lives of thousands of the city's dwellers. 'People who had never known what it is to live un-surrounded by cesspits, privies, night-soil pails, or ill-kept earth-closets, or other of the vile appliances I saw in Melbourne, will wonder how they could have existed under such conditions,' Mansergh promised.

Through initiatives such as the Mansergh project, Australian life spans were increasing. The average life span of those attending the gold rushes was somewhere in the early thirties, lower than that of Britain. While the deaths of children dragged the average down, the squalor, poor sanitary conditions and inadequate housing of gold miners also contributed to the low figure. By the 1870s the average had improved to thirty-seven years for men and fifty for females. As for child mortality, at least the infant in the bush was protected somewhat from contagion by distance from other humans. In 1874, in the Sydney industrial suburbs of Alexandria and Waterloo, however, infant mortality was up to 46 per cent of births. Over a long period, mortality in Sydney suburbs was 50 per cent higher than amongst the same age groups in the Australian bush. According to the *Illustrated Sydney News* of 13 July 1878, a visitor to Sydney would be astonished by the number of funerals that thronged the streets. 'But of what size are most of the coffins? It is the children, the little children, that are being borne so thickly to the grave . . . in what city (except Melbourne) could such havoc of the very young and the wholly helpless take place?'

Children who died in epidemic diseases were often buried half a dozen at a time and any person could simply enter a cemetery with a small coffin, give the grave-digger a few pence and have it deposited in a grave. A Brisbane fruiterer would bury a dead child for one shilling 'in a coffin made from a fruit box'. Middle-class funerals were far more formal and some of them were organised through the Masonic and Friendly societies, which buried the deceased with solemn care after a considerable procession. As late as the 1880s Sydney people were still burying their dead in the Devonshire Street cemetery, where in rainy weather decay would ooze through the stone walls into Elizabeth Street. In 1886, after an outbreak of typhoid in the Sydney suburb of Balmain, it was found that the well of a dairy was contaminated from 'so foetid a soakage' from the nearby cemetery.

By the time Mansergh and other sanitary engineers had finished their work, and the Federationists had united Australia, Australian men could expect to live an average of fifty-five years and women fifty-eight.

Tuberculosis would still be a great curse, but tonics prescribed for it were laced with as-yet unbanned opium. Every year some thousands of pounds of opium were legally imported into New South Wales, Victoria and other parts of Australia. Holloway's Pills and Holloway's Ointment were laced with laudanum. The temporary relief it gave the sick person was taken as proof of the efficacy of the patent preparations.

THE FRONTIER WOMEN AND INFANT DEATH

The archetype of women's hardship in the bush is a literary one, 'The Drover's Wife', by Henry Lawson. It is easy to argue that Lawson's woman, running a farm while her husband is absent droving, having given birth to six children, the second born with the aid of an Aboriginal midwife while her husband was away trying to persuade a doctor to ride out and attend to her, is the authentic experience of real women of the bush. When one of her children died while her husband was again away, the drover's wife of the story rode 19 miles for help, carrying the dead child. These conditions of life and death would have been familiar to many Australian families, even after Federation.

In 1867 at Benayeo, beyond Ballarat, Louisa Geoghegan recorded the death from fever of a twelve-year-old child named Bessie Hinds, whom doctors did not reach for two days. Mrs Hinds seemed thereafter to take refuge at her piano, an item from Europe, somehow removed from the hard country in which her eldest daughter had died.

Mrs C.C. Richards from South Australia landed with her husband and four children at Albany in Western Australia in 1885. She lived under canvas in an environment of dust and flies and under conditions of questionable sanitation. One morning in 1886 one of her sons carried the body of his brother home, and the only clue to cause of death was that the elder brother saw blood on his younger brother's legs. A month later Mrs Richards gave birth to a baby girl and thirteen months later the child, Ella, died from the same complaint, beginning with diarrhoea and ending with bleeding from the anus. A doctor told Mrs Richards he could do little to help the child as 'the lining of her stomach was coming away'. But the acute fever that was killing the Richards' children was caused by the water, she said. 'After that, I felt I just wanted to die—our two lovely children taken from us in just over a year.'

There were so many ways parents could lose children, yet the fear of it became fixed on the statistically least likely cause—that children would become lost either in thickets of forest or in bare, waterless landscapes. Frederick McCubbin's 1886 painting *The Lost Child* epitomised this fear that the settler's child might be devoured by the environment if not epidemic disease. McCubbin's painting was possibly based on the 1885 finding of a child named Clara Crosbie, who had been lost for three weeks in the bush near Lilydale in Victoria. In fact the incidence of lost children was small but stood as a token for the other ways children might be taken. When Elizabeth Anne O'Rourke of North Gippsland, Victoria, wandered away from the family home in March 1866, she had been trying to follow her father, David. The riveting detail for other parents who heard of the tragedy was that when Aboriginal people found her body a year later, she was still in her pink dress, at the bottom of a rock from which she had fallen. Mary O'Rourke moved away from the station where her child had died of exposure and buried her daughter on her father's station at Black Mountain. Mary's dutiful husband David transported his homestead from his run and re-erected it near his daughter's grave.

The peril to children was real enough in dry regions. In the early 1890s Walter Allender, aged about eleven, died from exposure in the bush near Mullewa, Western Australia, and Darcy Ives followed a dog from his parents' home in Mukinbudin into the bush in 1893. It was April but still ferociously hot, and he perished in the hinterland. Recently orphaned four-year-old Johnny Carney also wandered away from a relative's farm in the Mullewa region. It was popularly believed when his remains were found with Aboriginal help that he had been cannibalised after death, but there is no evidence to prove this. At Pender Bay near Broome in 1912 Bertha Clarke of Wyndham, 'half Aboriginal', wandered off from a picnic party. Her body was found after two weeks.

Yet it was the bacterial thickets which claimed most children. And the death rate amongst child-bearing women themselves did not improve much between 1871 and 1905—it was roughly 6.5 per cent in 1871–80 and a little over 6 per cent in 1901–05. If these odds were acceptable for one birth, they mounted with each new child a woman bore, becoming over entire lifetimes of child-bearing a casualty rate equivalent to that of modern warfare. Puerperal fever, a form of sepsis of the birth canal or urinary tract following delivery, was the most common cause of such deaths and killed many mothers as well, and the figures did not much improve in the twentieth century until the arrival and use of antibiotics in the 1940s.

To have a doctor in the house at the time of birth was seen as an exceptional luxury by women in the bush. Ada Cambridge, an Australian novelist and wife of a Victorian Anglican clergyman whose postings took him to work in Wangaratta, Beechworth, Yackandandah and Williamstown, never forgot her own experience of giving birth to two children in the bush and observing the travails of other women. She wrote in 1903, after her novels had given her entree into the colonial aristocracy, that 'the majority of bush women prefer to stay at home and make shift with the peripatetic gap [midwife], old and unscientific as she always was'. Lady Dudley, the beautiful, intelligent and forceful wife of a governor-general of no particular talents, was shocked by the conditions in which women gave birth in the bush, and in 1909 she founded Lady Dudley's Bush Nursing Scheme, a project which was not as successful as she had hoped. Rose Lindsay, Norman Lindsay's wife, remembered that when, at the time of Federation, her sister gave birth at Gosford without a midwife, the baby died. The father was sent to fetch the undertaker but instead spent the money on drink, so the baby had to be buried in a deal box near the shack. Perhaps that, as well as Norman Lindsay's fast talking, persuaded the beautiful Rose to pose for Lindsay's scandal-making drawing, *Crucified Venus*.

A young immigrant, Matilda Wallace, had a not-uncommon history. She married in 1861 and soon after wrote 'we buried our first little baby'. Her husband was a wanderer, an amateur explorer, and so they travelled to Queensland in a wagon, an exceptional journey but not utterly abnormal for the time. While she was running the station and living in little more than a camp on a pastoral lease at Mount Murchison, inland from Gladstone, Matilda lost a second child while her husband was away hawking to supplement their income. Two more sons died in infancy in the mid-1860s. In 1868 she moved to a nearby town which no longer exists, remarking that it was her first sight of 'civilisation' in seven years. Her husband announced he must go to Burra in South Australia to take delivery of 5000 sheep, and now she complained that her health would not let her run the property without his presence. So she travelled with him that prodigious distance and drove the sheep along a long track on which her young daughter contracted sandy blight, the blinding eye disease. From that point Matilda disappeared from recorded history.

Constance Jane Ellis described in her autobiography the death of her premature baby girl in North Queensland in 1890. Her husband Tom was out ploughing when she went into labour, and the couple discussed whether he should seek help at the nearby station, but it was a day's ride away and nobody there would be medically equipped anyhow. The child was delivered, but died within four days. Tom went to the nearest station for timber for the coffin. 'Well,

Tom chose a pretty spot beside the jungle and dug a grave and we buried our baby . . . about the saddest time we ever had.'

To add to the grief of the mothers of stillborn children, the Anglican and Catholic churches would not let them be buried in consecrated ground, since they had not been baptised. The stillborn baby of Henry and Laura Box was buried in 1913 on top of a hill behind the old orchard at the Popanyinning Pod Farm in Western Australia; 'the Church would not bury him in the cemetery because he had not been baptised'. A Mrs Carmichael, living on marginal land at Wellington Mills near Bunbury, gave birth to a stillborn baby in 1915 and three years later delivered twin boys who lasted only eight hours. A doctor said, 'The cause of death was through malnutrition as a consequence of his mother's sickness and overwork.' At the finish of the war to end all wars, it was still the norm for many pregnant farm women to be overworked and frequently malnourished.

MARVELLOUS MELBOURNE

In the 1880s Melbourne had the character of a great city of the Empire which had transformed itself from squalid village to urban wonder in a little over thirty years. In Collins Street, around the Italianate Stock Exchange, the worldly top hat and morning suit were de rigueur. The Crimean shirts and clay-streaked pants of the 1850s were but a memory, or not even that, for Melburnians on the make, who were a considerable crowd. Collins Street was the epicentre of fortune, and the privileged of the city considered the colonial legislature up the road, nearly every member of which was a director and investor in the banks and building societies of the city, as a mechanism for making easier still the inflation of bank shares and property prices.

For Victoria had no limit. The decade had begun with the triumph of the International Exhibition of 1880, for which the Exhibition Building was erected, and to which the world came. It showed up the less-than-brilliant Sydney Exhibition of 1870 by having the whole world of new technology and merchandise on display, and was followed by a further exhibition in 1888, this one astonishingly lit by its own electric generating plant. There were visitors from other states and the Victorian countryside who had had their first exposure to that new, intense, electric beam in the Exhibition Building in Melbourne.

James Munro, Presbyterian, Scottish-born temperance leader, the man whose acumen drove the exhibition of 1880, a cabinet minister and premier

(1890–92), had founded in the 1860s the Victoria Permanent Property Investment Building Society. With the funds in hand he developed entire regions of the city. By 1882 he also founded the Federal Bank and the Federal Building Society and, to bolster them when his personal withdrawals or outside investments made them unstable, the Real Estate Mortgage and Deposit Bank, shares in which were sold to bolster the concealed losses of his other companies. The brilliant young lawyer and legislator Alfred Deakin was himself a director of a building society, though he did not play the games Munro played with his institution, lending investors' and depositors' money to relatives and friends on the loosest possible terms, in the expectation that endlessly inflating land prices would, like a rising tide, cover all sins. James Munro had, on the strength of his financial companies, acquired great pastoral stations and leaseholds in the Northern Territory, Queensland and Western Australia. The Munro of the 1880s was not a born criminal. The times made him. Escalating wealth unhinged him. On the floor of the House he was a political progressive. He sought female suffrage because he believed that women voters would support temperance legislation. In the pro-pub electorate of Carlton he had been denied a hall in which to address electors, and so built his own. He also built a number of what were called 'coffee palaces'—hotels which had considerable grandeur and comfort but which did not serve liquor. The Windsor, a famous Melbourne hotel, began its career as the Grand Coffee Palace.

In the 1880s banks and financial institutions like Munro's mushroomed up with titles designed to imply solidity and permanence, indeed 'Permanent' was a favourite. So were 'Imperial', 'Australian', 'Premier', 'Federal', 'Scottish-Australian' and 'Metropolitan'. What the building societies did was to finance 'spec' builders who ran up thousands of cottages in the inner suburbs. David Mitchell, the father of Nellie Melba, was building the mammoth Equitable Insurance Building at the corner of Elizabeth and Collins streets. The new hydraulic lifts made the building of such larger offices possible. As well as creating suburbs, David Munro was building bridges across the Yarra. There was no overestimating the impact of the telegraph on the works of Munro and others—now the Australian colonies knew what was happening in London virtually on the day it happened, and so did London investors see each day at rising what a gold mine Melbourne was, whether in bank stocks or in real estate.

The boom 1880s were an era of great stability in Victoria. Duncan Gillies and Alfred Deakin had formed a coalition which united liberal factions and brought in a long phase of political stability as well. This government would not fall until

November 1890, when the collapse of shares and property prices exposed the scale of what they had been borrowing from British investors for public work, including roads and sewerage and railways. These borrowings had certainly helped their friends and associates down in Collins Street, and also created a modern network of rail which made it immensely easier for wheat growers to get their produce to market and thus help the good times roll along in the bush as well as in the city. The writer of a private book of prayers, Alfred Deakin was himself a modest presence at the table of Mammon, director of a building society, an investor of his own and his father's money in a range of societies and banks run by fine temperance men. He, however, possessed a genuine spirituality and sought no more than affluence. It was Victoria's unlimited future which was his drug. Like thousands more, he lost his own investments and—more scarifying to his conscience—his father's as well.

CHAPTER 4

The last colonial decade
1890s

THE WAY THE MONEY GOES

James Munro had been leader of the Opposition for some time when the long rule of the railway-building Berry–Deakin ministry ended, making him premier and treasurer in November 1890. There were some problems with his banks and financial institutions, along with those of other folk, but no one believed the 1880s boom was not only about to end but to implode. There had been industrial unrest—the Maritime Union strike of 1890 had brought other unions into a savage class battle—but by the time Munro came to power in November 1890 the unions were beginning to run out of funds.

Along with Victoria's collapsing fortunes however—its old friends and financiers from overseas now stung by them and letting them hang—Munro's own apparently unassailable fortune began to evaporate. Almost instantaneously shares worth pounds descended to the price of a few pence, bewildering and impoverishing many middle-class families and hurling the mighty down from their thrones. Amongst those whose thrones were wobbling was Munro. After a year of trouble, a Voluntary Liquidation Act was passed on 3 December 1891 with the supposed aim of stopping mischievous speculators from forcing companies into compulsory liquidation against the will of the majority of shareholders. But above all, it prevented small shareholders from making any inquiry into a company's affairs, and enabled the companies to wind up their affairs privately, by 'secret compositions', often by paying their shareholders and depositors one penny in the pound. (There were, by the way, 240 pennies to a pound.) That is, the fortunes of many people, including the modestly affluent, were reduced to about 0.4 per cent of what they had been worth a few months before.

Munro did not initiate this legislation but he agreed to it, and his Federal Building Society and Real Estate Mortgage and Deposit Bank availed themselves of it very quickly. Munro, pursued down Collins and Bourke streets by shareholders wondering where their money had gone, or abusing him for the declining value of shares, was pleased to hand over the reins of government to his deputy, William Shiels, and to plan to go to London to replace Sir Graham Berry as agent-general. There was a huge public protest at the appointment, and the *Age* and the magazine *Table Talk* lambasted him. He was called back from London by an embarrassed government. Sixty-one years of age, he was walking along Collins Street as a private citizen reduced in rank and wealth when a labourer named George Davis accosted him and shouted that investment in Munro's Real Estate Bank had cost him all his money, reduced him to the status of labourer, and left him with 'nothing but the Yarra'. That being so, he thought that he might as well kill Munro and go to the scaffold instead. He stopped short of murder but was charged with assault. He was fined £5, but the magistrate hearing the case said that it was remarkable, given the times the city had endured, that the citizens had behaved with such admirable composure. He almost implied that it was excusable for Davis to hit an old man.

Sir Matthew Davies, born in Geelong in 1850, was Minister of Justice in James Munro's cabinet from November 1890 to February 1892 and was largely responsible for the Voluntary Liquidation Act which allowed those 'secret compositions', that is, the winding up of banks and building societies without the principals ever having to face their creditors. Davies was lawyer to many of the so-called 'land boomers', the men whose companies attracted the citizens of Victoria and the other colonies and of Britain to invest in ever-inflating Victorian real estate. Spacious in his gifts to charity, Davies lived in a splendid Toorak mansion. Much of his early legal work was connected with the property dealings of one of the most notable of the land boomers, Charles Henry James, and Davies himself began speculating in land, forming his first land company in 1882, buying and selling real estate on the basis of investment from the public. By 1887 he owned a network of about forty companies.

The great crisis for Davies came in 1892 when his Mercantile Bank declared an 8 per cent dividend for its shareholders in February but then suddenly suspended payment of it in March. He was forced to resign from Parliament in

April. Secretly he boarded a ship named the *City of Chicago*, bound for London, where, by the wonder of the Overland Telegraph, he had organised a meeting with his British creditors and shareholders. At it he hoped to raise money to keep the bank afloat. But his ship was wrecked on the Irish coast on 2 July 1892, and Davies was forced to scale a cliff on a rope ladder to escape the wreck. He reached London too late for the meeting of his depositors and found they had applied for liquidation of his bank. They attacked him bitterly at a reconvened London meeting, and refused to save him.

When he got back to Melbourne he found most of his other companies in difficulty. In January 1893 he was committed to trial for fraud for issuing a false balance sheet. The young, aggressive solicitor-general, Isaac Isaacs, Federationist son of a Yackandandah draper, meant to get him. The attorney-general, Sir Bryan O'Loghlen, withdrew the charges, but Isaacs pursued Davies with new writs. Davies fled Australia before he could be arrested, but a Victorian detective followed on a later ship and arrested him in Colombo.

At his fraud trial in Melbourne, he was acquitted but forced to file his schedule in bankruptcy in 1894. All his companies collapsed and were wound up, and a then fabulous sum of £4 million invested by others was lost. To shareholders and other creditors he was permitted under his own pernicious legislation to pay one quarter of a penny in the pound, that is, less than 0.01 per cent of what they had invested. Losses of this nature, and accusations of fraud, were by then so common in Melbourne that his personal shame was diluted, and he would stand for Parliament again—though unsuccessfully—and still manage to be elected Deputy Grandmaster of Freemasons. He was also permitted to go on practising law.

The spectacle of reduced circumstances, of families moving to smaller homes, of once prominent persons leading somewhat less visible lives, was so common that both those guilty of fraud, and those who had acted as negligent directors of companies in which they had shares, were able to console themselves that they were not the sole examples of the great cleansing. But they could not always avoid paying the price for what had happened; Matthew Davies and James Munro suffered depression and self-doubt, and so, most acutely, did Alfred Deakin, a director of the City of Melbourne Building Society, who devised special prayers of repentance to help him through his dark night, the weight of his burden of responsibility and the bite of his own loss and shame.

Deakin's old schoolmate Theodore Fink, member of the Yorick Club, friend of writers such as Marcus Clarke and Jules François Archibald of the *Bulletin*, and artists like Charles Conder, Arthur Streeton, Frederick McCubbin and Tom Roberts, suffered from the collapse of the land boom too. By 1891 Deakin owed £70 000, a massive amount in those days but small compared to the debts of others. He resolved his own financial differences by arranging a secret composition.

His younger brother Benjamin had a more notable crash. Benjamin was a speculator and developer who owned the Collins Street land the stock exchange of Melbourne was built on. With the crash his Mercantile Finance Company, just one of his companies, would lose £1 million. He made a secret composition with his creditors and his estate realised a halfpenny in the pound. At least two attempts were made by investors and institutions to have Fink's composition set aside, since large assets of land had been moved into the name of his wife Catherine. As late as 1909 his wife was still subdividing and selling this land. In 1899 she was able to buy back the freehold of Fink's buildings in Collins Street, which Benjamin had lost in the bust.

CLEVER DEVICES

There was a cleverness of a less pernicious variety operating in the bush. Some of the best places for success for smaller agriculturalists from the 1870s were the wheat growing areas of South Australia and western Victoria, where in both cases the railway connected the farmers to the ports and farm machinery made production so much easier. The South Australian government offered a £4000 prize with a closing date of 1879 for a stripping and winnowing machine. By December 1879 twenty-four machines had been entered and trials took place on a farm at Gawler. The government did not award the major prize but smaller sums were shared between a number of South Australian and Victorian inventors.

In 1884 Hugh Victor McKay, a young man of twenty-three, tried out a machine which, with its drive belts, cogging and bagging, promised to do everything. Throughout his childhood his wheat-farmer father used the horse-drawn South Australian stripper and the manual winnower—what the Americans were beginning to call 'combination harvesters'. It was in 1885 that McKay's prototype, which would do all that mechanically, was tried in the field and patented. Hugh persuaded the plough makers McCalman Garde and Company of North Melbourne to manufacture his machine. James Morrow had exhibited a stripper harvester more than a year earlier and had won a prize at a government trial in December 1884, but the manufacturers spread the myth that McKay was the true begetter.

The McKay Harvesting Machinery Company, established in 1890, purchased McKay's patents back along with the manufacturing rights. The depression came close to sending him broke. When he married in 1891, he was down to £25. But with a syndicate's help, he was able to begin business as the Harvester Company and to market his harvester under the name Sunshine. By 1901 he was selling 500 a year, but then he began to sell in South Africa and through an Argentinean agent, who marketed the machines under the name La Australiana, in South America. By 1905 he was selling 2000 a year.

McKay would be known for something other than mechanically enhancing the harvest process. A paternalistic employer who underwrote his workers' choirs, drama groups and cricket teams and who did not—to his own mind—work them for inhuman hours, he detested unionism and threatened to replace workers with machines if they dallied with it. He avoided the decisions of wages boards by moving his business, and Tom Mann, the Labor leader, called him a free trader in humans.

He became concerned that the stripper harvester, which he believed had been pirated by Americans, was being dumped cheaply in Australia by the International Harvester Company of Chicago. McKay wanted higher tariffs and applied for exemption from excise duties, and came to the attention of Justice Henry Higgins, who selected this as the test case to decide whether McKay was paying the fair and reasonable wages justified by the levels of protection put in place by the new federal government. In his celebrated Harvester judgment of November 1907, the Sunshine Harvester works, ruled Higgins, was 'a marvel of enterprise, energy and pluck', but the normal needs of an average employee 'regarded as a human being in a civilised community' dictated that an unskilled labourer should be paid a minimum of 7 shillings for a day of eight hours. As some wage rates at Sunshine Harvester were below this, McKay could not be exempted from excise. Thus a resonating legal judgment arose from the romance of golden grain promptly harvested.

In 1911 the Agricultural Implement Makers' Union called a strike to enforce the closed shop but also to bring the industry under a federal award. Led by McKay the employers responded with a lockout of all unionists, whether they were striking or not. McKay refused Prime Minister Andrew Fisher's offer to mediate. The strike lasted thirteen weeks and left the union defeated and fundless, and it also helped poison industrial relations. McKay's paternalism had been replaced by new stratagems and new dissensions. He decided to take his grievances to the federal parliament and stood for the seat of Ballarat in 1913, but a Labor candidate won in a fierce campaign.

A CHANGED WORLD

Striking shearers had gathered in Wilcannia in 1890, turning the world of jointly shared pastoral endeavour into a conflict. Their activism was not as lost on Edward 'Plorn' Dickens as that of the Harvester workers was on Hugh McKay, but he was on the government's side. 'Any demonstration made by the government,' said Plorn, concerning the intervention of police troopers, 'has not been made against trade unionism. The government have simply done their duty in protecting society against these ruffians and blackguards who always rise to the surface during a time of popular excitement.' However, he said, with somewhat more wisdom, Parliament should not pass hasty repressive legislation. 'In the excited state of public feeling the people are hardly fit to record their votes without temper or prejudice.'

A new force had entered the field, derived from Labor Leagues set up throughout Australia. For the election of June 1891 the New South Wales Labor Party for the first time nominated candidates and selected J.H. Cann against the sitting member for Sturt, which included Broken Hill. Labor won the seat. But in Wilcannia Plorn was returned unopposed. The *Sydney Morning Herald* noted that at his pre-election political meeting 'he received a splendid hearing and was frequently applauded'. It was generally thought that no one had a chance of successfully standing against him.

Parliament met and Sir Henry Parkes continued to hold office until October, when Sir George Dibbs came back into power. Now Edward told the Minister for Public Works that secession had been 'seriously entertained' by the press and the people of Broken Hill. It is not remarkable for a man of his era that he would never, however, as party to the compact with Macquarie Street which he now foreshadowed breaking, mention the Barkindji people, tall desert people, of the region of Wilcannia. He would have seen the Aboriginal as stockmen and as town drifters, and in so far as he considered them at all they were as to most men of his class either cheaper labour or a hindrance to the progress of the region.

In 1893 Edward rose to speak against a suggestion made by Premier Dibbs to raise £94 000 for railway building by imposing tolls on the Darling River. Edward pointed out that £80 000 had been spent on trying to keep the Darling open in a losing struggle against the climate. 'The Premier reminds me somewhat of a gentleman named Micawber . . . In this case the Premier wants to make up his figures and he waits for something to turn up.' But in his general ineffectuality at least Plorn reached for a visionary argument.

If there is one thing that could possibly retard Federation it would be the tolls which the Premier proposes . . . there is no doubt that the whole principle of the proposal is retaliation against the adjoining colonies of South Australia and Victoria, because owing to their position and certain facilities of nature, they are able to carry our produce and bring produce to us, at a far cheaper rate than we can ourselves.

The proposal to levy river tolls was abandoned, though whether it was due to Plorn one does not know. But there was never to be a railway to his town.

Back in his lodgings in Gresham Street, his marriage to Connie Desailly was not going well. The couple was childless, and Plorn's political career was doomed. His defeat in 1894 was the result of the further development of class war in the minefields.

The Amalgamated Miners' Association created by William Guthrie Spence in 1878 was strong in Broken Hill. A handsome, driven and charismatic young union leader, Richard Sleath, had risen to the presidency of the organisation before the age of twenty-three. The son of a Fifeshire ploughman, he was a Briton, but another kind of Briton to Edward Dickens. Sleath had succeeded in making the Broken Hill Proprietary Company accept a 'union shop'. He sat on a board of inquiry into lead poisoning of miners working the BHP silver-lead deposits.

By 1892 he was speaking in favour of nationalisation of the mines, and came into collision with BHP management, who—because of the collapse in world mineral prices—were devoted now to reducing wages and introducing individual contracts with workers. In June 1892 they told Sleath that they would not be paying the miners a flat wage but would vary it according to the ore they mined. The 'Big Strike' of July 1892 lasted eighteen weeks and brought Sleath frequently to the rostrum throughout Broken Hill, and the miners felt a communal power in his presence—a sense of power which grew dimmer, however, the hungrier their children got. He spoke ferociously about mining conditions at the BHP shareholders meeting in Melbourne. When the company brought in non-union labour from Sydney and Melbourne, there were battles between the police and the union men, and Sleath counselled good order, though he was quoted by the *Herald* as saying that perhaps 'all the men should be armed and drilled'.

In September 1892 he was arrested with four others for supposedly inciting violence. The five men were committed to trial by a Broken Hill magistrate with the trial to take place in Deniliquin in the Riverina. They had to travel there via Adelaide and Melbourne, and were warmly welcomed by unionists in those cities. The trial in Deniliquin lasted five days and a guilty verdict was handed down. Sleath was sentenced to two years' imprisonment.

The strike wavered and collapsed for want of funds to support the miners. But when Sleath returned as hero-martyr to Broken Hill he was greeted at the Sulphide Street Railway Station by up to 2000 men, women and children, who began cheering from the time the train of the 'prodigals had crossed Bromide Street'. Sleath and other released miners were taken in drays drawn by miners to the Theatre Royal Hotel for breakfast. Wages had fallen by 10 per cent, and the working week had been increased, but the thousands of Barrier miners dreamed of sending Sleath to Macquarie Street. Labour could not win a strike, but Labor members could win elections. A month after his release from prison, Sleath had given a speech in Wilcannia on 'Land and Labour', and was cheered by the audience.

During the 1892 strike, Plorn Dickens had visited Broken Hill on his way to Sydney for a sitting of Parliament and seen the silent mines. When George Reid, a fleshy whimsical Free Trader, moved a motion to censure the strikers, Plorn told the House he had never seen men better behaved than the unionists on picket duty. Nor had he seen any aggressive police acts, he said. He praised his colleague, J.H. Cann, the Labour Member of Parliament for Bourke, and said that Cann had done as much as he could to settle 'this unfortunate dispute' by recommending the unions remove the pickets, since removal was one of the pre-conditions of a meeting between the mine owners and the miners' representatives. But the union would not do so. Plorn appealed to members to put nation before party interests and vote down the motion. The motion was indeed defeated.

But after a boundary distribution, the west was now suddenly full of Labor candidates ready to tap into the anger over the failure of the miners' strike in Broken Hill. In 1894 Cann was to be the candidate for Broken Hill, and Sleath was selected to oppose the relatively easy target, Plorn Dickens. By 1894 several Wilcannia banks had suspended payments for the duration of the financial crisis, and citizens had at various times found themselves without ready cash for simple household needs. A number of municipal employees had been sacked, and were ripe for change. So were the shearers. On one station the manager had had to send for the police to keep the peace between those willing to work for the cut rate of 25 shillings a week and those who refused to take less than

30 shillings. Because of his genial and sympathetic attitudes, Plorn was given a warm welcome by the workers at that and other stations. But he did not have a vision of organised fraternity to present.

In Dickens' last speech in Parliament he made his final attack on the land laws. According to the *Barrier Miner*, this was no more than a poor attempt to make himself 'solid' with his constituency. When Parliament recessed for a new election in early 1894, a committee was formed in Wilcannia for Dickens' re-election. In the meantime Sleath was speaking in the mining towns of White Cliffs and Tibooburra. He and Dickens coincided in their belief that there should be no further influx of 'Asiatics', and both candidates urged the extension of the telegraph to the remote communities. They both also advocated locks along the Darling to keep its length navigable.

The *Miner* also turned Plorn's own arguments against him, as if only Labor folk thought of the issues of the region. Broken Hill was caught between the 'inter-colonial cut-throatism' of South Australia and New South Wales, with South Australia regulating her railway tariff so as to make it cheaper for the mining companies to ship to Adelaide. 'Broken Hill people suffer both ways. It is they who have to pay Customs duty if they buy South Australian goods, and it is they who have to pay carriage for the long journey by sea and land if they buy Sydney side stuff.' There were no inducements and no reduction in costs from New South Wales—a cry Plorn had also raised in Macquarie Street. Many, though not all, remotely placed people in Australia looked, like Plorn, to Federation, for it would bring free trade between the colonies.

The *Barrier Miner* concluded before the election between glamorous young Sleath and plodding Dickens that 'labour can be transferred so rapidly from one place to another and the prosperity of one colony means prosperity to the labourers of another colony. West Australia's prosperity improves the position of workers in New South Wales. The Labor party is therefore the only true Federal party.'

Dickens returned home early from Parliament because of the pressure from Sleath. At his election meeting, one of his supporters, Quin, said that the new relationship between labour and capital meant that the electorate needed a moderate man. In fact the electorate was ready for a new, passionate model. As a sign of Dickens' liberality, he had voted for the Bank Notes Bill George Dibbs' government had legislated, decreeing that only the bank notes of four major reputable banks could be circulated, giving people certainty (Quin said) and a better deal than many Victorian depositors had got. He claimed the bill had 'saved the country, as otherwise the storekeepers and businessmen could not carry on'. But it had created want and inconvenience in country areas, where often only small banks operated, and it was not likely that Dickens would be forgiven for it.

At a meeting at White Cliffs, the voters passed a unanimous vote of no confidence in Dickens and ended by giving three cheers for Sleath. When Dickens rode out across desert to speak at Tibooburra, a motion was carried in the hall that he was 'not a fit and proper person to represent the electors of Wilcannia'. In June 1894 the *Barrier Miner* revived the old slur that 'the most interesting thing about you is that you are the son of Charles Dickens . . . If the theory is true, we ought not blame children born late in their parents' life if they do not attain the brilliance of these parents at their best.' It then estimated the size of Plorn's inheritance from his immortal parent and drew the conclusion that he had squandered it.

As the election drew near, the *Barrier Miner* mentioned that many Broken Hill miners were leaving for Western Australia, and every day that passed further batches reduced the voting power of Labor. Some correspondents believed that squatters and others were deliberately sending their station workers away to other electorates to prevent them voting Labor. On 7 April 1894 the paper gave an idea of the practical difficulties of democracy in such a huge region. The Darling had flooded and the two policemen stationed at Mount Browne had to travel through flooded country for 150 miles (240 kilometres) east and 70 miles (over 110 kilometres) west to deliver the ballot papers. Said the *Miner*, 'These back country people most certainly ought not to be disenfranchised.' Premier Dibbs, 'the dictator of this colony and not merely the premier of it', had nonetheless extended the election date to the end of May, but this was not long enough, said the people of western New South Wales.

After the election, final figures were not known for a week, but it became apparent that the militant Sleath had won against the merely liberal Plorn with a majority of over 60 per cent. George Reid's Free Trade Party had won half the seats and would have to go into a coalition with Labor's twenty-three members, these including, as well as Sleath, the Balmain shopkeeper and future prime minister Billy Hughes.

Sleath's career in the Labor Party would prove turbulent. He would hold the seat until 1904 but would end by standing as an independent, since he was not amenable to party discipline.

TRANSPORTED GENTLEMEN DECLINE

From now on Australia increasingly failed the late great novelist's dream that it would be the making of his sons. Plorn was left to seek appointments from old parliamentary friends. From the general nature of his written applications it is sometimes hard to gauge just what post he is seeking. On 20 September 1895 the Speaker of the Legislative Assembly, J.P. Abbott, wrote that he was sure that a certain appointment would be made to Edward Dickens. It does not seem, however, that it was.

Meanwhile, possibly in the hope of finding mineral deposits, Plorn was becoming interested in the geology of the west. A mineral destiny, like the pastoral one, flickered on Plorn's horizon, as it did for so many colonials, and then died. By May 1897 Plorn, back in Sydney, wrote again to Abbott asking for his help in securing a post. Abbott replied that he was very sad to hear that Plorn had been unwell, but explained that he was bombarded with such requests and hoped that Edward's wishes regarding employment in Western Australia would come to fruition. The job he sought was that of Secretary to the Department of Aborigines in Western Australia. He asked G.W. Rusden, 'my oldest friend in Australia', to recommend him to Sir John Forrest, Premier of Western Australia and legendary explorer, who was in Melbourne for the Federal Convention. Plorn told Rusden, mentioning the other race for the first time visible in the record of his life, that in his years on the Darling 'I saw a great deal of the Darks, and in fact took a great interest in them.'

Edmund Barton, handsome lawyer, furiously busy campaigning for Federation, and the venal and Rabelaisian George Reid, Premier of New South Wales, wrote Plorn testimonials. They were on their way to future prime ministerships of a federated nation. Sir John Forrest wrote a letter to Edward the day after he heard from him. 'I will be glad to place your application with others for consideration—but seeing that there are many applicants in the Colony having also special knowledge of the Aborigines, I cannot hold out much hope of your application being favourably considered.' Edward did not get the job.

It would be June 1900 before he was given an appointment as an inspector in the Moree Land District, around the Gwydir River. The job involved visiting properties purchased under the new Land Act of 1895 to see that the contracts of occupation were being kept. If Connie joined him in Moree, where he lodged at the Criterion Hotel, she did not stay long but went to reside with her mother in Adelaide. Obliged to travel long distances on horseback over rough country roads, in the early days of Federation Plorn's health declined. His drinking became heavy. The landlady of the Criterion Hotel, Mrs E.C. Everingham, was a kindly woman who let Edward owe her rent. Plorn also won the affection of a young man staying at the hotel, Roland James Rudd. When Rudd's mother sent him some quail, Rudd thanked her and declared, 'I would like some more for my friend Mr Dickens who has been on the sick list this last month and we can't get him to eat anything hardly.'

Henry and Kitty in England heard of their brother's illness and sent him £100, which did not arrive until after his death on 23 January 1902. He died, said the doctors, of 'acute phthisis exhaustion' during a very severe summer where the night-time temperature did not fall below 80 degrees Fahrenheit (27 degrees Celsius) and the daytime temperatures were 105 degrees Fahrenheit (40 degrees Celsius) or more. One of Edward's other friends in Moree was a Methodist clergyman, the Reverend F.W. Hynes, who conducted the burial service in the Methodist portion of the Moree cemetery. So ended Plorn's attempt to come to terms with Australia.

For many years the situation of the grave was not known. Money was collected by the Dickens Fellowship in Sydney and a memorial tablet was placed in the Church of England in Moree. Over sixty years after Plorn's death, his grave was correctly located and a memorial stone erected above him. Many other gentlemen exiles achieved even less than that.

Alfred Dickens had continued to manage E.B.L. Dickens and Company in Melbourne in the 1880s, but like other Victorians seems to have invested in the land bubble. In 1888 he married again, a young woman named Emily Riley. A year after Alfred and Emily moved to Hawthorn, the depression struck and Alfred was so short of money that he remembered a reading of his father's works that he had performed in Hamilton in the Western District ten years before. He decided to take to the road lecturing on his father's life, and performing readings of his work. His first Melbourne lecture, addressed to the Bankers' Institute, was a triumph. He next played at the beautiful Athenaeum Hall in Melbourne, then went on to Geelong, Ballarat and Sydney. There he wrote to Sir Henry Parkes, inviting him to extend his patronage to the opening lecture in Sydney. Sir Henry Parkes agreed to preside at the 18 March 1892 performance, but did not in the end honour the event, since the weather was so bad on the night. A second lecture was delivered under the patronage of the Governor of New South Wales, the Earl of Jersey.

The firm of J & N Tait, theatrical producers of Melbourne, would much later organise tours of the United Kingdom and America. Alfred was glad to go, in part because of his unhappy relationship with his new wife. According to his American producer, he never mentioned her, though he often spoke of his first wife and his children. In 1910 he toured the English counties for three months, including in his program two lectures in London. He then rested before sailing for America. He was now over sixty-five years old and the tour of sixty-six lectures must have exhausted him, even though he received warm receptions everywhere. Agents received invitations for him to return to nearly every town in which he had given his lectures and readings.

He returned to Melbourne somewhat more affluent than he had left it. Soon after arriving in England again he told a journalist that Australia was a magnificent country with 'a fine future for an immigrant with little means'. He said that the advance of socialism in Australia would never destroy the imperial and British spirit there.

Alfred left England for America in the autumn of 1911 in a weakened state. He lectured in New York, St Louis and elsewhere, including Cairo, Illinois, which had been visited by his father and lampooned in Dickens' *American Notes*. Lectures elsewhere continued to exhaust him, though he sometimes received over $1000 for a single lecture. In New York on 30 December 1911, staying at the famous Astor, he felt particularly ill and collapsed in the hotel lobby. He cancelled that night's lecture, and died that afternoon in his hotel room. Again neither the Australian earth nor the society of Melbourne, which through its economic depression had helped drive him on this deadly circuit, had served him well. He had told Mrs Johnson, the New York governor's wife, how he had loved his beds of red geraniums in Melbourne and how his daughter Kathleen wore them in her hair. On 6 January 1912 his body was buried at renowned Trinity Church in lower New York, finding there the valuable earth he had never found in Australia.

WHAT THE *BULLETIN* DID

Established in 1880, the *Bulletin* found itself of a mind to exploit the disunion, uncertainty and class mistrust of the 1890s. John Archibald (a Victorian by birth who sometimes went by the name Jules François Archibald) saw his magazine, which he founded with an older journalist, John Haynes, as a means of focusing a new nationalism—radical, populist, republican, contemptuous of supposed nobility and pretension, anti-Semitic yet at the same time opposed to the sectarianism between Catholic and Protestant. Archibald had had an important experience on the Palmer goldfields in Queensland, and believed he had found in the miners there, in their ruggedness, humour and their abomination of Asiatics, the essential and admirable Australian. Thus, though he and Haynes had spent most of their lives in the city, the *Bulletin* was called 'the Bushman's Bible', appealing to the mining prospector, the drover, the shearer, the self-educated, robust, new species. The Australian.

Ballads had been sung in the Australian past to combat the immensity and silences of the Australian interior. So ballads played a large part in the life of the *Bulletin*. In some ways the *Bulletin* celebrated a world already passing, at least closer in to the cities and wherever the railway reached. 'Those golden days are vanished', Henry Lawson grieved in the *Bulletin*'s pages,

> And altered is the scene;
> The diggings are deserted,
> The camping grounds are green;
> The flaunting flag of progress
> Is in the west unfurled,
> The mighty bush with iron rails is tethered to the world.

Shearers were riding bicycles instead of horses, or were humping their swags, to reach their shearing sheds. But beyond the railways and the good roads lay the Australia the *Bulletin* sought to honour and set up as a template of the national soul. So did its readers and contributors, from John Farrell, another journalist friend of Archibald's who wrote the mocking, nationalist 'Australia to England', to the gentleman stockman Barcroft Boake, very much an Adam Lindsay Gordon sort of man, and Lawson and Paterson.

Paterson and Lawson are themselves interesting contrasts. Paterson was the grazier's son. A Sydney solicitor, he wrote ballads of the bush. It never happened the other way, that people who lived in the bush wrote ballads of city life. The politics some people read into 'Waltzing Matilda'—itinerant swagman against landed capitalist—was entirely unintended by Paterson. 'The Man From Snowy River' has no politics. Paterson personally expected justice from the station owner, who should be a man who worked with his shearers, paid high wages and was sympathetic to unionised labour.

Henry Lawson wrote of the city, but as a bitter place, and the bush as a test for the soul and an arena of struggle and quest for justice. His father, Niels

Hertzberg Larsen, native of the Norwegian island of Tremoy, had jumped ship in Melbourne to go gold seeking. His son Henry Lawson, born in 1867 in a tent on the goldfields at Grenfell, and taken at four by his questing Norwegian father and tough young Australian-born mother to the Gulgong rush, mourned for and mythologised the old goldfields, squalor and all, even though—or perhaps because—he could barely remember them.

> *Oh who would paint a goldfield,*
> *And limn the picture right,*
> *As we have often seen it*
> *In early morning's light;*
> *The yellow mounds of mullock*
> *With spots of red and white,*
> *The scattered quartz that glistened,*
> *Like diamonds in the light;*
> *The azure line of ridges,*
> *The bush of darkest green,*
> *The little homes of calico*
> *That dotted all the scene.*

By the time Lawson was six, his father had given up looking for gold and had selected 40 acres near Gulgong. Lawson never found the selector's life romantic. He was a proletarian, one in heart with the itinerant shearer or agricultural worker, the drover and the doomed, scrabbling selector of the kind his father had been. But he also pitied the city working class, what he called 'the armies of the rear', because when not haplessly itinerant in the bush, he became one of them. He lived a harsh life from 1867 to 1922, and though many thought him a balladist beyond compare, he wrote for sixpence a line, so that his quality came and went with his thirst. His verses at their best were also a cry to anger and action in the white dispossessed of the cities who were required in their poverty to listen to city fathers blather on about the classlessness, the equality and prosperity of Australia. 'They lie, the men who tell us, for reasons of their own, That want is here a stranger, and that misery's unknown.'

Working men and women thrilled to such verses as:

> *That the curse of class distinctions from our shoulders shall be hurled.*
> *An' the sense of Human Kinship revolutionise the world;*

There'll be higher education for the toilin-starvin clown
An' the rich an' educated shall be educated down.

This vengefulness sprang directly from Lawson's heart, for he had been a put-upon and ill-paid worker, had suffered social contempt for his drunkenness and his unsatisfactory performance as an employee and, above all, had suffered poverty.

Lawson, like his mother Louisa, was a republican too.

The Queen has lived for seventy years, for seventy years and three;
And few have lived a flatter life, more useless life than she;
She never said a clever thing or wrote a clever line,
She never did a noble deed, in coming times to shine;
And yet we read, and still we read, in every magazine,
The praises of that woman whom the English call 'The Queen'.

Far different in tenor and politics from Lawson was John O'Brien (Monsignor John Hartigan, parish priest of Narranderra). In 1906 he would do for Irish Catholics what Paterson did for the community at large—he depicted the Irish-born or first-generation Irish cockie in all his contradictoriness, his amusing if excusable ignorance, and his capacity to endure. The famous Hanrahan, who complained in drought or flood that 'we'll all be rooned', was his creation, as was the bush kid of Irish parentage who could not tell a visiting bishop the importance of Christmas but suddenly remembered, 'It's the day before the races out at Tangmalangmaroo.'

In fiction the *Bulletin* wanted a terse style. 'Grit not gush' was Archibald's motto—it was certainly the attitude of literary editor A.G. Stephens, a Queensland journalist who, during his stint at the *Bulletin* up to 1906, was the comptroller of the magazine's literary taste—with a dazzling record in that role. Other writers Stephens published included Edward Dyson, Ernest Favenc, E.J. Brady and Price Warung. Price Warung, whose real name was William Astley, did the *Bulletin* the service of depicting the convict days in a way that justified contempt for the British and provided ammunition for the supposedly coming republic. Louis Becke's tales of blackbirding in the South Seas appeared there too.

In this atmosphere A.G. Stephens published a literary phenomenon, a good-natured book as strong as Lawson in its respect for the unlanded, the despised. It was *Such is Life*, written under the pseudonym Tom Collins by Joseph Furphy. In its gritty, eloquent bush discourses all human questions, including free will and predestination, class and democracy, are canvassed. It concerns itself with 'the art of riding horses and the art of swapping them, the modes of spinning yarns and of telling whoppers, the varied crafts of the bushman and the formidable mnemonic power which they demand, the reticent loyalties of mate and dog, the eccentricities of bush-scholarship, the curiosities of bush-etiquette, and the firm pattern of bush-ethics'.

Joseph Furphy had been a drought-struck selector from the Riverina area of New South Wales who, finding the terms of Australian agriculture had defeated him, had to walk away from his farm. He became a bullock driver, but uncharacteristically of the stereotype of such a man, was a non-swearing practitioner of temperance. The drought of 1883 destroyed even the bullock-driving career. During the depression of the 1890s, he worked in his brother's ironworks at Shepparton in Victoria, and had a little shed in which he read devoutly and prepared to write a book in which the ordinarily despised bullockies and swagmen would be depicted as possessing a certain voice, rough and democratic, the voice of the humble of the earth waiting to be exalted and worthy of it, while the finance men who had seized their marginal land from them were creatures of the devil.

At the head of his book Furphy promised that his rambling tale would be in 'Temper, democratic; bias, offensively Australian'. The bush made living a crude and rough existence. But the novel worked against the idea that the bush made utterly brutal, unthinking men. 'Yet he has thoughts that glow, and words that burn, albeit with such sulphurous fumes that, when uttered in a public place, they frequently render him liable to fourteen days [imprisonment] without the option. Yet this futureless person is the man who pioneers all industries . . . whose heavy footprints mark the waterless mulga, the wind-swept plains, and the scorching sand.'

He was encouraged throughout the process of writing by a friend, Kate Baker, a County Waterford-born girl twenty years younger than him. (Furphy's own people came from Northern Ireland.) Furphy, who was married but found his wife an inscrutable being, admired Kate Baker's intellectual capacity, and there is no indication that the admiration went further than that. She was, he boasted of her, 'the only girl in the Eastern Hemisphere who knew who Belisarius was'. Tom Collins, as he called himself for the purposes of publication, finished his book in March 1897, sent it to Alfred George Stephens of the *Bulletin*, and had it published in 1903 by that magazine.

Such is Life was not successful in its day, and Furphy, retiring from work, took his wife and sons and went and lived in Western Australia, where he died in September 1912. As he had written in his unsuccessful verse,

This dictum you may safely trust –
Growl you may, but Go you must.

Kate Baker then bought up the remaining print run of *Such Is Life* and republished it with a foreword by the Melbourne writer Vance Palmer. She would also publish Furphy's poetry and, with Miles Franklin, a biography.

Miles Franklin, who at the age of sixteen wrote *My Brilliant Career* (1901), and Steele Rudd were others published by Stephens. Bernard O'Dowd, born in Melbourne in 1866, brought his powerful intellect and gifts to lay on the altar of the *Bulletin* tradition. For most of his life he was a Supreme Court librarian and parliamentary draftsman. Having renounced the Catholicism of his childhood, he was a socialist and founder of the left-wing magazine *Tocsin*. To him Australia was 'the whole world's legatee', inheritor of the best aspects of humankind and its institutions, and rejecter of the worst. In other words, Australia was the last chance of humanity.

She is the scroll on which we are to write
Mythologies our own and epics new.

O'Dowd and the young Christopher Brennan in Sydney were the first poets of serious ideas. Brennan was only thirty when he wrote his great inconclusive poem 'The Wanderer'. It was unique in that although it was written in a house full of children's nappies, and with a disgruntled wife, German mother-in-law and mentally disturbed sister-in-law hanging over his endeavours, it was influenced not by shearers but by the French imagists as filtered by a young man with a classical education. All he shared with Lawson was a tragic thirst for liquor.

O'Dowd was Alfred Deakin's favourite and one can see why: he thought that the poet's work was central to society, in that it should deal with politics, religion, science and reform in general. There was a need for 'the permeator poet, the projector of ideals, the poet militant . . . in this virgin and unhandicapped land of social experiments, embryonic democracy, and the Coming Race, Australia!'

He raised the famous question of whether Australia would be 'a drift Sargasso where the West in Halcyon calm rebuilds her fatal nest', or 'Delos of a coming Sun-God's race?' For all progressives of the time, and for Australians since, the question had resonance—were we to be citizens of not just another unjust little province but a utopia, a vision for the world to behold?

His vision, if not his belief in the central nature of poetry, was a very strong and common one amongst the Australians of his era. Every issue, from Federation to the unionism of shearers or seamen to the Empire and Boer War to suspicion of Jews and the abomination of Asians to the whimsy, misery or grandeur of the bush kept the pages of the *Bulletin* flowing with verse.

BANJO DOESN'T CARE FOR MATILDA

Australia's national song derived from a man whose character was built equally by the experience of being the son of a pastoral manager, but as an adult was an urbane city dweller of a democratic temper. He was educated at Sydney Grammar School and the University of Sydney, yet began his education in a bush school at Binalong amongst the children of shearers and selectors. As a young balladist he used the name Banjo, after a family racehorse, and one of his own enthusiasms remained thoroughbred horses. He frequently rode them as an amateur jockey at Randwick and Rosehill racetracks in Sydney.

The story of the writing of 'Waltzing Matilda' is a matter of Australian oral rather than documentary history, but the ABC's research on the matter in the early 1960s received the imprimatur of Banjo's son. A family known as the McPhersons were party to it—they had overlanded to Queensland after Victoria's Berry government's Land Acts, which they felt threatened by. They had entertained the bushranger Mad Dog Morgan on their property, and Mrs McPherson had played the piano for him.

At the time of the origin of 'Waltzing Matilda', young Robert McPherson and his brothers were managing Dagworth Station on the Diamantina River north-west of Winton, and in 1894 the widowed Ewan McPherson, the patriarch of the family, brought his daughters north to join his sons on the station. The story goes that before she left for Queensland young Christina McPherson attended the races in Warrnambool in April 1894 and heard the Warrnambool Militia Artillery Band playing an arrangement of an old Scottish tune named 'The Bonnie Wood of Craigielea'. The tune stuck in her head. When Christina reached Winton she met an old school friend, Sarah Reilly, and invited her to come out and stay at Dagworth. Miss Reilly had a young male companion, however, a small, cock-sparrow sort of man, a solicitor from Sydney, Andrew Barton Paterson. Paterson was on sabbatical from his law practice. Bring Mr Paterson as well, said Christina.

Paterson came to Dagworth and delighted in going on long rides around the property with Robert McPherson. Christina took on the task of entertaining the company with music in the evenings, and though the homestead did not boast a piano, she was able to borrow an autoharp, a sort of zither, patented in the 1880s and popular in the new world, from the station bookkeeper. Young Andrew Paterson heard her play 'The Bonnie Wood of Craigielea' on that instrument. According to Paterson himself, he asked, 'Why don't you sing the words to that?' Christina replied that it had no words.

Robert McPherson told a later researcher, Sydney May, perhaps a little too neatly, that as he and Banjo rode around Dagworth in the next few days, three disconnected events occurred. They came across a dead sheep with a forequarter missing, and McPherson explained that itinerants, swagmen, often took the forequarter for their meals. Then the two young men visited a waterhole on the western boundary and McPherson told Paterson that a man had drowned there once while attempting to escape from troopers. Then one of the jackaroos mentioned to McPherson and Paterson that he had seen 'a couple of men waltzing matilda down in the billabong'. Paterson did not know what 'waltzing matilda' meant, and he was told that it meant carrying a swag. The usage delighted him.

A family named the Ramsays of Oondooroo Station now invited the McPhersons to come look at some new fire-fighting equipment they'd acquired. Paterson drove over from Dagworth with the family. At Oondooroo they found a piano and a Ramsay family member, Herbert, who had been trained as a baritone. Christina played 'Craigielea' on the piano and Paterson began writing down his lyrics for it in short bursts, passing them to Herbert Ramsay, who sang them. And so the offspring of station owners and managers assembled around a piano creating a song which one commentator would call 'a treason song' of stock theft by an itinerant worker.

A month later, in May 1885, the Winton Races were held. The McPhersons of Dagworth and the Ramsays of Oondooroo and their guests went along, where on pub pianos they performed their new song. Paterson then packed his copy of his lyrics in his luggage but seems to have forgotten it when he returned to Sydney. For some reason, perhaps involving his thwarted attraction to Christina McPherson, his memories of Dagworth were unhappy, and his regard for 'Waltzing Matilda' was coloured by that memory. He sold it with 'a lot of old junk', shorter bush poems, to Angus and Robertson in 1903, the year of his marriage to Alice Walker of Tenterfield. Between its creation and publication he had been away at the Boer War as a correspondent, and had become a famous figure for his ballad 'The Man From Snowy River'. Angus and Robertson tried to sell the musical rights to 'Waltzing Matilda' to Inglis and Company, the proprietors of Billy Tea, as a marketing tool, but the idea did not come to anything. Mrs Marie Cowan, however, wife of the general manager of Inglis and Company, set her hand to an arrangement of the music. Mr Cowan contacted Paterson with a copy of text and music and Paterson wrote back, 'Your song received, very satisfactory. Marie Cowan has done a good job, good luck to her.'

'Waltzing Matilda', with minor textual variations, would in the end be fitted, as well as to 'Craigielea', to entirely different music altogether, the tune of another folk song. The two versions, the most popular and the more esoteric, exist to this day. What is certain is that the phenomenon developed, the text being spread, the song being performed, without any encouragement from Paterson himself. May, who wrote an early account of its genesis, recalled himself hearing the song sung far from Paterson or the McPhersons and Ramsays, on a station in New South Wales, in 1899. Banjo Paterson would survive his time as a field ambulance driver and re-mount officer in World War I and live until 1941, by which time the song had been—to say the least—popularly adopted.

FEDERATION, PROTECTION, DESTINY

It seems to the reader of nineteenth-century Australian politics that Free Trade and Protection, though seriously divided camps, were often flags of convenience for politicians. No more principled shift from one to the other was the case of the young lawyer-journalist Alfred Deakin. Deakin had made friends with the powerful but reclusive David Syme, editor of the *Age*, a liberal progressive like himself and a Protectionist, that is, one who chose to design society by making foreign exports too expensive to compete with local factories, whose owners in turn nurtured a sane society by paying appropriate wages.

Deakin remembered the night he was converted by Syme's arguments to become a Protectionist, in line with the growing protectionist bent of Victoria, 'as we crossed the old Prince's Bridge one evening'. He was brought around by argument, not by workshop owners begging for such favours, especially not by those workshop owners who were fellow members of the Legislative Assembly. Syme brought him from Free Trade to Protection by holding out the concept that Deakin could do more to design society by Protection than Free Trade would permit him to do. It did happen that the Free Trade faction was always in the minority in Victoria and that to continue a Free Trader would have cramped his path in politics. Yet Deakin was genuinely pure-spirited enough to have a conversion like that of St Paul.

Federation became his other major dogma. Many colonial politicians paid lip service to Federation, like the people they represented, thinking it inevitable and not worth getting in a lather over. Along with Parkes and others, Deakin was one of those who tried to drive it. One of the few groups actively engaged in Federation in the early 1880s was the Australian Natives Association, a largely Victorian group of Australian-born, founded in 1871, largely from the children of the post-gold rush generation, many of them born in the canvas towns of Melbourne or the goldfields. Deakin was a member of the Prahran branch of the ANA.

In the matter of Federation, he was also influenced and was to an extent a follower of Premier James Service, another of those thoughtful but deft Scots who was a Free Trader but, unlike most free traders, a liberal. When Sydney and Melbourne were linked by train in 1883, Service said: 'I decline to subscribe to the doctrine that I am to die before the grand Federation of the Australian colonies.' (Sadly, he would die in 1899.)

Earlier that same year, 1883, the Queensland–German New Guinea crisis had occurred. In an attempt to prevent German expansion in the Pacific, the minute naval force at Queensland's disposal was sent by Premier McIlwraith to seize the southern half of Eastern New Guinea. Side by side with genuine concern that Australia and Britain were being trumped was a desire to keep for Queensland the trade across the Torres Strait and to blackbird in New Guinea if they wished. When, before ranks of sailors and a crowd of fascinated but bemused natives, the new colony was proclaimed in Port Moresby, Britain was embarrassed. It chastised Queensland for its presumption. It would, in fact, formally take over the area and its adjoining islands a year later, once it had cleared the business with its friend Bismarck, the German chancellor. But in the meantime there was a feeling in the Australian colonies that their interests in the Pacific were being betrayed by Whitehall. Service suggested a Convention of Colonies to consider the possibility of some form of federal action on both New Guinea and the future of the New Hebrides (Vanuatu). 'Federation and all the islands,' he had cried. The convention met in Sydney in December 1883, and a Federal Council was created, a small body made up of two politicians (later four) from each of the colonies to frame laws on a few matters of common interest. But the New South Wales delegation refused to join the council because many thought it a Victorian plot to impose Victorian-style protectionist laws on them. Even Parkes, who was out of office and had no part to play in the convention but who had earlier suggested a similar council, now said it would delay Federation.

Left: Mark Jeffery, a Tasmanian survivor from the days of transportation, veteran of Port Arthur's 'separate' prison, was for a time a convict grave-digger on the Isle of the Dead, where he claimed to have come face-to-face with 'His Satanic Majesty'. He would see Federation and die in 1903. (National Library of Australia) *Right:* Western Australia began to receive convicts in 1850 and the last transport ship arrived in 1868. Sad-faced William Stewart, former Western Australian transportee, pictured in 1900, bears the mark of many former convict males—loneliness, a sense of exile and a hard life as a labourer. (State Library of Western Australia, 066191PD)

Left: Convicts did not expire and vanish with the end of transportation. Long-living and handsome, former Van Diemen's Land convict and blanket-thief Mary Witherington in her later incarnation as Mrs Herbert. Her husband, a convict stonemason, carved her face in the multi-faced bridge at Ross. Though transported in 1835, she lived until 1890. (State Library of Tasmania, PH30-1-264) *Right:* Daniel Herbert, stonemason husband of Mary Witherington, in his post-convict, mid-Victorian Sunday best. (State Library of Tasmania, PH30-1-263)

BROTHER HARRY RETURNS FROM AUSTRALIA—GREAT SENSATION IN BAKER STREET.

Young men of the British gentry sent to Australia to remake themselves were characteristically expected to return rich, informal in manners and clothing. Rendered uncouth by their colonial experience, they were capable of appalling even the liveried servants who opened their English family doors to them. (State Library of Victoria, MP00/00/56/38)

 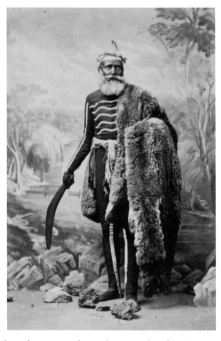

Left: Edward Bulwer Lytton (Plorn) Dickens, less than gifted student, was a boy whose study of Latin was cancelled by his father Charles so that he could apply himself to 'a general improvement of his acquaintance with the properties of the things he will have to subdue to his use in a rough wild life' in Australia. (The Dickens Museum, London) *Right:* A successful Englishman G.W. Rusden, friend of Charles Dickens, clerk of the Victorian Parliament and pamphleteer and columnist under the Aboriginal named 'Yittadairn', whose persona he adopts in fancy dress for this photograph. (State Library of Victoria, H29562)

Momba Station, north-east of Wilcannia, at which Plorn Dickens arrived before the age of seventeen, provided the beginning of a hard Australian education for him, and of expectations which turned out to be less than great for the young English son of the great writer. (National Library of Australia, nla.pic-an 24460098)

Wool being washed on a creek of the Darling River in a year of good flow. But here as elsewhere in remoter Australia, water would prove to be an occasional blessing, and drought would determine individual and national fortunes and put limits on population. (National Library of Australia, nla.pic-an 24473329)

Thomas Bungaleenee, son of a man detained for the supposed abduction of a woman who never existed, became inflamed with the tragic desire to be identified as white. He was the first of his race to be inducted as a member of the Independent Order of Oddfellows. (State Library of NSW, Mitchell Library, ML Q059/13)

The first overseas war in which Australians fought was in New Zealand against the Maoris. These Australian volunteers were photographed one quiet day in 1864 outside their redoubt and signalling post at Kaitake near New Plymouth. Some of them stayed on to take up land grants as a reward for service. (Alexander Turnbull Library, Wellington, New Zealand, ref: PA1-q-177-07)

The arrival of neighbouring squatters, and the disposal of the bodies of the nineteen massacred members of Horatio Wills's party at Cullin-La-Ringo, inland from Rockhampton. The Aboriginal people would pay many times over for their murders here. (State Library of Queensland, ACC 8085)

Sir Samuel Wilson, previously 'Bullocky Sam', in knightly uniform. A land-hungry Ulsterman, he began small but acquired properties in the Wimmera and New South Wales, lived in the mansion of Ercildoune in Victoria and endowed the University of Melbourne. (State Library of Victoria, H38849/4983)

Dad (Thomas) Davis, Steele Rudd's father and model for Dad in *On Our Selection*, stands on the right in the second row with sons and grandsons outside the Davis homestead on the Darling Downs in 1896. The family wanted it known that this structure was not the original 'old shingle hut', but a house moved from elsewhere. (National Library of Australia, nla.pic-vn 4903038)

Alfred Deakin, future statesman, as a child of Golden Melbourne in the 1860s. The visionary, questing quality he would bring to his adult face has not yet appeared in this sunny, suburban childhood which seems a planet removed from that of contemporary small landholders' children such as Ned Kelly. (National Library of Australia, nla.ms-ms 1540-19-613-s7-a1

Tom Wills, Rugby Old Boy and permanent schoolchild. An inter-colonial cricketer, he was the survivor of a massacre of his family by Queensland Aborigines, gathered a team of Western District Aborigines to tour England, and would be credited with founding Australian Rules football. (State Library of NSW, Mitchell Library, ML A927.96)

A team of Western District Aborigines, the first sporting tourists Australia would send abroad. Here, in the summer of 1866–67, they pose by the Melbourne Cricket Ground Pavilion with their selector and fellow player Tom Wills in the middle back row. (State Library of NSW, Mitchell Library, a128392 /MPG/113)

HOW NICE!

Brown, in his anxiety to avail himself of the new telegraph line, some few day sago announced to his friends in England, the pleasing fact of his approaching marriage. He has since got married, and this is only the fourth time on his wedding night that he has had to go down stairs to receive congratulatory messages in reply to his communication.

It is 1872, the Overland Telegraph is in operation and Brown, Australian settler, businessman and bridegroom, leaves his bed for the fourth time on his wedding night to receive congratulatory telegrams from London friends. Previously he would have had to wait weeks if not months for these salutations. (State Library of NSW, Mitchell Library, *Sydney Punch*, 7 November 1872 p. 466)

In this illustration of 1869 entitled 'Slave Trade in the South Seas', Captain Palmer RN of HMS *Rosario*, appointed by the Admiralty to interdict the blackbirding trade, seizes the schooner *Daphne* and liberates the South Seas natives from the ships' hold. Palmer despaired, however, of the colonial court system, which regularly found even murdering blackbirders not guilty. (National Library of Australia, nla.pic-an 10267974)

Left: While dying in 1892 William Brookes, a friend of the Anti-Slavery Society, was carried into the Legislative Council of Queensland on a stretcher to argue for an hour against a law re-introducing Kanaka recruiting. The bill passed but the practice came under increasing pressure from the advocates of White Australia. (State Library of Queensland, 94376) *Right:* Kanakas, supposedly voluntary labourers for the sugar plantations of Queensland, are photographed on a recruiting vessel in the New Hebrides (Vanuatu) in the 1890s. Regulations to return them home after a specified time were often ignored, there were notorious cases of on-board brutality and murder, and patchy diet and medical care meant that Australia was often their burial place. (National Library of Australia, nla.pic-an 24494646)

Louis Becke in 1900. A supercargo on a blackbirder and crew mate of the notorious 'recruiter' 'Bully Hayes', he became a literary star of the *Bulletin,* in which his stories of serving on blackbirding expeditions were first published. (National Library of Australia, nla.pic-an 23193911)

Left: Mrs Charles Rasp, wife of the boundary rider who came to Australia for the health of his lungs and who, while out mustering in the Barrier Ranges during the shearing season of 1883, took ore samples from 'a broken hill'. Rasp became a mineral grandee and did not die until 1907. Mrs Rasp then remarried and became Countess von Zedtwitz. (State Library of South Australia B28306) *Right:* A young, intellectually inquisitive South Australian desert Aboriginal named David Unaipon, son of the first Ngarrindjeri lay preacher, was the protégé of the missionary the Reverend George Taplin. As an adolescent Unaipon would study science and anthropology in the museums and libraries of Adelaide. (National Archives of Australia, A659, 1945/1/1470, folio no. 85)

Just before Christmas 1867, Prince Alfred, the first of the Queen's blood to visit Australia, shoots rabbits on the estate of Thomas Austin, Barwon Park, a house and grounds fit for any prince. Brought in from Western England for such sport as this, the rabbits would colonise Australia and become an ally of drought in destroying pastures and pastoralists. (State Library of Victoria Ian20/12/67/4)

Louis Buvelot, a Swiss immigrant and mentor to Tom Roberts and Julian Ashton, was considered by them a forerunner in the struggle to bring a true eye to the Australian landscape, which in this photograph he seems to approach confidently. (National Library of Australia, nla.pic-an 24230088)

Louis Buvelot's *A Summer Afternoon near Templestowe* was thought to be 'thoroughly Australian' by Frederick McCubbin and other members of the Heidelberg School, although it appears to be an idyllic English scene to the modern eye. (Louis Buvelot, Swiss 1814–1888, worked in Brazil 1835-52, Australia 1865-88, oil on canvas 76.6 x 118.9 cm, National Gallery of Victoria, Melbourne, purchased, 1869)

This often reproduced photograph of Ned Kelly's lieutenant Dan Byrne, strung up dead in the doorway of the Benalla police barracks, has added significance because the man in the bowler hat on the left walking away with his sketch book is the asthmatic immigrant artist, Julian Ashton. At this time he worked as a magazine illustrator, but would live on to found an art school and provide a link from the age of bushranging and the age of the Australian impressionists. (State Library of Victoria, H13587)

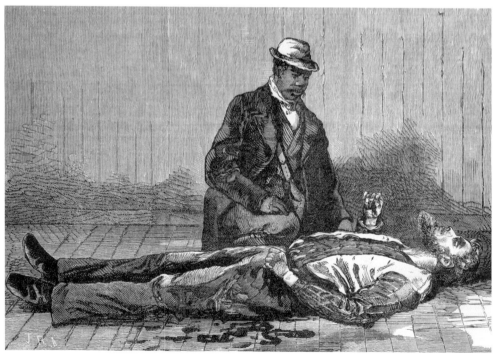

This magazine depiction of the finding of Byrne's dead body in the Glenrowan Inn has none of the frenzy and fire of the events. The body was first discovered by Father Gibney, but the figure leaning over Joe seems to be a police blacktracker. This rather stiff wood engraving is based on the work of Julian Ashton. (State Library of Victoria, IAN03/07/80/105)

In 1883, Germany had ambitions to acquire the north-eastern coast of New Guinea. In answer to these fears the Queensland government of Thomas McIlwraith used its small military resources to seize pre-emptively the south-eastern coast in the Empire's name. The Empire was appalled at this colonial arrogance. (State Library of NSW, MitchellLibrary, SPF /2752, e)

Left: The talented Russian scientist and explorer, Count Nicholai Nicholaievich Miklouhoi-Maklai, was in his early thirties when this photograph was taken in about 1880. Petitioning the Pacific High Commissioner to protect the land rights of New Guinean natives, he would later make the same appeal to Count Bismarck of Germany. (State Library of Queensland, 195877) *Right:* Immigrant girls were housed in barracks on arrival in Australia, in this case in the old convict barracks at Hyde Park Sydney. The more commodious and faster steamships, travelling through the Suez Canal from 1869 and reaching Australia in as little as thirty-three days, allowed immigrants to bring more fashionable clothing with them and to arrive in robust health. (State Library of NSW, *Australian Town and Country Journal*, 19 July 1879, p 120 TN 115)

Infant mortality: a South Australian mother mourns her child circa 1875. Bush children did not die of epidemics as the city children, and this tragic burial was better provided for than those of the children of city slums buried for a few pennies in coffins made of fruit boxes. (State Library of South Australia B39315)

Chinese fossicker 'Ah Sin', Aboriginal 'Jack' the blacktracker, and 'Harry' the white digger play cut-throat euchre for pennyweights of gold on a remote goldfield somewhere in Northern Australia. This degree of fraternisation was considered inappropriate and depraved in politer regions. (National Library of Australia, nla.pic-an 8927787)

Louisa Lawson, future Sydney feminist, republican and mother of Henry, stands before her home in Gulgong with her son Charles William. The vertical logs of the structure give little promise of protection from wind or rain, a reality of which many selectors complained in their own cases. (State Library of NSW, Mitchell Library, ON 4 Box 4 No 18410)

A mixed race family run a rudimentary boarding house on the gold field of Home Rule near Gulgong in New South Wales. Next door is the butcher's shop where no doubt, according to the practice of pre-refrigeration, butchers carved patterns in the meat carcases to appeal to purchasers. (State Library of NSW, Mitchell LIbrary, on4_38 950)

This engraving of Beath, Schiess and Company's clothing factories in Melbourne gives some sense of the industriousness of workers and the physical conditions under which they worked but offers the viewer little information about the abysmal wages and long hours under which such workers lived. (State Library of Victoria, IAN13/05/82/69)

Veterans of the strikes of the 1890s face the camera in the new and utopian version of Australia founded by William Lane in Paraguay. Soon after the visionary but tyrannical Lane established Nueva Australia in the jungle in 1893, the colony split in two. The writer Mary Gilmore joined Lane's second fore-doomed settlement, where staples were rice and monkey-meat. (State Library of NSW, Mitchell Library, a1188003 PXD 905 / no. 13)

He wanted faster, more definite action. He was willing to join a Federation, he said, but not 'a pipsqueak council'. But as Deakin said, the very existence of the council gave him hope of better things.

But in the meantime there was already extant the question that would bedevil all Australian politics for another half-century or more—to what extent was Australian policy to be a mere echo of imperial policy? It is sometimes believed that Australians did not push independence in this area until the fall of Singapore in 1942. But already in Deakin's young manhood, the colonials wanted in many areas, not all of them praiseworthy, to live by their own policies. And one of the problems would always be that the British, from Salisbury to Churchill, could never understand why they just didn't go along with the Empire.

In 1886, the British Colonial Secretary was Lord Stanhope, a trim Conservative dandy, a former cricketer, and—above all—a man interested in saving imperial expense by encouraging the Australian colonies to federate (particularly on defence) and create a centre for their own combined strength. He called an Imperial Conference for the coming year, and Deakin, the young native-born Liberal leader in a Coalition in which he served as Chief Secretary, was nominated as the leader of the Victorian delegation. When appointed, his wife, Pattie Brown, had recently given birth to a second daughter, and their house in Walsh Street, South Yarra was being built. Despite all, he must go.

The conference met from 4 April to 9 May in 1887 in Whitehall. Other delegates were Samuel Griffith from Queensland and John Forrest of Western Australia, who had travelled on the same ship as Deakin and had discussed their own feelings on issues including Federation. The Victorian delegation was backed by Graham Berry, retired Victorian statesman and agent-general in London.

The 1887 conference was opened under Stanhope's successor Sir Henry Holland, who invited Tory Prime Minister Salisbury to attend. The occasion provided, said Sir Henry, with a touch too much of the schoolmaster, 'a good opportunity of mixing a little wholesome bitter with the sweet, by pointing out that cases must arise in which strict colonial views clashed with the necessities of imperial policy, and that in such cases, H.M. Government, with every desire to uphold colonial interests, have a right to expect concession from the Colonial Governments'. Holland begged Salisbury to attend sessions to do with the Pacific Islands and point out 'that the colonists must not try and set up the Monroe doctrine over all the Pacific islands', seizing them for the sake of creating a defensive wall.

On 26 April Prime Minister Salisbury made a speech which was particularly aimed at the Australian colonies and provoked a hostile response from them.

The speech told the Australians not to try to interfere with imperial intentions for the Pacific. Salisbury knew a little about the Australian colonies. Educated at Eton and Cambridge, Salisbury—Robert Arthur Talbot Gascoyne—had made a sea voyage in the 1850s to cure a nervous debility and had visited Australia and the diggings, wearing a jumper because he had been warned the diggers would laugh at him if he dressed like a gent. At Castlemaine and Bendigo he was treated with respect, approved of the observance of the Sabbath by miners and said that there was less crime on the diggings than in a large English town. But his Australian experience seemed far away from him by the time the colonial conference took place. At one stage during it, he thought the colonists 'the most unreasonable people I have ever heard or dreamt of'.

Deakin himself disagreed that 'for reasons of imperial policy' a colony had to sacrifice its aims. But for colonial politicians the trap was always baited with honey, and Deakin was treated, like the others, to dinners and visits to country houses—that is, he went through the process of being 'duchessed', as Australians called seduction by the British establishment. He was immune to it. He was offered a knighthood but refused. In his own time he ran off to Edinburgh and heard Annie Besant speak on Theosophism, saw Oxford and Cambridge and visited the graves of his grandfather and grandmother in Witney in Oxfordshire. He also took former Premier Berry's children to see Buffalo Bill's version of the Wild West.

Far from being overawed, Deakin's opening speech was the antithesis of Salisbury's. He said he intended to raise matters that challenged imperial policy, including the presence of French convicts in the Pacific. The wishes of colonial people, he said, no matter how many thousands of miles away from Westminster, should move the Colonial Office, the Foreign Office and 'that mysterious entity, the Cabinet'. In that way there would be no difference between colonial and imperial interests—Australian interests in the Pacific islands should, he implied, also compel the interest of the imperial government in the exact same way, not in a different way.

The Earl of Onslow, undersecretary to Holland, remembered later that on one side of the table were the rulers of England, and on the other the representatives of the colonies, 'grave and reverend signors' who delivered themselves of many platitudes, in excellent language—particularly in regard to loyalty to the Empire. 'But Deakin was different. He told us at once what Australia thought of England. He said that when he took up the paper [at home] he learned that Mr Gladstone had a cold, or Lord Salisbury the gout—but when he took up the . . . papers in England he could find nothing from Australia except that one man had won a sculling race, or a pugilist had beaten another.' He complained with total frankness about how the British had given the islands of the Pacific to the French, and Samoa to the Germans, and 'he told it with such bonhomie that we could not help realising that we had before us a real live man'.

It is said that in secret session Salisbury, prime minister and foreign secretary at the same time, chastised the Australian delegations for their anxiety about French designs on the New Hebrides, and declared that France might be allowed to annex them, and if so, the Australians should accept it. The New Hebrides were far from Australia he said, and if France could not be dissuaded from occupying the islands, Britain could not go to war over it. Therefore the colonials should let Salisbury do a deal: if the French would agree not to introduce convict transportation to the New Hebrides, they could have the islands in return. This was a settlement the French had already offered Salisbury, and Salisbury thought it a jolly fair thing. According to Deakin there was humble acquiescence by one New South Wales delegate and implied acceptance by Griffith of Queensland, but Berry and Service, the Victorians, both spoke out. Deakin himself followed with an angry, passionate and rational rejection of every point.

Though no transcript exists, we know that Deakin and others raised the matter of Scottish Presbyterian missionaries in Vanuatu who had appealed to the Victorians in particular for help in the face of a French occupation. Both Premier James Service, who in his Scottish youth combined zealous lay preaching with progressive politics, and his successor Duncan Gillies, a successful Ballarat miner in the 1850s but again a devout Presbyterian, had been galvanised by their pleas. The Australians believed too that France could be a potential enemy in the Pacific. Already French colonists and British colonists, or more exactly Scottish Presbyterian colonists, were locked in a battle to get their home governments to settle the issue. And now, in 1887 in London, it was largely settled by Deakin's vehemence. The Foreign Office was at least edgy if not angry that the Australians wanted them to frighten the French, a valued neighbour, over obscure little islands which men in Whitehall and at Westminster had never seen before, were never going to, and might even be hard put to find on a map. But as a result of Deakin's protests official instructions were given to the British Ambassador in Paris to say that no concessions would be given to the French in regard to their taking over the New Hebrides.

The most significant decision arising from the conference was the recognition by Salisbury and his cabinet that on Britain's behalf the Australians should take responsibility for administering British New Guinea, the south-eastern coast of that huge island, along with the whole of vast New Britain, now Rabaul.

In other matters, the British also wanted financial contributions from the colonies to the Admiralty for their naval defence. The Admiralty would provide an auxiliary squadron of cruisers and torpedo boats for the Australian station in return for a payment by the colonies towards maintenance and the interest on the cost.

Deakin would come back from the colonial meeting in London a definite promoter of Federation, chiefly because he had been appalled at the timidity and disunity of the various Australian colonial delegates. They went to London without any preparedness to speak with one voice. If disputes were ever to arise between Australia and Great Britain, they would be much more quickly settled and in accordance with the approval of the people 'when we are united in voice and in aim, if our representations went home [to Great Britain] backed out by the high authority of a Federal Parliament and a Federal Government'.

THE TRAIN TO TENTERFIELD

Parkes would suggest that what further sparked him to campaign for Federation in the late 1880s and early 1890s was the 1899 report of Major General Sir James Edwards, a British officer who made a tour of inspection of Australian defences and fortifications and argued that the Australian colonies could create a basis of defence only if the colonies agreed to a federal system to organise it. But in a visit to Melbourne in 1889, down the railway line to Albury in his fine-fitted saloon carriage—in part to see another great exhibition in a Melbourne not yet fallen to rags and ashes—Parkes lambasted Victorian politicians who wanted union between the colonies but who put fierce taxes on imports from New South Wales and other states. The attack was sincere but also motivated by a heightened sense of destiny. The Governor of New South Wales at that time, Baron Carrington, had suggested to Parkes that it would be a climactic act of Parkes' life to lead the colonies to Federation. It was the sort of talk Parkes found inspiring. Bereft of all economic success, he had also recently lost Clarinda, the immigrant girl from Birmingham who had suffered a steerage passage and bouts of poverty with him before and after their arrival in Australia in 1842. He had his eye on another woman, Eleanor Dixon, but he also had intimations of bad health and mortality. However, a great destiny could compensate for all.

Duncan Gillies, the Victorian premier, former goldfields partner of Peter Lalor, Eureka rebel, was suspicious of Parkes. Why should New South Wales pose as the great Federation state when men like Service had made the running until now? And if Parkes was so keen on Federation, why didn't he join the Federal Council? 'Honest Tom' Playford, a former market gardener from South Australia, attacked Parkes in Melbourne for not having belonged to the Federal Council and thus not being sincere and loyal to the idea. Western Australia also suspected Parkes' motives. Parkes would soon advance the issue, however. On a visit to Queensland to speak to the cabinet and legislators there he received a more sympathetic hearing. Then, returning home, he spoke at a banquet at the Tenterfield School of Arts on 24 October, urging that the colonial leaders should be summoned to a convention to devise a federal constitution.

It is interesting that, although his speech had a potent impact, there is no grand ringing phrase remembered from it. He asked '[w]hether the time had not now come for the creation on this Australian continent of an Australian government', as reported in the third-person in the manner of nineteenth-century news reports. 'Australia,' he said, 'had now a population of three and a half millions, and the American people numbered only between three and four millions when they formed the great commonwealth of the United States. The numbers were about the same, and surely what America had done by war the Australians could bring about by peace, without breaking the ties that held them to the mother country.'

The Australian Federation Conference was convened and met in Parliament House, Melbourne, for eight heat-frazzled days in February 1890. 'Parkes too ill', said Deakin's diary. But he had been well enough to frighten some delegates with the fact that his resolutions did not include the words 'under the Crown' and to create suspicion that his old republicanism might be rearing its head again. New Zealand sent two representatives, but it became apparent to the Australians even as early as this that while New Zealand would not be opposed to federation of the Australian colonies, it would not yet be considering joining itself. Parkes was not so ill either as not to give the conference his broader thoughts on the Federation issue. 'Make yourself a united people, appear before the world as one, and the dream of going "home" would die away. We should create an Australian home . . . we should have "home" within our own shores.' (Two years before that appeal to fraternity he had led attacks on Irish Catholics and raised the bogey of their potential disloyalty. Did he consider them part of the 'Australian home'?)

It was proposed by Parkes and seconded by Deakin that the next step should be a National Australasian Convention, to be held in the following year, at which the first complete draft of a constitution was to be written and adopted.

At the end of February 1891, Deakin, out of office, occupying the back bench and secretly tormented by the part his overconfidence might have played in his own losses, his father's and Victoria's, had just returned from a journey to India, where he had been commissioned by Syme of the *Age* to study irrigation projects and where he went as a student of religion. He was suffering from carbuncles and was run down and took a holiday in the Blue Mountains, spending a lot of time in the company of an urbane American he had met on the train from Sydney, Josiah Royce, a Harvard don who was on a Pacific voyage to aid recovery from overwork. Deakin was well placed to attend the National Australasian Convention in Sydney as a delegate appointed by the Victorians. Beginning in March 1891 the convention ran for five weeks. Although Parkes was in the chair, he did not take as active a role as others, in part because of a recent carriage accident. But he emphasised the name 'Commonwealth' to an extent that it became the accepted title of the proposed Federation. Over those five weeks, to the astonishment of many including themselves, the delegates came up with a draft constitution not far from what would be adopted later in the decade by the Australian people. The House of Representatives, Senate and High Court to interpret the constitution were all created by various sections of the document. Most delegates did not want to follow the American model of a cabinet separate from the legislature. The House of Representatives, the lower house, was to be the House the cabinet was responsible to, though senators could be cabinet ministers. The big argument was on the question of whether the Senate could alter money bills, bills passed in the Lower House to finance government itself, or could merely recommend changes. The smaller states wanted the Senate to have more control over money bills, since they would have the same numbers in the Senate as the large states would. And underlying everything, even the Victorians—such as Deakin, to whom protectionism was the map of a just society—were nervous about giving up customs and tariffs to a federal government who might lower them.

Between the conference of 1890 and the convention of 1891, the air had gone out of these seemingly limitlessly expanding colonies. Many formerly middle-class men were contemplating suicide rather than the culminating glory of Federation. And the leading Federationists, Parkes, Deakin and Samuel Griffith of Queensland, had all been sworn in special constables to thwart the unions during the strikes of 1890. Griffith, in the midst of drafting the constitution in 1891, was directing the movements of police colonial troops armed with— amongst other weapons—Nordenfeldt machine guns to protect strike-breaking, non-union shearers and the properties they worked on. The cry of many, including members of the Labor Leagues and the nascent Labor Party, was that the governments could readily arrest and gaol strikers but were unwilling to arrest the speculators and fraudsters who had left Australian homes desolate. Thus Federation became at best a sideshow to Labor men and women, a distraction from the main issues, a toy of the privileged.

Anti-federalists were formed at the other end of the political scale too. 'Dickie' Haynes, a cranky individualist and member of the Legislative Council of Western Australia, declared that being a British subject was a higher calling than being Australian. As well as these problems, Federation would have to occur without external pressure. In Canada it had been stimulated by the Irish Fenian invasions of Ontario in 1866 and 1867, after which confederation and a federal defence system seemed wise. Despite hysteria to the contrary, it was unlikely that the Yankee Fenians would oblige by invading Australia.

Parkes would write of the early period of the Sydney convention, 'Poor Mr Playford came to our good city evidently bent on mischief. His dominant idea was to pick a quarrel . . . there will be more Playfords and more Lees [Lee Steere of Western Australia], and we shall be fortunate if we do not meet more awkward creatures than either.' Deakin wrote back saying that he expected Steere, who was dubious about Federation for Western Australia but whose amiable spirit made him what Deakin would call 'a general favourite', would be more cooperative when the process got going. That it would get going, Deakin never doubted. Sir Samuel Griffith, a leading draftsman of the first constitution bill and a Queensland premier, declared, 'Every lesson of history teaches us that the manifest destiny of Australia is to be one people . . . those who oppose union are opposing an irresistible force.' But in 1891 it seemed more a gentle tide than an irresistible force.

THE FEDERATIONIST WALTZ

There had been another Federation movement. The imperial Federation movement was in force throughout the late nineteenth century from the mid-1880s onwards. The aim of imperial Federationists was to make Australia one state amongst others in a federation of the English-speaking Empire. Radical nationalists such as the Australian Natives Association thought imperial Federation a conservative plot against Australian nation-making. The imperial Federationist movement would always be a minority enthusiasm. There were, despite the slowness of the pace, many more harbingers of Australian than of imperial Federation. Not only did Edmund Barton utter the famous and memorable adage that Federation would create 'a nation for a continent and a continent for a nation', but there had been, as narrated earlier in this account, a development of culture that was purely Australian and sometimes republican by impulse. And sometimes there was a crossover between the cultural and the political ideas of Federation, which did not occur with the imperial Federation cause. Price Warung, an author of stories from the convict era published in the *Bulletin*, the populist and national journal, was really William Astley, organising secretary of the unofficial Bathurst People's Federal Convention in 1896. Constituted of citizen enthusiasts, Bathurst would be significant in that Cardinal Patrick Moran spoke there in favour of Federation, thus bringing many of his flock with him into that camp. Robert Garran, secretary of the Drafting Committee at the 1897 Federal Convention also published in the *Bulletin*, and John Quick, who with Garran would later write the exhaustive *Annotated Constitution of the Australian Commonwealth*, had tried to write a history of Australian literature. The native population of artists also tended to cement the colonies. Arthur Streeton, the artist, declared later that it seemed to him 'as though federation were unconsciously begun by the artists and national galleries'.

Utopian novels were written about the coming Federation, about an Australia transformed by female franchise, just wages and peace. Catherine Helen Spence wrote a novel in 1888, *A Week in the Future*, in which a woman who is dying is offered the chance to spend a week in the federated Australia of 1988. She finds the working day shortened to six hours, accommodation organised collectively, disease and inebriation conquered, women liberated through equal education, the Empire vanished. Spence was an incarnation of that connection between cultural and political yearning which created Federation. She had been born in Scotland but brought to raw South Australia in 1840 as an infant. She became a leading campaigner for proportional representation in Australian parliaments and would become Australia's first female political candidate when she stood for election as a delegate to the 1897 Federal Convention. She was defeated in great part by the belief amongst many males that just because women could by then vote in South Australia (though not in any other colony), it did not mean they could necessarily be elected to Parliament. In Western Australia, under the influence of the same nexus of women's organisations that had won women's suffrage in South Australia, Western Australia also granted women the vote. Her advocacy for the Hare-Spence form of proportional representation (in part by having a number of candidates per electorate) was supported by the early Labor Party, since it gave them the best chance of penetrating the colonial legislatures.

Spence was a leader in the fight for female franchise in South Australia, achieved in 1894, and was interested in Federation for its possibility of delivering the franchise for women. Working with her had been the Australian Women's Suffrage Society, formed in 1889, and the Women's Christian Temperance Organisation. These bodies would all support Federation, since Federation would create the possibility of giving the vote to women nationally, and reluctant states would have to follow. The Women's Temperance Organisation throughout Australia believed in far more than mere control of drinking, and thus preventing male brutality and family poverty. Women's petitions for the vote and equal rights in marriage and property were presented to the 1897 convention, including that of the Womanhood Suffrage League of New South Wales, signed by, amongst others, the formidable and eloquent Rose Scott, cousin and soul mate of David Mitchell, from whom the famed library would derive. Another campaigner for women's suffrage and thus Federation was Maybanke Wolstenholme, who had learned her feminism from being married to a shiftless man. She kept a boarding-house to support her children, many of whom died in infancy.

A petition from the Women's Suffrage League addressed to the delegates of the crucial 1897 convention asked that in a new federal constitution the women of all colonies be empowered to choose their representatives 'so that United Australia may become a true democracy resting upon the will of the whole and not half of the people'. (In the event, the Commonwealth would accede to the franchise demand not in the constitution itself but the year following Federation.)

There were predictable reactions to women's activism, not least from the *Bulletin*.

Pray, lovely Woman, cease to tease
The Candidates with tearful pleas
About your suffrage matter.

Give us a chance pray, if you please,
To federate the colonies
Without your endless chatter.

There were many at the convention of 1897 in Adelaide who supported female franchise but did not want to see it in the draft constitution for fear that in the coming referendum on the constitution some men would vote no specifically because it guaranteed the female vote. Apart from primitive male supremacists, there were socialists and libertarians who feared that women's votes would create a society run by clergymen. The compromise was the proposed Section 41, which said that no adult person who had the right to vote in state elections would be prevented from voting federally. At the time South Australian women had the right to vote in their state, and since it would be an absurdity for women of merely one state to be empowered to vote in a federal election, the other states would be forced to introduce women's franchise. The right of all women to vote federally would be covered by any eventual Franchise Act.

Rose Scott wasn't happy with that. In her house in Woollahra, which had been a salon for all the best colonial minds, she let furious ink flow. 'We don't want any "ifs" in a matter in which our absolute rights are concerned!' Not trusting the all-male framers of the constitution, she began to campaign against it, becoming what was called an 'anti-Billite'. The Golding sisters, Annie and Belle, girls from the bush, schoolteacher and public servant, more socialist and less affluent than Rose and often clashing with her in the suffrage movement, also saw the draft constitution as a men's plan to 'rivet chains on generations yet unborn, chains that will gall, chains that will drag them down, and never, never break'.

GOING FOR GOLD

Gold still possessed the power to compel men into deserts when it was reported in the 1880s from the Kimberleys, the Pilbara, the Murchison River and Southern Cross. It was a matter of mania and besottedness. Copper seemed a plainer mineral. It did not evoke images of men galloping out of the wilderness to register claims in town, though. The South Australians had nonetheless enjoyed the steady success of copper mining at Moonta, Kapunda and Burra, where Cornish miners considered themselves lucky and prosperous, for decades. In 1871, for example, South Australia produced one-tenth of the world's copper despite having a settler population of a little less than 200 000. But they were willing to bring to copper the same speculative habits as operated with gold speculation companies. A former Scots opium trader between China and Calcutta, Captain (later Sir) Walter Watson Hughes, had founded the copper operations at Wallaroo on a station of his near the sand dunes of Spencer's Gulf as early as 1861. Hugh's mine at Wallaroo had, as happened with most mineral booms, been discovered by a shepherd named James Boor, and the shaft site was chosen for Captain Hughes by Cornish miners, who are said to have used the old Cornish process of standing on likely deposit areas, swinging a pick over their heads and beginning to sink a shaft where it landed. And there *was* galloping, Hughes sending stockmen on fast horses to Adelaide to register his finds. He also went looking for copper on another property of his, Moonta, south of Port Pirie, inland a few miles from Port Hughes.

All Adelaide entrepreneurs, including William Finke, patron of John McDouall Stuart, were able with as much panache as any eastern entrepreneur to offload their mining leases in London. Such companies as the Great Northern Copper Mining Company of South Australia appeared. When the governor himself, the difficult, dogmatic and spiky Sir Richard MacDonnell, rode out to see the site of the mine in whose London prospectus his opinion had been falsely quoted, and whose shares were being sold for enormous profit in London, he found an abandoned shaft.

South Australian wheat and produce fed the Victorian and New South Wales goldfields, but that did not bring in the masses of people gold had brought to New South Wales and Victoria. In 1863 the government had sought the services of Hargreaves, the man reputed to have found gold in New South Wales. Moaning about rheumatism in his hand, he fossicked to little effect in country out beyond Port Augusta.

South Australia, as mentioned elsewhere, became exuberant and speculative about mining leases in their Northern Territory, and later about the desert finds in Western Australia. The Coolgardie Gold Mining and Prospecting Syndicate was Adelaide-based. Those who raised money by company float to invest in mining had a speculative streak as big as the individual, pioneering prospector. They were often men who loved and gambled on horse-racing. They were often the ones, not the discoverers such as Paddy Hannan of Kalgoorlie and the strapping Arthur Bayley of Coolgardie, who profited from the rushes others began. In many cases, they were profiting not with mineral realities, the only way a prospector could profit, but—as Sir Richard MacDonnell discovered—with rumours and feverish dreams.

In the far south of the country the Mount Lyell copper mine in Tasmania had become famous by the 1890s. Mount Lyell was on the west coast of Tasmania and it too had begun as a gold-mining lease. All equipment needed to be brought in by way of the town of Strahan, and the difficulty of moving supplies over that most rugged of terrains kept the original gold-mining company a modest operation. In 1892 two Adelaide immigrants, A.E. Bowes Kelly from Galway and William Orr from Fifeshire, both of them original shareholders in BHP, tried a silver claim at Zeehan, on Tasmania's west coast, which failed, but then bought out the Mount Lyell lease and began copper mining. Ultimately a railway would be built to Strahan and a brilliant metallurgist named Robert Sticht would build a smelting plant and have eleven blast furnaces operating. An appalling fire in 1912 killed forty-two men in the chambers of the mine, but as the war began in 1914 the company had built its own hydroelectric system to bring power to the mine and settled down to supplying a considerable portion of a murderous world's appetite for the metal.

The 1887 gold rush at Croydon, Queensland, south-east of the Gulf of Carpentaria, had found uncertain success in a tropical but water-starved landscape of humpies, desolation, typhoid fever, puerperal fever in women who gave birth there, and dysentery. It survived on the misery of its diggers. But Charters Towers, south-west of Townsville, had become so massive a source that its proud miners and citizens referred to it as 'The World'. The legend is that in 1871 a twelve-year-old Aboriginal boy named Jupiter Mossman discovered the first nugget while chasing horses stampeded by a flash of lightning. But it was only when commercial mining began that Charters Towers became the second most important town in Queensland, many of its buildings, including its stock exchange, as grand as those of the Victorian goldfields. It would become profitably connected with the stock exchange in London, with the more knowing brokers operating in Charters Towers, whose earth and possibilities they had a sense of, rather than in London where it was merely a promise and a name.

In 1886, a Colonial and Indian Exhibition was staged in London and was visited by 5 million Britons. The Queensland display consisted of a stamp mill demonstrating the crushing of a hundred tons of gold-bearing rock from Charters Towers. A Charters Towers mine owner named Thomas Mills had raised up above the heads of the visitors to the exhibition a lump of gold worth £6000. He was able to float a new mine on the basis of the investment money he raised from those who stood beneath it and gawped up at it. Charters Towers residents, delighted at the sudden and unreal escalation of their own various shares, could not invent enough companies to satisfy the British frenzy for them. Many owners of useless Charters Towers leases simply took them to London and sold them for massive returns. The stockbrokers of Charters Towers employed large numbers of sales representatives, who went about selling to investors in other cities. Charters Towers was throughout the early 1890s the richest goldfield of all, even more so in that period than Mount Morgan. Its gold was deep, but in entire reefs.

Many gold rushes began with a short period of secrecy followed by a fevered announcement to the world. News of gold mining at a hill known as Ironstone Mountain, inland from Rockhampton, was kept secret from the 1860s by a stockman named William Mackinlay. It was hard for him to do more than wash the alluvial soil at the base of the hill whose ironstone cap seemed to declare that there was no gold of much worth to be had there. Frederick Morgan, the owner of the Criterion Hotel in Rockhampton, was taken to the hill in 1882 by Mackinlay's son-in-law, Sandy Gordon. Frederick Morgan had a speculative streak in him and had already received returns from a goldfield at Galawa near Mount Wheeler, and Sandy Gordon had been under threat of sacking from that mine. His wife promised that if the Morgan brothers would keep Gordon on, she would make him lead them to a silver mine near Rockhampton. An alcoholic saving himself from the sack was the trigger for the richest Australian gold mine of all.

For they did not find silver at the Ironstone Mountain, soon to be renamed Mount Morgan, but there were signs of gold within the crevices of the ironstone cap. After three days' work, they sent Gordon away on horseback with stones for assay, but he turned in to the Dairy Inn on the way and was not seen again by the Morgans. Frederick Morgan and his brothers, Thomas and Edwin, acquired the lease for the hill and took out a number of nearby mineral claims. The Morgans were, however, uncertain about prospects, and invited in as half-partner Thomas Hall, the manager of the Queensland National Bank in Rockhampton. Capital he provided—was it the bank's, or was it Hall's own?—made it possible to begin commercial mining at the hill. Secretly bringing the ten-head battery for crushing stone from Rockhampton by wagons was enormous work for bullocks and men, and once it was erected, the mercury on the battery plates, designed to attract the gold, failed to do so, since much of the precious metal extracted at Mount Morgan had a patina of iron oxide. But what was extracted was a good enough promise of better things.

And still the gold of Mount Morgan remained a secret. The people of Rockhampton did not know that saddle bags of gold were being ridden into town by the Morgans and their men to be accounted for, sold by telegraphic dealings and shipped out by T.S. Hall at the Queensland National Bank. It was the better part of two years before a reporter came out to the hill and discovered the meaning of all the activity. The Morgans nonetheless always remained dubious about the place. Edwin Morgan, the manager, dug a shaft to see how deep the gold went. He was deceived by the fact that the gold seemed to bottom out at about 500 feet (150 metres), and he did not know it slewed away underground, plentifully and deceptively for an indefinite, rich distance, from his shaft. The Morgan brothers offered to sell their remaining half-share, and this was bought up for £93 000 by a young red-haired Rockhampton graduate of the Westminster School, William Knox D'Arcy, a solicitor in the port. Through D'Arcy, Mount Morgan would have an impact on more than the gold market but also on the geopolitics of the twentieth century.

It proved to be the deal of D'Arcy's life, enabling him within three years to return to England and never again lay his eyes on Rockhampton and Mount Morgan. He remained a director of the Mount Morgan Gold Mining Company and chaired its London board, but lived a princely life with a London house, a shooting estate in Norfolk and a stand of his own at Epsom race course.

Thomas Hall, the Rockhampton bank manager, invited Walter Hall, his brother, to join the syndicate, which by now was having to fight off claims on it by other speculators and hence needed further capital. Two of the claims had to be contested not only in the Queensland Supreme Court but ultimately in the Privy Council in Britain. The new partner, Walter Hall, was a remarkably unpretentious man even after Mount Morgan made him unassailably rich. Like the other members of the syndicate and the Morgans themselves, he was a passionate racing man and would be a committee member of the Australian Jockey Club for nearly forty years. He had married the daughter of a wealthy pastoralist, and after his death his estate was worth close to £3 million. His widow, Eliza, devoted one million of it in his honour to create a Walter and Eliza Hall trust which, in Victoria, would be spent in establishing the Walter and Eliza Hall Institute for Research in Pathology and Medicine.

By the early twentieth century Mount Morgan was producing copper as well as gold. In 1907 and 1908 a number of miners died in roof collapses. Others were saved because they were standing in the lift well. But the casualties of the war beneath the earth did not delay D'Arcy from his speculations and the ultimate sinister mineral boom of 1914–18. In the 1920s copper prices fell, and men went on strike when wages were reduced. In the midst of the strike the mine caught fire. The directors dreamed up the idea of running it as an open-cut mine but this was derided, shares crashed and the liquidators were called in 1927. Mining families drifted away to the sugar fields, looking for work.

In the Alaska gold rushes prospectors died of hypothermia. The prospectors of Australia, particularly of Western Australia, were likely to perish of thirst or, more commonly, of the diseases produced either by a lack of water or the pollution of what water was available.

In 1890 J.F. Connolly, a draftsman from the New South Wales railways and an amateur ethnologist, had been brought over to Western Australia to work as a prospector for the Western Australian merchant F.C. Monger. East of Geraldton, he split his search party for further reconnaissance. Two of his men became lost and died of thirst, but Connolly safely returned to a station named Annean where some stockriders had pointed out a few traces of gold to him earlier. When he got there, he found others had already pitched their tents and were working the field. They had found the gold there plentiful, and the water supply from the nearby Murchison River more than adequate. It was only when a miner turned up in Geraldton looking for medical attention after a brawl that the word about Mount Murchison really got out.

Gold had earlier been found in the Kimberley and in the Pilbara but a location inland from Geraldton, like Mount Murchison, was a much better proposition than the tropics. Alluvial gold was mined, miners could also pick up or extract visible, small pebbles of gold. But obviously this would ultimately be a field for commercial mining. The limitation of the Murchison field was that the water was unsafe and enteric fever killed diggers, who were buried in coffins made out of grocery cases advertising Coleman's Mustard and Condensed Milk.

Further south, gold was found in 1887 at Yilgarn, east of Perth. These finds were welcome at least in some ways, as distracting as they were for the sons of farmers and for agricultural workers, in that they promised an inflow of capital and population. The Western Australian Stock Exchange was now created in Perth to speculate in shares. These were the sorts of events which caused Western Australians to cry of their colony, 'At last she moves.'

The Sydney merchant Anthony Hordern, whose famed Palace Warehouse and Palace Emporium sat in George Street, Sydney, had a passionate interest in Western Australia and devised immigration and railway schemes, even one, which did not eventuate, running as far as the Kimberley where overlanding clans like the Duracks were settling down to make cattle stations. His plans for the west, which seemed even closer to reality now that goldfields were operating, would soon be snuffed out when, in 1886, he died of 'brain fever' aboard a ship.

There was considerable excitement about reefs south of Yilgarn named Southern Cross. Southern Cross seemed the limit though. East of it lay the great desert plain. Even so, some men, using Aboriginal guides to take them to water-holes and camels driven by Afghans to carry their gear, went gold seeking beyond, towards the arid and dangerous east. There was indeed so much demand for camels that the elegantly and princely Afghan Faiz Mahomet, who had managed a desert camel operation for Elder Smith in South Australia, would arrive with his brother Tagh and three steamers full of camels, and with another two shiploads on order from India, to supply freight to Southern Cross and beyond.

Arthur Bayley was a fellow who seemed genetically designed for mineral frontiers. He was a twenty-seven-year-old prospector and athlete who competed for prize money in foot races, and was a champion hammer thrower. He had already mined gold in dismal Croydon in the Gulf of Carpentaria, in the Palmer River in North Queensland near Cooktown, and at Mount Murchison. His friend, William Ford, had known him in Croydon and had seen him triumph in bare fist fights. Ford felt certain that Bayley was equipped by his previous experience to survive the wilderness to the east of Southern Cross. They put together a team of ten horses, and supplies adequate for a long winter of prospecting, rode out 120 miles (200 kilometres) into the desert, and were doubling back because of lack of water when near the site of what would be the town of Coolgardie they found a waterhole. The following morning, Bayley went rounding up horses and saw at his feet a nugget. He fetched Ford, and by noon they had picked up 20 ounces (over 500 grams) of gold. In a month they had collected £800 worth, rode secretly to Southern Cross to get rations, and then turned back towards their discovery. But there was a miners' strike in progress in the Southern Cross commercial mines, and a number of young strikers had the time to try to follow them. One of them, Tommy Talbot, described his arrival at the basin of earth where Bayley and Ford were working. 'We could see it [gold] glittering in the sunlight for at least twenty yards in front of us.'

There was immediate and hard-handed conflict between Bayley and the newcomers. Bayley knew he would have to register his claim with the warden at Southern Cross, and galloped back to that settlement on 17 December 1892. The news was out now, and it seemed unprecedented news, as if this were the Western Australian find of finds. When interviewed, Bayley's friend Ford said, 'We gathered nuggets like spuds in a paddock.' This image had the power to stampede the imagination. Men from Murchison, and young men from Perth and other coastal towns, moved towards Southern Cross now, but only because it was the jumping-off point for Coolgardie. In the depressed eastern colonies, men and some women took ship for Western Australia. The population of Western Australia would increase fourfold between 1891 and 1901.

The report of gold still had the capacity to turn young men into adventurers who would leave comfortable but suddenly boring jobs to suffer intense discomfort and danger on a long shot. Albert Gaston was a youth who worked in a sawmill in the town of York, east of Perth. Serving the boiler of the big saw, when the news came through of a find at Coolgardie he nearly failed to let off steam and ran the risk of blowing up the boiler. In the tradition of gold seekers forty years past, he left work instantly and at dawn trekked east with a billy and water bag and a few clothes. He had 300 miles (500 kilometres) to cover, and farms and fencing and other signs of adequate water gave out a little over 12 miles from town. When he arrived at the first waterhole out of Southern Cross he had to take his turn at filling his water bag to boil up some tea. He claims that one day he was forced to walk 38 miles to reach the next waterhole. Reaching the field, he found a lack of food except expensive tinned meat and, of course, a lack of water. An infestation of flies energetically spread gastro-enteric fever.

Most prospectors built a hessian hut or pitched a tent in Coolgardie and went ranging up to 60 miles (100 kilometres) or more from town looking for their own lode. Eventually, after finding only two pennyweights of gold at a site 50 miles north of Coolgardie, Albert Gaston, hard up for water and passing groups of men similarly traipsing who had stopped to bury a friend who had died on the track, at last managed to return to the new settlement.

Paddy Hannan, a secretive and gnarled little Irish troll now in his early fifties, had worked on the Victorian fields and fossicked in South Australia, and was camped at Southern Cross when Bayley's news got out. Adept at desert travelling, he immediately marched to Coolgardie. By June 1893 Hannan and two other Irishmen, Flanagan and O'Shea, found gold near the surface of a red soil plain 25 miles (40 kilometres) further east of Coolgardie, and set about working it in the normal early secrecy. But ultimately miners had to come to town for supplies and to register claims, and in June 1893, when Paddy turned up in the tented town of Coolgardie carrying with him 100 ounces (nearly 3 kilograms) of gold for sale, a great proportion of the desert horde heard and began yet another move east.

Hannan, like Bayley, was not the sort of man who had the capital to develop such goldfields. In the future he would sometimes prospect under contract for syndicates, but in the early twentieth century fell back on a compassionate pension of £150 a year from the Western Australian government. It was justly earned. That so-called Golden Mile between Coolgardie and Kalgoorlie would be an engine for Western Australian wealth and growth. The Garnbirringu natives of the area, whose word for the desert food silky pear would give the Kalgoorlie goldfield its name (just as Coolgardie derived its name from the words for mulga wood and waterholes), might have been justified in thinking that their home region, in which only they had the key to the water, would remain forever unvisited. Now they found their home full of grasping, ambitious, thirsty and squalling white fellows who struck out in all directions, spreading their chaos.

The possibility of waterholes being emptied by thirsty miners would lead the government in the end to build small reservoirs along the way. Cobb and Co began to operate a service and small corrugated-iron and hessian stores and shanties appeared along the track. Faiz Mahomet's camel teams, working from depots in Geraldton, Coolgardie and other centres, carried freight and water. Faiz Mahomet also founded stores at these places and had a reputation for staking miners, which spread his reputation as a 'good darkie'. Even so he petitioned the government for protection against goldfield hostilities which were directed not only against him but also at the southern European so-called 'tributers', who worked not by union rules but by receiving a share (tribute) from what they mined. His 1896 request for naturalisation was turned down. That year too, in a dispute whose origins will probably now be never known, his brother Tagh was killed by another Muslim while praying in the rudimentary Coolgardie mosque.

The Adelaide stock exchange, which had been founded by South Australia's appetite for Broken Hill shares in the 1880s, took to the Western Australian gold-mining stocks with great enthusiasm. George Brookman was a forty-three-year-old Adelaide financier who appointed his brother William and Sam Pearce as a syndicate's prospectors. The Irishman Paddy Hannan thought little of the claims taken up and made by Brookman and Pearce, but in Adelaide their Coolgardie Gold Mining and Prospecting syndicate raised capital, and their chief source of wealth, Great Boulder, would produce in present values something like $3 billion of gold. Because of the decline in South African gold mining and the economic collapse in eastern Australia, British investors had money to send Coolgardie's way. In 1894 a group of speculators led by Colonel J.T. North, who had made his fortune promoting Chilean nitrate on the London stock market, now earned further riches by floating the Londonderry and Wealth of Nations mines. The Londonderry was floated for £700 000, of which only £50 000 was devoted to working the mine, the rest going to the promoters and vendors of the shares and, of course, the directors of the company. The mine produced barely anything.

But Brookman and Pearce's Great Boulder, efficiently run by a young engineer named Richard Hamilton, flourished. A British company named Bewick Moreing introduced a similar professionalism when it took over a number of leases. Its goldfields staff included a young mining engineer from Iowa, a graduate of Stanford named Herbert Clark Hoover, a future and undistinguished American president. Part of his job was to assess possibilities beyond Coolgardie and Kalgoorlie, and he was the engineer who pressed upon his seniors the possibilities of the Sons of Gwalia mine near Leonora. He would be superintendent of that mine for some months in 1898 and would be called back to America later in the year. He took with him a reputation for being an excellent engineer and, in a foreshadowing of his crushing of American veterans' protests at the beginning of the Great Depression, for sacking miners according to the fluctuations of the market.

The problems of the old world reached Coolgardie when there was a fight between Catholics and Protestants during an Orange parade in Coolgardie in July 1897, and a few years later police had to draw their revolvers to quell an even worse Irish disturbance at Southern Cross. But both sides of the sectarian divide suffered equally for lack of the refining influence of women. Nor did enteric fevers discriminate between them. And the countryside became even more desolate and dry as wood for pit props was cut down.

C.Y. O'Connor, an Irish engineer, had been daring enough to offer Premier Forrest, the new and first Western Australian premier, a man of progressive vision, a 350-mile (560-kilometre) pipeline from Mundaring in the Darling Range behind Perth all the way to the goldfields. It was a phenomenal proposition and its critics not only declared that no pipeline of such length existed anywhere on earth but resorted to what would prove to be lethal ridicule.

O'Connor's creation of a harbour at Fremantle had similarly been attacked, yet its success would become obvious. The network of railways surveyed and devised by him, including a line to Southern Cross and then ultimately to the towns of the Golden Mile, were built throughout the 1890s, and as with Fremantle, were achieved with the support and admiration of John Forrest. Forrest was an enthusiastic enabler of O'Connor's plans for the pipeline, and both men saw it not simply as servicing the goldfields but as creating farming in the intervening zones. The Irish engineer made an interesting boss by the standards of his day. He told Forrest's bureaucrats that the workers of the Fremantle railway workshops were overworked, underpaid and laboured in squalor. His improvements in conditions produced energy in the workshop and great profits for the railway.

Some claim that O'Connor overstated the water shortage at the goldfields to justify his world-beating project, and that Kalgoorlie and other towns were already building watertanks, and even considering desalinating the water found at depth in the mines. And it might have been above all in the name of serving the steam engines with water that O'Connor promoted a pipeline. But even then a number of rock catchments were discovered and ground-water tanks had already been built along the railway line to deal with the problem of human and mechanical thirst. In any case, responsibility for water supplies on the goldfields was placed permanently in O'Connor's hands in November 1893 and his water engineers reported to him that, despite all the canards about adequate water already being in place, every device that could be used to conserve water on the Golden Mile would still yield no more than a gallon (4.5 litres) per person per day.

To make the pipeline work, water from a catchment on the Perth side of the Darling Range would need to be raised 1000 feet and then pumped over 300 miles (500 kilometres) to its reservoir at Coolgardie. Only Forrest could have convinced the Western Australian Parliament to seek the capital in London to build the thing, and the contracts for the steel pipes were signed in October 1898.

While the early work was still in progress, in February 1901 Forrest entered federal Parliament and became Minister for Defence, under which portfolio he invited O'Connor to present plans for a transcontinental line linking Kalgoorlie to Port Augusta. Forrest's absence in Melbourne, however, left O'Connor without his chief ally. Overworked and close to nervous collapse, O'Connor had to face his attackers alone. On 8 March 1902 a preliminary pumping test raised water over the Darling range for about 6 miles (10 kilometres) into the hinterland. This showed there was no reason why, having ascended 1000 feet, the water could not now be pumped on to Kalgoorlie. But the ruin of O'Connor's soul had already occurred. On the morning of 10 March 1902, when he should have felt validated by what had occurred two days before, he took his pistol when he went for his early morning ride. He was usually accompanied by his daughter, but that day she was ill. He rode along the beach at Fremantle, took with him his horse into the surf and killed himself with his revolver. In his suicide note he had written, 'The Coolgardie Scheme is alright and I could finish it if I got a chance and protection from misrepresentation but there is no hope of that now.' At the end of the same year the work was finished within budget, and on 24 January 1903 Forrest turned on the water at Coolgardie and Kalgoorlie before enthusiastic crowds. He was full of praise for O'Connor.

BUILDING AUSTRALIA—ANYWHERE BUT AUSTRALIA

The enormously popular 1886 American book *Looking Backward*, by the American journalist and author Edward Bellamy, had a massive impact on Australian socialists. It was, with *Uncle Tom's Cabin* and *Ben-Hur*, one of the great bestsellers of the Victorian age. A utopian fantasy, the novel was also a political argument. The protagonist, a man named Julian White, falls into a trance in 1887 and wakes in a utopian 2000. Unlike Marx, the genial Bellamy saw no contradiction between religion and socialism, and envisaged socialism arriving by peaceful means, through consent between all reasonable humans and by the force of its own argument—Bellamy's character Dr Leete believed 'the whole mass of people would embrace it'. Capitalists themselves would give up control of the means of production.

Amongst other things, in the ideal Boston of Bellamy's tale, women possessed political equality with men—an equality not all socialists in Australia or elsewhere were willing to accord them. In *Looking Backward*, women had the support of the state in raising children and were not reliant on the goodwill of husbands or lovers. Communal dining rooms and disposable plates replaced women's normal domestic drudgery, and clothing and carpets were also disposable. Clothing was unisex, and conventional beauty was not an objective, since it had always been used by men as a tool for oppressing women.

The Brisbane journalist and young firebrand William Lane, influenced like others by Bellamy, had already himself written one of the futuristic novels so favoured by the times. It was entitled *White or Yellow? A Story of the Race-War of AD 1908*. It was published in 1887 in serial form in his newspaper *Boomerang*, and showed that his concept of utopia depended on the republic of Asians. Lane had come to Brisbane in 1885, arriving at a time of high unemployment in the city, which enhanced his sense that there were good jobs up country which had been taken by Kanakas. The gulf between labour and capital had not yet developed into the class war of the early 1890s, and Lane found that premiers Griffith and McIlwraith also spoke of farmers' cooperatives, land reform and the compatibility of religion and socialism, the very subjects he canvassed in his newspaper *Boomerang*.

Lane believed in isolated utopianism. 'We want to be left alone. We don't care whether Canada loses a fishing monopoly or not; or whether Russian civil servants replace the British pauper aristocracy in Hindustan offices; or whether China takes missionaries and opium-dealers together and sends them packing; or whether the sun sets on the British drum-beat or not—so long as the said drum-beat keeps away from our shores.' The Old World was Australia's enemy, and so were the Chinese. In 1890, with backing from a number of unions, he became first editor of the *Worker*, whose oratory was designed for the whole mass of workers. The paper quickly acquired a circulation of 20 000. It was read in every shearing shed, mining camp and railway-construction settlement in Australia. Like William Guthrie Spence he came from outside the labour movement, but while some, such as Spence, thought him a prophet, others, such as Victorian cabinet ministers, called him the most dangerous man in Australia. Lane, who had been lame since childhood and had a North American accent from some years spent in Canada and Detroit, had become a seer to the shearers, his articles beloved by the strikers, some of whom learned them by heart. According to Vance Palmer, being quoted like scripture gave Lane a Messiah complex.

Energised by Bellamy's book, Lane soon wrote his own analysis of Australian wrongs and of how they might be righted, *The Working Man's Paradise*, published in 1892 to raise money for those who had been given gaol sentences in the shearers' strike. *The Working Man's Paradise* featured Nellie Lawton, a selector's daughter, and Ned Hawkins, a man of the bush, rather like those who would have gathered discontentedly in the shearing camps of the west in the early 1890s. Nellie, however, is the passionate unionist in this case, and in the spirit of Lane's own puritanism she harangues men out of the pub and into the unions. It is not only the sufferings of the bush that Lane takes on in his novel. Ned is sickened to the core by the slums of Sydney. Typically, one of the characters hopes that marriage will put Nellie in her place, but Nellie is too interested in the mission of equality between humans to marry. Besides, she sees that in these slums men are emasculated by humiliating drudgery. Similarly, seamstresses stitch sixteen hours a day, servant girls are on constant call and housewives struggle and scrape and penny-pinch behind closed doors. As for prostitution, it is also a form of industrial oppression.

Lane desired to make a perfect Antipodean garden from which the rest of the world's vileness could be excluded. If the perfect place could not be Australia, then perhaps it could be something smaller and elsewhere. His disillusionment after the strikes of the early 1890s led him to turn his gaze to Western Australia, and then to South America. There would be a perfected Australia, even if it had to be on another continent. Three of his agents received a warm welcome and an offer of assistance from Paraguayan authorities. A place for settlement was chosen and the government offered to give free entrance to everything the settlers brought with them and to transport them to their new home. They would be exempt from customs duties for ten years, but in return the New Australia Settlement Association undertook to settle 800 families on the land in four years.

This project drew away a great deal of visionary talent from Australia. To those who accused Lane of abandoning Australia, he said, 'In this new Australia movement, we exchange empty patriotism to a country in which we have no share, for the solid possession of a great tract of good land, secured under terms which could not possibly be secured here.' Those recruited were shearers unable to get work or enough of it, free selectors living in rural squalor, skilled workers finding it hard to have their skills rewarded, small capitalists ruined by the depression, and intellectuals such as young schoolteacher-poet Mary Gilmore. The vessel chartered to take Lane and his followers to Paraguay, the *Royal Tar*, sailed from Sydney on 21 July 1893 carrying the first 220 emigrants. In a group photograph, the children of the new Australia are arrayed in the front row in smocks and Sunday suits. The *Royal Tar* was followed out of the harbour by boats and launches full not of mockers, but of those who had at least a vague regard for the new endeavour. For New Australia was not meant to be simply a gesture of disgruntlement, but to be a bold example for people of all nations to follow. It was, in other words, to have a world-revolutionary effect. The colonists could give an example of the principles of an ideal Australia, but do so from somewhere overseas.

Lane took one of the smallest cabins on the *Royal Tar*, worked at potato peeling, and was called Will or Billy by the others. With intellectuals such as

John Sibbald and Harry Taylor, and women such as a forthright Mrs McNamara, wife of a Sydney socialist bookseller, he prepared a manifesto on education in New Australia. 'It is our unanimous and earnest opinion [that] the system of education at present existent in the competitive civilised world, is as brutal, degrading and unsatisfactory as competitive civilisation itself.'

Rancour began to divide the colonists by the time they hit the cold seas around Cape Horn, and served as an omen of coming conflict in New Australia. As the novelty of participating in domestic efforts wore off for him, men and women began to complain that Lane was despotic and unfair. Everyone was pleased when the *Royal Tar* reached Montevideo in Uruguay and the journey to neighbouring Paraguay could begin.

Mary Jean Cameron, a young teacher posted to Stanmore Public School in 1891, would serve as the Sydney contact for Lane's enterprise in its early phase. She had met William Lane on a discussion evening in 1892 above McNamara's bookshop in Sydney, the venue for the meetings of the Australian Socialist League. Mary's politics had been influenced by a teaching stint at Silverton which had shown her, in BHP's treatment of miners, that the ideal, the fraternal and the cooperative was the way of the future.

At McNamara's she also met Henry Lawson, two years younger than her, deaf and troubled. Their relationship—Mary claimed that Henry proposed both marriage and an elopement—would delay her own departure for New Australia. She also met Louisa Lawson, editor of the *Dawn*, the feminist journal, and convenor of the Dawn Clubs, which were made up of its readers and who campaigned for women's suffrage. Before moving to Stanmore, Mary Cameron became for a time a boarder at Louisa's house. Louisa had come a long way since she had married the shiftless Neils Larsen and endured life as a young mother and drudge in the tents of Gulgong and the Weddin Mountains, and at the small selection at Eurunderee. Louisa's house in North Sydney contained the printing press which produced the *Republican*. Lawson's 'Song of the Republic' would resonate with many,

> *Sons of the South, make choice between*
> *(Sons of the South, choose true)*
> *The Land of Morn and the Land of E'en,*
> *The Old Dead Tree and the Young Tree Green,*
> *The land that belongs to the lord and the Queen,*
> *And the land that belongs to you.*

Lane's own wife, Ann, returned from the hardships of Paraguay to Mary's new lodgings at Marrickville. It had been everyone's hope, including Mrs Lane's, that Mary would marry Lane's lieutenant, David Russell Stevenson, a cousin of Robert Louis Stevenson. Her other potential husband, Henry Lawson, had returned from Western Australia as hard up as he had left, had visited Bourke, and had spent eight months in New Zealand. When he presented himself at Mary's door he was often staggering. He saw her off at the dock in 1895 on the journey to join Lane not at Nueva Australia, but at his breakaway settlement at Cosme.

For New Australia had already split in two, and utopianism had foundered on the rock of Lane's astringent personality. It had begun with William Lane expelling three men for returning tipsy after a drinking session with the local priest. They also spoke of seeing a Paraguayan woman rolling a cigar on her naked thigh, and were accused of breaking another pledge they had taken about fraternising with the locals and crossing the 'Colour Line' so significant in Lane's brand of socialism. In 1893 William Lane affixed a notice of expulsion of the men, Brittlebank, White and Westward, to the door of the store in Nueva Australia.

This autocratic expulsion divided the colony, since the constitution called for a vote by the members and a five-sixths majority before anyone could be expelled. The named men refused to leave, and Lane went on refusing a ballot, disappeared, and returned later with a squad of Paraguayan soldiers, riding into the settlement with a revolver in his belt, like an autocrat rather than a socialist leader. 'Why could he not come down to the campfire and tell us as man to man, as one mate among a crowd, what he wanted?' wrote one. Another settler declared, 'Lane does the thinking and the colonists do the work—result, barbarism.'

Eighty individuals left Nueva Australia and presented themselves in Asunción, the capital, begging the British Consul to ship them back to Australia. A diplomat was sent to reason with Lane but found him to be intransigent. When his colonists moved a motion of no confidence in him, Lane and sixty-three of his followers migrated to a new land grant 80 miles (130 kilometres) away in Cosme, to the south-west and in thicker jungle. Here Lane felt renewed, even though his title to the new land was questionable. A land grant was at length offered by the Paraguayan government. Lane had to pay for the leasehold with money raised in Australia by true believers.

Mary made her way from Asunción towards the breakaway settlement Cosme by paddle-steamer and steam train. At a siding in the forest, transport arrived for her from Cosme: a horse led into town by Lane's brother. When Mary reached Cosme she saw thatched huts and found not only that the chief diet consisted of beans and sweet potatoes, monkey or deer meat, but also that she was only the third single woman in a colony heavily populated by unmarried bushworkers, veterans of the 1890–91 strike. Her potential husband Stevenson rebuffed her, and though there was a welcome dance for her in the social hall, it was a poor affair and most of the men were scared off by her frankness and, by the standards of the day, superior education. Nonetheless she wrote to W.G. Spence, 'I am satisfied with my own lot.' Mary even wrote to Henry Lawson asking him to 'come while the field is new . . . PS I didn't get married'. Lawson did not write back—he had himself just impetuously married the daughter of Mrs McNamara, Bertha Bredt.

The Cosme settlement still believed it would stand as an example to the world and its members, as Mary Gilmore noticed, deliberately swallowed all complaint about things and avoided factions. People grew haggard, however, and though they did not complain they became cheerless. The women became rundown. A school was opened in which Mary taught, and the engineer of the party, McLeod, built two bridges over streams nearby for the benefit of both settlers and local Indians. In November 1897 the population reached 131, but the newcomers began to express discontent. Gradually the dream that they would influence the whole world into accepting Lane's communist model was replaced by a desire to survive as what Lane called 'a small settlement of 100 people, where brotherhood was, [rather] than a huge state of a 100 million, where brotherhood was not'. Soon, as men came to concentrate on the wants and standard of health of their individual families, people began to leave Cosme. Lane had not become less dictatorial. A man named Petrie wrote to Spence, 'Whiffs of dogma; stacks of selfishness, yards of words and absolutely no liberty.' Lane himself became ill and sad and even more difficult. In September 1896 he went to England to recruit a proposed 3000 Britons. He managed to enlist only forty to fifty people. While Lane was at these endeavours, nine dissenters turned up in England from Cosme and denounced him publicly.

In the end, Mary Cameron was courted by a tall and rather gentle bushman named William Gilmore, with whom she took strolls in the rainforest. She married Gilmore in the clearing and he gave her a ring fashioned out of a shilling with the middle cut out. She wrote for the colony's journal, the *Cosme Monthly*,

And us two don't want nothing
To make life good and true,
And lovin'-sweet, and happy,
While us two's got us two.

It would become, through eventual Australian publication, a sentimental favour-ite, but Mary wanted a great deal more than 'us two'.

In August 1898, heavily pregnant, she travelled by third-class carriage to the regional centre of Villarrica, and there she gave birth to a son, William. The colony of Cosme, having already split off from New Australia, was by now itself split into factions. William Lane still enforced the 'Colour Line', and fraternis-ing with local Paraguayans, particularly women, was totally prohibited. When men yielded to the temptation, there were further expulsions, and sometimes the offending male's friends and supporters marched from the colony with him. William Lane himself ultimately gave up on his own people and left with his family in 1899. He would go to New Zealand, perhaps not willing to display his broken dream in Australia, and as a journalist in Auckland came to edit the *New Zealand Herald* as a new-born conservative imperialist.

Utopia had failed and William Gilmore, without the fare to take himself and Mary and their son home, went instead to Argentina, to work on the sheep stations of Patagonia. At the end of July 1900, Mary herself left the *colonia* in Paraguay and went to Patagonia to be with her husband. Her eventual return to Australia, whenever the Gilmores managed to raise the money, was now assured, though many of the Australian idealists would be stuck in the country in which they had chosen to remake Australia anew.

By March 1902 Mary, her husband and Billy had the money for third-class tickets across the Atlantic for Liverpool. On arriving in Liverpool a message was waiting for them from Henry Lawson and Bertha, his wife, temporarily in London: 'Bed's made, and cot's ready for the little fellow, come at once, am simply mad for the sight of an Australian face.' The interlude was short. Henry and Mary were two Australians whose voices were confused by the London experience. Back in Australia, the Gilmores lived in a slab hut in rural Victoria where Mary raised Billy during Will's absence on itinerant work. The marriage virtually ended in 1911, after the publication of her first volume of poetry—ironically entitled *Marri'd and Other Verses*—when she was given a job writing a women's page for the trade union paper, the *New South Wales Worker*. Will took a small farm in Queensland, and Mary wrote him a weekly letter for the next thirty-four years. But her potent voice far transcended his humble farming destiny.

In 1914–15, some of the young of the two South American Australian utopias would return to Australia to join the First AIF. It was particularly in the 1930s that tragedy overcame the English and Spanish-speaking grandchildren of those who made up New Australia and Cosme. In 1932, a three-year war of considerable savagery was fought between Paraguay and Bolivia over a disputed, barren region known as the Chaco. Control over the region was for the Paraguayans essential for the production of mate, a caffeine-rich drink made of the desert yerba plant, of great commercial value in South America. For Bolivia, the control of the Paraguay River and possible oil deposits provided motivation. In the jungles many soldiers lost their lives to fevers, in the dryer area they lacked water. One hundred thousand men were lost from both countries, including the flower of the descendants of New Australia and Cosme.

LEMURIA

Lemuria was an ancient continent which connected India to Madagascar, since both Madagascar and India were home to the same species of lemur. But Madame Blavatsky, the co-founder of the Theosophical Society, argued that it was Australia that was the remains of Lemuria and that the Aborigines were the leftovers of its sub-humans. Theosophy had considerable impact in Australia, not least for its mysticism and sense of the immanence of spirits in all nature and amongst the living—an idea which appealed to Alfred Deakin—but also for its teaching that Aryans were the highest Root Race to emerge on the development path of humanity, and that they were descended from the inhabitants of the Lemurian civilisation of Atlantis. The idea that Australia was the remains of Lemuria gave Australia a significance which transcended the colonial, and inspired writers to create novels which redeemed Australia from its aridity, its withered antiquity and its Aboriginality. All these novels involved lost superior races, pre-Aboriginal golden societies which were the remains of Atlantis.

In the 1891 novel *Golden Lake* by Carlton Dawe, a prolific Australian writer, the fantastically named Dick Hardwicke looks at the surface of Central Australia from the security of an oasis and says, as millions of Australians would say, 'Ah, what a country this could be if only it had more water.' But Dick discovers wonderful subterranean waters and, beneath the Aborigine of the surface, an Atlantean race, people who pre-dated history but whose racial superiority was a beacon for White Australia. The lost race and hidden waters characterised the genre. The famous Rosa Praed, Queensland-born (1851), with a soul tempered early in her marriage by two years spent on a remote station near Gladstone, was soon taken by her husband to an affluent life in London in her mid-twenties. Apart from her belief in Madame Blavatsky and the concept of Lemuria, she was a public advocate of Irish home rule, left her husband to live with a medium named Nancy Harward (whom she believed to have been a Germanic slave in ancient Rome) and in 1902, still in London, echoed the preoccupations of her fellow countrymen in a novel named *Fugitive Anne*. In this work the characters encounter, in the uninhabitable country below the Gulf of Carpenteria, an underground world blessed by water, and a noble race named the Aca. Much of her material on the surface world of colonial pastoral life in the Gulf came from her sister Lizzie Jardine, a pastoralist's wife in the region. Fugitive Anne and her rescuer-pursuer, a naturalist named Hansen, penetrate a hole in a great stone to enter a 'small Switzerland', and 'mountains, some covered with tropical verdure; others, bare granite peaks and humps, barring the horizon as far as the eye could see'. Hanson 'knew that he had found here in the unexplored heart of Australia—that continent which had been declared to have no previous inhabitants but the degraded Aboriginals found there on the first explorers' landing—ruins which proclaim the fact of a civilisation'. The Aca who are then encountered even fulfil Mr Deakin's dream of irrigation, producing 'plantations of cocoa, bananas, palms'.

Thus Rosa Praed tried to redeem Australia from its limitations of race and climate.

WAR IN NORTHERN AUSTRALIA

It was on the surface, not in some mythic underworld, that Australians continued their lives. In some places in northern Australia a war between pastoralists and natives would continue for decades. Squatter George Sutherland recorded how in the 1860s he had arrived at Lake Mary in Central Queensland to confront the local people and 'rob them of their country', by means of carbine fire. After later assault upon others in the Barclay and Gregory river areas of the Gulf country, he wrote that his party 'kept trotting behind them to . . . make them understand we were their masters'. Another squatter concluded, 'They are a hard-used race but we have to occupy the country; and no two races can inhabit the same country but the weaker must go to the wall.'

It was calculated in 1861 that in the southern districts of Queensland Aborigines had killed approximately 250 Europeans. Deaths on the native side were not calculated. Newspaper accounts detail seventy-six instances of raids on stock as well, though these are only the reported cases. Similar casualty rates probably occurred in the rest of Queensland during the European advance and consolidation. The war seemed to become more intense the further north and west it moved. There was an energetic resistance in the Mackay and Bowen regions, and Governor Bowen in late 1866 believed that 600 whites had been killed by Aborigines. In 1869 the *Port Denison Times* reported, 'Our own town at least had its foundations cemented in blood.' The Cardwell district, the Palmer River goldfields and the Atherton Tablelands were venues for many fierce and bloody skirmishes and battles between settlers and natives. At Battle Camp south-west of Cairns in November 1873 the natives attacked the diggers' barricades and were shot down by the increasingly sophisticated and high-muzzle velocity bullets from rifles such as the Snider and the Martini-Henry, which made it possible to fire ten rounds a minute, more than three times the quantity of fire the indigenes of south-eastern Australia had faced.

Early in 1873 George Dalrymple, explorer and land commissioner, reported that the 'high, wild, broken conglomerate tablelands and ranges about Gilberton had suffered ten murders', and that nearly the whole Chinese population 'which formed the valuable alluvial diggers of the field had left the district, leaving the valley of the Gilbert in undisputed possession of the Aboriginals'. One miner, W.B. Kininmonth, reported of the Palmer natives in 1874: 'They seemed to be long, lanky fellows, more of a copper colour than the Southern blacks and having by far more pluck—as when we pointed our guns at them, they stood still, as much as to say, "Fire away".' George Dalrymple believed in firmness. Finding a group of natives on Shaw Island off Port Denison (Bowen), he told them through the medium of a Fitzroy River Aborigine, one of the six native troopers with him, that his party had come to return 'blood for blood' and his message was backed up with rifle fire from other native troopers on the slopes behind the beach.

At Gilberton the next year four white men were speared and all their property put to the torch. Mr William Hodgkinson MLA, after failing to obtain some compensation for the men and their families, raged that the events 'would show the people in the North—those people on whom the prosperity of the country so much depended—that they must shoot every black fellow they found, in spite of the pseudo-philanthropists'. Indeed, a northern squatter reported in 1877 that the Warrgamay-speaking clans along the Herbert River were 'disappearing one by one and sometimes in larger numbers by the aid of powder and ball . . . I heard today of the massacre of four blacks including a woman, a boy of eight and a girl of twelve.'

Posses of squatters and of native police were involved in pursuing the so-called Kalkadoons of the inland Gulf region, 'the Plains of Promise'. Kalkadoons were recklessly brave and often turned and charged the muzzles of the carbines. In the Gulf country, the Cape and along the western borderlands with the Northern Territory and South Australia, guerrilla warfare against Kalkadoon and the Waanyi-Garrwa people continued into the 1880s. The lessees of Gregory Downs, the Watson brothers, writing to the colonial secretary on 18 June 1880, testified that 'sub-inspectors [of Native Mounted Police] and their troopers go into the bush, round up the blacks and shoot them indiscriminately and kidnap the gins and the little boys'. The Native Mounted Police used in the north were recruited from along the Murray and elsewhere in New South Wales and Victoria and had no fellow feeling for these strange tribes they were ordered to attack. In 1884, at Battle Mountain, in far-western Queensland near the site of Mount Isa, as many as 600 Aboriginal warriors confronted settlers and Native Mounted Police commanded by a future Queensland police commissioner, Frederic Urquhart, in one of the largest and bloodiest confrontations of the frontier wars, in which as many as 200 natives were killed and the rest pursued and 'dispersed'. The white officers who led the Native Mounted Police used those words, 'dispersal' and 'disperse', to cover a number of sins.

Covert state involvement in this forced displacement was more open and prolonged than elsewhere in Australia, and the government of Queensland supported the Native Mounted Police as a 'force of extermination'. The Martini-Henry rifle came into operation in the 1880s and the Native Mounted Police were armed with it. It was claimed to be twice as accurate as the earlier Sniders. But in the 1880s the Winchester repeater rifles also became popular and could discharge fifteen-round magazines as fast as the trigger was pulled. There was no fighting against such weapons with clubs and spears. This reality is reflected in one sweep of the Yungaburra district near Cairns in 1884, when Yidinji people were slaughtered at Skull Pocket along the Mulgrave River, and at Waree. One of the pursuers, Jack Kane, recalled 'they were easy running shots. The native police rushed in with their scrub knives and killed off the children . . . I didn't mind the killing of the "bucks" but I didn't quite like them braining the kids.'

The struggle between races in northern Australia, like a similar conflict in the prairies of the United States, was a struggle for control of waterholes. Given the scarcity of water in Australia, the conflict was intense. One of the most militant figures in this struggle was Constable William Willshire, stationed at Alice Springs in the 1880s and then at Victoria River. During the 1880s up to 1000 Aborigines were killed in the Alice Springs pastoral district. Amongst desert populations these amounted to huge losses.

Recounting one engagement between, on the one side, his Native Mounted Police squad, recruited from other parts of Australia and armed with Martini-Henry carbines, and on the other the 'mischievous' local natives of the north, Willshire wrote in an eloquent but sinister phrase that his party's weapons 'were talking English to the silent majesty of those great eternal rocks'.

Willshire was a man of physical courage and psychological sturdiness, and—without excusing his euphemism for slaughter—was a man of his time implementing policy with which pastoralists and governments were content. He was the armed herald who proclaimed, and was the instrument of, racial theories harboured not only by himself but by many other participants in popular racial science. His memoirs read deplorably now, a Petri dish of noxious attitudes, but they were presented to the gaze of his generation in the confidence that they would be enthusiastically applauded. 'Racist' has become almost too flimsy a word to encompass all that exhibits itself in his book.

Given the realities of remote Australia, and the war indigenes were fighting to retain land sites, there is no reason to doubt Willshire when he asserts that 'many sleepless nights and weary anxious days have been gone through in doing duty amongst wild tribes, who during the writing of this book committed murders and killed the settlers' horses and cattle; and the author, being a police officer in charge of native constables ... and those acts being exigencies of the service, he had to go out with his trackers and deal with each case respectively as the law provided'. In the dedication of his 1896 memoirs, he honoured James Logan Ledgerwood, a Territory pastoralist. 'I was prompted to select you for this Dedication as you thoroughly understand the scheming designs of Aborigines who contrive to take the heart's blood of white men.'

The lamentations and the tears belonged not to the punished natives but to the relatives of the dead pioneers alone. 'Oh sorrowing, oh, sorrowing mothers and sisters true, your sons' and brothers' bones lay bleaching in scenes of wildest desolation, and in scenes of picturesque beauty, at various waterholes on the Overland Telegraph Line, at dozens of places in the Northern Territory, especially its rivers.' There is no denying that individual travellers, or small parties, had reason to be fearful of attack. Patrolling the Katherine, Daly, Gregory, Roper and Victoria rivers in the mid-1880s, Willshire claims he did not know when he lay down at night when the attack would come, and if this is so it could not have added to his kind thoughts. According to him the marauding natives often sheltered between murders at mission stations now beginning to spread across the north, run by Trappist monks, Presbyterians, Jesuits, all of whom he mocked. Their attack made, he said, they then retreated, reassuming the garments of the mission and its pieties. His energy was employed by contrast as missionary of the carbine, and he was relentless in spreading that light.

His memories are full of ambiguity towards his enemy. The Aborigines, he said, were 'beautiful liars', and like many Europeans he showed a certain respect for the full-blood Aborigines, and a genuine interest in their culture, even presenting a vocabulary of the Victoria River language in his book. Indeed, he confessed his initial weakness for the natives.

> I lived with the natives for sixteen years. I spent hundreds of pounds to ameliorate their condition, and in return they attempted to murder me. I was exceedingly kind to them. I incurred the displeasure of white men, who said I was spoiling them through my liberality. My kindness was rewarded with the blackest of ingratitude . . . when I saw my mistake and altered my hand, I became firm, and the natives then respected me with that fawning civility so characteristic of a low degraded race.

Like many Europeans, he despised fringe-dwelling half-castes, even though it had been through the sexual adventures of the settlers that half-castes were born.

He was involved in the pursuit of evildoers, for example, when in August 1885 a prospecting party was attacked by blacks and a man named Walker killed. The offending group 'were tracked up by an avenging party [police and others], and sic transit Gloria mundi!' In January 1892 Charles Deloitte and George Clarke were murdered at Creswell Downs Station, and again Willshire took to the field with his Native Mounted Police. Then in April 1892 six Malays were massacred by the natives at Bowen Straits east of Palmerston. Altogether, 1892 seems to have been a bad year for attacks, since Mr W.S. Scott, manager of Willeroo Station, was camped for dinner out on his run when speared to death on 11 October. In all these cases Willshire's 'carbine spoke', and carbines were the superior weaponry of the day.

There was a strange racial ambivalence in Willshire when he pursued a group of Aborigines who had been spearing cattle on the Victoria run in August 1894. He came upon them camped in a gorge off the north bank of the Wickham River. The men picked up their spears and commenced climbing the precipitous sides of the cliff while the females and children crawled into rocky embrasures. Willshire does not say what happened in detail—he merely records that 'when we had finished with the male portion we brought the black gins and their offspring out from their rocky alcoves. There were some nice looking boys and girls among them. One girl had a face and figure worthy of Aphrodite—had she dwelt in a Grecian sculptor's brain?' He treated a pregnant mother with kindly attention, and when she gave birth to a child he reflected, 'The newborn babe turned out to be a boy, the nucleus of a cattle-killer.'

His adventures were diverse. He told the tale of a 'civilised black boy' belonging to a Justice of the Peace in the lower Victoria district who was murdered by 'the wild natives of the Gregory River'. Pursuing them to Gordon Creek, they saw a beautiful 'savage maiden' running screaming to give warning to the miscreants, but the black trackers were already at the spot before she could do it. The only reference to what happened when his party descended upon the group was 'when all was over my boys brought her and some others to our camp'. A number who survived the fire fights of the frontiers became the servant-companions of native troopers.

Obviously there were black women who were not even as fortunate as that.

A WORKER'S PARADISE?

Though work was hard and wages low, the idea was fostered in Australia, not merely at the level of civic orations but in the suppositions of ordinary folk, that—by comparison with the factory squalor immigrants encountered— Australia was a working man's paradise. This belief has been a potent and enduring Australian legend. The decade of the 1870s, said the *Sydney Morning Herald*, reminiscing in September 1890, was one during which workers were 'the most fortunate, the best paid and the most prosperous in the world'. The truth was that Australian working conditions in the later nineteenth century were often as bad and occasionally were harsher than those of the Old World, particularly in the way people were worked in country areas but also in the manufactures of the cities. In the mid-nineties, before she went to Paraguay and New Australia, Henry Lawson would take the young schoolteacher Mary

Gilmore to see the misery of Sydney. 'He used to take me out to see the wrong things, the things repressive of the rights of Australia; the things like a blot upon her and which prevented her being herself. The low-wage workers, the Chinamen working at treadle-saws in underground cellars lit only by a grating in the street, the huddled houses . . . the pale seamstresses . . . the neglected children of the Quay and elsewhere.' It is significant that young Mary also saw Australia as of its nature a paradise and that it was only 'the things which prevented her being herself' that stood in the way.

In the 1890s depression, the working man's paradise thesis came under acute pressure. There was a high level of burglary, babies were abandoned on doorsteps, in the slums there were evictions, and the number of people applying for charity doubled. According to the lively South Australian premier, Charles Kingston, a radical, 'Australian society set high standards for individual self-sufficiency', and sometimes people simply could not reach them. Only South Australia and Western Australia had state-subsidised Benevolent Asylums, the equivalent of British and Irish workhouses, and these asylums, said the visiting Irish home rule campaigner Michael Davitt, 'had at least some of the much-dreaded atmosphere of Poor Law Institutions in England'. On the other hand, he continued, workers who had gone to the wall were not treated like semi-criminals, and there was no hereditary pauper class, as in England. And the richest investors in Australian enterprise often lived overseas, like Mount Morgan's Mr D'Arcy, and this helped the development of the myth of Australian equity.

And yet . . . In the 1870s, Dr. J.E. Neild, public health expert, wrote, 'I know from experience something of the chronic domestic dirt which prevailed among the lower classes in the manufacturing towns of England, but nothing that I ever witnessed in the West Riding of Yorkshire and in South Lancashire equalled in repulsiveness what I have found in Melbourne.' Though housing conditions were generally better than in the slums of London or Manchester, it was a matter of mere degree. On the other hand, even in the depression of the 1890s the average family's spending power in New South Wales was £38 per head of population per year, compared with £30 in Britain. Did that £8 difference create the basis for awarding Australia the crown as a working man's paradise? Similarly, the New South Wales statistician Timothy Coghlin found that the average Englishman had to work 127 days to earn the cost of his food, but the average Australian achieved the same result after 119 days of labour, and ate far better food in the process. The far better food was a considerable factor in the belief in the Australian industrial nirvana. To the European working class, meat and tea were luxuries, but were standard in the diet of the Australian working class. There was a chance that because of a better diet, the more successful of Australian working men and their wives and children developed into a distinctive physical type, taller and leaner but generally stronger. That this was not always the case is obvious from any reading of our history, but Rolf Boldrewood, the author of *Robbery Under Arms*, certainly believed in a better destiny making a better kind of human being, always envisaged as a male. 'His limbs are muscular and sinewy; his chest is broad; his shoulders well spread.' According to Boldrewood, the Australian could 'generally do manual labour after a fashion and at a pace that would astonish a Kent or Sussex local'.

Politicians and society in general had held out the vision of the working man's utopia, and now unions intended to hammer down the conditions which would ensure it. The first attempts had been made in the late 1850s by the Operative Stonemasons' Societies of Melbourne and Sydney, who were transforming these cut-rate ports into modern urban glories. They were like the young Parkes, influenced by Chartism, and believed in the previously forbidden right to 'combine' (a right for which Chartists and earlier British and Irish protesters had been transported as convicts). British masons usually worked under shelter and a milder climate, but here in Australia there were few workshops or other awnings to protect the stonemason from the sun or the wet. They believed that the sixty-hour week then in place was far too long. On the cusp of the 1860s, the Printers' Union was also campaigning for an eight-hour day.

In 1866 Farmer and Company, the large Sydney store, which like British firms had been willing to work their shop assistants ninety hours a week, became the first in New South Wales to close for the Saturday half-holiday. When Anthony Hordern died in 1868 his sons brought back the Sydney emporium's closing hours from 10 p.m. to 7 p.m. David Jones adopted even shorter hours during the 1870s and abandoned Saturday-night trading. All this was in part due to the progressive spirit in some of the major Australian shopkeepers. In Brisbane in 1879 the Dublin-born draper Thomas Finney pioneered 6 p.m. closing at his department stores, Finney Isles and Company, and he followed it with early Saturday closing in 1885. The idea of co-ownership appealed to Finney, and he subsidised a staff fund on a £1 to £1 basis. Profit-sharing as a means to motivate and elevate workers was a world phenomenon and many company owners adopted it. In 1888 Peter Johns, formerly a workman on the Crystal Palace in London, and owner of a large engineering works in Melbourne, gave more than half his own shares to employees, an arrangement which helped him, in collaboration with his workers, to survive the 1890s depression almost without damage.

In South Australia the owners of the Burra and Moonta copper mines built cottages for their employees and introduced compulsory medical benefits schemes at low weekly rates. These paid half-wages to disabled men, and at Moonta in 1873 introduced a minimum wage of £2 a week in bad years. (Previously there had been no bottom to the lowering of wages in hard periods.)

George Marchant, a man from Kent who had arrived in Brisbane in 1874 'friendless and practically penniless', had not only worked in the bush as a station hand. To earn a living in town he collected empty bottles and he and his wife Sarah opened a soft drink business which spread from Brisbane to branches in other states. The company was based on his invention and patenting of a bottling machine which came to be used all over the world. Like many such self-made men, he had begun his career as a staunch anti-unionist, but began to fraternise with Labor thinkers such as fiery William Lane, editor of the *Boomerang*, and during the 1890 shipping strike chaired meetings which raised funds to support the strikers. He too practised profit-sharing in his factories.

The expectation that things would be better in Australia (whether they always were or not) was a powerful motivator for workers. W.H.S. Blake, a tailor employed by Alston and Brown in Melbourne who became a leader of the Early Closing Association, said that in his youth in England he had to start work at seven every morning and usually work until midnight—a working week of nearly 100 hours. To be employed in Alston and Brown's factory or showroom, which always closed at 6 p.m., made him ecstatic. Extra time gave working men a chance to raise themselves; in Collingwood, Joel Eade, Cornishman and a former gold miner in California and Victoria, attended drawing classes at the Melbourne Mechanic's Institute and was able to 'lift himself' from carpenter to town surveyor. He later founded the Collingwood School of Design for 'rising operatives'.

It was still true that most businessmen, from the ports to the remotest pastures, saw the unions as the serpent at society's breast. And a sacking or an industrial accident could still impose acute misery and hunger even in the house of a skilled worker. Families tried to invest in 'friendly societies' which would support them through the illness of the injured worker, and in insurance against his death. One of the 'friendly societies' was the Independent Order of Oddfellows, open to all craftsmen. By 1865 there were 106 lodges in Victoria, forty-six in Sydney and sixty-four in Adelaide. Lodges often employed their own doctors to look after members.

*

For unskilled workers, living and working conditions were much more squalid, unhealthy and hopeful than for the 'rising operative'. When Henry Lawson went to work at Hudson Brothers' railway carriage works at Clyde in the 1880s, he had to rise at 5 a.m., walk across the city to catch the train at six from Redfern, and go to work painting and rubbing down carriages with 'blood coming from finger ends and trickling over the pumice stone'. He would return home at 6.30 p.m. in a stupor of weariness. He knew what it was to wander from job to job and have the 'furtive and criminal-like' shame of his position. Such was his experience of the working man's paradise. Later, in the midst of celebrations for the Queen's Jubilee, he would write about workers with a personal fury:

> I listened through the music and the sounds of revelry
> And all the hollow noises of that year of Jubilee;
> I heard beyond the music and beyond the royal cheer,
> The steady tramp of thousands that were marching in the rear…
> I heard defiance ringing from the men of rags and dirt,
> I heard wan women singing that sad 'Song of the Shirt',
> And o'er the sounds of menace and moaning low and drear,
> I heard the steady tramping of their feet along the rear.

Employees in newspaper and general printing offices were amongst the most misused. Indeed, many journalists in the 1880s received only 30 shillings a week. Compositors worked ten-hour night shifts with only a meal snatched while they worked. Their wages were about 27 shillings for the standard fifty-four hours' work. Boys were employed sometimes for 2 shillings and sixpence a week, and in 1883 the *Melbourne Herald* and the *World* newspapers each employed about thirty boy compositors to every four tradesmen. A compositor who complained could quickly be replaced. The Typographical Society succeeded in banning boy labour from night work at the *Age* and *Argus*. But twelve-year-old boys were still being employed this way on other presses and in the larger regional towns. Here they worked from 3 p.m. until 3 a.m.

The first Factory Act in Australia was passed by the Victorian Parliament in 1873, initiated by William Collard Smith, son of a Cheshire cotton factory owner who had come to Australia for the gold rush. Smith, living in Ballarat, had also been a pioneer in mine safety inspection. He was appointed chairman of a Royal

Commission to investigate working conditions in 1883, ten years after the first Factory Act, and found that for thousands of workers 'a system of forced labour, repugnant to every sense of justice in humanity', was in place. Many employees were obliged to work beyond the limits of physical endurance. Smith and his fellow commissioners reported that the worst abuses occurred in companies whose growth had been encouraged by protection: high tariffs. Deakin would always believe such industries should be able to afford high wage levels—high profits and high wages were the rationale of protectionism. But in many factories, protection as an engine of prosperity for workers was failing.

In textile and clothing factories, men earned an average of 35 shillings a week, women only 10 shillings, boys about 7 shillings and girls 4 shillings. The mills secretly agreed to employ entire families so that pittances could be combined. Truant officers were supposed to extract child labourers from these factories, but were not always able to—the child's own parents often worked there too and pleaded with the truant officers that they needed the child's wages. According to the report of the Victorian Royal Commission 1882–84, to keep a child labourer in work the parents sidestepped the compulsory Education Act by putting their children's names on a private school roll, such as that of a Catholic school, which were not available to the department's inspectors. Inspectors might then lie in wait and catch the children as they went on their lunch break. But although the parents were fined, they would sometimes send the children back to work under different names.

Nine- to twelve-year-olds also worked in the tobacco industry. At Feldheim, Jacobs and Company in Melbourne, nine-year-olds earned 7 shillings for working six days a week from 8 a.m. to 6 p.m. producing 50 000 cigars a week. Needless to say, their conversations were said to have been of 'the most filthy description'. A sign at the workshop door read *All hands are liable to be discharged at one moment's notice* over the signature of the chairman, John A. Wilson.

At one of the best mills, the Victorian Woollen and Cloth Manufactory in Geelong, all hands worked a sixty-hour week for which twelve-year-old boys were paid 8 shillings. The Victorian Royal Commission in 1883 visited some of the better clothing factories of Melbourne, and disapproved of many of them. Even twenty years later, at a further Victorian Royal Commission of 1900–03 on the Operation of the Factories and Shops Law, a woman who had an apparently invalided husband testified that she worked in a clothing factory from twelve to sixteen hours a day, six days a week, for which she was paid 12 shillings and sixpence weekly, and only survived because the employer took on two of her children to work the same hours at 5 shillings a week each. 'I consider we are nothing lesser than white slaves with our employers,' said one woman to the Victorian Royal Commission.

The Tailoresses's Union struggled with the issue for years. A coat machinist employed on piece work by Cohen & Lyon of Melbourne testified that she worked all day in the factory and another three hours each night at home but could rarely earn more than 17 shillings a week. A Mrs Adams and her two daughters, who sewed moleskin trousers at McIvor and Lincoln's, worked from 8 a.m. till 11 p.m. each day, assisted at home by another child when she came home from school. Between them, these four females earned £3 a week. The desperation of workers to continue receiving wages caused them to turn up to work even when they were ill, spreading diseases like typhoid fever.

A witness quoted in the Report on the Condition of the Working Class, New South Wales, 1859–60, described living conditions as 'worse than in any part of the world that I have seen—worse than in London'. The Benevolent Society and St Vincent de Paul handed out small amounts of bread and meat, salt and soap in cases of need. A Royal Commission on Public Charities in New South Wales, entering a slum off Gloucester Street in Sydney, found entire families trying to live off less than £1 a week. And in a house they visited there was merely 'some bread, and a small quantity of pumpkin and turnips'. Even in Adelaide a slum developed from the 1850s near East Terrace in tenements built in the mid-nineteenth century. The landlord was the Adelaide entrepreneur and self-proclaimed radical William Peacock, MLC.

At work the health conditions mirrored the slums where the worker lived. In the 1880s, at Mitchell's Brush Factory in Lonsdale Street, Melbourne, there was no privy at all for male employees. At F. Joseph and Company Clothing Factory in Flinders Lane, employing men and women, the same conditions prevailed. At some Sydney engineering works men had to walk as much as half a mile to the nearest public privies to urinate or excrete and lost wages in the process. As in Britain, there were diseases caused directly by work but for which there was no compensation. Watchmakers suffered a disease of the bones because of the use of phosphorus in their trade. Grocers suffered a skin disease—'grocer's itch'—from a mite which infested sugarbags, dried fruit and grain. Painters contracted painter's colic, a form of crippling lead poisoning. Even knife grinders developed lung disease from the clouds of metal particles their machines generated. Children who were sent into confined spaces to service machinery often suffered accidents. A boy of twelve was crushed to death between the rollers of printing machinery. Machinery had no safety guards, and neither did sawmills or joineries have guards to prevent a bandsaw flying off the wheel.

The safety and health inspectors put in place by safety laws such as the Deakin-inspired Shops and Factories Bill of 1885 were, by the time the law was chopped about and amended, under the authority of the municipal councils, many of whose aldermen owned factories. On the basis of the 1883 Royal Commission, and with the support of a number of manufacturers, Alfred Deakin introduced a strong bill, but he was only able to force limited changes through. He had wanted all workshops with two or more employees brought under the Act and the registration of companies, sanitary requirements, limits on the hours minors could work and compensation for injury. The Legislative Council diluted the bill so much that the question of closing hours was handed over to local Shopkeepers' Associations and councils for separate decisions to be made in each suburb. So few changes were made that the trade unions began to found Labor Leagues with the goal of putting workers into Parliament, since well-meaning liberals like Deakin had failed them.

In any case, when health inspectors prosecuted businesses, the workers were too frightened to give evidence for fear of dismissal, and magistrates were often manufacturers themselves.

In 1896 Victoria established Australia's first wages board, in which employers and employees' representatives convened to agree upon minimum wages. The Shops and Factories Act was further strengthened in 1896 and 1900, though there was no overall reform. Victoria was considered to lead the world in enlightened legislation. By the end of the century, most Melbourne shops adopted standard hours of 8 a.m. to 6 p.m. on weekdays and 8 a.m. to 1 p.m. on Saturdays. Packers, however, continued work for long hours behind the shopfront. Enoch Nickless, managing director of Mayne Nickless and Company Limited, which delivered parcels for most of Melbourne's big stores, was unable to see how his carters' hours could ever be shortened. Some ladies would wait up till one o'clock for a hat. 'It would be impossible to work our business in sixty hours, not less than seventy hours per week are required.'

While Victoria battled its way towards reform, other states did very little. In South Australia, a Royal Commission reported in 1892 on working conditions for the protection of women and children, but the first reform bill was thrown out by the South Australian Legislative Council in 1893. It was accepted the following year on condition that children of thirteen would still be legally permitted to work a forty-eight-hour week. Adelaide shops remained open at their discretion. Eight-hour bills were rejected in Queensland. Though Western Australia passed early closing and factory laws in 1897, Tasmania went without industrial legislation at all.

In New South Wales, whether the government was led by the Free Traders Henry Parkes and George Reid or the Protectionist George Dibbs, industrial conditions were left to market forces. Only in 1896, when George Reid became dependent on a few Labor Members of Parliament to retain power, was the first attempt at a Factories and Shops Act made. All the scandals revealed in Melbourne in the early 1880s were current in Sydney up to Federation. There was no regulation of outworkers—women in the clothes industries who were given piece work to do at home were often deserted or widowed wives. A *Daily Telegraph* reporter visited a Surry Hills tenement just before midnight on 16 August 1901 to see 'a tired looking woman busily working with her needle finishing the trousers, which her husband was machining, while two little eight- and-ten-year-old girls sewed the buttons on another pair of trousers'. William Lyne got a New South Wales Early Closing Act through Parliament in 1899 under pressure from the Toynbee Guild, an association of reforming university men. But as long as shops closed on Wednesday or Saturday afternoon, they were allowed to stay open as long as they liked on Friday and Saturday nights and employers were still allowed to work their carters any number of hours they liked. The fact was that shopkeepers could work their employees up to sixty hours a week without any extra pay.

A number of wages boards existed under the legislation, but of five workers who became members of the Jam Industry Wages Board and voted in 1900 to increase adult wages from 30 shillings to 35 shillings a week, four were immediately sacked. Similarly, all five operatives on the Fell-mongers' Board were warned what would happen if they voted against their employer's wishes. William McVicars, owner with his brother of the Sydney Woollen Mills and president of the New South Wales Chamber of Manufacturers, declared in 1901 that 'Shops and Factories Acts, that is, regulating the conditions of employment, was carrying legislation too far'. Many employers argued that lack of regulation allowed them to keep on slower workers at less wages who under fixed-wage situations would be thrown out of work and die of disease. By the birth of the Commonwealth, there was a lack of shared wealth amongst many bush and urban citizens of the new Australia. It is therefore easy to see why the new-born Labor Party and the trade unions did not consider Federation the primary issue.

THE GODLY RADICALS

A Staffordshire coal miner, Joseph Cook, like many early Labor men, combined socialist vision with religious orthodoxy. In his English youth he was a lay preacher of theology for the Primitive Methodists, whose eschewing of all sin suited his dour soul. Being the breadwinner for the family—his father had been killed in a mine accident—he did not emigrate to Australia until the age of twenty-five, after his siblings had grown up and were self-sufficient.

He was, like a young shopkeeper of Balmain, William Morris Hughes, a Free Trader to begin with, and believed that there should be but a single tax, and that on land. Married to a schoolteacher, he lived and worked in Lithgow. In August 1890, during the Maritime Strike, he served on the Labor Defence Committee at a time when the Lithgow mines were being worked by non-unionists, all under the protection of the New South Wales' small permanent army. The following year this honest, glum fellow was elected to the New South Wales Parliament.

At a Labor conference in March 1894 a resolution was passed that members had to bind themselves to espouse the official position reached by a vote in caucus. Cook and a number of others refused to sign this 'solidarity pledge', and he was voted as a Labor Independent. He would almost immediately take a cabinet position in George Reid's conservative Free Trade government, and would be increasingly abominated by his former fellow workers in the solidarity movement, including William Morris Hughes. But only fourteen members of 'solidarity Labor' were elected to that Parliament in 1894.

If the election of Labor members was noticed in the broader world, and it was by many people, it was often suspected by conservatives to be the appearance of a dogmatically socialist clique instead of the bunch of pragmatists the party was from the start. It disappointed radicals by showing little interest in the overthrow of society and too much in improving lives of working men and women by degrees—a shorter week here, a few more shillings in pay packets there, an improved safety law somewhere else. And in that vein the vivid Billy Hughes became a potent operator from the start. Elected to the New South Wales Parliament in 1894, a solidarity man, this amusing cynic looked with a little bemusement at the religious devotion of his fellow Labor men—five were lay preachers, James McGowen was a Sunday school superintendent. 'As a set off,' he wrote, however, 'I ought to let you know that two of the most notable of our members have been in gaol as a result of their activities in the Broken Hill strike.' They were idealists but ready to make a deal. They quickly understood that they held the balance of power between Sir George Reid's Free Traders and Sir William Lyne's Protectionists. The Labor Party in Parliament had supported Reid because he had in turn introduced legislation which favoured their interests—early closing of shops and navigation bills. The time was, as Hughes said, 'rotten ripe' for the working hours to be cut. Reid made the mistake of promising to limit the hours of shop assistants, but not to shorten the hours that the shops stayed open. Believing that the shop workers would be under pressure from their bosses to keep working the long hours they always had anyway, Billy Hughes went as an emissary to see lanky, amiable Sir William Lyne. Lyne promised that if Labor came over to him he would pass an Early Closing Bill as drafted by Hughes. Labor members, through Billy, then assured Sir William Lyne that they would support him if he moved a No Confidence Bill. The No Confidence Bill against George Reid was promptly proposed and was passed; Lyne came to power and early closing became law.

Sir William Lyne now considered that the best thing he could do was subsume the Labor Party into his own group. He offered them two ministerial positions, but they refused to accept them—no member of the party was to take office in any government other than one it had formed itself. The Early Closing Act was 'welcomed with glee by those who stood behind the nation's counters'. It clipped, said Hughes, twenty-five to thirty hours off the shop workers' week and gave them their lives back. But there was great resistance from the small shop owners of the kind he himself had recently been. He claims he went around Redfern visiting small shopkeepers, soothing them, and being amused by an Irish woman sitting on a chair in front of her closed shop. He asked the woman how her customers liked the new arrangement. 'O-thim! Sure they don't bother a scrap; they just go round to the back.'

When bubonic plague broke out in Hughes' own electorate in 1900, spreading from a ship from Mauritius which had moored at Sir John See's wharf—See being one of Lyne's ministers—Hughes began to pressure Lyne about public health. Hughes had visited the slums around Darling Harbour and saw impacted filth everywhere and heaped pyramids of offal, garbage and putrefying dogs in backyards. The harbour walls around Darling Harbour were 'daubed with excreta, and thousands of rats poking their heads out of holes in the wall'. It was something Sir William Lyne did not seem to be aware of and he was appalled. Hughes claims to have said to Sir William, 'But do you know that some, if not all, of these filthy dens are owned by Aldermen of the City Council . . . the men who own these unspeakable hovels live in fine homes in the best parts of Sydney.' The problem was that people who lived in squalor had no votes in local elections because they were not rate-payers. Thus, Sir William devoted himself to altering the local electoral laws. It seemed that Hughes was becoming an igniter—what people would later call 'a fiery particle'.

Hughes was also outraged by the conditions of labour on the waterfront. The Wharf Labourers' Union had been smashed by the Maritime Strike of 1890, and members of the union were blacklisted. Work was very irregularly granted on the waterfront generally, and when they got it, men would often work a forty-eight-hour shift in a ship's refrigeration hold stacking meat, and then get no more work for a few weeks. The revival of the union began in 1896 with the Fiery Particle pushing it. Friends outside the union willing to give it help included Archdeacon Langley of St Phillip's church, who made his school hall available for union meetings, and Jack Kilbeg (Manchester Jack), owner of Mann's Hotel on the corner of Kent and Grosvenor streets, a pub frequented by wharf labourers. The reinvigorated union was launched at Federation Hall in 1899. Due to his alliance with Hughes, the premier, W.J. Lyne was willing to attend. So was the Minister for Works, E.W. O'Sullivan, along with nine other members of parliament, as well as Archdeacon Langley and the Reverend Father Albury, whose parish was full of the impoverished dock workers of Darling Harbour. The waterside workers and their families predictably adored Hughes for organising this display of strength. But he was no firebrand. An industrial realist, before he left for Melbourne to serve in the federal Parliament in May 1901, Hughes urged the members 'to avoid any rash and ill-considered measures'.

CHAPTER 5

Seeking Federation, and having it
Late 1890s to 1914

AND BE ONE PEOPLE

At Largs Bay, a beach near Adelaide, on a late summer day in 1897, two young men could be seen amongst the waves. They were both native born and willing to be as strenuous in the sea as elsewhere. One was the youngish, industrious lawyer, legislator and journalist Alfred Deakin, tall and with a trim beard. The other was a much shorter but indomitable fellow with water dripping off the end of his wax moustache. He was the attorney-general of Victoria, Isaac Isaacs, son of a draper from Yackandandah who had come from Russian-occupied east Poland. His mother, born in London, had been ambitious for her son, who had not disappointed her with his talents, any more than Deakin, the other surfer, had disappointed his. Isaacs had studied law at university part time, graduating with first-class honours thirteen years before this swim at Largs Bay. It was claimed he had a photographic memory and could read law reports at a speed close to their handing down, and by 1890 he was an accomplished advocate, representing banks, land and finance companies and, on one occasion, the stock exchange.

Both of these men were elected delegates to a Federation Convention which was about to meet in Adelaide, though very few of the convention's other venerable members could have joined them in this sport. Isaacs had other gifts few delegates had. He could speak Russian, French, German, Italian and Greek to varying degrees. As Solicitor-General he had insisted on pursuing those associated with the failed Mercantile Bank for conspiracy to defraud. Forced to resign from the Victorian Parliament over it, Isaacs won back his seat overwhelmingly in the next election, and became attorney-general in the Turner Liberal ministry which he held from 27 September 1894 till the end of 1899.

Isaacs was, however, not as trusted or respected as Deakin, for he did not have an appeasing temperament and he possessed the naked ambition instilled in him by his mother. He had also to suffer anti-Semitic attitudes of the kind so popular with the *Bulletin*, yet had much public support because of his interest in reform. And he had told the Australian Natives Association that he looked forward to the day when he could say, because of Federation, 'I am an Australian.' He had the broadest knowledge of other constitutions of anyone who was about to meet to finalise the Australian version.

Deakin saw that there was a plot in place to keep Isaacs off the Drafting Committee of the Federal Convention, but that was not to do with his Jewishness as much as his propensity to lecture other members on constitutional minutiae. Isaacs did not think that the future Senate should have equal membership for all states and wanted to exalt above all the House of Representatives. He did not want a broad right for those whose claims were defeated in the High Court to appeal to the Privy Council in London. And he was opposed to a Bill of Rights. On the Senate issue he would be defeated, but on the other two he would have some success.

Deakin saw Federation as an urgent task. How close was Federation to God's will in the mind of Alfred Deakin? Much closer than it was for the sensualist George Reid. 'Grant O God,' went one of the prayers Deakin composed, 'that I may have sufficient clearness of vision or sufficient antagonism to failure to avoid injuring the cause of true progress towards Thee and Thy kingdom on earth.' The way to the kingdom on earth lay through a federal Australia. In a speech to the Australian Natives Association at Bendigo towards the end of the three 1897–98 conventions, in March 1898, Deakin strove to express the piety he felt for Federation.

A Federal Constitution is the last and final product of political intellect and constructive ingenuity; it represents the highest development of the possibilities of self-government among people scattered over a large area . . . Do not every year and every month exact from us a toll of severance? Do not we find ourselves hampered in commerce, restricted in influence, weakened in prestige, because we are jarring atoms instead of a united organism?

He answered these questions by quoting the poet William Gay, with whom Deakin had corresponded and who was already dying of the tuberculosis he had come to Australia in 1888 to cure. His nurse, Mary Simpson, was a schoolteacher and also a familiar correspondent of Deakin's and burned with the same order of flame as William Gay himself, sustaining in him the visionary fire. Gay had, however, died late in 1897, but he cast his shadow forward over the coming Federation.

> *Our country's garment*
> *With hands unfilial we have basely rent,*
> *With petty variance our souls are spent,*
> *An ancient kinship underfoot is trod:*
> *Oh let us rise,—united,—penitent,—*
> *And be one people,—mighty, serving God!*

The crucial Federation conventions were held in Adelaide in March 1897, in Sydney in September the same year and in early 1898 in Melbourne. Ten delegates from each state were elected to travel to the three connected conventions, but Western Australian attendance was erratic, and the Queensland Parliament had not passed the legislation to make the election of their delegates possible. New Zealand decided not to send delegates. In Sydney the ascetic Cardinal Moran stood as a delegate for New South Wales to represent Catholic interests, but Protestant bodies campaigned successfully against him. The Adelaide and Melbourne meetings were characterised by heatwaves, the Melbourne meeting coinciding with bushfires which caused the Englishmen facing the Australians led by Harry Trott at the Melbourne Cricket Ground to complain that the smoke was making things impossible for them in the field. All this was endured also by the delegates to the convention, men wearing formal suits, having travelled a great distance by train and ship, and slipping off some afternoons, still in those fustian clothes, to get a little of the last session of play. (Australia won the Ashes, four Tests to one, another omen of Federation.)

The fact that the first of these serial conventions was held in a smaller state was a success for the South Australian premier, Charles Kingston, a rambunctious fellow whose character seemed at odds with the 'city of churches'. When he was admitted to the bar, a young man opposed his accreditation on the grounds that he had seduced the young man's sister. Kingston, an Australian Rules player for South Adelaide, beat up the brother and married the girl, Lucy McCarthy. When in 1892 a conservative member of Parliament, Sir Richard Baker, attacked him as a disgrace to the legal profession, Kingston sent Sir Richard a pistol and an invitation to meet him for a duel in Victoria Square, Adelaide. Sir Richard told the police, who arrested Kingston. A magistrate bound him over to keep the peace, and he was still keeping it when elected premier as a popular radical in 1893. His reform program included arbitration for industrial disputes, the legitimisation of children born out of wedlock, the creation of a state bank, and the extension of the franchise to all adults—to women, that is. After lambasting the South Australia Co., Adelaide's foundation company, as premier he was attacked with a horsewhip by its manager, an assault which occurred in the street and drew blood. Kingston asked, who could now deny he had bled for South Australia?

The delegates who travelled to the first session in Adelaide by way of Victoria—the New South Welshmen and Tasmanians—were impressed by the welcome they received along the way. Ballarat honoured them, and a crowd at Albury had greeted the blasé and unreliable George Reid. It was in Victoria that the interest in Federation was most intense, but Deakin saw New South Wales as dominant at the convention, since its premier, Sir George Reid, Free Trader and political opportunist, was hostile to Protectionist Victoria, lukewarm about Federation and suspected New South Wales might lose economically. Despite the presence of Edmund Barton, the Sydney lawyer and true successor of Parkes in the Federation campaign, New South Wales had the most power to destroy the whole plan. Victorian delegates were treated by Reid as ideological enemies, at best dreamers and at worst plunderers of New South Wales by the customs they collected from goods flowing between the colonies in the gimcrack Victorian customs house along the Murray and in the grander ones in larger ports. Though under the draft constitution the collection of customs duties was to be awarded to the Commonwealth and the states were to lose the power to collect them, Reid was uneasy about it all, foreseeing a Victorian-dominated Federal government soaking up most of the customs revenue raised by the Federal government, driving up prices through high tariffs, rewarding the obedient smaller states with more than their fair share of revenue and starving New South Wales.

'The chief and almost the sole offender was Reid,' wrote Deakin, 'who, having failed in all his attempts to induce the Victorians to wrestle with him upon their several rivalries, turned upon the South Australians, the Tasmanians and the Western Australians in turn with studied offensiveness and vulgar jibes until he who had entered the Convention at Adelaide its most popular, most influential, and most generous leader, left it the most unpopular, the least trusted and least respected of all its members.' Reid, said Deakin, 'was neither federal nor anti-federal but either at need and as far as possible both at once.'

Deakin thought the men who brought home Federation at that convention sitting serially in three cities were Barton, Barton's fellow New South Welshman Richard O'Connor, Charles Kingston and Frederick Holder of South Australia, George Turner and Isaacs of Victoria, and John Forrest of Western Austra-lia. Reid nonetheless let the Constitution Bill be drafted, the clauses which explained it and the sections themselves, and committed himself to present the bill, as did the other premiers, to his parliament and, if accepted by them, to the people of New South Wales at a referendum. This was the process devised by Dr John Quick at an earlier people's convention in Corowa. Quick was respected by all for watching over the bill in its infancy, 'as if it had been his own child'. He was not an Australian native but had been born in Cornwall of one of those mineral-divining Cornish families who had emigrated to Victoria in the 1850s and gone to the Bendigo goldfields. He began work at the age of ten in industrial mining, became an adolescent reporter on two Bendigo news-papers, then moved to Melbourne and by twenty-five had graduated in law. His concern would always be that the public should be informed enough to be able to vote at referendum on the Federation issue. He had no doubt that to be an informed citizen would be to vote Yes.

Not everyone in the smaller colonies was as informed as Quick would have wished, but saw instead a number of reasons to be nervous of having their economies swamped by those of Victoria and New South Wales. Sir Edward Braddon, Premier of Tasmania, proposed in Adelaide that the Commonwealth return to the states three-quarters of the customs revenue it raised. Edward Nicholas Coventry Braddon had spent many years in India, where he had run indigo factories and plantations, before moving to Tasmania and ultimately becoming Premier. In his youth he had served in a volunteer force to fight the Indian mutineers. As well as admiring his distinguished looks, Deakin would say of him that 'he was a most amiable cynic, an accomplished strategist and an expert administrator . . . Beside the massive Kingston, the podgy Reid . . . and the bluff Henry-the-Eighth appearance of Forrest, he looked like an attaché from Paris surrounded by the fat burghers of a Flanders city.' But Braddon saw the small states as potentially the poorer owners in an apartment block whose wealthier neighbours might embark on communal extravagances which could ruin their less affluent brethren.

Reid and Barton both opposed Braddon's idea that a guaranteed sum be raised by the federal authorities. New South Wales threatened to walk out over it. They were Free Traders and if Braddon had his way the Commonwealth would be prevented from going Free Trade, and would be forced to raise tariff barriers just to make enough revenue to run itself. Braddon's motion ultimately having been carried after midnight on the last Friday of the Melbourne session, it was blasted as 'the Braddon Blot'. Having the states rely on the Commonwealth for funds violated the central principle of federalism, it was argued: the principle that each government should be independent in its own sphere. Largesse on one hand, begging and haggling on the other, should not characterise the relation between federal and state governments. In the end, Section 87 of the constitution, Braddon's proposal, was amended before Federation so that the arrangement was to last only for ten years.

The constitution as framed had now to be accepted by the colonial houses of parliament and submitted to the people for acceptance at referendum. In New South Wales the sturdy-hearted Barton had backing from Bernhard Ringrose Wise, Oxford graduate and an exemplar of the Victorian-era man, being scholarly, passionately interested in the arts—he entertained Robert Louis Stevenson during the famed Scottish writer's Sydney visit—and a member of a number of sporting bodies, such as the Harriers Athletics Club. Another ally was Richard Edward O'Connor, Irish Australian, a rare New South Wales Protectionist like Barton and a Catholic of broader interests than those of the Cardinal.

Bernard O'Dowd, nationalist poet and Labor man, was an early opponent of the bill because, like others, he believed it undemocratic and a distraction from the struggle for justice.

They daze us with 'Our Destiny'
With blare of 'War' and 'Fame':
To part us, shriek out 'Unity'
And drug us with a Name.

Nonetheless, Barton, O'Connor and Wise, wrote Deakin, 'though poorer in funds and richer in scruples than their antagonists, travelled New South Wales getting out the Yes vote'. There was hostility to them, but above all, a yawning Australian apathy. But there were also a pleasing number of enthusiasts. In New South Wales most of the opposition still came from business, the Labor Party and so-called New South Wales patriots. Federation, said the Nays, meant New

South Wales would be plundered to pay for the benefit of its neighbours, and dictated to by senators from small states. The Senate issue—that little Tasmania and under-populated Western Australia would have the same number of senators as New South Wales—was an important argument for the 'anti-Billites', as the opponents of Federation were called.

When the New South Wales Parliament voted for the bill and passed enabling legislation for a referendum, their stipulation was that the Yes vote, even if greater than the No, must total 80 000 or more. Voting was not compulsory, and many would declare it all bloody nonsense and stay away from the poll. Were there 80 000 enrolled Federation enthusiasts in New South Wales? The politically engaged gathered outside the *Sydney Morning Herald* office on referendum day, 3 June 1898, where the voting figures delivered by telegraph were posted on a sort of scoreboard. Many of the No party, however, preferred to make a crowd outside the *Telegraph* office, since the *Telegraph* was so furiously anti-bill. That morning the *Telegraph*'s headlines had read: THE MOMENTOUS THIRD, THE BILL SHOULD DIE TONIGHT, KILLED BY AN OUTRAGED DEMOCRACY . . . VOTE FOR THE BILL AND THE STEP IS IRRETRACEABLE. At eight o'clock that night, the *Herald* posted the Yes vote at more than 80 000, and Barton emerged from the hotel where he had been waiting and was carried shoulder-high through the streets. The Federation flag, a white ensign with the Union Jack in one corner and with a blue cross punctuated by the stars of the Southern Cross, was broken out.

But the numbers were wrong; the *Herald* revised them, anti-Federationists yelled at Barton that he'd been a little too previous, and the *Telegraph* mocked. The final figures were 71 595 Yes, and 66 228 No. The Yes vote did not reach the 80 000 required for success. The anti-Billites rejoiced that Federation was stymied. That same day Tasmania and Victoria had voted powerfully in favour. The next day, so did South Australia. In South Australia the Yes vote had been 67 per cent, in Tasmania 81 per cent, and in Victoria 82 per cent, so that the mere technical failure to reach 80 000 Yes votes in New South Wales seemed a tragedy at the time. There would need to be another series of referenda, and New South Wales could again spoil it! And all the Federationists knew who to blame, that walrus-moustached George Reid who was seen as having interposed his enormous body between the hope and the realisation of Federation.

The Federalists of New South Wales, led by Barton, kept fighting. Reid also came to realise that if he fell from power in New South Wales, and another Federation referendum was held and, under the influence of what had happened in other states, was won, he would be handing to Barton and his crew all credit. He would be giving them entitlement and moral claim to represent New South Wales in a national house of Parliament. Besides, the majority who had voted Yes had shocked him. He began to see himself as history might see him—a pure spoiler. Mr Barton, Mr O'Connor and Mr Wise might achieve a triumph in which he had no share. He therefore plumped for the idea of the bill, with appropriate amendments.

Barton stood against Reid in his own seat in July 1898, advocating three changes to the constitution bill: the federal capital to be located in New South Wales, the Braddon clause to be removed, and the necessity of three-fifths majority at a joint sitting of Parliament to resolve a deadlock should also be excised. He was narrowly defeated in a campaign which Reid made vicious. But in September Barton was elected for the Hastings and Macleay in a by-election and became leader of the opposition. His supporter, the larrikin politician William Crick—racegoer, alcoholic and defender of Dean O'Haran of St Mary's Cathedral, who was, wrongfully it seems, accused of having had sex with a married woman in the confessional—carried on a fierce campaign against Reid in the New South Wales Parliament. A desire to replace Barton as both potential future prime minister and leader of the Federal movement led Reid to conduct a second referendum campaign with energy and his normal populist wit. A new referendum was to be held on 20 June 1899.

The *Bulletin* concentrated what Deakin called 'its unrivalled wealth of ridicule against the opponents of the bill'. The *Telegraph* was still the opposing voice. On the day, however, 107 420 New South Welshmen voted for Federation by a majority of nearly 25 000. So other colonies, except for Western Australia, passed new enabling acts for a second referendum, and Queensland for a first one. In South Australia Federation was reaffirmed by an even greater vote than before. Victoria and Tasmania voted in July, and in Victoria over 150 000 people voted for the bill and less than 10 000 voted against. In Tasmania the No vote was less than a thousand.

In Queensland, as in other parts of Australia, to the despair of democrats, plural votes still existed—that is, as well as having a vote as a citizen where he resided, a propertied man also had a vote in every electorate in which he possessed property with an annual value of £10. On top of that, in the enormous Queensland hinterland there was a large population of nomadic bush workers who were not registered as voters. The Queensland Federationists proposed that every man over the age of twenty-one should be allowed to vote, whether registered or not, but the Queensland opposition voted it down, just as they did the proposal that each citizen should vote once only. Various politicians wanted to amend the bill but the leaders of all the parties pointed out the futility of taking a vote on anything but the same constitution as the other states. So the referendum in Queensland was set to be held on 2 September 1899.

In Queensland there had not been much discussion of Federation in the press or politics or in the community, so that those in favour—men like Samuel Griffiths—had to work hard and cover great distances to explain it. They found that Federation was most popular along the southern border, where producers looked forward to free access to Victorian markets, amongst sugar growers for the same reason, and in the north and centre of the state, where there was a passion for seceding from Brisbane, which people thought would be easier to do under a Federation. But in Brisbane itself, and the south-east, opposition was strong; manufacturers were worried about open competition with Sydney, and so were many farmers. The result of the poll was 38 488 in favour to 30 996 against. In the end Rockhampton polled against the bill because Section 124, though it provided that there could be new states, declared it possible only with the consent of the parent state.

Western Australia was yet to accept the bill. At the Premiers' Conference of 1899, Sir John Forrest, who had had to spend the greatest amount of choppy time at sea going to and coming from conventions, showed unease about aspects of the bill. Though there was no referendum held in Western Australia in 1899, Clause 3 of the Commonwealth of Australia Constitution Act allowed the admission of Western Australia to the Federation, 'On or after a day . . . not being later than one year after the passing of this Act . . . if Her Majesty is satisfied that the people of Western Australia have agreed thereto.'

Unlike New South Wales, Western Australia had belonged to the Federal Council set up in 1883 and involving, as well as the Australian colonies, Fiji and New Zealand. But many Western Australians felt now that in Federation they would be too far away from the centre of political and financial power in the east. So the Western Australians—including Sir John Forrest, the Western Australian who had made a great contribution in the various conventions, who wanted the federal Parliament to have the power to legislate the building of a transcontinental railway—desired to be able to impose their own customs duties on the other colonies and on the world in general for the first five years of Federation, and an exemption for the same period from the jurisdiction of the Interstate Commission, the body which would police interstate free trade. The Western

Australian Parliament wanted to give their electors a choice between the bill the other states had passed and the bill with the Western Australian amendments. This was opposed by eastern federalists, who were confident that though there were few members representing the goldfields in the state Parliament, there were plenty of goldfields people who would vote Yes. In the Legislative Council of Western Australia, the idea of presenting either bill, the one as amended by Western Australia or the one passed in a referenda in the east, was obstructed.

On the goldfields the miners, damned elsewhere in Western Australia as 't'othersiders' and 'ancient colonists', had by now been enraged by new mining regulations, and had driven Premier John Forrest back to his railway carriage when he visited Coolgardie. Now they held meetings to call for their separation from Western Australia and their inclusion in the Australian Federation. 'Separation for Federation' became the goldfields slogan, and preliminary meetings to send delegates to London to organise separation were held. Compared to pastoralist areas, the goldfields returned less than their share of members to the Parliament in Perth, and the miners bitterly resented it, as they did the prices they paid for freight on what they believed was the overpriced railway, and so for goods in the stores. The young journalist Frederick Vosper, who would found the *Sunday Times* in Perth, campaigned for miners' rights *and* Federation and was a potent voice for goldfields secession if necessary. (Elected in the end to the first federal Parliament, where he would have made an interesting impact, he died of peritonitis before the Parliament met.) The Colonial Office did not seriously entertain the separation idea, but the intention of the miners did make other Western Australians think that it might be better to vote for Federation than face the loss of their gold lodes.

Forrest tried to meet the mutiny against Perth by reducing customs on imported food, by introducing an industrial arbitration act, and by giving women of twenty-one years and older the vote. But the mining districts even looked askance on these reforms, since there were more women in the pastoral electorates than on the goldfields. And even Frederick Vosper now began to wonder aloud if social justice might not be better achieved by an independent Western Australia than within a federation.

In January 1900 John Forrest went east to Sydney for the conference of premiers and abandoned three of the Western Australian amendments, but would not yield on the right of Western Australia to go on imposing customs for five years. To accept that would have been to make the people vote on Federation all over again, said some of the easterners, particularly New South Wales, but on legal advice an amendment to the bill was managed for the sake of getting Western Australia into the great federal tent.

Since the convention of 1891, New Zealand had taken no part in the framing of the federal constitution. New Zealand was mentioned, however, in Clause 6 as a possible state. In July 1899 a Federation League had been formed in Auckland, and the idea was discussed by politicians, the press and the people. New Zealand's distance of 1200 miles (1900 kilometres) by sea from eastern Australia dampened enthusiasm for Federation. Sir John Hall, former Prime Minister of New Zealand, who legislated to give New Zealand women the vote in 1893, had said at the 1890 Melbourne conference that the 1200 miles of the Tasman Sea were 1200 reasons why New Zealand should not join an Australian union. Federationists pointed out that this was a very poor argument since steamships connected eastern Australia to New Zealand faster than to Western Australia.

New Zealand and Australia were, in the days of the Federation debate, united economically and socially by the large numbers of people who moved both ways across the Tasman, by the same banks and insurance companies, by trade unions, churches and professional organisations. The network of connections was stronger across the Tasman than it was across the Nullarbor. Yet the reason the Federation cause arose at all in New Zealand was fear of losing access to the Australian market, and Prime Minister Richard Seddon of New Zealand, who as a pockmarked youngster had mined in Victoria for gold, therefore appointed a Royal Commission on Federation. It found that there was no overriding sense that union was the New Zealand destiny. Seddon's commissioners did not believe in the visionary idea that union would bring a higher form of existence to New Zealanders, and were more interested in the fact that New Zealand would always need its own individual defence force, and that with Federation there would be a loss of independence to create one. Seddon answered the imminent arrival of a Commonwealth by increasing efforts to acquire Samoa, Fiji and Tonga and so make New Zealand the head of an island dominion rather than merely part of an Australian one. He still watched closely the progress of the Australian Constitution when it was brought to London, and his representative there would give the Australians a great deal of trouble.

Ultimately, on 17 May 1900, three days after the Commonwealth bill was introduced in the House of Commons in Westminster, the Western Australian Parliament passed an enabling act by which the constitution bill would be submitted to a referendum. On 23 May, Sir John Forrest moved the second reading and said he would vote for Federation, even though he was uncertain about the benefits it would bring to Western Australia in the near future. All adults—men and women—who had been twelve months in the colony would be entitled to vote. The referendum was fixed for 31 July, and Sir John Forrest argued hard for a Yes vote, since he knew that to join the Commonwealth was an inevitability for the Western Australians, and they were better off joining now and helping to form policy. Western Australia would, after all, have as many senators as the big states. The anti-Federalists argued that federal control of customs would wreck the finances of Western Australia, and that Section 95, allowing Western Australia to retain intercolonial duties on a reducing scale over five years, was a mere token. On the day of the vote, Yes won by a majority of 25 109. Though country electorates voted against the bill, Perth and Fremantle voted for it by a small margin. On the goldfields, however, 26 000 voted Yes against less than 2000 No. The goldfields would thus be forever praised or blamed for hauling Western Australia into the Federation.

BOER WAR

And, as the colonies contemplated Federation, they were at war, and if the war lasted long enough would pass it on to the new nation they were making. Famously, when Britain declared war on the Boers of South Africa on 3 October 1899, it was native-born Sir George Turner, Deakin's friend, a little man in a shabby brown suit and soon to be first federal treasurer, who declared that 'if ever the old country were really menaced, we would spend our last man and our last shilling in her cause', a sentiment which would be echoed by Andrew Fisher at the beginning of World War I. In Perth, John Forrest turned on a member who asked questions about the justice of the British cause in South Africa, which seemed to be nakedly expansionist to many throughout the world, and declared, 'We do not want to know.' William Morris Hughes, Labor man, spoke for a sizeable Australian minority when he accused Great Britain of engaging in a cowardly undertaking to bully the Boers out of the gold and diamonds of the Transvaal and the Orange Free State.

Australia sent an extraordinary patchwork of troops to the Boer War, and there were in fact five waves of the Australian contribution. The first were the contingents raised by the Australian colonies after the outbreak of war in 1899 from the militia in the various colonies. The second were the 'bushmen' contingents, paid for by public subscription or wealthy individuals. The third were the 'imperial bushmen' contingents paid for by the government in Britain. Then there were the 'draft contingents' raised by state governments after Federation on behalf of the new Commonwealth government. And towards the close of the war Australian Commonwealth Horse Contingents were recruited by the federal government itself. The 4th Tasmanian, 6th Queensland, South Australian and Western Australian contingents did not reach South Africa until March–April 1901, just over a year before the end of the war. The Commonwealth's contingents did not embark until 1902 and most did not arrive in time for the war.

The Boers had early success, but the first Australians, between four and six contingents from each of the colonies, arrived in South Africa between November 1899 and March 1900. These men were in place in the Orange Free State to fight in the British counter-offensive of 1900. During the campaign British professionals complained of the poor training of Australian officers, though the men themselves rode and shot well. The officers were generally squatters' sons, and the troopers were generally shearers, station hands, farmers or a few as yet unelevated squatters.

The first Australians arrived in Cape Town in December 1899 after the 'black week' of 10–17 December when the British lost three engagements with the Boers. By February, with Australian mounted regiments—the South Australians on the left, the Western Australians and the Tasmanians on the right—were defending a semi-circular position, connected by farmhouses and small hills, at Colesburg, hundreds of miles up the Central Railway in the Northern Cape. Two Australian newspaper correspondents, Alfred Smiler Hayes, former boxing promoter, writing for the *London Daily News* and Jack Lambie, weathered correspondent for the *Age*, were amongst the first shot dead, but the Australian troopers, fiercely attacked by confident Boers, just as adept in the saddle and with a rifle as the Australians, fell by the dozens. A regiment of the Wiltshires came up in support, the line was held, and an officer said of the confused action that he did not know whether the Australians had saved the Wiltshires or the Wiltshires the Australians.

Meanwhile, in February 1900, 500 Queenslanders and New South Welshmen were riding and marching towards Kimberley in the Orange Free State in a great British column led by Lord Roberts. It was tough and thirsty going. 'We killed our horses and almost killed ourselves to relieve the Diamond City,' wrote *Sydney Morning Herald* correspondent Banjo Paterson. He saw many falling over with enteric fever, then the common name for typhoid. Medical facilities were scarce. Banjo wrote, 'Passed some infantry that had been on the march for days and were pretty well exhausted. It was pitiful to see them, half delirious with heat and thirst, dropping out of the ranks and throwing themselves down in the sun, often too far gone to shelter their heads from the sun, but letting their helmets roll off and lie beside them'. The Scot's Greys were next to the New South Wales contingent and were well mounted, 'but their big English horses were not standing it as well as our leathery Walers'. When the column reached the Modder River, they cleared the Boers away from the crossing by a charge-cum-stampede initiated by the horses sniffing the water.

The cock-sparrow, Banjo, was aware that the war was internationally unpopular. 'The German emperor was sending messages of congratulation to Kruger [the Boer general] and the American Press were roasting the war for all they were worth.' But, amongst all his reporting, he had the mental space to engage in an argument with Colonel Haig, the future field marshal, about whether the horses of the tin bellies, the Life Guards, were better than the Australian horses. Paterson had something of a last word in his less than distinguished but popular 'To Kimberley with French':

And in the front the Lancers rode that New South Wales had sent,
With easy stride across the plain their long lean walers went.

General French's column drove the Boers away from the outskirts of Kimberley, into which the troops rode to a 'howling, shrieking, cheering crowd'. With the off-handed anti-Semitism of his day, Paterson mentioned that French was officially received by a Jewish gentleman 'who probably owned a gold diamond mine', and whose opening words were, 'Veil, general, vy didn't you come before?' The Boers withdrew and the troopers sat down in the streets of the city to eat horse soup.

Field Marshal Roberts' advance on Bloemfontein and Pretoria from the west was fascinating in detail, especially as recounted by Banjo Paterson. He brought to the deeds of the Australians the same romantic view he had expressed in 'The Man from Snowy River'. For example, he wrote of the cool-headed courage of a Sydney barrister, Captain Robert Lenehan, soon to command the famous Bushveldt Carabineers, of which Breaker Morant was a lieutenant. Genuinely remarkable was Trooper Lawrence Palmer of the Australian Horse, who was shot in the head and kept riding and fighting till he fell from his horse from loss of blood. The unworthy joke went around amongst the British that you couldn't stop an Australian by shooting him where the brain was supposed to be.

Men of the New South Wales Mounted Rifles had a part in what was to be their last major battle at Paardeberg in Cape Province in the same month. The Boer army became fragmented thereafter, forming commando units. Mounted troops were suitable for the pursuit of these groups. But enteric fever (typhoid) wiped out so many troopers that it—rather than determined Boer skirmishers fighting for their homes—became the major killer. During a period of rest in the newly captured town of Bloemfontein a further typhoid epidemic broke out because of corpses and human waste in the water supply. The Australians, given that so many of them had experience in the bush, were better than the British, often urban, soldier at boiling water and excreting at a safe distance from water sources. But at the hospitals in Bloemfontein, full of typhus cases (arising from lice bites), Australians were also amongst the dying, and amongst them was yet another correspondent, Horace Spooner, who wrote for two Sydney newspapers. The Anglican Reverend Frederick Wray, 'the sporting chaplain', accomplished Australian Rules footballer, spent all his days soothing the dying and burying the dead. Here as elsewhere a lack of wood meant that men were buried in sewn-up blankets. As ever, the military had an interest in the fighting soldiers but were skimping on the 'in-effectives', that is, the wounded and dead.

On 28 July 1900 in the Caledon Valley in the West Cape, Banjo Paterson saw the Boers caught 'like sheep without a shepherd. They had thousands of cattle and sheep with them.' Also in their retinue were 'women, children and Kaffirs . . .'. Another time, travelling with surgeons under a truce to collect a wounded British soldier the Boers had captured, Paterson found his party right in the middle of a Boer commando. 'We saw a lot of rough, dirty, bearded men, just like a crowd of shearers or farmhands.' But these Boers were self-supplying. 'Each man was his own ordnance, supply and remount department.'

One of Paterson's fellow campaigners was a young English journalist considered both brash and reckless, who would have a massive impact on Australia's future without ever setting foot there. This was Winston Churchill, who had already reported on Kitchener's revenge campaign in the Sudan. Paterson and the young Winston Churchill travelled together, though a lot of their time was spent hanging around headquarters. According to Paterson, writing at a time before Churchill had achieved any status as a great politician, the young Englishman said to him, 'This correspondent job is nothing to me; but I mean to get into

Parliament through it. They wouldn't listen to me when I put up for Parliament, because they had never heard of me. Now I am going to plaster the *Morning Post* with cables about our correspondent, Mr Winston Churchill, driving an armoured train, or pointing out to Lord Roberts where the enemy is.' The man was a curious combination of ability and swagger, said Paterson, and the army could neither understand nor like him.

From September 1900 Australian troops were sent to sweep the countryside and enforce the severe policy of cutting the Boer guerrillas off from the support of their farms and families. It was a long, weary, not particularly meritorious guerrilla phase which would last until 1902. It was in the latter phase that Breaker Morant, feeling he had implied authorisation to do so, executed a number of Boers and was himself tried and executed as a result of his actions. The attitudes to the Boers did not improve the behaviour of Australian and other troopers on the veldt. The burning of farms, the confiscation of horses, cattle and wagons and the rounding up of the inhabitants, usually women and children, made up a great part of soldiers' activities. So also did the long night rides, followed by an attack on a Boer farmhouse or encampment at dawn. The Boers were generally quickly overwhelmed or flitted into country they knew well. Guerrilla war hardens the soul, and moving with his contingent on the village of Bethel in May 1901 a Queensland trooper, George Horsburgh, felt no remorse when the village was set fire to and its inhabitants moved to one of Kitchener's concentration camps. In the last five months of 1901, the New South Wales Mounted Rifles trekked over 1800 miles (3000 kilometres) and were involved in thirteen skirmishes for the loss of five dead and nineteen wounded. They reported killing twenty-seven Boers, wounding fifteen and capturing just under 200.

A majority of people at home became disenchanted as the conflict dragged on, especially as the effect of the war on Boer detainees was reported on by an outraged international press. For by mid-1901 General Kitchener had copied the Spanish procedure for pacifying Cuba and removed women, children and old people from farms, along with any male who surrendered his rifle and took the oath of loyalty. The first two camps Kitchener ordered opened were at Pretoria and Bloemfontein. Some 28 000 Boers died in the camps, of whom 22 000 were children. 'It is a war,' complained the Liberal politician Lloyd George, 'not against soldiers but against women and children.' Over 100 000 black Africans were also detained to prevent them from being of use to the Boers.

Two hundred and eighty-two Australians died in action or from wounds, while 286 died from disease, from a total of at least 16 000 men engaged. Without belittling those deaths, the casualty rate caused the public and the authorities to expect a similar lenient death rate in a future great war in Europe.

THE LONDON STRUGGLE

By the time Western Australia voted Yes, a number of Australian delegates who had taken the bill to London, especially Barton and Deakin, were at the frazzled end of battling the British cabinet to have it passed without amendment in Westminster. The British Colonial Secretary, Joseph Chamberlain, had earlier suggested a team of Australian delegates should come to London to help him oversee the bill's passage through Parliament. Some thought it an unwise move to accept the invitation, since the presence of Australians as the watchdogs of the bill might actually encourage Chamberlain to seek amendments. Chamberlain was a high Tory and in some ways a monocled incarnation of imperial arrogance. He gave very little weight to the fact that Australians, colony by colony, had ratified this bill as it was, and decided it would be necessary to amend it for its passage through the British Parliament. There was also the possibility that further amendments might be moved in either the House of Commons or the Lords. So he must be dealt with if the bill as approved by colonial citizens was to be ratified by Westminster.

George Reid and William Lyne were disgruntled that there was only one man the public in New South Wales would want to see appointed to go to London—Barton. The New South Wales delegate and unofficial leader of the federal team, Barton, was much in need of the fee attached to this work, and dearly wanted to go. Barton had, said Deakin, an 'inability to live within his income' and an 'indifference to resulting embarrassments'. The Victorian government of course appointed Deakin. Charles Kingston would represent South Australia and James Dickson Queensland.

Dickson was a Brisbane merchant, not native born like the others but born in Plymouth, and was interested in Federation chiefly because Queensland could not risk either isolation nor being written off later as a non-founding state. Although he would ultimately be appointed Minister of Defence in the first federal cabinet, he was a diabetes sufferer, and would become ill at the Federation ceremonies in Sydney on 1 January 1901 and die there on 10 January after only a week in office. But for the moment, in 1900, he was more interested in the Empire than in Federation, and would side with Joseph Chamberlain over the idea that there *should* be enshrined in the constitution a broad right of appeal to the Privy Council of Great Britain against decisions of the High Court. Should, for example, a British company, or indeed any person or body in Australia, lose its case before the Australian High Court, a final appeal could be to the Privy Council of Great Britain, an appeal which had been available to litigants in the colonies.

Sir Philip Fysh, Agent-General for Tasmania, would act as that state's representative in negotiations with the British government, and Sir John Forrest appointed S.H. Parker, a Perth lawyer with a large family to support, was delegated to get special concessions for Western Australia, a task at which, despite his charm, Parker failed.

In March 1900, having resigned from the colonial Parliament, Barton and his wife Jeanie arrived in London. He was to be, with Deakin's emphatic endorsement, the leader of the Australian delegation. In the published journal he would keep, Deakin would write subtle and clear-eyed assessments of his fellow Australians and of the British leaders and nobility they met and dealt with. Deakin was far from being seduced by the supposed splendour and superior wisdom of the British ministry. The Tory Prime Minister Robert Cecil (Lord Salisbury), a member of the famous family of Hatfield House, was a man of over seventy years. He seemed to Deakin the 'idol that middle-class philistinism most love to rest upon ... His speeches contained indiscretions enough to have ruined a dozen Cabinets in the colonies but scarcely shook him in the estimation of his countrymen.'

Deakin believed that many of those he met would not be in politics except for the circumstances of their birth. Arthur Balfour owed his position, said Deakin, to the fact that he was Lord Salisbury's nephew. Indeed the term 'Bob's your uncle' is said to have derived from the relationship between Lord Salisbury and his nephew. He was the member responsible for pursuing the war in South Africa and had lost a great deal of credit from the exercise. Chamberlain, says Deakin, was by contrast the classic businessman—'Neither student nor philosopher nor man of culture'. The opposition Liberals, by contrast, were more to his taste and had merited their positions to a great degree.

Joseph Chamberlain probably walked into his meetings in Whitehall with the delegates from Australia with the idea that they would be as divided as had been the various colonial delegates at the first imperial conference of 1887, and would be concerned chiefly with ceremonial matters as were the delegates of 1897. Mr Chamberlain and his officials sat on one side of the table and the Australians upon the other, 'both parties preserving a polite antagonism to each other'. Chamberlain knew that he had an advantage over them—they needed him to guide the bill through Parliament—and he was willing to use that lever. He could delay the introduction of the bill to the British Parliament as long as he wanted. He possessed, said Deakin, 'the consciousness of all the means of coercion he enjoyed'. There were a number of sections of the constitution which the ruling Tory ministers would have liked to have seen eliminated, including Section 51, which gave the Australian Parliament control of foreign affairs and of the relations of the Commonwealth with the islands of the Pacific. Chamberlain, however, pushed none of those amendments. Even though in the end the British government, who were at base in favour of Federation, decided not to hamper the bill, Chamberlain had other issues to fight on.

At that first conference on 15 March, Chamberlain welcomed the delegates and said that the British government had decided not to ask for any amendments except those it deemed absolutely necessary. One of these amendments was to Covering Clause 2, and its objectionable declaration that 'This Act shall bind the Crown'. The claim that the laws of the Commonwealth should be binding upon British ships whose port of clearance or whose port of destination was in the Commonwealth should also be removed. Above all, Section 74, which denied appeals from the Federal High Court to the Privy Council of Britain, could not be permitted, Chamberlain said. 'He could not conceive of any refusal [by the Australians] as warrantable or possible and although without arrogance, spoke as a lord paramount or at least a predominant partner.' Chamberlain wanted it clearly stated too that the Colonial Laws Validity Act, a British act, would apply to all federal legislation. That is, he wanted British legislation to override Australian legislation in the case of any conflict between the two. He also confused the delegates by expressing surprise that the Australians should send troops to the Boer War, a war which had little to do with their own interests. But, he told them as well that he objected to the idea that the Colonial Office should be a mere registry bureau for decisions already made by colonials.

All the delegates now spoke in reply. Barton made the point that the bill should be accepted with no alteration, but then seemed to yield and say that there should be as little alteration as possible. Chamberlain would later use that concession against him. Deakin seems to have been more direct and confessed his amazement that amendments should be requested so late in the day, when the British could have commented on the bill before it was presented to the Australian people. If any changes were forced on the delegates, then they would need to be referred back to the Australian people, delaying Federation indefinitely. James Dickson, on the other hand, told Mr Chamberlain that the entrance of that colony in the federal compact depended on the Colonial Office interfering to make the constitution acceptable to Queensland, and that the Premier of Western Australia, Sir John Forrest, was only hesitating in calling a referendum because he hoped the Colonial Office would change the bill in Western Australia's favour. If the British government did not interfere, Forrest would have no option but to accept the bill as it stood.

The Australian delegates asked that the amendments be presented in detail the next day. It was, said Deakin, an 'unpropitious beginning'. The delegates, however, met up privately at their hotel, and Deakin and Barton argued that there should be unity at all costs, that they had everything to lose and nothing to gain by each colony making its own statements and variations through their individual mouths, and that they must oppose any amendment. This argument was aimed at stopping Dickson from breaking ranks. The next morning, Deakin, Barton, hulking Kingston and the rest were back in front of Chamberlain demanding again that the draft Australian Constitution, the bill, should be accepted without criticism or further consideration and that 'legislative independence [should be] recognised as amply as was that of the United States after their separation'. This was exactly the brand of colonial impudence Chamberlain hated. He confided to one of his British colleagues that if the delegates thought that they were going to get their bill through without amendment, 'he'd see them damned first'. He was determined to insist on some amendment, however small, simply to show them that he was their imperial master.

One night during the negotiations, the delegates attended a dinner held by the New Zealand Agent-General, William Pember Reeves, a former journalist and New Zealand politician. Despite Deakin's disregard for Reeves' 'restless ambition and cold temperament which rendered him incapable of loyalty', he was a brilliant speaker. After the meal, Reeves rose to attack Australian Federation and urge its delay not only because of the Privy Council argument, on which he sided with Chamberlain, but because of the damage it would wreak on New Zealand trade. The amendment of the bill to secure totally unrestricted rights of appeal from Australian courts to the Privy Council should be presented all over again to the Australian people at referendum, as part of a new Federation bill. 'Nor should there be any hurry to pass the bill as it stands ... Australian federation which we all desire, may wait a short twelve months more.' The delegates would not like this, he admitted. 'They naturally wish for their own Australia.' The entire Reeves speech was reproduced in the *St James Gazette* the next morning, along with a report of a Reeves interview, in which he admitted that New Zealand did in fact desire the privilege of coming into the Federation at any time after it occurred but by her own will and at her pleasure. After the article appeared, Reeves sent a message to the delegates asking them for a meeting. Deakin, Barton and Kingston told him that to have New Zealand and Western Australia asking for the same amendments as the British government made a meeting pointless.

The three Federation champions now decided that Deakin, with his direct, pungent but accurate style, should be the one to frame the delegates' memoranda on the bill. These were to be presented to the British cabinet and should have some impact. To help Deakin, Kingston prepared his own energetic notes, and so did Barton in his scholarly but long-winded style. At the same time, Deakin had to acknowledge Dickson's position and the uncertain Western Australian views.

The reply of the British ministry to the first memorandum was in the same tone as that of Chamberlain—'Peremptory,' said Deakin, 'incisive, clear and in the nature of an ultimatum.' A second memorandum was prepared now in which the delegates politely declined to abandon their position. Dickson from Queensland, however, 'went boldly over to the enemy' and would not sign it. Kingston refused to go on with any discussion in Dickson's presence, and Dickson withdrew from the delegation. The proposed parties to Federation had split in two right in front of their imperial hosts. There were reasons. The Queensland Chief Justice, Sir Samuel Griffith, had been writing to Dickson, stiffening his resistance to the others. The atmosphere over the breakfast table of the delegates, with Edmund Barton's wife Jeanie frowning at Dickson as solemnly as did her husband, must have been less than easy. Dickson received many telegrams from the Queensland government, upon whom, he implied to other delegates, the blame lay for the position he was in. But Dickson after all was a colonial British businessman who did not want his commercial interests entirely at the mercy of an unpredictable Australian High Court which did not yet exist.

On 5 April, a conference open to all interested parties was held at the Colonial Office. Chamberlain knew that four of the delegates—the Western Australian Parker feeling he must be solidly with Deakin and the others despite his doubts—would not waver but that there were two, the Tasmanian Fysh and Queensland's Dickson, who were on his side and who could be persuaded to stay on it. Dickson in particular would take notice if Chamberlain threatened that the attitude of the others would cause a dangerous and unbrotherly split between Britain and

Australia. These two, said Deakin, 'had a deeper deference towards the authorities ... They were visibly apologetic.' Chamberlain began with an attack on the delegates' position. He said the case of New Zealand's trade would need to be assessed and that the desire of Forrest and Parker that Western Australia should go on collecting its own customs duties was a pressing one. He told Deakin, Barton and the others that if they did not give way on this minor point, federation of the states would be delayed. But under the bluster, Chamberlain himself was starting to retreat. He was willing to let the Australians have their way on controlling British shipping. But the Colonial Laws Validity Act would need to be accepted as applying to every law the future federal government would pass, and then, the old point, appeals to the Privy Council from decisions of the High Court should be as broadly allowed as they were under the laws of the various colonies.

The responses of the delegates were predictable. Barton answered that it was not within the rights of delegates to consent to an amendment of a constitution already voted on by the Australian electors, and that the delay and expense of a third referendum would be odious to Australians. Kingston declared that he had his instructions from South Australia and he was not intending to ask for further ones. The convention of 1891, he told Chamberlain, composed of representatives from the whole of the colonies, had voted to prohibit any appeals of any kind to the courts of Great Britain. The Australian courts were the Queen's courts just as much as any who sat in Britain. He then answered Chamberlain with Chamberlain's own brand of blackmail—he said that the good relations between Australia and the mother country should not be disturbed by harmful delay and useless debate.

Now it was Deakin's turn. The main interest of New Zealand, he said, was to go on exporting her goods into Australia, and these goods would be subjected to Australian customs if New Zealand did not join. As for the Western Australians, the concession asked by them was small, but it was the fault of their representatives to the conventions and at the premiers' conferences that this issue had not been worked out then. The issue of the Privy Council and Section 74, the relevant section, was not raised by Britain before the first referendum was held, and this led the Australians to think there was no objection. Deakin then rang the changes on Kingston's threat: the generosity of the British Parliament towards the Australian Constitution would, he felt sure, 'be repaid by an immediate endeavour in the Australian legislature to meet their wishes as far as possible'.

By now, the three champions of the constitution, Barton, Kingston and

Deakin, had written home suggesting that any reply to the British government sent by a new conference of premiers held to consider the issue should be sent to the delegates first so that they could refine it. That was done. Deakin and company wanted to insert further and more aggressive sentiments, such as, 'The Premiers feel it their undoubted duty to strongly represent that either of these courses [amending the constitution or postponing it] would be distasteful and harassing and try the patience of the people.' In the fourth paragraph the premiers urged that the voice of the Australian people should receive 'favourable consideration'. But the big three begged them to state their abhorrence for amendments. Each of the three privately telegraphed his own premier urging him to stand up against amendments.

Indeed, Deakin, Kingston and Barton were told that at home they were getting only tepid support, while the London press could not understand why they were holding out on such a small matter. So they decided to take on public opinion themselves and preach 'the gospel of the Bill without amendment'. When members of the Tory government, arguing with them in conference, also invited them to visit the palaces, country estates and clubs of London privilege, the three hard-core delegates, instead of being overwhelmed by their lush surroundings, began to lobby people. On any evening or weekend they could be found arguing their case at the residences of Lord Landsdowne, Lord James of Hereford, Lord Hopetoun (the future first governor-general of the coming Commonwealth), Lord Windsor and Lord Rosebery, as well as those of Sir Charles Dilke and other leading Liberals. Quite a number of Chamberlain's colleagues now became convinced of the rightness of the Australian case. Even Chamberlain's seniors, Arthur Balfour and the Duke of Devonshire, began to ask him whether his stubbornness was wise.

In London one night that spring the British Empire League brought the Prince of Wales and his son, the Duke of York, to hear Mr Barton speak. The National Liberal Club, the City Liberal Club, the Constitutional Senior and Junior Clubs, the Press Clubs, the Anglo-Saxon Colonial Clubs, the Fishmongers' Guild, the National Conservative Union and the London Chamber of Commerce, along with many others, served as venues for the three. Sir Julian Salomons, Agent-General for New South Wales, had undermined Barton and his friends by arguing against Clause 74, and at the City Liberal Club Barton and Sir Julian had an angry exchange of opinions. But the overall effect was that Chamberlain, in making the delegates so welcome as promising colonial vassals, had given them platforms from which they could attack him.

At last Chamberlain told the delegation that the final conference was to be held on 8 May 1900, before the bill was introduced to the House of Commons on 14 May. The meeting began. 'Coldly, with impassive demeanour and sententious deliberation, Chamberlain stated his case.' The argument was still the Colonial Laws Validity Act matter, which of course the delegates saw as an intrusion on Australian sovereignty, and the right of appeal to the Privy Council. Chamberlain accused the delegates, in a voice that vibrated, of not having given proper attention to the amendments. He declared that he was 'disappointed and pained at the tone of the last memo'. No British parliament could be coerced in this fashion, he said.

The three companions had already decided that if Chamberlain did not move they would threaten to leave London since their presence there could no longer serve any purpose. But Barton spoke and forgot to say so, sitting down prematurely to prevent himself completely losing his temper. As for Kingston, he was almost 'inarticulate with suppressed vexation'. Dickson, said Deakin, 'was brief and triumphant'. When Deakin's turn came, he accused Chamberlain and the Colonial Office of having omitted to take notice earlier of the draft constitution which had been extant in various forms since 1891. The only way he could see out of the dilemma was to create the federation and leave it to the federal government to alter the parts of the bill the British wanted altered, but even so he believed the Colonial Laws Validity Act should not apply at all. But, he said, for the British government to insist on the amendments at the expense of the Commonwealth bill 'was a fatal mistake likely to be fruitful of ill will'. The bill was dear to them all, said Deakin, not only because they were amongst its begetters but because it had been so dearly bought. 'The pride in it and the love of it which the Australian people cherished were sentiments to be studied and not ignored, and to be satisfied, not offended, and might be rendered a motive power of perpetual gratitude.' If Chamberlain and the British cabinet would just accept it!

The announcement of the disagreement with the delegates, and the determination of the British government to insist upon changing Section 74, created little press interest or sympathy. Chamberlain invited the delegates to dine with him that night. For the three great Federalists it was a wistful, half-amiable dinner. Deakin left early. Barton, Deakin and Kingston met the next day to look at a proposed Section 74 as it was now reframed by the law officers of the Crown. The accepted new Section 74 declared in layman's terms that no appeal should be made to the Privy Council ('the Queen in Council') upon any question which challenged the powers of the Commonwealth, or on any conflict concerning the constitutional powers of states, unless the High Court certified that it should happen. The constitution would not intrude on the Queen's prerogative to give special leave of appeal from the High Court to the council, but the Australian Parliament had the power to limit the matters in which leave could be asked. In other words, the whiphand belonged to the Australian High Court and to the Australian Parliament. They realised at once that they had won. The new clause suggested appeals to the Privy Council on constitutional matters and those involving British interests be allowed only by the consent of the respective governments of Australia and Great Britain. And it left Australian laws immune from imperial revision. This gave Australia the effective sovereignty it sought.

The delegates were delighted, while Chamberlain himself pretended to have prevailed. After the meeting with Chamberlain had ended and 'the door closed upon them [the delegates] and left them alone, they seized each other's hands and danced hand in hand in a ring around the centre of the room to express their jubilation'. It was easier to imagine Kingston dancing better than Deakin, but it seems to have been the truth: two whiskered men and a clean-shaven one doing the Federation waltz. The proposed amendment was wired to the premiers and when no reply came the delegates signed a short note accepting the new arrangement and taking entire responsibility for it on their shoulders. The settlement was announced to the crowded House of Commons by Chamberlain. Chamberlain's speech was, Deakin admitted, masterful. The passage of the bill was assured.

Yet Dickson's wrath and mortification at what had happened was, according to Deakin, undisguised. Dickson, Griffith and the Queensland government attacked the compromise Section 74 which put the control of judgments on the constitution back in Australian hands. It was now the preserve of the Australian Parliament to permit appeals to the Privy Council if it chose. The Australian Natives Association applauded the delegates as did the South Australian politicians Symon and Downer and the New South Welshman Dick O'Connor, but the rest of Australia, said Deakin, 'shrieked censure upon the daring delegates'. The influential classes of the Australian colonies and the press were determined to strike out the new Clause 74 and leave an unrestricted right of appeal to the Privy Council on all matters. But when the bill passed through the British Parliament, the argument was all at once over, and the naysayers accepted it.

Deakin left London and travelled on the Continent, suffering from a rash of carbuncles, no doubt brought on by the stress of the experience he had been through. He said he was still pelted with telegrams every day, but some of them were from Kingston denouncing the Chief Justices around Australia who were all attacking the new Section 74.

Australia would federate, and the founding documents of the Australian community were signed in Sydney on 1 January 1901. It was time to reach for the bunting and the protocol books.

THE BIRTHDAY

The first Governor-General of the new Commonwealth, part of his task being the exercise of the reserve powers under the Constitution (the giving of royal assent to the bill, the ceremonial headship of armed forces, the invitation to the leader of an electorally successful party to try to form a government, and so on), was a trim little fellow of more charm than charisma, the Earl of Hopetoun. In his care also was put the duty of seeing that Australian legislation did not damage imperial interests. Though the British government did not expect this to be likely to happen, there was after all a Labor Party, better developed than that of the United Kingdom, some of whose members espoused classic socialist aims.

Hopetoun had been born in 1860, a Scot educated at Eton and Sandhurst on the basis of an enormous family estate on the Firth of Forth. Its management had absorbed him until he became Conservative Whip in the House of Lords in 1883. He was a known quantity to at least some Australians. He had been Governor of Victoria during the 1890s depression and, in that hard-up age, had entertained extravagantly in Melbourne's Government House, a matter of admiration to some and shock to others. But he went on impromptu rides around Melbourne and made friends easily with citizens he encountered. The *Bulletin* claimed he had more broken bones from riding horses than any man in Australia.

In 1898 he declined the post of Governor-General of Canada and became Lord Chamberlain, but in 1900, for whatever reason, he accepted the governor-generalship of the Commonwealth of Australia. On the journey to Australia he became ill with typhoid fever, and Lady Ethelred Hopetoun, a more imperious being than her husband, fell ill to malaria.

Tall, robust Premier William Lyne of New South Wales, a Tasmanian originally but a dubious Federalist who had, in alliance with Labor, passed an impressive list of reform bills regarding arbitration, work hours, and factory reform, had begun to charm Hopetoun as soon as his ship, the *Royal Arthur*, reached Jervis Bay. Like Lord Hopetoun, Lyne loved thoroughbred horses and was a cheery fellow with an infectious laugh. For the ship's arrival in Sydney on 15 December 1900, Lyne organised a great harbour spectacular. On 18 December Lord Hopetoun asked the advice of a number of men, including the Chief Justice and George Reid, about who should be invited to form a cabinet and, if successful, become prime minister. He did not seem to consult any Federalists. But Lyne was native born, premier of the senior colony, and so was eligible in Hopetoun's eyes, and he issued a commission to Lyne to form a government. There was outrage amongst Federationists but a narky feeling from others that it served men like Barton right for being such zealots.

Deakin wrote to Barton from the Australian Club in Melbourne on 20 December, telling him that the *Age* had accepted Lyne, and the political advisers to the Victorian government were settling down to accepting him too. 'The whole business makes me sick with disgust.' Deakin's opinion of Lyne was not informed by Christian charity either: 'A smooth, sleek, suspicious, blundering, short-sighted backblocks politician,' was Deakin's assessment. But Lyne now seemed an inevitability, and by 21 December Deakin was admitting to himself that his objections to Lyne were personal. Accepting him for now would give Barton greater moral and political power, Deakin thought. 'I wrote last night in bitterness,' he told Barton. 'I write this morning in sorrow. I have braced Turner [the premier] up and will try . . . in an hour or two to secure you the leadership, but even failing that in my judgement it is your duty to join Lyne . . . Australia will suffer if you refuse to crucify yourself.' Richard O'Connor, in a letter to Barton, declared, 'Hopetoun's surroundings have obviously been too much for him, they have been all Lyne and his government.'

Lyne now consulted the premiers of three other states—Queensland (Robert Philp of the famous shipping, trading and blackbirding company Burns Philp), South Australia (Frederick Holder) and George Turner of Victoria, all in Sydney for the celebrations. Forrest of Western Australia, an admirer of Barton's, was still in transit. The three premiers told Lyne they believed that Alfred Deakin and a number of leading Federalists would never agree to serve in a Lyne cabinet. Therefore, they said, Lyne could not form a credible government, and so he should advise Lord Hopetoun to send for Barton, who could. When Deakin's and Barton's friends O'Connor, Bernhard Ringrose Wise and Charlie Kingston refused to accept cabinet positions under him, Lyne rode to Government House, returned his commission to Hopetoun, and suggested Barton be immediately called on.

Barton had no trouble in finding a cabinet (always allowing that each of them managed to win a federal seat in coming elections). He wanted a largely Protectionist cabinet, raising its revenues from tariffs and protecting its people with them. But he sought one which represented all the states. He invited each premier to take a cabinet position. Philp did not want to leave Queensland, and so the sick and soon-to-die Dickson had to serve. Lyne had to be invited in and, to his credit, never became viperous towards Barton. Though his ambitions to be prime minister remained, they would never be fulfilled. Turner of Victoria and Forrest of Western Australia accepted at once, but Holder of South Australia was away on a holiday and could not be reached. So the recent premier and congenial soul Kingston was invited in. Holder would be desolated, but was promised the post of first Speaker of the House. Likeable Neil Lewis, Premier of Tasmania, accepted but would resign in April before elections took place. And then Deakin and O'Connor, not premiers of the moment but great federal leaders, men dear to Barton, were offered cabinet posts.

Gathered together in the Sydney Domain on the humid New Year's Day of 1901 were mounted Australian troops who had returned from the Boer War, as well as Australasian lancers, infantry and cadets. The colonial troops were to march beneath ten arches between the Domain and the entrance to Centennial Park with detachments of British troops (no doubt pleased to be allotted to these duties rather than to the dreary, typhoid-ridden and deadly war in South Africa). Here in their highly coloured uniforms were representatives of the Royal Horse Artillery, squadrons of various lancers and hussar regiments, the Royal Field Artillery, the Coldstream Guards, the Royal Fusiliers and a detachment from the British army in India.

Yet the procession did not have a predominantly military tone. Billy Hughes, Labor Party member of the New South Wales legislature, decided he would gather 'a goodly bunch of shearers—all mounted, each man with a packhorse, carrying his swag'. The horses would be provided in Sydney, but were to be of the sort met in the back country of Queensland and New South Wales, which Hughes knew well from his early wanderings as a young immigrant looking for work. To gather this corps of horsemen Hughes got in touch with the Australian Workers' Union, who selected the men, all union-card shearers. Hughes met them when they arrived by train at Central Station. Their mounts had been supplied by that boozy, landslide rigging member of parliament W.N. Willis, the member for Bourke, and at first meeting with the horses the shearers found them 'pretty much uncontrollable'. As Billy Hughes related it, they bolted at full gallop, some towards Camperdown, some up Regent Street, and others for the Quay. Billy himself claimed that he narrowly avoided being thrown by one of them at the mortuary station near Redfern, from which the funeral trains departed for Rookwood cemetery. Ultimately Mr Hughes, having marshalled a band to train with the riders, got the horses used to noise and musical instruments. The shearers and their mounts became his contribution to the great federal nuptials.

For the procession route there was an arch to welcome the Governor-General, there were American, French, German and other community arches, a Citizens' Commonwealth arch, a Melbourne arch, a Chinese arch and so on. Miners wielding picks stood ready on the walls of the coal arch. Beneath these arches would travel the 'allegorical cars'—floats, including ones representing the Canadians, Japanese and Italians.

An Aboriginal arch was attended by sixty Aboriginal men, women and children. The Aborigines had no place in the Constitution except in Section 127, which read, 'In reckoning the number of people of the Commonwealth, or of a state or other part of the Commonwealth, Aboriginal natives shall not be counted.' While the clause might have been motivated by a desire to keep down the contribution per capita of population that the states with large Aboriginal populations, such as South Australia, contributed to initiating the Common-wealth, it would nonetheless continue as a noxious and ambiguous presence within the document.

Two hundred policemen marched with the troops that day, as did silver miners wearing lamps and carrying picks, coal miners, gold miners and tin miners, all in white with sashes. They were joined by house painters, timber-getters, seamen and maritime engineers, bakers, furniture makers with miniature pieces of furni-ture on the end of sticks, and so on. Then came two carriages with presidents and secretaries of the Labor Leagues, the executives of major unions and the New South Wales Labor Council. After these came members of lodges and friendly societies. Fire fighters and church leaders preceded the politicians (including those who had opposed the bill), judges and senior academics. Cardinal Moran, who had spoken up for Federation at a Bathurst convention and thus secured many Irish-Catholic Yes votes, would not accept the idea that he should march in front of, and thus have lower precedence than, the Anglican Archbishop, William Saumarez Smith. A cardinal trumped an archbishop, Moran argued. The organisers asserted that their choice was in no way sectarian, but that the Anglican Archbishop represented the largest body of adherents in Australia. Wesleyan, Presbyterian and Methodist leaders also boycotted the procession over order of precedence, but other Christian and Jewish clergy did take part. Though Moran withdrew from the procession, he chose to stand alongside the choir of 2000 Catholic schoolchildren on the steps of St Mary's to wave and chorale the procession on its way.

Despite a stormy previous night, it was a characteristic hot and humid midsummer day. In fact, some soldiers collapsed from the heat—one newspaper declared that some of these were 'sweating Tommies' but others were Australians. A policeman was killed by a runaway horse and several horses were burned to death in a city police station when decorative Chinese lanterns set the building alight. But in Darlinghurst gaol a Mr Choice, awaiting execution for the murder of his wife, had been given back his life for Federation's sake, his sentence being commuted to life imprisonment. Where people felt remote from the colonial capitals there were processions too, a large one at Rockhampton, even though the Chinese came close to destroying their decorations when they heard that they were excluded from a march to the Rockhampton football ground.

At last, in Centennial Park, under a temporary canopy, at a place now marked by an undistinguished little pagoda, the Anglican Archbishop recited the Lord's Prayer, a prayer for the Commonwealth and a prayer for the Governor-General. The Declaration of the Commonwealth and the reading of the Letters Patent of the Governor-General, Lord Hopetoun, then occurred. The Oath of Office was administered to the new Prime Minister and his cabinet. Deakin shook with the weight of the moment. Barton was Prime Minister and Minister for External Affairs, Lyne was Minister for Home Affairs, Deakin and Turner were Attorney-General and Treasurer respectively, Charlie Kingston was Minister for Trade and Customs, Forrest from Western Australia was Postmaster-General, Dickson of Queensland was Minister for Defence—a gesture to cosset that state—and Neil Lewis the Tasmanian was Minister without Portfolio. The table on which Queen Victoria had signed the Act the previous year had been brought to Australia and was set up under the pavilion in Centennial Park. As commissions were signed by the still-sickly Lord Hopetoun, a hot wind blew some realistic grit in through the flaps to take pretension out of the moment. Papers flew off the table and officials ran around picking them up off the ground. Some of the ministers sworn in on 1 January wore the official dress of members of the British cabinet—the so-called Windsor uniform of silk breeches, stockings and braided and gold-buttoned coat. Barton wore a morning suit, however, and Deakin a normal suit of business. 'God Save the Queen' was sung, as was the Hallelujah chorus, 'Advance Australia Fair' and 'Rule Britannia'.

Australia's first Federal day had been hard on the Governor-General and his wife, Ethelred, and this explained their absence from the official banquet on the night of Australia's inauguration. Even so, Hopetoun's future would not be glittering. He would spend two and a half years in the post, annoying Barton and a number of other people, including the Australian Natives Association, by criticising Australia's delay in sending further troops to South Africa. He would die before the decade was out of pernicious anaemia. But on Australia's natal day he had been a presence in a cocked hat, which was all that was needed.

It was a matter of celebration, thought Deakin and others, that the Federation of Australia had been achieved without much external pressure and the lack of immediate threat. Australia was now, as one historian says, 'a nation, but not yet a nation-state'. But it was imagined as such by its members, and subscribed to by a mass of Australians as a special combination and community, at least a potential utopia, and as a secret well-kept.

Edmund 'Toby' Barton was in his early fifties when he became the first Prime Minister of Australia, and he was, appropriately, native born—at Glebe in January 1849. (Equally to be weighed, perhaps, in that era, was his lack of convict background.) He had been a dazzling student in the classics at Sydney University and went on to do his Master's, and he learned to debate at the Sydney Mechanics' School of Arts. He had organised several intercolonial cricket matches and umpired in some major games, including New South Wales versus Lord Harris's English XI, a game interrupted by a riot when the star Australian batsman, Billy Murdoch, was given out by a Victorian accompanying the English XI.

Barton was admitted to the bar in 1871 and entered the Legislative Assembly eight years later representing the seat of Sydney University. He was well read and handsome, and loved Shakespearean theatre and the opera. In 1882 Barton, with his considerable knowledge of constitutional law, was appointed Speaker of the House, the youngest yet. But he was able to control such rowdies as Adolphus Mudgee Taylor. Mudgee Taylor was a perpetual mover of points of order, was regularly suspended for abuse, and had even been removed from the floor by the Sergeant-at-Arms. To gain political advantage, Taylor was not above publishing the names of members who—so he claimed—were drunk in the House.

Payment of members, introduced into Victoria in 1870, would not be enacted in New South Wales until 1889, and even after he had become a minister, Barton went on representing clients in legal matters. He became affluent through his work at the bar until a devotion to the Federation cause depleted his finances in the 1890s.

He was a convivial man who spent much time at the Athenaeum Club, frequented by John Archibald, founder of the *Bulletin*, by William Bede Dalley, artist Julian Ashton, writer Louis Becke and James Fairfax of the *Herald*. Throughout the 1890s he set up several Federation Leagues. His allies included his secretary, Queenslander Atlee Hunt; Robert Garran, a classicist and author of *The Coming Commonwealth* who would act as secretary of the drafting committee of the crucial 1897 convention; and a young lawyer and future Premier of New South Wales, Thomas Bavin. It was Garran who would record Barton's great aphorism uttered in a speech at the Sydney suburb of Ashfield: 'For the first time in history, we have a nation for a continent and a continent for a nation.'

At last all that colonial in-fighting had ended. Barton would afterwards describe how ordinarily the government of the Commonwealth began. All the early business was done at a table in a closed-off verandah of a government building, where he was assisted by Hunt (who dressed so well that people often mistook him for the Prime Minister), Garran, who was to be secretary of the attorney-general's department, and one messenger. The Governor-General would come over daily from Government House to keep up on the planning for elections and for the first opening of Parliament in Melbourne. When Barton moved to Melbourne the state government there gave him similarly cramped quarters to work in.

Barton's first task was to arrange for the federal elections to be held. In the House he would represent the electorate of Hunter, and that January, as the indomitable Jeanie Barton prepared the household for a move to Melbourne, he gave his policy speech to an excited audience in the West Maitland town hall, with both Deakin and Lyne in attendance. He declared that this was 'the first time in history in which it is allowed to one body of men to govern a whole continent'. He promised to find a site for the federal capital as soon as possible, to create a public service and a High Court, and an Interstate Commission to decide revenue disputes between states and the federal government. There must also be federal conciliation and arbitration if there was a national industrial crisis. There must be a federal railway network—he undertook to build railways to Western Australia and to Broken Hill. Female federal franchise would be legislated early, and so would a federal system of old age and invalid pensions. (As it turned out, these would not be introduced until 1908.) And, he told his enthusiastic listeners, he would introduce laws to prevent an influx of Asiatic labour and any further importation of Kanakas.

The customs department had been pre-recruited and had needed to begin operations from 1 January as the chief source of income for the federal government. 'The power of direct taxation of the Commonwealth I agree is a power not to be lightly or rashly exercised.' Since they had lost customs, the states could now only raise money through income tax. It would be, he said, 'an act of insanity' to do anything to disadvantage the states. However, it would take £700 000 to set up and run a federal government and all its activities, and therefore the Commonwealth tariffs collected by the customs department must be a high one. Within two years of the inauguration of the Commonwealth all intercolonial duties were to be dropped, and the states would immediately reap the advantage of intercolonial free trade. Western Australia could collect at a diminishing ratio over five years. In the meantime, the states should be certain that the tariffs imposed by the new government would suit their people and 'be thoroughly liberal and at the same time of a purely Australian character. The Ministry will not take any action that will have the effect of destroying State industries, and the Commonwealth will not be issued in by the pattering of the feet of people driven out of employment.'

The first elections were held on 29 and 30 March 1901. The Free Traders—city merchants and squatters and others—did well enough, especially in New South Wales where George Reid led the charge, to be confident that it would not be possible for Mr Barton to raise too high a tariff. A complex tariff system, involving different charges for various imported goods, according to their supposed capacity to undercut local products and manufacturers, would be put in place before the first session of Parliament ended in 1902. It would define Australia—managerial wages were in the age of tariffs no more than four or five times those of skilled craftsmen, and the skilled craftsman earned well, and even the labourer would be guaranteed 'frugal comfort' by the introduction in 1907, through the failure of McKay's Harvester case in the High Court, of the basic wage. This would be all the work of liberal conservatives in combination at various stages with Labor Party blocs. It did not produce as equal a society as the visionaries wanted. It did not redeem the ratty squalor of working-class suburbs (where bubonic plague had broken out in 1900), or save all the debt-ridden farms, their walls caulked from the cold with wadded newspaper and their floors made of stamped-down termite nests. The historic irony, whose force is not to be underestimated, is that the liberal conservatism of men like Barton and Deakin, influenced by the realities of Labor's parliamentary presence, would create better social conditions than would the more doctrinaire systems of industrial equality which came later here and elsewhere in the world.

OPENING BUSINESS

After Parliament was grandly opened at the Exhibition Building in Melbourne on 9 May by the Duke of York, the first session was held in the Victorian Parliament building and taken up with procedural matters. There were three distinct groupings in the first Parliament—Barton's Protectionists, Reid's Free Traders and the Labor Party led by the congenial Chris Watson. Billy Hughes was elected to the first federal Parliament as a Labor man. Alderman J.C. Beer stood against him in the West Sydney electorate, supported by local shopkeepers who disapproved of Hughes's part in legislating for early closing. Reasonably enough he declared, 'I'm afraid the Federal Parliament will have very little to do with fixing the hours of labour and levelling-up wages by means of minimum-wage acts—that will mostly be left to the states.' And then, a sure vote-winner: 'Our chief plank is, of course, a white Australia. There's no compromise about *that*. The industrious coloured brother has to go—and remain away.' Hughes polled nearly 7000 votes and Mr Beer a little over 2000. Hughes remained a Free Trade Labor man. The Labor Party was still divided along those old lines. In the meantime the tariff served very nicely as a source of finance and he would ultimately be won over by it.

There was no federal organisation yet for the Labor members who were elected to the federal Parliament in Melbourne. The caucus would come from a meeting held two days before Parliament opened and attended by eight Labor senators and fourteen members of the House of Representatives, a meeting at which the federal Labor Party was established.

None of the parties controlled Parliament on its own. And for the first but not last time in Australian history, the Prime Minister lacked the numbers to control the Senate. Whatever laws were passed came from a consensus amongst the members, but consensus was quickly achieved in May 1901 when laws were passed to create a public service for the various departments, appointment to be subject to competitive public examination. By the end of 1902 the Parliament adopted 'first past the post' voting as well as universal female franchise, thereby indirectly forcing those states who had not already given the vote to women to do so on the basis that those who had the right to vote federally also inevitably were entitled to exercise it at the state level. Women could also be candidates for election.

The unlimited franchise for Aborigines was debated and voted down. Only those natives already registered for voting in the states—that is, a minority—could vote in federal elections. There were grounds on which Aboriginal franchise could have been guaranteed. By the early 1890s Aborigines could exercise the vote in four colonies, New South Wales, Victoria, South Australia and Tasmania, and in the Northern Territory. Missionaries urged them to enrol. Western Australia and Queensland excluded Aborigines from voting because they were a high proportion of the population. But the Commonwealth Franchise Act of 1902 originally proposed giving Aborigines the unlimited franchise, but opposition came from a number of directions. The Labor leader Chris Watson feared that if the 'thousands upon thousands' of Aborigines in Queensland and Western Australia were enfranchised it would lead merely to their being 'manipulated by their employers and delivered to the anti-Labor side'. The Victorian radicals H.B. Higgins and Isaac Isaacs declared that Aborigines lacked the 'intelligence, interest or capacity' to exercise the vote. An amendment excluding them at federal level was easily passed.

Already and most pressingly, in that first year, the Parliament looked to achieve as soon as possible a White Australia through the framing, and passing in September, of an Immigration Restriction Act aimed at ending a Chinese presence, and a Pacific Islands Labourers Act. The states, which as former colonies had restricted Pacific Islanders and Chinese and non-Europeans in general from owning or leasing land or vessels, and from public works and railway building, were moved to impose further restrictions even after the federal government's legislation had passed.

It was true that the federal parliamentarians had overwhelming support for their laws concerning race, including and perhaps especially the twenty-two members of Labor. The Laborites were a mixture of Protectionists like Chris Watson and Free Traders like Billy Hughes, the midget dynamo from West Sydney, but all agreed on this. One of them, Andrew Fisher, a Scottish miner from Gympie, believed passionately that white Australians could flourish in the tropics, and no other race was needed. In the Queensland Parliament he had earlier argued at length against the use of Kanakas, and now in the federal House of Representatives he was in favour of both the acts that created White Australia.

Deakin, Attorney-General, the first speaker in the immigration restriction debate, declared that the Commonwealth did not want to offend foreigners, and did not argue racial superiority. It was purely a matter of protecting the equity of white Australians in their country. Deakin confessed an intellectual interest in Buddhism and Hinduism, but he wanted to avoid for Australians the poverty he had seen in India. Deakin argued that the Chinese and Japanese immigrants to Australia were the lesser of their races, 'the least educated and least informed of their countrymen'. Yet his arguments were contradictory; the Japanese, he claimed, 'because of their high abilities . . . are the most dangerous because they most nearly approach us, and would, therefore, be our most formidable competitors'.

There was also the issue of shared values:

> The unity of Australia is nothing, if that does not imply a united race. A united race means not only that its members can intermix, intermarry and associate without degradation on either side, but implies one inspired by the same ideas, and an aspiration towards the same ideals; of a people possessing the same general cast of character, tone of thought—the same constitutional training and traditions—a people qualified to live under the constitution.

Underlying the question of exclusion of Asians from Australia was the problem that Britain devoutly desired friendship with Japan, had already made a trade treaty with it, and that Chamberlain, the Colonial Secretary, had warned the Australians who attended the Colonial Conference of 1897 to celebrate the Queen's Jubilee that 'to exclude, by reason of their colour, or by reason of their race, all Her Majesty's Indian subjects, or even all Asiatics, would be an act so offensive to those people that it would be most painful . . . to Her Majesty to have to sanction it'.

There were in that first Australian Parliament members who wanted to try to accommodate the British by an indirect method of excluding undesirable races, a method which did not explicitly invoke racial difference but was based on the immigrant's ignorance of English, and perhaps of other European languages. Others, John Forrest from Western Australia amongst them, thought that Chamberlain's directions were imperial impudence and ought to be ignored, letting the Japanese think whatever they chose to.

The government proposed in the end to adopt an indirect version, a euphemistically named natal test, under which an immigrant considered undesirable could be prohibited from entering Australia if he failed to fill out in any European language an immigration application, and to write out a passage of fifty words in English dictated by an immigration officer. The test was at the official's discretion—British and other Northern European immigrants would in practice not be subjected to it. The Labor Party's handsome Chris Watson, his blue eyes blazing, his height and build—which had made him a notable rower and rugby player—seeming to bespeak a model of White Australia, wanted on behalf of the workers of Australia an even stronger test—dictation to be administered in any European language. Watson's amendment was defeated, however. As Deakin's mentor Henry Higgins had said, 'We feel in regard to these people—whether their skins are black or copper—that if only they had the same standard of life as we had, we would be glad to have them by our side.'

There were a minority of politicians who attacked White Australia. Henry Dobson, a lawyer and Tasmanian senator from 1901 and for the rest of the decade, declared, 'Australia cannot be perfectly white. Is it not now white enough for anyone?' Bruce Smith, another lawyer and member for Parkes until 1919, opposed White Australia as an hysterical policy. The federal government was there to prevent socially unsatisfactory acts by legislation, but not to legislate against cultural tendencies 'inherent in another people, and on that account make them such great opponents'. New South Wales Senator Edward Pulsford predicted that Australia might ultimately be ashamed of the White Australia policy for 'its brutal disregard of the susceptibilities of other nations'. He had earlier opposed Henry Parkes' immigration bills in the state Parliament. Neither Dobson, Smith nor Pulsford were radicals. They had in common that they were all devout Federationists, and Pulsford was an expert on international trade—in 1903 he published an influential book, *Commerce and the Empire*, in which he argued for open markets and attacked the delusion of Australia's 'preferential trade' with Britain. As he believed in open markets, he believed in open worlds. In 1905 he wrote a pamphlet supporting Japanese objections to White Australia.

John Langdon Parsons, the South Australian minister responsible for the Northern Territory and South Australian government resident in Darwin from 1884–1890, a former Baptist pastor who had lost his faith but retained his oratory, also wanted closer relationships with Asia and a rail link between Port Augusta and Darwin to service it. In 1901 he was brave enough to tell an Adelaide audience, 'Australasia is South Asia.'

After the Immigration Restriction Act was passed, Barton needed to soothe the Japanese Acting Consul-General, who claimed that there was a conflict between the Act and a protocol permitting Asian immigration to Queensland that the British had somehow made Queensland sign as part of the Anglo-Japanese Treaty in 1895. But the Act stood. Parliament sought to clean up some of the irregularities which had characterised states such as Queensland, South

Australia—which would control the Northern Territory until the federal government took over in 1911—and Western Australia.

While the members of the new parliament argued in Melbourne about excluding the Japanese and other Asians, the Asian presence in much of northern Australia would continue for some years. Japanese were delayed in their arrival in the Northern Territory and Western Australia by the 1877 revolution of the old military caste of the samurai against the modernised Japanese army, for which many young men were conscripted into the armed forces. Pearling ultimately did bring Japanese to Australia, just twelve divers to begin with, in June 1884. The Darwin pearl shell beds were soon cleaned out but a Japanese diver, Hamaura, later found more shell on the Northern Territory coast and called on other Japanese divers to come across from Western Australia. By the end of 1892 three Japanese-owned pearl luggers were working from Darwin. Having survived with their white fellow-residents the Darwin cyclone of 1897, nearly 300 Japanese lived in the Darwin area by 1898, most of them pearlers, some domestic servants and shopkeepers, some running boarding houses, and one of them a doctor.

As a community of men, they had done well enough now to import their own prostitutes. It had become a practice with the Japanese resident in Hong Kong to smuggle girls from poor families out of Japan, generally to work in brothels. In 1899 a visiting Japanese official, H. Sato, reported that a male pimp named Takada had arrived in Darwin with five girls from Nagasaki.

The Japanese brothels attracted condemnation, of course, and fuelled the pre-Federation White Australia fervour; though a correspondent wrote in the *Bulletin* in 1895 that the Japanese women transcended the services of their white rivals. They were 'particularly clean, modest, sober, exceedingly polite', and they did not steal from their customers.

Japanese shopkeepers in the north meanwhile were considered courteous and fair in prices. But even after the early race legislation of the Commonwealth, Japanese divers remained in the pearl industry, and were considered essential personnel by whites in the north. Since the young Commonwealth government saw them as a lesion in the outer shell of White Australia, it decided in 1911 to replace them with Royal Navy-trained divers. This resulted in catastrophe; three of the divers died of the bends, and the others left Broome in protest. The import of Japanese divers continued despite the Immigration Restriction Act. Further divers from the south coast of Honshu were recruited for work in Broome until the eve of World War II. Many died in diving accidents, going too deep or staying down too long. Wakayama Prefecture thus lost many of its young men to the Australian pearling industry.

Broome in particular remained a blot on White Australia. It had communities of Manilamen (Filipinos), Malays, Javanese (Indonesians) and Timorese. The pearling luggers were owned by European Australians but employed Japanese, Malay and Aboriginal divers. Offensive to all proper racial feeling, there were wild bars where the Japanese played cards, and South Sea Islanders, Filipinos and Timorese and white men involved in the pearling industry pursued their various pleasures.

Many of the Aborigines had children by the Indonesian and Malay divers, in what seemed to be quite genial relationships like the one which had existed between Makassan (Indonesian) trepangers—harvesters of the meat of bêche-de-mer—and the Yolngu people of Arnhem Land from the seventeenth century. Henry Prinsep, the Chief Protector of Aborigines, noticed that Asian men who married native wives treated them very kindly, although he regretted that these unions produced a mongrel race.

Some things were impervious to race laws. Others were not. As a result of the Immigration Restriction Act, Chinese wives were not allowed to join their husbands as permanent residents, and the hope was that the Chinese would become extinct. In the 1920s and 1930s Chinatowns were cleared for lack of population and for want of any public sympathy. In 1922 the mayor of Cairns was congratulated by his constituents for his 'splendid attempt to wipe China-town off the face of the map of Cairns'. In Atherton, the last keeper of the Chinese temple in its Chinatown would die in 1948.

As twin to the Immigration Restriction Act, the Pacific Island Labourers Act was passed under which Kanakas would be returned to their South Sea islands. This pleased Labor, since it meant an expansion of the job market in Queensland. As part of the cleansing the Pacific Islanders were to be repatriated to the New Hebrides and other former recruiting grounds during 1906 and 1907. Intervention from the Colonial Office in Whitehall and from islander supporters in Queensland who did not now want to see these people simply ejected irrespective of their ties to Queensland meant that some remained. Men already married into other racial groups often lay low as the police rode the Queensland hinterland looking for islanders. Some 4300 islanders, families severed or not, were returned to the islands. A man known only as Louis, who had been working in the canefields of the Burdekin River, wrote to his woman, Rosie, just before he was deported, 'I sorry that I can't come see you before I go home. Government he hurry up along we fellow.'

*

The new government soon had to greet not only soldiers returning from the Boer War, but the 451 men of the naval contingent who returned from the Boxer rebellion in China on 25 April 1901. After the incursions of Westerners from the Opium Wars onwards Chinese nationalist societies emerged, the most radical being the I-ho-Ch'uan, The Righteous and Harmonious Fists, nicknamed Boxers by Western journalists. Sensing the power of the movement, the Dowager Empress T'zu-Hsi sent Imperial Chinese troops to support the Boxers.

The Victorian naval reservists, trained in the manner of marines, were quartered in Tientsin (Tianjin), south-east of Beijing, and were in the force allocated along with troops from eight European nations with interests in China to help capture the Chinese forts at Peitang to the north of the city. Though the Australians marched with German, French, British and other forces for seven days to assault the fortress of Pau-ting Foo, where the Chinese government was believed to have sought refuge after Beijing was taken by Western forces, they found it had already surrendered.

Having arrived too late to lift the siege of the Embassy section of Beijing, the New South Wales contingent performed police and guard duties. Disappointed that their campaign had offered none of the confrontations young men were then innocent enough to desire, the Australians left China in March 1901.

TOBY ABROAD

Edmund Barton displayed considerable powers of tact and conciliation in both cabinet and in the House, but he was disorganised in administration and had never had a gift for political tactics. He needed to cobble together a different majority for almost every piece of legislation. When he delayed putting to Parliament the question of an £8000 allowance for the Governor-General, Hopetoun resigned at the delay. But when he went to England to attend the coronation of Edward VII and the Colonial Conference of 1902, he negotiated a new naval agreement with the UK. Believing an Australian navy was not yet viable, he pledged £200 000 to keep a British squadron based in Sydney. Barton now accepted a knighthood, having refused one three times before, and he received an honorary doctorate from Oxford. But Australian sectarianism burst forth when he visited the Pope and was given a Papal Medallion. Not only was the Vatican the Whore of Babylon, but Catholics in Australia were contributing money to support those arguing for Home Rule, Irish self-government, in the Parliament in Westminster. Barton was attacked in particular by the Reverend Dill Macky, a famous sectarian, who organised a petition of condemnation signed by 30 000 Protestants.

In 1901 Barton had said that Australia would have no foreign policy of its own separate from that of the Empire in general, but that was more piety than reality. It had long been apparent that Australia was interested in the Pacific in a way British statesmen were not. After a quarter of a century of argument, there was still a dispute with the French over the New Hebrides, the islands from which so many of the Kanakas had been 'recruited'. The French had landed troops there to protect French businesses. In August Barton sent a French-speaking agent, Wilson le Couteur, to the New Hebrides as Australia's first spy. In the meantime the Colonial Office did nothing to settle the matter. In 1903 Barton refused the British compromise on a joint protectorate, British and French, and urged the Colonial Office to take the New Hebrides either by purchase or treaty. He offered to subsidise their acquisition and the costs of administration.

Back home in January 1903 Barton clashed with the new Governor-General, Lord Tennyson. Son of the renowned poet, Lord Tennyson had already made enemies while Governor of South Australia by speaking out independently, and not on his ministers' advice, on the business of appeals to the Privy Council. Now, through his official secretary, he was commenting adversely on confidential communications with the Colonial Office over the New Herbrides and other business. Barton had to visit Government House in Melbourne and remind the Governor-General that it was his duty to accept the advice of his ministers.

The Naval Agreement Act, to pay for a British naval squadron based in Australian waters, was carried in the House, but in July Kingston, Barton's fellow warrior from the Whitehall battles of 1900, resigned over differences in cabinet about whether the Conciliation and Arbitration Bill he had worked so energetically to frame would apply to foreign seamen in Australian ports, as he had argued it must. The British government did not want it to, and neither did Forrest. These issues might seem small but one cannot take out of them the personal bitterness that was often invested, and in this case Kingston's opponent was Sir John Forrest who, though a supporter of Federation, had caused Kingston and other delegates a great deal of heartache in their days of fighting with Chamberlain. Barton sided with Forrest and, in poor health, Kingston departed the ministry. Given Kingston's radical tendencies, Chris Watson, the first federal Labor prime minister, would in 1904 offer him a place in his ministry, but Kingston was by then too sick, and would suffer from strokes until his death in 1908.

Two months after Kingston left the cabinet, in September 1903, Barton himself resigned, sick of trouble over the same bill which had driven Kingston out but also attracted to another post offered him. It is hard to say whether Barton was designed for the prime ministership. His secretary, Atlee Hunt, would complain about Barton's lack of application, his willingness to waste his own time and that of others, and his weakness for perception-clouding drink. Deakin took his place, though it would only be until the election of April 1904, when Labor under Chris Watson would be able to form government. Within a few days of his resignation Barton was appointed a judge of the new High Court of Australia. Sir Samuel Way, a hostile commentator, said that Barton went as a means of saving his wife and children from want and because his Protectionist party was growing dissatisfied with his leadership. Barton's disciple Bavin had said he was 'impatient of questions of detail', but once away from politics he made a good judge. He served on the High Court with his friend Richard O'Connor under the leadership of Samuel Griffith of Queensland, on whose scholarship he depended. Following Griffith's idea of balancing state and federal interests, the High Court overturned Deakin's plans to include state employees in federal arbitration. The judges of the High Court also devised the doctrine of 'implied immunity of instrumentalities', which prevented the states from taxing Commonwealth public servants, but also prevented the Commonwealth from arbitrating in industrial disputes in the states' railways. On the way they settled compensation for a man on whom a federally owned awning had collapsed.

When World War I began, Barton was still on the High Court and agreed with the Commonwealth's defence power and its extensive control of the civilian economy during the war. Barton enjoyed life even then. He liked to dine and go to the races, and went to Tasmania for the summer law vacations. His closest relationship was with his eldest daughter Jean. His son Wilfred was the first New South Wales Rhodes scholar and was serving in the British army in France when Sir Edmund visited England with his wife and daughter. On 10 June 1915, in the midst of the Gallipoli campaign and the generals' plans for summer slaughters on the Western Front, he was sworn into the British Privy Council, the same body of appeals which had been so fiercely argued over in 1900. In 1919 he was disappointed at not succeeding Griffith as Chief Justice, but a heart attack the following year quieted all ambition, and led to the sudden death of Australia's first prime minister.

BY NAME ALONE

For most of us the early Australian prime ministers survive chiefly as a muddle of names. Except for scholars, even Deakin is an uncertain presence. In explaining him, as in explaining Australian politicians of the early twentieth century, we learn of what formed them from their childhoods, which were in the case of Barton and Deakin native Australian but in other cases, such as that of the first Labor prime minister Chris Watson and peppery little Billy Hughes, were often spent in other parts of the world prior to immigration to Australia.

The future Australian Labor prime minister Andrew Fisher had a background similar to that of 'the fiery particle', the Welshman William Hughes, except that Andrew Fisher was born in Scotland—in 1866 in Cross House, a coal mining town near Kilmarnock. He grew up in a family of seven, the children and grandchildren of militant coal miners. His grandfather, John Fisher, had for outspokenness been victimised by colliery owners, and his father was also a trade unionist and one of the founders of the local co-operative society. His own suitability for mining was diminished by impaired hearing, which would plague him his entire life. During his childhood his father grew fatally ill with pneumoconiosis, commonly known as 'dusted lungs'. Thus, Fisher's formal education lasted only until he was ten. From that point, his mother needed his wages, and he began to work the typical twelve-hour day in the pits. He nonetheless managed to attend night school in Kilmarnock and use the library of the local co-operative, and was particularly influenced by the works of his fellow Scots, Robbie Burns and Thomas Carlisle, and by the American Ralph Waldo Emerson. At seventeen, he was elected secretary of the Cross House branch of the Ayrshire Miners' Union. James Keir Hardie, illegitimate son of a Scots housemaid and a miner and later credited with being the founder of the British Labour Party, held the position of general secretary of the union for some years, and Fisher was obviously influenced by him.

Fisher had a gentle demeanour and was, like so many progressive Australian politicians, a devout Presbyterian. But he was effective enough as an organiser to have been twice blacklisted by pit owners because of his union activities. A powerful influence on him would be an 1881 strike, the so-called 'tatty strike', during which miners lived off potatoes given or sold on credit by friendly farmers. A bitter winter sent the miners back to work ten weeks later. The local Ayrshire organisation was destroyed by the strike, and it was then that the National Mine Workers' movement, in which Keir Hardie was so prominent, took over its interests.

At the end of the tatty strike, perhaps because he was open to mine owner vengeance, Fisher began intense discussions with his family about migrating to Australia. Accompanied by his brother James, he arrived in Queensland on the *New Guinea* in August 1885. After unsettled beginnings, and unlike many other immigrants, he found the promises inherent in Australia fulfilled. He was involved in the sinking of a new mine at Burrum for the Queensland Colliery Company, and became the manager of the pit. By 1887 he was a miner but also shareholder of the Dudley Coal and Investment Company. He left Burrum to settle on the goldfields of Gympie. Here, too, the miners were shareholders, and were considered by miners on other fields to be too conservative in industrial matters. But working as a miner at North Phoenix Number One field, and serving on the committee of the Australian Miners' Association, he was involved in an 1890 strike for half-holiday Saturdays for miners, and was sacked. He had acquired his engine driver's certificate and went to work on the surface of another mine. Fisher had every chance to enter the ranks of management and capital, but consistently sided with union decisions.

Though still a moderate, a Presbyterian Sunday School teacher who, like William Lane, considered that it was drink as well as bosses that kept the working man down, Fisher was subject to further black listings for union activity. Again, there existed in his mind no contradiction between Fisher the banned miner and Fisher the superintendent of the Presbyterian Church, the member of the Independent Order of Oddfellows, the shareholder in the Gympie Industrial Co-Operative Society he helped found, and the member of the local unit of the Colonial Defence Force. Christianity was no enemy of wage justice, industrial safety or collective action. By 1891, he was also was president of the Gympie branch of the Amalgamated Miners' Association and president of the Gympie branch of the newly formed Labor Party. In Britain his old mentor Keir Hardie, scandalising other MPs by appearing in cloth cap and working man's suit in the Commons, had arrived at Westminster as the first British Labour member of parliament.

Fisher and other Labor candidates in Queensland first stood in the 1893 Legislative Assembly election, and Fisher won Gympie and held his seat for three years. A bystander described him as having a 'charming though unobjectionable self-confidence'. He was also an open-faced handsome man. He spoke in a strong Scots accent and was considered a good fellow, fond of cricket and chess. But he was a poor orator. He lost his seat in 1896, and because he attributed a great part of his loss to the lies of the *Gympie Times*, as well as starting a new job as an engine driver, he established a newspaper, the *Gympie Truth*.

He wrote a great deal of the copy but had a bout of typhoid in 1897 which forced him to concentrate purely on the paper's management. When he won his seat back in 1899, he was a member of the first Labor government elected anywhere in the world—however transitory, unstable and minority it was—a phenomenon which seemed to convince many in the outside world that Australia must be the working man's utopia. The momentary Labor premier was Anderson Dawson, a native-born miner from Rockhampton whose weakness for alcohol would ultimately destroy him. Fisher was meaninglessly appointed Secretary of Railways and Minister for Public Works—the government lasted only from 25 November to 7 December, and fell due to the failure of a coalition with Liberals, or as they were sometimes called Ministerialists.

Fisher, who would later so fulsomely support the dispatch of troops to the Great War, was opposed to sending Australian troops to the Boer War but, relatively rarely for a Labor man, devoted his mental energies to campaigning for the proposed Commonwealth before the Queensland referendum of 1899. He would then, as later, be a believer in broader rather than narrower powers for a federal government. In the first federal elections in March 1901 he won the seat of Wide Bay, and in May met in Melbourne with the other newly elected Labor parliamentarians to form a Commonwealth Labor Party. The new federal Parliament was, like colonial parliaments before it, composed of many immigrants—sixteen members came from Scotland, twenty-five from England, eight from Ireland and one from Wales. Other notable Scots in this parliament were George Reid, Alan McLean, promoter of arbitration and conciliation, Labor senator Gregor McGregor of South Australia, and handsome Western Australian Labor senator Hugh de Largie.

In 1901 Fisher married Margaret Irvine, his Gympie boarding house land-lady's daughter. Margaret's people came from the Shetland Islands, and her father had been killed in a Queensland mine accident. She was a Sunday School teacher in the program of which Fisher was superintendent. In her late twenties—an advanced age for marriage according to the perceptions of the time—she was marrying a man near forty. In the midst of a drought Margaret's younger sister, Elsie, had to walk some miles to a local mine to get sufficient water for the non-alcoholic drinks at the wedding party. Margaret, who would be an active supporter of women's suffrage, took part in street marches organised by the Alliance for Women's Suffrage and would become a friend of the feminist leader Vida Goldstein.

Vida is more than worth lingering on, and not just because Andrew Fisher was an acquaintance. If Fisher was characteristic of Labor's origins, the charismatic Vida was equally characteristic of the energetically pursued women's politics of Fisher's era. She attracted many renowned friends, including Miles Franklin. She was the daughter of a Cork-born Jewish immigrant named Jacob Goldstein, a devout Unitarian who devoted himself to creating a scientific structure for charity and the relief of poverty. He encouraged determination and independence in his four daughters. In the 1890s he involved them in forming labour colonies, notably at Leongatha, but like many visionaries he was hard to live with and his wife found him irritable and advised her daughters on what a trap marriage could be. Vida and her sisters opened a co-educational preparatory school in St Kilda, and ignored many proposals of marriage to work for women's suffrage with the curiously named National Anti-Sweating League, and for reforms in women's prisons.

Vida became a very accomplished and witty public speaker. In 1902 she would take a ship to the United States to speak at the International Women's Suffrage Conference, and on being elected secretary gave evidence in favour of women's suffrage to a committee of the US Congress. Since the federal government would that year extend the vote to women, on her return from America she became in 1903 the first woman in the British Empire to be nominated and stand for election to a national parliament, in her case as an independent candidate for the Senate. She was supported by the Women's Federal Political Association, a body formed to organise the women's vote for the first federal elections. There was public ridicule of her candidacy but she polled 51 000 votes. Whatever she thought of Margaret Fisher's marriage, Vida was the friend who persuaded Miles Franklin to leave the cramped literary and political pastures of Australia and go to the United States.

The same year that Andrew Fisher married Margaret, one of his brothers died in the north of England. Another had been killed in a mining accident in India in 1893 and yet another in a railway accident in Canada in 1895. Andrew would have a kinder time of it in Australia, but his social reticence might have owed something to the deaths of three robust brothers in nine years. In the meantime, Margaret Fisher bore five sons and one daughter, with another child stillborn.

In April 1904, during a debate on the Conciliation and Arbitration Bill, Fisher would have a part in activating the first Labor government of the new federation. He moved an amendment designed to include state employees under the terms of the conciliation and arbitration legislation. Deakin, the prime minister, opposed the amendment, but in the following vote it was carried and Deakin resigned and Chris Watson, born in Chile, raised in New Zealand, took office, with Deakin's Liberals now the junior side of the coalition. Fisher had never wanted the alliance Chris Watson had made with Deakin's Liberal Party, but thought it could be tolerated while ever Deakin's men supported Labor projects. Watson and others even discussed whether Labor should actually consider a formal coalition with Deakin's Liberals. So a minority Labor government, led by Chris Watson with Fisher as Minister for Trade and Customs, came into being. The administration did not last long. Its collapse came in August as a result of Watson's version of the same Conciliation and Arbitration Bill being voted down.

Earlier, in August 1905, Fisher had been elected deputy leader of the party, defeating Billy Hughes by one vote. Hughes was a man for long, rancorous grudges and never forgave Fisher, and in return the sober, un-flamboyant Fisher despised Hughes for his duplicity and outrageous ambitions. David Low, the *Bulletin* cartoonist, described Hughes in 1916 as 'too small to hit, too deaf to argue with and too tough to chew', and Fisher early found that this was the case.

Chris Watson suddenly resigned as leader of the party in October 1907, pleading ill health but making people draw their own surmises, including the fact that his wife did not like the long absences in Melbourne that being the leader of the party imposed on him. This time Fisher, a Labor protectionist, defeated the Labor Free Trader Hughes for the leadership. He was able to neutralise Hughes's ironic bitterness through the respect even his opponents in caucus had for him.

Up to now Fisher had been on the left of his party, had moved that the ownership of all means of production, distribution and exchange should be part of the party platform, and saw society as a rift between the workers and the 'speculating classes'. Nonetheless, mutual appeasement was possible. In a presidential address to the ALP in 1908, he said: 'No more sneers and scorn for Socialism! ... There are two ways open—the universal strike, and the other way of providing the necessary courts to see that the worker gets his remuneration. I am for the latter ... we can do in parliament for the workers what we could not accomplish by the universal strike.'

In November 1908 Labor, which was again in unofficial coalition with the Deakin government, defected from its alliance because it thought a set of Deakin's proposed tariff laws too weak to protect the workers. Deakin's government collapsed. In part, the Labor members had been influenced by a cohort of fifty unemployed Melburnians who broke onto the floor of the chamber and accused the Labor members of loafing away their time while men lacked breakfast and dinner. Fisher was invited to form a government and so became prime minister and Treasurer in Labor's second minority government.

The emergence of Labor governments at federal level in Australia had an impact on labour movements everywhere else on earth, and Keir Hardie was one of many British Labour MPs who sent congratulations. The press reaction was anti-Labor, but Fisher himself, a confusing figure as socialist church goer, was treated with a sort of patronising respect. His hold on government was tenuous, since the party always had to come to terms with its Liberal partners.

Under Fisher's prime ministership an amendment to the 1904 Seat of Government Act stipulated that the Yass-Canberra area would be the site of the new federal capital. Fisher himself had voted for Dalgety, near Cooma, to be the capital location. As we will see, none of this settled the matter anyhow. One of his cabinet, the exuberant American-born King O'Malley, the Minister for Home Affairs, would suggest that the capital be called Fisher, to which Fisher replied, 'We don't want any Yankee jokes, Mr O'Malley.'

None of this was as important as giving the Commonwealth more power over wages and prices, measures Fisher was unable to get through the House. He wanted a people's bank, the Commonwealth, and standard banknotes issued by the government. Like Deakin before, he was a promoter of the necessity for a navy to protect the shores of a White Australia. He believed that fast 'torpedo destroyers' were better protection for Australia than the massive dreadnoughts many conservatives wanted. In the end he reluctantly accepted the idea of acquiring a dreadnought, a symbol of a serious navy, from Britain. He ordered three torpedo destroyers and, to the disgust of some radicals, having been a militiaman himself, he introduced, at the suggestion of British general Kitchener, a scheme of compulsory military training.

In May 1909, when Parliament resumed, Lord Dudley, the less-than-gifted Governor-General, read his speech about the coming legislative plans of the government, with his beautiful, talented, traduced and reformist wife Lady Dudley reduced to watching from the gallery. But Deakin's Liberals were tired of being dragged along by Labor's cries for more social reform than they desired, and Deakin had made a secret alliance with Joseph Cook, a former Lithgow miner and Labor man, soured by years of unsuccessfully pushing the Free Trade barrow. The new group, known as the Fusion Party, was led by Deakin and Cook, with

Deakin as prime minister. People did not approve of the opportunism Deakin and Cook had shown and in April 1910 the Labor Party won at the polls and for the first time had control of both Houses of Federal Parliament. Deakin would remain in the House but slowly fade. He had always had a tendency to work to the point of nervous or physical breakdown, and he now suffered from this over-exertion. He retired from Parliament in 1913, and lived reclusively near Ballarat, occasionally active, occasionally travelling, always haunted not by his successes but his failures, always arguing with God about the value of existence. From 1916 a mental fog engulfed him and he would die an isolated death, watched over by his wife Pattie, in 1919.

With his mandate at the polls in 1910, Fisher was able to make his own policies for a trans-continental railway and new levels of social welfare. He created the Commonwealth Bank, of which he was the first depositor, a bank 'directly belonging to the people and directly managed by the people's own agents'. His government also legislated for the establishment of an Australian note issue for the whole Commonwealth, instead of the blizzard of individual bank-based notes with which people then did business. The new notes were at first mocked—according to the habits of Australian cynicism—as 'Fisher's flimsies'. He was presented with the first £1 note printed by the government. Other acts gave preference to unionists, lowered the criteria for pensions, provided workers' compensation for industrial accidents and disease, and introduced a maternity allowance granted to the mother on the birth of her child, 'the baby bonus'. He saw these reforms as a recognition of rights rather than a granting of privileges. Not 'the slightest stigma of charity [is] attached to this allowance proposal'. He knew that 'many women go through the most trying period of their lives, ill-fed, ill-clad, ill-equipped, without assistance, and with nothing left of them but a proud spirit'. The government owed something to sustain that pride and relieve that want.

Fisher's house in Dinsdale Street, Albert Park, was now well peopled with his sons, his beloved daughter Peggy, his wife, and her mother and sisters. He found refuge in the company of a family of Scots painters, the Patersons, and—quite innocently—with their artist sister Esther. Through them he developed a sense that Australia was not a wilderness for higher sensibility but a venue for the arts.

On a visit to Britain on official business in 1911, Prime Minister Fisher was informed he had been appointed a Member of His Majesty's Most Honourable Privy Council. Apart from its judicial section, which was the final court of appeal in the Empire, and to which Australians could make appeals from High Court decisions with the High Court's permission, membership of the Privy Council had diminished in importance since the time of James II. But most Britons would still kill for the honour of being a member. Fisher, awkward about the offer, and perhaps knowing the appointment would not impress many of his Australian followers, begged off attending a Privy Council meeting convened to swear him in, using the excuse that he had an engagement in Kilmarnock—as he did, to meet members of the family. Correspondence between the Privy Council and Fisher became increasingly terse as it became clear that he hoped to leave the country without ever taking the oath and joining the Council. Eventually he was told that the King had consented to his being appointed to the office by an 'Order in Council', an edict no Briton could disobey. He was warned that the next time he came to England he would have to be sworn in. It is unlikely that anyone else in history put up such a struggle to reject such an honour. Fisher's secretary, M.L. Shepherd, would remember his refusal to wear lace on his court dress for the coronation of George V. Yet Shepherd says that he insisted on every proper protocol while prime minister—in part, he did not want a Labor prime minister treated with any less respect than a conservative prime minister.

But Fisher was also something of an Empire loyalist, although he would say that same year, 1911, that he 'would not hesitate to haul down the Union Jack if Australia's interests required it'. He also reflected that in a way the conservatives, who had initially accused the Labor Party of profound radicalism, were now often following in Labor's wake when it came to their own policies. Yet he was not radical enough for everyone. In 1912, during a bitter strike in Queensland which began over the right of Brisbane Tramways workers to wear their union badges, both the strikers and the state asked Fisher to send federal troops—the state wanted them to maintain order, the unions to protect the workers from the roughshod mounted police led by the ruthless old frontier policeman, Commissioner Urquhart. To the disgust of both sides, Fisher refused the request, but sent a personal donation to the strike fund.

Such was the earlier career of an Australian politician now nearly forgotten. It would take on added significance when as a result of his government's legislation, though after Joseph Cook came to power in 1913 by a majority of one in the House of Representatives, the Australian navy emerged out of the Pacific. Appearing before the eyes of the public, the heavy cruiser *Australia*, launched by Lady Reid, wife of Sir George, in Glasgow, accompanied by the light cruisers *Sydney*, *Melbourne* and *Encounter* and the destroyers *Warrego*,

Parramatta and *Yarra*, made their formal entry into Australia one early morning in October 1913. The heavy cruiser was 18 800 tons, and happened to be of the species of warship the escalation of whose numbers on both sides were commonly believed to have helped bring on World War I. Lining the heads and foreshores, people had greeted her arrival as if she were 'a living sentient thing'—a validation of the new nation. The *Sydney Mail* wrote that here were 'ships of defence bought in love of country and Empire'. Though they were officially greeted as, to quote the *Herald*, 'harbingers of peace', the sailors and the public were aware of a formidable German East Asian Cruiser Squadron operating in the Pacific and led by Admiral Graf Spee. Billy Hughes would say of *Australia* and its flotilla that but for it 'the great cities of Australia would have been reduced to ruins, overseas trade paralysed, coast wide shipping sunk, and communications with the outside world cut off'. In the next year, and in the months leading up to the declaration of war in 1914, *Australia* had visited all the chief ports to show herself to a national audience, and a feature film, *Sea Dogs of Australia*, was shot aboard her and opened just after war was declared in August 1914.

The war having begun, Cook used his loyalty to Britain as a stick with which to beat a popular Labor Party, but the fact was that Fisher was as engaged in the issue as Cook was. In Benalla the day war was declared, Fisher told an audience, 'In a time of emergency there are no parties at all. We stand united against the common foe.' Most of his party were with him, although some saw the war fervour as a potential underminer of workers' welfare. But the Australians, as South Britons, lived in a society which in any case saw a declaration of war as a matter for the King, not for the Parliament of Australia. There were reasons of self-interest to participate (getting the Germans out of the South Pacific, for example). And, in any case, the coming conflict was not envisaged as the cataclysm it would prove to be. The idea of war held by most politicians and by society was based on the fleeting Franco-Prussian War of 1870, or else on the Boer War, in which typhoid was more lethal than bullets. British and Dominion politicians should perhaps have consulted the mayhem of the American Civil War, and added on another fifty years of technological development, for a clue as to how bloody the war would be.

In September 1914 Cook deliberately brought on a double dissolution by trying to push through the Senate legislation to abolish preferences for union members. Hughes, Fisher's deputy, demanded that the election be postponed and that the Parliament support Cook for the duration of the conflict. Hughes wrote to Fisher, 'All ideas about having an election at the moment when our very existence is at stake, must be set aside.' If Labor renounced its almost certain victory at the polls, argued Hughes in a slightly serpentine manner, Cook's carping and attacks on the loyalty of Labor would merely show he was putting his 'wretched party interests' above those of the nation. But the people wanted to hear only about the war and government existed only to deal with the war, and it should be one government.

Hughes's argument was an omen of the little Welshman's ultimate identification with the war, his intense sense that Australia should be involved not only for love of Empire but to make Australia safe from German ambitions and German warships in the Pacific and Indian Oceans. It is hard to recapture the urgency of that hour, the sense of threat at home Australians felt as well as the intimate sense of the threat abroad to the Empire.

But Fisher proceeded with the election campaign because he felt it impossible to work with the difficult Cook. Labor won. Although he had hope for diplomatic solutions, Fisher was now prime-minister-at-war. Under his aegis the AIF (Australian Imperial Force) would sail off to its various conflicts and the Australian navy take to seas from Northern Europe to the South Pacific.

With the war, and intimations it would not quickly end, came the introduction of federal income tax and the War Precautions and War Census Acts. Fisher was early presented with demands for conscription, which he avoided since he knew it would split the party and its followers. Hughes complained from the start that Fisher was not aggressive enough to lead a nation in wartime. But Fisher was one of the first recipients of the real news from Gallipoli. His naval representative in London, Captain Muirhead Collins, told him both that the Australians had won universal renown but that the operation itself was a blunder. He adapted to the casualties rather as Lincoln did to Civil War casualties—each list eroding him a little more. He was particularly distressed by the mortal wounding of his friend General Bridges by a Turkish sniper's bullet. In the meanwhile, Hughes' discontent was broadly expressed, and the little Welshman spread news of the imminent resignation of the more phlegmatic Scot, even telling the Governor-General that Fisher was finished.

The premiers of the states fought Fisher's plan to standardise the rail system as a first step in Australia's defence. But he held out to Australians his belief, which Hughes would never share, that when the war ended there could arise 'a great international tribunal' to resolve conflicts. He told his party that the 'great war was taking place because we were in a transition period from an era of capitalism, where there was commercial greed, to an era when the toiling masses of the world would have more control over international affairs'. Under pressure from such delegates to the Labor Party conference as young John Curtin of the Timber Workers' Union, who wanted protection from wartime 'price brigands', Fisher wanted to hold a referendum to give the federal government power to fix prices. But the states would undermine the proposition and the referendum was never held.

After the failure of August offensives on Gallipoli, a young journalist named Keith Murdoch wrote a damning 8000 word report on the Gallipoli campaign and sent it to Fisher and a number of leading British politicians. In London, the Australian High Commissioner, Fisher's old leader Chris Watson, was urging that Australia send its last man into the battle, a concept that alarmed and haunted the Prime Minister. Empire loyalists attacked him for not doing enough for the war effort, while his faithful attacked him over war profiteering, and he bore the knowledge that Australia's finest children were being uselessly killed or maimed beyond repair on Gallipoli. In poor physical and mental condition, Fisher nonetheless came to agree with Hughes on the conscription issue, even though he despised the man. His feelings were contradictory on Billy. He thought that the quick-footed Hughes might be better equipped to save the Labor Party from breaking up over the issue of conscription which, he believed, would inevitably arise. At one time, however, he tried to get him out of the way by offering him the post of High Commissioner in London, which Hughes declined. Now Fisher was being offered that role should *he* resign. He did so on 30 October 1915. His war minister, Senator Pearce, would claim that walking down the steps of Melbourne Parliament House that day, Fisher declared the members of the party could all go to hell.

The sacrifice Fisher made in resigning, at least in so far as it was a sacrifice, would prove futile, since the Labor Party would split on conscription. Fisher worked for Australia's interests in London and in support of the AIF. He had established a working relationship and friendship with General Birdwood, the Commander-in-Chief of Australian and New Zealand forces in Europe. When, through Birdwood, he was offered the *Legion d'Honneur*, he refused, according to his vow never to accept such honours.

Fisher returned to Australia in 1921 and made a few gestures towards entering Parliament again, but he already had health problems and the onset of dementia. He returned to live in Britain in 1922, and tried but failed to get British Labour endorsement for a Scottish seat. He died in London in 1928.

SURF

Federation coincided with the emergence of a new relationship between Australians and the ocean. From 1810 there is evidence of Australians using their surf beaches for picnics, particularly the natural lawns and bush behind the beaches. But when, as early as 1877, surf-bathing began there were outcries about beach rowdy-ism and immoral practices. A bill was debated in the New South Wales Parliament in 1894 which sought to legislate for minimum legal public clothing, since there were bathing costumes that left 'the larrikins of Sydney with their abdomens bare and exposed to the view of females'.

The nineteenth-century ideal Australian, despite all evidence of hardship, was the selector. Coastal people, especially in the cities, were not as noble as those who were being tested and ennobled by the bush. In the poetry of the now largely urban Paterson and Lawson, figures such as Clancy of the Overflow transcended the urban mob, Clancy having 'the vision splendid of the sunlit plains extended' while city people had 'stunted forms and weedy' since they had 'no time to grow'. Henry Lawson similarly confessed, in part with a political sting Paterson lacked,

I look in vain for traces of the fresh and fair and sweet
In sallow, sunken faces that are drifting through the street.

Those who went surf-bathing in the late nineteenth century were not culture heroes but larrikins, a word which then had the same meaning as 'lout'. And larrikinism was a product of all things mean, including Catholicism and slums. A correspondent had written to the *Bulletin* in 1887: 'Larrikinism is a disease begotten of sacerdotal slavery, hypocrisy, poverty, destitution, ignorance, bad housing, class oppression, and environment, and want of rational and elevating amusement.' And the larrikin might intrude on your beach picnic and certainly did not elevate the beach with the remnants of his masculinity. He degraded it. Respectable people who wanted to bathe in the surf rented the bathing machines, small private huts backed down to the beach into the shallows by horses and from whose steps families, and particularly women, could bathe without being seen from the beach.

By 1900, however, the surf was becoming the place that in some minds gave fibre to the city dweller. As the popular, illustrated *Sydney Mail* wrote, the 'combat with the curling breakers . . . and the exultant feeling of physical energy actively exerted in the open air vibrates through this summer seaside'. Surf-bathing and 'breaker-shooting' at Manly, Bondi, Coogee, Long Bay and elsewhere were quite suddenly not only a national pastime, but a rival to the bush myth. Paterson's city people of pallid face and nervous haste were soon rushing for the trams to Bronte or Bondi or Brighton. And a ferry trip to Manly could release the city-dwellers from their urban greyness.

In 1902, on a hot morning when nearly two hundred men could be seen bathing at Bondi, the Waverley Council brought in the police who, uncertain about their power, could not prevent bathers from entering the water but tried to intimidate them out of it. Fifteen men persisted, though, and policemen took down their names. It turned out that none of them were larrikins and one of them was even the local Bondi clergyman. Only two of the men were wearing neck to knee costumes, with the rest wearing only trunks. Senior Constable McKenzie and Constable Roach reported to the Commissioner that the bathers had not been disturbing anyone, they were not, as reported, running along the beach naked, and 'there are only two houses within view of the beach'. The police suspected that the attack on surfing was being led by a man named Farmer, who had leased an enclosed bathing area from Waverley Council which was not now so well patronised any more.

By 1905, Manly presented itself, in an age blighted with consumption, as being a sanatorium as well as a place of recreation, but that year up to a thousand surfers a day of both sexes—'families and friendly parties'—were seen in the surf on hot days. Many, including councillors and clergy, were scandalised, and they and the mayor of Waverley, R.G. Watkins, were still fighting a rearguard action against surf-bathing when the 1907 swimming season began, and were particularly exercised about surf-bathers and sunbathers. 'After contact with water, the V-trunks favoured by many of the male bathers, show up the figure . . . in a very much worse manner than if they were nude.' The effects on the outline of the female bathers, however, 'are worse than [with] the men'. The chief anxiety seemed to have been the embarrassment of women visitors to the beaches caused by male nakedness rather than male lust caused by brazenness amongst the young women bathers.

But by now surf-bathing was not only believed to be healthy and invigorating, and a blessing to 'thousands of the toilers in the metropolis', but surf-bathers were becoming middle-class heroes. In 1907 the *Sydney Morning Herald* described a gathering of surf-bathers at Bondi Beach as 'decidedly handsome, Roman centurions'. The beach was at the same time a venue for human equality, open to all, free of payment. 'The surf is a glorious democracy—or else it represents the adjustment of all the classifications that history and politics and social conditions ever brought about', one commentator, Egbert T. Russell, wrote in January 1910. 'Plain primitive manhood and womanhood are the only tests the surf-bather applies to distinguish one from another.' The beach was even preparing Australian men for future national conflicts. It was a venue for a sun-kissed Australian *herrenvolk*. A.W. Ralph, in the *Sydney Morning Herald* of 26 September 1908, wrote, 'When Australia needs them, as someday no doubt she will, these men, training athletes, tan with the sun on the beaches, strong and brawny with the buffeting in the surf, will be well-fitted to take up their trust and do duty for their country.' Surf lifesaving clubs began to form, taking on themselves the duties of safety and rescue but also of keeping good order. In 1909 the prodigiously successful novelist Jack London, visiting Manly, was astonished to see a lifesaver stop two youths from dragging another one into the water.

The beaches of Gallipoli were another matter, though men swam there for relief and hygiene. By the 1920s Harvey Sutton, former Olympic athlete and Professor of Preventive Medicine and Director of the School of Tropical Health at the University of Sydney, was helping the popularisation of surfing for its eugenic benefits for men and women. For the healthiest girls met the healthiest boys on the beach. In the post-war suburbs, the idea that the surf could produce a better race was solidly entrenched as a sport and an engine to produce a better, unique race. The women who participated in the Silver Reel Competition, said Professor Sutton, proved that Australian women were gaining their freedom from traditional drudgery.

While Australian climatic conditions and post-war changes in commodity prices would increasingly render the bush a more ambiguous place of redemption, the surf would not lose its charm or power, and the march-pasts and reel competitions of the young gods and goddesses of the beach showed promise of what Bernard O'Dowd had raised as a possibility years before in his famous poem on Australia, that Australia might become the 'Delos of a coming Sun-God's race'.

ACCENT ON THE 'CAN'

'I name the capital of Australia, Canberra,' declared young Lady Denman, wife of the Governor-General Lord Denman, good friend of Andrew Fisher, in an Australian paddock one blustery hot day in 1913. 'The accent is on the "Can".' Lord Denman suffered from hay fever and the Australian pollens, particularly the wattle, set him off. He may have asked his wife to make the announcement so that his own speech should not be interrupted by sneezes. Thus a spot on the Canberry Plains of the Monaro was consecrated to this high national purpose, and a considerable contest between competing locations came to an end.

A 'prohibitory arc', mentioned in Section 125 of the Australian Constitution, ran north, west and south of Sydney. The federal capital when chosen could not lie within it. Beyond it, bush municipalities of New South Wales and their politicians competed for some years to become the federal capital. Bathurst, for example, formed its own Bathurst Federal Capital League in 1900 in its desire to become the capital. A local man, Price Warung, notable anti-imperialist and opponent of the Boer War, author for the *Bulletin* of convict stories emphasising British colonial savagery and a man who had advised Andrew Barton on how to handle the provincial press on the matter of Federation, was employed by Bathurst to write a booklet entitled, *Bathurst, The Ideal Federal Capital*. In his words, Bathurst was desirable for its 'centrality and accessibility; salubrity; and capacity for impregnable defence'. Bombala, a timber and wool town in the south-eastern mountains of New South Wales, had its passionate local promoters pushing the idea that it could be capital and Eden its port. The similarly upland village of Dalgety would prove to have great endurance as a possible site. Commonwealth Commissioners appointed after Federation to consider the location of the capital suggested the region of Albury. So did Sir William Lyne, former Free Trade premier of New South Wales, originally an anti-Billite but nearly the first prime minister and, as the member for Hume, a founding member of the federal Parliament. He had also, as Minister for Home Affairs, guided the legislation enfranchising women through both Houses in 1902. He would relentlessly push for the Albury area, and in particular Tumut, within his electorate, to be the capital of the new Federation. He was sure that the Victorians would be happy with a capital closer to Melbourne than to Sydney. George 'Yes-No' Reid likewise promoted his electorate round Carcoar and the village of Garland, serviced by the small train station at Lyndhurst. Queensland, however, wanted the capital to be as far north as possible rather than down on the Victorian border, and some therefore liked the Armidale area.

One remarkable member of the new federal Parliament was particularly passionate about building an august capital. This was King O'Malley, born—he claimed—in Canada in 1858, a circumstance which if true gave him automatic British citizenship. In reality he seemed to have been born in Valley Falls, Kansas. O'Malley would later claim, however, his Canadian-resident father was killed in the Civil War and thus he went at an early age from Canada to live with an aunt and uncle in Kansas. O'Malley sold insurance throughout the United States and also became a successful real estate agent. He was interested in fundamentalist religion and avoiding tax and so founded an elaborately entitled sect, the Waterlily Rockbound Church, the Red Skin Church of the Cayuse Nation, of which he was sole bishop. He married a good-looking young adherent, Rosy Wilmot.

O'Malley was a temperance man, but could speechify and tell anecdotes as if he were filled with what he called 'stagger juice' liquor. He claimed, for example, to have been a journalist for a paper called the *Arizona Kicker*, and that when he arrived in Brisbane around 1888, suffering from tuberculosis, he had shipped his own coffin with him. In Australia, his health rebounding, he tried selling insurance in Melbourne and western Tasmania, and then in Western Australia, before settling in Adelaide. Here he became a successful insurance agent and, by emphasising his Canadian origins, was elected to the House of Assembly in 1896. Having been rejected by the voters at the next election, he returned to Zeehan in Tasmania and stood for a seat in the new federal House of Representatives. In 1901, a month after the federal Parliament first assembled, he joined the Australian Labor Party. On 19 July that year, O'Malley moved in the Parliament a bill to set aside an area of not less than a thousand square miles (approximately 1600 square kilometres) for the ultimate federal capital. His thousand square miles was larger than some had previously envisioned.

Members of the House of Representatives and Senators, including the irreverent Labor sprite William Morris Hughes, made a number of tours of possible sites from March 1902 onwards. On their first expedition they travelled out into drought-stricken regions near Albury and then to Tumut, in both of which places people told them the conditions were not normal and therefore that they could expect better things in the future if they put the capital there. Later in the year, when the delegation rolled up the coastal range into Bombala by enclosed wagon, a fierce mountain wind blew all day and the coaches became, said Hughes, 'perambulating refrigerators'. The local policeman did not help by telling the visiting politicians that he had lived in Bombala for fifteen years 'and

I declare to God this is the warmest winter I have ever known'. But it was only at Bombala, they would report, that they saw enough water to support a new city. Billy Hughes, travelling with the party, found nearby Dalgety, west of Bombala in the Snowy Mountains, a 'frozen waste, where the half-dozen houses seemed to have been washed up and left on the bank during a flood'. He tried to swim at Dalgety in the 'liquid ice' and claimed he had 'never been the same man since'. Descending into the Monaro region, they found that the drought-stricken Lake George, pushed by local pastoralists, an unreliable environment.

Deakin was realistic in his acceptance of what it was possible to achieve in most of these bush sites. 'The seat of government would certainly not be more than a mere township for many years . . . Without descending to the modesty of the wattle and the daub, anything that will shelter the honourable members from the inclemency of the weather should be good enough for us.' This was wise advice given that Bombala had been the most recent recommendation of the Common- wealth Commissioners, appointed to report independently of the politicians' reconnaissance. And if not Bombala, they had said, then Orange or Tumut.

At last, a non-preferential ballot took place in the House of Representatives at eleven o'clock in the evening on 8 October 1902. In this first ballot one site was to be marked by each member and Bombala got sixteen votes and Lyndhurst (the whistle-stop village almost halfway between Bathurst and Cowra) and Tumut fourteen each. On the final, fourth ballot, Tumut beat Lyndhurst by thirty-six votes to twenty-five. In Tumut, the town crier went through the streets shouting the wonderful news and Madigan's Oriental Hotel kept an open bar.

George Reid and many Sydney members of the House were appalled that the capital would end up so much closer to Melbourne than to Sydney. The tenor of the debate over the capital is shown by the fact that when the bill resulting from the ballot was sent to the Senate, the New South Wales senators described the selection of a site a dog show, one small town after another being promoted by this or that senator and Tumut being the final result. One of the members called his opponents 'political dingos', and a Victorian senator said the New South Wales speeches against Victorian interests were no better than 'the outpourings of a sewer'. The Senate sent the bill back to the House of Representatives for re-consideration of the location of the envisaged capital and, believing this would be the pattern time after time, Prime Minister Deakin dropped the matter.

In 1903 Lyne prepared a seat of government bill which involved proposing an act with the name of the chosen site as a blank, but members said they 'did not feel inclined to stand up and discuss a blank'. He suggested that a ballot be held amongst members of both Houses, and a preferential voting system be used to select the capital. This was arch cunning on the part of a man who more than any other politician wanted the capital in his own seat. Preferential voting meant that those who wanted Albury or Tumut (the majority, he believed) would put Bombala last, and vice versa. George Reid, Free Trade prime minister now and destined to last in office only eleven months, opposed the proposal and it went down.

For characteristically eccentric reasons, there was a phase in which King O'Malley wanted Bombala. 'The history of the world shows that cold climates produce the greatest geniuses . . . How big is the state of Maine? That state is not as big as Bombala, and yet it gave birth to Longfellow.' Mesopotamia, Egypt and Greece thus counted for nothing with O'Malley. Indeed, he thought that if you put the greatest men into places such as Tumut or Albury instead of Bombala, in three generations their descendants would be degenerate. 'I found them [that is, similar types] in San Domingo on a Sabbath morning going to a cock fight with a rooster under each arm and a sombrero on their heads.'

Chris Watson was the next to try to finalise the issue. In 1904, as prime minister, he introduced a new bill which called for the federal territory to be within a square thirty miles (48 kilometres) in length and breadth. As a result of a new parliamentary ballot Bombala was now chosen, replacing Tumut, but not definitively. In the bill, now moved successfully through both Houses, the nine hundred square mile (approximately 1500 square kilometre) capital territory was confirmed, although still no one knew where it would be. During the debate Tumut had been considered too low-lying, so Lyne scoured his electorate and came up with a salubrious mountain not far from what he called the 'world famous Tumba-rumba Creek'. The name of the place was Tooma.

In despair and self-interest, others argued that Sydney and Melbourne should host alternate sessions of federal Parliament. On 9 August 1904, there was yet another House of Representatives ballot and Tumut mourned yet again as the Dalgety site near Bombala was voted in. Even as this ballot took place, the New South Wales principal engineer, L.A.B. Wade, had been surveying the region between Yass, Goulburn and Queanbeyan and found it satisfactory, and the federal leaders showed no interest in rushing their parliament up to the wild environs of Dalgety.

The next potentially significant stage occurred some years later when, in early 1907, John Forrest, acting prime minister while Deakin was away attending a Commonwealth conference in London, visited the pastoral area Wade had nominated, a region which had been named Canberra or Canberry since it was settled. Forrest knew it had its advocates but declared it possessed 'Nothing of particular importance in either scenery or great natural features ... There are no rising knolls for public edifices'. The summer of 1907–08 dried up most of the water in every site other than the Canberra region, however, and so Canberra passed an important test.

So by March 1908 Deakin, in his second prime ministership, wrote to Wade for copies of all reports on Canberra and its region. He delayed the bill until April, and then muddied the waters by saying, 'The supremacy of Dalgety is un-challengeable.' The urgency which had fuelled him towards Federation did not possess him when it came to choosing the national capital. He was, after all, a Victorian, and how convenient it was for him and the other Melburnite members to catch a tram to the federal Parliament in Spring Street instead of finding their way to a paddock in Monaro. The argument rolled on, with the New South Welshman Reid still pushing his barrow for Lyndhurst in his electorate, Lyne pushing Tooma near Tumut, and others urging consideration of an array of places in the mid-west of New South Wales as well as in its north and south.

Sir John Forrest, however, urged his fellow members on 'because Federation will never be complete', he said, until the choice was made. In fact, a bill called generally the Dalgety Bill, reflecting Deakin's preference, was before Parliament, and when the House resumed at the end of September 1908 the debate began again. There seemed to be anxiety amongst members about the choice of Dalgety, its inaccessibility and its severe winters, and a growing enthusiasm for Canberra could be detected. 'If we go to Dalgety,' said William Morris Hughes, 'the climate will kill half the older men in parliament.'

On the evening of 1 October 1908, the House of Representatives agreed to have a new ballot. Austin Chapman, the member who had most pushed the Dalgety option, had suffered a stroke and gone to Maryborough to recover—at which some in the House said it was strange he did not go to Dalgety if the place was as healthy as he had so frequently argued. By the seventh round of the ballot Canberra was emerging as the choice. On the next ballot Canberra gained further support from those whose favoured locations had been eliminated, particularly from George Reid's Lyndhurst and Lyne's beloved Tooma. On the ninth and last ballot 'Yass-Canberra' beat Dalgety by thirty-nine votes to thirty-three.

In the Senate, which needed to confirm the decision, Canberra won against Dalgety by nineteen votes to seventeen. So when Andrew Fisher became Labor prime minister in November 1908, he took the Seat of Government

(Yass-Canberra) Bill to its second reading and got it through both Houses. The argument about seats, municipalities and pastures was over.

Town planning was a barely established genre in 1910 when the first international conference in London was attended by an Australian architect, John Sulman, who gave a paper on the desirability of the radial ring system of roads instead of the traditional checkerboard. To Sulman, the architectural inheritance of Australia was pitiful and his spirit expanded to the idea of a new city to be built from the pastoral soil up. Some of his ideas would ultimately be incorporated in the new capital, and indeed he would design the famous Canberra Civic buildings.

Meanwhile, between November 1908 and April 1910, Australia had three prime ministerships—Fisher, Deakin for a third time by creating a Fusion Party out of the three non-Labor groupings, and then Fisher for a second time by election, the first prime minister to have a majority in both Houses. Fisher had not had time to do much in his first term and now had much on his mind, not least the creating of an Australian navy, of a people's bank named the Commonwealth, of price-fixing legislation. King O'Malley, as Minister for Home Affairs, was left to pursue the capital issue. But having begun as a great supporter of a bush capital, he had by now come to doubt the sanity of any member who would want to leave Melbourne, where the rents were low, the people prosperous and healthy, 'and where we have libraries, great newspapers and the best of society'. His being appointed Minister for Home Affairs nonetheless gradually revived his federal capital fervour and he decided that Australia must build the finest capital city in the world. The Federal Territory as marked out on the Canberra plains by a new act had only two small villages, Thawa and Hall, and its population was less than two thousand. The Aboriginal populace had been long banished from the pasturelands along the Molonglo, and the last full-blood was claimed to have died in 1897.

But this was now, in O'Malley's mind, the consecrated site. Early in 1911, when Fisher's government announced the competition for the design of the city, he claimed for himself the right to make the final choice of three designs put forward to him by the selection board. O'Malley, like Billy Hughes, was a believer in the idea that Australia had a huge population growth ahead of it, and the conditions of the prize were that the city designs should be for an initial population of 25 000. By the closing date at the end of January 1912, seventy-two entries had arrived in Melbourne in large crates, and a display of the entries was organised at Government House.

The highest-placed of the Australian entrants was a design by three Sydney architects, W. Scott Griffiths, Robert Coulter and Charles Caswell. Design twenty-nine came from an architect in Illinois, Walter Burley Griffin. It and a design by Eliel Saarinen of Finland, and another by Professor Alfred Agache of Paris, were the finalists. Agache would receive a commission that year to re-design Dunkirk and would plan extensions of Paris suburbs. He saw the Molonglo as a potential mini-Paris and his was the only design to include an airport. Saarinen's Canberra was highly formal and classical, with major water features. It demanded cutting the hills and filling lower ground. Of these designs, that of the thirty-five-year-old Walter Burley Griffin was selected by O'Malley, as it had been by two of the three man board. Griffin's technique involved simple, well-balanced designs, such as that of his proposed federal Parliament. All official buildings were to share the same scale and principles of size so that, looked at from any direction, they 'worked together into one simple pattern'. There was to be a lack of great towers.He argued that if you took up neo-classical architecture and built to reflect the great buildings of Europe, the results would be not grand but bizarre. And there were to be radial roads as favoured by the Australian architect Sulman. He also wanted to retain vistas of the surrounding mountains. Lakes were to run at right angles across the main road system.

In the Australian style, there were immediate attacks on the winning design in most major newspapers. Many wanted grand classical buildings of the kind Australia lacked, and Palace of Versailles fountains. O'Malley himself sought to pick what he considered the best aspect from all three designs. He claimed that the conditions of the contest gave the government the right to use whatever it liked from all the entries. O'Malley referred the final designs to a departmental board for its advice and it produced a hybrid in which Griffin's plans were dominant but not totally pursued. When Griffin saw its recommendations in Chicago he suggested the board meet him in Canberra, but the Australians were not keen on that.

On 20 February 1913, construction of the city was formally commenced at a stage when the disappointed Burley Griffin was far away in Chicago. On a warm day on which the women who attended wisely kept their parasols fully deployed, O'Malley drove the first survey peg into open ground amongst gum trees. It was on 12 March that the chief ceremony, involving the naming of the city officially and celebrating the beginning of construction, would be held. Trains from Sydney and Melbourne came to Queanbeyan and brought, amongst other citizens, motion picture cameramen. The visitors moved in long lines of automobiles, cabs, sulkies, buggies and bicycles from Queanbeyan to the ceremonial site within the Capital Territory, inside whose margins O'Malley had prohibited 'stagger juice'. 'Canberra' was of course expected to be the name announced. But as a result of government invitation, there had been 750 suggestions for the capital's name. They included Sydmelbane, Sydmelperadbrisho, Wheatwoolgold, Kangaremu and Eucalypta. Others included Reveneulia, Gonebroke, Swindleville and Fisherburra. Further suggestions included Maxurba and Victoria Deferenda Defender. Those who did not like the prohibition on alcohol gave it names such as Thirstyville.

A scatter of tents appropriate for a militia exercise appeared on the pastoral flats around the site before the official naming. From Duntroon marched the first class of cadets, to be inspected by Andrew Fisher and the sneeze-prone Lord Denman. Andrew Fisher, King O'Malley and Lord Denman laid three stones for a proposed Commencement Column which would never be built, and then the current Mrs O'Malley, Amy Garrod, a New Zealander, gave Lady Denman an ornamental gold case with the name in it, and at noon Lady Denman opened the case and made her statement: 'I name the capital of Australia, Canberra.' In a great marquee near the site a celebration banquet was then held for those fortunate enough to be invited.

In the end Griffin would be brought to Australia to work on the scheme, but constant intrusions by bureaucrats drove him out by 1920. Early Canberra, according to Burley Griffin's plan, hunkered low in the Molonglo Valley presenting very little of the greened aspect the city would later have. Cynics called it a good sheep station spoiled. On 9 May 1927, the federal Parliament would gather for the first time in the long, plain three-storey parliament building, but there had been something less than a rush to come to Canberra. Even by 1941 its population was barely 10 000, mainly bureaucrats and their families. The capital's airfield was a rustic grass strip which had to be tested for firmness before planes could land there.

But it was the capital.

THE TRICK OF AVIATION

Even allowing for the enthusiasm with which the rest of the world took to powered aviation, the Australians seized upon it with a prodigious vigour based on the size and unnegotiable nature of much of the interior and the ability of a flying machine to nullify distance. But aviation first appeared in Australia as a kind of magic trick, an extension of conjuring. Harry Houdini, the renowned magician, son of a rabbi, had bought a box-like aircraft named the Voisin in Germany, and had made some sort of brief wild flight in it there. Now he brought it with him on his tour of Australia. It was a biplane, its wings covered with fabric and lathe and connected by sections on which the word 'Houdini' was emblazoned. Houdini had been performing at Melbourne's Opera House, but he slept in his hangar at Digger's Rest with his plane each night waiting for the perfect morning to take off. When it came on 18 March 1910, he got himself airborne and made what was claimed to be the first 'controlled' flight in Australia. In fact Colin de Fries, an Englishman, had flown a Wright Model A aircraft about 115 yards (105 metres) at Sydney's Victoria Racecourse on 9 December 1909. But it was indeed a modest hop compared to Houdini's.

Houdini flew three times on that morning of 18 March and on the second flight nearly crashed on landing. But the third flight at 7 a.m. was flawless. He took off in front of thirty witnesses, and though hampered by a cross current of wind he reached a height of from 90 to 100 feet (27.5 to 30.5 metres) through-out, and remained in the air for three minutes and 37 seconds. Houdini's rival aviator, Ralph C. Banks, had bought a Wright Flyer and set it up at Digger's Rest too, and had tried to fly on the morning of 1 March, but he crashed, the plane suffering minor damage. He would later sign the witness statement verifying Houdini's flight.

Despite Houdini's association with show business, he did warn spectators that day that this was something more than a stunt. It was more, he said, than the sort of 'minor modification that is perpetual in any art'. This was something beyond even art. Later in March he flew the plane at Rosehill Racecourse in Sydney for over seven minutes.

The previous year, the Commonwealth government was motivated to offer a prize of £5000 for a flying machine suitable for military purposes. The Victorian John R. Duigan won with a Wright-style glider which flew on a tether rope and by early October 1910 could travel nearly 200 yards (183 metres). Again, the achievement was a lesser one than Houdini's, although Duigan would lead a squadron of the Australian Flying Corps on the Western Front, and be awarded the Military Cross on 9 May 1918 over Villers-Bretonneux.

There were rumours that Houdini was encouraged to fly by a British friend, Lord Northcliffe, the newspaper magnate who was urging the creation of a

British Ministry of Munitions to give publicity to the possibility of air power, for Northcliffe was alarmed that Japan was already building an air corps. Houdini's flight thus fitted in well with Australian concerns. In fact, the Japanese air force consisted mainly of hot air balloons deployed in the Russian Japanese War of 1904–05, and it did not purchase its first aircraft, a Farman biplane, until 1910. But its very existence was motivation. The suspicion that Japan was slyly adopting new technologies was now very strong in the West.

The establishment of a flying corps in Australia began in October 1912 when orders were placed for two BE (Blériot Experimental) -2As, two French Duperdussin aircraft, and a Bristol Box Kite. Though primitive by later models, the Australian Flying Corps was acquiring the most up-to-date equipment available. It was, in its first year of existence, more technologically modern than it would be for most of its peacetime existence thereafter.

LIVE SHOWS AND FLICKERS

As Federation arrived, there were five boys in the Tait family in Richmond, Melbourne. Was it Federation that helped spark entrepreneurship in men such as them, canny children of a Shetland Islander who combined a capacity for bespoke tailoring with a passion for the theatre? If so, it was exactly the result Deakin had hoped for. Charles Tait, the eldest of the theatre-struck brothers, began work in 1879 at the age of eleven as an usher at Saturday night concerts in the Exhibition Building, the Athenaeum Hall and the Melbourne Town Hall. His younger brother, John, studied as a lawyer's clerk but gave it up to manage Nellie Melba's return tour of Australia in 1902. Nevin Tait also began with solid employment with a financier but by the time of Federation was working for J.C. Williamson's theatrical company.

In 1902 John, Nevin and Frank founded J & N Tait, and Nevin went to London to attract a number of famous artists to tour Australia, including the Welsh Male Choir, the violinists Haydn Wood and Mary Hall, and the renowned actress Dame Clara Butt and her husband Kennerley Rumford. Other excursions would net John McCormack, the fabulously loved Irish tenor, and the equally adored Scots music hall comedian Harry Lauder. Thus Australian theatre audiences were knitted into the entertainment stream of the larger English-speaking world.

Then, in 1906, the brothers produced the first extended narrative film in the world. *The Story of the Kelly Gang*, directed by Charles Tait, caused a sensation by running for an entire hour. Most of the film was shot on his wife's family property at Heidelberg, but it was in other ways as well a family affair. His wife played Kate Kelly, his children, his brothers and their children all took part. The production cost £1000, but the film was said to have returned the company at least £25 000.

Throughout, they eyed their rival, James Cassius Williamson. J.C. Williamson was an American who had come to Australia with his wife Margaret Virginia Sutherland in a play named *Struck Oil* in 1874. They went home afterwards but returned with the Australian rights for *HMS Pinafore*. Williamson, with partners Arthur Garner and George Musgrove, formed a theatrical company that took over the Theatre Royal in Melbourne and which was often accused of swamping a healthy Australian repertory system. In 1886 they opened the luxurious Princess Theatre in Melbourne with *The Mikado,* and they brought the superstar Sarah Bernhardt to Australia in 1891. Williamson's wife, an entrepreneur in her own right, still acted under the name of Maggie Moore, and travelled to America a great deal, to the extent that she became estranged from James Cassius. He obtained an injunction against her in 1894 to prevent her from reviving *Struck Oil* with her new lover, Harry M. Roberts. Williamson himself was living with another woman (an actress, Mary Weir), and in 1899 Maggie divorced him and in 1902 married Harry Roberts in New York. But Maggie would perform again for some years in Australia under the aegis of her former husband's company. She famously kept a menagerie at her Rose Bay house. In 1925, when she went to live with her sister in San Francisco, she was run down by a cable car, underwent a leg amputation and died.

Meanwhile Williamson and J & N Tait were between them responsible for the visits of all the stars—as well as the Melbourne-born diva extraordinaire Nellie Melba, they contracted Russian singer Feodor Chaliapin, violinist Jascha Heifetz, pianist Ignacy Jan Paderewski and dancer Anna Pavlova, along with the native-born and eccentric composer-performer Percy Grainger. They also signed up local talent—the Geelong boy John Brownlee, for example, who had been discovered in 1922 when Melba heard him sing Handel's *Messiah* at the Albert Street Conservatorium in Melbourne.

Raymond Longford, born in 1878, was the son of a warder at Darlinghurst gaol. Though a seaman holding a third mate's ticket, he had an impulse for theatrical performance. After beginning his career in an English theatre in India, he came back to Australia to tour country towns with humbler theatrical companies than those of the Williamsons and the Taits. He was tall, had long features and a fine voice.

Lottie Lyell, the daughter of a Balmain estate agent, wanted to join the company Longford worked for, the Popular Dramatic Organisation, and in about 1906 her parents placed her in his care; he was a man who could hypnotise parents as well as daughters. Lottie had great vivacity and natural gifts of stagecraft and her oval face and large eyes were considered exemplars of beauty for her time. In 1911 Longford and Lottie met Cosens Spencer, a former rail splitter and drover born in England, who began screening moving pictures in New South Wales under his reversed name, Spencer Cosens. He had married a Scots girl, Mary Huntley, who became his chief projectionist and business partner. In 1905 they opened the Great American Theatrescope at the Lyceum Theatre in Sydney, and it became a permanent picture theatre from June 1908. It was Spencer's company which commissioned the young Raymond Longford to direct films. Longford made the business of being a film director a profession instead of a sideline. (In this case too it will be necessary to go beyond 1920 to deal with the entirety of his career.)

He had already acted in a number of Cosens' films, including *Captain Midnight* and *The Life of Rufus Dawes*, based on Marcus Clarke's novel *His Natural Life*, but now he directed *Australia Calls*, a film depicting invasion from Asia, in which Lottie starred. Indeed she acted only in films he directed and was by now his de facto wife. Longford made the first version of *The Mutiny of the Bounty* in 1916, and he and Lottie were surprised that their 1918 film, *The Woman Suffers*, was banned in New South Wales. The triumph for both of them was *The Sentimental Bloke*, made in 1919, in which Lottie played the Sentimental Bloke's girl, Doreen. She then played Nell in Longford's *Rudd's New Selection*. In the early 1920s Longford and Lyell formed their own production company, but Lottie was already suffering from 'the white plague', tuberculosis, and after working on *The Bushwhackers* in 1925 she died at the age of thirty-five. The company absorbed Longford's fortune but he continued to direct for wages through the 1920s and into the era of the talkies. His last film as a director was in 1934, though he appeared as a minor character in the films of others until 1941.

He was the first director to find himself fighting for a quota system to ensure a just distribution of Australian-made films. He would claim before a 1927 Royal Commission on the moving-picture industry that though the outstanding figure in the business, he had been subjected to persecution by the distribution combine Australasian Films. But he would have to leave that unwon battle to later filmmakers, for World War II saw him working as a tally clerk on the

Sydney wharfs. When he died in 1959, his second wife organised his burial in the same grave as Lottie Lyell.

GOD'S WORD IN THE NORTH

In the late nineteenth and early twentieth centuries, missionaries had begun to move into remoter Australia, in a process hard to narrate meaningfully unless, as with early films, we take the story to the end of the 1930s. When Robert and Frances Wilson, a Presbyterian missionary couple, appeared in their lugger in Port George near Derby, Western Australia, in 1912, the Worora people, according to their oral tradition, had a debate which echoed that held in the Sydney basin 124 years before. An elder named Ambula argued for killing them, but another, Indamoi, cried, 'No! They are not trying to harm us. They do not hunt our food. They have given us food and gifts. We have nothing to fear from them.' By the 1920s more than twenty Christian missions had been founded in northern Australia. The arrival of such missionaries was based in part on the idea of rescuing Aboriginal peoples before the impact of European settlement could destroy them. It was also, of course, to evangelise. At worst this involved a belief that the natives were vessels for noxious spirits and satanic traditions, and that the vessels must be cleansed and refilled with Christianity's decent oils.

The latter was often a problematic process. The Jesuit mission at Daly River in the Northern Territory was flooded out three times, and finally abandoned in 1899. At Beagle Bay in the Kimberleys, Spanish and French Trappist monks set up a mission in 1892. They founded a school and conducted classes in French, since the monks did not know English, and in the Nyul-Nyul language. Daisy Bates visited this mission and said that its condition seemed hopeless, given that the gardens, once dug, were smothered by native bushes, and the paperbark huts fell down in storms. But she was astounded to hear natives singing Gregorian chant. The Trappists tried to run the mission while keeping to the severe rules of their order—silence, unless they were engaged on missionary work, a plain vegetarian diet, and meditation and the singing of the Office from 2 a.m. till dawn, followed by a full day of work. In the case of the Beagle Bay mission the monks' diet consisted of pumpkin and rice and beer they brewed from sorghum.

The Trappists were joined by a former Broome policeman, who would become Brother Xavier, but all his rigour, and that of the other monks, could not prevent girls being traded to Filipino luggers which put into the bay. Ultimately, in 1901, due to the ageing of the Trappist community, they handed the mission over to the Pallottine Fathers, founded by St Vincent Pallotti, an order whose rule of life was less rigorous.

German-born Father Francis Gsell, future Bishop of Darwin and member of the Sacred Heart Order, established the mission at Bathurst Island, off the coast of the Northern Territory, in 1911. He had the wisdom to try to 'learn gradually their habits and customs so as to penetrate into their minds without hurt or shock'. Disturbed by native polygamy, he claimed to have bought more than thirty wives to save them from the practice. He declared in the end that after thirty years he had not made a convert.

When the Benedictine monks settled at Draper River in the Kimberley in 1908, although they hung presents and food in the trees, which were always taken overnight, no Aborigine came in to talk to them until 1912. In 1913 the mission was attacked by the local natives and two friars were wounded by spears. Right through World War I the Benedictine monks maintained their presence, but chiefly by turning their mission into a fortification. There was similar hostility in other places. In 1917 the Reverend Robert Hall, a Presbyterian missionary from New Zealand who had served two years on Mornington Island, where he worked with his wife Catherine, was speared by a native named Burketown Peter.

Some Aborigines were attracted by the claim of missionaries that they had special powers. The Benedictines at Draper River were able to cure cases of the skin disease yaws, and their supplies of food made them a desirable stop on the general circuit of Aboriginal life. Gradually the mission became a welcome sanctuary for those in trouble. These included men under the threat of tribal vengeance, young women escaping punishment for unfaithfulness to an aged husband and those fleeing from pastoralists or their stockmen. Slowly there was a 'coming in' to the mission.

Some missionaries tried to adjust the Christian message and endeavour to fit it to Aboriginal requirements. At the Trappist mission, Daisy Bates was surprised to see a girl of about twelve married to a much older man according to the Catholic rites—such marriages were normal in Aboriginal society, and it was better in the monks' view that they occur according to the sacrament and within a framework of monogamy. Robert and Frances Wilson, at Kunmunya, consulted with the Aborigines over marriage law problems, and their successor, a remarkable Ulsterman named Robert Love who served there from 1915–1940 and translated two of the Gospels into Worora, declared, 'In this mission we will never tolerate paternalism. These people are our equals in intelligence and our superiors in physique.' Some missionaries saw that to have Aborigines queuing up for food each day was degrading, and George and Jessie Goldsmith of the Methodist mission on Goulburn Island introduced a cardboard money system to allow Aboriginal members of the mission to buy food and goods of their choice from the store, and to cook it themselves.

Not all were as liberal-minded. Since missionaries understood that the older people were unreachable, they concentrated on the children, and enclosed dormitories for the children were a common feature of missions. If the parents protested at being separated from their children they were threatened with the withdrawal of rations. But in some cases they were happy to leave their children at the mission in the dormitory in the belief that they would be well fed. Dick Roughsey, a twentieth-century Aboriginal leader, remembered being put into the dormitory at a Presbyterian mission in the Gulf of Carpentaria. 'Then one morning I stood waiting under the dormitory, held back only by the enclos-ing wire netting, while my parents, also crying, vanished into the bush on the way back home.' The dormitories were run according to strict regimens, and although some skills such as mining, engineering, carpentry and shearing were taught to the boys, there was nowhere close by where they could seek a job based on these skills.

There were instances of severe discipline. The Anglican Reverend E.R. Gribble used pack drill to punish boys at Yarrabah in Queensland, until he was withdrawn in 1928 for fathering a child to an Aboriginal girl of the mission. He was also irregular with his financial bookkeeping, contemptuous of Aboriginal culture and had an obsession with sexual morality. He had, however, two years before sent the world news of a Forrest River massacre of natives by police.

Some were more liberal than others in permitting traditional culture to operate alongside the Christian and European virtues they were preaching. The Trappists and the Pallottines at Beagle Bay tried to end Aboriginal ceremonial. Trappist Father Alphonse had manhandled an elder at a ritual war ceremony in an attempt to stop it occurring, without understanding that such an assault was worse than any ritual bloodletting. The attitude of the Pallottines changed through the work of Father E.A. Worms, a member of their order who happened to be an internationally respected anthropologist and who arrived at Beagle Bay in 1930 to study the ceremonies of the Yaoro. Of these he wrote, 'Aboriginal religion penetrates all facets of life and has little to fear from distinctions which are both abstract and disunitive, and which we with a philosophical education often make.' That is, Aboriginal religion was inherent in the daily practices of the Australian Aborigines, of whom he would ultimately show a knowledge of twenty-six language groups. Long before, in 1914, the Ulster Presbyterian Robert Love wrote of a ritual cleansing and feeding ceremony carried out by the Worora warriors to welcome visiting tribesmen and saw a connection between this and Christian sacraments, and indeed the Last Supper.

The liberal-minded missionaries, however, remained in a minority. Indeed, missionaries were often driven not by a Father Worms or Robert Love-style respect but by their belief that a great imperative existed that their dogma replace all tribal darkness. They were yet another European legion, but empowered by a general benevolence rather than by a Snider rifle. This difference meant little to Aborigines who suffered on individual missions, who lost pride, who were bullied. The contrasts between missionaries remained, and wisdom came at its own pace to the missionaries. Dr Charles Duguid, a veteran of the Medical Corps in the desert battles of World War I and a lay moderator of the Presbyterian Church in South Australia, came to Ernabella in Central Australia and was appalled by the mistreatment of Pitjantjatjara men and women on surrounding pastoral runs and reserves. With his wife Irene he opened a Presbyterian mission in 1937 and ran it on the principle that there should be no intrusion on the traditional way of life and that, except for the Presbyterian stricture that corroborees not occur on Sundays, no compulsion. The local language should be spoken, and responsibility for managing the community's business should be passed to the people who came to the mission. Even as late as the 1930s such ideas were considered revolutionary, but they had an impact on the Ernabella people, who requested that on his death (which did not come until 1971) Duguid's body be buried in their midst.

UNFEDERATED AT PLAY

Australian Rules football, operating in Victoria as a device for civic and tribal identity, did not attract widespread support in New South Wales and Queensland, though the game did take hold in Broken Hill and along the Riverina. It is often argued, though there is no ultimate explanation, that the increasing eminence of Melbourne made this further form of Victorian inventiveness unwelcome. As Federation came, and Melbourne people looked forward to the first Federal Australian Rules season, New South Welsh people looked forward to a season of rugby.

The first Australian rugby club, based on the running game then played at Oxford and Cambridge, had been founded at Sydney University in 1864, and a Southern (New South Wales) competition was formed at the Oxford Hotel in Sydney ten years later with the Wallaroos, Balmain, University and Waratah the foundation clubs. In this game the emphasis was not on goals kicked but on tries scored. On that basis, in 1882 the first Queensland–New South Wales match was played—a son of the Irish political convict Kevin Izod O'Doherty played for Queensland. Two years later a New Zealand team toured Australia and won all its matches. In 1899 when a British rugby team toured, and played a test series against Australia, highly nationalist Australian supporters filled the venues, though Britain won the series. The high water mark year for rugby was in many ways 1907—crowds for each match in a series against New Zealand were always in excess of 30 000 and reached 52 000 in Sydney. But a rival league was about to arise.

The issue had already been raised in rugby clubs in England, especially in the industrialised north, that men injured in games would lose pay while they were recovering. The Rugby Union offered no injury compensation to such men. In 1895 at the George Hotel in Huddersfield, a Northern Union, which took account of the fact that most of its players were not Oxbridge gentlemen of independent means but rather miners and mill workers, was formed. It proposed paying allowances to rugby players to cover their potential injuries. This Northern Union, abhorred by British rugby officialdom, departed the official union in 1895 and became the Rugby League. The number of forwards in the new game was two less than in rugby, allowing for more open, running play and, it was hoped, fewer injuries. A brisk process known as the play-the-ball replaced the endless rucks and mauls of the Rugby Union form of the game. Since most rugby players in Australia were working-class men, the principles of the British Rugby League appealed to them. The crowd of 52 000 who had seen them play the rugby test against the New Zealanders in Sydney made them aware that someone was making a lot of money out of their efforts.

Champion player of the Australian rugby team was Dally Messenger, a friend of the great cricketer and rugby follower Victor Trumper, who had earlier that year helped defeat the English cricket team with an innings of 166 runs at the Sydney Cricket Ground. Trumper and the entrepreneur and noted cricket umpire James J. Giltinan asked the working-class Messenger whether for a fee of £50 he would cross to a new code if it were founded. The inauguration of this new code occurred in 1907 at Bateman's Crystal Hotel in Sydney. So many players followed

Messenger over that by the code's first day of play, 20 April 1908, the League was able to field eight teams. It was the almost immediate popularity of rugby league which further prevented the spread of Australian Rules into Eastern Australia.

South Sydney were the first premiers, and an Australian team, 'the Kangaroos', was selected to leave for England to play in the northern winter of 1908–09. Dally Messenger was the star of that first touring team. One test match against England was played and drawn at Everton. James J. Giltinan, the backer of the English tour, ran out of money and was not able to return all of his players to Australia. Some of them, like Jim Devereux from North Sydney, who scored the first try in the first game of the Australian Rugby League, played for the English club Hull, and it would be 1918 before he returned home.

'I would be idle to deny that the League made a spectacular display,' wrote Gordon Inglis, a sporting commentator, but 'neither schools nor university are likely to waver in their allegiance to Rugby [Union]'. Indeed, many splendid players stayed with the Union and represented the national team, the Wallabies, across the world. So eastern Australia retained twin rugby obsessions which would, for the time being, drive out what the Victorians thought of as the true national game.

In the meantime, though the League continued to poach players from union, union officials in Australia increasingly looked upon the playing of even one rugby league game as a loss of amateur virginity and a transgression of gentlemanly principles and amateurism. The adherence of the private schools and the university to rugby helped create a class difference between the two games. At a schoolboy level, rugby league was played not by the Great Public Schools but in the main by state schools and Catholic parochial and brothers' schools. Often in eastern Australia when a person said, 'I support rugby union myself', he was not stating necessarily a sporting preference but the fact that he had been to one of the better schools.

No such distinction existed in Melbourne, where everyone, from the chairmen of banks to factory workers, were crazy for their game. But when it came to football, Australia remained unfederated.

CATTLE STATION BLACKS AND DROVERS' BOYS

In remote Australia, there were other games afoot. Aborigines sometimes worked for European dingo hunters, crocodile and buffalo shooters, for the snakeskin and possum-skin collectors and gold and tin miners, the latter at such places as

Bamboo Creek south of Darwin, and in small camps in the Pilbara and Kimberley. Tin miners used Aboriginal women to 'yandy' the tin, that is, to use the normal plant-collecting coolamon to wash light soils away from the heavier, remaining flecks of tin. The use of Aboriginal women in gold and tin camps was sexual as well, and their treatment varied. One witness said that in the early 1900s at the Starcke River tin and gold mine north of Cooktown in Queensland, two brothers named Webb maintained a rough code of honour in the camp, and beat severely a man who attempted to have sex with an Aborigine without her consent.

Sometimes Aboriginal men employed to wash soil brought in only enough mineral to keep the European prospector happy, and sold the residue themselves. In Western Australia, at the Shaw tin fields in 1906, Aborigines washed tin out of the soil quite profitably. Early in some of these relationship with Europeans, the Aborigines were negotiating as equals.

Once the mustering of cattle or the shearing of sheep had been attended to, Aboriginal stock workers were sometimes put to work diving for shell and pearls off the coast on behalf of their pastoral bosses. Those on the tropical coasts of Australia found that working on a pearl lugger was adventurous but hard, and involved great risks to health. During the 1880s the diving suit was introduced, but even where it was used Aborigines still did not want to work as deep-sea divers, even though experienced divers could have a share of the profits and a cash advance of up to £100. In Darwin many Aborigines worked as servants— by the end of World War I one out of every five local natives was a Darwin domestic, retiring in the evenings to humpies in the mangroves of Frances Bay or elsewhere. Most European children in the north of Australia were raised by Aboriginal domestics and were sometimes suckled by them.

But the vast majority of native peoples employed in the Northern Territory worked in the cattle industry, where their wages were lower and their living conditions more squalid than those of white stockmen. Various acts passed between 1897 and 1911 in Queensland, Western Australia and the Northern Territory set down rations, clothing, medical care and wages as essential obligations for those who attained a permit to employ Aborigines, but the regulations, over such reaches of space and bad roads, were hard to police and did not specify minimum wages. Payment was in fact often in rations, which attracted stockmen and their families but took them away from traditional food sources.

Many Aboriginal men and women, however, liked working on the cattle stations, riding stock, chasing cattle which broke away from the herd, mustering, and exercising all the skills that went with it. Their capacity to track also allowed them to find stock in remoter parts of the enormous stations. All this earned them a respect not easily extended to them elsewhere in Australian society. In the case of just bosses, native stockmen came to admire the station boss who worked so closely with them. There were some bosses who in the off-work season helped their stockmen and women to travel back to their country for ceremonies and even to their ceremonial sites. Often, though, after a time in the bush, they found that they were not the hunters their parents had been, and so came back to the station for rations. One Aborigine would eventually complain to author and boundary rider Bill Harney, 'Having no clothes to change into [they were issued only one set of clothing at a time] we were always dirty . . . our hands were our plate, our pannikin was a used tin from a rubbish heap.'

Women, sometimes domestics in the station, were also cattle workers themselves. They dressed the same as the stockmen and were equally good riders. The institution of 'the drover's boy' came into being. The bush aphorism declared that, 'Women drovers work all day in the saddle and all night in the swag.' At Hermannsburg mission west of Alice Springs, the German Lutheran mission-aries criticised the pastoralists for luring young Aborigines away, using the women to drove cattle and for sexual partners. Women were kept for purposes of sex on all stations, the missionaries asserted, and syphilis was widespread amongst both white stockmen and Aborigines.

Sometimes Aboriginal stockmen decided to escape the station. In 1905 Pierce Smith, who managed Hodgson Downs (near Minyeri) for the Eastern and African Cold Storage Supply Company, was beginning to set up in his own right on the edges of that property, and recruited a Marra couple named Tiger and Jenny. One night in 1906 the pair absconded from the station and made a camp on a high hill. Smith tracked them down next morning and tried to talk them into returning. Tiger declared that he wasn't going back. 'By and by you shoot me there longa house.' Smith now raised his rifle in any case and shot both Tiger and Jenny. Tiger died quickly, but Jenny was wounded and crawled up to Tiger's side. Other Aboriginal stockmen with Smith rode up the hill and comforted her, and then helped to cover Tiger's body with leaves and branches. Jenny was taken away for treatment. In distant Melbourne the Commonwealth of Australia was legislating for an entire federated system, but up in the north each station boss was his own unconfederated master of the locals.

FOR FEAR OF JAPAN

Australians became galvanised by the Japanese success against the Russians in 1905, and would not cease to be alarmed by them until their overthrow as a world power in the 1940s. It is hard to imagine now the shock to the whole world of the defeat of Russia by an Asian nation—and not merely the defeat, but the near obliteration of the Russian navy. Japan and Russia had clashed in 1904 over control of Korea and Manchuria. The war had begun with a Japanese attack on the Russian naval base of Port Arthur (Lu-Shun), which the Russians had leased (by duress) from China. The Russians had also been attacked in Manchuria and forced to withdraw. But the greatest shock to the status of white men came when two-thirds of the Russian Baltic fleet, which in October 1904 had sailed around the world to confront their enemy, was sunk in Tsushima Strait between Korea and the coast of Japan. Despite Australia's immediate apprehension, the hope remained that the British navy would always protect Australia from the Japanese, but the British had recently renewed the naval treaty they had signed with the Japanese in 1902. The treaty agreed that Korea should become Japan's sphere of interest and China remain Britain's, but it bespoke a certain unease as to whether Britain could hold the Japanese in the northern Pacific.

Australian concern generated the popular 1909 book by C.H. Kirmess, *The Australian Crisis*. Kirmess was the nom de plume of Anglo-Australian newspaperman Frank Ignatius Fox, a friend of Deakin and a subscriber with him to the doctrines of Protectionism and White Australia. The fear men such as he harboured was that Britain might not take adequate action to support Australia in a clash with Japan, and this was eloquently expressed in the novel. Downing Street does not react strongly when Japanese forces invade northern Australia. Britain has to choose between its Pacific ally, Japan, and its Australian kinsmen. 'For immense issues were at stake: on the one hand, the estrangement of a proud nation [Japan] whose alliance was invaluable in Asia; on the other, fierce colonial resentment. British interest, paramount to all other considerations, demanded dilatory treatment of this awkward complication.' And dilatory and evasive treatment is what the British give in Kirmess's novel. While British diplomacy applies itself to Japan, the invader establishes himself, opposed only by the Australian White Guard, on the four-square but embattled resistance front. When, at the novel's close, the White Guard have been defeated, the British put an imperial garrison into the Northern Territory, and 'the excellent relations between the garrison and the invaders increased the disgust of the Commonwealth patriots'.

Worst of all, white women, British and Australian, breed with the invaders and beget 'little brown babies . . . and the white heirs of the continent had to stand by impassively condemned to look on and to record the event'. Apart from a frenzy over miscegenation, there emerges in the novel both an admiration and a fear of Japanese ingenuity, social cohesion, engineering and hygiene. The Japanese are at the same time too clever and too debased to have a right to Australia.

The Big Five, by Ambrose Pratt, a Sydney Bohemian lawyer and former super-cargo on a blackbirder, was another novel of Australian dread, published in 1911. It begins with the British doing what Australians had always feared they would do—withdrawing their fleet from the Pacific. The result is the establishment of a large colony of Asians in the Northern Territory. At this the Australians form, again, a 'white guard' to fight the Japanese, but at the close of the novel they are overwhelmed.

CHAPTER 6

The Great War
Onset and early gambits

ALIENS?

The Australian colonies cherished Britishness to the extent that in South Australia in 1856, legislation had been passed to exclude non-British settlers and naturalised aliens from membership of the legislature. And even being a naturalised alien was a limited good. Until Australian Federation, a naturalised subject of one colony did not become a formerly foreign naturalised subject of the United Kingdom or another colony unless he went through a legal process. Thus one could be naturalised in, say, South Australia but revert to being an alien as soon as you crossed the border to Victoria. This was a constant grievance in the colonial German press. But colonial Britons pointed to the Lutheran schools in South Australia and along the Murray in New South Wales where classes were conducted in German, and based on the Prussian system of education, and declared that the German settlers felt superior to the Australo-British. Lutheran church services were entirely in German as well. But the desire for a naturalised form of citizenship which would be good for the whole continent was probably one of the reasons the German community would vote for Federation.

Martin Basedow, born near Hamburg, was the owner-editor of the *Tanunda Deutsche Zeitung*, founded in 1863, which became in time the *Australische Deutsche Zeitung*. He was interested in German community issues but also social questions, the Labor movement and Australian Federation. He declared that the Germans, with their 'honour, sentiment, *gemutlichkeit*, obedience to superiors', were natural collaborators with the British. Such talk was partially lip service, because some in the German community rather hopefully foresaw Australia and New Zealand breaking with Britain. His father-in-law, the reforming Lutheran pastor Dr Carl Wilhelm Ludwig Muecke, who often wrote for Basedow's paper, had said in 1875, 'Not Germans, not Englishmen: we want to be Australians.' Basedow himself argued that if the British government empowered Australia to make treaties with foreign countries, then only the monarchic link would remain and the colonies might be neutral should the United Kingdom go to war. But German ambitions in New Guinea and the Pacific in general in the 1880s put the German–Australians at odds with the British-derived Australians. German society believed that the British Empire was on the wane, and so to an extent did the German community in the United States and Australia, and that it was a mere inevitability that the German Empire would replace it.

The dreams of Martin Basedow would be subverted by world events. Once war broke out, naturalised Germans were immediately suspected of collaborating with intelligence-gathering networks based in the consulates. Consular officials and German businessmen were interned under the Trading With the Enemy Act, 1914. Unhappily, the spread of anti-German hysteria resulted in the reporting of innocent people of German origin or background. Some Germans might even have sought internment as a means of survival. Any German reservists who happened to be travelling in Australia or passing through when war began were also interned, as were the sailors on German vessels in Australian ports. Once rounded up, German colonial officials, and nationals and their families in New Guinea and elsewhere, were also brought to camps in Australia. But to intern German-born naturalised citizens, and native-born Australians of German ancestry, required a special act of Parliament, which was quickly passed as the War Precautions Act, 1914. Nearly 7000 enemy aliens were interned from 1915 to 1919, and of these 4500 were residents of Australia before the outbreak of war. This included some 700 naturalised British. Thousands more lived under suspicion in the wider community and were not interned. Did the authorities act in relation to aliens on the basis of genuine information, or were they behaving as frenzied British jingoes?

The argument could go either way, but things could have been much worse for local Germans and Australians of German descent. At the opening of hostilities there had been a public desire for more sweeping detention than that. War committees had been set up in Australian universities, and Professor Archibald

Strong of Melbourne was the eloquent spokesman of the university intellectuals when he argued that for a generation Germans had been schooled in the belief that Germany's destiny was to dominate Britain and seize all its colonies. Perhaps he was overstating the issue when he declared: 'Australia still has to learn, or still to feel acutely, that she has even more stake in the present war than has England.' But he was certainly voicing a popularly held belief.

Many academics toured Australia warning that German *Kultur*—German achievements and the way they underpinned German destiny—was a great threat, and so young men should enlist, and trade unions should not hinder the war effort. The Bryce Report on German atrocities in Belgium—named to honour its chairman, Viscount James Bryce—arrived in Australia soon after its publication in Britain and America in early 1915, and it featured highly coloured accounts of German savagery in Belgium and sharpened Australian anti-German fury. As a result, German Australians such as Dr Eugen Hirschfeld, who had worked to spread the German language in schools, and Carl Zoeller, a prominent businessman in Brisbane, together with various Lutheran pastors, were interned and afterwards deported. German clubs whose name or program included that fatal word *Kultur* were closed down.

Britons, now uppermost on the local council, or able to control and compel the alarmed naturalised German Australians, proposed that the name of Germanton, a prosperous farming town north of Albury, should be changed. The name Germanton had arisen, people pointed out, only because John Christopher Pabst and his family ran a hotel store on the Great South Road around which the town had coalesced. The undersecretary of the Department of Lands proposed to the citizens of Germanton the names Kitchener and Holbrook, and the council chose Holbrook, the latter name being that of the commander of the submarine *AE2*, who had won a Victoria Cross for sinking Turkish shipping in the Dardanelles in December 1914.

The German-born felt a natural sympathy for their motherland, probably all the more so as their adopted country treated them with scorn. In May 1915 Paul Schmoork was arrested after mentioning German military superiority in a hotel in Jindera. August Heppner from Gerogery was arrested in an Albury hotel for basically the same crime. F.W. Scrimes, the teacher at West Gerogery, claimed that German parents were punishing their children if they praised the valour of the Australians at Gallipoli or if they sang the soldiers' song 'It's a Long Way to Tipperary'. Some local Germans sported pictures of Germany and even of the Kaiser and Bismarck in their houses. There was by now such a fury against Germans that when fifty members of the Albury militia battery marched to the railway station to catch a train and become part of the AIF, some of them were asked to fall out of the ranks and remain behind. They were all young men whose parents were natives of Germany.

In June 1916 the New South Wales state government held a referendum on hotel closing hours, and during the campaign electoral officers were given the discretionary power to confiscate and annul the votes of people of enemy origin *and* their sons and daughters. The German Edward Heppner threatened to resign from Culcairn Shire Council, saying that the King himself had German parentage and was not prevented from voting. There had been an hysterical story that the cast-iron verandah posts of Heppner's house were really deployable German cannon.

Later, when the second conscription referendum was in prospect, those born in foreign countries were barred from voting even if they had taken out British citizenship, and so were their children. Postmen were paid one and a half pence for each name they submitted that could lead to a removal from the electoral roll. People of German origin were, along with the Irish, blamed for the defeat of the first conscription referendum in 1916. A Wagga bank manager, E.A. Carruthers, accused Germans of holding secret meetings in Walla Walla, north of Albury, to keep down the recruitment rate. One Hermann Paesch chaired a public meeting in Walla Walla to protest. Amongst other things he bemoaned the sentiments of Billy Hughes, who had said that there would be no Germans in the Australian forces because they might shoot the Australians in the back.

Members of the military Intelligence Division visited Walla Walla to make inquiries about German activity. In March 1918 four Walla Walla men—Hermann Paesch, John Wenke, Edward Heppner and Ernest Wenke—were arrested and taken by military police to Holsworthy concentration camp. No charge was brought against the men kept in Holsworthy. All the men arrested were Australian born but of German descent, and two of them were members of the Culcairn Shire Council. Heppner was an agricultural tool maker employing eleven men. He and Paesch and John Wenke had certainly been vocal in the anti-conscription movement. The secret services considered Paesch to be 'the most disloyal and highly dangerous . . . the above is confirmed by Mr Carruthers J.P., the local bank manager'. Yet Paesch and his wife Anna had raised or donated themselves over £1200 towards the war effort. His son said that they had given him permission to join the armed forces, though his enlistment was rebuffed by the army.

Left: The striking, sculpted face of Henry Lawson is clear-eyed yet melancholy in this photo portrait of the early twentieth century. A.G. Stevens of the *Bulletin* paid him sixpence a line for verse that inevitably varied in quality because he was always hard up. (State Library of NSW, Mitchell Library, a2005230/ ON 186/228-232)
Right: Catherine Helen Spence came to Adelaide in 1840 as an adolescent immigrant. Electoral reform, the vote for women and proportional representation left her no time for more novels (the last written in 1894). She was combative and beloved, and much mourned when, after publishing her autobiography, she died in 1910. (National Library of Australia, nla.pic an14617296)

Left: Brilliant young lawyer and Federationist Isaac Isaacs was capable of running a law practice and a distinguished parliamentary career both in the Victorian Parliament and, after Federation, in the national house. Deakin wrote of him that 'his will was indomitable, his courage inexhaustible and his ambition immeasurable'. (National Library of Australia, nla.pican21399820-34) *Right:* While other premiers watch bemused from a distance, plump and opportunistic George Reid of Free Trade New South Wales claims all the Murray, along which Protectionist Victoria had its customs houses and on which it depended for irrigation. (State Library of South Australia, *The Critic*, 5 February 1898)

George Reid, Prime Minister Edmund Barton, Sir William Lyne, Alfred Deakin and other members of the House toast robust Australian woman, who holds high the franchise she has achieved. (National Library of Australia, nla.pic-an 6222116)

The Womanhood Suffrage League of New South Wales organised at the Protestant Hall in Sydney a September 1902 demonstration of women's gratitude to Sir William Lyne and Sir John See, parliamentarians who had been active in the federal campaign to provide the franchise to women. See would also achieve some note as a slum landlord. (State Library of NSW, Mitchell Library, a928828 /MPG 149)

Federation was a matter of passion for these citizens who marched in its favour at Summer Hill in Sydney in 1898 on the evening before the first New South Wales referendum, which would fail to reach the 80 000 Yes votes the New South Wales Parliament had insisted on. (State Library of NSW, *Sydney Mail*, Saturday 11 June, 1898, p. 1229)

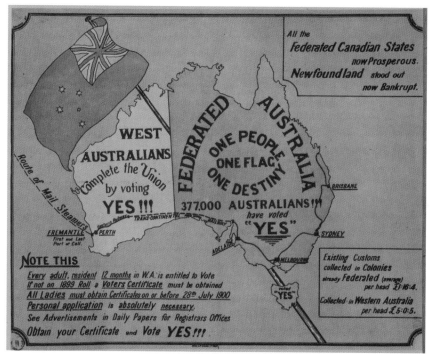

A poster urging Western Australians to choose Federation. On 31 July 1900, the state was the last to hold a poll on Federation, and it was won overwhelmingly by over 44 000 to 19 000. There would ever after be a tendency to blame the Easterners on the goldfields for the Yes vote, for they had loudly threatened to secede from Western Australia if Federation was defeated. But in fact, people in Perth and Fremantle voted solidly in favour as well. (National Library of Australia, nla.pic vn3302372)

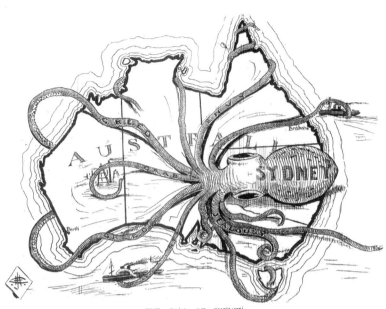

THE GALL OF SYDNEY.

Big states feared that under Federation they would need to support smaller ones, especially since smaller states would have as many senators as they did. But this South Australian anti-Federation cartoon in the magazine *The Critic* was concerned that New South Wales, within whose boundaries the federal capital was to lie, would dominate and squeeze the smaller states. (State Library of South Australia, *The Critic* 18 March 1899)

To accommodate an amended Constitution Bill, which needed a second referendum, the South Australians (like the Victorians, Tasmanians and New South Welshmen) voted again in April 1899 and gathered here outside the *Advertiser* office waiting on the figures. The number of 'Yes' votes in South Australia exceeded 'No' by 48 000. (State Library of South Australia B8821)

The three federal champions, clear-eyed Deakin, hard-up but determined Barton and rambunctious Kingston take the Constitution Bill to England where Secretary for the Colonies Joseph Chamberlain, harbouring ideas of his own and with amendments in mind, awaits their arrival. He would find that these three, however, could not be 'duchessed' into compliance. (State Library of South Australia, *Quiz*, 8 February1900)

On the hot night of 1 January 1901, the Sydney Town Hall was illuminated by fireworks boasting 'One People, One Destiny', while on the other side of the city the frail Lord Hopetoun recovered at Government House. (State Library of NSW, Mitchell Library,a186005h /PXD 760, 62)

The Imperial pharmacist, Secretary of State Chamberlain, accepts a prescription written by 'my doctor at home', the Australian electorate, but would prefer to change a clause to give the British government, by way of the Privy Council, a form of direct control over Australian High Court decisions. (National Library of Australia, *London Punch*, 23 May 1900 p 371)

THE IMPERIAL DISPENSARY.

In Brisbane an Aboriginal arch was built outside the Lamington Hotel to celebrate federal events, to which native men with spears and shields added their presence. Since many of those who passed beneath the arch believed, on evidence offered by popular science, that the Aborigines were regrettably but inevitably a dying race, Federation would fail to deliver any added status or leverage to Australia's indigenes. (State Library of Queensland, 149581)

The Chinese citizens of Melbourne were very much in the sights of White Australia legislation likely to be passed during the first session of the new parliament in May 1901. Nonetheless, they raised one of the ornamental arches so loved by Melbournians to celebrate the opening of the session by the Duke of Cornwall and York. (State Library of Victoria, H96.160/651)

This photograph of the Centennial Park Pavilion where, on a sweltering New Years Day, the Federation was instituted, conveys little of the furnace-breath wind which blew commission and constitution documents off the table, and grit into bystanders' eyes. But the woman on the right, sisterly hand on another's shoulder, and the cane chairs moved awry, give the picture a humane informality. (National Library of Australia, nla.pic-an13 117)

Women Aboriginal stockriders, Warramungu and Walpiri, at Alexandria Station on the Barkly Tablelands in the Northern Territory in 1916. Nicknamed 'drover's boys', 'lady stockmen' were described as riding all day in the saddle and working all night in the swag. (State Library of NSW, Mitchell Library, ML PXB 81, 47b)

A group of forty-three Chinese men about to be shipped home from Darwin in June 1914. White Australia's intentions in this case were bolstered by unsanitary conditions in Darwin's Chinatown. Some observers would claim that the removal of such men as these, and especially of their more entrepreneurial fellow Chinese, brought stagnation to Northern Australia. (National Archives of Australia, A3, NT1915/1028)

Sir William Lyne, so nearly first prime minister, gets temporarily stuck on a fence while showing a 1902 touring group of parliamentarians the suitability of his electorate around Albury for a national capital. On the left, in a bowler, Deakin seems a little amused, while on the immediate right Billy Hughes and Chris Watson gather themselves to follow Sir William. (National Library of Australia, nla.pican24553118)

This is the first recruiting poster produced in Australia, designed by an illustrator named Jim Hannan. It contrasts the dilemma of an Australian soldier on Gallipoli with a heedless football crowd at the Melbourne Cricket Ground. The idea that sport caused young men to tarry at home was one pursued not only by posters but by politicians and generals in two world wars. (Australian War Memorial, ARTV07583)

This Melbourne recruiting poster of 1915 carries the face of Lieutenant Albert Jacka, who won the Victoria Cross on Gallipoli in July 1915 for his exploits at Courtney's Post. The idea of a Sportsmen's 1000 (which did not exist as a military unit) would revive after the defeat of the first conscription referendum and be used, for example, to urge footballers to be in for the last quarter, and tennis players to let their racquets stand. (State Library of Victora, H2001.34/3a)

On the Island of Lemnos to which Gallipoli's wounded came and where survivors had occasional rest, Nurse Clarice Daley marries the light horseman Sergeant Ernest Alfred Lawrence. Nurses who married were meant to resign and go perhaps to nurse with the Red Cross as volunteers. (Australian War Memorial, P01360.001)

Private William Sing, light horseman, photographed here in Egypt after Gallipoli was evacuated. He had been decorated for being a pioneer of sniping on Gallipoli. The Turks he was confirmed as shooting numbered 150 but probably exceeded 200. The marriage of his Chinese father and English mother had not been as highly approved of as was the marksmanship of their son. (Australian War Memorial, P08403.001)

Left: At Number 1 Australian Auxiliary Hospital in Harefield, north-west of London, a recuperating digger does his best, perhaps jokingly, to write a letter. Both hands and one leg are gone, and the gameness of his features, and his willingness to be in on the joke, do him honour. (Australian War Memorial H16947) *Right:* Australian wounded from Gallipoli reach Wandsworth Hospital where Tom Roberts, Arthur Streeton and George Coates, who painted this well-ordered scene, were medical orderlies. Though Wandsworth was far from the shock and anguish of their original wounding, the patients were not yet necessarily free of the risk of septicaemia or gangrene, and the shock of battle that still reverberated in their dreams. (Australian War Memorial)

Jovial mutineers, obvious veterans, who believed that the Australians had been over-used and been asked to 'do other men's work' on the Western Front in 1918. The card they sent is addressed to the Assistant Provost Marshal. '*Nous jamais regardez vous encore* (We will never see you again.),' they say. '*Au revoir. Nous.*' It was believed none of these men were caught, or if caught, they were unofficially returned to their units for minor punishment. (Australian War Memorial, A03862)

Left: Near Gueudecourt on the Somme in the winter of 1916–17, the war historian Captain C.E.W. Bean encounters the mud in Gird Trench. Mud at its worst delayed the movement not only of supplies but of wounded, and could swallow men alive. It also caused casualties from the condition called trenchfoot, against which soldiers were urged to anoint their feet with whale oil. (Australian War Memorial E00572) *Right:* Vera Deakin founded and administered the Wounded and Missing Inquiry Bureau. Since its purpose was to provide families with greater information about the fate of their men, the military did not approve of her. But the thoroughness of her investigations gave great comfort to families. (Australian War Memorial, P02119.001)

Iso Rae, Melbourne artist caught in Étaples in France by the war, worked as a volunteer in the huge British camp through which many Australian and British troops passed. For lack of materials, she used pastels. This 1915 work shows a soldier guarding a clump of tents occupied either by German prisoners or soldiers charged with indiscipline. (Australian War Memorial ART 19594)

Jesse Traill is said to have become an artist after meeting Tom Roberts painting on a Melbourne beach. An indomitable spirit, while still a young woman in 1911 she was one of the first Australians to go to the Dutch East Indies (Indonesia) to investigate Asian art, and would later be perhaps the first Australian artist to discover 'the Centre'. In World War I she worked for more than three years as a volunteer in a military hospital in Rouen where her chances to paint were limited by work hours and scarcity of materials. (State Library of Victoria, H2000.63/6)

John Monash, citizen soldier, his battles brilliantly won, poses for his post-war portrait in a London studio. His appointment as commander of the Australian Corps had been opposed by such notable men as C.E.W. Bean and Keith Murdoch, both of whom thought him opportunistic and self-promoting. But as he poses here, he has become a man of national renown and international repute. At home awaits high civil offices and an ambiguous marriage. (State Library of Victoria, H32848)

Left: Private Douglas Grant, left, discharged in 1916 under regulations restricting Aboriginal enlistment, re-enlisted in the 13th Batallion and was captured at Bullecourt in April 1917. Visited and prodded by German scientists and anthropologists, he was respected by fellow POWs who elected him to supervise the distribution of relief parcels. (Australian War Memorial P01692.001) *Right:* In the River Somme sector in Picardy on 20 September 1918, Australians of the 5th Division's 59th Battalion, recruited from rural Victoria, play Australian Rules football. Seven days later they would go into the line, be shelled with high explosive and gas for two nights, then fight their last battle along the St Quentin Canal. By their withdrawal from the line on 2 October, they would lose a further 202 men. (Australian War Memorial, E03354)

Standing on a supply box, Billy Hughes addresses men of the 4th Division at Daours east of Amiens. It is 3 July 1918, and although Billy does not know it, these men are about to go into Monash's highly planned 'model' battle at Hamel, in which more ground was gained in less than an hour than had been acquired in many other days, weeks and months-long campaigns. (Australian War Memorial E02651)

General Chauvel, Light Horse corps commander second from the left, visits airmen of Number 1 Squadron near Jaffa in February 1918. The young airmen will range far ahead of Chauvel's mounted infantry in the drive for Damascus and Beirut, and in many cases demoralise and harry the Turks before the British, Australians and New Zealanders of the ground forces reach them. (Australian War Memorial P03631.042)

Families waiting for their returned men as truckloads of soldiers from troopships roll up to the Anzac Buffet in Hyde Park, Sydney. The uncertainty has clearly been sufficient to put frowns on the faces of those awaiting reunion. (Australian War Memorial H11576)

The war is over, the Peace Treaty signed, and diggers awaiting transport home carry Billy Hughes, the Little Digger, shoulder-high along a London Street near Victoria Station, possibly Horseferry Road, Australian headquarters and site of the War Chest Club. He has been torn from his official vehicle for this rough but affectionate salute. (National Library of Australia, nla.pican23150756)

John Wenke was released from Holsworthy after the authorities discovered that his son, David, who had managed despite all to enlist, had been wounded and had recently been shipped back to Australia.

Perhaps the most engrossing case of a naturalised child of Germans at this time was that of John Monash, originally Monasch, a civil engineer in Melbourne and leading figure in the militia. The son of Prussian Germans, he was a graduate of Scots College and eminent in his profession, having served as president of the Victorian Institute of Engineers. In 1914 he had been likely to become Chancellor of Melbourne University and to be knighted for it. His marriage to a Jewish girl named Vic—Hannah Victoria Moss—was not entirely a meeting of souls but to all appearances was a properly run alliance. Yet though he had been married by a rabbi, his colleagues knew he was utterly agnostic, and he had had a long affair with another engineer's wife, Annie Gabriel. Thus here was a successful man who could be undermined by a number of factors, not least amongst them his Germanness and his Jewishness.

Appointed commander of the Fourth Infantry Brigade with the rank not of brigadier general but of colonel in September 1914, he had in fact a great deal to give up by enlisting, including direct control of his engineering business. 'I am virtual head of four large industrial companies, operating in Victoria and South Australia; also member of the University Council, and many of its committees, also Chairman and member of a number of scientific bodies.' These considerations would have given other men every reason to remain, but he opted to go.

By October 1914 the slanders against him began to arrive at the office of the Minister for War, G.F. Pearce. Much was made in these attacks on the 'c' which had been omitted from his name. General Kitchener even received such correspondence. The mutterings would not disappear entirely, but the 'success', the brio and endurance of his Fourth Brigade at Gallipoli, and its love for its brigade commander, would give his name such validity in Victoria that his mother's family, the Behrends, began to call themselves the Monash-Behrends, a practice that Monash himself ultimately asked them to cease.

RAISING THE FORCE

The Australian government had put in place a militia and cadet training scheme from 1911. The plan was that by 1919 these men and their units would be fully trained and able to wage war. Since the inspector general of the army, Australian-born General William Bridges, felt that no viable force could yet be built out of these units, given that they were too young and that what training they had was based on home defence, he advised that an entirely new force must be created consisting of a division and the Light Horse brigade. The home defence men could apply to be part of this force if they chose. There was government pressure on him to get the force together quickly. The Canadians were declaring they had 20 000 men ready to leave for the front on a few weeks' notice. It must be done quickly also because within five or six months the Germans would have been driven back across the Rhine, and Australia must be part of the force that did it. Some Australian officers began reading travel guides to the Rhine Valley.

It was Bridges who devised the name Australian Imperial Force. 'It's not an expedition,' he said. 'I'd want a name that will sound well when they call it by our initials.' (Even so, the force sent to New Guinea was expeditionary, made up of navy, naval reserve and militia.) Bridges and the staff officer Brundenell White had finished the planning for the structure of the AIF by 8 August. The recruited soldiers would be organised on a territorial basis, New South Wales to provide the first infantry brigade, Victoria the second, and the other four states the third. The Light Horse was also to be allotted by state, and individual battalions would be recruited not just from a state as a whole, but the particular region of the state. The second battalion, for example, came chiefly from the northern rivers of New South Wales or from the coal mines of the Hunter. The third battalion came from the West of New South Wales and its south coast. The seventh battalion was to a great extent from the town and district of Bendigo in Victoria.

This large force of over 20 000 men was to be created within a month, with 12 September the proposed date of embarkation. The recruitment process Bridges and White had devised before the war went into operation. Australian soldiers who were married would be required to sign a declaration agreeing to allot not less than two-fifths of their pay to their family. Pay rates were devised— five shillings a day for an infantryman, with a one shilling retrospective payment at the end of the sevice. The term 'six bob a day tourists' came almost instantly into use. Lieutenants were on £1 one shilling a day, while a brigadier general received £2 five shillings. For the recruits who presented at the nation's barracks, 'It was a game to be played and they were players by nature,' wrote Charles Bean. They were inheritors of 'the fine exalted British standard'. The recruits included 'Irishmen with a generous semi-religious hatred of the German horrors in Belgium.' Not all of the men of best British tradition were as keen to avenge

Belgium from the midst of the Australian ranks. Many British immigrants who had served in British Army regiments in the past were booking passages back to Britain to rejoin their old units.

Nor was every voice clamant for war. In the *Australian Worker* a letter writer declared that while there would be the profits for capital, 'It is we, the workers, who when mortally wounded are left to rot on the battlefield'. Patriotic funds were founded and contributed to in every municipality. But the Glebe Political Labour League held a carnival to raise money for the unemployed who had been sacked by nervous employers and hit with food prices that had risen by 20 per cent during August. Just the same, many shearers and station hands who were members of the Australian Workers' Union were enlisting—12 000 by April 1915. A number of clergymen enlisted in the ranks. Amongst them was the Anglican pastor Digges La Touche, graduate of Trinity College, Dublin. Men took extra-ordinary lengths to get themselves enlisted. One New South Welshman went all the way to Adelaide to present himself for the South Australian battalion of the Light Horse.

One natural brake on recruiting was the popular idea that the war would soon be over without the Australians getting there in time. But when the city of Liege in Belgium fell to the enemy in mid-August, it became obvious that the war might even become a matter of years rather than months, and there was a further rush to the recruiting offices. As the training began during August, many of the men could not be controlled by the normal methods used in the British Army. They laughed at regular officers whose accents of command were of the educated British variety. This was considered by Australian recruits to be a case of 'putting on the dog'. They did not like to be told that this or that area was 'out of bounds'. Fortunately Bridges had hardly any brigadier generals or regimental commanders who had not spent most of their life amongst the Australian populace, and so many senior officers understood how to appeal to the men in the ranks. The drab uniform the Australians were to wear, the lack of colour and decoration, was also deliberately chosen by Bridges, who had seen many a highly colourful and decorative British regiment in South Africa torn to tatters by Boer fire or typhoid fever.

Drilling now took place on the outskirts of cities, but it was obvious that if Australia was to rush to the battlefront, the balance of the training would need to be done over there, somewhere in another hemisphere.

GREAT AND URGENT SERVICE

Within hours of the declaration of war, the Australian goverment received a telegram from the Secretary of State for the Colonies asking the Australians to send an expedition to destroy radio stations in New Guinea, 'a great and urgent Imperial service'. Indeed, some of the radio messages transmitted from the German island capital of Rabaul in the New Guinean island of New Britain had already been intercepted in Australia. But the British were still nervous of Australian intentions, however, and urged that no formal proclamation of annexation should be made without communication with His Majesty's government.

The Australians, mindful of the formidable German East Asia squadron in the Pacific—at that stage consisting of the *Scharnhorst*, *Gneisenau*, *Leipzig*, *Emden*, *Nürnberg* and a number of light cruisers—began on 11 August 1914 to gather an expeditionary force of 1500 men, chiefly in Sydney. The Australian expedition was to be under the command of Colonel William Holmes, a citizen soldier whose normal work was as secretary of the Sydney Water and Sewerage Board and whose father had come to Australia in the 1840s as a member of the 11th Foot. Very few of the infantry enlisted by Holmes were regular soldiers, but many were members of the militia. After being cheered through the streets of Sydney, the party embarked a week later on the *Berrima*. Six companies of the Australian naval reserve would follow soon after.

On the Queensland coast, the *Berrima* was met by the light cruiser *Sydney* and put in to Palm Island, a remarkably beautiful island used by the Queensland government as a detention area for misbehaving members of the Bwgcolman and Manbarra Aboriginal peoples. Here the infantry trained in tropic bush as bewildered Aborigines looked on at the first military gestures of Australia in what would become known as the Great War.

The Australian expedition moved on to Port Moresby, where it met up with a Queensland citizen militia force waiting in its ship, the *Kanowna*. But Admiral Sir George Patey, the Englishman in command of the Australian navy, left them here, with instructions not to move, as he sailed off in his flagship to help the New Zealanders capture Samoa. That done, Patey returned, and the expedition left Port Moresby for Rabaul on 7 September. By now one of the German radio stations on Nauru had been destroyed by sailors from the *Melbourne*.

The chief landing parties on New Britain went ashore not at Rabaul itself, but east of the town, near Herbertshöhe, and elsewhere along the coast. The first party were fired on by a German force of three officers and a number of conscripted natives, but kept on and overran the whole force, taking them prisoner. Sixty sailors came ashore from an Australian destroyer as reinforcements. To clear the way, the Australians even used a wounded and captured German sergeant to announce to his emplaced comrades that resistance was useless. The German wireless station hidden in the jungle was found and destroyed after skirmishes along thickly forested jungle tracks. The Australians were helped by the fact that a German plantation manager whose property the radio wires crossed began cutting them in a panic as the Australians drew closer.

In September, the first Australian to die in battle in this war, which would in its extent far exceed these small colonial skirmishes, was a seaman named W. Williams, until recently an employee of the Melbourne City Council, who was wounded in the stomach by fire from the German trench line. He was retrieved by stretcher bearers, escorted to the rear by the medical officer Captain Brian Pockley and was taken aboard the *Berrima*. Pockley attended to Williams, and then, later in the day, returning to the front with a soldier, became aware that the fire from the Germans and their native troops was intense and so lent his Medical Corps brassard with its red cross to the soldier. Without it, he was fair game and was shot almost at once. Himself taken back to *Berrima*, he and Williams, the man he had treated earlier in the day, both died almost simultaneously. Three days after the deaths of Williams and Pockley, the Australian submarine *AE1*, commanded by Captain Thomas Besant, disappeared off Rabaul, probably trapped or holed on coral, its crew dying fearful deaths.

After further Australian confrontations with German officers and native troops, Ernst Haber, acting governor of German New Guinea, agreed to surrender. Many of his German—as distinct from native—forces inland had been stricken by malaria and dysentery, and shells from Australian ships such as the destroyers *Warrego* and *Encounter* were now falling onto the compound at Toma, to which Haber had withdrawn. On 21 September German soldiers and 110 native troops marched in from the bush, exchanged salutes with the Australians amongst the bungalows and casuarinas, and laid down their arms. Holmes had granted to the Germans the full honours of war, that is, the right to march with the colours displayed, the drums beating, bayonets fixed and swords drawn. He felt this was a concession he had to make to achieve the capitulation. In that country, he thought (prophetically, and of a war yet to come), in this jungle, a few soldiers could hold up a considerable body of men, and he did not choose to incur the cost of that. The conditions of the surrender proposed by Colonel Holmes also required that German civilians were to take an oath of neutrality, and Dr Haber was to be sent back to Germany after undertaking to engage no further in the war. In the meantime he was to be sent to Australia.

So control of what would prove to be a very important and strategic island in the eyes of both Australian and Japanese governments was passed to Australia with a minimum of human damage on the day the Labor government of Andrew Fisher took office. A proclamation read at the surrender told the New Guineans what the new realities were. 'All boys belongina one place, you savvy big master he come now, he new feller master, he strong feller too much . . . No more Um Kaiser, God save Um King.'

For Colonel Holmes, the next place to assert control was the port of Madang on the north coast of the New Guinea mainland. He left garrisons on New Britain, and a strong naval force escorted the *Berrima*, on which he travelled, to the new objective. He took along Lieutenant Mayer, a German officer, to interpret for him. As the Australian flotilla entered Madang, they did not know that the German raider *Kormoran*, whose orders were to attack Australian shipping, and the *Prinz Eitel Friedrich* were sheltering at Port Alexis, just twelve miles up the coast from Madang. The *Kormoran* would soon sail off to Yap, in the Caroline Islands in the North Pacific, to take on board the German garrison there for a reoccupation of Madang. But the German resident on Yap urged the *Kormoran* not to undertake the mission, since the acting governor of New Guinea and the German civilians of Madang had already surrendered. The *Kormoran* would ultimately be interned at the American base in Guam.

Indeed, at the landing of men from the naval reserve, the infantry and a medical unit, the German civilians ashore took the oath of neutrality. The storehouses of the New Guinea Company were taken over as a barracks for the troops.

Holmes had no instruction about what to do now—he was merely the commander and therefore had no direct orders to annex New Guinea. Haber's subtle argument against suspending all hostilities in mainland German New Guinea was that the capitulation applied only to the regions actually occupied, not to the regions which had as yet not 'experienced a contest of arms'. Eventually Holmes overcame Haber's point. Even so, a Lieutenant Detzner, a German officer exploring the mountainous border of British-held Papua, avoided surrender by remaining harmlessly at large in the jungle for the rest of the war.

The capture of German New Guinea would, by the end of the war, become the operation whose implications would be most argued about at an ultimate peace conference.

THE GAME AT SEA

While the Australians were engaged in occupying German New Guinea and New Britain as an opening gambit in their Pacific game, at the other end of the Pacific the Japanese were engaged in another phase of their Pacific intentions, in a battle that might have received greater attention had it not been swamped by events in Europe. It involved Britain's Pacific partner, Japan, and the enemy of the moment, Germany.

On 7 August 1914 the Japanese government had received an official request from Britain for help in destroying German raiders in the North Pacific, and sent Germany an ultimatum on 14 August demanding the withdrawal of German naval forces from the North Pacific. When this was not answered, Japan declared war on the Kaiser on 23 August 1914. The Japanese agenda in this war was not only to clear the German navy out of the North Pacific and seize its territory in the Chinese province of Shandong but also to end the German government's pretensions to the control of the Marianas, Caroline Islands and Marshall Islands. Above all, it hoped to force on China demands which would reduce it to the level of protectorate. Only international opposition, especially from the United States, prevented the Japanese government from achieving that aim for now.

In August 1914 Tsingtao (Qingdao) was a great prize. Japan went about the long-planned business of seizing it with exceptional energy and overwhelming force. Four dreadnoughts, four battle cruisers, thirteen light cruisers and all attendant ships were deployed. The first landing force was to consist of the Japanese 18th Division's 23 000 men. Great Britain despatched a small naval force to join them, as much to keep an eye on what was happening as to add strength. Under the command of Maximilian von Spee, Germany's East Asia Squadron, the same one which so troubled the Australian government, was ordered to leave Tsingtao before the Japanese fleet could trap it there. The Japanese blockaded the harbour and looked through their binoculars at the orderly military town, with wide streets and artillery redoubts which abutted the old Chinese town. Here 4000 German and Austrian troops were garrisoned. The Japanese landed, dug a siege trench and began operations, ultimately storming the hills and capturing fortifications. An omen of the future revealed itself to the sailors of the British dreadnought—a small number of aircraft were launched from a deck extended out over the sea on one of the Japanese battleships. These were reconnaissance planes, but they also performed bombing raids.

By early November the British wanted to put an end to the doomed defence, but the Japanese leadership chose to take the city by storm. They suffered great losses in their charge up the slope to the final fortification. The *New York Times* reported, 'The German garrison could not hold out, and the white flag was hoisted from Fort C, close to General Meyer Waldrick's residence'.

Tsingtao was the North Pacific bookend to Australia's success in New Guinea. While the Australian move could be looked at cynically too, enough had been seen by the British observers at Tsingtao to create unease about future Japanese intentions in the Pacific and certainly to reinforce Australian ones. It all echoed what Colonel Legge, the Dominion representative on the Imperial General Staff in England, had reported on 25 July 1913—that Japan possessed the capability to send off three divisions to Australia in under four weeks from the date of mobilisation, and without giving Australia any meaningful warning.

The Japanese would withdraw from Tsingtao in 1921 as part of the general post-war rearrangement of borders, and allocation of other protectorates and mandates over islands in the North Pacific they had also taken from Germany in 1914.

TRANSPORTS

The first 20000 Australian volunteers for the war in Europe, and a strong New Zealand contingent as well, confident that with a few weeks' training they were ready for any confrontation in the larger world, were waiting impatiently in barracks, frustrated and delayed. The British Admiralty was frustrated too, by the fact that no one on the British or Australian side knew where Count von Spee's Pacific naval squadron were. It had been suggested that the *Australia* and three small cruisers should escort the twenty-seven Australian transports, to which the New Zealand convoy was to be added, to whatever destination was assigned. But the *Australia* was still in New Guinea when in mid-September von Spee's cruisers, including the *Scharnhorst* and the *Gneisenau*, were sighted off Apia, Samoa. The German raider *Emden*, a cruiser disguised as a mere freighter, had also by now begun to sink a huge tonnage of British shipping all over the Indian Ocean.

The British Admiralty, under pressure to get the troops of Oceania to the battlefront, ordered the Royal Navy's *Minotaur* and, in the spirit of the Anglo-Japanese naval treaty of 1905, the Japanese cruiser *Ibuki* to meet any Australian–New Zealand convoy at Fremantle and escort them onwards. But the Australian and New Zealand politicians were worried about danger to the transports in the Tasman Sea and the Southern Ocean. A German wireless transmission was intercepted ordering a collier, from which German raiders could refuel themselves, to New Guinea, which meant that raiders might be slated to operate in the waters between Australia and New Zealand. The New Zealanders might have to wait for the second convoy because of the danger of crossing the Tasman. Prime Minister Fisher and the minister for defence, Senator George Pearce, urged a delay, while the commander of the troops, General William Bridges, a British professional of considerable courage and character, sadly to be killed by a sniper's bullet at Gallipoli, urged that the politicians should take a sturdier attitude and that transports should sail. The Admiralty persistently advised that the despatch of transports from New Zealand and Australian ports to the points of concentration in Fremantle was 'an operation free from undue risk'. But Fisher was haunted by the possibility of Australia's 20 000 finest boys drowning. At the Australian government's order, some troopships which had already embarked from eastern Australian for the rendezvous at Fremantle were fetched back to Melbourne and Sydney. The Australian cruiser *Melbourne* itself was sent southwards from Sydney to bring back stragglers. Meanwhile, the *Minotaur* and *Ibuki* reached Fremantle at the end of September. The captain of the *Ibuki* sent a message to the Australian Naval Board: 'We are grateful to Providence for the honour of cooperating with our Allies in the restoration of the peace of the world, and trust Providence will further honour us with an opportunity of cooperating actively and to some effect in the defence of a common interest in Far Eastern waters.'

When the German cruisers were found to have moved north in the Pacific and raided Papeete in French-controlled Tahiti, the Admiralty even more pressingly urged the departure of the Australian–New Zealand convoy. But the New Zealanders still delayed, concerned about the inadequacy of the escort across the Tasman. Finally, on 16 October 1914, ten New Zealand transports set out for Albany, and the eastern Australian transports began to move to join impatient troops from Western Australia. With the *Melbourne* standing off Gabo Island until the last transport from Sydney had safely passed, all Australian transports reached Albany by 28 October. On leaving Fremantle for the journey to the northern hemisphere, the Australian transports formed up three abreast, followed by the ten New Zealand vessels two abreast. The *Minotaur* led, the *Sydney* was on the port side to the west, the *Ibuki* to the east, and at the stern was the *Melbourne*. The concern was that they did not know where the *Emden* was, and if it sneaked amongst the convoy it could create mayhem, firing and torpedoing in both directions, drowning many Australians and New Zealanders and undermining their governments' resolve.

At the start of the war, the *Emden* had been stationed in the passage between the island of Tsushima and the Japanese mainland and had captured a Japanese cruiser, the *Riasan*, which it manned with a German crew, renamed the *Kormoran*, and turned into a fellow raider. The *Emden* then separated from the *Kormoran* and made for the Molucca Passage in Indonesia with her special coaling ship accompanying her. Cruising on the steamer route between Colombo and Calcutta, she sank twenty-one vessels within six weeks, bombarded the fuel depot of Madras in India and raided warships at anchor in Penang. In just five days of its rampage it captured or sank eight ships. Some of the surviving crew were transferred to her collier. Other ships were sunk off Ceylon (now Sri Lanka). One of the ships captured by the *Emden*, the *Exford*, contained 5500 tons of Welsh coal.

The captain of the *Emden*, Karl von Müller, was now attracted southwards to the Cocos and Keeling Islands. The *Emden*'s motive for coming south was to destroy the radio transmitters at this most remote of relay points and break British communications in the Indian Ocean. But it might also have intended to intercept the convoy. Trouble now broke out in South Africa with a pro-German Boer uprising and the *Minotaur* was ordered off to the Cape of Good Hope, leaving the *Melbourne*, with the *Sydney* and the *Ibuki*, in charge of the thirty-eight transports.

Early on the morning of 9 November, when soldiers were exercising on the decks of the troopships, Cocos Island wireless station transmitted the signal, 'Strange warship approaching'. An SOS was then appended with the news that a three-funnelled warship was landing a party in boats. That was the last transmission from Cocos Island. The *Melbourne* turned to the island but the captain soon swung back into his position, realising the convoy was his responsibility. He signalled the *Sydney* to veer away and find the 'strange warship' which dominated so many imaginations from Melbourne to the Admiralty in London. By 9.15 a.m., the *Sydney* was off the island and saw the enemy cruiser. The *Emden* began firing. Shot fell either side of the *Sydney*, and fifteen shells landed aboard her, of which only five burst. Two hit the after-control platform and wounded everyone there, another hit the bridge and killed a man but did not explode. Other shells hit a gun crew and started a fire in cordite charges. Aboard the *Sydney* that day were a number of boys of about sixteen years of age from the training ship *Tingara*, and they fortuitously were all at their battle stations when a shell destroyed their mess. They were especially praised for coolness. When a German shell tore off the range-finder operator's leg, a *Tingara* boy named Roy Millar, thrown to the deck, rose, shook himself and asked, 'Where's my bloody telescope?'

The *Emden* fired at such a hectic rate because she knew she must disable the *Sydney* before her guns got their range. But soon the *Sydney*'s shells had smashed the wireless room aboard the *Emden* and wrecked the steering gear. The forward funnel went over the side of the ship. A shell fell into the after-ammunition room, which von Müller ordered flooded. As his third funnel was blown away, von Müller saw that he was three miles closer to North Keeling Island than the *Sydney*. The *Emden* drove itself up onto a reef by the island. This accomplished, Captain John Glossop then turned the *Sydney* away to chase the collier *Buresk*, which had left the *Emden* earlier in the day. When the *Sydney* overtook the *Buresk* the German captain surrendered, making the point that there were many non-combatant Chinese aboard from the German possession of Tsingtao. Before sinking the *Buresk*, Glossop allowed its crew to take to boats, which he then towed back to North Keeling Island.

He arrived there about four o'clock in the afternoon and saw that the grounded *Emden*'s flag was still flying. His claim, and that of other *Sydney* officers, is that von Müller temporised and pretended he had no signal book to answer the *Sydney*'s question, 'Will you surrender?' The official historian maintains that German officers captured on the *Buresk* told Glossop that von Müller would never surrender. After the message was sent again and went unanswered, the *Sydney* ran in to about a two-mile range and fired two salvos. Later, von Müller would claim that the men who were hit by those shells and then died, or who dived overboard and drowned trying to swim ashore, could have been saved.

When the *Emden* was boarded by a crew from the *Sydney*, the ratings, who had never seen war's mayhem before, were shocked at the sight of men lying in heaps, by the damage their shells had done to the deck and the superstructure. The wounded were not in good condition since they had only one surgeon to work on them, the assistant surgeon having been blown overboard and then died ashore. Captain Glossop borrowed the wireless staff doctor, H.S. Ollerhead, to help the medical officers of the *Sydney* and the half-deranged doctor of the *Emden* treat and operate on the wounded of both the *Sydney* and the *Emden*. The *Emden*'s killed and drowned numbered 133, including three Chinese laundrymen.

Earlier in the day a party of German officers and men had also been landed on Direction Island, near North Keeling, to destroy the cable station there. They would now be captured, but the landing party on Cocos commandeered a small ship named *Ayesha*, on which they would ultimately sail all the way to Arabia, connecting up there with the Turkish railway system which would take them to Istanbul and then, through friendly country, home.

*

The Anzac convoy was by now approaching the Dutch East Indies on its way to havoc such as would dwarf any damage the *Emden* could have done it.

The Australian navy's role in the war from then on was divided between the Indian-Pacific region, the Mediterranean and as part of the Grand Fleet in the North Sea. Fortunately perhaps for many young sailors, a collision with a New Zealand vessel disqualified the *Australia* from participation in the huge Battle of Jutland in 1916. This did not mean that for its sailors the war was not an education in geography and—to an extent—politics, or that the life of a naval rating in the North Sea was delightful. The sailors were, however, saved the mud and the gas and the horror ashore.

HUGHES, GERMANS, MINERALS

After Fisher came to power in late 1914, one of the first issues that Billy Hughes faced as attorney-general was the question of minerals—lead, copper and zinc in particular—and the fact that at the outbreak of war the control of much of the mining and export of these minerals in Australia was in the hands of a small group of German firms. Hughes had been unaware of the issue when the war began but, finding out, took up the matter with characteristic zeal. The whole output of zinc, for example, was sold in the form of concentrates to metals-trading firm Henry R. Merton (HRM) of London or to the Australian Metal Company of Melbourne, both of whom were subsidiaries of Frankfurt's Metallgesellschaft AG. The German agencies which sent metals to Germany shrouded their identity under that disarming name Australian Metal Company, and shipped considerable quantities of lead and zinc to Germany through various channels, but mostly via America.

The export of metals was now embargoed, but workers at Broken Hill, Port Pirie and Port Kembla were put off and appealed to the Labor government over their lost jobs. Indeed, the methods used by Billy on all mining and metal-trading companies were at first heavy-handed, and on 8 November, at his order, raids were mounted by police and customs officers on the offices of all the main firms producing and exporting metals, including Broken Hill Proprietary.

Hughes now employed a technical adviser, John Higgins, a metallurgist who had retired to the country after being driven out of business by German competition. Higgins does not seem to have been vengeful but advised Hughes that there were extant contracts that would be revived after the war to give Germany effective control of the industry for many years thereafter. Governments, especially that of Asquith, the British prime minister, were loath to interfere with these contractual relationships—contracts were in some eyes a supreme consideration—and Billy Hughes inveighed against possible 'paralysis of zinc production during the war, and the renewal of German control afterwards'.

W.S. Robinson of BHP was offended by Hughes' fervour on the matter, but Hughes won him over and asked him if he would be so kind as to give advice when the attorney-general needed it. He told Robinson he wanted a metals exchange to control and register all dealings in metals and ores and so ensure that none found their way to Germany. But he also wanted results which would enrich Australian and British companies—a substantial increase in the Australian output of refined lead; a plant for making copper wire; and a scheme for the treatment of zinc concentrates.

In the middle of the year, when the Gallipoli campaign was in full bloom, Hughes accused the Mount Morgan Mining Company, the biggest copper producers, of continuing to sell through HRM, and Goldsborough Mort and Company of having applied for permission to act as Merton's agents. This brought on a further brawl with the miners. He boasted now, 'The Australian Metal Company was closed and its presiding genius, a plausible gentleman named Franz Wallach, put into cold storage.' Wallach took a writ of habeas corpus in the Supreme Court of Victoria. The War Precautions Act, however, said Hughes with some pride, 'clothed the executive with authority that barely stopped this side of absolutism'.

The hearing of the matter in the Victorian Supreme Court attracted great interest. Hughes puts his bias against Wallach in these terms: 'Tens of thousands were being killed or wounded by bullets and shells made from lead and zinc mined and smelted in Australia and shipped through devious channels to Germany by the Australian Metal Company.' The Commonwealth had to appeal to the High Court to get Wallach interned, but Sir Samuel Griffith came down on the side of the minister of defence and Wallach was locked up for the duration of the war.

Hughes brought to his later narration of some of his endeavours in wartime an amused tone, even levity. He would tell the story of Mr Johnson, a competent businessman, to whom he gave the task of producing canned fish for the Australian market so that less money and cargo space were spent on salmon imports. Johnson produced cans with salmon labels on them, but they fell foul of the Chief Commonwealth Health Officer, Perry Norris, who claimed they were not salmon. 'Of course it's not salmon,' Johnson admitted. 'There are no salmon in these waters.' It was jewfish, he confessed.

'Holy Moses,' Hughes said. 'But it's pink!'

'Yes, I know,' said Johnson. 'We had to give it a touch of cochineal!'

But by now it was the casualties from Gallipoli who were having the profoundest impact on Hughes, and dampened even his taste for satire. The idea for conscription was already forming in him.

THE BLOOD MYTH UNASSAILABLE

Though enthusiastically godfathered by Churchill, Gallipoli was an example of the work of the Easterners, those in the War Office and Admiralty who wanted to attack Germany through her supposed underbelly, her allies in the East. The Westerners, those who wanted to defeat Germany in Western Europe, sneered at the operation as if it were a sideshow and, given its mismanagement, it was indeed a frightful sideshow. And in the overall plan, the Anzac landings of 25 April were subsidiary to the main British landings at Helles in the toe of the peninsula. The Anzacs were meant to cross the peninsula and capture the heights which overlooked the Dardanelles, the approaches to Istanbul, in the area known as the Narrows. The British and French, sweeping up from Helles, were to connect up with them there. Once these heights across the Gallipoli peninsula were secured, the British navy would have some chance of sailing up through the Narrows to seize the Golden Horn and Istanbul.

Australians, supposedly a non-poetic race, turned Gallipoli into *their* legend, and pegged out the entirety of it. This was quite an act of national assertion. The British, for example, sent over 450 000 into the battle on the Gallipoli Peninsula, of whom 33 500 were killed. But the modern British contemporaries of the young Australians who descend on Gallipoli each year probably do not even know such battles occurred on the Gallipoli Peninsula, or where Gallipoli is. The Australian imagination has seized the campaign as if it had been predominantly fought by Antipodeans.

The claim on Gallipoli is all the more remarkable given the unruly and, according to British officers, disreputable behaviour of the Australians in Egypt. E.G. Halse, an Australian stretcher bearer, quoted Kitchener with glee as having said that it took him twenty years to make Cairo what it was, and the Australians had undone it in twenty minutes. The Anzacs, for example, had set fire to the brothel area of Cairo, the Wazzir, when one of their number was knifed there. Halse also observed the reckless amateur archaeology of Australian troops around Zeitoun and Heliopolis. 'They bring into camp bones and skulls which their entrenching tools have unearthed.'

They penetrated cafes and bars reserved for officers and showed no conventional respect for their superiors. Halse recorded: 'Sensation in Cairo yesterday. An Australian saluted an officer.' There is a widespread story which encapsulates the attitude. A British officer (variously a colonel, major or captain, depending on who told the story) stops an Australian who has not saluted. 'Do you know what I am?' asks the officer. 'No.' 'Well, I'm a colonel.' The Australian says, 'That's a bloody good job. I'd keep it if I was you.'

At Gallipoli, says the legend, Australians showed that true discipline was not parade ground discipline, but the endurance tempered in the furnace of Australia's hard bush labours, skills, traditions and misadventures. (Again, the suburbs were downplayed.) And then the obvious fact that this peculiarly Australian vigour and panache was let down by the incompetence of British generals who, like General Hamilton, stayed snugly offshore on his command ship! In the Australian version the Anzacs were superior to all other forces, but in fact they were also quaking boys—if they had inherited stoicism from their forebears (and many, many of them had) it does not mean they felt no fear. To depict them as supra-human is in fact to diminish the bravery of the mass. There was a sizeable number of men who suffered from what they called at Gallipoli 'DAH', disordered action of the heart, a form of shell shock. And that there were self-inflicted wounds is dealt with frankly by the official medical history of the campaign. It was a mere human outfall that there be such wounds, 'a crude and instinctive reaction against a psychic impasse' to quote a surgeon, Colonel Butler. From 26 May onwards, special instructions were issued by the authorities: men guilty of self-maiming should not be evacuated unless it were absolutely necessary, but treated until it was time to return to duty. These cases serve to emphasise the heartbreaking tenacity of the majority. Since no military victory seemed possible, fortitude itself became the victory and the national triumph.

The health problem on Gallipoli is de-emphasised in the myth. But threat arose not merely from the direction of the enemy but from an early lack of sanitation and from the flies which bred on excreta and the bodies of the dead and then landed and sat like a layer of black across every plate of biscuit, bread and bully beef a man ate. Typhoid, paratyphoid and dysentery struck down the brave, and many Australian mothers and wives, without knowing it, owed their menfolk's survival to the sanitation officers who created proper latrines and imposed sanitary order in the crazy ravines and on the escarpments of Gallipoli.

Most Australians know of the misfortunes of the first day. The Australians and New Zealanders were to have landed on smoother terrain a mile or so further south, and any visit to Anzac Cove shows how the vagaries of the offshore currents damned them to land beneath intimidating heights, broken by ravines, where losses were guaranteed, where the chances of penetration seemed impossible—though Anzacs did that day nearly take the heights while they were under-defended by the Turks.

Since the story of Gallipoli from a campaign point of view has in the past been so brilliantly written by others, it is instructive to look at how it appeared to the rescuers, the Medical Corps, their doctors, orderlies, and stretcher bearers. A member of the Australian Army Medical Corps aboard ship saw landing parties going ashore on destroyers 'packed like sardines', with the destroyers towing barges no less packed. 'Many of these fellows, before they reached the shore, were shot and tumbled overboard—picked off by snipers . . . one lot of ambulance men were picked off in this way. They were WA boys.' The field ambulance men and doctors were confronted with the sheer cliffs and prickly scrub, and murderous machine-gun fire and shrapnel. The pebbly beach was described by many as not being wider than a cricket pitch, and the wounded had to be treated in the shelter of three-feet-high overhangs by men of the 1st Australian Field Ambulance. Some of them were killed by fire retrieving wounded. 'Talk about mixed bathing,' said one field ambulance man. 'Men and bullets.' The ambulance men could see a boat lying aground packed with dead, and on the beach a piled heap of twenty men, dead and wounded, half in and half out of the water. Because of enemy fire, it would be three days before anyone could reach them.

Further forward a regimental aid post had been established and those wounded in the chest, abdomen and head, and others with severe leg wounds, were being carried back while others walked or limped to join the crowd on the beach, where a casualty clearing station had been set up. A white label was attached to light wounds and a red to those who had suffered grave wounds. But it was dangerous and close to impossible to create field ambulance hospitals out of view of the Turks. The doctors and hospital orderlies had never expected anything like this level of mayhem, and triage—the sorting out of casualties— was near hopeless because of the scale of wounded. Many men who were killed or hit on boats heading for the shore were offloaded to passing minesweepers and destroyers to lie wherever they could be fitted on steel decks before being taken to the initial Gallipoli hospital ship, the *Sudan*.

On 25 April, one field ambulance reported its casualties as two killed, eighteen wounded and four missing. Yet they had cleared more than 3000 wounded. All urgent operations were done, including necessary amputations, tying of arteries, and attending to abdominal wounds, compound fractures of the skull, bladder wounds and compound fractures of the thigh. All these necessitated anaesthetics, which were administered in nearly every instance by non-commissioned officers or by privates.

After dark the wounded were placed on anything that would float them out to the hospital ships or the transports. It was cold that first night at Gallipoli and there was some rain. In the rain and the dark, one transport was hailed by a boat from shore and asked to take ninety Australian wounded on board. The men had been towed around in a small boat for hours seeking accommodation. Forty stretcher cases were swung on board by means of cargo nets lowered over the sides. Several of the casualties died shortly after being put on board.

At four-thirty the next morning, men of the 3rd Australian Field Ambulance landed, some of them immediately becoming victims of sniping, but the rest setting up under an embankment and bringing in the wounded from nearby country. The landing units were scattered groups so it was not easy to find the wounded. The only hospital ship off Anzac Cove at that time, the *Gascon*, rapidly filled up with wounded. Two transport ships were set aside for the lightly wounded. Private Gissing on the transport *Seang Bee* described the ship's hospital being filled almost instantaneously. 'The mess tables were ripped up from below, blankets spread down and the men were laid here as closely as possible.' The *Seang Bee*, its decks already crowded with 900 wounded by 26 April, could not leave the area yet, since her hulls were still full of unloaded ammunition.

An Australian orderly with Number 2 Australian Stationary Hospital, while off Anzac Cove on a transport which had suddenly taken aboard nearly 700 wounded men, 'the majority of them in an awful state', was offered a bribe of 5 sovereigns by one desperately bleeding man to fetch a doctor. Yet a ship full of medical equipment named the *Hindu* had been ordered away on the evening of 25 April without having unloaded its medicines and medical equipment onto the ships where casualties might be carried. The medical situation at Anzac Cove between 25 April and 5 May was also affected by delay and shortage of supplies.

One of the first sets of women's eyes to look upon Gallipoli belonged to Daisy Richmond of the hospital ship *Guildford Castle* as it edged in to collect wounded on the morning of 26 April. Until recently Daisy Richmond had worked in

Boorowa, New South Wales, and she had volunteered for the Australian Army Nursing Service. Unlike the British and Canadian nurses the Australians lacked official rank and status, and were sometimes bullied by traditional army regular medical officers who, against much evidence to the contrary, believed nurses had no place close to the battlefront. The first casualties—eighteen men—came alongside at 2 p.m. on the deck of a destroyer but within hours hundreds more arrived. The nurses had to adjust to a new and unimagined scale of damage to young flesh. 'It was terrible. Badly wounded men kept crawling in from the barges. At times we worked for thirty-six hours without stopping.' The ships were as yet not equipped with the quantities of morphine and dressings needed for the magnitude of events. Surgical instruments were sterilised in water boiled over one or two inadequate primus stoves in a converted pantry.

Because of the possibility that the military operation might be cancelled and the troops withdrawn, there was great anxiety to get wounded men away from Gallipoli as soon as possible. Indeed, General Birdwood, commander of the Australians, a man of considerable courage, suggested a withdrawal. It is interesting to speculate what would have happened if he had persuaded the others, who were in some cases more obtuse men, such as the overall commander General Hamilton. Birdwood would certainly have saved his men in the short term, but only to have them committed all the earlier to the great mincing machine of France and Flanders, or to other poorly planned campaigns in the East.

Dr A.G. Butler, who wrote the medical history of the war, said that the interests of the medical service—to get the severely wounded and amputees away from the primitive and pestilential Gallipoli to fit environs elsewhere—was often at odds with the interests of a ruthless martial machine. Early in the campaigns there was less prompt loading of the badly wounded onto hospital and transport ships than later. According to original orders no ship was to leave its position off Anzac Cove for forty-eight hours. But by 27 April a number of vessels carrying 2800 wounded, below and on their decks, had left for Egypt. Medical units slated to land were broken up so that there were sufficient orderlies to go with the wounded on the transports. Colonel J. Maher of the Royal Australian Army Medical Corps was made Deputy Director of Medical Services Lines of Communication, to control evacuation from Anzac Cove. Under him the flow of the damaged men out of that lethal peninsula improved.

In a conventional war the regimental aid station was furthest forward, just behind the frontline, then the dressing stations and field ambulances a further distance back to give primary aid, and then, ideally three or four miles back, the casualty clearing station, where emergency surgery was performed, wounds were treated, dead flesh cut away and sepsis, wound infection, warded off with antiseptics and cleansing. Patients were also assessed and had labels attached to them according to the severity of wounds. But the casualty clearing personnel, doctors and orderlies at Gallipoli had no more protection than the field ambulances when they first landed.

Dressing stations and field ambulances were eventually set up in the more protected gullies, often dug into the sides of hills and covered with corrugated iron and camouflage, and then the wounded were carried down to the casualty clearing station closer to the beach but similarly concealed. From there, those who could be safely moved to a ship were so moved. Not all of this could happen by night. Casualties lying on the beach waiting for a barge to take them out to the ships were sometimes wounded again or killed by fire from above. Major John Corben of the overworked 1st Australian Casualty Clearing Station was ultimately, in August, put in charge of clearing the beach promptly, but several of his orderlies were put out of action by shrapnel and bullets, and a shelter shed erected to protect waiting wounded was pierced by a huge high explosive shell, which killed a sick man lying on a stretcher, wounded another 'and so shattered the leg of a member of our unit that it had to be amputated two days later on a hospital ship'. The man did not survive.

The Australian surgeons operating competently on the wounded were not meanwhile themselves free from danger. Late in the Gallipoli campaign one casualty clearing station surgeon, Captain H.F. Green, a citizen of Daylesford before medical practice took him to Melbourne, was, wrote Lieutenant George Bell, 'operating on a man when a shrapnel shell from Beachy Bill Battery burst overhead and a pellet went right through his chest and Green fell into the arms of the doctor who was administering the anaesthetics'.

Private H. Chichenani, an Australian orderly, wrote that during the first fortnight abdominal wounds were predominant but as the men got better entrenched, abdominal wounds lessened and head injuries were more noticeable. These wounds must have shocked members of the Australian Medical Corps, who had rarely seen such damage before. But Private A. Gordon remarked on the new respect stretcher bearers received. 'Some of the fellows before this had looked upon the AMC men as cold footers—easy jobbers, etc.'

Many found the Dominion hospitals, generally run by citizen-soldier medical staff, much preferable to the British army hospitals more likely at this stage to be headed by professional military surgeons. John Monash, commanding the

4th Australian Infantry Brigade, was critical of the British hospitals which operated on the nearby island of Lemnos, in Malta and in Egypt. 'It's about time too that somebody asks about the treatment of Australian soldiers in Tommy hospitals, for it's the absolute dizzy limit. Nothing could be better than our Australian or New Zealand or Canadian hospitals, but as to the British hospitals here, well, the sooner they hang somebody for gross mismanagement, the better.' The food supplied to the wounded and ill was poor and insufficient 'to ensure rapid physical restoration of the personnel', as Monash put it.

For the first three months after the landing and that early close call for the Turkish defences above the beach, the campaign was a matter of consolidating, but doing it in daily peril—even in the rear—of being sighted by snipers and artillery and killed or wounded—not in a charge, but in doing simple, homely things such as unloading crates of canned beef or strolling on the beach. The August offensives, when the British attempted to capture Krithia while the Australians assaulted Hill 60 and the New Zealanders were slaughtered on the slopes of Chunuk Bair, were the next great attempts to break out, and again the impossibly confused terrain prevented it all. Some generals blamed Monash for mistaking his objectives and getting his men lost, but the maps were inadequate, the darkness of the night of the attack confusing, the advice of guides ambiguous, while once again the valour of Monash's brigade was admirable. The critics were the same men who had failed to possess or provide adequate maps and lacked the capacity to read them competently, who did not know about the coastal currents of the Dardanelles and who—aboard their floating headquarters—had no topographic imagination. There had already been three ferocious battles for the village of Krithia inland from Helles, the toe of the peninsula, and some of the Anzacs were thrown in there as well. The French lost particularly heavily at Krithia in the infamous Ravin de la Mort. But after these August failures, simply hanging on to the beachhead at Anzac Cove, Suvla Bay and Cape Helles became the issue.

THE NURSES AT LEMNOS

Sister Kit McNaughton, from Little River in Victoria, who had trained as a nurse in the Geelong Infirmary and Benevolent Asylum, was now serving at Number 2 General Hospital in Cairo, dealing with the wreckage of the August offensives on the Dardanelles, when she found out she had been accepted as a volunteer to work on the island of Lemnos. She and twenty-four other army nurses travelled by train from Cairo to Alexandria and sailed aboard the SS *Assaye*—650 miles across the Mediterranean to Lemnos in the northern Aegean, only a two- or three-hour journey from Gallipoli.

By now the wind-scoured, if mythic, Greek island of Lemnos had been taken over as the centre of medical activities in the area, the clearing station for all casualties. In September and October alone these casualties amounted to 50 000 men. The guns of Gallipoli, only fifty miles away, were quite audible, and the deepwater harbour was full of 'ships by the hundred', many of which had delivered the wounded and sick.

The nurses served in tent cities to the north-east and west of the harbour—East and West Mudros. It was stony earth. As a staff member, Sister Aitken, commented, 'At one period or other it seemed to have rained stones.' Nurses were always cheered ashore by soldiers and sailors in the surrounding ships, but their experience once they got to their nursing stations was more ambiguous. A number worked in the Number 2 Australian Stationary Hospital under the courtly Lieutenant Colonel Arthur White who, on their arrival, had escorted them in motor cars up to the hospital site on Turk's Head Promontory in West Mudros. Unlike some of his colleagues, he respected their work. Nearby, the Number 3 Australian General Hospital also had its lines, along with two Canadian and a British stationary hospital, and a convalescent depot with accommodation for 2000 men. Across the inlet was a rest camp newly created to give relief and recreation and rotation out of the line for some of the Anzac Corps.

Though they failed to stress it in their journals because of the traditions of stoicism they had acquired in their Australian girlhoods, indications of the slighting treatment some nurses received emerge nonetheless. 'At times our presence was ignored by an officer, with the result we had little control over the orderlies,' wrote Sister Nellie Morrice. She declared that the patients thought otherwise because they lay there inadequately treated, 'dishevelled and dirty . . . looking more like wild men . . . unshaven, long haired and weeks of dirt and vermin on them'.

Prior to 1914 military officers had not necessarily been used to working with nurses, since military nurses worked only in the largest medical units, the general hospitals, usually situated about 150 miles behind the front. The presence of Kit McNaughton and her fellow nurses in a stationary hospital in a military camp at an advanced place was therefore beyond the experience of some of the professional military doctors. Sister Neeta Selwyn Smith of Number 3 General Hospital wrote in her post-war report to Colonel Butler, the official medical historian, that 'I believe the OC said he would rather have a hospital without sisters'. Captain Deakin, a medical officer, reading a paper for the New South Wales branch of the British Medical Association in December 1916, declared that in the high summer of 1915, when the slaughter on Gallipoli was intense, 'all the nursing had been performed by our male orderlies, who by this time had become expert nurses and could take temperatures and pulses, give hydrodermic injections, enemata and "bowel washouts" as well as any nurse'. His recommendations were that male orderlies should be made efficient to make the presence of female nurses unnecessary in a stationary or general hospital.

Deakin's confidence in an all-male staff is contradicted by Sister Morrice. She says that on arrival on Lemnos in September the nurses found men lying on muddy mattresses on the ground, and that dysentery patients were forced to hobble outside, dressed only in their nightclothes, to use commodes in the icy wind. 'It did not take the sisters long to get the beds raised . . . [we] kept the men in bed and ordered that bed pans should be given to them.' The Australian nurses were also aware that the nurses in the Canadian hospitals nearby were paid more, and better treated and appreciated, and to be efficient they needed to battle their resentment about that.

As the autumn came on, heavy dews attacked the fabric of the tents and penetrated the canvas walls to the extent that sisters had to huddle in the same cot for warmth. Gales swept over the island for the whole autumn, creating cold sandstorms. The women lacked warm clothing and Colonel R.J.H. Featherston, Acting Director of Medical Services for Australia, ordered that they were to have gumboots, trousers and warm clothes even if that meant wearing men's clothing. Featherston cabled back to Melbourne that the women would break down if their situation wasn't improved, and that 'if the sisters were not better treated he would take them off the island'.

For an island designed to treat men with typhoid, paratyphoid, dysentery and other plagues, as well as the severely wounded, water was still scarce. Men and nurses had to balance the laundering of clothes against the need for bathing. The nurses regularly brought lice from the hospital tents and the foul uniforms of the sick back into their sleeping quarters, and Sister McNaughton took a cold sponge bath at eleven o'clock one freezing night to 'keep the creepy things away'. Food was primitive, but sometimes naval officers from ships on the harbour sauntered up and invited them to a rare afternoon tea or dinner aboard, and the young women rushed to accept the invitation. Some men from the Australian Field Artillery on the island sent over a hamper to them, but generally, as Sister Olive Haynes wrote in October 1915, they could not get a boat to go out to the ships to fetch food for them 'and the MOs won't help us'.

As in every other hospital in that theatre of war, nursing units were dealing with greater numbers than had been foreseen. In France it was believed that a stationary hospital should take only 240 patients and be staffed by twenty-seven sisters. Number 2 Australian Stationary Hospital had 840 patients, and this multiplied both the work and the infection rate. The flies of summer were only beginning to die off and dysentery afflicted patients and nurses. As autumn came on and the weather cooled, paratyphoid and jaundice took over.

Dr Featherston meanwhile claimed that Australian nurses, working under Imperial Regulations as 'honorary officers', were subjected to 'threats of personal violence' as well as 'petty annoyances and insults', arising from continual disputes with NCOs and orderlies about the nurses' authority. In a hospital where the commanding officer did not like female nurses—Number 2 Stationary seems to have been such a place—the position of the nurses was nearly as testing as the campaign at Gallipoli itself. Featherston recommended that Australian nurses be given commissioned rank to wear, and in 1916 this would become the case.

Staff Nurse Tilly was discovered at Number 3 Australian General Hospital at Lemnos sitting in a dark ward on a mattress on the floor with a private soldier. Though she argued her innocence, Colonel de Crespigny, the commanding officer, wrote that, 'I am of the opinion that her conduct cannot be condoned, on account of the example to other members of his unit.' Nurse Tilly was sent home and asked to resign. But under the intense conditions, potent feelings, maternal, sisterly and amatory, were released. Kit McNaughton said that she was 'fast losing her heart' to an ill soldier, 'but he is just like Corry [her brother] so I can be excused for loving him'.

Yet as hostile as some of the orderlies and officers were, the nurses were welcome as visitors to the rest camp. Sister McNaughton wrote of going to a concert where she and her friend were the only two sisters in a crowd of 2000 men and were cheered to the front seats. It must have been a welcome contrast to their treatment in the wards. By October Kit McNaughton was showing some signs of exhaustion, depression and withdrawal—she could no longer identify with every individual in the mass of suffering and remain sane. In December she wrote, 'Saturday—life much the same, one big bustle and no one prepared for the invasion of patients—not enough to eat for anyone.' The next day they were expecting another 200 patients, of whom she wrote, 'God help them.'

Later, on the Western Front, her dissatisfaction and anger would emerge in what she called a 'brush-up' with imperious British matrons and medical officers. She would be told by an imperial matron not to speak to Australian soldiers while treating them. She became angry at an Australian medical officer for his treatment of a soldier. She had such a quarrel with one medical officer in 1917 that she thought she might be sent home, and in the end had to apologise for not obeying his orders.

Nurses from Queensland and Victoria formed union-like bodies to agitate for better wages and conditions than the very poor ones they had enjoyed in their pre-war nursing and their early war experience. After the war it would be predominantly former AIF nurses who took part in the Trained Nurses' Guild activities. Yet the women were also liberated by the war from the strict social controls and demands of civil society. On Lemnos Olive Haynes, along with some other nurses, simply cut off their long hair rather than go to the trouble of looking after it. By now they all dressed like soldiers and went out so dressed to pursue a social life, including an excursion to the hot baths at Thermos in the company of artillery officers from the rest camp. On the way up the switchbacks to the spa they undertook target practice with the officers' revolvers.

In December 1915 the Gallipoli Peninsula was evacuated. Sprained ankles suffered in the last withdrawal down the slopes to the beach were the almost-benign final Gallipoli injuries the nurses would deal with on Lemnos. They returned by hospital ship to Egypt in January 1916, 'the funniest looking crowd of weather-beaten and toil-worn women one could imagine—hats of various shape, coats ditto. And boots and gloves beyond description.' Sister Tev Davies wrote, 'We are being supplied with riding pants, tunics and gumboots. Golly, won't we look tragic?' They were different women now, quietly proud of what they had done, and sufficiently haunted and educated by experience to have risen above the style of submission in which they had lived at home. But in Egypt they were now broken up and sent to various units—some to return to Australia on hospital ships, others to go to England and to France.

THE BLOOD MYTH UNASSAILABLE II

The withdrawal from Gallipoli in December 1915 seemed so brilliantly managed that for generations of Australians it would have the weight of a victory, not a retreat. Somehow the Anzacs were able to get away over a number of nights while an ever-shrinking number of troops held the line. The same process would occur with the British, Indians and French at Helles but would not be completed until 8 January 1916.

Even so, the British General Monro estimated that a third of the men would become casualties during the withdrawal, and many of the wounded would not make it off. As well as that, in late November when the planning meetings for the evacuation had just been held on the island of Imbros (the Turkish island of Gökçeada) and on the *Aragon*, where General Monro had his headquarters, cold rains fell so torrentially that at Suvla Bay, north of Anzac Cove, men were drowned in trenches. The flooding was followed on 29 November by snow, and the Anzac evacuation was delayed by a sudden tide of casualties suffering from both frostbite and gangrene of feet and hands.

From the Anzac area over 40000 men had to be withdrawn. From 8 December onwards the first 20000 left by dark, and by 17 December just over 20 000 held the line, but would in their turn creep by squads down the ravines to the beach over two nights, and be taken off by cutter and barge to the troopships waiting to return them to Lemnos and Egypt. Amongst the troop transports were three of the largest liners then afloat: the *Britannic*, the *Aquitania* and the *Mauretania*, which between them could take some 8000 wounded and sick, had been commissioned as hospital ships for the evacuation.

The terrain and the methods used helped maintain secrecy. One unnamed Australian wrote of making his way up to the line through a sap when his path was stopped by descending mules carrying stripped-down mountain artillery. 'I thought at once, "My goodness, if the Turks don't see all this as it goes along they must be blind."' But when he had trudged on another two hundred yards or so, the sound and sight were all lost in the broken ravines of Gallipoli. Taken off too were the Egyptian and Maltese labourers who had helped carry burdens and had built the piers, and the little railway which ran goods ashore from Williams Pier.

Harold Edward 'Pompey' Elliott, the Melbourne lawyer and citizen soldier whose brigade would be one of the last to leave, told his men that anyone who was heard to mention the word 'evacuation' would be court-martialled. At the centre of the legendary cleverness of the withdrawal was a device which was brought to General Elliott's attention early in the evacuation process. A twenty-year-old architectural modeller, Bill Scurry, who had been at Gallipoli only a few weeks but who had served as a lieutenant with Pompey in the Essendon Rifles, had designed a system by which water in a higher placed container dripped gradually into another beneath it, which was attached in turn to a rifle trigger. In the end the lower container pulled the trigger and fired the rifle, creating an appearance that the thinning lines were in fact still heavily manned. On the second last night, 20 December, 10 200 soldiers made their way down to the beach leaving 10 000 to endure a final day in the lines opposite the Turks. Then, on the last night, the men left at spaced intervals, down the hills to the transports, headed for the rest camps of Lemnos. In Australia the withdrawal was not seen as a defeat, nor did the soldiers involved seem to look upon Gallipoli as a fiasco. Or if they did, some of their morale had been restored by the triumph of the withdrawal.

The last on the Gallipoli Peninsula, willing to stay there and be captured if necessary, were to be the 13th British and 1st Australian Casualty Clearing Stations. Supplies adequate for 1200 men for thirty days were left at these clearing stations. It was hoped that the Turkish military would respect the wounded and allow them to be eventually repatriated by the Red Cross. On the final night of the withdrawal, the seriously wounded were not to be transported but their wounds were to be dressed, and they were left behind with a volunteer force of doctors and orderlies. In the end, Captain Alan Barton of the Australian Army Medical Corps, a man still only in his mid-to-late thirties who would become an expert on battlefield anaesthesia and wound closure, volunteered to stay with the wounded. He was kept company by a small party of Australian Medical Corps personnel and was left with a letter written by the head of the Australian Medical Services—the formidable Neville Howse VC, a veteran of the Boer War and Taree surgeon—addressed to the Principal Medical Officer of the Turkish army. 'I am leaving Captain Barton of the Australian Army Medical Corps and a small party of AAMC personnel. I have every confidence that our wounded will be treated with the same care and kindness as we have treated yours.' It was even hoped that after the 1st Australian Casualty Clearing Station was captured by the Turks, the enemy might allow the wounded to be collected by British transports under flags of truce. But Barton was able to begin moving out his last casualties on the night of 20 December, and then, before dawn, he and his party left that scene of so much agony and fear and went out to the last transport. To considerable relief on Colonel Howse's part, Captain Barton and his volunteers turned up at Mudros, the harbour of Lemnos. One of his orderlies had been hit in the arm by a spent bullet and Bartlett believed him 'probably the last Anzac casualty'.

Death amongst his fellow professionals had not been uncommon. Captain G. Mathison of 2nd Field Ambulance had died in May of wounds received at Helles, Captain S. Campbell in July of wounds received at ANZAC, and Captain J. Buchanan of 2nd Light Horse, rescued from Gallipoli, would die on Mudros in December 1915. Nor was that anywhere near the full toll of stretcher bearers, orderlies or doctors Gallipoli claimed.

INTERLUDE: PATERSON AND WORLD WAR I

Without formally being a correspondent, Banjo Paterson enlisted for the Great War on an apparently voluntary basis. A dashing fellow such as he, though now fifty years old, could not but take part in the collision between the Man From Snowy River and the Prussian Lancer. At the extraordinary Australian Voluntary Hospital on the Normandy coast at Wimereux, he volunteered to drive an ambulance during the French and Belgian campaigns of 1914–15. On the way, in Egypt, he had taken note of the Anglo-Australians landing, looking to join their old English regiments and 'wearing as many ribbons as prize bulls ... Any one of them who would sooner be shot as a private in the Coldstream guards than get a decoration in a nameless Australian force.' In reality, some of these Yorkshiremen, Cousin Jacks and Cockneys, rebuffed by their old units, would fall in numbers in Australian units at Gallipoli.

At Wimereux the institution mentioned above, the Australian Voluntary Hospital, was run by Lady Rachel Dudley, a beautiful 'shop-girl', a former fashionable milliner, and the estranged wife of the former Australian Governor-General, the Second Earl of Dudley, George Humble Ward, a philanderer and man of limited gifts whom Andrew Fisher had despised. Appointed in 1908, within little more than six months he refused Fisher's request for a poll. Deakin, who was the beneficiary, nevertheless did not feel any sense of loss when Dudley returned to England in 1911. The more gifted Lady Dudley, appalled by the lack of skilled help for women giving birth in the bush, founded the Lady Dudley Bush Nursing Scheme.

Her hospital at Wimereux, established when she was in her early fifties, existed as an exercise in well-intentioned willpower. For its comfort and less formal atmosphere, many an Englishman recommended it as the place to get into if you could. 'She's a Quaker by birth,' wrote Paterson. 'Comes from that Gurney family of bankers; and if you want a real good stubborn fighter get a Quaker.' Others, predictably, described the Australian Voluntary Hospital as a 'petticoat-ridden outfit'. But the Royal Army Medical Corps, which disapproved of the Australian nurses on Lemnos, reserved an especial hostility for Lady Dudley, who was nonetheless too well connected not to be obeyed. It is a sad after-note to this remarkable woman's history that she would drown while swimming in Western Ireland in 1920.

Meanwhile, Banjo returned to Australia in 1915 and was commissioned in the Second Remount Unit, an appropriate posting given his passion for horses. Promoted to captain, he served in the Middle East, was wounded in April 1916, but rejoined his unit in July. He was promoted to major and commanded the Australian Remount Squadron.

CHAPTER 7

War and peace
From France and Flanders to the peace

I DIED IN HELL

In Australian memory the war in France is seen as a series of tragedies fought in a hellish, shell-hole-dimpled morass. It was, as Siegfried Sassoon, the British soldier-poet, wrote, 'The place where youth and laughter go.'

For many Australian troops, though, it began as an idyll. Marseilles and the south of France were a delight after the blasted landscapes of Egypt and Gallipoli. It was, said the Australian Medical Corps man W.C. Watson, a 'treat to be greeted by our own kind, the girls and women do give us a hearty reception'. In Marseilles the Fort Saint-Jean and Notre-Dame de la Garde seemed prodigiously grand and old to boys from a new country, as was the Chateau d'If, which was the setting for Dumas' still massively popular *The Count of Monte Cristo*. 'My eyes are sore,' Watson wrote on the troop train heading north, 'trying to see too much of this lovely southern France.' But the sight of German prisoners at the railway junction of Laroche was sobering as well as fascinating; 'it is really cruel to see the train loads of wounded coming in and their broken limbs etc. Nearly every woman here is in mourning for a relative of some sort.'

Settled into billets (barns, stables) behind the lines at Steenbecque in the north of France, George R. Faulkner of the 15th Field Ambulance attended the saying of the rosary every evening at the village church, until on 7 July the unit was marched out to a position closer to the front. Here a barrage of gas shells was laid down and they were ordered to move through it quickly, wearing their masks. And now death arrived. The first experience of it for Faulkner was when Captain McKenzie of the 8th Field Ambulance came out from his first-aid post to look at a German bombardment and was immediately blown to pieces. It was an early lesson that the impersonal outweighed the personal in France. But they were young and it was payday and what had happened to McKenzie was just bad luck. Faulkner and three other boys celebrated their pay with a bottle of champagne, for which they pooled five shillings each.

Such was one side of the French experience.

Despite many superb modern histories, for the lay reader the various battles blur, separated by ill-defined stretches of churned French and Belgian country-side, involving foul trenches, inhuman bombardment, satanic gas and night-hour raids on enemy lines, some involving an entire battalion, others a company, often a platoon. Even these raids left young men dead out there in the enemy trenches, or in intervening earth and mud. In histories of World War I, the mud rises, the impersonal torrent of shells fall, and geography is swamped. In the trench line stretching from the north coast of Belgium down to the Swiss border—a trench line five hundred miles long—the British sector was less than one hundred and fifty miles, a minute distance by Australian standards. The British sector, in which the Australians would fight at various points and at various times, ran up from south of the Somme River, skirting Paris to run north-east up into Flanders—the lethal western province of Belgium—and thence to the North Sea.

Even though it was written of a specific battle, Pozières, in late July 1916, perhaps the best generic Australian evocation of the dismay of participation in that loathsome business was produced by Lieutenant J.A. Raws of the 23rd Battalion, a Victorian battalion of the 2nd Division. Raws was an English immigrant and Melbourne *Age* journalist who would be killed by the end of August 1916. His brother would also be killed in the furious and bloody mess of Pozières. The region of Pozières was, said Raws:

nothing but a churned mass of debris with bricks, stones and girders, and bodies pounded to nothing. And forest! There are not even tree trunks left, not a leaf or a twig. All is buried and churned up again and buried again. The sad part is that one can see no end of this. If we live tonight, we have to go through tomorrow night, and next week and next month. Poor wounded devils you meet on the stretchers are laughing with glee. One cannot blame them—they are getting out of this ... we are lousy, stinking, ragged, unshaven, sleepless ... I have one puttee, a dead man's helmet, another dead man's gas protector, a dead man's bayonet. My tunic is rotten

320

with other men's blood and partly splattered with a comrade's brains. I have had much luck and kept my nerve so far. The awful difficulty is to keep it. The bravest of all often lose it—one becomes a gibbering maniac. Only the men you would have trusted and believed in before proved equal to it.

He then mentioned one or two of his friends who stood like granite rocks.

But many other fine men broke to pieces. Everyone called it shell-shock but shell-shock is very rare. What 90% get is justifiable funk due to the collapse of the helm—of self control. [And then, under bombardment] I was buried twice and thrown down several times—buried with dead and dying. The ground was covered with bodies in all stages of decay and mutilation and I would, after struggling free from the earth, pick up a body by me to lift him out with me, and find him a decayed corpse. I pulled a head off—was covered in blood.

But through it all was the undeniable shining star of brotherhood, of what Australians called 'mateship'. Major J.C. Toft wrote, 'When one gets close to rough chaps as some of these men were, one finds hidden qualities. All these men were wicked in the Church sense. All had a keen sense of humour . . . one was particularly impressed with the fact that those of Irish descent loved most a scrap . . . One standard of honour was demanded. Each should do his fair share.' All sects, creeds and types were in the trenches with Toft, he said; 'men from Hobart to Lismore to Cairns, from Emerald, Barcaldine, Longreach, Winton, Cloncurry and Charters Towers . . . men of different habits and thought saw much in each other to love.' There was a feeling that if such fraternity could be applied in civil life after the war, the world would be redeemed.

The Australian campaigns began first with the AIF's 5th Division under the unpopular but ambitious General McKay in front of the French village of Fromelles, north of the Somme, in July 1916. It was a deadly and failed attack of the kind military men called 'a demonstration', designed to stop German forces from moving southwards towards the Somme front. One Gallipoli soldier said of Fromelles, 'We thought we knew something of the horrors of war, but we were mere recruits, and have had our full education in one day.'

The casualties were about 6000, and the shattered division would be marched out to be replenished by new troops who would need training. Soon after, on

23 July 1916, three Australian divisions, the 1st, 2nd and 4th, were at various stages thrown against the German line at the village of Pozières in the Somme Valley. The 1st Division captured the village on the first day, but hanging on to it was deadly. The 2nd Division took over and mounted two further attacks, and then the 4th Division went up into the line and beat off the final German counter-attack. The three divisions suffered in excess of 13 000 casualties. Mouquet Farm, on the ridge north-west of the wrecked village of Pozières, was by 3 September 1916 attacked nine times by these same three Australian divisions, resulting in another 11 000 Australian casualties. Surrounded by the Allies, it would fall in September 1916. There followed a freezing winter on the Somme, which at least cemented the mud in place but was the coldest the native-born Australians, and probably the immigrant diggers as well, had ever endured.

Again, it would be wrong to think that casualties would cease to be inflicted both at the front and in the reserve lines between major assaults. In early October 1916, for example, the 19th Battalion was in the line near Ypres in Flanders and on 4 October undertook a raid led by Lieutenant Heath and two second lieutenants and fifty other ranks. Even though retaliation directed by the German artillery on the Australian lines was very light, it killed one man and wounded four others. On 14 November, the 19th had been moved south again to the Pozières region, in front of the villages of Flers and Eaucourt L'Abbaye, and went into action accompanied by the Northumberland Fusiliers to take at least temporarily part of the enemy's first line, capture prisoners and assess German strength. In this sadly forgotten operation there were Australian casualties of twelve officers and 369 other ranks—about a third of the Australians committed.

In the spring, the fortified French village of Bullecourt, between Cambrai and Arras, was the target for an Australian 2nd Division offensive between 3 and 17 May 1917, which though partly successful produced a number of ferocious counter attacks. The Australian casualties at Bullecourt amounted to 8000 men.

Entrained for the north that same spring, the Australians took part in a successful assault on a ridge running between Messines and Wytschaete. Australian tunnelling companies had, like similar British units, dug saps under the enemy lines—such as the deep tunnel dug by the 1st Australian Tunnelling Company under Hill 60—and at the start of the assault nineteen underground accumulations of high explosives were detonated, causing instantly an estimated 10 000 German casualties. British and Anzac troops took all their objectives on 7 June, but German counter attacks continued until 14 May. Messines was the opening battle for the 3rd Division, led by John Monash, part of the Anzac Corps and of General Plumer's British Second Army, and unjustly mocked for their lack of involvement until now as 'deep thinkers', contemplators rather than actors. In this battle the 4th Division was led by Major General William Holmes, who had commanded the New Guinea expedition. Within a month, he would, unluckily, be killed by a shell while escorting the tall, urbane Labor Premier of New South Wales, William Holman, on a tour of the front. But every day there were unlucky shells for some members of the AIF. And in terms of objectives reached, Messines was considered a success.

'I died in Hell, they called it Passchendaele,' wrote Siegfried Sassoon. In that battle, near Ypres in late July 1917, when the French army was beginning to mutiny on a serious level, the 3rd Division struggled through acres of mud against furious machine-gun fire. A number of Australian divisions were then committed throughout September in the same campaign—known as Third Ypres—fighting either side of the Menin Road and in the gas-drenched Polygon Wood, where cement strongpoints held them up. The gain of a few miles and the straightening of the salient seemed to satisfy the generals, but the Australian losses in just over a week in September were 11 000. With the provisos given above about minor raids and offensives and artillery barges, the campaigning for the autumn closed and another bitter winter began. On 2 February 1917, Private John Keneally wrote to his brother: 'Supposed to be the coldest for fifteen years . . . when you want a wash or shave you have to get a bucket of ice and put it on the stove. You said in your letter you would like to have a bit of this life. Get that out of your head . . . If you ever come near the front I'll shoot you myself rather than let you go in the trenches.'

With the Russian revolution of February 1917, the Russian army had become first rebellious and then mutinied. Lenin and his Bolsheviks accomplished the revolution later in 1917 by telling the army he would make a separate peace with Germany. In the meantime, the Russians undertook no offences in the east. The Germans now had many extra and rested divisions to hurl against the British in March 1918. Ludendorff, the German commander, hoped to smash his way through Amiens, dividing the French and British armies, and swing north to capture the Channel ports, thus encircling the British. The three major attacks on the Western Front from late March, throughout April and into May were known as the *Kaiserschlacht*, and soon after they began the Germans' intention seemed to switch from capturing the Channel ports as a chief objective to simply smashing an irreparable wedge between British and French and—something that now looked possible—the destruction of the British army before the Americans were ready to fight. The attack on the Somme Valley was known as Michael, another a little to the north was Mars, and the smaller offensive in Flanders was codenamed George. The collapse of the British front on the Somme early in the offensive seemed to be catastrophic, with men stampeding rearwards through villages once won by rivers of blood, heading towards Amiens. Moved down from Flanders, where they had been posted during the winter, the Australian Corps of five divisions (the 4th Division being, however, a mere shadow held in reserve) was now commanded by the Australian civil engineer and citizen soldier John Monash. The AIF advanced through the melee of British Fifth Army retreat, and in the villages they marched past British stragglers by the thousands retreating westwards, some of whom called to them, 'You won't hold them.' The sight of the British, many of them new and untried soldiers who had been given a job for which they were not ready, escaping in such numbers and in such disorder would create an ultimate belief, justified or not, that the Australians were asked to do more than their fair share, a perception which would generate mutiny amongst the diggers later in the year.

There is no doubting the morale or the determination of the men of the Australian Corps at the stage of the German attack. While the 3rd Division took a rest in its advance in the village of Heilly, on its way to hold the angle between where the Ancre River entered the Somme, the historian C.E.W. Bean claims that a digger, cleaning his rifle, called to a village woman suffering obvious distress and anxiety, '*Fini retreat, madame. Fini retreat—beaucoup Australiens ici*.' Townspeople west of Bapaume, loading up farm wagons and lorries to join the stream of refugees from what seemed like an unstoppable German attack, saw the diggers and cried, '*Les Australiens. Pas necessaire maintenant*.' An Australian was told, '*Vous les tiendrez*': You'll hold them. And that was indeed what happened.

On the Ancre the Australians could see German reinforcements pouring from buses in the background. The entire effort along the front involved ferocious fighting, shell and machine guns and all the rest of the horrors. For now, however, the Australians stopped the German advance on the Somme. This was a point at which all that Australia would come to believe of the diggers was validated. In Australian minds ever since, the idea has been that the four divisions of the Australian Corps saved the West, though many modern historians dispute that idea, claiming amongst other things that the Germans had by now overstretched themselves.

Characteristic of the Australian morale was a letter from Private John Keneally of the 19th Battalion in the 2nd Division written on 14 April 1918.

Things in this part of the world have livened up a good deal since old Jerry started his offensive, but his little game will soon come to an end . . . His losses are terrible. They come over massed and it is quite a treat for our gunners to get going on them in the open, quite a change to get him out of his dugouts. All you can see is dead Fritzes lying about in scores . . . I think it is his last dash and it won't be long before the boys are all coming home again . . . I'll settle down in some quiet spot when this bit of a squabble is over.

On the eve of Anzac Day the Germans took the village of Villers-Bretonneux. The Australians had earlier captured it, but it had been lost by the two battle-weary British divisions placed there to hold it. Now the orders were to recapture it. In innumerable horrifying conflicts during night assaults, Sergeant Charlie Stokes and Lieutenant Clifford Sadlier of Subiaco in Western Australia decided to take the German machine guns in front of them which were killing and maiming the men of the 51st Battalion. Their crazed assault, throwing bombs or grenades as they went, was successful. This was just one of many such furious encounters that night of face-to-face fighting when Australian young men struggled so intimately with German young men that they could smell the other's sweat and terror and the accretions of mud and blood and brain matter in uniforms.

Here ended the German offensive and the historian of the 5th Division, which had been so savaged at Fromelles, was able to declare, 'Thereafter, no German ever set foot in Villers-Bretonneux, save as a prisoner of war.' The town, if not captured, would have provided a position from which Amiens could be reduced to ruins by artillery.

In the summer of 1918, the Americans arrived in numbers. According to Bean, the Australians were still heavily used: 'The Anzac fronts provided a quite extraordinary proportion of the news in the British communiqués,' he wrote. On 10 June, under Monash, the Australians seized the latest German front system at Morlancourt, south of Albert. Now the Battle of Hamel, a village just south of the Somme, was planned with great intensity by Monash and his staff, and according to Monash was meant to serve as a model of what could be done on the Western Front by collaboration between aircraft, artillery, tanks and infantry. The story of Hamel will be told later in this narrative, but this eminently successful assault gained in less than an hour more than many previous attacks had managed to gain in a month. Amongst the successes of the day was the capture of the enormous rail-borne 'Amiens gun', capable of pounding the city of Amiens from a distance of 15 miles (25 kilometres). The account of the Australian plans to blow it up and then to souvenir it instead is told in homely fashion by Corporal John Palmer. 'Les Strahan one of our sappers in the party had been a driver in the Western Australian railways, and he found there was still a head of steam, he asked for a fair go, instead of blowing the gun up he got the engine going, we were told then to try to get it back if possible into a cutting so it could be camouflaged.' This sort of collision between world history and Antipodean dryness and practicality is one of the aspects of the Great War which would fascinate Australians of future generations. Despite the triumph of the day, there were over 2000 casualties. One of them was Private Edward Wylie who, with his comrades of the 59th Battalion, captured a sunken road. It was, however, partly within range of a machine-gun position. Sergeant G. Robertson wrote: 'Wylie lifted his head to look at a machine-gun position opposite when he was hit right in the throat. Within a few minutes Wylie, a man named O'Mara (shot through spine and killed instantly), Davies (through back) and Curly Hendry (through head instantly) were killed.'

In coming days the Allies continued forward, with the Australians making the pace, but by now the shortage of tanks left the infantry less protected. On 23 August 1918, Private Albert Golding wrote, 'The French are pushing Jerry back down south, and we tell each other that the war is just about over, but each one knows that it won't end for three or four years yet.' On the last night of August the Australians crossed the Somme River to assault a mound named Mont St Quentin which overlooked Péronne. Mont St Quentin was like all the hills and ridges of this war—just high enough to give an inordinate advantage to those who held it and barely noticeable as a rise. By 7 a.m. the Australian troops had captured the slope and summit. They had taken 14 500 prisoners and 170 guns since 8 August, and the guns would be repatriated to Australia and donated to municipalities for display in such places as public parks, where they can be seen to this day.

The Germans were forced out of Péronne by 3 September, and retreated now to the Hindenburg Line. Throughout September 1918, the Australians attacked that line, the last and best prepared of the German trench systems. They were frequently in the open, advancing across fields which had not been ploughed to hellishness by artillery, and their casualties were still high. 'By the way I lost one of my old mates Barney Heffernan,' wrote Private John Keneally to his mother. 'You have his photo I think I sent on which we had taken when we first arrived in England. He had a fairly hard knock and died of wounds.'

At 5.20 a.m. on 18 September Monash's troops went forward against a fiercely defended Hindenburg Line. They were escorted by only eight tanks, but Monash had ordered the construction of fake tanks to undermine German perception. The Australians penetrated quickly and could thus boast of being the first into the Hindenburg Line, where that day they took 4300 prisoners. Some days later, Australian and US troops were the first to advance against the centre of the Hindenburg Line at Bellicourt. There were heavy losses, not least amongst the untried 27th American Division. After four days the third section of the Hindenburg Line was breached. The Australians broke beyond and slept in the comfortable reserve German trenches and ate German supplies.

The last attack was against Montbrehain village beyond the Hindenburg. There were a final 430 Australian casualties. It was the last battle for the Australians. The Americans replaced them. Most of the Australians had been fighting for six months without a break, and eleven out of sixty battalions had been amalgamated into other units for lack of men. In the Australian army, there had been 27 000 casualties since 8 August. Captain Francis Fairweather wrote, 'Unless one understands the position it would seem that the Australians have been worked to death as we have been going continuously since 27 March, but they are the only troops that would have the initiative for this type of warfare.'

After the Armistice, the landscape opened up. On 27 November 1918 John Keneally wrote, 'We are today about 20 Kilo from the Belgian border. The French towns we have come through which were recently held by Fritz are in a bad way. No one could believe what a hard time the civilian population have had under the Hun . . . they are all practically starving but the Jerries will pay dear for it all.' Billy Hughes thought the same way.

The Australian forces engaged throughout the war totalled 417 000 which, though much less a number than the armies of the major powers, was a massive commitment for a population of 4 million. The casualty rate was nearly 65 per cent wounded, prisoners of war or stricken with serious illness related to the war. Nearly 60 000 would die. This was a higher rate of casualties than those of the British forces, and much, much higher than those of the Americans. Billy Hughes would remember this as well.

THOMAS KENEALLY

THE CATEGORIES OF MISERY

In popular imagination, World War I has become predominantly a war of mud. Mud intruded in sundry ways. In front of the village of Lagnicourt in March 1917, the ground had begun to thaw so that the rifles of a South Australian battalion were choked with mud within 50 yards of the German line. Seven of the South Australians' Lewis machine guns also clogged, and a man spent all his time running from post to post, trying to clean them with strips of German blanket. Combine that degree of liquefaction with the cling of mud upon uniform, boots and other equipment and one gets the picture of the wallow of France and Flanders. 'In every depression,' wrote C.E.W. Bean, 'the flooded craters lay brim to brim like the footprints of monstrous animals.'

W.C. Watson, a stretcher bearer, describes entering the recently thawed and thus nearly uninhabitable British trenches on the Somme near Bapaume in the spring of 1917. The mud of the region added pounds of clag to the boots, equipment and arms of men marching up to the line. This was the muck in which the dead of the previous summer had been buried, and their putrefying bodies liberated from the grave again, in whole or part, by endless artillery barrages.

A man's native susceptibilities had to be deadened by the effect of walking over the dead body of some poor Tommy lying scarcely covered in the bottom of the trench or here and there to observe a limb, boot or hand or a piece of khaki sticking out from the side of the trench with no other legend than 'an unknown British soldier'... here an arm was exposed, here a hand, just a sodden remnant of bone and muscle, there a leg and there two Blucher boots, pointing skyward, suggesting their Hun owner had been buried head downward, or had been thrown that way by a subsequent explosion.

Watson had a fear of being buried while sheltering in undercut holes in the sides of trenches. Here men slept like dogs, he said, but whenever high explosive shells began to arrive, he would come out. 'I felt always a horror of being buried alive.' Five men were one night lying 3 or 4 yards from him in such holds when an explosion brought tons of heavy wet earth down on them. Three of the men were quickly dug out, but one of the diggers hurled his shovelfuls of mud over the parapet, and this attracted increased German shelling on that part of the trench. An older man was still buried, and when at last dug out with Watson's help he was immobile. Whether he was at that stage dead or not Watson would never know, since a shell now exploded and a spear of shrapnel ripped the man's back open.

Men learned, however, that the old shell holes were like quicksand and were advised to shelter in the fresher ones. Near some duckboards men sank and smothered. In October 1917, near Westhoeck in Flanders, an Australian motor ambulance skidded off the road and sank roof first into the bog.

It was a terrible element for those who were casualties. On 13 October 1917 stretcher bearers were trying to find the wounded in front of the German lines in the morass of Passchendaele. The Germans mercifully refrained from firing and in some cases, seeing the bearers wallowing in the mud, even directed the bearers to wounded Australians who had become barely visible in the mire. But finding a wounded man was merely a beginning. Carrying the wounded back to the trenches and down the rearwards communication trenches to the nearest form of medical attention, the regimental aid post, was a labour with mud, and a struggle with traffic of other mud-encumbered men that could take half a day. At the aid post areas themselves men were laid down in mud, still under shelling, which filled the air with falling body parts and mud.

Crown Prince Rupprecht, aware of the impact of mud on the Allies, wrote in his diary: 'Most gratifying rain; our most effective ally.' General Haig said after Passchendaele, perhaps with too much complacency, that Flanders mud was famous in the history of war and had defeated more armies than his. The alternative was the freezing of the terrain, which replaced trench foot with frostbite and froze men's mufflers to their face. Thus there were only two seasons at the front—mud and ice.

General Monash, like other generals on both sides of the line, was willing to use gas. In military terms it could be so effective since in human terms it could induce such terror. Near Ypres in late February 1917, Monash combined smoke and gas shells in the preparatory bombardments of his divisional artillery. When the Australians attacked, smoke shells alone were fired in the final bombardment so that the Australians would not be subject to the poisonous effects, but German defenders, seeing the smoke, would continue to wear their incapacitating gas masks. This method of deception would be used by both sides in World War I since it was taken as axiomatic that men could not fight a battle in gas masks, and that they hated wearing them only a little more than they hated the blistering, choking range of gases used by both sides. By the time the Australians reached the Western Front, gas was still released in clouds from cylinders when the wind was right and would be even in the last phase of the war, when the Germans were holding on to the Hindenburg Line.

The first Australians to encounter a gas cloud of this nature were an advance party of 2nd Division troops in June 1916. They had already trained in a released gas practice behind the British line so they seemed to have survived it well—except for a cyclist-messenger who had left his gas mask behind and suffered an acute dose as he pedalled rearwards to find it. As the war continued, gas arrived chiefly by shells which landed not with a bang but a thud. For another two decades, Australian families would hear the racking and wheezing of the gas victims. The gases they had been poisoned by included the damaging and often fatal lung irritants such as chlorine, phosgene and diphosgene, which could make a man choke to death by attacking the pulmonary system and bursting apart the walls of the air sacs in the lung. When phosgene and the other lung irritants were inhaled, the victim's lungs would flood with oedema fluid. After the most acute torture, death would result by choking and drowning. At the casualty clearing stations oxygen was given to those men whose panicked eyes and blue skin betrayed the symptoms of gas damage. The patient often became semi-delirious.

The last category were the vesicants which irritated or burned the skin—the most famous being dichlorethylsulphide or mustard gas. Mustard gas could slough away the membranes of the trachea. The dead skin served as a breeding ground for secondary infections and men could die of bronchopneumonia and other diseases. Men who sat on ground that was contaminated by mustard gas would often be burned through their clothing and develop blisters.

There were rarer cases of hydrocyanic gas, which attacked the central nervous system, but attacking troops of the side who used it were themselves unwilling to advance into such a lethal cloud. This notorious gas would later be used in concentration camps in World War II.

It was militarily useful also to use the less deadly but disorienting 'lachrymators', tear gas, such as benzyl bromide, or sneezing gas, which the troops called 'smokes'. The chemical officers of both sides mixed and matched all these ingredients at any given time. If an irritant gas could get to a man's mouth and nostrils a second or two before he got his clumsy mask on, it could cause such acute irritation of eyes or nose that he was likely to rip it off again and become subject to something more deadly. For the convenience of their gunners, the Germans marked their shells with a yellow, blue or green cross, to signify the main contents.

Australian nurses such as May Tilton, working in September 1917 in a ward for gas victims at a casualty clearing station several miles behind the lines in Belgium, noticed how, unlike the other wounded, the gas victims wore 'such frightened expressions'. (It is a matter of the incidental cruelty of the situation that May Tilton's fiancé was killed while she was working in the gas wards that October.) She bathed the victims' eyes with sodium bicarbonate, put cocaine drops in them, and relieved the outer flesh and inner membrane pain of mustard-gas burns with morphine. She and other nurses administered oxygen from a device named 'the octopus', an oxygen cylinder to which many tubes and masks were attached, allowing a number of soldiers to benefit from the cylinder at the same time. But she and the other women could work in the ward only for a certain time, since the gas fumes rising from the men and their uniforms would begin to attack the nurses' throats and eyes also, and they would go out into the open to inhale air and drink tea before returning. Sister Topsy Tyson declared after working in a ward permeated by the residue of a gas attack at Messines, 'My throat and eyes were smarting and I felt awfully sick.' Elsie Cook (daughter-in-law of the prime minister Joseph Cook), an Australian volunteer nurse working in a hospital near Amiens in April 1918, wrote, 'Hundreds of gas cases coming in all night . . . they were quite blinded and suffering.' Sister Tev Davies found that even when the gas victims got as far from the front as Boulogne, their condition was still pitiable. 'Mum, such cruel stuff it is . . . one runs all day with inhalations, gargles, douches, eye baths. Mercy me! Fritz is fiendish alright. Not warfare at all, it is slaughter absolutely.'

Adolescent Fritzes, of course, suffered as badly from the same causes as did the British and Australians. Near Messines in May–June 1917 a mixture of explosive and gas shells were fired at the German batteries to force the gun crews to wear their masks continuously and so deny them sleep. In reciprocation, in July the artillery of the 2nd, 4th and 5th Australian Divisions at Ypres were shelled with mustard gas and, at a breath, the 4th Division's artillery lost four officers and 117 men. Near Polygon Wood, close to Ypres, the Australian Pioneer Squads, whose job was to lay down the duckboards leading to the frontline, continually suffered from burns due to the mustard gas oil which settled into the soil of shell holes and impregnated their clothing. These were considered minor problems compared to those visited upon the troops by explosive shells. But gas so terrified the troops and so impregnated the air and soil that Colonel Butler, the official historian, mentions cases of men disabled by the sincere belief they had been gassed when they had not. Gas lingered in the air in any case and reduced men to speaking in croaking voices.

The back areas were regularly shelled with gas as a means of preventing reinforcements and supplies from moving, and to disable the gunners. In the summer and early autumn of 1917, the German chemical officers were favouring shells named Blue Cross, which released what was called a 'sneezing gas' penetrating the respirators, then they changed over to Yellow Cross mustard gas to catch those who had taken their masks off. On the night of 28 October, at Passchendaele, the officers and men of the 5th and 6th Batteries were put totally out of action by gas. On 2 November, two battery commanders were gassed and died within forty-eight hours. Even in the support line, the 25th Battalion, six officers and 202 men were gassed and bivouacs had to be changed again and again because of mustard gas impregnation of the soil.

Particularly from 1917 troops found the bombing of front and rear areas unnerving, the bombers coming in low and releasing their high-explosive bombs by a lever and to great effect. 'Fritz is a constant visitor over these parts nearly every night,' wrote a soldier from hospital. In the dark of the night, casualty clearing stations and hospitals ran the risk of being bombed. In July 1917 the 3rd Australian Casualty Clearing Station was near a railroad at Passchendaele and close to an observation balloon unit and suffered accordingly, one tent of patients disappearing. Every bottle of anaesthetic in the operating theatres was shattered. The mortuary was hit with grisly results. One stretcher case was found deeply embedded in the earth, dead of concussion, still on his stretcher. The attrition from bombing continued for two months, and the wounded, immobilised on their beds, felt very exposed during these attacks. Nor were nurses immune. One nurse, Alice Ross King, winner of the Military Medal, found it hard to be ordered away from her wounded into a dugout as bombs fell. In late 1917 another Australian nurse, Eileen King, serving in a tented field hospital in France, had her left thigh broken when a stick of bombs fell. She continued to work, getting patients out of a burning marquee. For this she was also awarded the Military Medal.

SHELL SHOCK

There were cases of war-induced 'madness' even at Gallipoli, and the 287 cases ultimately evacuated from Gallipoli were only the worst instances. Some men who landed at Gallipoli were already suffering from mental disease. One of Australia's senior medical consultants, Dr Harry Maudsley, claimed that some of these soldiers had been specifically advised by their practitioners to enlist, for the transportation to the battle zone and a bracing involvement in combat were seen as potential cures for their condition.

Even so, the possibility of psychiatric problems arising at Gallipoli had not occurred to the military beforehand, and the system for recording the causes why men were evacuated were crude. In aid stations on the slopes running down to Anzac Cove, regimental medical officers began to see tremors, stammering, speechlessness (mutism or aphonia) and paralysis. Previously brave young men who, without being physically wounded, were obviously unfit to carry on were taken off the beach to the island of Lemnos or to Malta or Alexandria to recuperate.

At Gallipoli there was never relief. There could be no going AWL, ducking back to a village for wine or the company of women, as the Australians in France became notorious for. Only on a rare leave on Lemnos or Imbros was such release from pressure possible. Neuroses and mental breakdown were not the preserve of the private soldier. From 25 April 1915 Lieutenant Colonel W.T. Paterson amazed other officers by his behaviour, hunting around with a revolver in his hand 'looking for General Bridges to kill him'. Paterson was shipped out to Lemnos and eventually to Egypt with 'nervous instability'. Of men like Paterson, the commander of the 4th Field Ambulance, L.J. Beeston, wrote, 'The number of officers clearing out is not commendable. One cannot wonder at the men's squibbing it, one is more and more surprised at officers in whom we would have placed every confidence before the war and they are so bare-faced about it.'

But was everyone who went 'squibbing it'? The nurse May Tilton remembered nursing a twenty-year-old who regained his reason but had lost his ability to talk in more than nearly inaudible murmurs. 'He told me in the faintest whisper that he saw his two elder brothers killed one day on the peninsula. He went mad and wanted to rush the Turks' trenches; remembered being prevented; then knew no more.'

Major Alfred Campbell, who would serve in Egypt and run the first 'nerve hospital' for diggers at Randwick in Sydney, wrote of the trigger for mental disorder that 'in most the cause was a severe shock, such as a shell explosion close at hand, lifting them in the air and burying them with debris'. One man had been rendered blind due to psychic shock within a few minutes of landing at Anzac Cove. He made a rapid recovery and returned to the front but the first nearby shell explosion brought the blindness on again. 'These were not necessarily wanting in courage,' said Campbell. 'Many of them possibly self-goaded continued on duty for weeks . . . some were finally knocked out, but not wounded, by an explosion of some kind.'

Campbell took particular note of a case of the condition named hemi-chorea in a young man who had done considerable trench fighting at Gallipoli. 'Movements of face, trunk and limbs on one side so violent that the subject was unable to walk, use a bed pan or take food unassisted.'

In 1916, as the Australians went into action in France, the British military were still avoiding the term 'shell shock'. They divided all such cases diagnosed in the field into two categories—one was 'shell concussion', the symptoms of concussion of the brain or spinal cord of a severe nature, and the second was 'nervous shock'. Soldiers in the first category were to be evacuated as wounded, and the second as sick. The latter were directed to special clearing stations behind the lines.

In France, the men in the frontline did not doubt the reality of shell shock. Doomed young Lieutenant Raws saw the officer commanding the 23rd Battalion go 'temporarily mad' and desert his men. References to temporary madness stud soldiers' letters, and later—even in civilian life—the madness and the torment could return and become more permanent. Raws mentions in a letter to his sister dated 8 August 1916 that 'the strain had sent two officers mad'. But comrades do not seem to blame other men for this temporary madness from which men often recovered; nor, in the case of those with whom a range of symptoms became more permanent, did they despise. The term 'poor fellow' was often used for those who were sent back to the rear with manifestations of more long-running mental disorders. W.C. Watson saw men crazed by shells bursting near them. 'It was pitiful to see the nervous wrecks of men being led out by the hand crouching in terror at the sound of every passing shell.'

How temporary madness and ultimate shell shock might arise is suggested by Corporal Archie Barwick, who wrote, 'As the ground heaved under the frightful bombardment any amount of men were driven stark staring mad and more than one of them rushed out of the trenches towards the Germans, any amount of them could be seen crying and sobbing like children, their nerves completely gone. How on earth anyone could stand it God alone knows. We were all nearly in a state of silliness and half-dazed.' Captain G.D. Mitchell, a young man who would later write a book on his experience, *Backs to the Wall,* admitted that at the beginning of the winter of 1916 a nearly disabling terror overwhelmed him. It was probably a delayed reaction, he believed, for the night was quite still, there was no bombardment and he was on listening duty—listening in particular for enemy activity and patrols. 'In that hour was born in me a fear that lasted throughout the whole winter. It was the dread of dying in the mud, going down into that stinking morass and though dead being conscious throughout the ages. It was probably a form of claustrophobia.' Indeed, one of the common triggers of 'madness' or shell shock was burial alive in soil impregnated with gas, rats and body parts. Sergeant J.R. Edwards of the medical detail attached to the 27th Battalion wrote almost cheerily of the experience of being buried alive. He and a friend were lying together in a recess of a trench running alongside the road between the village of La Boisselle and Pozières. At one o'clock La Boisselle came 'under attention' from the German gunners.

> A 5.9 landed fair on the parapet above our 'possie'. It broke down the 3 or 4 feet of earth above the recess, and buried us . . . I tried to raise a cry but the earth was over my face and my hands were pinned across my chest by the weight . . . I struggled like hell but could do nothing. All of a sudden the pressure became heavier; it was irresistible, and I was blotted out. I recollect thinking, 'I'm gone', and knew nothing more until coming to in the colonel's dugout sometime later.

Two soldiers named Bert and Jim were the rescuers, and had begun work with shovels almost at once. They dug with shells falling all around them and at last got Edwards' companion, Telfer, out. To get to Telfer, however, they had to pull out a wooden strut and that caused the further collapse of dirt on top of Edwards. When he was excavated, 'It took four swaddies [orderlies] to hold me on the stretcher. I believe I yelled and screeched like mad. Evidently resurrection is a tougher ordeal than death.' He said that 'something had been jarred inside my tough old nut, and my memory was affected'. Telfer and he were taken back to an auxiliary dressing station at Bécourt and were admitted to the base hospital. But Edwards, an extraordinarily robust soul, was discharged a week later, rejoined his battalion and served in it till the war's end. Other men, through no fault of their own, would have been affected for life—indeed, we do not know whether or not Edwards himself was.

It had been at Pozières on the Somme in late July 1916, said the psychiatrist Lieutenant Colonel J.W. Springthorpe, that for the first time shell shock 'fell like an avalanche' on thousands. Gunner Butcher, who had enlisted in mid-1915, was blown up three times during the campaigns of 1916 and was evacuated to England suffering from stabbing pains in the head. He was excitable, shook and perspired, and often felt as if the bed was being pulled from under him to pitch him over a precipice. Private A., a minor from the 17th Battalion who had been blown up twice in three days, was admitted to hospital in England and was still suffering in May 1918. On the Somme in September 1916, Lieutenant Colonel E.A. Harris was brought in by a stretcher party 'blown up by a shell', said C.E.W. Bean, 'and suffering from shell shock', and told Brigadier-General Pompey Elliott that he doubted he could face another battle. Bean would also write, 'The genuine shell shocks were a feature of Pozières.' Private Longford Colley-Priest, a stretcher bearer with the 8th Australian Field Ambulance, wrote of his experiences at Fromelles in July 1916, 'A chap has just been brought in and is sitting by my side, poor devil, his whole body is shaking, one would think he was shivering from the cold. His nerves must be shattered.'

By 1917 Springthorpe had established a network of sympathetic English families who were willing to host his Australian hospital patients. But military bureaucracy intervened. Springthorpe angrily asked why his patients could never be allowed sick leave since 'I have continuously and repeatedly made use of sick leave for selected shell shock patients'. But the director of Australia's services, Major General Neville Howse VC, wrote that there seemed to be no sufficient reason to allow it.

C.E.W. Bean admitted he had been appalled 'with the look of the men' in general. He had passed an Australian battalion without seeing a single smile on any man's face. The Somme had wrought this. Doctors attributed some of the problems to the passive and impersonal nature of the warfare when, as official historian Lieutenant Colonel Butler wrote, 'after each minor advance the troops must sit tight in sectors of the front system which the enemy then pounded to dust'. With this went lack of sleep, poor food, unrelenting anxiety and acute physical discomfort. As Charles Bean wrote, the Somme sector left the Australians 'facing the storm with no other protection than the naked framework of their character'.

The numbers who suffered the conditions should not be exaggerated nor underestimated. Between October 1915 and August 1918 nearly 20 000 sick and wounded casualties were sent home to Australia. Of these 878 were considered to be suffering from the freshly diagnosed condition named shell shock, but 1400 from disordered action of the heart (DAH), a diagnosis often deployed by surgeons to save brave men from the stigma of mental disease, for which the high command had little sympathy. Indeed, merciful Australian regimental medical officers were frowned on for diagnosing men as suffering DAH or the curiously named Effort Syndrome rather than shame their patients by tagging them with a mental condition. The use of the diagnosis DAH as a cover for shell shock would be banned by the British high command in late May 1918. Many surgeons were in any case sending men back labelled NYD, or Not Yet Diagnosed. NYD (W) became the notation written on the labels attached to the fragments of men's uniforms when they were sent back down with shell shock and wound, NYD (S) was the diagnosis of shell shock without a wound. Later in the war medical officers became confident enough to write 'Shell shock W'. The W stood for 'wound' but also for 'windage', which would come to be called 'blast'.

As well as the figures for shell shock and DAH amongst those transported home, however, there were the thousands more Australians who could not be moved yet from British hospitals entirely or partially devoted to the treatment of the condition. And shell shock was often associated with being wounded, and it was the physical wound rather than the mental one that made it into the list. One historian argues from the details provided for casualties that 16.96 per cent of the Australians on the Western Front suffered from shell shock at some time or other, though many recovered with treatment. But any attempt to work out how many soldiers suffered shell shock in combination with wounds is an impossibility.

Some validly argue that a remarkable solidarity between men could itself act as a preventive of shock. In the Australian army this solidarity often arose between officers promoted from the ranks or respected in their own right and their men, and operated on an intimacy which would not have been tolerated in other armies. Captain J.G. Croft, a Queensland officer, wrote of himself that 'I was one of a mob'. Major G.D. Mitchell would later write that the post-war hit play *Journey's End*, which featured British officers sitting in a dugout utterly separate from the men, could never have been written about the Australian army. Instead of 'solitary glory' the Australian platoon officer fed from his mess tin amongst his men. 'I have often had my rum issue swiped by some dissolute private when my back was turned. And cigarettes—blazes! When I had one left, the platoon considered they had an option on it.' Indeed, men commissioned in the field felt such an egalitarian desire to validate themselves in front of their friends in the ranks they were frequently killed doing it, giving rise to the saying, 'One star, one stunt [battle].'

Yet sometimes this safety net of brotherhood was not enough. The damage from shell shock could be long-term. Nineteen-year-old Private John Hargreaves, a tall and sturdy young man, had enlisted in the AIF in July 1915, and in 1916 the family received official notification that he was returning home because of his wounds. The Hargreaves family travelled by train from Ararat in western Victoria to meet the hospital ship *Karoola* in Melbourne, which carried a number of the men who had been wounded at Pozières five months earlier. The Hargreaves could not find their son amongst the disembarking soldiers, and tracked him down to Caulfield Hospital. Their son sat before them in 'mental stupor'. He had been buried alive by a shell at Pozières, an experience which was a common trigger of shell shock. He could not move or acknowledge anyone, or recognise his family, although he did squeeze the hand of his favourite younger sister Teddy. The family found out that on the way back to Australia John needed to be hand-fed by one of the ship's cooks. He suffered, amongst all else, from aphonia, the inability to speak. Men with such symptoms had already been shipped home from Gallipoli in 1915, and their relatives had begun to agitate for special hospitals to treat them, instead of seeing them sent to civilian lunatic asylums and sanatoria.

There remained a suspicion that those who succumbed to shell shock were morally or genetically inferior. Even Lieutenant Colonel Arthur 'Gertie' Butler, an accomplished Queensland surgeon, Cambridge athlete and graduate, an obstetrician and gynaecologist before the war, and brilliant writer of the three-volume official medical history of the AIF afterwards, found the condition both complex and mystifying. It was not for lack of encountering what soldiers called 'madness'. He had been one of the first to land at Gallipoli on 25 April, and in France had run field ambulances and the 1st Division's main dressing station at Bullecourt and on the Menin Road in Flanders in 1917. Butler wrote, 'Shell-shock was a term used in the early days to describe a variety of conditions ranging from cowardice to maniacal insanity.' Butler gave his study of shell shock the chapter heading 'Moral and Mental Disorders in the War of 1914–18'. 'At the other end . . . comes the problem of the line between "cowardice"—a military crime—and "nervous breakdown".' Butler argued, however, that Australian soldiers were more 'constructively "democratic"' than other troops, and thus were more influenced by what they saw around them in the trenches than by any diktat on 'madness' or 'funk' coming down the line from the staff. They knew what they knew about other men and themselves, and what they knew was the inhuman strain of it all. This knowledge, too, might account for the fact that the Australian authorities would impose but never carry out the death penalty for desertion, despite British pressure to do so.

POWS

Only 3800 Australians surrendered to the Germans, and such a small proportion of all the Australians engaged is itself a sign that war in the trenches was a bitter affray in which high explosives, gas, machine guns and bacteria imposed the great majority of casualties.

Prisoners of war are not often mentioned in the popular record of World War I. Perhaps it was difficult to find them a place in the Anzac legend. Five hundred were taken at Fromelles, the opening Australian engagement, another 1200 the following spring at Bullecourt and more still at Villers-Bretonneux in 1918. The imprisonment of these latter men was relatively short. But a document entitled *How the Germans Treated Australian Prisoners of War*, produced by the Department of Defence in Melbourne in 1919, seemed to place a measure of blame for a failure of esprit on the captives' part. 'In such a situation men so entrapped could minimise their chances of being killed by becoming passive and presenting a non-threatening attitude to the enemy or fleeing. When large numbers of men have been captured, it is certain that a moment is reached, almost collectively, in which they forfeit their aggressive instincts and opt for survival.' Yet often enough they had had no choice in the matter, having been left wounded on the field.

Private G. Davidson, captured at Fromelles, later remembered a reasonable level of treatment. 'I was taken to Douai hospital [behind German lines in France] and I remained in hospital there until October ... was then sent to Munster. I was in hospital until April 30 1917 and was then transferred to the Lager. I remained in the Lager until December 7 1917. Then I was moved to Mannheim where I passed the Medical Board for internment in a neutral country.' Davidson's Fromelles wounds, which had kept him in hospital for nine months, made him no further threat to the German state and so he was sent to Holland under the care of the Red Cross and ultimately repatriated.

Not everyone thought fondly of the Douai military hospital. Lance Corporal Alder went through four operations on his arms and legs there but was at one stage left for twenty-three days without fresh bandages. 'My wounds were covered in maggots. I complained to the doctor through the interpreter ... he replied to catch them would be a good pastime for me.' Private Marrinon, shot through his arm and both thighs, found that after his operation he was neglected and his wounds dressed only every ten days, and on one occasion after a delay of sixteen days. Private Wait says he often saw a German under-officer named Marks ill-treat the men, and when they cried out in pain behave even worse.

'He was brutal in his handling of the patients . . .' In some cases men became aware of the shortages of everything from food to bandages that were occurring due to the blockade of Germany by the Royal Navy and which might explain some of the neglect of prisoners. Anaesthetics became rare commodities, and paper bandages began to replace cloth ones.

The story of the neglect and misuse of Australian POWs by Germans must be balanced against the experience of Alice Ross King, an Australian nursing sister at Number 2 Casualty Clearing Station near the front, a veteran of bombings and the shelling and gas-shelling of the little sump where the station was located. In November 1917, on her way back to her own tent, she heard the cries of men from beneath a tent she had not noticed before. Inside, she found fifty-three wounded German prisoners who had been forgotten for the past three days, a period during which the clearing station had been flooded with wounded. She found their condition horrifying and, though everyone on the staff was 'dead beat', she called the doctor and they went to work, getting orderlies to remove the thirteen who had died and treating the other forty patients. Similarly, George Faulkner of the Medical Corps confessed that when a German plane which was constantly bombing the frontlines, communication trenches and dressing stations crashed, and a surviving airman, wearing an Iron Cross, came to the dressing station, 'I gave him as much pain as possible, felt like knocking him out.'

Those unwounded who were captured at Fromelles had been marched to a collecting prison, Fort MacDonald in Lille, known as the Black Hole. But again the later reports of prisoners varied. Some complained of inhumane treatment and starvation. Private S.E. McGarvie of the 30th Battalion remembers his march to Fort MacDonald as brutal, with the Uhlan (lancer) cavalry lowering their lances to ride down a French crowd who emerged to look at the Australian prisoners.

The War Department was skimpy in the details it sent to relatives of such men, and did not see taking much further interest in them as its chief business. One of the most meaningful and informative points of contact between the Australian prisoners and the home front was provided by an Australian volunteer, Miss Mary Elizabeth Chomley. Mary Chomley, a woman in her mid-forties, was the daughter of a Victorian judge. She had been involved in the Australian arts and craft movement, and in 1897 had served as secretary of the Australian Exhibition of Women's Work. Chomley had gone to England as a Red Cross volunteer worker early in the war and worked in a British hospital until in 1916 she was given an office in Red Cross headquarters as Secretary of the Prisoner of War Department of the Australian Red Cross. In appearance, she was a rangy woman wearing on each lapel of her uniform the rising sun of Australia, and the badge of the Red Cross on her tie and hat band.

One of her first steps after Fromelles was to discover from the Red Cross the location of prisoners taken in that battle and to write to them. Private W. Inwood of the 28th Battalion would write to Miss Chomley in July 1917, 'I have just received your letter of March 4th ... it gives me great pleasure to be able to write to such a staunch friend.' Miss Chomley's new department not only gave the wider Red Cross organisation the names and prison addresses of POWs so that comfort parcels could be sent, but it received about 20 000 letters a month from Australian prisoners and relatives, all of which Chomley and her small staff attempted to answer. The department also catalogued personal details of prisoners, such as clothing and shoe size, and medical requirements, so that they could assemble personalised comfort parcels for the prisoners. Prisoners wrote to her asking for toothpaste, books and boxing gloves. Many of the letters thanked Miss Chomley and told her of the regular arrival of parcels, or else reported on their failure to turn up. Robert Duff of the 43rd Battalion told Miss Chomley that the arrival of the parcels 'lets a chap know that he is not forgotten'.

She received a great deal of information on the post-capture experiences of soldiers. Private Nelligan, one of Miss Chomley's correspondents, remembers being hit by a bomb (in World War I parlance this generally meant a grenade) after witnessing 'an ugly tragedy'. Two of the men of his battalion were badly wounded by fragments and lying not far away. One of them, leaving his wounded comrade 'in a restful position', went to the German lines to get help. A German soldier, believed by Nelligan to be a member of the enemy's medical corps, shot him through the head. Private John Bolton, wounded, was treated badly after capture. He was taken with other captives through a communication trench full of Germans soldiers who kicked and knocked them about. At the dressing station, none of his wounds or those of other Australians were dressed. According to John Bolton, a wounded man with him died of the rough handling in the communications trench. By contrast, a Private Donovan, suffering shrapnel wounds and a bullet through the left hip, was wrapped up in a sheet suspended from a pole, and carried by German bearers behind the lines to have his wounds dressed. A Private White was taken to a dressing station and 'treated kindly and given some coffee, bread and cheese'. Since Nelligan, Bolton and White were captured at approximately the same time, and their experiences were polar opposites, Mary Chomley was left to contemplate, if she had time for it, the range of human impulses in time of war. Some Australians wrote that the Germans were particularly vengeful towards them for fighting so far away from their homes, in a war that—in German eyes—was none of their business.

The winter of 1916–17 was known as 'the turnip winter' and brought starvation in German cities, and the onset of rickets amongst German children. Private White declared that 'the Germans do not seem to have the food to give us'. Private T.E. Gippsland wrote that for fifteen months he and his fellows had been given barely sufficient food to survive and had 'been forced to gather weeds and herbs for sustenance'. While in parts of Germany civilians were pursuing that option as well, there was a strong sense in the testimonies of prisoners that the German guards were deliberately starving them. One of the camps most complained about was at Schneide-Mühle, in what is now western Poland. Dinner, said Private Storey, was a ladleful of horse beans and water with occasionally a square inch of some 'mysterious flesh'. Breakfast consisted of a cup of acorn coffee. It is easy at this distance of time to look at the effects of the British blockade upon Germany in general. It would have been harder then to endure slow starvation in a prisoner-of-war camp.

But even then the food ration varied from camp to camp. Hunger does not seem to have been a systematic tactic, though the Australians suspected that in some camps it was applied as a means of keeping them docile. On a three-day journey from Dülmen to Schneide-Mühle by train, Private Noll was fed only one meal and a cup of coffee. Private Thomas, who was held in Dülmen prisoner-of-war camp in western Germany, said that those in his section were fed less than those in other sections. If that is true it means that the ration was not uniform even within the one camp. Thomas said that when moved to a camp in Erkrath, again in good farming country in western Germany, the food was a feast by comparison, and cheese, sausages, bacon, vegetables and the occasional stewed apple were available.

Prisoners' rations could be supplemented by food packages from Australia and Miss Chomley's Australian Red Cross POW Department, which sent food parcels every fortnight containing meat, tea, jam, butter and tobacco. Some repatriated prisoners, including Private W. Mayo of the 53rd Battalion, said they would not have survived without the Red Cross parcels. But often the packages were plundered or German guards would tease prisoners with their contents and then withdraw them. In Lechfeld camp, Sergeant Batteram said that for the first ten or eleven weeks 'the Germans robbed us of our parcels', but when the distribution of parcels continued, they were mutilated or smashed. Private

Patrick Regan wrote, 'Prisoners tended to be as much resigned as resentful at having items pinched knowing as most did that the guards had little to eat themselves.' The guards also received letters from home complaining of food shortages, and the fruitcake and preserves from Australia were better-quality food than any of them were getting. The battle cruiser *Australia* and the light cruisers *Sydney* and *Melbourne* were operating in the North Sea as part of the Grand Fleet preventing neutral ships from carrying goods to Germany, and thus contributing to the discomfort of Australian and other prisoners, and of their guards and their guards' families. The Australians pitied fellow prisoners—Italians, Russians—who received no such relief as Miss Chomley offered at all. Private J.P.V. Marrinon claimed that many Russians and Italians simply died of starvation or misuse. From pity, the Australians gave some of the food that arrived by parcel to prisoners from other countries.

Many prisoners were sent in groups or 'commandos' to work in salt or coal mines or lime quarries. Here hours were long and food even more basic. Private W. Grant performed a variety of 'commando' work, from railway building at Halle to timber-cutting near Dülmen camp. He claimed that when he was sent to a labour camp in a quarry, he experienced delayed parcels and brutality, the guards driving men along with the butts of their rifles. Men who were considered disobedient or lazy had a period in what Private White called the 'silly stand', standing at attention for a period of hours at the guard's discretion. Private Noll was flogged with a whip at a quarry. 'Threats to shoot us were frequent and we were starved,' he declared. But some of the prisoners went to work on farms and factories and had a better time of it both as regards labour and rations. Just the same, Private Meyers was sent back from a hospital before he had properly recovered from an infection and was put to work in a timber yard. He asked to see a doctor. 'I was made to stand to attention for two and a half days and during that time I was kicked by four guards and slashed about with a rifle and bayonet.' Even so, the Australians were appalled by the condition of foreign 'prisoners of respite' who were used for labour close to the enemy lines. 'During October 1917,' wrote Private White, 'I saw fifteen hundred prisoners of war who had been working behind the lines since April 1917 . . . they were practically skeletons, helping each other along.'

POWs asked Miss Chomley to write to their mothers and wives and reassure them, and she obliged. Her work hours must have extended into the long English twilight of summer and the dour early nights of winter.

A Lance Corporal Baird tried with other Australians to escape the prison depot in Lille. Miss Chomley was able to verify for his family that he had not been shot on recapture but had received fourteen days' solitary confinement. Indeed some families had been initially informed of their soldier's death, and then received the welcome news of his being a POW. Sadly, some of these died of disease, often as a result of the impact of wounds on the immune system. Private Bisset was initially reported as having been killed in action, again through the work of Miss Chomley and Miss Deakin was found to be a POW, only to die in captivity in the late months of the war or early months of the peace. Lieutenant Arthur Dent's family received a notification that their son had been killed in action in November 1916 in the final days of the Battle of the Somme, but then Mary Chomley's office was able to tell Mrs Dent that her son, though badly wounded, was alive and a POW in Germany. Dent would ultimately write a letter of glowing gratitude to Miss Chomley and her staff. 'Untold sufferings are alleviated by their prompt attention to the prisoner's requirements.'

'My dear friend,' Private Clare addressed her in a letter. 'The winter here is very severe, snow and ice, but thanks to your society, I do not feel the cold.' The 1917 Christmas parcels arrived in packaging which displayed Australian wattle and a map of the continent, and came at a time when the prisoners were yearning for a blazing Australian summer.

But Mary Chomley was not always praised. Sometimes the frustrations of prisoners were directed at her. She received a letter of complaint from a group of NCOs about their unfulfilled needs, although one Sergeant Alex Campbell was quick to write her a letter of apology. Watt Finlay wrote to her in July 1918: 'Ask any Australian here what he is going to do directly he arrives in England—and what do we hear? "Go direct to the Red Cross and meet Miss Chomley . . . She's the goods."'

A similar body, the Australian Red Cross Wounded and Missing Bureau, was founded and run by Vera Deakin, the daughter of the former prime minister Alfred Deakin, from London Red Cross offices, and collaborated with Miss Chomley's office in matters to do with POWs. For the sake of families in Australia it scoured the hospitals, base depots, war front and POW camps for news of individual Australian soldiers. During one month alone in 1917, Miss Deakin and her staff had to attend to 4000 inquiries. Eva Collins, for example, wrote to the Australian Red Cross about her brother, Private John Collins, who had been reported wounded and missing at Fromelles. Two of his friends, Vera Deakin reported, had seen him stricken with 'a couple of machine gun bullets

in his side'. Yet Miss Chomley's and Miss Deakin's departments, working in coop-
eration, were able to confirm by December that Private Collins was a prisoner
in Germany.

On thousands of others no definite news was ever received, there being none.
They were many who simply vanished, children and brothers and husbands
who had been torn to gobbets by heavy artillery, or whose bodies, gouged by
machine-gun bullets, sank into the mud of France or Flanders.

An Australian army nurse, Alice Ross King, wrote to Vera Deakin, concerned
about the disappearance of her fiancé, Harry Moffitt. She had met him in Egypt
just after he had been evacuated with all the others from Gallipoli, but he had
disappeared at Fromelles while serving as the adjutant of the 53rd Battalion
of the AIF, a position held in peacetime by officers in their forties but in the
Great War by boys. Vera's pursuit of the truth in this matter, as in others, was
admirable. On 28 October 1916 she wrote to the anxious Alice, now serving
at Number 1 Australian General Hospital in Rouen, that an eyewitness had
seen Lieutenant Moffitt killed by a shell, the same shell that had killed his
remarkably young battalion commander, Colonel Norris. Vera would write a
further series of letters to Alice based on the bureau's remarkable breadth of
research amongst survivors of Fromelles, and other sources such as the Red
Cross. When Harry Moffitt's name appeared on a German-released death list
it meant, as Vera Deakin told Alice Ross King, that the Germans had found his
pay book and identification disc, very likely on his dead body. Alice absorbed
this and continued to nurse at Rouen, amongst other things roasting chestnuts
on the stoves in her ward as a treat for the wounded. Even then, Vera Deakin
did further research, and in January 1917 wrote again to say that a sergeant in
the 53rd Battalion reported that he saw Major Moffitt suffer a head wound and
die instantly. Given the deaths she had seen occur at Rouen, and the intractable
wounds that presented themselves there and often went septic or gangrenous,
Alice could console herself with the idea that Harry Moffitt's death had been
instantaneous. His grave was never found.

The admirable Miss Chomley returned to Australia after the war, but then
later went back to London to pursue a career as an emigration official. In
December 1918 Vera Deakin's office was visited by young Australian airman and
escaped POW Thomas White, who had absconded from Istanbul by steamer in
the later summer of 1918. They were engaged within three weeks. Later Thomas
White would stand for the National Party and serve in the cabinet of Stanley
Melbourne Bruce throughout the mid-1920s.

BEARING STRETCHERS

Stretcher bearers' journals show something of the shambles of the frontline and—given that their job was not primarily to fight but they still took heavy casualties in their own ranks—provide a particular lens on the war in France. Even before the first official action there were, said W.C. Watson, 'Several cases of noses blown right off, to say nothing of fractures—shock, etc.' At the field dressing station where he worked as part of the 5th Division, George Faulkner treated a Private Brice of the 57th Battalion who 'was in great agony, died in our arms, as soon as we lifted him off the ambulance car'. On 19 July 1916, the day the Battle of Fromelles was to begin, it was Faulkner's turn to go up to the trenches. He thought that the brigade going into the trenches had 'a sort of heavy, dull manner, not usually like our Australians'.

By the end of the next day, 'My back and loins are as tho broken from carrying our good brave lads . . . The regimental stretcher bearers who without a doubt are as brave as any men in the army were either shot, fagged out or gone in the nerves.' As a result not many wounded were arriving at the dressing posts and field ambulance stations during the day the battle waned. On the night following a dozen volunteers, including Faulkner, crawled out into no-man's-land and brought back eight cases. Their priority, retrieval, was not the chief priority of men on either side of the line. 'The snipers made it too hot, so we had to give it up. All day today we can see on to No Man's Land by periscope at least five cases trying to move to give us a signal they are still alive.'

They brought in three during the following day by throwing them first a water bottle and then a rope they could attach to themselves and be dragged to safety. After withdrawing from the enemy positions they had temporarily held, Faulkner said, 'all the lads were emphatic on two points'. One was the lack of reinforcements, the other was that their own 5th Division artillery had—for lack of practice—killed and wounded many of their own men. Back at the field ambulance station, 'as near as we can estimate we have since Wednesday midday till Friday midday treated nearly 3,400 cases—the majority of these were carried in'—there not being sufficient motor ambulances. Around the dressing stations a little further forward many dead were being buried. On 24 July, a Monday, Faulkner and his friends heard a faint voice over the parapet and leaned over to drag in a Private Morris from Sydney who had been out there since the Thursday morning before.

Back in the reserve line, no one was safe. Even while pumping water into a bucket by a disused convent wall, a sniper's bullet came close to finding Faulkner.

Artillery was wreaking great damage either side of the line and Faulkner could hear the Germans' trumpet playing, a signal for the need for stretcher bearers. It was a good day when he could write, 'Not many casualties.' And, Faulkner observed, one of the wounded made the men in the dressing station laugh hysterically when he clapped the doctor on the back and said, 'Give us a tot, Doc—never mind the wound.'

The rebuilt 5th Division had returned to the front at Bapaume in the late spring of 1917. The stretcher bearers found they could not force their way back with the wounded through the crowds of reinforcements, ammunition carriers, ration bearers, runners, etc. 'As it is impossible for us to convey the wounded down the saps, we have to do it all over the top and we are under observation from Fritz on his slight elevation . . . it is very evident a lot of us will never leave the Somme. I am sadly afraid our infantry are also disheartened and as great things are expected of them they are not getting a fair show.' He believed their rations were poor to the point of dispiriting them. In these conditions, too, a dozen of the stretcher bearers were out of action through 'Blightys', wounds for which they would be taken out of the line and perhaps sent to England. Some of them were suffering shell shock—the fact that Faulkner uses the term in a journal in late 1916 shows that the soldiers believed in it as a distinct condition.

The bearers at Bapaume felt they were under observation from the steeple of the church. To collect the wounded they had to hurry across a hundred yards of open ground. Faulkner describes a very tragic coincidence when three of the twelve men detailed from the infantry to help them in the stretcher bearing were hit by a shell while taking a spell in a dugout. One was killed instantly. 'The other two had both legs blown off from the thighs and they were in great agony, we could not do much for these poor fellows . . . We were all completely done in from ploughing knee deep through the stiff mud.'

In early February 1917, Faulkner became close to one of the wounded men who had multiple wounds in his right leg and side. 'Absolutely the best patient I have yet handled—he died while in our charge from secondary haemorrhage and I had the painful duty of taking charge of his personal belongings.' He extracted a promise from Faulkner that Faulkner would write to Miss R. Edwards of Stanmore, Sydney to whom he was engaged.

On 17 March the Australians took Bapaume. They were exhilarated and it was probably the best day for the AIF in what would be a fierce year on the Western Front. Moving up to tend to wounded, Faulkner 'saw a captain hung up on the entanglements—also a lance corporal who had died but not without his victim, who lay alongside him—many souvenirs in the form of photos, postcards etc were offering'. Faulkner preferred to leave it all alone.

Though there was no doubting Faulkner's bravery, when General Birdwood came and visited the field ambulances and invited the stretcher bearers to attend an officers' school, the stretcher bearer declined. 'Twenty volunteered. I was nearly going to apply but I thought it better to be a live coward than a Lance Jack Lieutenant with a DCM and wooden cross.' It was a curious observation given the number of stretcher bearers who died and that his chances of acquiring a wooden cross in the field ambulance were very good.

The subsequent Australian attack on Bullecourt on 2–4 April 1917 would be greeted by Faulkner with the cry, 'horrors and more horror'.

Afterwards he went looking around the village of Ligny-Thilloy and the bloody crossroads near to Factory Corner where not only the recent dead but the Australian remains from an action the previous November were scattered. He was searching for the body of a friend named Hubert O'Kelly, 'who I am sure fell just about there'. He knew O'Kelly's family would want to know where. 'My friend, Les Bowden, who was looking for a friend had the very good fortune to identify him by some papers strewn about.' There is an unutterable poignancy to the picture of these two young searching a spring meadow for the dead. Faulkner somehow worked out from the Royal Engineers' survey post that O'Kelly had fallen one and a half miles from Ligny-Thilloy. 'I would like to put up a cross, about fifty metres from either the right survey post or the big mound where some dozen Tommies are buried.' On Anzac Day 1917 he struck out across country from a rest area to try to find the grave of another friend, Percy Single, near Mouquet Farm.

Meanwhile, he expressed something close to envy of a wounded friend. 'Poor old Reg Wood's got a nice Blighty, got a nice little piece of HE in the thigh that missed the femoral artery.' Carrying a man, he found himself hit on the head by shrapnel, which made a hole in his steel helmet. 'Captain Young or Captain Beard would easily have given me a Blighty ticket—if I had been less honest—all I had to say was that I couldn't carry on and had a headache, but I couldn't pretend.'

Suddenly something more serious befell him. The copybook handwriting now vanished from his journal, and was succeeded by handwriting like that of a child. Obviously, his writing arm has been lost. He confided to his journal that he was wounded at Bullecourt on 15 May. 'Arm amputated on

18th. Stayed at Number Eight Rouen till 3.30 am on 25th, lay on troop ship E812 till 10.30 on 27th.' Queen Alexandra Hospital at Millbank received him. 'Great kindness everywhere.'

THE MODEL GENERAL MAKES THE MODEL BATTLE

John Monash was not particularly liked by C.E.W. Bean, the lanky redhead official correspondent and, later, historian. Monash in return believed that both his 4th Brigade at Gallipoli and then his 3rd Division in France received inadequate praise in the pieces C.E.W. Bean wrote for the *Sydney Morning Herald*. Bean depicted Monash on 3 May 1918, during the German spring offensive, as talking of a 'disaster', of seeming shaken. He reserved the strongest criticism he had of any general for Monash. To what extent Bean's attitude was based on what he saw—with some justice—as Monash's powers of self-promotion, and to what extent on Monash's German heritage and Jewishness, is hard to say.

The Australian government—in the absence of Prime Minister Billy Hughes, who was travelling in the United States—had approved the appointment of Monash as commander of the new Australian Corps on 18 May 1918. Monash was delighted. It was, he said, 'the finest corps command in the British Army' and also one of the largest, consisting of 166 000 men. General Birdwood himself, administrative head of the AIF—or, in title, General Officer Commanding—was almost simultaneously invited by the British to take over the shattered British Fifth Army, which had caved in under the German spring offensive, and re-form it. At the same time he was to continue in his job as GOC of the Australians. From the beginning of Australian campaigning in France, Lieutenant General William Birdwood, an English soldier appointed to overall command of the Australians and New Zealanders at Gallipoli, had left his staff in London under the industrious and clever Australian General Brudenell White and gone amongst the troops. He became a favourite with the Australians, and instinctively understood the difference between their military casualness and genuine indiscipline.

Bean was shocked not only at Monash's elevation to command of the corps, but also appalled to learn that Birdwood intended to send Brudenell White to take over full time as chief of staff of the Fifth Army. He thought the corps command should go to White. On 16 May, when Birdwood's recommendation of Monash was still only a rumour, Bean confided in Will Dyson, the official war artist, and Hubert Wilkins, the famous photographer. 'We had been talking of the relative merits of White who does not advertise and Monash who does.'

Bean declared that Dyson said, 'Yes—Monash *will* get there—he must get there all the time on account of the qualities of his race; the Jew will always get there.' Bean and Dyson went to London to conspire with the influential Australian journalist Keith Murdoch, and the plotting would continue through the rest of May and early June. Keith Murdoch cabled Hughes to tell him that the opinion of the AIF was that Birdwood should not retain administrative command as General Officer Commanding while also commanding the Fifth Army, and Monash should not have been appointed field commander of the Australians over White. Their combined message was that Monash's 'genius' was for organisation and administration, but that he lacked 'the physical audacity that Australian troops were thought to require'. Even Andrew Fisher, now Australian High Commissioner in London, thought Monash the wrong man, but did not become a plotter.

In response, Hughes asked long-suffering George Pearce, Minister for Defence, to postpone the decision. But he found the cabinet had already ratified the appointment. This did not deter Murdoch, who even telegraphed Hughes' old sparring partner over the German mineral companies, W.S. Robinson of BHP, asking him to lobby the government along these lines. The Australian censors held up news of Monash's appointment for almost a month because they suspected the decision might be reversed. Bean still believed that Monash had worked to get the generalship of the Australian Corps 'by all sorts of clever, well hidden, subterranean channels', but nearly forty years later he wrote in the margin of his diary, 'I do not now believe this to be true.' At the time, though, he presumed to groom General Brudenell White for the job which could still be taken from Monash. He wrote to White that 'our men are not so safe under Gen. Monash as under you'.

On 6 June, Murdoch sang his siren song to Monash, suggesting he take the London administrative role Birdwood had had: 'You as a full General with supreme authority . . . would be the solution of many of our country's difficulties.' He also offered both as bribe and threat the news that his cables went out to 250 newspapers, Australian and foreign. The implication behind this could only have been that he had the power to exalt or pillory Monash, and Monash had better give up the Corps and go to London to take Birdwood's job. Bean kept on confiding to his journal that Monash 'cannot inspire this force with a high chivalrous patriotic spirit . . . there is no question where the interest of the Australian nation lies. It lies in making White one of its great men and makers.'

Murdoch was so relentless that Brudenell White had to make it clear that he would not accept command of the Australian Corps if offered it. Monash was aware of the plots against him and certainly saw them as due at least in part to his Jewishness. 'It is a great nuisance to have to fight a pogrom of this nature in the midst of all one's other anxieties.' It was a rare reference in his life to anti-Semitism. Birdwood would say in any case that he had absolute confidence in Monash, as did General Rawlinson, the British general within whose Fourth Army the Australian Corps was the jewel, and who declared that Murdoch was 'a mischievous and persistent villain'.

But even as Monash planned campaigns, particularly a battle near the village of Hamel, he did not believe his position secure. When Billy Hughes and Joseph Cook came to review the troops, not knowing that the Battle of Hamel was afoot, Monash said to them, 'I am bound to tell you, quite frankly, that any arrangement which would involve my removal from the command of this corps would be, in the highest degree, distasteful to me.' Hughes put his hand on Monash's shoulder and gave him some ambiguous reassurance. That night, at corps headquarters, Bishop G.M. Long, who was in charge of adult education for the soldiers, spent hours trying to persuade Bean and Murdoch that they were wrong. Hughes, as the argument went on, did not get steadily more angry with Murdoch and Bean but with Monash himself for being importunate. But the Battle of Hamel, narrated below, partially put paid to the plotting, and the 8 August 1918 offensive against the Germans, a triumph for the corps, closed the issue. Much later Bean spoke of his and Murdoch's 'high-intentioned but ill-judged intervention'. That it resulted in no damage to the AIF was probably due to the magnanimity of both White and Monash.

From early June 1918 Monash had been talking with Major General Sinclair-Maclagan and Major General Gellibrand, two of his divisional commanders, about an attack to straighten out the German bulge in the Australian lines at the extreme southern end of the British army in France. Maclagan was a Scot who had been recruited for the early Australian army in 1901. He had been so exhausted, mentally and physically, by the first two days of Gallipoli that he had needed to be rested, but he soon returned to action and was a great critic of the lack of planning which went into some of the Gallipoli operations. Gellibrand and Monash were critics not only of Gallipoli but Western Front tactics and planning. Monash believed that it was time that 'some commander on our side of No Man's Land' should begin to think creatively about an offensive. At the Fourth Army, of which the Australian Corps was part, there arrived a new kind of tank, and Monash thought they could be used against the German bulge in which lay the Somme village of Hamel, whose capture would straighten the line.

Monash took the tank with an intense seriousness, to the extent that some of those who admired him would attribute to him the founding tactics which would later be used by the Germans in France in 1940, a position perhaps mocked by British historians but strongly upheld by much Australian opinion. Monash believed that the tank, by drawing fire onto itself and providing cover, would reduce infantry losses. Monash's idea was that 'each tank was, for tactical purposes, to be treated as an infantry weapon', and advance level with the men. The young staff officer Thomas Blamey was one who felt uneasy about putting such reliance on tanks. The tanks had let down the Australians, he said, at Bullecourt in 1917. But Monash's plan was different. For the first time in history each tank would be assigned to and controlled by an infantry officer. The battalions were bussed back to rear areas daily to drill with the tanks, and even to go for joy rides in them. But not only was Monash banking on the tank corps, but the tank corps were banking on him. They had never before been taken quite so seriously.

Monash also wanted attacks by aircraft to be coordinated with the ground assault. He presented a plan for a 4th Brigade dawn assault using artillery and tanks and aircraft in an intense collaboration not previously achieved. Monash had also depended very strongly on reconnaissance by aircraft of the enemy positions and of night bombing and strafing to exhaust the men opposite the Australians. Each day until the attack a gas and smoke shell barrage would be fired, but on the day of the attack only smoke shells would be used, so that the advancing men would be uninhibited by gas masks though the Germans would probably be wearing theirs.

Rawlinson asked whether Monash would like Americans to join the battle, and Monash asked for 2000 men of the US 33rd Division, organised in eight companies. On 2 July, two days before the attack, Billy Hughes made his visit to Monash's sector. He was a disappointed man in that the Australian people had voted down his conscription referendums to prevent these fine men from receiving numbers of reinforcements who would reduce the wastage of Australia's bravest. Many of the troops he visited had voted against conscription—they did not want their little brothers thrown into the furnace, they did not want their morale vitiated by unwilling young men, and the Irish Catholics amongst them were possibly influenced by opinions from home about the futility of such sacrifices for an unloved imperial government, particularly so after the execution of the leaders of the 1916 Dublin uprising. Private John Keneally had written late in December 1917 that 'we are all waiting for the result of the referendum to see what sort of a time Mr W Hughes has got for his trouble. He won't get a yes from the boys over here that's sure.'

That day in July 1918, though, Hughes seemed relaxed. While Cook addressed the troops, Hughes lay on the ground chewing a stalk of grass, looking up into the faces of the heroes. 'I talked to the boys who were going into the Hamel stunt just before they started,' said Hughes later. 'Words are poor things to describe them, but as they stood there thousands of them armed cap-a-pie: helmets [and] full kit ready for action their bayonets glistening in the sun: an enemy aeroplane overhead being attacked by our anti-aircraft guns ... I thought that with a million of such men one could conquer the world.'

On the day before the battle, half the Americans were withdrawn, to their great chagrin, but then later in the afternoon Monash learned that General Pershing did not want any American participation—the motivation seeming to be an unwillingness to have Americans commanded by anyone but Americans. As Monash said, 'The whole of the infantry destined for the assault at dawn next morning, including those very Americans, were already on its way to its battle stations.' Withdrawing the Americans would mean abandonment of the battle, he argued. Monash asked Rawlinson, the Fourth Army commander, to stand firm. Rawlinson replied, 'Do you want me to run the risk of being sent back to England? Do you mean it is worth that?' Monash claimed to have responded, 'It is more important to keep the confidence of the Americans and the Australians in each other than to preserve even an army commander.'

The withdrawal of a thousand of the men from the 33rd American Division was beyond his control, but it challenged his belief that once a plan was finalised it should not be interfered with. A thousand Americans remained, distributed by platoons amongst the three Australian brigades that would be making the first assault. In the small hours of 4 July the Australians and their intermixture of Americans went forward into an as yet un-churned no-man's-land and lay down in the grass and the crops which had been sown there. A ground mist which mixed with the smoke shells helped create an even greater screen for the advance. At the appointed second, the infantry rose up—many of them lighting cigarettes—and with the tanks behind them walked forward behind the creeping barrage.

It was all over in ninety-three minutes, Monash would later exalt. It was the perfect set piece battle of the war. One participant wrote, 'It wasn't a battle at all—just a Sunday morning stroll through the park. No rifle fire, no machine gun fire, no shell fire, no casualties, nothing at all.' But it was not so in all parts of the line. There were 1400 casualties—tragic enough, but light for France—and 800 of these Australian and American casualties were walking wounded. The tanks came back festooned with cheering wounded. The forests of Vaire and Hamel woods had fallen to the 4th and 11th Brigades, the first line of the advance, and the 11th and their tanks captured Hamel village itself. Sixty tanks were sent forward and only three were temporarily disabled. The advance 'gave us possession of the whole of the Hamel Valley, and landed us on the forward or eastern slope of the last ridge, from which the enemy had been able to overlook any of the country held by us'.

Hamel became the model for all other operations of the corps. It was the first battle in which the experiment of using aeroplanes for the purpose of carrying and delivering small-arms ammunition was tried. Until then it required two men to carry one ammunition box of a thousand rounds which a machine gun in action would expend in less than five minutes. These carrying parties had to travel probably not less than two or three miles, often across country open to fire. Each plane carried two boxes of ammunition as well as bombs (grenades), and they could be released by hand lever, and thus dropped by parachute. Captain Lawrence Wackett of the Australian Flying Corps trained the fliers on how to make such a drop. Each machine-gun crew, upon reaching its appointed locality, spread upon the ground a large V-shaped canvas—V for Vickers machine guns. After some training, the pilots could drop the ammunition from a height of at least 1000 feet to within 100 yards of the appointed spot. Wackett's method introduced what Monash called 'an obvious economy in wounds and lives'.

The Supreme War Council in Versailles were riveted by this victory. French Prime Minister George Clemenceau visited the 4th Division and told them how they had astonished the continent of Europe by their valour, and when they cheered, declared, 'Des jolies enfants.'

The Australians followed up the victory by relentless patrolling. In case the Australians felt they were being overused—and they began to suspect it—Monash addressed every brigade in the Australian Corps, explaining how by comparison with other soldiers their workload was not excessive. Monash, not a modest man, declared that the effect of Hamel 'was electric . . . it stimulated many men to the realisation that the enemy was, after all, not invulnerable, in spite of the formidable increase in his resources which he had brought from Russia. It marked the termination, once and for all, of the purely defensive attitude of the British front.'

WAR AND ART

There were a number of official war artists appointed to the AIF, all Australians who happened to be in England. They included Will Dyson, George Lambert, John and Will Longstaff and Arthur Streeton. But one fine unofficial artist, Iso Rae from Melbourne, was caught in France by the war, in the art community of the coastal town of Étaples.

One of those children of the gold rush, Iso had been born in Melbourne in 1860 and became a student at the National Gallery School of Melbourne. There she became friendly with Tom Roberts, John Longstaff, Frederick McCubbin and others. In 1887 she moved to Paris with her mother and sister, and there was influenced by the work of the post-Impressionists. Her work would resemble theirs, with bold dark outlines and flat areas of colour. In 1890 the three Rae women moved to Étaples, a fishing port at the mouth of the River Canche in Picardy, where there was an artist's colony of Australians, British and Americans, ultimately frequented also by a much younger and notable Australian artist, Emily Hilda Rix from Ballarat. Rix was also accompanied by a sister and their mother.

Iso and Emily drew and sketched the Picardy landscape over which the coming horror of the war would play out, and were both exhibited in the Paris Salon and in London. But the outbreak of war drove most of the Australians out of Étaples. The Rix women moved to London, where in 1916 Emily married Major George Nicholson, an Australian soldier who was killed later that year. Iso Rae's mother was sick, however, and it was considered best not to move her. As the first winter of the war spread its gloom over the Channel Iso's sister wrote, 'We are, I believe, the only English in this town now . . . many women went.' In that grim Channel town now transformed by the demands of the war, and in France in general, Iso Rae would become one of only two Australian women artists to document the war in France. The other was Jessie Traill, who was working in the military hospital in Rouen.

The British army base camp at Étaples, in which Iso worked for the Voluntary Aid Detachment of the British Red Cross in one of the YMCA huts, was enormous and was served by railways, roads and canals and, above all, by cross-Channel transports connecting camps in England to the southern and eastern battlefields of France. Through Étaples travelled British, Canadian, Scottish and Australian forces. Wilfred Owen, the war poet, described it as 'a vast, dreadful encampment. It seemed neither France nor England, but a kind of paddock where the beasts are kept a few days before the shambles'. But in Iso's hands it became almost attractive.

She had little time now for studio work. Canvases and oil paints were difficult to obtain. So she resorted to pastels on paper to record the unearthly camp and all the men, anonymous, hugging themselves in overcoats, who passed through it. One of Iso's 200 or more superb pastels of the place shows troops arriving at the Anzac camp in June 1916, another troops queuing in front of the rudimentary camp cinema at night. She also depicted German POWs working in the Anzac camp, building a new station platform, Tommies playing football, and men bound for Blighty whose pyjamas were marked NYD for 'Not Yet Diagnosed'—shell-shock cases, in other words. In 1916 Iso's mother died, but her daughters stayed on in Étaples until 1932 when, alarmed by Hitler, the sisters moved to England.

Jessie Traill was born in 1881 to an affluent family who lived in Brighton, Melbourne, and is said to have decided to become an artist after meeting Tom Roberts painting on Black Rock Beach. She had studied French at a school in Switzerland and was a rugged young woman, travelling alone by boat to Java via New Guinea in an attempt to achieve an artist's perspective on Asia. She and another graduate of the National Gallery of Victoria Art School, Jessie Evans, volunteered in the Great War as Red Cross Princess Alexandra Voluntary Aid Detachment nurses in France, and they worked in hospitals around Rouen for three and a half years. Here Jessie Traill had the same problem as Iso Rae—the volunteer nurses were worked hard, and for long hours. But in her free time, Jessie depicted life in the rear area, damaged young men emerging from the killing machine and fresh young men about to be fed into it. She was also an activist, raising money for the reconstruction of a small village near Rouen. She would later be described by the art historian Sandra Lanteri as 'a bridge to the Australian modernists of the post-war era', and in the 1930s would make extraordinary etchings of the building of the Harbour Bridge, which stand honourably beside the more famous paintings of the unfinished structure by the Australian Impressionists Grace Cossington Smith and Roland Wakeland. She would also paint in Central Australia a decade before it was considered a fit place for artists, let alone women.

Tom Roberts, in Britain when war began, served in the British army Medical Corps, as an enlisted man with the rank of corporal, at the 3rd London General Hospital in Wandsworth, where he became an orderly to the dentists and witnessed some of the work the dentists did with shrapnel and bullet wounds to the jaw. He would sketch an Australian soldier, his eyes full of pain, whose lower jaw had been shot right through, leaving the two sides working independently. Roberts explained that a splint was put in to hold the whole jaw firmly together while the chin was built up 'and looks almost normal', said Roberts, offering his sketch to prove it.

In another Roberts drawing, a large part of a man's lower jaw has been shot away, leaving an external wound 'which was the size of a hen egg'. The remains of the jaw slewed away to the right side of the man's face, said Roberts, but the dental surgeon slowly brought it back into position. 'A case now being treated had the whole upper jaw and left eye carried away, leaving only one thing human looking, on a strange front to a man's head, an eye—an eye that, through the pain, the operations, stayed bright.' With what Roberts calls a queer voice, the man muttered, 'It'll be alright. I never was a Don Juan.'

For some reason Roberts was not one of the official war artists appointed in 1918, but his fellow Wandsworth orderly Arthur Streeton was, and would paint grander mayhem on a grander scale.

FLYING AS A WAY OF DEATH ON THE WESTERN FRONT

As Monash and others had grasped, the airplane made this war a war of three dimensions. Where other wars had been a matter of back and forth, this one was increasingly a matter of back, forth and up. The Australian Flying Corps operated three squadrons over the Western Front. The purposes of the squadrons, as well as fighting enemy aircraft, were the mapping of trench systems, the directing of artillery and giving support to infantry operations. For the young fliers on the Western Front, death was almost assured. Sometimes it was a freakish matter, as in December 1917, when Lieutenant J.L. Sandy and Sergeant H.F. Hughes, observing fire from a battery of 8-inch Howitzers, were attacked from above by six Albatross fighters. Sandy turned to engage the enemy, and shot one of them down. Another Australian Number 3 Squadron plane came in to help, and to the other pilot Sandy and Hughes seemed to be unharmed. But they did not return to the airfield. An armour-piercing bullet had passed through Hughes' left lung then buried itself in the base of Sandy's skull. The plane flew itself in circles before crashing in a field.

In another fatal incident, in mid-air over the British lines at Wytschaete in the winter of 1917–18, an RE-8 reconnaissance plane on its way to the German lines and flown by Lieutenants Streeter and F.J. Tarrant was obliterated by a British shell. On 16 August 1918, after the German front began to crumble, Lieutenant E.P.E. McCleery, a coach builder and engineer from Berrima, took off with eighty other Australian aircraft, two entire Australian squadrons, from their field at Bertangles north of Amiens to attack German airfields at Haubourdin and Lomme. Clearing the German hangars by only a few feet, they destroyed men and buildings and messes and aircraft. The mission was a complete success for the Australians and there were robust celebrations that evening in the mess at Bertangles. The next morning Lieutenant McCleery was still tired from the stress of the day before and the evening celebrations. Back for a second attack on the Germans, the low-flying Australians met fire from anti-aircraft guns and other weapons. McCleery's plane was shot down by a German machine-gun post he attacked. His Sopwith Camel smashed into the airfield pavement and the twenty-five-year-old pilot was killed.

Australian fliers were involved in the downing and death of the Red Baron, when two of their RE-8s, on a photographic reconnaissance mission, were intercepted by members of Captain von Richthofen's squadron. The Canadian captain A.R. Brown is generally credited with this victory but in fact the Baron was shot down by Australian ground fire, since the fatal entry wound was eight centimetres lower than the exit wound and Brown was above or level with the Baron. Thus the aristocrat was buried with military honours by slouch-hatted Australians from the suburbs and the bush, representatives of the least aristocratic race on earth, in a field at Poulainville.

During the German offensive in March 1918, Sopwith Camels of the Australian Flying Corps Number 4 Fighter Squadron flew below 450 feet (150 metres) in rain and fog, avoiding enemy fighters and the fire of German riflemen and machine gunners from the trenches, to attack enemy troops with machine guns and drop 25-pound Cooper bombs.

When they moved to Villers-Bocage in France, Australian airmen instigated a number of technical and training innovations. (Arthur Streeton, the great painter of the gum tree, painted an excellent picture of the airfield there.) Captain L.J. Wackett had already modified the bomb racks so that ammu-ni-tion could be dropped to troops in action. This bombing had an element of intimacy between the plane and the victims below. It created terror in the victims, but it also meant that many fliers, amongst them Australians and the Baron, were brought down by small-calibre arms, as well as by the fledgling 'Archies'—anti-aircraft guns.

A CONSCRIPT NATION

When Labor prime minister William Morris Hughes put the conscription issue to the Australian people, he was accused of being a moral coward by those who wanted conscription. They did not fully understand the difficulties he would have forcing it through the Senate, or the determination of many Labor members and the unions to oppose it. But by mid-1916, Hughes was not the only man in his cabinet to believe conscription necessary to make up for the Australian losses suffered on the Somme. Senator George Pearce, the war minister, former Coolgardie miner and carpenter, was simply one of the cabinet in favour. Their motives were subtle—they were under moral pressure from other Dominions, such as Canada and New Zealand, both of which had introduced conscription. They may even have felt that trade with Britain might be dependent upon Australia's going this step further because distance from Britain put the country's trade in a difficult situation. During his visit to Europe in 1916, Hughes had needed to chase up and purchase a flotilla of fifteen cargo ships to bring Australian wheat to the British market. But he also genuinely desired that more reluctant Australian youths should be sent to reinforce the remaining elite of volunteers, and thus increase the chances of survival of all Australian soldiers.

The first referendum was on 28 October 1916. In most Protestant churches worshippers were urged to vote Yes, since the war was a holy conflict and thus the necessity of enlarging the army was depicted as a moral rather than a political issue. Not all of the Protestant community, however, voted as the pastors would have wished them to. The proposal was narrowly defeated, with a majority against it in three states. In a poll of over 2 500 000 voters, conscription was defeated by a mere 72 000. At a Labor conference in Melbourne in December 1916, Hughes and all those who had been in favour of conscription were expelled from the Labor Party. Hughes was both aggrieved and wistful, and never again quite at home in politics. He had not left the party, he declared. The party had left him. He had hoped to govern in his own right in a form of the Labor Party which would continue the campaign of nationalism and victory. In the end, he was forced to join the opposition in a combined National or 'Win the War' Party, of which he was elected head and thus became prime minister. He won an election in May 1917, even though Archbishop Mannix of Melbourne had declared from the pulpits of Melbourne that a vote for Hughes was a vote for conscription.

Indeed, Hughes felt forced to revive the conscription issue now. He argued that Australia needed 16 500 recruits each month, but in the early months of

1917 there were not more than 5000, dropping to 2500 in the second half of the year. By the end of 1917, as the second referendum approached, Australians seemed emotionally exhausted. There was not only a sense that conscription would kill not save more boys, but also a fear that Australia, because of its losses and its class divisions, would never be the same again.

The second referendum on 20 December 1917 was lost by a larger majority than before. This time the No vote widened by a majority of 166 000. It was not such a majority, however, that it failed to show how split Australia was. There were all manner of reasons cited for the defeat, including rumours about the prevalence of venereal disease in the AIF, which voters thought conscription would further spread. But the campaign had aroused the most furious political and sectarian passions. A handbill produced by the Reinforcements Referendum Council to condemn the No voters read in part: 'I believe in the IWW [Industrial Workers of the World or Wobblies], I believe in Sinn Fein, I believe that Britain should be crashed and humiliated, I believe in the massacre of Belgian priests, I believe in the murder of women, and baby-killing . . . I believe in burning Australian haystacks. I believe in German mine laying in Australian waters. I believe in handing Australia over to Germany. I believe I'm worm enough to vote NO.'

In reply the *Australian Worker* declared that conscription 'is the most immoral of all forms of gambling. It is fraught with tragedy; red with murder and foul with abomination.'

To many Australian workers the priority was not to win campaigns in France, but to improve their wages in the face of ever rising prices for food. By August 1917, a strike would begin at the Randwick Tramway workshops, ostensibly over rosters, and would eventually enlist the state in a crisis involving fuel, food and transport workers. To middle-class men and women all this was a betrayal of their sons at the front, and the defeat of conscription soon after seemed to justify the suspicion that the Catholics, the unions and the Wobblies were all in it together.

A tale of some of Billy Hughes's frenetic campaigning for conscription will be related elsewhere, but the public rancour of the time was shown by a conscription rally held on the Melbourne Cricket Ground on 10 December. Anti-conscriptionists invaded the ground, and hurled eggs, road gravel and glass bottles at the speaker, including Hughes. A large stone came close to hitting the Prime Minister, and a witness claimed that a soldier knocked a knife out of the hand of a man attempting to throw it in the direction of the rostrum. Even as a rumour, this was a sign that the debate was poisonous.

THOSE IRISH

In regard to conscription and most other issues, the Irish and their children remained a source of unease, even though many soldiers of Irish ancestry had joined the ranks. The Easter weekend uprising in Dublin in 1916 was directly linked, in the minds of the suspicious, to the anti-conscription activities of the 'Rasputin of Australia', Daniel Mannix, the Catholic Archbishop of Melbourne. Most Irish in Australia did not favour the Irish uprising when it first occurred. Britain had as good as guaranteed Irish Home Rule, a form of Irish independence akin to that of a self-governing Dominion, at war's end. The Easter rebels were seen as having jumped the gun to a provocative extent. But when the British executed many of the captured Irish rebels in Dublin's Kilmainham gaol, Irish opinion turned against Britain. William Butler Yeats put it best: a terrible beauty was born. And Irish people in Australia asked themselves was this an Empire worth sacrificing their sons for?

Indeed, the St Patrick's Day procession in Melbourne in 1918 would feature a float depicting the 'martyrs' of the Easter uprising. The Governor-General, Sir Ronald Munro Ferguson, a Scotsman who would have preferred to have been Viceroy of India, believed that, partly due to the defeat of conscription, the mob was now ruling Australia. Seven members of the Irish National Association, which was seen as a front for the Irish Republican Brotherhood and its political wing Sinn Fein (Ourselves Alone), were arrested under the War Precautions Act. The Irish National Association had in fact run a small camp in the Blue Mountains, a cluster of tents, to train men to infiltrate Ireland and fight for her independence. It produced not one Irish fighter, but when it was discovered the entire Irish Catholic community were depicted as subscribers to the darkest sedition and rebellion.

To loyalists, one of the great Satans of anti-conscription and disloyal sentiment was Archbishop Daniel Mannix. Son of a County Cork tenant farmer, born in 1864, Mannix had been a turbulent figure in the politics of the Catholic Church in Ireland and some were pleased to see him hived off to Melbourne in 1913 as coadjutor (deputy) bishop. The Australian establishment saw him as a promoter of Sinn Fein, the political wing of Irish rebellion. But Mannix had not opposed the declaration of war in 1914, and in 1916 no Catholic bishop in Australia other than Mannix opposed conscription. When through the death of his predecessor Archbishop Carr he became Archbishop of Melbourne in May 1917, he became more vocal. He was the sort of Irishman who in opening new Catholic schools would announce that they were designed to lift the children of the Irish out of the impotence and ignorance to which Cromwell, and successive British administrations, had tried to consign them. He refused Hughes' offer to support conscription—the execution of the Easter uprising martyrs, notably that of the leader Padraig Pearse, had made him weep and rendered Britain perfidious in his mind as well as that of others. Though he spoke only twice on the issue in the first conscription campaign, in the second he became a frequent speaker in condemnation of conscription, and said at a church fete that the war was 'simply an ordinary trade war'. Hughes saw Mannix and the Industrial Workers of the World (a radical movement imported from Chicago with wide support among unionists), who were in their turn depicted as the major creators of the 1917 strike, as working in lock step.

In the second conscription debate, Archbishop Michael Kelly in Sydney remained a pro-conscriptionist, even though he received chiding letters from Catholic labour men. Patrick Cunningham, a Catholic layman, complained that Kelly was on the side of the lord mayors, the Members of the Legislative Council and the judges. After the second referendum was lost by an even bigger majority, Mannix would thank the Catholics of New South Wales 'for saving Australia'. When Mannix visited a working-class school in Balmain, the faithful rushed up to kiss his garments and do him homage.

With some justice, Prime Minister Billy Hughes believed he had personally experienced the anti-British passion of the Irish. Campaigning for conscription in 1917 in towns along the railway network of Queensland, speaking briefly but furiously at railway stations during the 1917 conscription debate, Hughes was often pelted with rotten eggs and overripe fruit by anti-conscriptionists. Not all of them were Irish, though; having failed to legalise conscription in the referendum of 1916, his eloquent convictions ran wildly and even offensively against anyone who doubted conscription's transparent necessity. Town by town in Queensland, he attacked the Labor state government ferociously and they, particularly Ted Theodore, struck back. Theodore, the Queensland Treasurer, declared that behind conscription lay not only slaughter on the Western Front but an attempt to destroy unionism by compelling its membership into the forces. At Warwick, Hughes was therefore ready to rant against the leftists and the Irish, and as he crossed the platform from the train to do so, one of the eggs thrown at him shattered on his hat. Sergeant H.B. Kenny of the Queensland police refused to arrest the marksman, Pat Brosnan. Kenny's argument was that Hughes, who had by now jumped down into the crowd ready to take on anyone, would not lay a charge under Queensland law, which was the only law Kenny was authorised to enforce, but demanded instead that he arrest the violator under federal law. A constitutional argument took place right there in the crowd in the railway forecourt, with Hughes declaring that he represented the Commonwealth, that the laws of the Commonwealth overrode those of the state, and Kenny must now uphold the former. After thirteen minutes of insult and argument between Hughes and sections of the crowd, no arrest was made and, Hughes' train continuing on its way, Kenny's view was endorsed by the Queensland government. In a telegram on the incident addressed to the Governor-General, Hughes wrote that he was trying to make the Queensland government of T.J. Ryan 'realise that this is *not* Ireland as Sinn Fein would have it.'

One reaction to the egg and the disobedience of Sergeant Kenny was the prompt creation of a Commonwealth police force. For, as Hughes said in a letter to the Governor-General urging he give assent to the new law creating the force, 'The [state] police is honeycombed with Sinn Feiners and IWW . . . There are towns in North Queensland where the law, State or Federal, is openly ingnored and IWW and Sinn Fien run the show.'

BRINGING THE FABRIC DOWN

To radicals of all kinds, and there were many kinds, the war seemed the beginning of the end for capitalism. Capital was so grossly visible in the profits of companies and in the blood of workers-turned-soldiers that world revolution seemed close, and in 1917 began to manifest itself in Russia.

During the war the Industrial Workers of the World (IWW) had affrighted public opinion with their combination of strikes and sabotage. The Wobblies were anarchists and believed that the sole structure required to bring the peace and plenty to the earth was not corrupted government but One Big Union (OBU) involving all the workers of the earth in unconquerable combination. This objective was given the name *syndicalism*, and in the pubs where the few true Marxists drank, believers in a coming Marxist state which might not even need unions, the words 'syndicalist bastard' was an insult for Marxists did not believe that the Wobbly OBU would deliver the earthly paradise. This did not mean there were not plenty of conversions of Wobblies to Marxism and vice versa. A normal wharf labourer or Hunter Valley coal miner understood his own discontent, rising prices and fixed pay that meant that his wife and kids ate poorly a number of nights a week. But he was not up on either Wobbly or Marxist dogma and did not care which doctrine improved the conditions of his life. The Wobblies were, however, very visible and, during the height of the war, scared Australia not only by their involvement in strikes but by their anarchist appetite for arson.

Hughes blamed the Wobblies for orchestrating a waterfront strike in February 1916, and was all the more furious since he had just managed to achieve the first federal award for the industry and had been pleased by the patriotism which had kept industry humming through 1915. Soon the Wobblies would encourage wildcat strikes on the waterfront, in the North Queensland sugar mills, the Government Clothing Factory in Melbourne, the railways workshop in Sydney, and amongst railway construction workers in South and Western Australia. The *Sydney Morning Herald* declared, perhaps with a little hysteria, that the IWW had twenty to thirty thousand supporters in all the unions, and that they had worked in the campaign to defeat the conscription referenda.

Many admired this side of the Wobblies' activities. But the IWW were avowedly advocates too of 'direct action', sabotage and the 'propaganda of the deed', also referred to as 'the black cat' and 'the wooden shoe', all designed to erode conventional government. *Direct Action* was in fact the name of their newspaper. Russian anarchism had involved attacks on government figures from Tsars to policemen. Tsars were scarce on the Hunter Valley coalfields, while constables were tragically available. A police constable in Tottenham in the Hunter Valley was murdered through an open window in October 1916. Herbert Kennedy, one of the two brothers arrested for the murder, declared that the IWW did not believe in assassination. Kennedy might have been innocent, since the IWW had become the whipping boy for all unrest. But what is certain is that, whether they believed in murder or not, they certainly believed in arson.

Fires had broken out in a number of buildings in Sydney, allegedly through the use of 'fire dope', a phosphorus incendiary much favoured by anarchists. During June and July 1916, there had been five spectacular fires in central Sydney commercial buildings, one of them being set in the Co-operative Building. The IWW was not backward in telling the world it was their work. 'Far better to see Sydney melted to the ground than to see the men of Sydney taken away to be butchered,' said Peter Larkin, brother of Irish revolutionary James Larkin, now released from gaol, at the Sydney Domain. Twelve Wobblies were arrested for arson, and in the subsequent court case the Crown witnesses, including the brothers Davis and Lewis Goldstein, gave evidence about the secret purchasing of fire dope, the instruction of Wobblies in its best use and the drawing of lots to decide who would set fires. Simultaneously with the Sydney trial there were arrests of Wobblies in Western Australia on the charge of seditious conspiracy.

When one of the Wobbly leaders, Tom Barker, was imprisoned under the War Precautions Act there was open Wobbly talk of rescuing him from prison by the 'wooden shoe'. Barker was author of a famous early World War I poster which urged, 'Let Those Who Own Australia Do the Fighting. Put the wealthiest in the front rank'. At about the same time, in December 1916, Franz Franz and Roland Kennedy, Herbert's brother, were found guilty of the murder of the constable at Tottenham and were sentenced to death.

Meanwhile, in the incendiary trial in Sydney, each of the twelve accused declared themselves innocent. The judge, Justice Pring, was a passionate enemy of union or leftist activism, and passed a range of sentences. Eight of the Wobblies received fifteen years. Whether they were the actual fire-setters or targets of convenience is not known.

On 15 December 1916 Hughes had introduced an Unlawful Associations Bill designed to make the IWW illegal, but the body continued to exist within the trade union movement under the mantra, 'The IWW has no present intention of being closed up.' Indeed, some members chose another form of sabotage, counterfeiting. In 1917, F.J. Morgan, a printer of *Direct Action*, had been arrested with other men for producing forged £5 notes. The two Goldstein brothers were worked on by the police to inform on Morgan, but would not do so. IWW premises in Sussex Street were raided by the police, and amongst those arrested was Peter Larkin. The charge was that he and Morgan and others 'did compass, imagine, intent, devise or intend to levy war against the King'. Eight more Wobblies would be arrested.

The Wobblies were seen as being behind all strikes, such as the great strike that occurred in August 1917 when some 6000 railway and tramway employees in New South Wales walked away in protest against the introduction of a work recording system. One of the strikers was far from being a Wobbly—the junior engine-driver and future prime minister Ben Chifley. The strike lasted eighty-one days and had by then been joined by 76 000 other workers, most of them not Wobblies. Forty thousand unionists marched through Sydney. J.C.L. Fitzpatrick of the Legislative Assembly of New South Wales saw the events as due purely to the influence of German agents and the Wobblies—the 'I Won't Work and the I Won't Wash crowd'. The Riot Act was read in military camps to warn soldiers who might think of siding with the strikers and 1500 special constables were sworn in to guard trams, trains and workshops.

Stories of attacks by non-combatants on the fabric of the society for which they had fought greeted soldiers on their homecoming in 1919. Many former officers in particular would begin to form their own 'secret' paramilitary groups to fight against Bolshevism. Their stories will be told soon. But even as the 'secret' armies mustered, the reality was that the Australian candidates for genuine Bolshevism were few in number.

KEEPING THE FABRIC UP

A Legion of Frontiersmen, a version of the 'white armies' which had fought off Asian infiltration in the novels of the day, had existed in Australia since 1906. But under pressure of the 1917 strike and of the divisions produced by war, a 'farmer's army' was also forming and by 25 September 1917 the Farmers' and Settlers' Association and the Primary Producers' Association had put together a group of 7300 strike breakers. The training camps of this unofficial force were openly held at the Sydney Cricket Ground and at Taronga Park. The Royal Agricultural Society provided stables for 3000 horses and storage for ammunition and even larger weapons, some of which had mysteriously turned up from AIF sources of supply. The businessman Henry Braddon formed a committee of New South Wales commercial leaders to give accommodation, provisions and evening entertainment for these 'loyalists' from the bush. Such was the leniency of the authorities to this unauthorised army that Braddon liaised daily with the state government and the Commissioner of Police. The force's medical officer at the Cricket Ground told the gathered farmers, 'We are here to do our duty to our country and our king, if we allow mob rule in Australia, then God help us.'

Far from the onset of revolution, however, by October 1917 the unions gave way on the strike and the men returned to work not having extracted any concessions. The acting Premier George Fuller sent a message to the Farmers' Army thanking them for their services on behalf of himself and the members of his cabinet. 'You left your ordinary calling and at loss and inconvenience undertook whatever duties were assigned to you.' They had enabled the sustaining of responsible government, said George Fuller. So the idea of private armies became normalised at the higher levels of government. Left-wing, 'Red', military mobilisation, always suspected to be in progress, did not occur on any scale like that of the Farmers' Army.

In late 1917 Prime Minister Hughes sent his friend, the Victorian businessman and future senator R.D. Elliott, to the United States to investigate the American Protective League, a secret network of volunteers supervised by the US Justice Department. The American League had begun a nationwide war against the IWW, destroying offices and beating up Wobblies before passing them onto the police. The League had its corruption problems, however. These ranged from members using their badges for free entry to theatres and free meals, to embezzling funds and bootlegging liquor. Elliott omitted all mention of these practices in his positive report to Hughes. On 29 May 1918 Senator George Pearce, Minister for Defence, who had followed Hughes out of the Labor Party, met with the Chief of the General Staff, Major General James Legge—back from Gallipoli and from France where he had commanded the Second Division at Pozières—and with leading businessmen, lawyers, bankers, insurance company men and academics in a Melbourne cabinet office to consider the founding of an Australian version of the League. Archibald Strong, Professor of English at the University of Melbourne, warned that if ever there was a national crisis from a Bolshevik-style insurgency, the only way to oppose it would be organising a counter-wave, something like the Protective League.

A week after the first meeting, a further meeting was held in the business centre of Melbourne which formalised the Citizens' Bureau of Intelligence and Propaganda. Various worthies, including the historian M.H. Ellis, were appointed to the Bureau. In Sydney there was a pre-existent group of leaders named the Round Table and it was their support which helped get the Bureau off the ground there and elsewhere. On military advice, the Bureau was now named the Directorate of War Propaganda.

One of the leaders in this process was Herbert Brookes, the escapee aviator Tom White's unwilling brother-in-law (he did not like White), an industrialist in Melbourne and a member of the Commonwealth Munitions Committee. He was a leading anti-Catholic campaigner, a cause revived, as if especially for his convenience, by the 1916 uprising and Catholic anti-conscriptionism. He combined this with an admirable progressive streak. Though not a mining magnate, he was particularly engaged in matters of the welfare of miners; at the Hollybush Coalmine he established schools out of his own pocket, and he campaigned for conditions designed to prevent miners' lung diseases. In one of his own businesses, Australian Paper Mills, he introduced profit-sharing in 1917. He was a founder of the Australian Red Cross, and ran the Australian Comforts Fund which put everything from writing paper to fruitcake parcels into the hands of Diggers. Soon after joining the Board of Trade in 1918 he would demand information on European social insurance and profit-sharing and he believed managers' wives on his sheep stations should be paid for the work they did. He was also a supporter of the arts and of the Melbourne Symphony. He was friendly with Rupert Bunny and E. Phillips Fox until the latter's death in 1915, and opened his house to visits by musicians, notably Sir Bernard Heinze.

But though Brookes admired his father-in-law Alfred Deakin, he had a tendency to fanaticism. After addressing a group of supporters in March 1918, he wrote, 'It was a glorious experience to feel yourself not yourself, but an instrument in the hands of that Power that works for righteousness.' A month or so after the Armistice, Brookes met up with Pearce and others, including F.C. Urquhart, the Queensland Police Commissioner, who was present without permission of the Queensland government. Urquhart had been disturbed by the socialism of the Queensland premier, P.J. Ryan, a premier who offended free enterprise by fostering state-owned butcheries to sell cheaper meat to the populace.

Through Brookes in particular an Australian Protective League was gradually cobbled together. Brookes nominated various citizens to lead the state branches of the organisation. There already existed in New South Wales a similar group named the King's Men, of whom Sir Edmund Barton, long-living first prime minister, was president and Lieutenant Colonel Reginald Rabett, recently returned from France, Honorary Secretary. Professor Mungo MacCallum was one of the vice presidents.

The Protective League placed a series of spies within the Victorian Railways Union, the Wobblies' organisation, the Melbourne Trades Hall and the Police Department. M.H. Ellis was able to send good intelligence from Brisbane, in that his brother, A.T. Ellis, was secretary to Premier Ryan. In Melbourne, by late 1918, the forces behind the Directorate of War Propaganda had already laid plans to blow up bridges across the Yarra if there were an uprising. But the activities of the League, like those of the Directorate, diminished with the coming of peace. Just the same, early in 1919 Billy Hughes had sent a consignment of machine guns and rifles to Brisbane in piano cases marked 'Furniture' for use by the Protective League.

The mutinous streak that had emerged in many Diggers late in 1918, and even more notably after peace was declared, with men refusing to drill in the manner of regular soldiers, added to the concerns of the authorities and of the leaders of society. On troopships returning to Australia there was hostility or else a live-and-let-live attitude between the soldiers and the officers. A young Englishwoman named Angela Thirkell, who married her husband Captain George Thirkell in London in December 1918, describes in *Trooper to the Southern Cross* her voyage to Australia on the troopship *Freidrichruh* as one in which the soldiers' decks became no-go zones for most officers. Such hostility had occurred elsewhere—in St Petersburg in 1917, when officers became victims of their men. In fact, on one Australian troopship a circular was discovered which called on AIF troops not to fire on their own people when a general uprising began. Already, in Melbourne in July 1919, returned soldiers invaded the office of the Conservative premier H.S.W. Lawson and threw an ink stand at him. This thrown ink stand represented in the minds of conservatives an act worthy of the fall of the Winter Palace to the Bolsheviks in 1917.

In March and April 1919, the so-called 'Red Flag Riots' were a further sign of volatility. After display of red flags at a march organised by the Queensland Trades and Labor Union Council (in which a number of Russian radicals fled from Tsarist prisons to Brisbane participated) loyalist forces, returned soldiers prominent amongst them, counter-marched on the Russian quarter in South Brisbane. There was a three-hour siege on the Russian Club, the storming of the offices of the ALP newspaper the *Daily Standard*, and the marshalling in early April by the RSL of a returned soldiers' army with 2000 members. Also co-operating were a group known as the United Loyalist Executive, a body Herbert Brookes had been involved with. Police Commissioner F.C. Urquhart was not at all dampened in his enthusiasm for the Red Flag Riots by the fact that outside the Russian Club on 24 March 1919 he had been accidentally but seriously wounded by a bayonet wielded by a loyalist returned soldier.

Everywhere from the establishment Union Club in Sydney to the Masonic lodges of Toorak, there was an expectation that something dire would happen in mid-1919. By mid-winter ex-servicemen were called together to form up in the gardens near Victoria Barracks in Melbourne, taking their place in their old platoons ready to be drilled by their former sergeants. They were addressed by six generals, three lieutenant-colonels and other officers. Brigadier General Grimwade, a Melbourne chemical company executive who had commanded the artillery of the Third Division in France, urged the men to organise themselves in small bodies to operate against law-breaking and disorder, and Pompey Elliott declared, 'Forces of disorder were arising in this country . . . they [the soldiers] must unite, as they had united before, to defend the Government and to maintain order.'

WESTERN FRONT MUTINY

In late September 1918 General John Monash and Major General John Gelli-brand, Commander of the 3rd Division, had a passionate exchange, in which

Gellibrand complained that battalions of only 200 men were being pushed into battle and the diggers were exhausted. Monash found it hard to believe that the troops were approaching the end of their strength. 'Six days' rest and a bath restores the elasticity of a division,' he said, even though he himself was exhausted.

On 21 September Australian soldiers of the 1st Battalion became restive. Three days before they had attacked the Hindenburg Line near Bellicourt and their brigade had taken over 4000 prisoners. They had been due to be relieved the day before but had been disappointed to have to stay on another night in the trenches and then to learn that the relief had been cancelled, and that they were to go back into the line to support an attack by the British to their north. This order was resented by the men, who even complained that they were being called again to do 'other people's work'. There was a strong sense that they were being kept in the line because they were more effective than British units. Some men refused to draw their ammunition from stores and others started walking back along a sunken road to the rear. Officers established a straggler post to round up those going absent, but the soldiers ordered to man it mysteriously reported that they had not encountered anyone leaving the line. When the 1st Battalion moved to its start tape on 21 September, more than half the battalion was missing. The assault was nevertheless a success.

One hundred and twenty-seven Australians were arrested and tried, and received sentences ranging from three to ten years, which they served in grim Dartmoor prison in England. Some accused Monash of being too soft on these men but, in any case, less than a year passed from the end of the war before their sentences were suspended. Peace brought with it no need to set an example any more.

Pompey Elliott had also faced a 5 September 1918 rebellion by the 59th Battalion of his brigade, who refused to follow orders near Pèronne on the Somme. It occurred when soldiers of the 59th were about to leave the line for a rest, but before leaving were ordered back into the frontline. Sixty men refused to go. Elliott behaved with great understanding. He urged the men to reconsider, and uttered no threats, and the men rejoined their units and engaged in the operations that had been ordered. But later in the month there occurred another mutiny over the disbandment of old battalions and their amalgamation into new ones. Some men of Elliott's 60th Battalion refused to be absorbed into the 59th. These amalgamations and disbandments were not popular anywhere amongst the Australian troops on the Western Front, even though they were obviously necessary because of losses. This time Elliott became angry and warned soldiers that the death penalty could be used in the case of mutiny. He even threatened that one man in ten could be shot. There was a cry from a man in the ranks: 'We've got bullets too.' On 25 September thirteen men of the 3rd Australian Tunnelling Company refused to go forward to the frontline. They received sentences of one to two years.

When at last the men of the AIF did fall back for rest, it was apparent to Australian commanders that for the time being nothing more could be asked of them. This was a crisis for the Australian forces, as conscription had failed and recruitment was inadequate. No one knew that the war had only a short time left to run. The Armistice would come as a great relief to the commanders of the AIF.

SHRINKING THE OTTOMAN EMPIRE

The Australian Flying Corps flew a great number of operations in support of the British and Australian penetration of Palestine and Syria, and the Australian Number 1 Squadron was for a time intimately involved with the Arab force catalysed by T.E. Lawrence (Lawrence of Arabia) on the eastern or right flank of the Allied advance on Damascus. On 16 May 1918 the South Australian Ross Smith flew Lawrence from a conference at General Allenby's headquarters in southern Palestine to his base at El Kutrani on the famous Turkish Hejaz Railway in what is now Jordan, the railway the Arabs (perhaps too often called Lawrence's Arabs) continually blew up and ambushed. Australian airmen, some operating from Ramleh in the modern-day West Bank, others from El Kutrani, part of Lawrence's Arab northern army that struck across the desert to Azrak, attacked the important Dera Railway which ran into Damascus. Ross Smith and his squadron were overwhelmingly successful in shooting down German Rumpler and Albatross aircraft which attacked or drew near to Lawrence's column. The Australian Bristol Fighters also bombed Turkish railway repair work parties trying to restore the lines after Arab attacks, and their presence itself attracted Bedouin groups to the Arab cause. From the air, the Australians observed Arabs and Turks harvesting grain in the Jordan Valley but also saw the Turkish build-up at Amman, now the capital of Jordan, and so bombed that ancient city as well.

This activity in the air was part of the Australian involvement in the conflict with Turkey and of Turkey's Ottoman Empire, named after its first sultan,

Uthman. The Australians had encountered this threatened empire at Gallipoli, and it had rebuffed them in their attempt to clear the way to Istanbul. But the Ottoman Empire still stretched across the Turkish Peninsula, down through Palestine, Syria, Lebanon, Arabia and modern Iraq, and westwards into Sinai, where it sat gazing at the British in Egypt. Having previously held all of Egypt, the Turks, often but not always led by German generals, had at the start of the war intended to capture the Suez and Egypt. Their troops were in the Sinai south-west of Jerusalem and had advanced as far as Romani. Over the winter of 1915–16 the Turks were using three traditional and ancient routes to cross the Sinai Peninsula, the triangular desolation between Palestine and the Suez Canal.

As British resistance to the Turkish movements in Sinai began to mature, Australian units of the Imperial Camel Brigade rode twice to Akaba to liaise with the Arabs of the Hejaz. Unlike the Lawrence depicted in David Lean's film *Lawrence of Arabia*, they found the route quite viable for camels and supplied with a number of watering places, though often of alkaline quality. Meanwhile the British were beginning to build a water pipeline and a railway to service their men on what would need to be an ultimate advance into Palestine. The central road through the Sinai was one taken by the Queen of Sheba, and Joseph of the Coat of Many Colours, and—according to tradition—Joseph, Mary and the child Jesus fleeing from Herod. The Turkish general Djemal used this central road for his advance towards Egypt in 1915.

Sinai was a place which from the time of the Hittites and then the Egyptians was to be briskly traversed before a fight could be staged. The systems and wells dug into the beds of wadis in Sinai had been reconditioned by the Turks for their advance on Egypt. But the water supply on this central route was too limited for an army. The coastal one was better, though the sand dunes and rocky earth were very hard on horses, guns and wheeled transportation. Anyone invading Egypt, or marching out of Egypt to invade Palestine, had to secure the wells at Katia, near the coast twenty miles east of the present Suez Canal. This was an eternal rule. Alexander had had to do it, and Napoleon had also seized them so that they could water ambitions which for him never came to fruition. By January 1916 the Turks had 25 000 men in Sinai. It was decided that they must be denied the Katia wells. If the Turks occupied Katia waters they were only a one- or two-day march from the Canal. Some of the Australians and other forces that winter had been engaged not against the Turks, but in Libya against the Senussi tribesmen galloping out south and west into Cyrenaica. But now, a year after Gallipoli, all the pressure was turned against the Turks in Sinai. The German aim in all this was that if the Turks could keep a permanent army around Katia, that in itself would tie up a lot of British troops guarding the Suez Canal. On the other hand, the Russians were also attacking the Turks from the direction of the Caucasus and had captured the Turkish city of Erzurum on 16 February 1916, and this news cannot have been pleasant for the Turkish troops in the Sinai.

The British had their own problems. For the two Light Horse divisions, one problem was that while a day's ration for a man consisted of only 2 or 3 pounds, that of a horse weighed 20 pounds. The daily water ration for a man washing economically and drinking was at most 1 gallon, but horses required 5 gallons. In order to supply not only the Australians but the entire British force, it was essential to push a new railway out into the desert.

The Light Horse was made up chiefly of men from the bush. It was not a cavalry force because its members were not armed with sword or lance. They were mounted riflemen, a few of whom had served in South Africa only twelve years earlier. Their Australian childhoods had tempered them, making them adept with horses and skilled with rifles. The horses they rode—though generally Walers—were not uniform in appearance. Some Australians rode on stocky, powerful ponies, and so did the New Zealanders, while others rode cross-breeds from draught Clydesdale mares to three-quarter thoroughbreds.

The heat of Sinai was for most of the year—except in the peak of summer— no worse than the heat of many parts of Australia in summer, and both men and horses were used to such conditions. The Australian saddle-horse, according to the official historian H.S. Gullett, was used to a hard life, 'seldom fed in a stable, and little time is given to its grooming. When an animal is wanted it is usually brought in from a small paddock near the homestead, cleaned, perhaps, of mud or falling coat, saddled, and ridden. The ride finished, the procedure in most seasons was to remove the saddle and bridle and turn the horse back at once into the paddock without grooming or hand feeding.' It was in this spirit that the light horseman dealt with his mount, and his mount lived. The light horseman himself had survived a raw upbringing and his qualities, as an historian remarks, 'rendered him impatient of that side of discipline which may be termed purely ceremonial'. He saw military formalities and etiquettes as irrelevant. The British general staff in Egypt and Palestine had complained often enough about it.

The light horsemen referred to the Turk as 'old Jacko' and did not get the point pushed by various journalists, British and Australian, that the campaign in Palestine was a 'new Crusade; to liberate the Holy Land from the infidel'. No Australian commander used such terms, and it is likely that if he had they would have been treated with derision. Similarly the idea that these operations might bring the Ottoman Empire unstrung was not mentioned, even though that was what was to happen very quickly. The chance to see the Holy Land and visit a captured Jerusalem and Nazareth was attractive to all of the Australians, but they did not see the hoped-for Turkish ejection from these places the way their medieval forefathers had.

Near Katia, the British Yeomanry and the Gloucesters of the British army were overrun by Turkish forces in April 1916 and attacked from the air by German aircraft. The British went reeling back through the village of Katia and the camp at Romani, and the Turks left the British wounded to their Bedouin militia, who circled them on horseback as they begged for water and cried, 'Finish British! Turks Cantara! Turks Port Said!'

The 2nd Light Horse Brigade of the Anzac Mounted Division, led by General Bull Ryrie, a Michelago grazier twice wounded at Gallipoli, rode up to Romani near Katia on 8 April, along with the New Zealand brigade and the headquarters unit of the Anzac Mounted Division, and covered the retreat of the British soldiers on the coast. 'The only entry into Egypt is by this desert,' Herodotus had written, and that entry was now about to be denied to the Turks by the undermanned Australian and New Zealand light horsemen. General Ryrie's brigade lacked ambulance transportation, except for a herd of seventy camels, to take the British wounded back to the rear from which the Medical Corps slung the badly wounded.

At the Romani sand dunes on the furiously hot night of 3 August 1916, Light Horse regiments lay under a quarter-moon on white sand. Their horses were tethered to horse lines further back. North of them, closer to the coast, were a number of British infantry regiments. Ahead lay hilly country which gave good cover for the snipers or raiders of the Turkish army. To their south a ridge of stone dubbed Mount Meredith dominated the country and General Chauvel, the Grafton-born horseman and Australian regular soldier who commanded the Anzac Division, had been suggesting to his superiors that infantry posts should be put on top, but had been ignored. The Turks themselves intended to occupy it and bombard the British railhead at Romani from it, a plan which was discovered by a light-horse patrol. The Turks subsequently found the entrances to the gullies were held by small parties of light horsemen sent out on their mounts by Chauvel. Many Australians were now bayoneted as they attempted to find their horses and retreat. Major M. Shanahan, out riding between these listening posts, came upon four Australians who had lost their horses and who did not know where the enemy was. He took two of the men up on his horse's back and had the two other troopers hang on to either stirrup and so was able to ride back through the Turks to the Australian lines. But Sergeant Bingham, a farmer from Tasmania, and Sergeant Tolman, who ran cattle on King Island, had both been bayoneted to death.

About one o'clock in the morning, closer to the coast, the Turks attacked the main Australian line, crying, 'Finish Australia! Finish Australia!' By two they were within 30 or 40 yards of the light horsemen. They could not be clearly seen and the Australians had to aim at rifle flashes. The Australians knew they could not hold this major Turkish attack that was now in progress because their own line was not continuous but ran in a series of posts over a number of sand dunes. The Turks had in many cases thrown away their boots to allow them to move with greater speed through the sand, for they were often country boys too, used to this sort of hardship, and they were attacking in particular now those scattered groups on the first part of the spur, Mount Meredith, on the extreme right. If the Turks could outflank the Australians, they could destroy Romani and prepare, with a British-built railway in hand, for an expedition against the Canal.

At 2.30 a.m. there was a large-scale bayonet charge against the Australians at Mount Meredith. The Turks tried to climb the almost-perpendicular southern-most slope and were held back by a small group of men under a young man from Gunnedah named Lieutenant Edwards, who would survive that night but die of disease brought on by desert campaigning before the year was out. Many officers and men were killed and others were driven back to a sheltered dip in the rock between Mount Meredith and its neighbour, Mount Wellington, where their horses were. A light horseman trying to lift a friend up behind his saddle found the man he held was in fact a Turk. The bullets meanwhile made spurts of flame in the sand, igniting the phosphorus with which it was naturally impregnated. Survivors were now retreating, many of them on horseback, towards Romani. But an order was heard above the racket. It was obeyed, a new line was formed. The Anzac front stood, and a flanking route which would have given the Turks the Romani rail and perhaps the Canal was blocked. Anzac officers yelled out promises of reinforce-ments at dawn, and men scooped out holes in the sand and settled down with the intention to stop the Turks again.

There were further attacks and as dawn broke the light horsemen could see the massed Turkish attack, and the Turks could see the thinness of the Aus-tralian defences. They again attacked the right, inland side of the Australian line, firing on men and horses. A retreat was necessary, but it occurred according to drill, troop covering troop, withdrawing from those holes quickly dug in the sand. Chauvel realised that he could not let hand-to-hand fighting break out, because the Turkish numbers were so great. Some Australians had been driven to Wellington Ridge, however, which the Turkish artillery swept with shrapnel and high explosives. By 7 a.m. the Turks had gained the ridge. But it was six hours too late for the Turks. Instead of possessing these vantage points in the cool of night they possessed them in a furnace-like morning.

Chauvel sent a message back that if a British rifle brigade could come up—an infantry brigade was nearly double the rifles of a light-horse brigade because so many men had to be kept behind to guard the horses—the Australians could draw back, water their horses, and then swing round the left of the enemy to cooperate with the mounted New Zealanders and yeomanry brigade in an attack which would envelop the Turks. General Royston, a South African who commanded the New Zealanders, assured them, 'You are making history today.' He swore to the New Zealanders and anyone within call that the Turks were retreating. He did not mind having his instructions overheard by Australians either, and they too were making history.

The Turkish troops were beginning to suffer from the heat. They were exhausted by forced marching and hours of fighting in the heavy sand. Most of the prisoners the Australians and others took had been without water for some hours and the food in their haversacks consisted chiefly of green dates they had gathered in the date groves. Many of them were suffering from dysentery.

Ryrie's Light Horse had by afternoon been fighting for twenty hours. But by nightfall they were incomparably better off than the Turks, who as well as everything else had heard that many layers of defence would block their advance to the Canal. There was only intermittent rest for the Australians that night. Ammunition and water were issued, and the orders were that there would be a bayonet advance at dawn.

Before the battle, a highly civilised message had been dropped by a German plane and happened to fall near Chauvel's tent. It asked the Australians to mark their ambulances more clearly so that they should not be bombed. Many of the wounded would owe their survival to this message. The arrangement for the transport of the wounded from the railhead to Kantara on the Canal, however, was appalling. No hospital trains were provided. The first lot of Australian wounded reached the railhead at Romani for transportation to Cairo, but found that the trains were to be used for the transport of Turkish prisoners, and so the light horsemen lay for some hours in the sun under artillery attack. They travelled to Kantara in open trucks and, though it was only a matter of 23 miles (37 kilometres), the journey took anywhere from six to fifteen hours. A number of officers and men who had left the ambulances in sound condition died from neglect and exhaustion. In Kantara some of them remained in hospital for nearly two days before being treated. There would be strong complaints from Chauvel and his senior medical men.

At dawn on 5 August, the 1st and 2nd Light Horse Brigades routed the Turks with a bayonet charge and the Turkish retreat was disorderly, as Chauvel unleashed the 3rd Brigade to pursue and harry them. So began a Turkish retreat which would not finish until Damascus and the end of the war.

A troop of Aboriginal light horsemen—nicknamed by some the Queensland Black Watch—arrived in Palestine to reinforce the 11th Light Horse while they were in the Jordan Valley. Major C.A.R. Munro wrote, 'Some of them were in the squadron of which I had command in May 1918 when the mounted troops, Australians and New Zealanders, charged through the Turkish lines in the Jordan Valley and rode about eight miles to their rear to cut the communication lines. I remember seeing some of the Aborigines well in the front of the advance.' One of them, Private John Johnston, died of his wounds on 1 June 1918. These twenty reinforcements of the 11th Light Horse was the only exclusively Aboriginal formation within the AIF. But though the numbers of Aborigines in the ranks of the AIF cannot be estimated, we know of many. Private Billy Elsdale, a full-blood Aborigine of the 47th Battalion, was killed in action at Fleurbaix on 7 November 1916. He is one of sixteen Aborigines identified as having been killed in action, though there were inevitably many more Aboriginal enlistees who came to harm.

Two days before Christmas 1916, at Magdhaba the Turks made a last stand to remain in Sinai. The Anzac Mounted Division, operating ahead of the infantry, were subjected to severe fire, but ended by driving the enemy off. The Imperial Camel Corps—made up of Australians, New Zealanders and British, with the major portion, two and a half battalions, being Australian—were also unleashed from the north-west. Soon after 1 p.m., Chauvel called off the attack. But the recall reached the commander of the 1st Light Horse Brigade, Brigadier General Charles Fox, just as his troops were preparing to assault the main enemy redoubt with bayonets fixed. He deliberately misplaced the message until the attack had started. The redoubt fell, and at four-thirty in the afternoon the Turkish garrison surrendered. The Australians set Magdhaba alight to prevent its use again and withdrew back to their camp at El Arish. The 1st Light Horse next captured Rafa, near the Sinai–Palestine border (now Ein Rafa), on the morning of 9 January 1917. The telegraph lines to Gaza were cut. Now the Anglo-Australian force could move to attack the main Turkish lines near Gaza on the coast. The first assault on Gaza on 26 March began well at 2.30 a.m. in a dense fog. Chauvel was given the Imperial Mounted Division as well as having his own men to attack Gaza from the north. But even as he was advancing and entering the outskirts of the town he heard to the east a battle to stop Turkish reinforcements arriving. Against his strongest protest he was ordered to withdraw and began the process. He ordered that badly wounded Turks be left close to the road for retrieval. At campfires that evening, the light horsemen were furious at being withdrawn.

Chauvel now became a lieutenant general in command of the Desert Mounted Corps, including the Camel Brigade. Of its nine horsed brigades, four were Australian, four British and one New Zealand. The artillery was mainly British. Another attack on Gaza was meant to distract the Turks while 9 miles (15 kilometres) inland at a junction named Beersheba the Mounted Corps was to make an enveloping attack from all sides. It was an irony that the comrades of the Light Horse lived in mud and ice in France and Flanders while all operations in Palestine involved control of water. The future of the advance in Palestine depended on the capture of the Beersheba wells. The Turkish Eighth Army garrisoned in Beersheba did not know that they, instead of Gaza, were the target. But if the wells could not be taken on the first day, Chauvel would have to pull his Desert Mounted Corps back. Chauvel's men made an assault on the height above Beersheba, Tel el Saba, at 3 p.m. on 31 October, and with the sun due to set at 4.30 he did not have a lot of time for the capture of the wells. But the hilly defence position was captured before Beersheba. Then, in waning light, the famous incident of the day occurred, the entirely successful charge of the 4th Light Horse Brigade.

Gaza fell in November and in December the British captured the ancient city of Jerusalem. The first Australians to ride in were from Western Australia, the 10th Light Horse. They were greeted by a nun who was repairing the tiles on the roof of a convent at the edge of town and ceased her task to wave to them. They were mud-splashed and unshaven and weary from their prolonged progress through the cold hills in the rain. 'Christ met each man on the threshold of the city,' says the official historian, Gullett. 'The influence was, perhaps, not lasting. War is not a Christian mission.' The populace—Greek, Armenian, Jewish and

Christian—had suffered under Turkish military rule and they were in a carnival mood by the time the Australians entered. The men were shocked by the dishevelled condition of the town. They had expected a golden city. They visited the sacred sites, the Church of the Nativity, the Garden of Gethsemane, as well as the Mosque of Omar and the Wailing Wall.

In Palestine the men were treated most cordially by the Jewish settlers, orange orchardists. The Australians thought they charged a lot for their wine but officers pointed out that the villagers had been through lean years. At Wadi Hanein an entire brigade was entertained at a feast and a dance to celebrate the capture of Jerusalem. A furious speech about deliverance was made by the village schoolmaster—in Russian. The Jewish matrons and girls wept at it. Afterwards the Australians danced with the women. This was the best time they had had, said some of the light horsemen, since they'd landed in Egypt.

There were many Turkish spies in Jerusalem, and when Fast's Hotel, an officers' club in Jerusalem, was suddenly emptied, the rumour started in the bazaars that the building was to become the Commander-in-Chief's advanced headquarters. So the Turks foresaw operations either along the main road to Nablus or on the western side of the Jordan Valley. That winter of 1917–18 the British forces began to operate on the other side of the Jordan Valley, in terrain now part of the state of Jordan. That was the centre line of the advance. On the western side they were well and truly within what would be the modern state of Israel, for that was where Beersheba lay. To the east, T.E. Lawrence and the Arabs were operating. For the force in the valley, the rain in the winter of 1917–18, combined with severe cold, was a trial to light horsemen operating in the open, though firewood was found and bivouac sheets and extra blankets were issued.

Chauvel advanced on Derra from Amman, the present capital of Jordan, with his two divisions and the camel brigade. At a place name Es Salt the Australians ran into a massive Turkish force. The Beni Sakr tribe around Es Salt had been persuaded to support the attack but wisely enough absconded. By midnight on 4 May, Chauvel's mounted infantry, including the Light Horse, retreated back across the Jordan, having lost fifteen hundred men.

The high command were a little embarrassed by this failure, but it could be blamed on the inadequacy and tiredness of the Australian, New Zealand, British and Indian troops engaged. Chauvel's corps was rested. When it set off again it overtook the Turks, and cut off their retreat through Nazareth. Otto Liman von Sanders, the German general who was now the enemy Commander-in-Chief, was very nearly captured in Nazareth, as Chauvel had planned. The supply situation became chaotic for von Sanders and the Hejaz railway was subject to attacks, not least by Lawrence. He also believed himself outnumbered and would not discover that he was wrong until the British and Australians captured more than 75 000 of his men in the late summer of 1918.

The Anzac Mounted Division was stationed by the Jordan River as a decoy. Many of its men were sick from bad water and sanitation, and exhausted. The division was supported by a composite body of Jewish infantry recruited in England and in Palestine itself, and the 20th Indian Infantry Brigade. Their job was to move around a lot and raise plenty of dust to keep Turkish forces arrayed in front of them.

New camps were built, 15 000 dummy horses were erected out of canvas, fake campfires were lit at night, and sleighs drawn by mules jogged about the sea of dust in the daytime. The Australian and British pilots were very active overhead and that helped the deception. While this was going on, T.E. Lawrence, with a strong Arab force, sent agents around the Amman district buying up all available horse feed, dropping hints that it was needed for the maintenance of British cavalry in the Jordan Valley. So in September 1918, while Allenby was massing his forces on the west, the enemy was kept in place in the Jordan Valley to the east by this display from Chauvel's corps. Most of the rest of the British force camped near the coast in the olive groves and orange orchards of Jaffa.

By 16 September 1918 Chauvel had secretly moved his headquarters 50 miles (80 kilometres) north, leaving the old camp standing, with a few men to keep the lights burning at night and kick up dust with dragged logs. Chauvel was to lead his corps across the Esdraelon Plain to Megiddo, which in ancient days had been called Armageddon. He was to capture Nazareth and then cut off the Turkish army held in place by the men he had left over in the Jordan Valley. Beyond the Jordan Valley Lawrence and the Arabs were advancing. A column assisted by Arab tribes and the Druze blew up a bridge and destroyed a section of the Hejaz Railway and then demolished further sections north and west. So as the general assault on Damascus under the British general Allenby was about to begin, railway traffic moving south towards three Turkish armies was suspended. Chauvel intended to take a line running from Haifa on the coast through Nazareth to Tiberias on the Sea of Galilee. A battle was fought at Megiddo and won. Allenby sent a cable to the government in Melbourne which read in part, 'The completeness of our victory is due to the action of the Desert Mounted Corps under General Chauvel.'

The plan for the capture of Damascus involved a swing to the east and an advance on the city by the Pilgrim's Road. The Arab Northern Army and Lawrence came under Chauvel's orders. The rest of his corps, with the Australian Mounted Division leading, would advance over the Golan Heights and make for Damascus. Despite facing a series of Turkish rearguards, Chauvel made the gates of Damascus by the evening of 30 September and cut the road on the other side through the Barada Gorge that led to Beirut. He entered Damascus next morning while the 3rd Light Horse Brigade continued to pursue the Turks northwards. Chauvel was now responsible for a city over whose control the political struggle had begun, involving not only Arab and Syrian leaders but his own liaison officer, Lieutenant Colonel T.E. Lawrence.

Chauvel was not politically informed enough to deal with these complications, or with Arab hopes or the relationship between Emir Feisal, the Arab leader, and Lawrence. When Chauvel dealt with the disorder in the city, which involved cracking down on the looting of the Arab militias, the action was lampooned by Lawrence as 'triumphal'. But Chauvel's job was an enormous one—to keep order on the streets of a city of 300 000 people, secure food, cooperate with the police, and care for a horde of sick and wounded Turks and the 20 000 prisoners his corps had taken in the city. His own troops were suffering from malaria and influenza at an appalling rate.

Various troops, including Australian Light Horse, pursued the Turks beyond Aleppo on the coast of modern Syria, which the Arab militias captured on 25 October. Five days later an armistice was signed with the Turks. Over six weeks, Chauvel's three divisions had marched and fought their way over 300 miles (480 kilometres) and taken well over 70 000 prisoners, all at a cost of only 533 battle casualties.

The secular Young Turks reformers who—in this acute Turkish crisis—had seized power from the Sultan in Istanbul tried to rouse the Arabs to a Holy War against all Christians in the Empire. The Arabs treated the call with indifference. Most of them had been only intermittent fighters under Feisal. Raids on moving trains on the Hejaz Railway and the annihilation of Turkish outposts were their contribution to the war. The British and Australian troops were contemptuous of them both racially and as soldiers.

After the Armistice the Australians and New Zealanders attacked an Arab village named Surafend. There had been attacks by Arabs on Australians, and a man from Surafend had certainly shot and killed a New Zealand trooper. Vengeful Australians and New Zealanders descended on the town, killing many men, beating others and putting the village to the torch. They also torched the nomad camp on the edge of town. The racial contempt of the era helped validate their actions in their own minds, but Allenby later addressed them with furious contempt and failed to send them a departing order of commendation as they shot their horses under orders—no room on the transports for livestock—and prepared to leave. An Australian pointed out to Allenby the injustice of his lack of commendation and he issued a glowing one as a result. But Surafend remained a taint on the general honour and extraordinary military performance of the Light Horse.

FLYING OVER PALESTINE, FLYING OVER FRANCE, FLYING TO AUSTRALIA

During the campaign in Palestine and Syria, on the morning of 21 September 1918, British and Australian bombers had discovered the main Turkish column in retreat in a gorge on Wadi Fara Road. Wadi Fara, a tributary of the River Jordan, is to the east of Nablus, and in modern-day Jordan. The Wadi Fara had been reconnoitred by a number of Australian aircraft, including one in which Hudson Fysh was the observer. Within a few years Fysh would be entering into partnership with three Queensland graziers and a fellow war flyer to create Qantas. Already reconnaissance planes like Fysh's had machine gunned a Turkish train arriving from the west at nearby Bisan, and dropped bombs on the airfields of Amman. Number 1 Squadron had sunk all Turkish vessels on the lake of Tiberias at the head of the Jordan River. At El Afule in Samaria, the land of the Samaritans, young Captain A.R. Brown, a draper from Tasmania, led a dawn patrol in which five machines dropped forty bombs and fired 4000 machine-gun rounds into retreating columns. Then at Burka and Jenin the Turks were similarly attacked—'They were closely packed,' wrote the official historian, 'and nearly every bomb fell plum among them.'

But what they were able to do at Wadi Fara surprised even the airmen of Number 1 Squadron. Here they bombed the lead vehicles of a large Turkish column and filled the neck of the defile through which the road passed with gutted vehicles and splintered wagons and concussed and burned bodies of men and camels. Clive Conrick, a young man whose family ran sheep and cattle on a station named Nappa Merrie on Cooper's Creek, recorded in his diary his machine gunning of the men caught below, some of them climbing the cliffs above the road to get away. He saw 'chips of rock fly off the cliff face and red splotches suddenly appear on the Turks who would stop climbing and fall and their bodies were strewn along the base of the cliff like a lot of dirty rags'. Then, when his pilot climbed again to escape the ridges, Conrick had an opportunity to strafe the trucks and the troops on the ground once more. During the day the Turkish survivors waved white flags but, wrote Conrick, 'It was quite impossible for us to accept the surrender of the enemy, so we just kept on destroying them.' This young flyer had been born at Australia's heart in 1891, at the station where, thirty years before, Burke and Wills had died. The Dig Tree stood on the property and was part of the landscape of his childhood. Before joining the Flying Corps he had appropriately been a member of the small and select Camel Corps.

L.W. Sutherland, an observer in another plane that day, recognised that on this battlefield the aircraft, which many still considered a novelty of military campaigning, was the dominant power. 'For the first time in the war, we, the newest arm of the service, had the most onerous work in a major operation . . . But oh, those killings! Only the lucky ones slept that night.'

Every day there were attacks on retreating Turks, organised to slow them down for capture by ground forces. Those who survived the air attacks and finished their march gave themselves up to the Light Horse in the hills on the southern fringe of the plain of Armageddon. British and Australian mounted divisions headed off these traumatised columns of the rearguard of the Turkish Seventh Army. They, like the Australians who had subjected them to a hellish day, knew that a new and lethal dimension had entered war. Aircraft were no longer a novelty.

So nothing was immune from the ruthlessness of young Australian airmen. In mid-August 1918 a large cavalry camp on the coast at Mukhalid was attacked. They strafed the horse lines and the tents and then swept along at 200 feet, machine gunning the beach where at least 300 men and many horses were bathing. Horses galloped and bathers rushed out of the water and into the gullies behind the beach.

Even when the Germans received new aircraft, the Pfalz Scouts, they were beaten out of the air over the desert. Sometimes, in the spirit of European (Australian) attitudes towards the wogs and Gyppos, the men of Number 1 Squadron would go 'felucca-ring', diving on the small lateen-rigged boats used by Arabs on the Sea of Galilee. There was a touch of civilised feeling, though, when Oberleutnant Gerhardt Felmey, the leading German pilot flying against Number 1 Squadron, in an excess of fellow feeling, dropped messages and photographs of recently captured Australian airmen on their home field, so that their fellow flyers knew that they were safe and their families at home could be reassured. A number of Australians began to do the same over German airfields.

By October 1918 the Turkish army was in such ragged and speedy retreat that only the aircraft could keep up with them. In France and Belgium too the German army was in retreat and in the open and at the mercy of aircraft.

Three Australian squadrons operated on the Western Front, and a further four training squadrons based in England served as replacements. This is a good indication of the short life of young airmen, often former infantry or Light Horse. In training, they lived a gracious life and went up to London to vaudeville and theatre. But casualties amongst them, even in the absence of enemy fire, were frequent and horrifying. One pilot wrote, 'A great pal of mine was on his very last flight—his last test before qualifying . . . a mist arose, he flew into the ground and was killed.'

There were other Australian airmen, the so-called Half-Flight, who served from the war's beginning. Lieutenant White, whom the nurse Vera Deakin would later marry, was captured by the Turks while his plane was on the ground in Mesopotamia (Iraq), having delivered an engineer beyond the lines to cut telegraph wires. Australian airmen of the Half-Flight were among those who surrendered in April 1916 in the besieged garrison at Cutt, eighty miles south of Baghdad. Few of them survived captivity, many being already weakened in health by the diseases rampant in Cutt.

As for battle, Australia's ace, Harry Cobby, who would later run the Civil Aviation Board in Australia, was just one who found the air very crowded over the Western Front—with up to a hundred aircraft in a melee. 'Hectic work. Half-rolling, diving, zooming, stalling, "split slipping", by inches you miss collision with friend or foe. Cool precise marksmanship is out of the question. Even more so in the somewhat more cumbersome reconnaissance aircraft.' A mix of vehemence and respect for their opponents characterised the young men who flew the planes—as was shown in the honours done to the Baron von Richthofen when he crashed in Australian lines. After an AIF honour guard had attended his burial, Australian airmen were very quick to rush to the lines at Morlancourt near the Somme to lay wreaths on his grave.

On 14 and 15 June 1919, two officers of the Royal Flying Corps, Captain J.W. Alcock and Lieutenant A.W. Brown, flew across the Atlantic from Newfoundland to Ireland in a Vicars-Vimy aircraft, a non-stop flight of 17 hours and

27 minutes. Both airmen were almost instantly knighted, though it would not be long before the young Alcock would be killed in an aircraft crash in Rouen.

The Australian government, composed of men who tended to look upon the Atlantic as a small pool, were motivated to offer a prize of £10 000 for the first successful flight from Britain to Australia. A number of Australian airmen in England immediately took up the challenge. They were required to land in Australia within the specified thirty days of taking off, and they would need to do so by midnight on 31 December 1920. The competing pilots must be Australian. The starting place was Hounslow aerodrome, or a seaplane station on the south coast of England, and the landing place was to be 'in the neighbour-hood of Port Darwin'. The pilots of the Australian squadrons who had survived the war took up the challenge in numbers.

The first to take off, in a Sopwith Wallaby, on 21 October 1919 were Captain G.C. Matthews with Sergeant T.D. McKay. McKay was a mechanical engineer, Matthews a master mariner and a Scot who had flown with the 3rd Australian Squadron. These aviators, forgotten to history, flew across the world before crashing at Bali on 19 April 1920 and being forced to abandon their flight. On 12 November 1919, Captain Ross Smith with his brother Lieutenant Keith Smith of Adelaide, and Sergeants Bennett and Shears, took off in a Vicars-Vimy supplied by the manufacturer. Ross had taken part in the attacks on Wadi Fara as well as defending Lawrence's Arab columns on their eastern campaign against the Turks. He was twice decorated with the Military Cross and three times with the Distinguished Flying Cross, and he had had the experience of flying a Handley Page bomber from Cairo to Calcutta in late 1918. Keith had been rejected for service with the AIF, took passage to England and there enlisted in the Royal Flying Corps. He was fully trained but did not see active service. He had been put on the unemployed list of the RAF the week before he started his flight.

On the day Ross Smith's successful flight from England to Australia began, the autumn air was frosty and the weather bureau forecast conditions unfit for flying, but at 8.30 they started their engines and took off from the snow-covered aerodrome. At the French coast they had to climb above snow clouds—the cold in the open cockpit was savage, 25 degrees Fahrenheit of frost. For three hours their breath froze on their face masks and the sandwiches they had brought were frozen solid. It took five days to cross Europe to Taranto in Italy. The next leg was to Crete, to Suda Bay, then to Heliopolis in Egypt. On 19 November, they took off for Damascus. The practical aspect of going to Damascus was that the journey directly south-eastwards would take them across the worst of the deserts of Arabia. Their route lay over the old battlefields of Romani, El Arish, Gaza and Nazareth and thus possessed a quotient of nostalgia for Ross Smith, who had flown over all those sites as a combatant.

A *simoom* wind nearly destroyed the aircraft in Damascus, and though they lashed it to the ground, they and a crowd of Indian Lancers had to hang on to it through the night. Taking off the next morning, they had their best day. They kept on across India, landing briefly at Delhi, then at Allahabad and Calcutta. They made Rangoon and passed the unofficial contestant, a French Lieutenant Poulet in his small Caudron machine. They had been advised to land at Singora in Thailand, which turned out to be a primitive aerodrome in the jungle not adequately cleared of stumps. But they survived it and reached Singapore on 4 December. At Surabaya, on an airstrip the Viceroy of Indonesia had ordered cleared especially for the race, their aircraft became deeply bogged as it rolled to a stop. The machine was dug out with the greatest difficulty. 'At one time I feared it would be impossible ever to start off from that aerodrome again,' said Ross Smith. Bamboo mats were laid down for 350 yards and the machine was hauled from the bog by Indonesians. The take-off was of course dangerous, with bamboo flying up and splintering into spears that came lancing backwards to them. When they landed in Timor, last stop before Darwin, 'Excitement kept us all from sleep that night.' The next day, 'A tiny speck upon the waters resolved itself into a warship, HMAS *Sydney*, in exactly the position we had asked her to be in, in case of need.' They arrived at Darwin on 10 December, beating the time limit of a month by two days, and won the prize. But even in their glory they knew something of the chanciness of aviation. Within eighteen months, former Sergeant, now Lieutenant Bennett would be killed in a crash.

Both Ross and Keith were knighted after the flight and the sergeants immediately commissioned. Democratically, the prize money was split four ways.

As for the Australians Ray Parer and John McIntosh, whose flight would inspire a poem by W.H. Auden, the British Air Ministry had forbidden them to take off because it considered their craft under-powered. The two airmen ignored this diktat, but it took them seven months to reach Darwin. They had left Hounslow on 8 January 1920, and arrived in Cairo on 21 February after flying over the crater of Vesuvius where heatwaves from the volcano caused the machine to fall out of control for 500 feet. They made two landings in the desert between Ramleh in Palestine and Baghdad, and their encounter with armed Arabs was the subject of Auden's poem. After four crash landings along the way, at Singapore Parer replaced his propeller for the fourth time. They crossed the Timor Sea and landed at Darwin in the evening of 2 August 1919.

Through these aviators, war aviation began to blend into civil aviation, and like the Overland Telegraph, into a creative assault on the challenges of time and size.

MAKING PEACE

Billy Hughes brought to the Peace Conference following the Armistice of 11 November 1918 a half-amused mocking tone, but one which involved a clear sense of Australian blood having been spilled on an altar at which world leaders could now strut and gesture. The conference was, in his eyes and with ironic inflection, the 'charmed circle [where] humanity but walked arm in arm and, defying the curse of the Confusion of Tongues, and the clash of colour, race and creed, held Communion one with the other on matters grave and gay'. Because of his increasing deafness, he brought his portable hearing machine to help him be party to discussion and eccentrically proposed that the Emir Feisal was 'the most striking and picturesque figure in the conference'. One Sergeant James, an Australian soldier who had served in the Middle East, translated Feisal's Arabic for Hughes, but Feisal and T.E. Lawrence would not come away from Paris as pleased as would Billy Hughes.

The British and French had huge delegations in Paris in 1919, and even the Germans had more than a hundred, while the American delegation numbered well over two hundred. When on 11 January 1919 Hughes travelled to Paris with Lloyd George and other British and Empire representatives, Hughes' party consisted of his secretary Percy Deane, Sir Robert Garran (his old friend from his attorney-general days and a senior public servant), Sir Joseph Cook and his private secretary, and the lawyer and politician John Greig Latham. On a less official footing, Melbourne barrister and member of the Round Table Group in Melbourne Sir Frederick Eggleston also accompanied the delegation, as did Henry Gullett, official war correspondent with the Australians in Palestine. Keith Murdoch was on hand to transmit news for his cable service.

The international intent was to make a new world which would be struc-tured by two influences—British and French desire for vengeance, and President Woodrow Wilson's glowing Fourteen Points, which were to provide the basis for a new level of negotiation between aggrieved nations, a new and peaceful mechanism for the resolution of warlike intentions, and self-determination for many minorities. The direction of the conference came under the Supreme Council, or the Council of Ten, a continuation of the Supreme Allied Council consisting of the presidents and foreign ministers of the United States, Britain, France, Italy and Japan. Before it, representatives of the smaller countries would be called to state their case on matters of special concern to them. Later, more informal decisions were resolved by a Council of Four: Wilson, British Prime Minister Lloyd George, French Prime Minister Georges Clemenceau and Vittirio Orlando, Prime Minister of Italy. Special committees or commissions were also set up.

Before leaving London for Paris, Hughes summarised his aims at a luncheon of the Australia and New Zealand Club. 'We do not want to exact an indemnity in excess of the cost of war . . . but up to her full capacity Germany must pay for the cost of the war.' Australia must also be given management of New Guinea and other South Sea islands. Hughes insisted that the Bismarck Archipelago and the German Solomons were inseparable from the Australian mainland strategically and administratively. Japanese infiltration of Rabaul, for example, would be just as serious as in New Guinea proper. All of them were 'necessary for our security, safety and freedom', he claimed. Lloyd George asked Hughes to take care of the Empire's case for the payment of indemnities by Germany. When Hughes went to see Clemenceau on this issue, he was warned of President Wilson's determined opposition and the Fourteen Points of 'the great man'. 'Wilson is the God in the machine to the people outside,' wrote Hughes. 'He is great on great principles. As to their application: he is so much like Alice in Wonderland.'

In President Wilson's Fourteen Points, there were to be no annexations, no indemnities, and freedom of the seas. Freedom of the seas was defeated by the self-interest of the various maritime parties; no indemnities was overturned in favour of Germany paying reparations; and to avoid on a technical basis the problem of annexations, the system of 'mandates' and 'mandated territories' was put in place, these to be supervised by the proposed League of Nations. Even so, President Wilson did not want the New Guinea mandate to be given to Australia unless a plebiscite on the matter was held amongst the New Guinea population. Hughes response, as related in his own narrative, was very much one of the time. 'Do you know, Mr President, that these natives eat one another?' Wilson, of course would have been offended by such an answer, and that would have been Hughes' genuine purpose. Lloyd George, however, held the alliance with America to be more important than Australia's desires, and therefore told

Hughes that if he insisted on the mandate, the British Navy would take no part in supporting Australia's control of New Guinea. Hughes would later say that he made some biting remarks to his fellow Welshman about politicians who, after the huge sacrifice the British peoples had made, now bowed in subservience before America, which had profited much and sacrificed little.

The conference was made up of a number of committees and the most important was the Covenant Committee of which President Wilson was chairman, and to which was delegated the task of drafting the Covenant of the League of Nations. The committee included Lord Robert Cecil and General Smuts of South Africa. The Covenant Committee, whom Hughes called the 'elect', were billeted in the Hotel Majestic, 'a magnificent caravanserai near the Arc de Triomphe where the food was excellent and the company even better'. (He should have known—he stayed there himself.) He became exercised by news from the Covenant Committee of a Racial Equality Clause designed to allow the members of any nation of the league free entry into any other nation of the league. 'Applied to Australia, it meant that Japanese might enter our country when and to the extent they desired. Our White Australia Policy would be a pricked bladder.' Hughes was again visited by Baron Makino, who urged a recognition by Australia of the Equality Principle, and told him both Lord Cecil and General Smuts were in favour of the clause. Africa and England were different, said Hughes in reply. Africa was already a coloured man's country. 'Australia, on the other hand, is very much a white man's country, sparsely populated by white men.'

Hughes lobbied the American press to fight against the clause, particularly journalists from the Pacific Coast states which had a Japanese minority. In the event, the unanimous vote President Wilson required to adopt the clause did not eventuate. In March there were direct talks between Hughes and the Japanese, and they seem to have been quite amicable, but Hughes had an immutable belief that the ultimate aim was Japanese immigration to Australia. 'Hughes alone persisted along his stubborn solitary path,' the Japanese delegation reported to their foreign minister. Yet, 'he was not unsympathetic to the Japanese stand'. Hughes, in an interview with a Japanese newspaper, declared that he did not want the Japanese people to believe that Australia was the only country who objected to the insertion of the amendment to the peace treaty proposed by Japan. As the representative of Australia, he claimed, he would 'give place to none in my respect, goodwill and esteem for the Japanese nation'. But as he did not ask the Japanese people to vary their domestic policy to suit Australia, he thought the Japanese would concede to Australia the same right. He hoped the two nations, the ancient one and the new one, could achieve their separate destinies and realise their ideals in their own way. But Wilson's chief aide, Colonel House, continued—conveniently—to put all the blame for the defeat of the proposition on Hughes.

For part of Hughes' battles and meetings with the Japanese, Wilson was absent in the United States, returning to Paris in mid-March 1919 with the intention of establishing the League of Nations as an integral part of the Treaty of Peace. He had been looking during his time at home at his chances of getting the peace treaty as it was proposed, including the idea of a League of Nations, through Congress. This hope would never be fulfilled. Returning to France a little daunted, Wilson was greeted sarcastically by Hughes. 'The heaven-born has returned from God's own country,' wrote Billy, who had spent part of the interval visiting Australian troops in Belgium, men anxious to be shipped home but for whom shipping had not been allocated.

Hughes ultimately stated his chief objectives to the Governor-General in a letter of 13 May 1919. 'I want (1) to get those islands on a satisfactory tenure; (2) to get our share of an indemnity; (3) to get the boys home; (4) to sell our wheat, lead, copper etc.; (5) to establish markets for our produce in Europe. If I do all these things I shall certainly deserve something better than to be hit on the head with an egg as at Warwick.'

Lloyd George was aware of the problem inherent in reparations—they could only be paid by allowing German industry to function and export, and thus be in competition with British goods. The Germans could not pay indemnities and at the same time be denied raw materials. But in late 1918, with grief and loss still upon them, people wanted Germany to suffer, and Lloyd George had an election coming up. So he proposed a committee of the Imperial War Cabinet to come up with a solution, and Hughes had been ultimately persuaded to act as its chairman. Perhaps Lloyd George thought that exposing Hughes to expert opinion would moderate his ideas. It did not. Hughes wanted to refuse to consider German capacity to pay reparations and simply concentrate on what she owed. The report of the committee was given to Lloyd George on 10 December, just in time for George to make a fire-eating reparations speech at Bristol.

The debate over the issue in the Peace Conference's Commission on Reparations, of which Hughes was a member, was a gruelling fight between Billy and the young John Foster Dulles, Princeton dropout, New York lawyer and special counsel to the American delegation. Hughes had originally opened on 10 February with a general statement of the British case. Reparation was a 'matter of compensation not a punishment'. The war had been a monstrous wrong inflicted by Germany. Dulles was willing to concede a certain obligation on Germany to compensate Belgium. Then what about the compensation of nations that came to Belgium's aid? Hughes declared, 'Those who have mortgaged their all to right Belgium's wrongs have suffered as much at Germany's hands as Belgium itself.'

The commission broke up with no decision and with Dulles' recommendation that it be referred to the Council of Four. Dulles had at least proposed the War Guilt Clause, an acknowledgement of guilt by Germany which would exercise the imaginations of German nationalists and be a useful tool for extreme German politicians. In the end, reparations would be settled on, but Australia would receive only £5.5 million, made up principally of ships seized in Australian ports and the value of expropriated property in New Guinea. Her total claim was close to £100 million.

As for such places as New Guinea in Australia's case or the Caroline Islands in Japan's, Wilson wanted to postpone these questions until after the establishment of the League of Nations. Clemenceau told Lloyd George to bring 'his savages', including Hughes and the New Zealanders with their claims on Samoa, to an afternoon session of the council. Hughes addressed the council and told them that the islands Australia had claim to 'encompassed Australia like fortresses'. New Guinea was only 80 miles (130 kilometres) from the mainland. Neighbouring islands could provide coaling and act as a submarine base to hostile powers unless Australia controlled them. Australia, he conceded, had no need for further territory, but these islands were essential to her peace, and Australia's sacrifices in the war entitled her to security. The US Secretary of State, Robert Lansing, would write, 'Hughes is a great bore.' Hughes didn't believe that the League of Nations should have the power to determine mandates—New Guinea should as of right be Australia's to administer. The Australian position, thought Wilson, came from 'a fundamental lack of faith in the League of Nations' as the ultimate defender.

Hughes got the chance to demonstrate on a map to the members of the council 'the narrow strip of sea that separated Australia from these strategic bases', which included New Guinea, Rabaul, Nauru and the Solomons. According to Hughes, Baron Nobuaki Makino, Japanese plenipotentiary and former foreign minister, approached him and told him he had made a good case, not only for Australian control of New Guinea but ultimately for Japanese control of the Marshall and Caroline Islands. Hughes objected that the Japanese had already occupied these islands, and it was therefore all the more important that Australia control New Guinea.

Hughes would claim that at one stage of negotiations Wilson asked him, 'And would you allow the natives to have access to the missionaries, Mr Hughes?'

'"Indeed, I would, sir," I replied, "for there are many days when these poor devils do not get half enough missionaries to eat."'

Even though it may only be an anecdote, it indicates Hughes' comtempt for what he saw as Wilson's moral posturing.

At a meeting with Hughes, Lloyd George suggested that he could see the case for a mandate for the mainland of New Guinea but was doubtful whether it could be applied to the adjacent islands, the Bismarck Archipelago (which included New Britain and the port of Rabaul, and New Ireland) and the German Solomons. Hughes made the argument that Rabaul was just as much a matter of concern, and a Japanese arrival there would be just as dangerous as one on the New Guinea mainland. Lloyd George lost his temper, told Hughes he had fought for Hughes' claims for the last three days but 'would not quarrel with the United States for the Solomon Islands'. Hughes did not back off when Lloyd George said that if Hughes persisted in his claim, he could not expect the British navy to help him enforce it. Hughes threatened 'to go to England and ask the people who owned the Navy what they have to say about it'. The meeting descended to Welsh cursing between Hughes and Lloyd George, and the latter was so distressed that that night, relaxing after dinner at a flat he had now rented, and playing Welsh hymns on the piano, he broke off and spat out the sentiment that he was not going to be bullied by 'a damned little Welshman'.

Finding the conference probably disinclined to agree upon the annexation of New Guinea by Australia and Samoa of New Zealand, Hughes and the New Zealanders agreed to Class C Mandates designed for claims on former German territories and areas that possessed 'remoteness from the centres of civilisation' or else had 'geographical contiguity to the mandatory state' and so could best be administered under the laws of the mandatory state, subject to safeguards for the native populations. Hughes realised that the C Mandate would not limit Australia's capacity to secure the Pacific Islands, and at the same time would put some limitation on Japan's right to fortify the northern Pacific islands to which they received a Class C Mandate as well. Hughes wanted the precise terms of the mandates settled before the treaty was signed, and had written to Colonel

House, Wilson's aide, that 'if peace was signed leaving Australia's position as regards the islands uncertain, there would be not only bitter disappointment, but grave misgivings . . . that both the territorial integrity of their country and the White Australia Policy, which is the cornerstone of our national edifice, were in serious danger'. But that was the minimum Australia and New Zealand would accept, and if that was not conceded definitely now they would not take part in an agreement at all. The US President asked if Australia and New Zealand were giving the conference an ultimatum. Hughes, who was deaf and depending on his hearing instrument, seemed distracted and was asked again whether he was laying down an ultimatum to the conference. He said that that was about it, but some thought that he had not understood the question. The less turbulent New Zealand Prime Minister William Massey assured Wilson it was not the case. 'Then, am I to understand,' Wilson continued, 'that if the whole civilised world asks Australia to agree to a mandate for these islands, Australia is prepared to defy the opinion of the whole civilised world?'

Hughes agreed pleasantly, 'That's about the size of it, Mr President. That puts it very well.' But again those present thought it possible that he had not heard properly. It was only when Wilson again asked whether Hughes set 5 million people against the 1200 million represented by the conference that Hughes replied, knowing that American losses were far lower than Australia's, 'I represent 60 000 dead.'

Wilson was not in a conciliatory mood, however. An article had appeared in the *Daily Mail* that morning attacking him as an impractical idealist, announcing that there was conflict between the Dominions and the United States, and that Britain was threatening the future of the Empire by siding with Wilson. Everyone believed that Hughes was the source of the article. Wilson said he would accept the idea of a Class C Mandate for Australia over New Guinea, subject to full discussion by the League of Nations when it was drawn up. The league could define each individual mandate, including that of Australia over the Pacific Islands, to 'fit the case as a glove fits the hand'. Hughes asked if he was really expected to tell the people of Australia that a mandate was to apply, but he did not know how except that it would fit like a hand to the glove?

When he later received the documentation of the Australian claims, President Wilson pencilled on it, 'I could agree to this if the interpretation in practice were to come from [South African Prime Minister] General Smuts . . . my difficulty is with the demands of men like Hughes and certain difficulties with Japan. A line of islands in her possession would be very dangerous to the US.' On the one hand Wilson believed in self-determination and the equal dignity of all men. On the other he was concerned about American interests and concerned too that if the Japanese had control over the islands of the North Pacific they could turn them into military bases that were closer to Hawaii than Hawaii was to the US. America's peace and security would be imperilled. The apostles of the war to end all wars were thus already aware of the danger of further ones. And Hughes, the most pragmatic of them all, certainly was. He dressed each morning at the Majestic with care, brushed his moustache before the mirror, snorted and was ready to put the man he referred to as the 'heaven-sent' in his place.

Hughes received a telegram from his cabinet expressing bitter disappointment over the Class C Mandate. It seemed to them (inaccurately as it turned out) that under it Australia would not have the authority to prevent Asian immigration to New Guinea and thus to the mainland. But Hughes knew that New Guinea and the other mandated islands were a long way from Paris and Geneva, and that in practice the Australians would run the mandate according to their own principles. That Hughes had stood up to the president was common knowledge throughout Paris and caused amusement in some cases, and in others was seen as an example of a smaller man standing up to a moral bully. Still others were outraged. Secretly, the Prime Minister of Canada, Sir Robert Gordon, apologised to Colonel House, President Wilson's aide and US delegate, for Hughes' behaviour.

The mandate issue was not fully settled because the Japanese objected, wanting an 'open door' clause under the Class C Mandates. They would rule out the right to fortify the Marshalls and Carolines if Australia would institute the open door. It would be a year before their objections were withdrawn and the mandates issued on 17 December 1920.

By the first week in May 1919 the draft of the immense treaty with its 439 articles was ready for approval by the Plenary Session. It was a mass of compromise. On 7 May the treaty was given to the German plenipotentiaries summoned to Versailles. They were allowed three weeks to provide a written response. During the meeting, Count Brockdorff-Rantzau of Germany protested that the terms contravened the Fourteen Points. He did so while seated, which brought an angry note delivered to Lloyd George by Hughes, who had moved along the table. 'Why does Clemenceau allow Rantzau to address him seated? He stood up and so did we all.'

The Allied reply to the German objections to the treaty was delivered on 16 June with an ultimatum demanding acceptance within a week. The signing session was fixed for the following Saturday, 28 June. The Dominions were to sign for themselves, and finding out on 26 June when he got to Paris after a visit to London that he needed a seal to set beside his signature, Hughes' staff searched the curio shops for something appropriate. Hughes particularly liked one of Hercules slaying the lion, but this was vetoed by Sir Robert Garran, who said, 'No, Mr Hughes, you are not in the least like Hercules.' Finally it was decided that an AIF tunic button could be shaped into a seal and it was the one that was used.

The signing occurred on the afternoon of 28 June in the Hall of Mirrors at Versailles. Clemenceau was in the position of honour, with Wilson on his right and Lloyd George on his left, and then the Dominion ministers, Hughes and his minister, colourless Joseph Cook, being seated between the Canadians and South Africans. Two German plenipotentiaries arrived at seven minutes past three and signed. That night there was a gala dinner and dance at the Hotel Majestic, and the British and Empire delegates returned the next morning to London. Billy met his wife and his daughter Helen at Victoria Station and their car was mobbed in the street by 500 Australian soldiers with shouts of 'Where's our Billy?' Hughes was pulled out of the car and hoisted shoulder-high by four of them, and Helen was carried off by another. He and his daughter accepted their rough treatment with good humour, as the prime minister's hat was knocked off and a soldier's hat jammed in its place. Mrs Hughes was more shaken. The car arrived at the Anzac Buffet in Horseferry Street and here Billy gave a speech, after which he was carried on a number of shoulders back to his car, still wearing the Digger hat. After all, he was the Little Digger.

The French prime minister had rather liked Hughes, since the French were cynical about the process and about the high-flown Wilson too. Clemenceau would later write, 'In the first rank, I should have placed Mr Hughes, the noble delegate of Australia, with whom one conversed through an acoustic box from which emerged symphonies of good sense.' He noticed that Hughes turned the machine off when he didn't like what he was hearing.

Australia's mandate over German New Guinea, including New Britain and New Ireland, would soon be officially confirmed, but Australia would need to share the mandate over Nauru with New Zealand and ultimately with Britain too, though Australia was in effective control. The Solomons remained with Britain.

Though Hitler would rise to power on the idea that the Allies had bled Germany white, the compensation for starting the war seemed small to Billy. 'All the indemnity we get will hardly pay for repatriation let alone the cost of the war and pensions. At least I fear so. It is *not* a good peace for Australia; nor indeed for Britain. It is a good peace for America.' His view was that Australia, with its 5 million people, had incurred a public debt of something like £300 million, which would need to be paid off by Australian taxpayers, while Germany, whose factories were unscathed, and the United States and Japan, who had made large profits out of the war, would all be at an unfair advantage.

In the trenches, men sealed together by the most extreme peril had dreamed of a peace in which they would apply the new level of brotherhood and cohesion they had achieved in war to Australian society in general. After all, this *was* the War to End All Wars and thus the war to bring about fraternity. Yet even the soldiers were divided—on conscription they had been split down the middle, as had been Australians at large. The strikes of 1917 had signalled to many of them that the Wobblies and others were fighting against them to shut down Australian ports and Australian mines. The idea was that what had happened in Russia that year, with the rise of the Bolsheviks, might now occur in Australia. The withdrawal of Russia from the battle, its signing of a peace treaty with Germany at Brest-Litovsk in the early days of March 1918, had enabled the massive German outbreak on the Western Front, which the Australians had had a large part in driving back and in finally extinguishing at significant cost of flesh and blood throughout 1918. The Bolshevik revolution had a great impression, one way or another, on both sides of the trench lines.

Yet others of the Australian troops had relatives who were unionised, and they understood exactly, from their own pre-war experience of hardship and food prices, what the people at home were upset about. And so the problem for the future was this: whether civilian or soldier, man or woman, some Australians wanted the war to transform society, put all the old pieties up for debate, and bring in a new era of social justice. Other Australians wanted to return to the same society which had existed before the war. These latter believed that the trade unions, the Wobblies and the socialists would try to deny them their Australia, and that therefore it would need to be defended by arms.

This division was potentially bitter. It was enhanced by the post-war slump, in which—as happens after every all-out war—prices of wheat and wool, metals and manufactures all fell, while food prices stayed high. Many Diggers who had been cheered home presented themselves for work at their old shop or factory and were told that times were too hard to re-employ them.

The common belief in a White Australia had nonetheless been validated by Billy Hughes amongst the international show ponies in Paris and Versailles. Good on him! And within that White Australia, there were estimated to be a mere 60 000 Aboriginal Australians. The belief that they and their culture would soon disappear remained as strong as it had in 1901, and the idea that they should exercise political influence was countenanced only by a few informed whites.

For those with jobs, meanwhile, the decade ahead looked glittering and tranquil, lit up by the pulse of modern music, by the sounds created by radio and, through open windows in the city and bush, by the melodies sent forth by record players. Modern consumerism was about to be born. The automobile was the most desirable consumer item and the young made it a venue for sexual experimentation deplored from pulpits and by their elders. The young were also enchanted by the seducing flicker of the cinema screen, and the long-lashed screen sirens stared and glimmered down the barrel of the camera in the darkened cinemas of the remotest towns, raising new expectations in the young.

But in the privileged parts of cities and in the countryside, solemn elders, particularly those who owned great pastoral or commercial enterprises, were already discussing the need to recruit and equip armies to protect Australia from the political calamity which seemed to be in play. The crisis had emerged in many European countries, in defeated Germany, and even in Britain, victorious though she was. There was a belief that though the battle in Europe was over, the battle for Australia itself was just beginning. The War to End All Wars was giving way to the war to rescue society.

TIMELINE TO 1919

1860	Burke and Wills' notorious expedition from southern Australia to the north began. At Cooper Creek, Burke and Wills, with two other men, left for the Gulf of Carpentaria. The fateful journey is one of the major upsets of Australia's history. In September 1861, after searching for Burke and Wills since June, the lone survivor of the expedition was found. Wills' grave and Burke's remains were then discovered.
1860	The Aboriginal Protection Board was established in Victoria. Nearly 11 000 hectares of land were turned into reserves for the 'temporary' residence of Victorian Aborigines. By 1900, most Victorian Aborigines had been placed on reserves.
1861	*June* Anti-Chinese riots broke out at Lambing Flat, a goldfield in New South Wales. None of the perpetrators were prosecuted despite Chinese people being killed.
1861	The New South Wales Robertson Land Act was enacted. The principles of free selection and conditional purchase were introduced in order to help the small farmer. The legislation, however, proved to benefit the squatters and large landowners.
1861	Nineteen settlers on the newly developed Cullin-la Ringo station in Queensland were killed by Aborigines. A party of men soon set out and a number of Aborigines were slaughtered.
1862	Explorer John McDouall Stuart successfully returns from crossing Australia from north to south on his third attempt.

1862	*4 November* Archer wins the second Melbourne Cup.
1863	*14 March* Goulburn given city status by Queen Victoria, thus making it Australia's first inland city.
1863	*11 November* Elizabeth Scott is hanged for the murder of her husband, making her the first woman to be executed in Victoria.
1863	South Sea Islanders brought to Queensland to work as indentured labourers in the sugar industry. Commonly known as Kanakas, later legislation attempted to prohibit their entry into the country.
1864	*17 February* Banjo Paterson is born.
1865	*26 January* Bushrangers Ben Hall, Johnny Gilbert and John Dunn hold up Kimberley's Inn in Collector, New South Wales. Dunn kills one police officer, Constable Samuel Nelson.
1865	Arnott's Biscuits is founded by Scottish-born William Arnott.
1866	*19 March* Sister Mary MacKillop founded the Sisters of Saint Joseph of the Sacred Heart at Penola, South Australia.
1866	*18 April* Australia's first Protective tariffs become law.
1867	A group of Irish political prisoners, known as the Fenians, transported to Western Australia.
1868	An Aboriginal cricket team toured England between May and September. It was the first organised group of cricketers from Australia to be sent overseas. The first game attracted a 20 000-strong crowd and a total of 47 games were played. The Aboriginal team won fourteen, lost fourteen and drew nineteen.
1868	After several debates over the ending of transportation to the Australian colonies throughout the 1860s, a decision was finally made to end transportation altogether. Declining crime rates in Britain prompted this decision. The last convict ship to Australia—the *Hougoumont*—reached Fremantle with 279 prisoners on 9 January. From the inception of transportation, almost 159 000 convicts were sent to Australia, the majority (80 000) to New South Wales, 67 500 to Van Diemen's Land (Tasmania) and 9700 to Western Australia.
1869	The Suez Canal was opened, enabling a more direct route between Europe and Australia.
1869	The opening in New South Wales of the Hawkesbury River Bridge linked the northern with the southern and western rail lines. It also connected Brisbane with Adelaide.

1870	Construction of the Overland Telegraph began.
1870	John Forrest, with his brother, led an expedition from Perth to Adelaide along the Great Australian Bight. John Forrest later became Western Australia's first premier.
1870	The last garrisons of British troops leave Australia. Each colony is now responsible for its own defence.
Late 1870s	The Kimberley was settled after the exploration of the area in 1879 by Alexander Forrest.
1871	After twenty years of assisted immigration there were 100 000 Irish settlers in Victoria.
1872	The Overland Telegraph, a 3200 kilometre telegraph line connecting Darwin and Port Augusta, was completed. It allowed fast connection between Australia and the rest of the world. This major engineering feat revolutionised communication and within the first year over 4000 telegrams were sent. In 1875 Western Australia joined the connection when a line was built across the Nullarbor Plain from South Australia.
1873	*19 July* Surveyor Willian Gosse renames Uluru 'Ayers Rock' after the premier of South Australia, Henry Ayers, despite it being called the former for thousands of years.
1873	Edward William Cole opened his first bookstore in Melbourne. It soon was claimed as the world's biggest bookstore, extending from Bourke Street to Collins Street.
1875	An art gallery was set up by the New South Wales government with the trustees from the Academy of Art. William Ford's 'Picnic Party at Hanging Rock' was displayed here.
1875	The South Australian government provided for 70 days of compulsory education each half a year for children aged seven to thirteen years. Absenteeism continued, however, because of the demand for child labour.
1876	A Tasmanian Aborigine named Truganini dies aged 73. The government falsely claims the 'last' Aborigine has died and therefore the 'native problem' was over.
1877	The first Test match between Australian and England played at the Melbourne Cricket Ground. Australia wins.

1878	Lawrence Hargrave began his research into birds, fish and insects in order to discover the movements essential for flight. By 1889 he had invented a rotary engine with revolving cylinders attached to propeller blades. It is said that the same rotary engines used on early European planes were appropriated from Hargrave's invention.
1879	The first time a parachute was used in Australia was after Henry L'Estrange deployed one when he lost control of his hot air balloon over Melbourne.
1879–80	The first successful shipment of frozen meat to Britain was made on the *Strathleven*. Australian James Harrison was a pioneering force behind refrigerated shipping, allowing the export of meat and dairy products.
1880s	The first land on the Cape York Peninsula was taken up to provide meat to the gold miners. There was an influx of pastoralists to the peninsula but few survived the harsh terrain.
1880	The *Bulletin* magazine is launched. Claimed to be a 'friend' of the bush and the workers, it was radical in its approach, republican and xenophobic. It was a continuous source of controversy, criticising conservatism in all facets of Australian society. It ceased publication in 2008.
1881	The first Australian Census was conducted. The non-Indigenous population was 2.3 million.
1882	The Australian cricket team defeat England on English soil for the first time. After this match *The Sporting Times* describes English cricket as dead, 'that its body shall be cremated and ashes sent to Australia . . .'. The Ashes was born.
1883	The New South Wales Aborigines Protection Board was established.
1885	The Broken Hill Proprietary Company, later to become BHP, Australia's largest mining company, was established.
1886	An article in the *West Australian* reported that the dispossession of 'blacks' would be the most 'effectual' course of action in order to settle the dispute with the white population. Dispossession of Aboriginal people from their homes became widespread. Protection legislation was enacted in Western Australia in this year.

| 1887 | Discoveries of gold in parts of Western Australia in 1885, notably Yilgarn and Halls Creek, opened up the discoveries at Kalgoorlie and Coolgardie which began Western Australia's gold rush. |

| 1887 | *May 3* A 'monster meeting' was held in Sydney to protest against Chinese immigration. Demonstrations led to the decision to limit the entry of Chinese immigrants based on certain categories, for example, merchants, seamen, students and officials. The colonies enacted legislation preventing the naturalisation of Chinese immigrants. Racial prejudice against Chinese people heightened and was cemented in the *Immigration Restriction Act 1901*. |

| 1887 | Henry Lawson's first printed poem, 'Song of the Republic', was published in the *Bulletin*. His first story, 'His Father's Mate', was published in the same magazine a year later. |

| 1888 | Angus and Robertson publishes its first book, *A Crown of Wattle*. |

| 1889 | Fosters Lager goes on sale for the first time. |

| 1889 | The bridge over the Hawkesbury River in New South Wales was the last link of the railway connecting Brisbane, Melbourne, Sydney and Adelaide. It was officially opened on 1 May. |

| 1889 | A.B. (Banjo) Paterson's 'Clancy of the Overflow' was published in the *Bulletin*, followed a year later by 'The Man from Snowy River'. |

| 1890s | This decade saw the proliferation of steam shipping over sail. By 1900, the tonnage of the world's steam ships was twice that of sail. |

| 1891 | The shearers' strike, which lasted from February to May in Queensland, erupted when pastoralists tried to cut wages and destroy unionism by employing non-union, often Chinese, labour. Many unionists were arrested for ransacking property and harassing non-unionists. The union defeat led to the formation of the Australian Labor Party. |

| 1891 | The Women's Christian Temperance Union of Australasia was formed in Melbourne. Campaigning against certain 'evils' of society such as alcohol and promiscuousness, the WCTU was also heavily involved in the campaign for women's suffrage. |

| 1892 | A miners' strike erupted in Broken Hill when employers broke an agreement with the unions. The Miners' Association was defeated and a number of strike leaders were gaoled. |

| 1893 | Major Australian banks were on the verge of collapse, particularly in Victoria, after the Federal Bank failed on 30 January. |

1894	South Australia grants women the right to vote and to stand for Parliament. These combined achievements together are a world first.
1895	The words of 'Waltzing Matilda' were first sung in public in a pub in Winton, Queensland named the North Gregory Hotel. It was set to the tune of an old Scottish ballad, 'Thou Bonnie Wood of Craigielea'.
1897	Essendon wins the first Victorian Football League premiership.
1897	Catherine Helen Spence is the first woman in the world to put herself up for election to Parliament when she stands for the Australasian Federal Convention in Adelaide. She has been named the 'Greatest Australian Woman' and is commemorated on the Australian $5 note.
1898	A re-energising of the Federation cause began when Alfred Deakin made a speech in Bendigo where he put to the people '. . . do we not find ourselves hampered in commerce, restricted in influence, weakened in prestige, because we are jarring atoms instead of a united organism'.
1898	A referendum to approve the draft constitution was passed with majorities in Victoria, South Australia and Tasmania, but New South Wales did not reach the statutory minimum.
1899	Another referendum was held and a majority vote Yes. Federation will go ahead despite Western Australia being reluctant to join in. A year later Western Australia decided to hold a referendum, resulting in a Yes vote.
1900	Two Aboriginal brothers, Jimmy and Joe Governor, killed seven white people in New South Wales because Jimmy had taken offence to slurs aimed at his wife. Joe Governor was shot dead and Jimmy was arrested and hanged.
1901	The newly enacted Commonwealth Constitution did not recognise Aboriginal people. It stated that 'in reckoning the numbers of the people . . . Aborginal natives shall not be counted'. The Common-wealth also declared that it would not legislate for Aboriginal people, therefore each state continued its power over Aboriginal affairs.

1901   The *Immigration Restriction Act 1901* was the first piece of legislation enacted by the newly federated Australia. The Act prohibited permanent settlement of non-Europeans. The 'White Australia Policy', as it was so-called, was enforced by a dictation test which was administered in a language that would ensure the applicant would fail. The restrictions were lessened in 1912 to allow Chinese students to stay up to one year without taking the test.

1902   The final year of fighting in South Africa against the Boers. Harry 'Breaker' Morant is executed for shooting unarmed Boer prisoners. The war ends on 31 May.

1902   Women are granted the vote in Australia and are permitted to stand for Parliament.

1904   The first national Labor government takes office with Chris Watson as prime minister.

1908   Rugby League comes to Australia.

1908   The *Bulletin* changes its slogan from 'Australia for Australians' to 'Australia for the White Man', which it keeps until 1960.

1909–10   Greater powers were established in New South Wales for the Protection Board to take Aboriginal children from their families. Half-caste, or 'mixed blood', children were taken and put into training as domestic servants or as labourers.

1910   Several unpowered aircraft flight attempts were made during the first decade of the 1900s. It wasn't until 1910 that the first powered aircraft flight was made. John Duigan made this flight in Spring Plains, Victoria. The aircraft had to be pushed from a shed, down a steep hill and across two creeks. The runway was only 800 metres long.

1911   The Dreadnought Scheme began in New South Wales.

1912   Prime Minister Fisher declares the wattle to be Australia's national flower and incorporates it into the coat of arms.

1913   Australia's national capital is founded and named Canberra.

1914   *16–18 July* Australia's first airmail was carried between Melbourne and Sydney by Maurice Gillaux. It took 2½ days.

1914   Britain declares war on Germany on 1 August. Australia follows almost immediately, with Prime Minister Fisher announcing Australia shall be there 'to the last man and the last shilling'.

1915	Australians land at Gallipoli on 25 April. The arrival was met with immense gunfire by the Turkish army and the battle was nothing short of slaughter. The Gallipoli campaign, which lasted until December, resulted in over 7000 Australian deaths and 20000 wounded.
1916	The first conscription plebiscite was put to the Australian people. Prime Minister Billy Hughes wanted to introduce compulsory male military service but the No vote prevailed. This caused not only a rift in Australian society, fuelling sectarian turmoil, but the decision caused the Labor Party to split. Billy Hughes is expelled from Labor and he takes his followers with him to form the first Nationalist Party of Australia.
1917	The two sides of the Transcontinental Railway between Kalgoorlie and Port Augusta, and stretching across the Nullarbor Plain, are connected.
1917	The General Strike of 1917 erupts in Sydney after New South Wales Railways instigated a card system to monitor and pinpoint 'inefficient' workers. Workers walked off in protest, beginning in Sydney and spreading to other states.
1918	*11 November* World War I ended and an Armistice was signed. Over 60000 Australians were killed and 153000 wounded. Approximately 330000 Australians served overseas.
1918–19	The 'Spanish Flu' epidemic kills over 12000 Australians.

NOTES

GENERAL HISTORIES OF THE PERIOD

In nearly all cases of individually mentioned Australians, the admirable online *Australian Dictionary of Biography*, founded and maintained by the Australian National University, was a most valuable resource throughout the writing of this history, though for the vast majority of Australians dealt with in this narrative other sources were also consulted. I shall not therefore mention case-by-case recourse to the *Australian Dictionary of Biography*, but acknowledge my enthusiastic thanks for it once and for all here.

Another highly appreciated reference which I acknowledge but mention once and for all here is Graeme Davison, John Hirst, Stuart Macintyre (eds), *The Oxford Companion to Australian History* (South Melbourne 2001).

There also exists a debt to general histories of Australia, including: Geoffrey Blainey, *A Shorter History of Australia* (Melbourne 1994); Manning Clark, *A Short History of Australia* (London 1964); Frank Crowley (ed), *A New History of Australia* (Melbourne 1974); David Day, *Claiming a Continent: A new history of Australia* (Sydney 1996); Beverley Kingston, *The Oxford History of Australia, Volume 3, 1860–1900* (Melbourne 1993); Stuart Macintyre, *A Concise History of Australia* (Melbourne 2004); Stuart Macintyre, *The Oxford History of Australia, Volume 4, 1901–1942* (Melbourne 1993); Ernest Scott, *A Short History of Australia* (Melbourne 1936); Frank Welsh, *Great Southern Land, a New History of Australia* (Melbourne, 2004).

CHAPTER NOTES

Abbreviations to the notes

ML	Mitchell Library, State Library of New South Wales
MS	Manuscript (MSS plural)
NLA	National Library of Australia
JRAHS	*Journal of the Royal Australian Historical Society*
JAS	*Journal of Australian Studies*
AWM	Australian War Memorial

CHAPTER 1 OLD AND NEW FACES IN A COLONIAL SOCIETY

Post-transportation convicts

A.G.L. Shaw, *Convicts and the Colonies* (London 1966).
Some Tasmanian convicts: Terry O'Malley, *The Sin Eaters: Post-colonial portraits from Van Diemen's Land* (Hobart 2006).
Australian sensibilities to convictism: Babette Smith, *Australia's Birthstain: The startling legacy of the convict era* (Sydney 2008).
On Fenians: Keith Amos, *The Fenians in Australia* (Sydney 1988); Thomas Keneally, *The Great Shame* (Sydney 1998); 'Personal and Other Descriptions, Acct. 1156, Volume 10, Convict Establishment, Convict Department No. 40', Western Australian Archives; 'Denis Cashman's Diary', MSS 1636, ML; Geoffrey Bolton, *Land of Vision and Mirage: Western Australia since 1826* (Perth 2006).

Desolate in the extreme

Michael Cathcart, *The Water Dreamers: The remarkable story of our dry continent* (Melbourne 2009).
John McDouall Stuart, *Explorations in Australia* (London 1863).
John Bailey, *Mr Stuart's Track: The forgotten life of Australia's greatest explorer* (Sydney 2007).
Griffith Taylor, *A Study of Warm Environments and Their Impact on British Settlement* (London 1947).

Senior Inspector Burke

C.M.H. Clark, *A History of Australia, Volume IV. The earth abideth forever, 1851–1888* (Melbourne 1978).

Sarah Murgatroyd, *The Dig Tree: The story of Burke and Wills* (London 2002).

Tom Bergin, *In the Steps of Burke and Wills* (Sydney 1981).

Tim Flannery (ed), *The Explorers: Stories of discovery and adventure from the Australian frontier* (Melbourne 2000).

Alan Moorehead, *Cooper's Creek* (London 1963).

Cathcart, *The Water Dreamers*.

Transported gentlemen

Mary Lazarus, *Two Brothers: Charles Dickens's sons in Australia* (Sydney 1973).

Charles Dickens, *David Copperfield* (London 1850) and *Great Expectations* (London 1860).

John Forster, *The Life of Charles Dickens: Two volumes* (London 1927).

Victoria Glendinning, *Anthony Trollope* (London 1992).

Henry Dickens, *The Recollections of Sir Henry Dickens*, (London 1934).

Being black and white

Don Watson, *Caledonia Australis: Scottish highlanders on the frontier of Australia* (Sydney 1984).

Richard Broome, *Aboriginal Victorians: A history since 1880* (Sydney 2005).

P.D. Gardner, 'A melancholy tale, Thomas Bungaleen, the civilised blackman', *Victorian Historical Journal*, volume 52, 1981.

Politics and bankruptcy

Charles E. Lyne, *The Life of Sir Henry Parkes* (Sydney 1897).

Peter Cochrane, *Colonial Ambition: Foundations of Australian democracy* (Melbourne 2006).

Sir Henry Parkes Papers, Consult Index, ML MSS 4312.

Sir Henry Parkes, Papers 1879–1896, ML MS S6072, microfilm C Y 4441.

Plorn tries to do a Magwitch

Lazarus, *Two Brothers*.

Glendinning, *Anthony Trollope*.

C.E.W. Bean, *On The Wool Track* (London 1910).

E.L. Dickens, Correspondence 1895–1898, ML MSS 1372.

The Wilcannia Times, 7 July 1881.

Social bandits

Social banditry: John McQuilton, *The Kelly Outbreak 1876–1880: The geographical dimension of social banditry* (Melbourne 1979); Russell Ward,

The Australian Legend (Melbourne 1978); Pat O'Malley, 'Social justice after the "death of the social"', *Social Justice*, volume 26, issue 2, 1999.
Ben Hall: John Bradshaw, *The Only True Account of Ned Kelly, Frank Gardiner, Ben Hall and Morgan* (n.d., nineteenth century); Susan C. West, 'The role of the "bush" in 1860s Bushranging', *JRAHS*, December 2005.

Cullin-la-Ringo
Greg de Moore, *Tom Wills: His spectacular rise and tragic fall* (Sydney 2008).
Oscar de Satgè, *Pages from the Journal of a Queensland Squatter* (London 1901).
H.H. Grundy, *Pictures of the Past* (London 1879).
Sydney Morning Herald, 16 November 1861.

The abominable crime
Lucy Chesser, 'Cross dressing: sexual miss-representation and homosexual desire, 1863–1893' in David L. Phillips and Graham Willet, *Australia's Homosexual Histories* (Sydney 2000).
Adam Carr, 'Policing the abominable crime in 19th century'; and Wayne Murdoch, 'Homosexuality and the Melbourne truth: an annotated listing 1913–1945', from Robert French (ed), *Camping by a Billabong* (Sydney 1993).

CHAPTER 2 TAKING FURTHER SHAPE

The squatter grandees
Douglas Stewart and Nancy Keesing (eds), *Old Bush Songs and Rhymes of Colonial Times* (Sydney 1957).
Michael Cannon, *Life in the Country* (Melbourne 1973).
Margaret Kiddle, *Men of Yesterday: A social history of the Western District of Victoria* (Melbourne 1961).
Max Barrett, *Ned Ryan: King of Galong Castle* (Sydney 1983).

The Duke, loyalism and pistols
Raelene Francis, *Selling Sex: A hidden history of prostitution* (Sydney 2007).
Patrick O'Farrell, *The Irish in Australia* (Sydney 1986).
Robert Travers, *The Phantom Fenians of New South Wales* (Sydney 1986).
Keneally, *The Great Shame.*
Amos, *The Fenians in Australia.*
Sydney Morning Herald, 13 March 1868.
Persecution of Irish employees: ML 4/7680/1.

Sectarian vituperation

O'Farrell, *The Irish in Australia*.

Keneally, *The Great Shame*.

Charles Gavan Duffy, *My Life in Two Hemispheres* (volume 2, London 1898).

Trevor McClaughlan, *Barefoot and Pregnant: The Irish orphan girls in Australia* (Melbourne 1991).

A childhood in the city

J.A. La Nauze, *Alfred Deakin: A biography* (Sydney 1979).

Michael Cannon, *Life in the Cities* (Melbourne 1975).

Al Gabay, *The Mystic Life of Alfred Deakin* (Melbourne 1992).

Making games

de Moore, *Tom Wills*.

Geoffrey Blainey, *A Game of Our Own: The origins of Australian Football* (Melbourne 1990).

Intercolonial cricket and tourists

Bell's Life in Melbourne, 10 July 1858.

Richard Broome, *Aboriginal Australians: Black responses to white dominance 1788–2001* (Sydney 2002).

de Moore, *Tom Wills*.

Rex Harcourt and John Mulvaney, *Cricket Walkabout: The Aboriginal cricketers of the 1860s* (Melbourne 2005).

Richard Cashman, Warwick Franks, Jim Maxwell et al. (eds), *The Cambridge Companion to Australian Cricket* (Melbourne 1996).

Overland telegraph

Gordon Reid, *A Picnic With the Natives: Aboriginal-European relations in the Northern Territory to 1910* (Melbourne 1990).

Geoffrey Blainey, *Black Kettle and Full Moon: Daily life in a vanished Australia* (Melbourne 2003).

Alan Powell, *A Far Country: A short history of the Northern Territory* (Melbourne 1982).

Henry Reynolds, *North of Capricorn: The untold story of the people of Australia's north* (Sydney 2003).

Goyder and all that

Cathcart, *The Water Dreamers*.

Derek Whitelock, *Adelaide 1836–1976: A history of difference* (Brisbane 1977).

Clark, *A History of Australia, Volume IV.*
Cannon, *Life in the Country.*

The enobling land
Humphrey McQueen, *A New Britannia* (Melbourne 1975).
Clark, *A History of Australia, Volume IV.*
Michael McKernan, *Drought: The red marauder* (Sydney 2005).
Cyril Pearl, *The Three Lives of Charles Gavan Duffy* (Sydney 1979).
Beverly Kingston, *A History of New South Wales* (Melbourne 2006).
Raymond Evans, *A History of Queensland* (Melbourne 2007).
Steele Rudd, *On Our Selection* (Sydney 1992, originally 1899).
Samuel Schumack, Memoirs, MS 1643, NLA.

The Asian south and north
G.O. Preshaw, *Banking Under Difficulties, or Life on the Goldfields of Victoria, New South Wales and New Zealand* (Melbourne 1888).
Geoffrey Blainey, *The Rush that Never Ended: A history of Australian mining* (Carlton 2003).
Reynolds, *North of Capricorn.*
Powell, *A Far Country*
Raymond Evans, Kay Saunders and Kathryn Cronin, *Exclusion, Exploitation and Extermination: Race relations in colonial Queensland* (Sydney 1975).
Queensland Punch, 1 December 1880.
Cooktown Courier, 3 October 1874.

On our selection
McQueen, *A New Britannia.*
Rudd, *On Our Selection.*
Steele Rudd, *Our New Selection* (Project Gutenberg Australia electronic book, originally published 1903).

Northern Territory pastorale
James Barry's account in *Brisbane Courier,* 16 September and 27 October 1874.
Tony Roberts, *Frontier Justice: A history of the Gulf country to 1900* (Brisbane 2005).
Henry Reynolds, *North of Capricorn.*
Powell, *A Far Country.*
Broome, *Aboriginal Australians.*

Kanaka dawn

Evans, *A History of Queensland*.

Michael Cannon, *Who's Master? Who's Man?* (Melbourne 1971).

Reid Mortenson, 'Slaving in Australian courts: Blackbirding cases, 1869–71', *Journal of South Pacific Law*, volume 4, 2000.

Brisbane Courier, 15 November 1867.

Louis Becke (ed), 'A Grove Day', *South Seas Supercargo* (Brisbane n.d.).

Sydney Empire, 6 October 1869.

Captain George Palmer, *Kidnapping in the South Seas* (Edinburgh 1871).

Kipling of the Pacific

Becke, *South Seas Supercargo*.

Nicholas Thomas and Richard Eves (eds), *Bad Colonists: The South Seas letters of Vernon Lee Walker and Louis Becke* (Durham, North Carolina, 1999).

Geoffrey Serle, *From Deserts the Prophets Come: The creative spirit in Australia, 1788–1972* (Melbourne 1973).

H.E. Maude, 'Louis Becke: The trader's historian', *Journal of Pacific History*, volume 2, 1967.

Steaming to Australia

Cannon, *Life in the Cities*.

Robin Haines, *Life and Death in the Age of Sail: The passage to Australia* (Sydney 2003).

C. Stretton, *Memoirs of Chequered Life* (London 1862).

Preshaw, *Banking Under Difficulties*.

The refrigeration wars

Cannon, *Life in the Cities*.

Ian Arthur, 'Shipboard refrigeration and the beginnings of the frozen meat trade', *JRAHS*, volume 92, part I.

Australian Society for History and Technology website.

Mineral dreams

Powell, *A Far Country*.

Blainey, *The Rush that Never Ended*.

Evans, *A History of Queensland*.

Reynolds, *North of Capricorn*.

Geoffrey Bolton, *Land of Vision and Mirage: Western Australia since 1826* (Perth 2008).

Geoffrey Blainey, *The Peaks of Lyell* (Melbourne 1978).

J.S. Battye, *A History of Western Australia from its Discovery to the Inauguration of the Commonwealth* (Project Gutenberg Australia electronic book, originally published 1924).

Social bandits II
John Molony, *Ned Kelly* (Carlton 2001).

John Molony, *I Am Ned Kelly* (Ringwood 1980).

John McQuilton, *The Kelly Outbreak, 1878–1880: The geographical dimension of social banditry* (Carlton 1987).

Max Brown, *Ned Kelly: Australian son* (Sydney 1980).

Colin F. Cave (ed), *Ned Kelly: Man and myth* (Sydney 1968).

Ian Jones, *Ned Kelly: A short life* (Sydney 2008).

Clark, *A History of Australia, Volume IV.*

Robert Macklin, *Fire in the Blood: The epic tale of Frank Gardiner and Australia's other bushrangers* (Sydney 2005).

CHAPTER 3 ONE HUNDRED YEARS COMPLETE

The Broken Hill
Blainey, *The Rush that Never Ended.*

Kingston, *A History of New South Wales.*

Peter Thompson and Robert Macklin, *The Big Fella: The rise and rise of BHP Billiton* (Sydney 2010).

W.R. Thomas, *In the Early Days: A faithful history of the Barrier Mines* (Broken Hill 1889).

More Kanaka scandals
Evans, *A History of Queensland.*

Evans, Saunders and Cronin, *Exclusion, Exploitation and Extermination.*

John Hirst, *The Sentimental Nation: The making of the Australian Commonwealth* (Melbourne 2000).

Reynolds, *North of Capricorn.*

Peter Thompson and Robert Macklin, *The Life and Adventures of Morrison of China* (Sydney 2004).

Jane Clary and Claire McLisky (eds), *Creating White Australia* (Sydney 2009).

Geoffrey Bolton, *Edmund Barton* (Sydney 2000).

John Reynolds, *Edmund Barton* (Sydney 1948).

Drought and Bishop Moorhouse

Michael McKernan, *Drought: The Red Marauder* (Sydney 2005).

Cathcart, *The Water Dreamers*.

Lazarus, *Two Brothers*.

Geoffrey Blainey, *A History of Victoria* (Melbourne 2006).

Clark, *A History of Australia, Volume IV*.

The end of Dickens' orphans

Lazarus, *Two Brothers*.

Hansard, New South Wales, 6 March 1889, Adjournment debate, Resignation of Government.

Hansard, New South Wales, 23 May 1889, Lands Bill.

Parkes Papers, 23 March and 17 May 1890, Consult Index, ML MSS 4312.

Hansard, New South Wales, Adjournment, 14 August 1889.

Hansard, New South Wales, Crown Lands Bill and Adjournment, 28 June 1889.

The great rabbit prize

Cannon, *Life in the Country*.

Stephen Dando-Collins, *Pasteur's Gambit: Louis Pasteur, the Australasian rabbit plague and a ten million dollar prize* (Sydney 2008).

Anthony Trollope, P.D. Edwards and R.B. Joyce (eds), *Australia* (St Lucia 1968).

Is art possible?

Serle, *From Deserts the Prophets Come*.

Kaye Harman, *Australia Brought to Book: Responses to Australia by visiting writers, 1836 to 1939* (Sydney 1985).

Joseph Furphy, *Such is Life* (Sydney 1903).

Henry Lawson, *The Ballad of the Drover and Other Verses* (Sydney 1918).

Miles Franklin, *My Brilliant Career* (Sydney 1901).

Jill Roe, *Stella Miles Franklin: A biography* (Sydney 2008).

Robert Gray and Geoffrey Lehmann (eds), *Australian Poetry in the Twentieth Century* (Melbourne 1999).

Cecil Hadgraft, *Australian Literature: A critical account to 1955* (Melbourne 1960).

Rolf Boldrewood, *Robbery Under Arms* (electronic edition, Project Gutenberg Australia).

Marcus Clarke, *For the Term of His Natural Life* (Electronic edition, Project Gutenberg Australia).

Robert Hughes, *The Art of Australia* (Melbourne 1970).

H.M. Green, *History of Australian Literature Pure and Applied*, Volume 1 (Sydney 1984).

Adam Lindsay Gordon poems (electronic edition, Project Gutenberg Australia).

Barcroft Boake poems (electronic edition, Project Gutenberg Australia).

Irrigation and the redemption of Australia

La Nauze, *Alfred Deakin*.

Cathcart, *The Water Dreamers*.

Cannon, *Life in the Country*.

Bushrangers, time, art

John McDonald, *Art of Australia Volume 1: Exploration to Federation* (Sydney 2008).

Serle, *From Deserts the Prophets Come*.

Bernard Smith, *Australian Painting 1788 to 1970* (Melbourne 1971).

A Russian in New Guinea

Anna Shnukal, 'N.N. Miklouho-Maclay in Torres Strait', *JRAHS*, volume 1998, issue 2.

John Daedemo Waiko, *A Short History of Papua New Guinea* (Melbourne 2007).

Celestials in southern Australia

Trollope, Edwards and Joyce, *Australia*.

Jean Gittins, *The Diggers from China: The story of Chinese on the goldfields* (Melbourne 1981).

Jan Ryan, *Ancestors: The Chinese in colonial Australia* (Fremantle 1995).

Henry Chan, Ann Curthoys and Nora Chang (eds), *The Overseas Chinese in Australasia: History, settlement and interactions* (Taipei 2001).

Barry McGowan, 'Reconsidering the Chinese experience on the goldfields of southern New South Wales', *Australian Historical Studies*, number 124, 2004.

Grandmotherly legislation and the privileges of disease

Geoffrey Serle, *The Rush to Be Rich: A history of the colony of Victoria 1883–1889* (Melbourne 1971).

Cannon, *Life in the Cities*.

Cannon, *Who's Master? Who's Man?*

Patrick Jalland, *Australian Ways of Death: A social and cultural history, 1840–1918* (New York 2002).

Victorian Parliament, Royal Commission into Sanitary Conditions of Melbourne (Melbourne 1888-90).
Victorian Parliament, Royal Commission on the Operation of Factories and Shop Law of Victoria, *1901–02.*

Frontier women and infant death
Bolton, *Land of Vision and Mirage.*
Jalland, *Australian Ways of Death.*
Colin Roderick (ed), *Henry Lawson: Short stories and sketches, 1888–1922* (Sydney 1972).
Constance Jane Ellis, *I Seek Adventure: An autobiographical account of pioneering experiences in outback Queensland from 1889 to 1904* (Sydney 1981).

Marvellous Melbourne
Michael Cannon, *The Land Boomers* (Melbourne 1966).
Cannon, *Life in the Cities.*
Michael Davitt, *Life and Progress in Australia* (London 1898).

CHAPTER 4 THE LAST COLONIAL DECADE

The way the money goes
Cannon, *The Land Boomers.*
Cannon, *Life in the Cities.*
Serle, *The Rush to be Rich.*
Blainey, *A History of Victoria.*
Maurice Brodzky, *Table Talk*, 20 March 1891, 19 May 1891, 9 June 1891.

Clever devices
Frances Wheelhouse, *Digging Stick to Rotary Hoe: Men and machines in rural Australia* (Sydney 1966).
Cannon, *Life in the Country.*
G.L. Sutton, *The Invention of the Stripper* (Perth 1937).
Vance Palmer, *National Portraits* (Sydney 1941).
Geoffrey Blainey, *Black Kettle and Full Moon.*
Harvester Case: Ian Turner, *Industrial Labour and Politics: The dynamics of the labour movement in eastern Australia, 1900–1921* (Canberra 1965).

A changed world
Sydney Morning Herald, 19 June 1891.

Lazarus, *Two Brothers*.

Vance Palmer, *The Legend of the Nineties* (Melbourne 1983).

Lloyd Ross, *William Lane and the Australian Labor Movement* (Sydney 2001).

Bruce Scates, *A New Australia* (Cambridge 1997).

C.M.H. Clark, *A History of Australia, Volume V: The people make laws, 1888–1815* (Melbourne 1981).

Graham Freudenberg, *Cause for Power: The official history of the New South Wales Branch of the Australian Labor Party* (Sydney 2000).

United Pastoralists Association of Queensland, *Some Facts, Principles and Opinions, The Great Shearers' Strike of 1891* (probably Brisbane 1891).

Rosemary Broomham, 'Planned warfare or accident in timing? The 1890 maritime strike revisited', *JRAHS*, August 1996.

Sean Scalmer, 'Labour's golden age and the changing forms of workers' representation in Australia', *JRAHS*, December 1998.

L.F. Fitzhardinge, *That Fiery Particle: A political biography of William Morris Hughes, Volume 1, 1862–1914* (Sydney 1964).

W.M. Hughes, *Policies and Potentates* (Sydney 1950).

H.V. Evatt, *William Holman: Australian Labour Leader* (Sydney 1979).

New South Wales Hansard, Diseases in Sheep Acts, 11 October 1892.

New South Wales Hansard, Debates, 8 September 1892.

Barrier Miner, 27 March and 29 June 1894.

Transported gentlemen decline

Lazarus, *Two Brothers*.

Dickens, *The Recollections of Sir Henry Dickens*.

Edward Bulwer Lytton Papers, 1895–1919, ML MSS1372, CY 1783.

Dickens to Parkes, date not known, ML, Parkes Papers, Consult Index, ML MSS 4312. *Sydney Morning Herald*, 14 and 16 March 1892.

What the *Bulletin* did

Serle, *From Deserts the Prophets Come*.

Manning Clark, *Henry Lawson: The man and the legend* (Melbourne 1995).

Clark, *A History of Australia, Volume V*.

Sylvia Lawson, *J.F. Archibald* (Melbourne 1971).

Lawson, *The Ballad of the Drover and Other Verses*.

Boake, Poems (electronic edition).

Furphy, *Such is Life*.

Francis Devlin Glass and Robin Eaden et al. (eds), *The Annotated Such is Life* (Sydney 1999).

Bernard O'Dowd, *Poems* (electronic edition, Project Gutenberg Australia).

John Hirst, *The Sentimental Nation: The making of the Australian Commonwealth* (Melbourne 2000).

Christopher Brennan poetry in Robert Gray and Geoffrey Layman (eds), *Australian Poetry in the Twentieth Century* (Melbourne 1991).

Banjo doesn't care for Matilda

J.S. Manifold, *Who Wrote the Ballads? Notes on Australian folksong* (Sydney 1964).

S. May, *The Story of Waltzing Matilda* (Brisbane 1944).

J. Meredith and H. Anderson, *Folk Songs of Australia and the Men and Women Who Sang Them* (Sydney 1968).

Federation, protection, destiny

John M. Ward, 'Charles Gavan Duffy and the Australian Federation Movement, 1856–70', *JRAHS*, volume 47, part 1, 1961.

La Nauze, *Alfred Deakin*.

Stuart Macintyre, *A Colonial Liberalism: The lost world of three Victorian visionaries* (Melbourne 1991).

Helen Irving, *To Constitute a Nation: A cultural history of Australia's constitution* (Melbourne 1997).

Hirst, *The Sentimental Nation*.

Clark, *A History of Australia, Volume V*.

Blainey, *A History of Victoria*.

The train to Tenterfield

La Nauze, *Alfred Deakin*.

Hirst, *The Sentimental Nation*.

Irving, *To Constitute a Nation*.

Parkes Papers, ML, see Index File.

Manning Clark, *Sources of Australian History* (London 1957).

Bolton, *Edmund Barton*.

Reynolds, *Edmund Barton*.

John Quick and Robert Garran, *The Annotated Constitution of the Commonwealth of Australia* (Sydney and Melbourne 1901).

Russell Ward, *A Nation for a Continent* (Melbourne 1977).

Stuart Macintyre, 'Introduction' in Alfred Deakin, *'And Be One People': Alfred Deakin's Federal Story* (Melbourne 1995).
Catherine Spence, *A Week in the Future* (electronic edition, Project Gutenberg Australia, first published 1888).
Susan Magarey, *Unbridling the Tongues of Women: A biography of Catherine Helen Spence* (Sydney 1985).
Joy Damousi, *Women Come Rally: Socialism, communism and gender in Australia, 1890–1955* (Melbourne 1994).
Judith A. Allen, *Rose Scott: A vision and revision in feminism* (Melbourne 1994).
George Reid, *My Reminiscences* (London 1917).
Scates, *A New Australia*.

Going for gold
Blainey, *The Rush that Never Ended*.
Evans, *A History of Queensland*.
William H. Dick, *The Famous Mount Morgan Gold Mine, Rockhampton, Queensland, Its History, Geological Formation and Prospects* (Rockhampton 1887).
Croydon Field in Keneally, *The Great Shame*.
Reynolds, *North of Capricorn*.
Bolton, *Land of Vision and Mirage*.
Powell, *A Far Country*.
Whitelock, *Adelaide 1836–1976*.

Building Australia—anywhere but Australia
Edward Bellamy, *Looking Backward, 2000 to 1888* (New York 1951 and electronic edition Project Gutenberg Australia).
William Lane, *The Working Man's Paradise* (Brisbane 1892).
Spence, *A Week in the Future*.
Bruce Skates, *A New Australia: Citizenship, radicalism and the First Republic* (Melbourne 1997).
Ann Whitehead, *Blue Stocking in Patagonia* (London 2003).
Ross, *William Lane and the Australian Labor Movement*.

Lemuria
Rosa Praed, *Fugitive Anne* (London 1902).
Bellamy, *Looking Backward*.
Lane, *The Working Man's Paradise*.
Spence, *A Week in the Future*.

John Docker, *The Nervous Nineties: Australian cultural life in the 1890s* (Melbourne 1991).

Cathcart, *The Water Dreamers*.

Evans, *A History of Queensland*.

Gabay, *The Mystic Life of Alfred Deakin*.

War in northern Australia

Cooktown Courier, 13 June 1874.

William H. Willshire, *The Land of the Dawning: Being facts gleaned from cannibals in the Australian stone age* (Adelaide 1896).

Noel Loos, *Invasion and Resistance: Aboriginal-European relations on the North Queensland frontier, 1861–1897* (Canberra 1982).

Evans, Saunders and Cronin, *Exclusion, Exploitation and Extermination*.

Evans, *A History of Queensland*.

E.M. Kerr, *The Australian Race, Volume 3* (Melbourne 1886).

George Sutherland, *Pioneering Days: Thrilling incidents across the wilds of Queensland,* (Brisbane 1913).

Queensland Parliament, *Royal Commission, Alleged Outrages Committed on the Aborigines in Queensland by the Native Mounted Police*, 1875.

Henry Reynolds, *Fate of a Free People* (Melbourne 1995).

Henry Reynolds, *The Law of the Land* (Melbourne 1987).

Henry Reynolds, *Dispossession: Black Australians and white invaders* (Sydney 1989).

Cathie Clement, 'Monotony, manhunts and malice: Eastern Kimberley law enforcement, 1896–1908', *Journal of the Royal Western Australian Historical Society*, volume 10, part I, 1989.

A worker's paradise?

K. Buckley and T. Wheelwright, *No Paradise for Workers: Capitalism and the common people in Australia, 1788–1914* (Melbourne 1988).

Cannon, *Life in the Cities*.

Palmer, *The Legend of the Nineties*.

J.E. Nield, *Dirt and Disease* (Melbourne 1872).

Elaine Thompson, *Fair Enough: Egalitarianism in Australia* (Sydney 1994).

Damousi, *Women Come Rally*.

Brian Fitzpatrick, *The Australian Commonwealth: A picture of the community 1901 to 1955* (Melbourne 1956).

Davitt, *Life and Progress in Australia*.

Daily Telegraph, 17 August 1901.

Victorian Parliament, *Royal Commission into Factories*.

S.F. Macintyre, 'Labor, capital and arbitration, 1890–1920' in Brian Head (ed) *State and the Economy in Autralia* (Melbourne 1989).

Stuart Macintyre, *Winners and Losers: The pursuit of social justice in Australian history* (Sydney 1985).

The godly radicals

Fitzhardinge, *That Fiery Particle*.

Freudenberg, *Cause for Power*.

L.F. Crisp, *The Australian Federal Labour Party, 1901–1951* (Sydney 1978).

Evatt, *William Holman*.

David Day, *Andrew Fisher: Prime Minister of Australia* (Sydney 2008).

Hughes, *Policies and Potentates*.

CHAPTER 5 SEEKING FEDERATION AND HAVING IT

And be one people

Irving, *To Constitute a Nation*.

Hirst, *The Sentimental Nation*.

Macintyre ('Introduction') in Alfred Deakin, *'And Be One People'*.

Gabay, *The Mystic Life of Alfred Deakin*.

Ward, *A Nation for a Continent*.

Bolton, *Edmund Barton*.

Reynolds, *Edmund Barton*.

F.K. Crowley, *Modern Australia in Documents, Volume 1* (Melbourne 1973).

Parkes Papers, ML, Consult Index File ML MSS 4312.

Argus, 2 January 1901.

Daily Telegraph, 10 January and 3 June 1901.

Boer War

A.B. Paterson, *Happy Dispatches* (Sydney 1934).

A.B. Paterson, *Rio Grande's Last Race and Other Verses* (Sydney 1902).

Craig Wilcox, *Australia's Boer War: The war in South Africa 1899–1902*, Australian War Memorial commissioned history (Melbourne 2002).

George R. Witton, *Scapegoats of Empire: The story of the Bushveldt Carbineers* (Melbourne 1907).

Clark, *A History of Australia, Volume V*.

M. Davitt, *The Boer Fight for Freedom* (New York 1902).

The London struggle
La Nauze, *Alfred Deakin*.
Bolton, *Edmund Barton*.
Reynolds, *Edmund Barton*.
Deakin, '*And Be One People*'.
Quick and Garran, *An Annotated History of the Constitution*.
Margaret Glass, *Charles Cameron Kingston: Federation father* (Melbourne 1997).

The birthday
As well as Federation titles already cited for 'The London struggle':
Sydney Morning Herald, 1 January and 2 January 1901.
Crowley, *Modern Australia in Documents, Volume 1*.
Clark, *A History of Australia, Volume V*.
Hughes, *Policies and Potentates*.

Opening business
Murray Goot, 'The Aboriginal franchise and its consequences', *Australian Journal of Politics and History*, December 2006.
Bolton, *Edmund Barton*.
Reynolds, *Edmund Barton*.
Fitzhardinge, *That Fiery Particle*.
Crowley, *Modern Australia in Documents, Volume 1*.
La Nauze, *Alfred Deakin*.
Turner, *Industrial Labour and Politics*.
Hirst, *The Sentimental Nation*.
Damousi, *Women Come Rally*.
Chan, Curthoys and Chiang, *The Overseas Chinese in Australasia*.

Toby abroad
Reynolds, *Edmund Barton*.
Bolton, *Edmund Barton*.
Clark, *A History of Australia, Volume V*.

By name alone
'Andrew Fisher: A proud, honest man of Scotland', *JRAHS*, volume 87, Part II, December 2001.
David Day, *Andrew Fisher: Prime Minister of Australia* (Sydney 2008).
Fitzhardinge, *That Fiery Particle*.

L.F. Fitzhardinge, *The Little Digger 1914–18: William Morris Hughes, a political biography* (Sydney 1979).
Crisp, *The Australian Federal Labour Party, 1901-1951*.

Surf
Grant Rodwell, '"The sense of victorious struggle": The eugenic dynamic in Australian popular surf culture, 1900 to 1950', *JAS*, 1999.
Sydney Morning Herald, 21 October 1907.
Cameron White, 'Picknicking, surf-bathing and middle-class morality on the beaches in the eastern suburbs of Sydney 1811–1912', *JAS*, issue 80, 2004. Leone Huntsman, *Sand in Our Souls: The beach in Australian history* (Melbourne 2001).
Douglas Booth, *Australian Beach Cultures: The history of sun, sand and surf* (London 2001).

Accent on the 'can'
Roger Pegrum, *The Bush Capital: How Australia chose Canberra as it federal capital* (Sydney 1983).
A.R. Hoyle, *King O'Malley: The American bounder* (Melbourne 1981).
Fitzhardinge, *That Fiery Particle*.
La Nauze, *Alfred Deakin*.
Reid, *My Reminiscences*.
Hughes, *Policies and Potentates*.
Hirst, *The Sentimental Nation*.

The trick of aviation
Crowley, *Modern Australia in Documents, Volume 1*.
Sydney Morning Herald, 10 December 1909.
Norman Brearley, 'Pioneering development of civil aviation in Australia', *Royal Western Australian Historical Society Journal*, volume 6, part 5, 1966.
Fitzpatrick, *The Australian Commonwealth*.
David Wilson, *The Brotherhood of Airmen: The men and women of the RAAF in action 1914 –today* (Sydney 2005).

Live show and flickers
Serle, *From Deserts the Prophets Come*.
Andrew Pike and Ross Cooper, *A Reference Guide to Australian Films, 1906–1969* (Canberra 1981).
Viola Tate, *A Family of Brothers: The Taits and J.C. Williamson* (Melbourne 1971).
Hal Porter, *Stars of Australian Screen and Stage* (Adelaide 1965).

God's word in the north

Broome, *Aboriginal Australians*.

Bob Reece, 'Introduction' in P.J. Bridge (ed), Daisy Bates, *My Natives and I: Incorporating the passing of the Aboriginals* (Perth 2004).

Anon, 'A journey back in time', *New Directions*, volume 11, issue 5, October/November 2007.

Michael Lambek, *A Reader in the Anthropology of Religion* (Melbourne 2002).

Ronald Murray Berndt, *Social Anthropology and Australian Aboriginal Studies: A contemporary overview* (Canberra 1988).

F.X. Gsell, *The Bishop with 150 Wives: Fifty years as a missionary* (Sydney 1955).

Cattle station blacks and drovers boys

Broome, *Aboriginal Australians*.

F. Stevens, *Aborigines in the Northern Territory Cattle Industry* (Canberra 1974).

Reid, *A Picnic With the Natives*.

Powell, *A Far Country*.

Reynolds, *North of Capricorn*.

Henry Reynolds, *With the White People* (Melbourne 1990).

Unfederated play

Richard Cashman (ed.), *Tales from Coathanger City: Ten years of Tom Brock Lectures* (Sydney 2010).

Ian Heads, *The Kangaroos* (Sydney 1990).

Richard Cashman (ed), *Australian Sport Through Time: The history of sport in Australia* (Sydney 1997).

Gordon Inglis, *Sport and Pastime in Australia* (London 1912).

Geoffrey Moorhouse, *A People's Game: The centennial history of Rugby League football, 1895–1995* (London 1995).

For fear of Japan

C.H. Kirmess, *The Australian Crisis* (University of Sydney electronic edition 2003).

Ambrose Pratt, *The Big Five* (Sydney 2011 and electronic edition Project Gutenberg Australia).

Fitzhardinge, *That Fiery Particle*.

Peter Spartalis, *The Diplomatic Battles of Billy Hughes* (Sydney 1983).

McQueen, *A New Britannia*.

Yoichi Hirama, 'Japanese naval assistance and its effect on Australian-Japanese relations' in Phillips P. O'Brien (ed), *The Anglo-Japanese Alliance, 1902–22* (New York 2004).

Ambrose Pratt, *The Big Five* (Sydney 2011 and Project Gutenberg Australia electronic edition).

CHAPTER 6 THE GREAT WAR

Aliens?

R.B. Walker, 'German-language press and people in South Australia, 1848–1900', *JRAHS*, volume 58, part 2, June 1972.

Michael McKernan, *The Australian People and the Great War* (Melbourne 1980).

Day, *Andrew Fisher*.

Fitzhardinge, *The Little Digger*.

Bill Latter, 'The night of the stones: The anti-German riots in Fremantle 1915', *Royal Western Australian Historical Society*, volume 10, part 4, 1992.

Raising the force

Chris Coulthard-Clark, 'Major-General Sir William Bridges' in D.M. Horner (ed), *The Commanders: Australian military leadership in the twentieth century* (Sydney 1984).

Guy Verney, 'General Sir Brudenell White: The staff officer as commander' in Horner, *The Commanders*.

C.E.W. Bean, *Anzac to Amiens* (Sydney 1946).

Day, *Andrew Fisher*.

Fitzhardinge, *The Little Digger*.

C.E.W. Bean, *Official History of Australia in the War of 1914–1918, Volume I: The story of Anzac from the outbreak of war to the end of the first phase of the Gallipoli campaign, May 4, 1915* (Sydney 1941).

Ernest Scott, *Official History of Australia in the War of 1914–1918, Volume XI: Australia During the War* (Sydney 1941).

Great and urgent service

S.S. MacKenzie, *Official History of Australia in the War of 1914–18, volume X: The Australians at Rabaul, the capture and administration of the German possessions in the Southern Pacific* (Sydney 1927).

Waiko, *A Short History of Papua New Guinea*.

Day, *Andrew Fisher*.

The game at sea
A.W. Jose, *Official History of Australia in the War of 1914–18, Volume IX: The Royal Australian Navy* (Sydney 2001).
Bean, *Official History of Australia in the War of 1914–18, Volume I.*
Phillips P. O'Brien (ed), *The Anglo-Japanese Alliance, 1902–22* (New York 2004).
Day, *Andrew Fisher.*

Transports
Jose, *Official History of Australia in the War of 1914–18.*
Bean, *Official History of Australia in the War of 1914–18, Volume I.*
P. O'Brien, *The Anglo-Japanese Alliance, 1902–22.*
Day, *Andrew Fisher.*

Hughes, Germans, minerals
Scott, *Official History of Australia in the War of 1914–1918, Volume XI.*
Fitzhardinge, *The Little Digger.*
Day, *Andrew Fisher.*
Hughes, *Policies and Potentates.*
Robert R. Garran, *Prosper the Commonwealth* (Sydney 1958).

The bloody myth unassailable
C.E.W. Bean, *Official History of Australia in the War of 1914–1918, Volumes I and II. The story of Anzac* (Sydney 1940).
Peter Hart, 'War is Helles: The real fight for Gallipoli', *Wartime*, issue 38, AWM.
Les Carlyon, *Gallipoli* (Sydney 2010).
Graham Freudenberg, *Churchill and Australia* (Sydney 2008).
Geoffrey Serle, *John Monash: A biography* (Melbourne 1982).
Coulthard-Clark, 'Major-General Sir William Bridges' in Horner, *The Commanders.*
Michael B. Tyquin, *Gallipoli: The medical war* (Sydney 1993).
E.G. Halse, 1 February 1916–4 May 1917, CY 4871, ML.

The nurses at Lemnos
Janet Butler, 'Nursing Gallipoli: Identity and the challenge of experience', *JAS*, issue 78, 2003.
Peter Rees, *The Other Anzacs: Nurses at war 1914–1918* (Sydney 2008).
A.G. Butler, *The History of the Australian Medical Services in World War I, Volume 1: Gallipoli, Palestine and New Guinea* (Sydney 1938).

The bloody myth unassailable II
Ross McMullin, *Pompey Elliott* (Melbourne 2002).
Bean, *Anzac to Amiens.*
Carlyon, *Gallipoli.*
Bean, *Official History of the Australians in the War of 1914-18, Volume II.*
Butler, *The History of the Australian Medical Services in World War I.*

Interlude
Paterson, *Happy Dispatches.*
Lady Rachel Dudley, AWM website listings.
A.G. Butler, *The History of the Australian Medical Services in World War I,*
Volume III: Special problems and services (Sydney 1942).
A.B. Paterson, AWM website listings.

CHAPTER 7 WAR AND PEACE

I died in hell
AWM, 4 Australian Imperial Force War Diaries, 1914–18 War Infantry, item
numbers 23/36/9 and10, Nineteenth Infantry Battalion, November 1916.
C.E.W. Bean, *Official History of the Australians in the War of 1914–18,*
Volume III: The AIF in France, 1916 (Sydney 1940).
C.E.W. Bean, *Official History of the Australians in the War of 1914–18,*
Volume IV: The AIF in France, 1917 (Sydney 1941).
C.E.W. Bean, *Official History of the Australians in the War of 1914-18,*
Volume V: The Australian Imperial Force in France during the main German
offensive (Sydney 1941).
A.G. Butler, *The History of the Australian Medical Services in World War I,*
Volume VI: The Australian Imperial Force in France during the Allied offensive
(Sydney 1942);
A.G. Butler, *The History of the Australian Medical Services in World War I,*
Volume II, The Western Front (Sydney 1940).
Butler, *The History of the Australian Medical Services in World War I, Volume III.*

The categories of misery
Bean, *Official History of the Australians in the War of 1914–18, Volumes III-VI.*
Butler, *The History of the Australian Medical Services in World War I,*
Volumes II and *III.*
John Keegan, *The First World War* (New York 1999).

Rees, *The Other Anzacs*.

Letters of Private John Keneally, 19th Battalion AIF, in author's possession.

Sister Elsie Cook, AWM File 49/22/46.

J.M. Gillings and J. Richards (eds), *In All Those Lines: The diary of Sister Elsie Tranter, 1916–1919* (Newstead 2008).

W.C. Watson, *Narrative of Experiences in France*, 1917, ML MSS 2949.

Shell shock

Michael Tyquin, *Madness and the Military: Australia's experience of the Great War* (Canberra 2006).

C.E.W. Bean, *Official History of the Australians in the War, Volume VI: The AIF in France, 1918* (Sydney 1942).

Butler, *The History of the Australian Medical Services in World War I, Volume III*.

Major Alfred Campbell, *Medical Journal of Australia*, 15 April 1916.

J. P. Lowson, 'The treatment of war neuroses by abreaction of the war shock', *The Medical Journal of Australia*, 6 November 1926.

Joanna Bourke, 'Shell shock and Australian soldiers in the Great War', *Sabretache*, Volume XXXVI, July–September 1995.

POWs

Josephine Kildea, *Miss Chomley and Her Prisoners*, Honours thesis, University of New South Wales, 2006.

Bruce Scates and Raelene Francis, *Women and the Great War* (Cambridge 1997).

Vera Deakin, AWM electronic biography.

Lieutenant George Howard Earp, IDRL/0254, AWM.

Bearing stretchers

Butler, *The History of the Australian Medical Services in World War I, Volume II*.

W.C. Watson, ML MSS 2949.

George R. Faulkner war diaries, 1916–1917, CY 4653 ML.

The model general makes the modern battle

Bean, *Official History of the Australians in the War of 1914–18, Volume VI*.

Fitzhardinge, *The Little Digger*.

John Monash, *The Australian Victories in France in 1918* (London 1920).

Peter Pederson, 'Maintaining the Advance: Monash, battle procedure and the Australian Corps in 1918' in Ashley Ekins (ed), *1918 Year of Victory: The end of the Great War and the shaping of history* (Wollombi 2010).

Serle, *John Monash*.

Tom Roberts and Maxilla Facial drawings, AWM website.

Butler, *The History of the Australian Medical Services in World War I, Volume III.*

War and art

Betty Snowden, 'Iso Rae in Étaples: Another perspective of war', *Wartime*, volume 8, 1999.

Jessie Traill, AWM on-line biography.

Sandra Lanteri, 'Celebrating Australia's bayside artists, Jessie C.A. Traill', *Brighton Historical Society*, Summer journal 2005–06.

Flying as a way of death on the Western Front

F.M. Cutlack, *Official History of the Australians in World War I, Volume VIII: The Australian Flying Corps in the western and eastern theatres of war, 1914–1918* (Sydney 1938).

David Wilson, *The Brotherhood of Airmen.*

A conscription nation

Fitzhardinge, *The Little Digger.*

J.M. Mann, *Conscription: The Australian debate, 1901–1970* (Melbourne 1970).

Jeremy Sammut, '"Busting" the anti-conscription legend', *JRAHS*, June 2006.

McKernan, *The Australian People and the Great War.*

Scott, *Official History of Australia in the War of 1914–1918, Volume XI.*

Those Irish

O'Farrell, *The Irish in Australia.*

Fitzhardinge, *That Fiery Particle.*

Mann, *Conscription.*

Sammut, '"Busting" the anti-conscription legend'.

Bringing the fabric down

Tom Poole and Eric Fried, 'Artem: A Bolshevik in Brisbane, including a translation of Artem Sergeiev's *Australia the Lucky Country*', *Australian Journal of Politics and History*, volume 31, number 2, 1985.

Turner, *Industrial Labour and Politics.*

McKernan, *The Australian People and the Great War.*

Scott, *Official History of Australia in the War of 1914–1918, Volume XI.*

Keeping the fabric up

Andrew Moore, *The Secret Army and the Premier: Conservative paramilitary organisations in New South Wales, 1930–1932* (Sydney 1989).

Andrew Moore, 'Writing about the extreme Right in Australian history', *Labour History*, volume 89, November 2005.
Kevin Windle, 'A Russian account of the Brisbane Red Flag riots of 1919', *Labour History*, number 99, November 2010.
Scott, *Official History of Australia in the War of 1914–1918, Volume XI.*

Western Front mutiny
Ashley Ekins, 'Fighting to Exhaustion: Morale, discipline and combat effectiveness in the armies of 1918' in Ekins, *1918 Year of Victory.*
Les Carlyon, *The Great War* (Sydney 2010).
McMullin, *Pompey Elliott.*

Shrinking the Ottoman Empire
Cutlack, *Official History of the Australians in World War I, Volume VIII.*
H.S. Gullett, *Official History of the Australians in World War I, Volume VII: The Australian Imperial Force in Sinai and Palestine, 1914–18* (1941).
A.J. Hill, 'General Sir Harry Chauvel: Australia's First Corps commander', in Horner, *The Commanders.*
'Aboriginal servicemen', *Reveille*, 30 September and 30 November 1931.

Flying over Palestine
Cutlack, *Official History of the Australians in the War of 1914–18, Volume VIII:*
Wilson, *The Brotherhood of Airmen.*

Peace treaty
Fitzhardinge, *The Little Digger.*
Spartalis, *The Diplomatic Battles of Billy Hughes.*
Hughes, *Policies and Potentates.*
C.D. Rowley, *The Australians in German New Guinea* (Melbourne 1958).
Waiko, *A Short History of Papua New Guinea.*
Scott, *Official History of Australia in the War of 1914–1918, Volume XI.*

INDEX

Page references followed by *t* indicate Timeline entries.